ACTIVE CORAL RESTORATION

Techniques for a Changing Planet

Edited by David E. Vaughan, PhD

J.ROSS PUBLISHING

Copyright © 2021 by J. Ross Publishing

ISBN: 978-1-60427-143-0

Printed and bound in the U.S.A. Printed on acid-free paper.

10 9 8 7 6 5 4 3 2 1

Library of Congress Cataloging-in-Publication Data
Names: Vaughan, David E., editor.
Title: Active coral restoration : techniques for a changing planet / edited by David Vaughan.
Description: Plantation : J. Ross Publishing, Inc., [2021] | Includes bibliographical references and index. |
Identifiers: LCCN 2021006281 (print) | LCCN 2021006282 (ebook) | ISBN 9781604271430 (hardcover) | ISBN 9781604278323 (epub)
Subjects: LCSH: Coral reef restoration.
Classification: LCC QH541.5.C7 A28 2021 (print) | LCC QH541.5.C7 (ebook) | DDC 333.95/53153—dc23
LC record available at https://lccn.loc.gov/2021006281
LC ebook record available at https://lccn.loc.gov/2021006282

Cover photo credit:
Thank you to Lisa Carne, Executive Director and Founder of Fragments of Hope, Ltd., for the photos on the front cover. The top photo is from October 2011 and shows degraded reef rubble with the first coral outplants of *Acropora palmata*, elkhorn coral, at sub-site #13 in Laughing Caye National Park, Belize. The bottom photo is of the same site in May 2016. Through active coral restoration, conducted by Fragments of Hope, this reef was successfully restored to a functional reef teeming with fish and invertebrates in just six years. Our gratitude to Lisa and her colleagues for sharing these photos, for telling their story in Chapter 11 of this book, and for their continued dedication to coral reef restoration.

This publication contains information obtained from authentic and highly regarded sources. Reprinted material is used with permission, and sources are indicated. Reasonable effort has been made to publish reliable data and information, but the author and the publisher cannot assume responsibility for the validity of all materials or for the consequences of their use.

All rights reserved. Neither this publication nor any part thereof may be reproduced, stored in a retrieval system, or transmitted in any form or by any means, electronic, mechanical, photocopying, recording or otherwise, without the prior written permission of the publisher.

The copyright owner's consent does not extend to copying for general distribution for promotion, for creating new works, or for resale. Specific permission must be obtained from J. Ross Publishing for such purposes.

Direct all inquiries to J. Ross Publishing, Inc., 151 N. Nob Hill Rd., Suite 476, Plantation, FL 33324.

Phone: (954) 727-9333
Fax: (561) 892-0700
Web: www.jrosspub.com

In memory of Dr. Ruth Gates, whose energy, enthusiasm, and dedication to the study and conservation of coral reefs has been a true inspiration—one that will lead us forward well into the future.

CONTENTS

Foreword..xv
About the Editor..xvii
Contributing Authors..xix
Acknowledgments..xxiii
WAV™ page..xxv

SECTION I: OVERVIEW..1

1 Introduction...3
    AUTHOR: David E. Vaughan
        References...5

2 History of Reef Restoration..7
    AUTHORS: Adam Smith, Boze Hancock, Nathan Cook, and David Vaughan
        Introduction...7
        Coral Reefs..8
        Coral Restoration..8
        Indigenous People and Reef Restoration........................10
        Scientific Pioneers of Reef Restoration.......................10
        Management Support for Coral Reef Restoration.................16
        Communication and Education on Reef Restoration...............17
        The Role of Private Business in Reef Restoration..............19
        Global Literature Review......................................21
        Discussion..26
        Conclusions...27
        Recommended Future Research and Goals.........................28
        Acknowledgments...28
        References..28

3 The Quandary of Active and Passive Reef Restoration in a Changing World...31
    AUTHOR: Buki Rinkevich
        What Is Ecological Restoration?...............................31
        Active and *Passive* Restoration—the Path of Silviculture...33
        The Path of *Active* and *Passive* Restoration in Coral Reefs.35

  Quandary and Solution for Active Reef Restoration....................37
  Acknowledgments 38
  References 38

4 Live Rock Farmer to Live Coral Farmer 43
 AUTHOR: Ken Nedimyer

  Introduction 43
  Early History: The Passion for Coral Reefs............................43
  Catastrophic Changes 44
  The Live Rock Farm 45
  The Coral Farm..48
  Coral Reef Restoration..51
  A Coral Farm Becomes a Coral Nursery................................52
  Starting the Coral Restoration Foundation..............................60
  Developing the Coral Tree Nursery Design 62
  Taking It to the Next Level 64
  Conclusions...65
  Recommended Future Research..66
  Acknowledgments 67

SECTION II: BIOLOGICAL CONSIDERATIONS AND METHODOLOGIES.... 69

5 Land and Field Nurseries...71
 AUTHOR: David E. Vaughan

  Introduction 71
  Locations for Nurseries 73
  Area Required..74
  Equipment..74
  Supplies and Materials..77
  Designs, Plans, Drawings, and Layouts.................................80
  Fouling—Maintenance and Cleaning 81
  Label Everything...81
  Measuring the Growth of Corals 84
  Production Capacity 85
  Vessels and Vehicles..86
  Safety Concerns 86
  Least Ecological Impact...86
  Discussion and Future Work...87
  Acknowledgments 87
  References 87

6 Asexual Coral Propagation—Fragmentation and Micro-Fragmentation 89
 AUTHOR: David E. Vaughan

  Introduction 90
  Micro-Fragmentation 95
  New Ways of Fragmenting 99
  Conclusions..101

    Recommended Future Research and Future Techniques 101
    Acknowledgments 102
    References 102

7 Coral Fusion: Harnessing Coral Clonality for Reef Restoration 103
AUTHORS: Z. H. Forsman, C. Page, and David E. Vaughan

    Introduction 103
    Coral Re-Skinning 104
    Natural or Artificial Coral Modules. 107
    Tiling the Reef. 108
    Coral Seedlings 109
    Fusion in Land Nurseries 110
    Fusion in Field Nurseries. 111
    The Fusion Process. 112
    Fusion or Confusion: To Fuse or Not to Fuse? 114
    Sexual or Asexual: To Clone or Not to Clone? 115
    Speeding up Sexual Maturity with Micro-Fragmentation 116
    Fusion for Genetic Crosses 117
    Conclusions. 118
    Acknowledgments 119
    References 119

8 Sexual Reproduction and Rearing Corals for Restoration 123
AUTHORS: Christopher Page, Nicole D. Fogarty, and David E. Vaughan

    Introduction 123
    Sexual Reproduction of Corals. 128
    Larval Culture, Settlement, and Post-Metamorphosis 129
    Larval Development. 130
    Settlement and Metamorphosis 132
    Multiple Settlement and Survival. 135
    Post-Settlement Care 136
    Grow Out to Juvenile Size 137
    Nursery Growth to a Juvenile and Raceway Ecology 138
    Managing Raceway Ecology 140
    Conclusions. 141
    References 141

9 Assisted Evolution and Coral Reef Resilience 145
AUTHOR: Hanna R. Koch

    Introduction 146
    Assisted Evolution Approaches: Acclimatization
        (Nongenetic) Processes. 154
    Experimental Evolution of Algal Endosymbionts (Symbiodiniaceae) 161
    Manipulating the Host Microbiome 168
    Interspecific Hybridization 177
    Intraspecific Managed Breeding and Genetic Adaptation 184

> Conclusions..200
> Acknowledgments..201
> References..201

10 Genetic Considerations for Coral Reef Restoration 221
AUTHOR: Hanna R. Koch

> Introduction...222
> The Need for an Evolutionary Perspective Within Coral
>   Reef Restoration..225
> Factors That Could Drive Reductions in Fitness During
>   Restoration Activities..229
> Recommendations..237
> The Coral Holobiont and Role of Algal Symbionts......................255
> Molecular Tools..257
> Conclusions...261
> Acknowledgments..263
> References..263

SECTION III: CASE STUDIES FROM AROUND THE WORLD................285

11 Belize: Fragments of Hope..287
AUTHORS: Lisa Carne and Maya A. Trotz

> Introduction...288
> Laughing Bird Caye National Park Experience........................288
> Current Techniques and Methods....................................304
> Community Involvement..308
> Next Steps...309
> Conclusion..310
> Acknowledgments..311
> References..312

12 Indian Ocean: Seychelles..313
AUTHORS: Sarah Frias-Torres, Claude Reveret, Phanor Montoya-Maya, and Nirmal J. Shah

> Introduction...313
> Large-Scale Coral Reef Restoration Project in Seychelles................315
> Small-Scale Coral Reef Restoration Projects in Seychelles...............324
> Biomimicry Applications and Inventions..............................326
> Capacity Building: Empowering the End User.........................333
> Summary..334
> Recommended Future Research......................................335
> Acknowledgments..336
> References..336

**13 Active Coral Reef Restoration In Eilat, Israel: Reconnoitering
the Long-Term Prospectus** 341
AUTHORS: Yael B. Horoszowski-Fridman and Buki Rinkevich

Introduction .... .342
Techniques and Methods. .... .345
Monitoring .... .349
Community Involvement, Volunteers, and Citizen Science. .... .351
Major Outcomes and Discussion .... .354
Conclusions. .... .360
Acknowledgments .... .361
References .... .361

14 Active Reef Restoration in the Mexican Caribbean: 15-Year Timeline .... .365
AUTHORS: Claudia Padilla-Souza, Jaime González-Cano,
Juan Carlos Huitrón Baca, and Roberto Ibarra-Navarro

Introduction .... .366
Techniques and Methods. .... .367
2004–2005 Period. .... .367
2005–2009 Period. .... .369
2009–2011 Period. .... .370
2012–2016 Period. .... .371
2017–2022 Period. .... .377
Monitoring the Effectiveness of Restoration Actions .... .386
Community Involvement, Volunteers, and Citizen Science. .... .387
Discussion .... .389
Conclusions. .... .389
Acknowledgments .... .391
References .... .391

15 Active Coral Reef Restoration in Australia. .... .393
AUTHORS: Adam Smith, Nathan Cook, and Johnny Gaskell

Introduction .... .394
Techniques and Methods. .... .394
Agincourt Reef, Cairns 2003. .... .397
Manta Ray Bay, Whitsunday Islands 2017 .... .397
Fitzroy Island, Cairns 2017–2019. .... .397
Blue Pearl and Manta Ray Bay, Whitsunday Islands 2018–2020 .... .400
Agincourt Reef #3, Cairns 2018–2020. .... .401
Lovers Cove, Daydream Island, Whitsundays 2019 .... .402
Vlasoff and Arlington Reef, Cairns 2018–2019 .... .404
Monitoring .... .404
Community Involvement, Volunteers, and Citizen Science. .... .407
Governance Overview. .... .410
Permits and Guidelines .... .411
The Reef Restoration and Adaptation Program .... .413
Discussion .... .414
Conclusion. .... .415
Acknowledgments .... .415
References .... .416

16 Reef Restoration in the Eastern Tropical Pacific, a Case Study in Golfo Dulce, Costa Rica ...417
AUTHORS: J. A. Kleypas, T. Villalobos-Cubero, J. A. Marín-Moraga, Á. Teran, J. Cortés, and J. J. Alvarado

    Introduction ...417
    Techniques and Methods ...420
    Monitoring ...422
    Community Involvement, Volunteers, and Citizen Science ...427
    Discussion ...427
    Conclusion ...428
    Acknowledgments ...428
    References ...428

17 Line Islands, Kiribati ...431
AUTHORS: Austin Bowden-Kerby, Taratau Kirata, and Laurence Romeo

    Introduction ...431
    Coral Nursery Establishment ...433
    Larval-Based Coral Recruitment ...436
    May 2017 Nursery Expansion Using Threatened *Acropora* Recruits ...438
    The Discovery of Regenerating Coral Colonies via Surviving Tissue Fragments ...440
    Tabuaeran Findings ...443
    Discovery of Surviving Staghorn Corals on a Kiritimati Reef Flat ...446
    Outplanting of Corals from the Nursery ...449
    Discussion ...453
    Proposed 500-Meter No-Go and No-Fishing Area Around Cook Islet ...455
    Coral Reef Restoration Strategy for Kiribati ...457
    Corals for Conservation's Coral Reef Restoration for Climate Change Adaptation Strategy ...459
    Acknowledgments ...461
    References ...462

18 Indonesia: Mars Assisted Reef Restoration System ...463
AUTHORS: David J. Smith, F. Mars, *S. Williams, J. van Oostrum, A. McArdle, S. Rapi, J. Jompa, and N. Janetski

    Introduction ...464
    The Restoration Site and the Specific Restoration Problem ...465
    The MARRS Approach ...467
    The Reef Stars ...467
    The Restoration Build ...468
    Monitoring the Performance of the MARRS Technique ...473
    Brief Overview of Ecological Response to Restoration ...477
    Future Restoration and Achieving Scale Through Catalyzing Action ...479

Contents

  Acknowledgments 481
  References 481

**19 Hurricane Impacts on Reef Restoration: The Good, the Bad,
  and the Ugly.. 483**
  AUTHORS: Jane Carrick, Caitlin Lustic, Diego Lirman, Stephanie Schopmeyer,
  Erich Bartels, Dan Burdeno, Craig Dahlgren, Victor Manuel Galvan, Dave
  Gilliam, Liz Goergen, Shannon Gore, Sean Griffin, Edwin A. Hernández-
  Delgado, Dalton Hesley, Jessica Levy, Kemit Amon Lewis, Shelby Luce,
  Kerry Maxwell, Samantha Mercado, Margaret Miller, Michael Nemeth,
  Carlos Toledo-Hernández, Claudia P. Ruiz-Diaz, Samuel E. Suleiman-Ramos,
  Cory Walter, Dana Williams

  Introduction 484
  Methods.. 485
  Results 492
  Lessons Learned: Damage Prevention Strategies...................... 505
  Conclusions.. 507
  References 509

**20 Bolstering Reef Restoration Efforts: A Multifaceted Approach
  from Reef Renewal Foundation Bonaire........................... 511**
  AUTHORS: Francesca Virdis, Bridget Hickey, and Ken Nedimyer

  Introduction 511
  Techniques and Methods... 516
  New Techniques: Boulder Corals and Larval Propagation.............. 521
  Monitoring 524
  Community Involvement, Volunteers, and Citizen Science
      (If Applicable) 528
  Discussion 530
  Conclusion—Words of Wisdom from the Case Study 533
  Acknowledgments 533
  References 534

21 Punta Cana, Dominican Republic 535
  AUTHORS: Jake Kheel and David E. Vaughan

  Introduction 536
  Coral Restoration in Punta Cana 537
  Center for Marine Innovation (CIM) 543
  Dominican Consortium of Coastal Restoration 544
  The Nature Conservancy.. 544
  The Marine Sanctuary Arrecifes del Sureste........................ 545
  Discussion and Conclusions....................................... 547
  Acknowledgments 547
  References 547

SECTION IV: THE FUTURE OF CORAL REEF RESTORATION 549

22 Emerging Technologies 551
AUTHORS: David E. Vaughan and Ken Nedimyer

Introduction 551
New Ways of Fragmenting 552
Revisting Fragment Size 555
Revisiting Fragment Growth Rate 555
Feeds and Supplements for Coral Growth 555
Increasing the Survival of Sexual Reproduction 556
Vessels and Vehicles Used in Active Coral Restoration 557
Substrates and Adhesives for Coral Attachment 557
Modules and Components for Transportation 558
Innovative and Emerging Coral Nurseries 558
Increasing Coral Production *at Scale* 561
Selective Rapid Growth Cycle 564
Conclusion 566
Acknowledgments 566
Reference 566

23 Making Restoration Meaningful: A Vision for Working at Multiple Scales to Help Secure a Future for Coral Reefs 567
AUTHORS: Les Kaufman, Ilsa B. Kuffner, Tom Moore, and Tali Vardi

Introduction 567
The Value of Restoration Efforts at Various Scales 569
Conclusions 576
Disclaimer 576
References 576

Epilogue 581

Appendix: Notes for Record Keeping 583
AUTHOR: Donna Vaughan

Why Keep Records? 583
Daily Environmental Records 583
Land-Based Nursery Records 584
Outplantings and Field Nursery Records 585
Costs of Operation 586
Conclusions 586
Acknowledgments 586
References 587
    Appendix 1A: Record of Daily Environmental Data 588
    Appendix 1B: Record for Daily Raceway Maintenance 589
    Appendix 1C: Monthly Record for Coral Growth and Health 590

    Appendix 1D: Record for Mechanical Maintenance at
        Land Based Nursery...................................591
    Appendix 1E: Record for Field Nursery/Outplant Site for
        Coral Growth and Health 592

Glossary 593

Index 601

FOREWORD

Philippe Cousteau Jr.

"If there is a *Garden of Eden* on earth . . . this must be it," I thought to myself as I stared in awe at the spectacle in front of me. It was a bright summer's day and I was floating in crystal clear water some 40 feet below the surface in front of a coral reef called Shab Rumi, a few hours boat ride off the coast of Sudan in the Red Sea. Every color imaginable could be seen stretching out along the contours of the reef. Fish of every shape and size, from gobies no larger than the head of a pencil to enormous groupers and shimmering reef sharks, darted all around me while enormous sea fans and sponges dotted the landscape—it was one of the most awe-inspiring things I had ever seen.

Of course, growing up exploring the ocean, I had seen many coral reefs before, but this one was special. Tragically, in just a few short decades, most reefs around the world, from the Caribbean to the Great Barrier Reef, had become a shadow of their former selves. This reef was different, due to its remoteness and the advantage it had by having evolved in such a historically warm body of water—it was thriving. For me, it was the first time I had ever seen a reef that was not ravaged by the effects of climate change, pollution, ocean acidification, destructive fishing, or a combination of all four.

Whenever I think back to that day when I was diving on Shab Rumi more than ten years ago, I am reminded of what's at stake. Though most reefs in the Red Sea are still thriving, that is not the case throughout the rest of the world. Indeed, coral reefs today continue to decline around the world and the critical function they play in maintaining a healthy ocean ecosystem continues to falter. Coral reefs, which cover less than 1% of the world's ocean (an area about the size of the U.S. state of Nevada) support nearly 25% of all known marine species. Their role in protecting shorelines, providing food to hundreds of millions of people, and as a source of important medical breakthroughs is vital not only to the health of the ocean but to the health of humanity as well. Despite all this, we have lost more than 40% of the world's coral reefs and it is estimated that, at the current trajectory, we may lose 90% by the middle of this century.

But there is good news, too, and that is why this book is so important. In the same way that humans are responsible for the destruction of these precious ecosystems, we can also become their saviors. This excellent book, edited by my dear friend Dr. David Vaughan, features both his ground-breaking work, as well as a collection of insights by a *who's who* in the coral restoration world. Starting with the early developers such as Austin Bowden-Kerby in the Caribbean, Buki Rinkevich in the Red Sea, and Ken Nedimyer in Florida and the Caribbean, it also includes many new and upcoming scientists who have forged reputations in their own areas of expertise such as technological innovation, genetics research, and assisted evolution. This clearly and inspiringly laid-out manual is a practical guide for today's practitioner as well as a roadmap for the future.

But, in some ways it is more than an exploration about active coral reef restoration; it is a guide for humanity to remind us that through innovation and determination, we can play an active role in returning the ocean to abundance. I have known Dave for 20 years and I continue to marvel at his dedication, humility, and brilliance. This book is a must-read for anyone interested in the exciting world of active coral reef restoration. This work proves that these *Gardens of Eden* need not be lost and that there is always hope for the future.

ABOUT THE EDITOR

Dr. David E. Vaughan has held positions in aquaculture research and development for over 30 years. He directed the Aquaculture Division at the Harbor Branch Oceanographic Institution (HBOI) for 17 years, including the design, build, and operation of the 60-acre HBOI Aquaculture Development Park—the world's only completely recirculating center for aquaculture training and demonstration. He is often cited with creating the R&D and scale-up of clam-farming technologies in Florida, and directing the training programs and operations of the nation's largest hatchery to produce clams that are used for the retraining of displaced fisherman. He founded and developed Oceans, Reefs, and Aquariums Inc. (ORA), a large marine ornamental production facility for producing thousands of reef fish as well as hard and soft corals for the aquarium trade. He also worked with Philippe Cousteau at Earth Echo International on international coral reef restoration initiatives.

Photo credit: Ian Shive

As Executive Director of the Mote Marine Laboratory Elizabeth Moore Center for Coral Reef Research and Restoration in the Florida Keys for 15 years, he started the Coral Reef Restoration Program. Through this program, he was heralded with being the first to develop the new technology of coral *micro-fragmentation*. Through micro-fragmentation, massive corals grow very quickly to reproductive size, which dramatically improves the rate at which coral reefs can be restored. In 2017, he received the Chicago Field Museum Parker/Gentry Award as *Conservationist of the Year* for his work with coral restoration, and served as an adjunct scientist at the Field Museum of Chicago.

Dr. Vaughan is now Founder and President of Plant a Million Corals Foundation and is actively helping people around the world to use micro-fragmentation as a scalable tool for reef restoration and is designing and building transportable land-based coral nursery systems that can be shipped to locations around the world in order to train others in this *game-changer* technology for restoration. Dave plans to continue sharing his discovered technologies and passion for coral restoration with the aim of fulfilling his goal of planting a million corals before he retires.

CONTRIBUTING AUTHORS

Juan José Alvarado, Centro de Investigación en Ciencias del Mar y Limnología, Universidad de Costa Rica, San José, Costa Rica *and* Escuela de Biología, Universidad de Costa Rica, San José, Costa Rica

Juan Carlos Huitrón Baca, Ancla Marina S.A. de C.V., Cancun, Mexico

Erich Bartels, Mote Marine Laboratory, 24244 Overseas Highway, Summerland Key, FL 33042, USA

Austin Bowden-Kerby, Corals for Conservation, P.O. Box 4649 Samabula, Fiji Islands *and* Teitei Livelihoods Centre, Km 20 Sigatoka Valley Road, Fiji Islands

Daniel Burdeno, Coral Restoration Foundation, 89111 Overseas Hwy, Tavernier, FL 33037, USA

Lisa Carne, Fragments of Hope, Placencia Village, Stann Creek, Belize

Jane Carrick, Rosenstiel School of Marine and Atmospheric Science, University of Miami, 4600 Rickenbacker Causeway, Miami, FL 33149, USA

Nathan Cook, Reef Ecologic Pty Ltd, 14 Cleveland Terrace, North Ward, Townsville, QLD Australia 4810

Jorge Cortés, Centro de Investigación en Ciencias del Mar y Limnología, Universidad de Costa Rica, San José, Costa Rica *and* Asociación Raising Coral Costa Rica, San José, Costa Rica

Craig Dahlgren, Perry Institute of Marine Science, 5356 Main St., P.O. Box 435, Rte. 100, Suite 1, Waitsfield, VT 05673, USA

Nicole D. Fogarty, University of North Carolina Wilmington, Center for Marine Science, 5600 Marvin K. Moss Ln., Wilmington, NC 28409, USA

Zac H. Forsman, Coral Conservation Genetics & Restoration, Hawai'i Institute of Marine Biology, University of Hawai'i, Mānoa, Coconut Island, Moku o Lo'e, 46-007 Lilipuna Road, Kāne'ohe, HI 96744, USA

Sarah Frias-Torres, Nature Seychelles, The Centre for Environment & Education, Roche Caiman, Mahe, Republic of Seychelles *and* Vulcan Inc., 505 5th Avenue South, Seattle, WA 98104, USA

Victor Manual Galvan, Fundacion Grupo Puntacana, Puntacana Resort & Club, Punta Cana 23302, Dominican Republic

Johnny Gaskell, Daydream Island Resort and Living Reef, Great Barrier Reef—Whitsundays, QLD 4802 Australia

David Gilliam, Halmos College of Natural Sciences and Oceanography, Nova Southeastern University, 8000 N Ocean Dr., Dania Beach, FL 33004, USA

Elizabeth A. Goergen, Halmos College of Natural Sciences and Oceanography, Nova Southeastern University, 8000 N Ocean Dr., Dania Beach, FL 33004, USA

Jaime González-Cano, National Institute of Fisheries and Aquaculture, Puerto Morelos, 77580, Mexico

Shannon Gore, Association of Reef Keepers, P.O. Box 3252, PMB 2106 Road Town, Tortola British Virgin Islands VG1110, UK

Sean P. Griffin, NOAA Restoration Center, 260 Guard Rd., Aguadilla, PR 00605, USA

Boze Hancock, The Nature Conservancy, C/O URI Graduate School of Oceanography, 215 South Ferry Rd Narragansett, RI 02882, USA

Edwin A. Hernández-Delgado, Sociedad Ambiente Marino, P.O. Box 22158, San Juan, PR 00931, USA

Dalton Hesley, Rosenstiel School of Marine and Atmospheric Science, University of Miami, 4600 Rickenbacker Causeway, Miami, FL 33149, USA

Bridget Hickey, Reef Renewal Foundation International, Kaya Gob Nicholas Debrot #85, Kralendijk, Bonaire, Dutch Caribbean

Yael B. Horoszowski-Fridman, National Institute of Oceanography, Tel Shikmona, P.O. Box 8030, Haifa, Israel *and* Department of Evolutionary and Environmental Biology, Faculty of Natural Sciences, University of Haifa, Haifa 31905, Israel

Roberto Ibarra-Navarro, Costa Occidental de Isla Mujeres, Punta Cancún y Punta Nizuc-National Park, CONANP, Mexico

Noel Janetski, Mars, Inc., 6885 Elm St., McLean, VA 22101, USA

Jamal Jompa, Hasanuddin University, 90245 Makassar, Indonesia

Les Kaufman, Department of Biology, Boston University *and* Pardee Center for the Study of the Longer-Range Future, 67 Bay State Road, Boston, MA 02215, USA

Jake Kheel, Fundacion Grupo Puntacana, Puntacana Resort & Club, Punta Cana 23302, Dominican Republic

Taratau Kirata, MFMRD, Line Islands, P.O. T609, Ronton Town, Kiritimati Island, Republic of Kiribati

Joan A. Kleypas, Climate & Global Dynamics, National Center for Atmospheric Research, P.O. Box 3000, Boulder, CO 80307-3000, USA *and* Asociación Raising Coral Costa Rica, San José, Costa Rica

Hanna R. Koch, The Elizabeth Moore International Center for Coral Reef Research and Restoration, Mote Marine Laboratory, 24244 Overseas Highway, Summerland Key, FL 33042, USA

Ilsa B. Kuffner, U.S. Geological Survey, St. Petersburg Coastal & Marine Science Center, St. Petersburg, FL 33701, USA

Jessica Levy, Coral Restoration Foundation, 89111 Overseas Hwy, Tavernier, FL 33037, USA

Kemit-Amon F. Lewis, Formerly of The Nature Conservancy, Post Office Box 531, Frederiksted, Virgin Islands 00841, USA

Diego Lirman, Rosenstiel School of Marine and Atmospheric Science, University of Miami, 4600 Rickenbacker Causeway, Miami, FL 33149, USA

Shelby Luce, Mote Marine Laboratory, 24244 Overseas Highway, Summerland Key, FL 33042, USA

Caitlin Lustic, The Nature Conservancy, Florida Keys Office, 127 Industrial Rd., Ste D, Big Pine Key, FL 33043, USA

José Andrés Marín-Moraga, Asociación Raising Coral Costa Rica, San José, Costa Rica

Frank Mars, Mars, Inc., 6885 Elm St., McLean, VA 22101, USA

Kerry E. Maxwell, FWC FWRI, 2796 Overseas Highway, Marathon, FL 33050, USA

Alicia McArdle, Mars, Inc., 6885 Elm St., McLean, VA 22101, USA

Samantha Mercado, Grupo Puntacana Foundation, Punta Cana Resort & Club, Punta Cana, 23302, Dominican Republic

Margaret Miller, Secore International, 2103 Coral Way, 2nd Floor, Miami FL 33145, USA

Phanor Montoya-Maya, Nature Seychelles, The Centre for Environment & Education, Roche Caiman, Mahe, Republic of Seychelles *and* Corales de Paz, Calle 4 No. 35A-51, Cali, Colombia

Tom Moore, National Oceanic and Atmospheric Administration, Restoration Center, St. Petersburg, FL 33701, USA

Ken Nedimyer, Nedimyer Reef Consulting, LLC, 212 Silver Palm Ave, Tavernier, FL 33070, USA

Michael I. Nemeth, ERT Inc., 260 Guard Rd., Aguadilla, PR 00605, USA

Claudia Padilla-Souza, National Institute of Fisheries and Aquaculture, Puerto Morelos 77580, Mexico

Christopher Page, The Elizabeth Moore International Center for Coral Reef Research and Restoration, Mote Marine Laboratory, 24244 Overseas Highway, Summerland Key, FL 33042, USA

Saipul Rapi, Mars, Inc., 6885 Elm St., McLean, VA 22101, USA

Claude Reveret, Nature Seychelles, The Centre for Environment & Education, Roche Caiman, Mahe Republic of Seychelles *and* CREOCEAN, Zone Technocean, Chef de Baie, Rue Charles Tellier, 17000 La Rochelle, France

Buki Rinkevich, National Institute of Oceanography, Tel Shikmona, P.O. Box 8030, Haifa, Israel

Laurence Romeo, Just World Partnerships, 117 Randolph Avenue, London, W9 1DN, UK

Claudia P. Ruiz-Diaz, Sociedad Ambiente Marino, P.O. Box 22158, San Juan, PR 00931, USA

Stephanie Schopmeyer, Fish and Wildlife Research Institute, Florida Fish and Wildlife Conservation Commission, 100 8th Ave SE, St. Petersburg, FL 33701, USA

Nirmal J. Shah, Nature Seychelles, The Centre for Environment & Education, Roche Caiman, Mahe Republic of Seychelles

Adam Smith, Reef Ecologic Pty Ltd, 14 Cleveland Terrace, North Ward, Townsville, QLD 4810, Australia *and* 1 James Cook Drive, James Cook University, Townsville, QLD 4811, Australia

David J. Smith, Mars, Inc., 6885 Elm St., McLean, VA 22101, USA *and* Coral Reef Research Unit, School of Life Sciences, University of Essex, Colchester, Essex, CO3 4SQ, UK

Samuel E. Suleiman-Ramos, Sociedad Ambiente Marino, P.O. Box 22158, San Juan, PR 00931, USA

Álvaro Teran, Asociación Raising Coral Costa Rica, San José, Costa Rica

Carlos Toledo-Hernández, Sociedad Ambiente Marino, P.O. Box 22158, San Juan, PR 00931, USA

Maya A. Trotz, College of Engineering, Department of Civil and Environmental Engineering, University of South Florida, 4202 E Fowler Avenue, ENG 030, Tampa, FL 33620, USA

Jos van Oostrum, Mars, Inc., 6885 Elm St., McLean, VA 22101, USA

Tali Vardi, ECS for National Oceanic and Atmospheric Administration, National Marine Fisheries Service, Office of Science & Technology, Silver Spring, MD 20910, USA

David E. Vaughan, Plant a Million Corals Foundation, 24215 Caribbean Drive, Summerland Key, FL 33042, USA

Tatiana Villalobos-Cubero, Asociación Raising Coral Costa Rica, San José, Costa Rica

Francesca Virdis, Reef Renewal Foundation International, Kaya Gob Nicholas Debrot #85, Kralendijk, Bonaire, Dutch Caribbean

Cory S. Walter, Mote Marine Laboratory, 24244 Overseas Highway, Summerland Key, FL 33042, USA

Dana E. Williams, University of Miami Rosenstiel School of Marine and Atmospheric Sciences, Cooperative Institute for Marine and Atmospheric Studies, 4600 Rickenbacker Causeway, Key Biscayne, FL 33149, USA

Susan Williams, Bodega Marine Laboratory and Department of Evolution and Ecology, University of California—Davis, P.O. Box 247, Bodega Bay, CA 94923-2047, USA

ACKNOWLEDGMENTS

We are living in an era where many have witnessed the rapid decline of coral reefs around the world. The before and after pictures of our favorite dive sites in the last few decades reveal startling photographic evidence that cannot be ignored. The realization that mankind has adversely impacted our oceans has led many to despair. Hope is not gone, however, because scientists and practitioners are continuing to move forward in addressing climate change and, at the same time, developing techniques and strategies to restore our coral reefs in what is now called *active coral restoration*. These practices will allow us to transition to large-scale culture coral production, using naturally resistant coral strains to restore the reefs. Scientists and practitioners have been working for years to get us to this point, and I am very pleased that many of them have contributed to this first comprehensive book on the subject. It is a valiant effort and there are many to thank. To the authors who have shared their experience and knowledge in chapters that will help the next level of coral restoration efforts take a *giant step* for mankind, you have my sincere gratitude. For those who shared their real-life experiences in case studies from around the world, I applaud you. I am humbled to be a part of this collection of *who's who* in active coral restoration, and I am thankful to all who generously gave their time to help bring this very important text to life. To my dedicated family, Donna and Dee Dee, who have joined me in this effort, I am forever grateful. Lastly, to Gwen Eyeington of J. Ross Publishing, who has been our guide to direct us along, I am indebted.

WAV Web Added Value™

This book has free material available for download from the
Web Added Value™ resource center at *www.jrosspub.com*

At J. Ross Publishing we are committed to providing today's professional with practical, hands-on tools that enhance the learning experience and give readers an opportunity to apply what they have learned. That is why we offer free ancillary materials available for download on this book and all participating Web Added Value™ publications. These online resources may include interactive versions of material that appears in the book or supplemental templates, worksheets, models, plans, case studies, proposals, spreadsheets and assessment tools, among other things. Whenever you see the WAV™ symbol in any of our publications, it means bonus materials accompany the book and are available from the Web Added Value Download Resource Center at www.jrosspub.com.

Downloads for *Active Coral Restoration: Techniques for a Changing Planet* include data sheets from the book in Excel format for record keeping.

SECTION I

Overview

1

INTRODUCTION

David E. Vaughan

People around the world are becoming more aware of the decline in the quality and quantity of natural resources and the impact this has on local and global ecosystem function, public health, and portions of the economy. Most are aware that these declining conditions also plague our oceans and affect all sizes of marine life, from the dinoflagellate to the blue whale. In this book, our focus is on coral reefs because they are the building blocks for the marine life in our oceans. Unfortunately, many of our coral reef systems have been degraded to such a point that we only have photos to remind us of what once existed. These photos that show how beautiful and diverse the coral reefs once were, are a dramatic reminder that we need to be proactive, right now, to save our oceans, and in turn—ourselves.

Coral reefs and their inhabitants are beloved by many due to their sheer beauty, which has been made known to the public through early television shows like "The Undersea World of Jacques Cousteau," published pieces in magazines like *National Geographic*, marine parks with spectacular aquariums, and current shows such as "Chasing Coral" on Netflix. Unfortunately, coral reefs have been in decline over the past few decades and are now a shadow of what they once were. Climate change from carbon emissions and other stressors such as habitat loss, overfishing (including dynamite fishing), nutrient runoff, plastics, and other pollution have caused disease, decline, and death in coral reefs around the world. These stressors are avoidable if mankind would refrain from the unrestrained consumption of natural resources and the excessive burning of fossil fuels. Losing half of the world's coral cover since 1970 (Intergovernmental Panel on Climate Change 2018) is a stark reminder that we must address these stressors, but this will take time. In the interim, we need new technologies to actively restore corals right now.

Restoration efforts on land first focused on the protection of natural areas from threats and stressors and then allowed nature to make a slow comeback on its own—essentially an *unassisted recovery*. For restoration of forests (reforestation), active methods are regularly used to cultivate and plant trees in order to return the area to a fully functioning forest more quickly than would occur if unassisted. Today, terrestrial and aquatic ecosystems can be restored through hydrologic alteration, invasive species removal, replanting of native species, pollution control, and so forth. Early efforts in coral reef restoration focused on repair and restoration of reefs from ship groundings, anchor damage, and other anthropogenic impacts that can be traced to a responsible party who would then be required to pay fines to support the recovery of the damage (Precht 2005). In many cases, the project only stabilized the reef structure itself while leaving natural biological recovery to occur over time. Over the last two decades, scientists, conservationists, and decision-making authorities have opted for *active coral restoration* tools, where unassisted recovery has failed to achieve the targeted goals. What initially started as *coral gardening* projects (Chapter 3) are now scaled to production projects where cultured corals are outplanted back onto the reef (Chapters 4 and 5). My passion and dedication to the restoration of coral reefs intensified throughout my unique career history that was both circuitous, fortuitous, and at times seemed divinely guided.

In 1966, I was privileged to be part of a science expedition to the Virgin Islands to sample corals in the area for the future West Indies Marine Lab in St. Croix. My job was to use a hammer to break off pieces of beautiful live corals to send back in formalin jars to the main laboratory at Fairleigh Dickinson University in New Jersey. Today, this practice would never be allowed due to the global decline in coral. Little did I know then, that many years later, I would be growing coral reef species. First, for the aquarium trade that started from a research project at Harbor Branch Oceanographic Institute (HBOI), which evolved into a new program and company called ORA (Oceans, Reefs and Aquariums); later, for the reef itself at Mote Tropical Research Laboratory; and now through the Plant a Million Corals Foundation.

During my early career at HBOI and through my projects at ORA, I grew a diversity of marine species including: clams, oysters, fish, shrimp, and ornamental corals using new large-scale sustainable recirculating technologies. In the year 2000, the success of the ORA project demonstrated that it was possible to produce both thousands of clownfish and over a hundred thousand hard and soft corals for the aquarium trade (so they did not need to be taken from the wild, predominantly the Pacific Ocean). On one occasion, Philippe and Alexandra Cousteau (grandchildren of Jacques Cousteau) were touring the facilities and said, "Dave, why aren't you growing corals for the reef?" We agreed to work together in this direction and our first effort was to start a new program within the Philippe Cousteau Foundation called the "International Coral Restoration Initiative" (CRI). In addition to my volunteer work with the CRI, I accepted a position at the Mote Tropical Research Laboratory in the Florida Keys (what is now the Elizabeth Moore International Center for Coral Reef Restoration and Research) as the Executive Director of the lab and manager of the Coral Reef Restoration Program. My entry back into the world of corals and reef systems hit me like a rock. The annual updates from reef monitoring efforts showed substantially less coral cover each year, more frequent bleaching events and increases in disease occurrences, which collectively made me feel like there was very little hope for these creatures. This catalyzed me to think about how to tailor the large-scale aquaculture technologies that I had used in the past, to improve coral reefs. My work with aquaculture system designs and the scaling up of the production of marine organisms would give me quite an advantage for producing and scaling up the growth of corals for reef restoration efforts.

During my tenure at Mote, I also managed the Coral Reef Restoration Program where we were starting to grow some of the massive species of corals into culture and from sexual reproduction. While trying to transfer a fragile three-year-old Elkhorn colony, I accidently broke it into several small pieces. This Elkhorn colony was one of the first ever cultured from sexual reproduction (test tube corals) and raised in the laboratory. What started as an accident, however, turned out to be what the *New York Times* called my "Eureka Mistake" in an article they ran in 2014 (https://www.nytimes.com/2014/11/25/science/a-lifesaving-transplant-for-coral-reefs.html). The breaking of this coral into tiny pieces or *fragments* stimulated them to grow faster than normal and was the foundation of a game-changing technology now termed *micro-fragmentation* (Chapter 6). Micro-fragmentation is a fast way to produce large numbers of smaller coral colonies that are suitable for outplanting onto restoration sites more quickly than we ever thought possible for the massive *reef-building* species. Furthermore, when these fragments from the same colony (clones) reach the size that is appropriate to be outplanted and are then planted near each other, they fuse back together again (Chapter 7). This "Eureka Mistake" led to the technologies of micro-fragmentation and fusion (or *re-skinning*), which are now two incredibly valuable tools for active coral restoration because they dramatically reduce the time it takes to grow the corals while also increasing the numbers of corals grown for use in restoration efforts. In late 2018, I retired from the Mote Tropical Research Laboratory and started my own foundation, Plant a Million Corals. I vowed, as in the frequently viewed AARP video (https://youtu.be/_0F5cQfke64), that "I would not retire until I planted a million corals."

While micro-fragmentation allows us to grow corals faster than ever thought possible, they still need to survive the environmental stressors once they are outplanted. Consequently, we need to culture sufficient numbers of corals that can survive these stressors through both asexual and sexual reproduction (Chapter 8). The selection for diverse genotypes that can better withstand the increases in water temperature and ocean acidification that is caused by global warming is paramount (Chapters 9 and 10). Observations of all the parameters of survival, such as resistance and resiliency, for the whole biome community must be the science that drives restoration—as well as emerging technologies and engineering that can scale it to make economic sense (Chapters 22 and 23). There are numerous scientists and leaders in the field who have also made big contributions in their areas of expertise (Chapter 2)—and they all agreed that the time is now to bring all of the information together into the first comprehensive volume on active coral restoration. Our collective work, energy, and passion for the coral reefs of the world is what inspired me to move forward as editor of this book.

This volume is divided into four sections. Section I: *Overview*—provides important foundational information on the history and evolution of active coral reef restoration. Section II: *Biological Considerations and Methodologies*—is complete with five chapters that provide in-depth discussion of current methodologies for the development of land and field nurseries, sexual and asexual coral propagation in the laboratory setting, coral fusion, and genetic selection for resistance and resilience. Section III: *Case Studies from Around the World*—provides eleven case studies that illustrate what has been successful and lessons learned of what has not. Section IV: *The Future of Coral Reef Restoration*—discusses emerging technologies in the field of active coral restoration and what we should look forward to in the years to come. As the editor, it was my absolute pleasure to collaborate with the dedicated scientists and practitioners who worked tirelessly—many in remote areas—to develop the technologies and manage the restoration projects that are discussed in this book. My hope is that this volume will inspire generations to come to continue the practice of active coral restoration and hope well into the future.

REFERENCES

AARP. 2016. "Saving coral reefs one coral at a time." https://youtu.be/_0F5cQfke64.
Intergovernmental Panel on Climate Change. 2018. IPCC Special Report on the Ocean and Cryosphere in a Changing Climate. https://www.ipcc.ch/srocc/.
New York Times. 2014. "A life saving transplant for coral reefs." https://www.nytimes.com/2014/11/25/science/a-lifesaving-transplant-for-coral-reefs.html.
Precht, W. F. 2006. Coral Reef Restoration Handbook. CRC Taylor & Francis. Boca Raton, FL.

2

HISTORY OF REEF RESTORATION

Adam Smith, Boze Hancock, Nathan Cook, and David E. Vaughan

ABSTRACT

This chapter collates historical information about the people and organizations who have contributed to active reef restoration over the past 40 years. We include indigenous people, scientists, managers, communicators, educators, and businesses. We also present results from a global literature review of reef restoration that covers 52 countries, with the majority of projects conducted in the United States, the Philippines, Thailand, and Indonesia (together representing 40% of projects). Coral restoration case studies are dominated by short-term projects, with 58% of all projects reporting less than 18 months of monitoring of the restored sites. Overall, 75% of the coral restoration projects focused primarily on fast-growing branching corals, 28% involved the coral genus *Acropora*, while 9% of studies included a single species—*Acropora cervicornis*. Overall, direct transplantation studies reported an average of 51% survival, with 20% reporting >90% survival of transplanted corals.

It is difficult to measure the number of people and organizations that are interested and involved in active coral reef restoration. In this chapter we shine the light on 20 individuals who have pioneered and contributed to global reef restoration. We make three recommendations to improve the history of reef restoration: (1) develop and maintain a global database of reef restoration knowledge, people, and projects; (2) develop and deliver a global reef restoration training and education program to one million people by 2025; and (3) identify 100 global priority reef restoration demonstration locations.

INTRODUCTION

The history of reef restoration has rarely been written, with the exception of Singapore (Chin Soon et al. 2017) and Japan (Omori 2010). We have conducted global reviews of scientific literature and practitioners that highlight major developments in the science and methods of those involved in reef restoration. The purpose of this chapter is to share the collective knowledge of a community of scientists and restoration practitioners who have been working both independently and collaboratively to restore populations of corals throughout the world. By sharing lessons learned from the people, organizations, and projects over approximately 40 years of experience of coral propagation and coral transplantation, we want to increase the success of others' efforts and accelerate conservation and restoration on a global scale.

CORAL REEFS

A coral reef is an underwater ecosystem that is characterized by reef-building corals. Reefs are formed of colonies of coral polyps held together by calcium carbonate. When alive, corals are colonies of small animals called polyps, arranged in diverse shapes. Reef-building or hermatypic corals live only in the photic zone (above 50 m), the depth to which sufficient sunlight penetrates the water. It takes approximately 10 thousand years for coral polyps to form a reef, and between 100 thousand and 30 million years for a fully mature reef to form.

Coral reefs occupy a small percentage (less than 0.1%) of the world's oceans, but they contain a disproportionately high share of its biodiversity. Coral reefs are vital for food, tourism, coastal protection, and many other ecosystem services.

Coral reefs are fragile, partly because they are sensitive to water conditions. Coral can survive short-term disturbances, but if the conditions that lead to the expulsion of the symbiotic algae (zooxanthellae) persist, the coral can die within a period of one day to two or three weeks. Mass mortality of coral reefs has increased in frequency throughout the world due to global warming, coastal development, declining water quality, and destructive fishing.

CORAL RESTORATION

Coral restoration is a term that is commonly used by scientists. Coral restoration is closely allied with (and often used interchangeably with) reef restoration, rehabilitation, remediation, transplantation, recovery, and intervention. In the United States and Australia, the terms remediation and intervention are more commonly employed in industry, the development of public policy, and the civil services. Coral farming, gardening, and coral nursery are often used by practitioners, divers, and the tourism industry.

In this chapter the authors consider coral reef restoration in a broad sense and include both active manipulation of reef building corals as well as activities designed to raise the profile and awareness of restoration and generate the social license needed to conduct active restoration.

The history of coral restoration can be categorized into distinct phases, which can be described as the addition of species and habitats or the removal of species (Figure 2.1). Early scientific pilot scale projects in the 1970s and 80s focused on methodology. Projects in the 2000s began to focus on increasing densities of endangered Caribbean corals and fast-growing staghorn corals. In the 2010s the global decline in coral reef health from climate change, cyclones, and coastal development resulted in great prioritization, communication, and action of coral reef restoration throughout the Caribbean, Pacific, and Indian Oceans including methods to *scale-up* coral restoration. Coral restoration has primarily focused on ecological aims such as coral growth and survivorship; however, more recently, social, economic, technological, and political outcomes have been seen as important factors.

Documenting the history of reef restoration is important because it allows us to understand our past and be more informed to take action in the future. We have approached this chapter by looking at key groups of active coral reef restorers: indigenous, scientists, managers, communicators, and educators. We have also provided our opinions on the leading individuals and organizations that have contributed to coral reef restoration (Table 2.1, Figure 2.2). The great men, women, and organizations in our history were innovators who were curious, responded

History of Reef Restoration

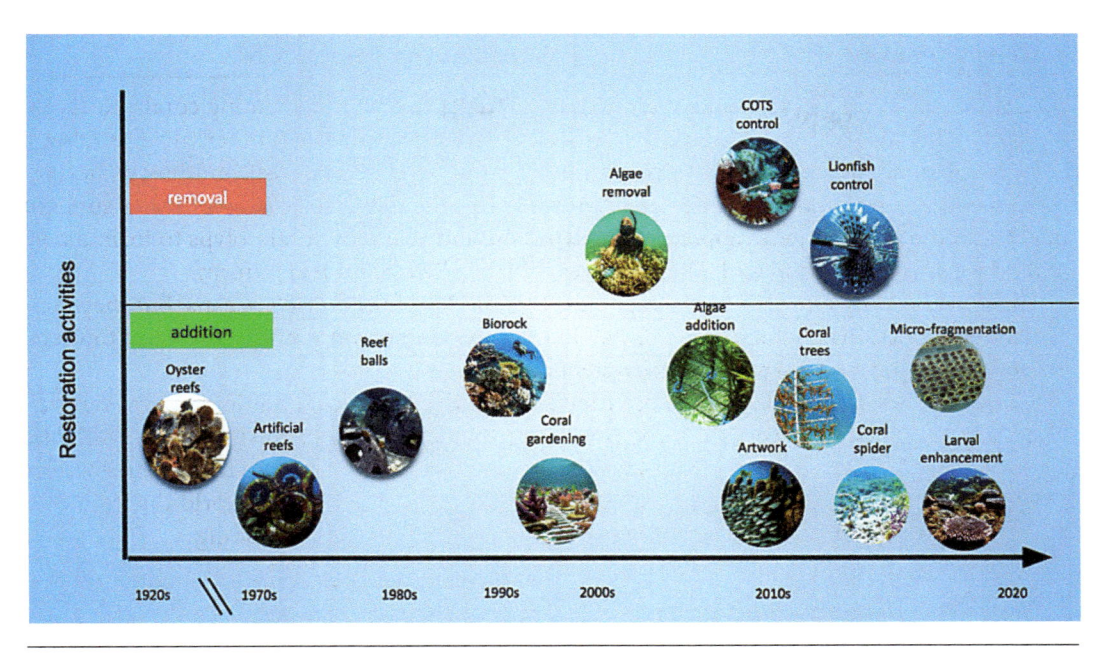

Figure 2.1 Chronology of the methods of reef restoration (Smith et al. 2018).

Table 2.1 Chronology of individuals and organizations and their contribution to coral reef restoration

Date	Name	Contribution
1979	Tom Goreau and Wolf Hilbertz	Biorock
1980s	Eduardo Gomez	Philippines coral and clam restoration
1984	National Oceanic Atmospheric Administration	Hawaii coral conservation lab
1987	Austin Bowden-Kerby	Coral farming
1988	Vicki Harriot and David Fisk	Coral transplantation—GBR
1990s	Chou Loke Ming	Coral restoration—Singapore
1993	Todd Barber	Reef Balls
1994	Baruch Rinkevich	Coral gardening—Red Sea
1997	David Lennon	Artificial reefs
2002	Ken Nedimyer	Coral Restoration Foundation
2003	Reef Resilience Network	Training
2006	Jason deCaires Taylor	Underwater sculptures
2006	Bill Precht	*Coral Reef Restoration Handbook*
2007	Mars Inc	Coral spiders—Indonesia
2009	ARRA Acropora coalition	NOAA, TNC, Mote, CRF
2010	Alasdair Edwards	*Reef Rehabilitation Manual*
2010	Margaret Miller	Sexual reproduction in coral

Continued

Date	Name	Contribution
2010	David Vaughan	Micro-fragmentation, Mote Marine Lab, FL
2011	Johnson et al.	Caribbean *Acropora* restoration guide: best practices for propagation and population enhancement
2011	Peter Harrison	Larval enhancement
2011	U.S. Navy	Restore reef after Port Royal ship grounding
2013	Lisa Carne	Fragments of Hope registered—Belize
2015	SECORE	Tetrapods—spawning coral restoration project
2016	Coral Restoration Consortium	Foster collaboration
2017	The Nature Conservancy	Caribbean Coral Hubs
2017	Great Barrier Reef Marine Park Authority	Reef Resilience Blueprint
2017	Australian Institute of Marine Science	Reef Restoration and Adaptation Program
2017	Ruth Gates	Assisted evolution of corals—Hawaii
2017	Mexican Government	Goal of 260,000 corals planted by 2022
2017	Reef Restoration Foundation	First coral nursery in the Great Barrier Reef
2018	Australian Government	Reef Restoration and Adaptation Program
2018	Reef Ecologic	Coral gardening—Great Barrier Reef
2018	Ken Nedimyer	Reef Renewal International—Bonaire
2018	Plant a Million Corals Foundation	Assisting ten Caribbean projects and TNC
2018	Coral Restoration Consortium	NOAA assisted working groups
2020	National Environmental Science Programme	Global review of reef restoration

to crises, made mistakes, and shared their knowledge. We acknowledge that our chronology is based on published and unpublished information, but is biased towards English-speaking countries and individuals.

INDIGENOUS PEOPLE AND REEF RESTORATION

There is no published information on reef restoration by indigenous people. The earliest confirmed indigenous planting of coral was the 1940s at Turtle Bay, Cairns (personal communication, Gudjugudju).

SCIENTIFIC PIONEERS OF REEF RESTORATION

In the early 1900s, *hard hat* diving was available for a few individuals to observe the underwater world. The earliest published research on coral transplantation methods was from the 1928–29 Great Barrier Reef Expedition on Low Isles. The scientists used hard hat diving helmets and glass viewers to conduct coral growth experiments. They published a book called *A Year on the Great Barrier Reef 1928–29 the Yonge Expedition*. The invention of the self-contained underwater

History of Reef Restoration

Figure 2.2 The pioneers of coral reef restoration. Top row: Tom Goreau, Wolf Hilbertz, Eduardo Gomez, Austin Bowden-Kerby; second row: Vicki Harriot, David Fisk, Todd Barber, Baruch Rinkevich; third row: Ken Nedimyer, David Lennon, Chou Loke Ming, Nathan Cook; fourth row: Bill Precht, Alastair Edwards, David Vaughan, Jason deCaires Taylor; fifth row: Peter Harrison, Frank Mars, Kirstin Marhaver, Ruth Gates.

breathing apparatus (SCUBA) in 1942 and subsequent commercialization of equipment and training opened up access to coral reefs for more people and scientists.

It is challenging to find who was the first modern scientific reef restorer. There were several pioneers in the Caribbean, United States, and Pacific. These pioneers included Tom Goreau and Wolf Hilbertz who patented Biorock®, a method using mineral accretion technology and steel and electricity to increase the rate of calcium carbonate deposition. Tom said, "No one believes what we do is possible until they see it themselves. Growing bright coral reefs that are swarming with fish in a few years in places that were barren deserts is something everybody thinks can't be done—but has been done in nearly 30 countries with only small donations, mostly from local people who remember how their reef used to be and realize they must grow more corals now." The team of Goreau and Hilbertz continued on a path of research and development that spanned over three decades, but ended with the untimely death of Hilbertz in 2007. Further development of the Biorock method continues through the leadership of Goreau as acting president of the Global Coral Reef Alliance.

Dr. Austin Bowden-Kerby (Figure 2.3) is a true pioneer and possibly the most published scientist in reef restoration (Figure 2.4). In his own words, he began:

> *Plugging broken frags into dead corals in the 1980s as it is was a natural no-brainer* (he planted his first corals in the Pacific in Chuuk in 1987). *I was apparently the first person to work on the Caribbean* Acropora *corals—starting in 1993* (he developed and adapted various reef restoration methods including A-frame, steel and wire mesh, cookies, and rope strung between two tables). *As far as methods: plugging broken frags into dead corals I began in the 1980s and the A-frame I developed in 1994 in Puerto Rico for my thesis. The steel frame coral nursery table design I copied from the ICLARM giant clam culture tables of the Solomon Islands, where I traveled for a coral farming workshop in 1997 at Marau Sound. The wire mesh tray was my invention from 1997, tying the corals onto sea shells with fishing line and weaving them into the mesh. This was improved when I learned from Simon Gower, a Solomon Island marine ornamentals trader, that you could make and use concrete discs, but he used solid ones without any eyes and he had not figured out how to keep them from tipping over. He had also used super glue instead of a cable tie or fishing line, so we joined the two ideas and made the first perforated cookies in 1997. The cookies grew in size over the years with my work to accommodate much bigger fragments and to grow a much larger coral before outplanting—that was much the focus of the Fiji work from 2000–2007.* (These turned out to be ideal methods for palmata coral in the Caribbean and the corymobose, digitate, and table form corals of the Pacific). *The rope method—strung between two tables—I copied pretty much from the seaweed farmers of the Philippines. The micro-fragmenting of staghorn tips—I had never called it that, but I had been doing that for some time, since 2005 or so—with multiple very tiny tips from the same mother colony that would otherwise die in the environment being plugged into a wet cement ball. The pegged rope method of outplanting I developed in 2009 for the Belize work. The places presently using these methods are Belize, Dominican Republic, Kiribati, and Fiji, but I have shared the manual with those in Thailand, Malaysia, the Philippines, and Indonesia. The manual was published by Punta Cana Ecological Foundation in Dominican Republic and is from 2014.*

Dr. Baruch Rinkevich is the godfather of reef restoration in the Red Sea. He completed a Science degree between 1972–82 at Tel Aviv University in Israel and a post doctorate at Scripps Institute of Oceanography in California, USA.

In our communication he wrote: *"I am pleased to hear about the reef restoration symposium in Australia and to see the developments in this discipline, something that 2–3 decades ago, was just a dream. It is unfortunate that I'll not attend this meeting, to meet my colleagues from Australia that till 2–3 years ago, many displayed reservations about the option of combining the phrases 'coral reef restoration' and 'Great Barrier Reef (GBR), Australia.'"*

Figure 2.3 Austin Bowden-Kerby with one of his early coral restoration experiments.

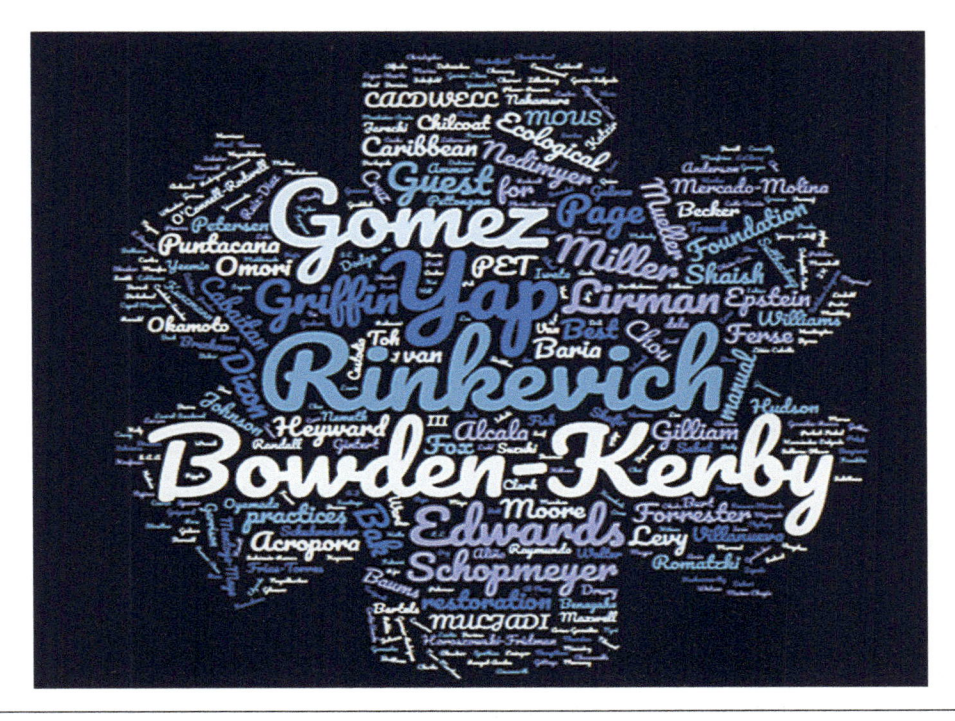

Figure 2.4 A word cloud of the scientists who have contributed to the academic literature on reef restoration (the larger the name the larger the contribution) (Smith et al. 2018).

According to Dr Rinkevich, coral reef restoration was guided by the notion of *gardening*, influenced by the silviculture discipline (forestation). The aims and methodologies were further distinguished between the two major phases in reef restoration: the nursery and the transplantation phases. Much of the literature has been devoted to develop and to support ideas and methodologies for both of these phases (Chapter 3). Dr. Rinkevich wrote:

During the last two decades, the 'gardening notion' as the cutting edge of coral restoration, and other approaches for reef restoration, have surmounted four major obstructions, all are currently satisfactorily deciphered:

    (a) Developing the needed credentials for farming a wide variety of coral species (now >100 species) from worldwide-distributed reefs in different types of nurseries

    (b) The ability to develop stocks of coral colonies: one of these methods is employing the use of coral 'nubbins' and another approach is growing coral colonies from larvae

    (c) Documentation that nursery farmed coral colonies perform well in their 'new homes,' following transplantation

    (d) Verification of the low-cost gardening approach (down to 0.17 and 0.19 US$/coral colony for farming and transplantation phases, respectively).

Now, this discipline is facing its fifth challenge—performing a large, ecologically profound, spatially relevant restoration act (hundreds of thousands to millions of coral colonies/site) to reveal the ecological impacts of large-scale transplantation acts. In the last five years we have been facing a new development: the employment of ecological engineering approaches and suggestions for genetic/molecular biology tools.

Ken Nedimyer (Figure 2.5) is the founder and former president of the Coral Restoration Foundation and Director of Reef Renewal International. By 1998, he saw that with climate change and ocean acidification, his Florida reefs were in serious trouble and he started to consider how to expand his live rock aquaculture into growing live coral reefs (Chapter 4). In 2002 he began an offshore coral garden in the Florida Keys. His years of experimentation involved developing better methods and improved coral nursery techniques, training volunteers, and developing effective ways to transplant the corals onto the nearby reefs.

Ken's persistence paid off and led to the formation of the nonprofit Coral Restoration Foundation in 2007 and the development of one of the world's largest offshore coral nurseries. In

Figure 2.5 Ken Nedimyer working on coral trees in the Caribbean.

2012, Ken began nursery programs in Colombia, South America and Bonaire (Netherlands Antilles) (Chapter 20); those programs are now producing thousands of corals per year that are being transplanted onto their local reefs. In 2014, Ken helped start the Coral Restoration Foundation International, to work on developing coral nursery and restoration programs throughout the Caribbean over the next five years. Ken's story and the results of his work addressing ocean issues have resulted in him being given several prestigious awards, including being named as a 2012 CNN Hero for "Defending the Planet" and SCUBA Diving Magazine's "Sea Hero of the Year."

It is important to recognize that individuals are parts of teams and collaborations. Ken's work was strongly linked with the National Oceanic and Atmospheric Administration (NOAA) and The Nature Conservancy (TNC) through the 2005 TNC-NOAA Community-Based Restoration Program (CRP) Partnership project and the 2009 NOAA American Recovery and Reinvestment Act (ARRA), with funding as part of a coalition of eight restoration interests.

Professor Chou Loke Ming has tested many reef restoration strategies in Singapore's sedimented waters. It started in the 1990s with the Marine Conservation Group of the Nature Society (Singapore) mobilizing over 400 volunteers to shift coral colonies and reef invertebrates. However, the early efforts were largely unsuccessful. Less than 11% of the transplants survived due to the poor choice of recipient site (a shallow area easily overgrown with algae and constantly subjected to surge and heavy sedimentation) as well as improper securing methods (transplanted colonies were only wedged between boulders without the use of adhesives, and were thus easily dislodged by wave action) (Chou and Tun 1997). This episode led to improvements in coral relocation techniques and subsequent mitigation projects. These included the relocation of corals from Labrador Park (for the installation of new power and water cables; Kesava 2007a), Sultan Shoal (for the construction of a mega container terminal; Chew 2014), and Pulau Semakau (for the disposal of incinerated waste; Tan 2015). Transplant survival rates for coral relocation projects are currently an estimated 70–80% (Chew 2014).

Coral restoration in Singapore has necessitated the use of specialized techniques to circumvent the problems of heavy sedimentation and unstable substrates. These strategies include the deployment of artificial substrates known as *reef enhancement units* to increase opportunities for coral recruitment, rearing of coral fragments on nursery frames, and transplantation.

Reef restoration in Thailand has had a long history with a number of key players experimenting with innovative ideas and implementing new projects to progress the marine conservation agenda. Nowhere in Thailand was this testing more active than on the small island of Koh Tao in southern Thailand. In the late 1990s, Thai groups such as the Thai Royal Navy and Khun Jintana, known locally as Queen of the Giant Clams, worked with local businesses to disseminate important knowledge about coral reef ecology and marine conservation in general. Small coral restoration projects including artificial reefs, and the islands first biorock project were implemented in 2005 by local community groups lead by Devrim and Kean Zahir and supported by the local community through the Koh Tao Dive Operators Club.

Since 2006–2007, Chad Scott of New Heaven Reef Conservation Program and Nathan Cook of Eco Koh Tao have implemented and expanded the scale and scope of reef restoration projects, including artificial reefs, coral nurseries, coral gardening, and biorock. Chad Scott, with Dr. James True of Prince of Songkhla University, conducted one of the first larval enhancement experiments on Koh Tao in 2010 and has been continuing reef monitoring while expanding. Many of these projects were conducted in partnership with the Save Koh Tao Community group.

Dr. David Vaughan's history in his own words: *"My career was in aquaculture production research and development and included scaling up hatchery production of clams, oysters, fish, shrimp, and marine ornamentals such as the clownfish (Nemo). I scaled up Pacific corals for the aquarium trade as well, under the development of Oceans, Reefs and Aquariums as its founder and president. While showing the grandchildren of Jacques Y. Cousteau around, Philippe mentioned to me that I "missed the point" of culturing corals for the aquarium trade, when I could be growing corals for the reef. In 2000, he and I founded the International Coral Restoration Initiative to do just that. I worked at Mote Marine Lab in the Florida Keys for several years and developed methods for restoration of the massive corals including micro-fragmentation and re-skinning, and now propose to not retire until I plant a million corals through my foundation, Plant a Million Corals!"*

Professor Peter Harrison is the founding Director of the Marine Ecology Research Centre at Southern Cross University. He was one of a consortium of scientists who *discovered* mass coral spawning in the 1980s and is currently leading research into sexual reproduction and larval enhancement of coral reefs with field projects in Australia and the Philippines.

MANAGEMENT SUPPORT FOR CORAL REEF RESTORATION

Management actions for coral reefs may be either in the form of passive or indirect measures, or in the form of active or direct interventions. The former generally involve improving the management of anthropogenic activities that are impeding natural recovery processes, and include many potential tools including legislation, policy, plans, and guidelines. One of the most effective tools for coral reef health is a well-managed marine protected area. Active physical restoration and/or biological restoration interventions may involve coral nurseries, transplantation of corals, and other biota to degraded areas.

There were two historical rationales for management support of reef restoration. The first reason was replacing declining coral reefs in the Asia\Pacific and Red Sea. The second reason, led by the United States, focused on restoring the damage, including both structural damage and the services lost from impacts to coral reefs from events such as ship groundings. The early leader in management of reef restoration was NOAA, which developed legislation in 1973 to protect and restore habitats. The legislation required companies to restore the public resources injured by discrete environmental incidents such as chemical or oil spills, the release of pollutants from an identifiable catastrophic event, or from physical damage to the habitat such as dredging for port expansion or land reclamation (e.g., NOAA 1997). The initial legislation was described in the Comprehensive Environmental Response, Cleanup, and Liability Act (1980) and the Oil Pollution Act (1990). For each incident addressed under such legislation, the damage first needed to be quantified, prior to designing restoration, in order to make the community *whole*. The acts dictate that restoration is undertaken to compensate the public for losses or injuries to natural resources under public ownership and held in trust by government managers, and that restoration includes the services that those natural resources would have provided. This legislation continues to influence the quantification of ecosystem services from multiple habitats, including bivalve habitat, and is being expanded in the U.S. section of the Gulf of Mexico through the *Restore Act* (2012), legislating the response to the Deep Water Horizon oil spill.

In the United States, the U.S. Coral Reef Task Force, established by Presidential Executive Order in 1998, leads U.S. efforts to preserve and protect coral reef ecosystems. The National Coral Reef Action Strategy was developed in 2002 based on the U.S. National Action Plan to Conserve Coral Reefs.

The Australian pioneers of coral transplantation and the links to management were Vicki Harriot and David Fisk. They published *Coral Transplantation as a Reef Management Option* for the Great Barrier Reef Marine Park Authority in 1988.

Edwards & Gomez (2007) concluded that *"there is little that managers can do in the face of the large-scale 'natural' drivers of degradation such as climate-change-related mass bleaching, storms, tsunamis, and disease outbreaks."* Some scientists and manager have recently argued that this message may be overly pessimistic in relation to large-scale drivers such as ocean warming and that the climate resilience of corals may be augmented through assisted evolution (van Oppen et al. 2015). Such innovative management methods represent a major change to our thinking about and approach to coral reef restoration (i.e., a shifting paradigm) and would increase the probability of survival of corals used for restoring degraded reefs.

In 2017, as a response to unprecedented coral bleaching and mass mortality, the Great Barrier Reef Marine Park Authority (GBRMPA) held a summit and published the GBRMPA Reef Resilience Blueprint (2017). This document identified 10 key initiatives that focused on actions to deliver maximum benefits for reef resilience. One of the initiatives was the broadscale implementation of active, localized restoration. This priority initiative focuses on three activity areas: testing, improving, and scaling up local-scale reef restoration methods—based on the best available science—for potential application across the resilience network facilitating opportunities for community and industry participation in local-scale restoration, and researching and developing large-scale restoration methods.

To achieve these initiatives and protect the reef, GBRMPA is working toward:

- Developing a policy to provide guidance on restoration activities in the GBR Marine Park;
- Establishing restoration demonstration site(s), with supporting communication material, to test, improve, and where appropriate, scale-up restoration methods; and
- Developing guidance for community participation in restoration activities, including *reef restoration toolkits* to support localized restoration activities and support the establishment of a research program on large-scale restoration methods.

COMMUNICATION AND EDUCATION ON REEF RESTORATION

Reef restoration communicators are authors of books, manuals, and scientific papers, as well as photographs, films, TED talks, and underwater art. The notable people in this field include Margos (1974), Jaap (2000), Precht (2006), Edwards and Gomez (2007), Edwards (2010), and Johnson et al. (2011), along with David Vaughan (2021) who wrote manuals for practitioners and scientists.

Jason de Caires Taylor gained international notoriety in 2006 with the creation of the world's first underwater sculpture park, situated off the west coast of Grenada in the West Indies. Now listed as one of the Top 25 Wonders of the World by National Geographic, the park was instrumental in the government declaring the site a National Marine Protected Area. In 2009, he went on to co-found Museo Subacuático de Arte, a vast collection of over 500 of his sculptural works that are installed between Cancun and Isla Mujeres in Mexico. He has since installed the Coralarium in the Maldives and is working on a project for the GBR.

We rely heavily on handbooks and manuals to collate the knowledge on coral restoration and translate it into projects. There are several reef restoration/rehabilitation manuals written by various professionals including: Precht (2006), Edwards and Gomez (2007), Edwards (2010), and Johnson et al. (2011). *Active Coral Restoration*, the book you are now reading, was edited by David Vaughan. The *Reef Rehabilitation Manual* (Edwards 2010) provides detailed, hands-on advice regarding how to carry out coral reef rehabilitation in a responsible and cost-effective manner. The rehabilitation project cycle was split into five main stages by Edwards (2010) (Figure 2.6).

It was only recently that sociocultural and economic considerations have been regarded as essential components of coral restoration effectiveness (Hein et al. 2017). They proposed 10 indicators to measure reef restoration projects, including six ecological indicators and four sociocultural and economic indicators (Figure 2.7).

The importance of educating professionals in proper reef restoration techniques is essential. Globally funded training programs such as the European Commission project "Developing ubiquitous restoration practices for Indo-Pacific coral reefs" in 2004 (Chou 2011) and the IOC/WESTPAC (Intergovernment Oceanographic Commission for Western Pacific) Workshop on Coral Reef Restoration Techniques in the Western Pacific Region in 2012 (Chavanich et al. 2014) have played key roles in capacity building for Southeast Asian marine scientists. German Mendez Cozumel developed the Cozumel Coral Reef Restoration Program in 2013 to help with restoring coral reefs and to conduct training programs. The Reef Resilience Network and Conservation Training have developed a short online course—*Advanced Studies in Reef Resilience*—which has a module for Reef Restoration.

There are popular (over one million views) TED talks by scientists such as Kristen Marhaver and artist Jason deCaires Taylor. Dr. Kristen Marhaver's work combines classic scientific

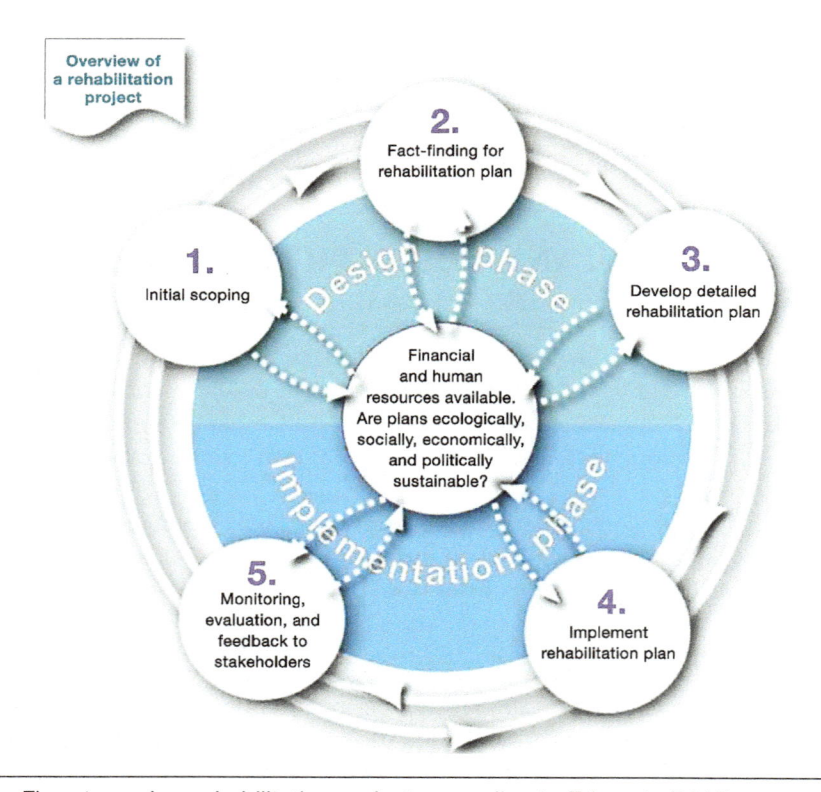

Figure 2.6 Five stages in a rehabilitation project, according to Edwards (2010).

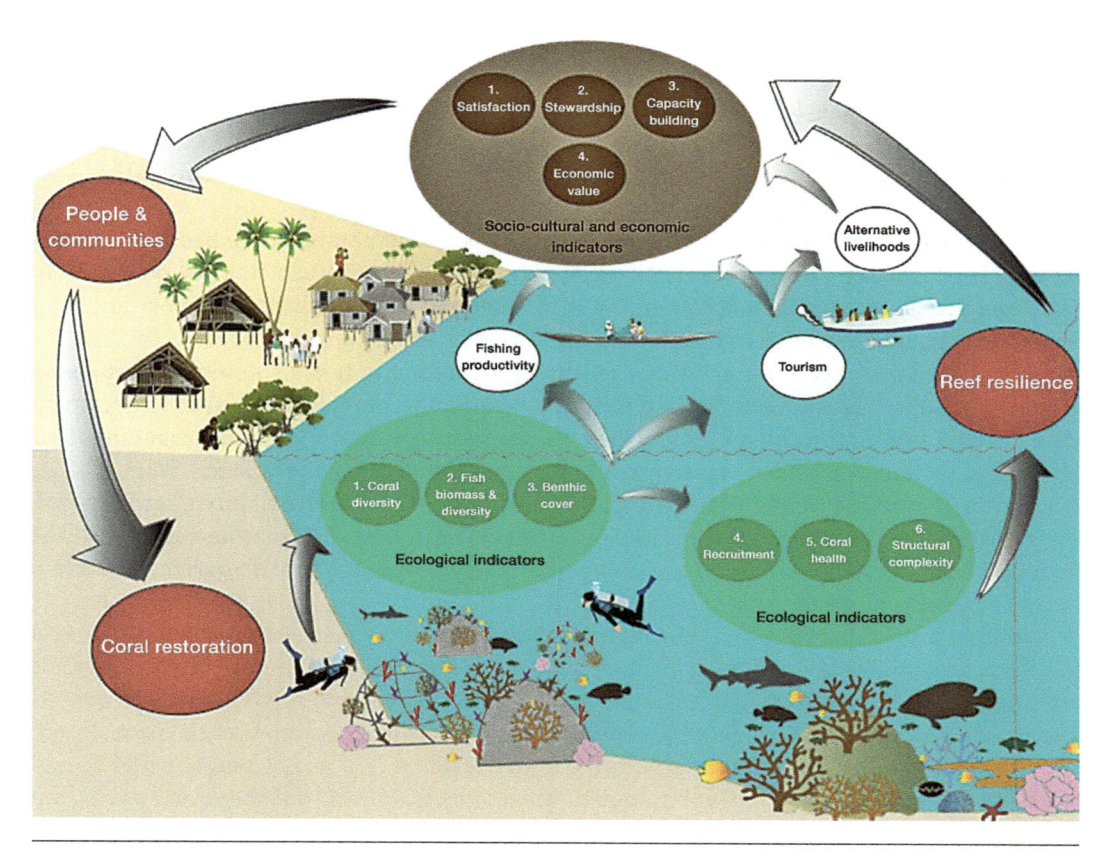

Figure 2.7 Illustration of the framework of positive interactions that link people and communities, coral restoration, and reef resilience. The six proposed ecological indicators are highlighted by green ovals; the four proposed sociocultural and economic indicators are highlighted by brown ovals (from Hein et al. 2017).

methods with new technologies to help threatened coral species survive their early life stages. She was the first person to rear juveniles of the endangered Caribbean Pillar Coral.

THE ROLE OF PRIVATE BUSINESS IN REEF RESTORATION

Private businesses and individuals have played an important part in the field of reef restoration. We describe a small number of businesses and people who have been important in the history of reef restoration.

Todd Barber's family had owned a dive store since 1979 and Todd naturally became an avid scuba diver with over 10,000 dives. After a high-flying career in computer and management consultancy, Todd returned to his first love, the *hobby and science* of marine reefs, in order to invent the Reef Ball and implement the concept in over 3,500 projects in 48 countries. A Reef Ball is a designed artificial reef that is used to restore ailing coral reefs and to create new fishing and scuba diving sites. Reef Balls are made of a special, marine-friendly concrete that is designed to mimic natural reef systems. They are used around the world to create habitats for fish and other marine and freshwater species. Reef Balls are made in many sizes in order to best match the natural reef type that is being mimicked. The most common sizes range from 0.1–1.8 m and 3–1,814 kg.

The business of reef restoration includes aquaculture, insurance, conservation, and tourism. The Nature Conservancy, Coral Restoration Foundation, Mars Foundation, Plant a Million Corals Foundation, Reef Renewal International, and SECORE are international leaders in coral restoration. In 2017, the Reef Restoration Foundation deployed Australia's first coral nursery using methodologies pioneered by the Coral Restoration Foundation (Nedimyer 2011).

David Lennon is an innovative businessman and has operated as a director of Reef Ball Australia since 1999. In 2008 he developed Sustainable Oceans International, and in 2012, Reef Arabia. He has designed ridge modules, seawall titles, and other interesting habitats and has been involved in industrial scale restoration activities in multiple countries.

A reef restoration project in North Sulawesi is one of David's favorite projects because the Newmont gold mine was closing, which meant their funding of hospitals, schools, and roads would end. Subsequently, they decided to fund construction of reefs that would replace reefs damaged by blast fishing and help boost the local commercial fishery. The positive result of this corporate, socially responsible investment is that this initial outlay contributes to producing fish for the locals indefinitely, even though the mine has closed. Newmont hired David to pick locations, design the reefs, and train the local fishermen in how to construct Reef Balls. The fishermen then went on to make over 3,000 units by hand; the coral growth proliferated and it is now a popular dive site.

Through his company Reef Arabia, David constructed a reef in Qatar from coral rubble that had been relocated from a shipping channel that was dredged for the new port. He planned the coral mitigation and offsets for the project and included relocation of 800 m^3 of coral rubble. People often overlook the value of the rubble, but it is wonderfully productive material and worth saving. As a resource, it is great to build with because it is already teeming with life.

David designed the prototypes of unique *ridge modules* specifically for the Arabian Gulf, but they are excellent for other areas and are about to be used in the United States. This concrete reef unit is designed to look more natural, provide substrate for attaching relocated or fragged corals, and has caves designed for local fish, such as grouper.

Off the coast of Indonesia, Mars Inc. has been working since 2007 to rebuild damaged sections of coral reef and to establish a marine protected area (Chapter 18). Frank Mars, one of the owners of the Mars Corporation, decided to implement a program to rehabilitate a coral reef in South Sualwesi. The villagers of Badi prepared *spiders* made from steel that were then coated in sand. The spiders are used as frames to place young coral in areas where the reef needs rehabilitating. Pieces of young coral are tied to the frame, which is then placed firmly on the sea floor. Each month the project will run for around three days, and each working day the Badi islanders will aim to place around 250 spiders around the edge of the island's reef flats. After a year, most places that have had spiders in place, show good coral regrowth. After two years the spiders are no longer visible, but covered by abundant new coral. This may be the world's largest coral reef restoration program with dimensions of over 8,000 sq. m and 8,645 spiders installed.

Not to be confused with the Mars Corporation, the Modular Artificial Reef Structure, a.k.a. MARS, was designed by Alex Goad in 2013 specifically to assist with the coral farming industry. Its ceramic surface is designed to house transplanted corals. Transplanted corals can be continually divided as they grow and eventually transplanted back to natural reefs.

Stewart Christie is the co-founder and CEO of the Reef Restoration Foundation, and in 2017 set up the first coral nursery at Fitzroy Island, Cairn, in the Great Barrier Reef Marine Park. Australia is stepping up efforts to help repair some of the damage the Great Barrier Reef has sustained, pledging over half a billion Australian dollars (around US$379 million) to an extensive recovery effort. Over $100 million of the funding is for reef restoration over a six-year period.

SECORE International is developing and testing techniques to raise and handle large amounts of coral offspring. SECORE and partners have designed small coral settlement substrates that self-attach to the reefs, enabling seeding coral recruits to join the reef in meaningful numbers. SECORE uses a multidisciplinary strategy combining research, active reef restoration, education, and outreach to help coral reefs. They work with a global network of scientists, public aquarium professionals, and local authorities, partners, and stakeholders.

GLOBAL LITERATURE REVIEW

To collate the latest knowledge of coral restoration, a global literature review was conducted (Boström-Einarsson et al. 2019; Boström-Einarsson et al. 2020) which assembled case studies and descriptions of coral restoration methods from four sources: (1) the primary literature (i.e. published peer-reviewed scientific literature), (2) grey literature (e.g., scientific reports and technical summaries from experts in the field), (3) online descriptions (e.g., blogs and online videos describing projects), and (4) an online survey targeting restoration practitioners (www.coralrestorationsurvey.com). We included only those case studies, which actively conducted coral restoration (i.e., at least one stage of scleractinian coral life-history was involved). The key dates from a historical perspective of scientific peer review literature are: in 1993, the substrate stabilization method was published; in 1996, substrate stabilization-electric was published; in 1997, coral gardening was published; and in 2002, larval enhancement was published (Figure 2.8). There was a massive spike in reef restoration studies in 2017 that was partially due to the survey methodology that included scientific and practitioner studies.

Coral transplantation is a commonly employed tool in reef restoration that involves securing whole colonies, fragments, or juveniles onto a degraded area with adhesives such as marine epoxy, concrete, and wires (reviewed by Rinkevich 2005; Edwards and Gomez 2007; Edwards 2010; Gomez et al. 2010; Omori 2010; Young et al. 2012). It hastens recovery processes of degraded reefs by increasing coral cover, biodiversity, and habitat complexity (Lindahl 2003). The coral *gardening* concept (Rinkevich 1995) involves corals reared in nurseries (on land or in water) to a suitable size before they are transplanted to degraded areas.

The earliest developed and most common method of coral restoration (used in 70% of reviewed projects, Boström-Einarsson et al. 2019) involves transplantation of coral fragments, which, in essence, could be seen as a simulation of asexual reproduction through fragmentation (Edwards and Gomez 2007). This technique is also called *asexual propagation* or *fragmentation*. Coral restoration involves many different approaches and technologies depending on the requirements of the situation. It can involve heavy equipment like cranes, graders, bulldozers, barges, or excavators, and also hand processes like the planting of corals. It can involve high-tech laboratory processes such as those applied in genetic engineering and micro-fragmentation.

In some situations, such as ship groundings, coral restorative work is handled entirely by professionals working with skilled operators and technicians. In others, ordinary local community members, divers, citizen scientists, and even tourists may do much of the work, acquiring skills as the project proceeds.

A total of 52 countries (Boström-Einarsson et al. 2019) (Figure 2.9(a)) were identified in which coral restoration projects have occurred, with the majority of projects conducted in the United States, the Philippines, Thailand, and Indonesia (together representing 40% of projects). We identified 329 case studies of coral restoration, of which 195 were from the scientific literature, 79 were sourced from the grey literature (i.e., reports and online descriptions), and 55 were responses to our survey for restoration practitioners (Boström-Einarsson et al. 2018; Figure 2.9(b) and (c)).

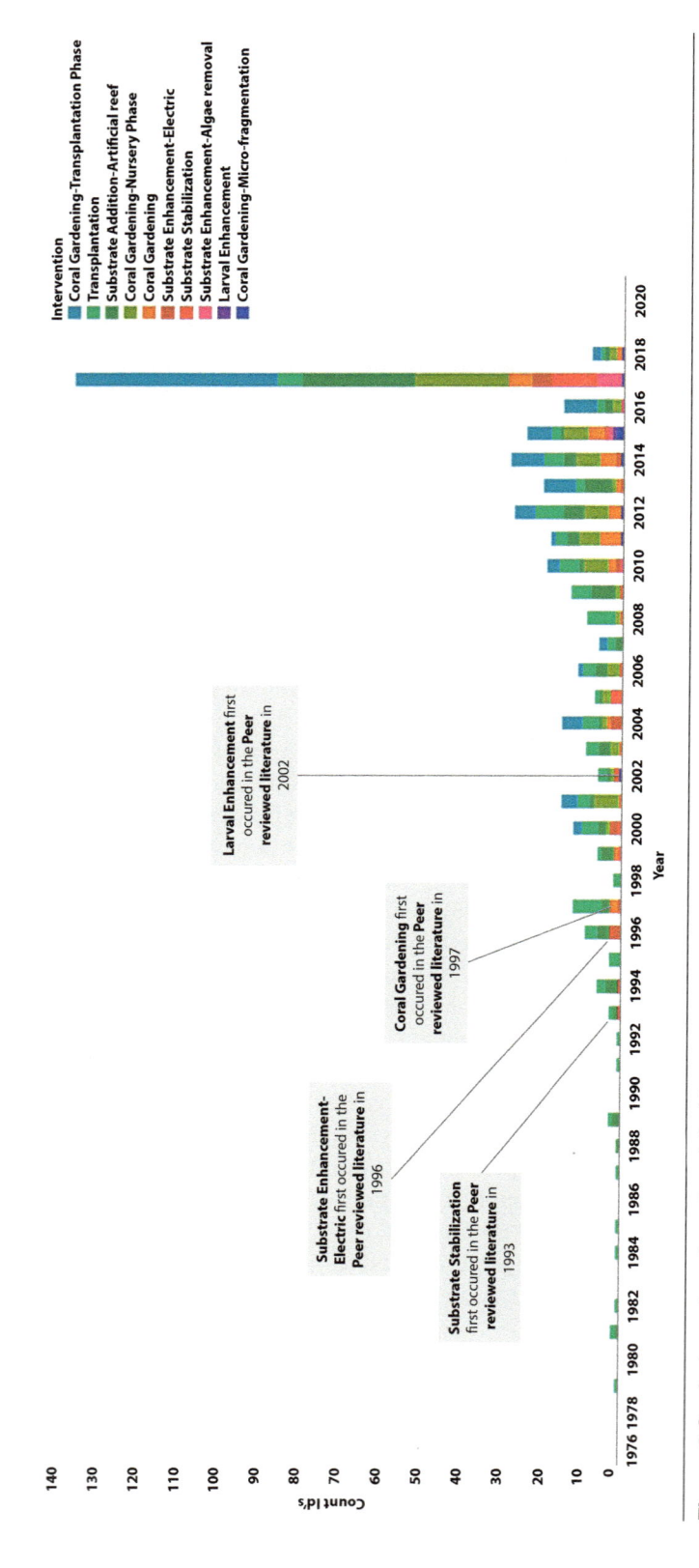

Figure 2.8 A chronology from the global literature review of the major developments in reef restoration and intervention. This included peer reviewed and practitioner surveys.

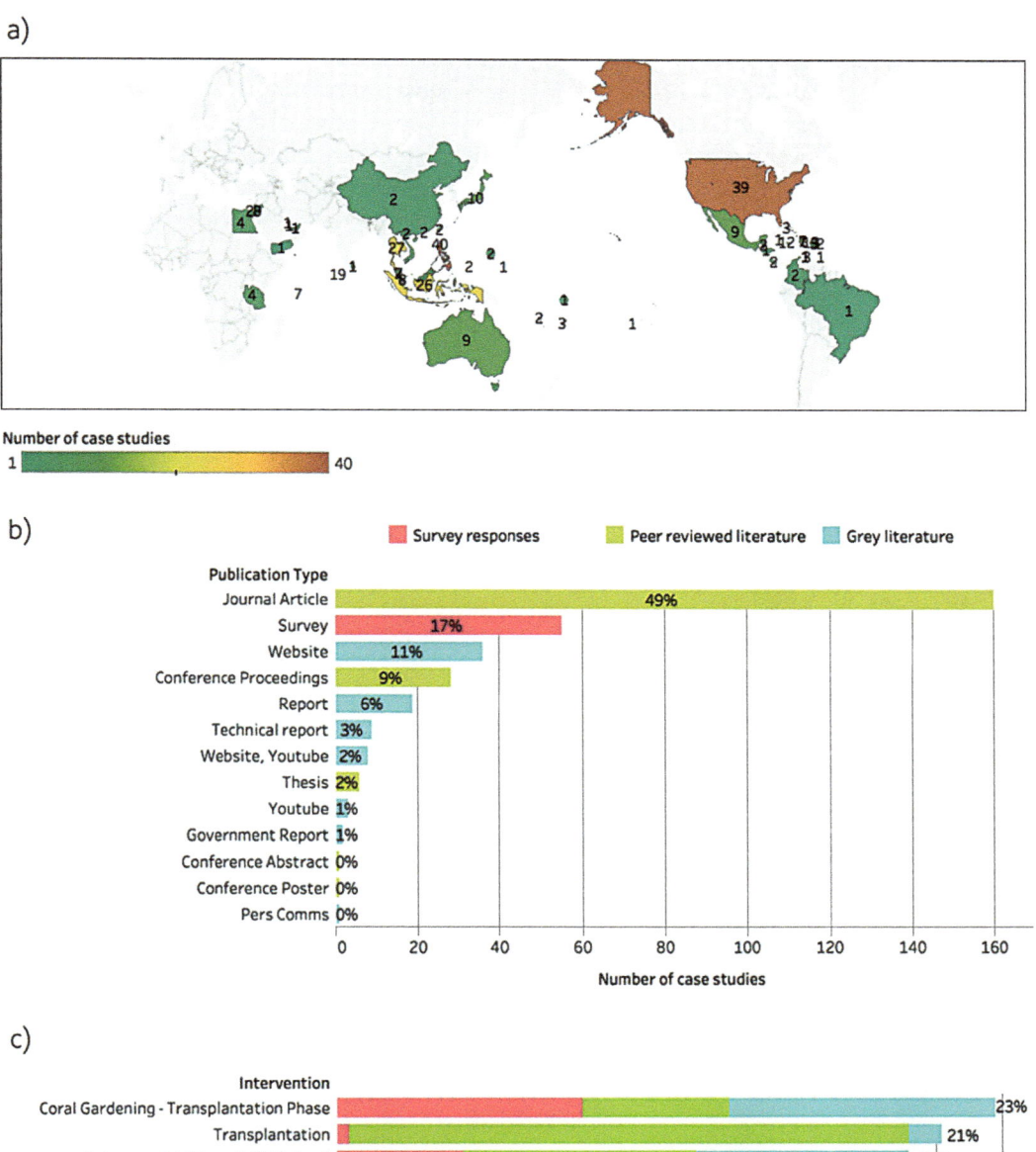

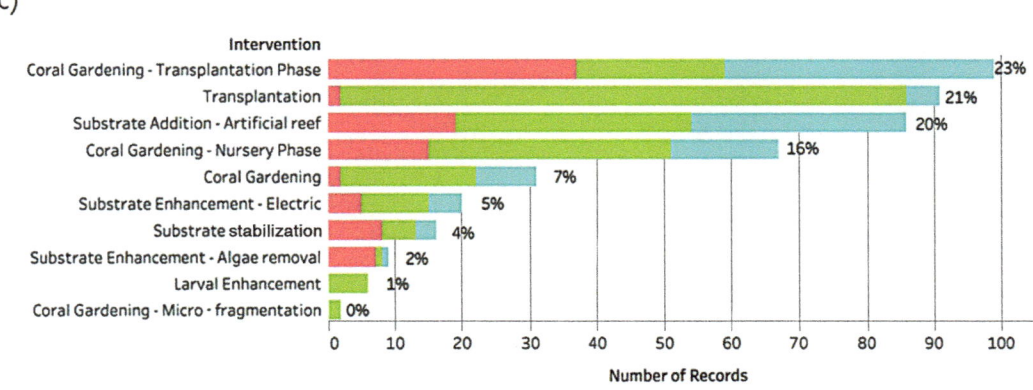

Figure 2.9 The (a) location, (b) source, and (c) type of intervention described in a global review of coral reef restoration methods (from Boström-Einarsson et al. 2018).

Coral restoration case studies are dominated by short-term projects, with 58% of all projects reporting less than 18 months of monitoring of the restored sites (Figure 2.10(a)). Overall, the median length of projects was 12 months. Similarly, most projects are relatively small in spatial scale, with a median size of restored areas of 440 m^2 (Figure 2.10(b)). The longest study monitored a transplantation project for 12 years (Garrison and Ward 2012), and studies that lasted 10 years or more (n = 5) tended to be monitoring programs on artificial reefs or restoration sites with transplanted corals; these also tended to be larger in spatial scale (>1,000 m^2) than the short-term studies.

Overall, coral restoration projects focused primarily on fast-growing branching corals, with 75% reporting using branching morphologies (Figure 2.11). Over a quarter of projects (28%)

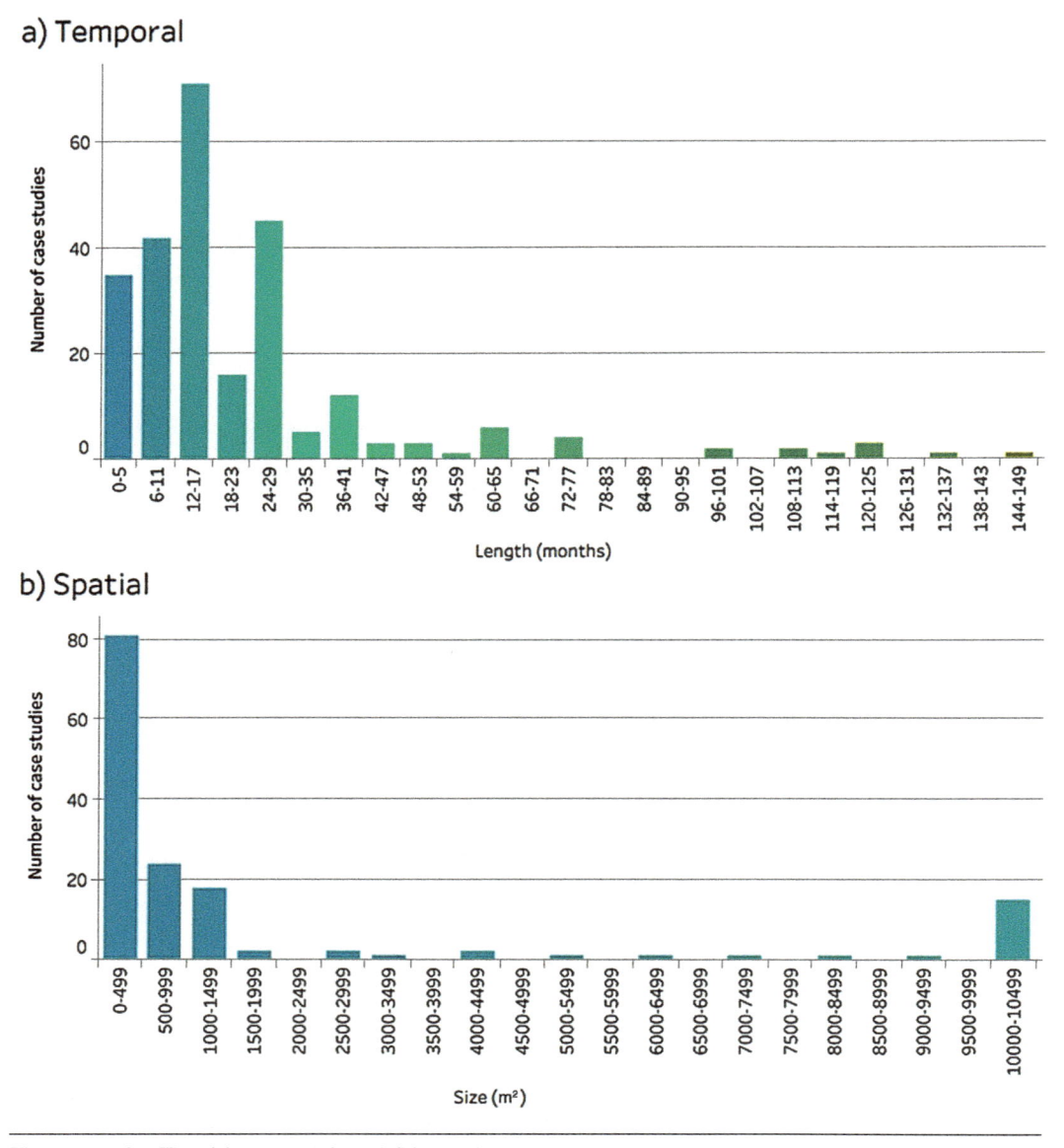

Figure 2.10 The (a) temporal and (b) spatial scale of coral restoration projects (from Boström-Einarsson et al. 2018).

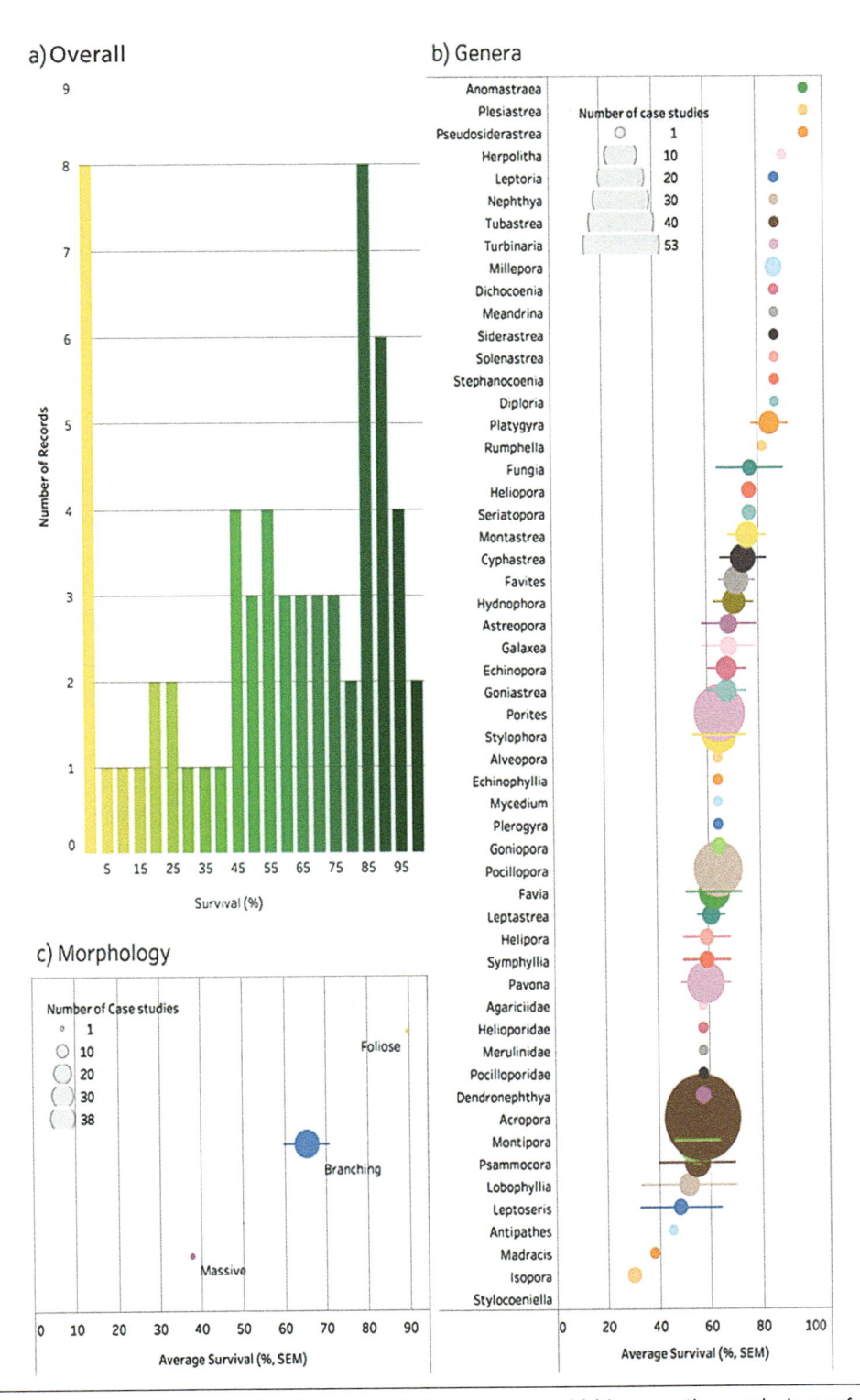

Figure 2.11 The average survival (a) overall, (b) by genera, and (c) by growth morphology of corals used in direct transplantation interventions. The size of each data point reflects the number of case studies supporting each calculation, the error bar represents standard error of the mean (SEM), and the different colors represent different species.

involved the coral genus *Acropora*, while 9% of studies included a single species—*Acropora cervicornis* (e.g., Bowden-Kerby 2008; Mercado-Molina et al. 2014; Schopmeyer et al. 2017). Among all the published documents, the top five species, represented in 22% of studies, were *Acropora cervicornis, Pocillopora damicornis, Stylophora pistillata, Porites cylindrica,* and *Acropora palmata.*

The success of direct transplantation depends on the size and health of the fragments, the method of transportation and attachment, and other extrinsic factors such as environmental conditions in the months following the transplantation, when coral fragments are stressed and vulnerable (van Woesik et al. 2017). Overall, direct transplantation studies reported an average of 51% survival, with 20% reporting >90% survival of transplanted corals.

DISCUSSION

Studying history is important because it allows us to understand our past, which in turn allows us to understand our present. If we want to know how and why our world is the way it is today, we have to look to history for answers. People often say that *history repeats itself*, but if we study the successes and failures of the past, we may, ideally, be able to learn from our mistakes and avoid repeating them in the future.

Modern reef restoration was pioneered by Tom Goreau and Wolf Hilbertz in 1979. The next wave of practitioners and scientists involved with reef restoration were Austin Bowden-Kerby, Vicki Harriot, David Fisk, Chou Loke Ming, and Baruck Rinkevich, who experimented with techniques for harvesting, growing, and transplanting coral. The drivers for their involvement with the new technique of reef restoration included concern for degradation to local coral reefs and the declining quality of scuba diving experiences as a result of cyclones, water quality, and coastal development.

Coral restoration involves many different approaches and technologies, depending on the requirements of the situation. It can involve heavy equipment such as cranes, graders, bulldozers, barges, or excavators, and also hand processes like the planting of corals. It can involve high-tech laboratory processes such as those applied in genetic engineering and micro-fragmentation.

Coral gardening is a simple and popular technique that is used in 70% of projects, and there is a major focus on fast-growing branching corals, with 75% of the projects showing the use of branching morphologies. The top five coral species being used in reef restoration were *Acropora cervicornis, Pocillopora damicornis, Stylophora pistillata, Porites cylindrica,* and *Acropora palmata.*

The global reviews of scientific literature and practitioners presented in this chapter identified 52 countries in which coral restoration projects have occurred, with the majority of projects conducted in the United States, the Philippines, Thailand, and Indonesia. Coral restoration case studies are dominated by short-term projects, with the median length of projects being 12 months. The longest study monitored a transplantation project for 12 years.

Reef restoration is about people and organizations who care about reefs. Non-governmental organizations such as The Nature Conservancy, Reef Resilience Network and Reef Restoration Foundation, Coral Restoration Foundation, Plant a Million Corals, and Reef Renewal International have been vital to partner with government and industry and involve the community on active projects. Scuba diving and consultancy businesses, such as Reef Balls, New Heaven Reef Conservation Program, Reef Arabia, and more recently, other businesses with a strong focus on sustainability, such as Mars Corporation and Reef Ecologic, have been involved in research, projects, training, and communication.

In the past five years, there has been an enormous increase in research and communication of reef restoration. Our global literature review documented an apparent 600% increase in published literature from 10–20 articles per year between 2000 and 2016 to over 120 articles in 2017.

It is difficult to measure the number of people and organizations interested and involved in reef restoration. An indicator of interest is the attendance of 300 people and multidisciplinary organizations at the Great Barrier Reef Restoration Symposium in June of 2018 that was held in Cairns, Australia, and the 450 people at the Reef Futures conference in Florida, USA, in December 2018. We recognize that the increased interest in reef restoration is linked to people who are willing to take action to help counter the global and local decline of coral reefs.

CONCLUSIONS

Coral reefs are under extreme pressure and it is necessary for people to share knowledge and take actions to reduce threats and improve reef health. The good news is that leading coral reef researchers, managers, tourism businesses, politicians, and stakeholders have recognized the challenge facing our coral reefs and are focusing on solutions. In 2018, reef restoration took another major step forward in terms of interest and funding when the Australian Government provided $6M to establish the Reef Restoration and Adaptation Program (RRAP). Over 18 months, RRAP conducted the world's most rigorous and comprehensive investigation into medium- and large-scale reef intervention, drawing on more than 150 experts from more than 20 organizations across the globe. The aim: to study the feasibility of intervening at scale on the Great Barrier Reef to help it adapt to, and recover from, the effects of climate change.

At the time of this writing, the consortium was embarking on a concerted, 10-year research and development program to rigorously risk-assess, test, develop, and if necessary, deploy a toolkit of novel interventions to help keep the reef resilient and sustain critical reef functions and values in the face of climate change (Figure 2.12).

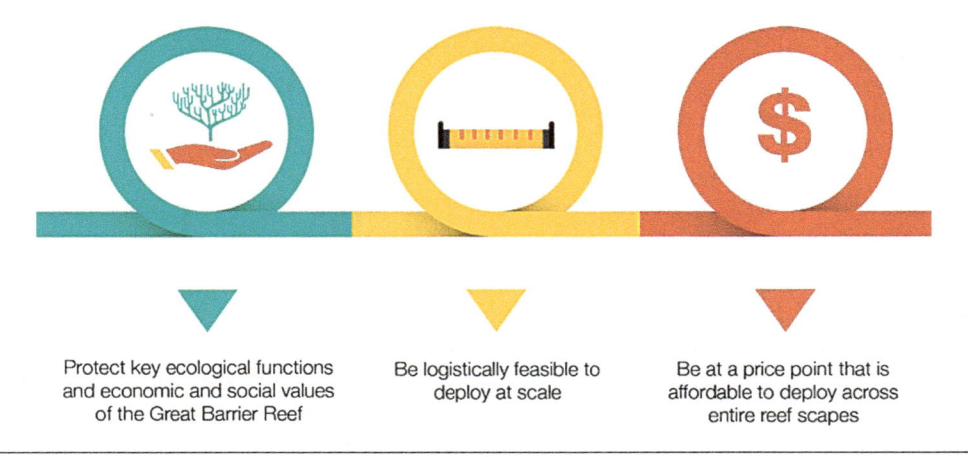

Figure 2.12 The ecological, social, logistical, and economic solutions sought by the RRAP (AIMS 2018).

RECOMMENDED FUTURE RESEARCH AND GOALS

We recommend a combination of environmental, social, and economic research projects and ongoing communication to share the history of reef restoration.

1. A global database of reef restoration knowledge, training, projects, practitioners, and funders to ensure that we work collaboratively, efficiently, and effectively.
2. A global training and education program for reef restoration. We estimate that there are approximately 1,000 self-taught people with demonstrated experience in active reef restoration and we recommend a target of one million trained people by 2025 in order to make a positive difference for coral reefs and communities. We recommend a global initiative where the people who rely on healthy reefs such as scuba divers, freedivers, snorkelers, tourists, and fishers participate in reef restoration training and donate at least one day a year or a small fee to a reef restoration project or foundation.
3. We recommend identification of 100 global priority reef restoration demonstration locations that implement best practice temporal goals of a 5–10-year project and spatial goals of 5,000–50,0000 m^2.

ACKNOWLEDGMENTS

The concept for a presentation on the history of reef restoration at the 2018 Great Barrier Reef Restoration Symposium was initiated by Adam Smith with co-authors Ian McLeod, Damien Burrows, Nathan Cook, Nadine Marshall, and Boze Hancock. We are grateful to Lisa Boström-Einarsson for the opportunity to include results from the global synthesis of coral restoration.

REFERENCES

AIMS. 2018. "Reef restoration and adaptation program. Helping the Great Barrier Reef resist, repair and recover." https://www.aims.gov.au/research/reef-recovery/RRAP.

Boström-Einarsson, L., D. Ceccarelli, R. C. Babcock, E. Bayraktarov, N. Cook, P. Harrison, M. Hein, et al. 2019. "Coral restoration in a changing world. *A global synthesis of methods and techniques.* Report to the National Environmental Science Program." Reef and Rainforest Research Centre Ltd, Cairns (63 pp.). https://nesptropical.edu.au/wp-content/uploads/2019/02/NESP-TWQ-Project-4.3-Technical-Report-1.pdf.

Boström-Einarsson L., R. C. Babcock, E. Bayraktarov, D. Ceccarelli, N. Cook, S. C. A. Ferse, B. Hancock, et al. 2020. *Coral restoration—A systematic review of current methods, successes, failures and future directions.* PLoS ONE 15(1): e0226631. https://doi.org/10.1371/journal.pone.0226631.

Bowden-Kerby, A. 2001. "Low-tech coral reef restoration methods modeled after natural fragmentation processes." *Bulletin of Marine Science* 69:915–931.

———. 2008. "Restoration of the threatened *Acropora cerviconiscorals*: Intraspecific variation as a factor in mortality, growth, and self-attachment." Pages 1194–1198 *in*. Ft. Lauderdale, Florida, USA.

Chamberland, V. F., D. Petersen, J. R. Guest, U. Petersen, M. Brittsan, and M. J. Vermeij. 2017. "New seeding approach reduces costs and time to outplant sexually propagated corals for reef restoration." *Sci. Rep.* 7(1):18076.

Chin Soon, L. and L. M. Chou. 2017. "Coral reef restoration in Singapore—Past, present and future: In: Sustainability matters: Environmental management in the Anthropocene." doi: 10.1142/9789813230620_0001.

Edwards, A. J. (ed.) 2010. *Reef Rehabilitation Manual.* Coral Reef Targeted Research & Capacity Building for Management Program: St Lucia, Australia.

Edwards, A. J. and E. D. Gomez. 2007. "Reef restoration concepts and guidelines: Making sensible management choices in the face of uncertainty." Coral Reef Targeted Research & Capacity Building for Management Programme: St Lucia, Australia.

Gomez, E. D., P. C. Cabaitan, H. T. Yap, and R. M. Dizon. 2014. "Can coral cover be restored in the absence of natural recruitment and reef recovery?" *Restoration Ecology* 22:142–150.

Hein, M. Y., B. L. Willis, R. Beeden, and A. Birtles. 2017. "The need for broader ecological and socioeconomic tools to evaluate the effectiveness of coral restoration programs." *Society for Ecological Restoration*. pp. 1–11. https://doi.org/10.1111/rec.12580.

Johnson et al. 2011. *Best Practices for Propagation and Population Enhancement. Caribbean Acropora Restoration Guide*. https://www.conservationgateway.org/Files/Documents/Johnson%20et%20al%202011%20Acropora%20Coral%20Guide.pdf.

Lindahl, U. 2003. "Coral reef rehabilitation through transplantation of staghorn corals: effects of artificial stabilization and mechanical damages." Coral Reefs 22:217–223.

Nedimyer K., K. Gaines, and S. Roach. 2011. "Coral Tree Nursery©: An innovative approach to growing corals in an ocean-based field nursery." *AACL Bioflux* 4(4):442–446.

Omori, M. 2010. "Degradation and restoration of coral reefs: Experience in Okinawa, Japan." *Marine Biology Research* 7:3–12.

Precht, W. F. (ed.) 2006. *Coral Reef Restoration Handbook*. CRC Press, Boca Raton, FL. 363 pp.

Precht, W. F., R. B. Aronson, S. L. Miller, B. D. Keller, and B. Causey. 2005. *The Folly of Coral Restoration Programs Following Natural Disturbances in the Florida Keys National Marine Sanctuary. Ecol. Restor.* 23(1):24–28.

Rinkevich, B. 1995. *Restoration Strategies for Coral Reefs Damaged by Recreational Activities: The Use of Sexual and Asexual Recruits. Restoration Ecology* 3:241–251.

———. 2005. *Conservation of Coral Reefs through Active Restoration Measures: Recent Approaches and Last Decade Progress. Environmental Science & Technology* 39:4333–4342.

Smith, A. K., I. McLeod, D. Burrows, N. Cook, N. Marshall, and B. Hancock. 2018. A history of reef restorors. Great Barrier Reef Restoration Symposium. July 16–19, 2018. Cairns, Australia.

Tunnell, J. W. 2007. *Coral Reefs of the Southern Gulf of Mexico*. Edited by John W. Tunnell, et al. Texas A&M University Press.

Young, C. N., S. A. Schopmeyer, and D. Lirman. 2012. "A review of reef restoration and coral propagation using the threatened genus *Acropora* in the Caribbean and Western Atlantic." *Bulletin of Marine Science* 88:1075–1098.

3

THE QUANDARY OF ACTIVE AND PASSIVE REEF RESTORATION IN A CHANGING WORLD

Buki Rinkevich

ABSTRACT

Coral reefs are under multiple anthropogenic and global change insults, altogether eroding reef diversity, goods, and services. The employment of traditional conservation protocols and measures, collectively known as *passive restoration* (where no constructive action is taken except to cease environmental stressors to allow unassisted, natural recovery), has failed to achieve target goals, while further decline of global reefs is the current forecast. Even though a consensus is yet to emerge, in the last two decades more and more scientists, conservationists, and decision-making authorities are opting for *active restoration* (where human intervention techniques that directly accelerate recovery or recuperate the ecosystems are implemented) that has been initiated under the rationale of *coral reef gardening*. The gardening tenet has a two-step restoration act—the nursery phase and the transplantation phase—and harnesses the principles, concepts, and theories used in *silviculture*. Active reef restoration succeeded, during its short life, to develop its own toolbox of methodologies while moving away from the traditional silviculture path. It adapts ecological engineering tactics and concepts, circumventing much of the ambiguity and debates generated in the forestation discipline. Active reef restoration is currently embracing the paradigms of developing *novel ecosystems*, without delving at this stage into the *functional* and *landscape* restoration issues, while also discounting topics like *reference site* and the costly *assisted migration*. Active reef restoration lays the foundation for the creation of coral populations that are best adapted to withstand global change impacts.

WHAT IS ECOLOGICAL RESTORATION?

Coral reefs possess an incomparable species diversity when compared to other marine ecosystems and thus, hold a vital role in the livelihood of hundreds of millions of human beings. They are also under multiple anthropogenic and global change stress factors, altogether directly and indirectly degrading their ecological properties (O'Neill et al. 2017; Eddy et al. 2018). A wide range of conservation management measures were suggested and implemented in attempts to resurrect degraded coral reefs, but the poor results shattered the then existing paradigms. Despite all of the conservation measures that were implemented, the global annual decline of reefs has not been halted (Bruno and Selig 2007), requiring a substantial revision of the employed management protocols while prompting the development of novel approaches (Rinkevich 2008). Out of all the new suggested approaches, the scientific discipline of active coral reef restoration has obtained increasing recognition lately as the most valid tactic to combat the continual decline in global reefs, primarily when aided by ecological engineering schemes (Rinkevich 2015; Linden and Rinkevich 2017; Lirman and Schopmeyer 2016; Rachmilovitz and Rinkevich 2017; Golomb et al. 2020; Table 3.1). This appreciation has emerged primarily following the understanding that coral reefs are not capable to naturally recuperate, without human intervention, and that even the best traditional management tools employed could not attain the desired conservation goals (Rinkevich 2008, 2015; Rachmilovitz and Rinkevich 2017). Further, the realization of the gloomy future of coral reefs was also swayed by the unexpected widely emerged ecological phase-shift phenomena, the transformations of coral reefs to algal reefs (McManus and Polsenberg 2004).

There is no consensus opinion yet among scientists, conservationists, and decision-making authorities about the preferable approach to reviving degraded reef areas, so they will evolve and adapt unassisted as long as no communal agreement exists about ubiquitous versus specific responses of bringing reef decline to a standstill. Views extend from broadening the traditional management methodologies, to radical solutions including the suggestion of moving species outside their current native ranges (Table 3.1, assisted migration; Hewitt et al. 2011; Benito-Garzón et al. 2013), up to the design of novel ecosystems that do not resemble past analogs (Miller and Bestelmeyer 2016). However, *ecological restoration* is still a common ground that is shared by many conservationists and decision-making authorities.

As a matter of fact, the term *ecological restoration* was lucidly defined just less than three decades ago in a U.S. National Academy of Sciences publication as "the return of an ecosystem to a close approximation of its condition prior to disturbance" (NRC 1992; Table 3.1). About a decade later, the definition of ecological restoration was further developed and fixed in the scientific field as "the process of assisting the recovery of ecosystems that have been damaged, degraded, or destroyed" (SER 2004; Table 3.1). More specifically this term stands for "an intentional activity that initiates or accelerates the recovery of an ecosystem with respect to its health, integrity, and sustainability" (SER 2004). Seemingly well understood, this term, however, represents a set of utopian goals since it is well recognized that by following existing anthropogenic activities and taking into account the foreseen climate change impacts, a complete return to the exact pre-degradation state is rarely, if ever, possible—even when the nine attributes of a restored ecosystem in the SER primer (2004) are well implemented (Alexander et al. 2016). Additionally, many of the suggested instruments in the ecological restoration toolbox adopt the goal of *assisting the recovery of ecosystems* (SER 2004) while targeting novel ecosystems that have little resemblance with past attributes (Harris et al. 2006; Benito-Garzón et al. 2013; Hobbs et al. 2013; Miller and Bestelmeyer 2016; Table 3.1).

The recovery envisaged by the ecological restoration tenet, while acceptable by ecosystems' stakeholders, ecologists, environmentalists, and conservationists, is guided by two classes of actions—*active* and *passive* restoration, each typified by a related body of notions and applied tools. While sometimes complementary in the applied tools employed, both classes of actions are fundamentally disparate and entail even conflicting conjectural approaches at their key benchmarks.

Table 3.1 Understanding ecological restoration and its core elements

Term	Core Element	Representative Citations
Ecological restoration	The return of an ecosystem to a close approximation of its condition prior to disturbance.	NRC 1992
Ecological restoration	The process of assisting the recovery of ecosystems that have been damaged, degraded, or destroyed.	SER 2004
Passive restoration	When no constructive action is taken except to cease or domesticate environmental stressors to allow human-unassisted, natural recovery.	Bradshaw 1996
Active restoration	Acts where human intervention techniques that directly accelerate recovery or recuperate ecosystems are implemented.	Bradshaw 1996
Landscape restoration	A process that aims to regain ecological integrity and enhance human well-being in a degraded landscape.	Maginnis and Jackson 2007
Functional restoration	Emphasizes the restoration of abiotic and biotic processes in degraded ecosystems.	King and Hobbs 2006
Habitat restoration	Restoring ecosystems for the specific purpose of providing habitat—either for the individual species or for the entire suite of species.	Miller and Hobbs 2007
Reference site	Historic conditions in a site that are believed to represent minimal human influence.	SER 2004
Novel ecosystem	A physical system of abiotic and biotic components (and their interactions) that, by virtue of human influence, differs from those that prevailed historically, having a tendency to self-organize and retain its novelty without future human involvement.	Hobbs et al. 2013; Miller and Bestelmeyer 2016
Assisted migration	The intentional translocation/movement of species outside of their historic ranges in order to mitigate actual or anticipated biodiversity losses caused by anthropogenic climatic change. Equivalent terms: facilitated migration, assisted colonization, managed relocation, assisted range expansion, and species translocation.	Hewitt et al. 2011
Gardening coral reefs	A strategy guided by a two-step restoration operation. The first step entails rearing coral stocks in mid-water floating nurseries, and upon reaching suitable sizes, applying the second step, the transplantation of nursery-farmed coral colonies onto denuded reef areas.	Rinkevich 1995, 2005, 2014, 2015, 2019, 2010
Ecological engineering	The design of sustainable ecosystems that integrate human society with its natural environment for the benefit of both.	Mitsch 2012; Rinkevich 2015, 2020

ACTIVE AND *PASSIVE* RESTORATION—THE PATH OF SILVICULTURE

Developing an effective toolbox to restore any degraded or altered ecosystem is imperative for the long-term survival and thriving of ecosystems. Originating from the discipline of silviculture, active and passive restoration reflect two disparate broad categories that environmentalists and conservationists consider as aiding the recovery of degrading lands (Bradshaw 1996). Restoration is deemed *active* where human intervention techniques that directly accelerate recovery or recuperate ecosystems are implemented, whereas *passive* restoration is when no constructive action is taken, except for stopping the environmental man-made pressure and allowing unassisted, natural recovery (Bradshaw 1996; Holl and Aide 2011; Morrison and Lindell 2011; Table 3.1). The literature reveals that active and passive restoration may lead to significantly different ecosystem-regeneration pathways and outcomes (e.g., Carnevale and Montagnini 2002; Florentine and Westbrooke 2004), even though restoration goals are similar. These goals in most *previous* forest restoration actions (current goals may differ, as mentioned later) were aimed toward a return to a close resemblance to intact reference sites (Table 3.1), or to a pre-degradation state in terms of structure and function at wrapping up phases of restoration (SER 2004). Otherwise, active and passive restoration may even augment each other (Scowcroft and Yeh 2013).

Active restoration in terrestrial ecosystems (primarily forest restorations), while generally less cost-effective than passive restoration and does not carry the passive restoration's typical *hidden costs* (Zahawi et al. 2014), is critical in reversing the path in habitats that are caught in a dilapidation trajectory (Clewell and Aronson 2006; Vyver et al. 2012). Further support for the previously mentioned conclusion are the troublesome, uncertain ecological upshots that are associated with the passive restoration acts, while also supporting numerous factors that may prevent a predictable ecosystem response to any restoration measure (Brancalion et al. 2016). At the same time, there is still doubt as to whether some of the employed *passive restoration* activities are advantageous to the compositions, structures, and functions of the restored areas, and whether or not these outcomes can be used as scientifically credible yardsticks. Following this rationale, most recent approaches to terrestrial restoration (silviculture-based activities) tend to apply the *active restoration* tactics but still include some traditional *passive* methodologies such as afforestation used in combination with new emerging approaches, such as assisted migration (Williams and Dumroese 2013).

In active forest restoration projects, the initiative for restoration is determined by the state of degradation, and is defined and mapped in accordance with the accepted criteria (Clewell and Aronson 2006). The leading challenge, then, is to set forth the most suitable strategies and tactics for forest restoration under current and foreseen climate change and increasing anthropogenic impacts. Clearly, pre-degradation states or historical references are less and less central in either the plans and/or the targeted goals, as no common ground exists with current/future scenarios (Stanturf et al. 2014).

Following Stanturf et al. (2014), active restoration was initiated as *revegetation* endeavors (simple forestation undertakings) by targeting the revegetation of empty land plots without contemplating the species localization or structural diversity, emphasizing renovated forest yields (e.g., trees for the logging industry) or forest functions (e.g., easing of soil erosion). Active restoration acts powered by ecological restoration theories (Bradshaw 1996) were then attempted, advanced by the establishment of the principles for ecological restoration (SER 2004) that moved from contemplating past conditions (primarily by the appraisal of reference sites) into novel ecosystem paradigms (Hallett et al. 2013; Hobbs 2013; Miller and Bestelmeyer 2016). Stanturf et al. (2014) further defined two developmental steps in the evolution of active forest restoration. The first, *forest landscape restoration* ("a process that aims to regain ecological integrity and enhance human well-being in a deforested or degraded forest landscape," Maginnis and Jackson 2007; Table 3.1), targeted the restoration of ecological processes at landscape-level scales, integrating human provisions. The second, *functional restoration* (Table 3.1), emphasized the restoration of the dynamic ecosystem's decayed fundamental functions, regardless of the structural ailments, but still trying to restore interactions between the ecosystem's functions and structures (King and Hobbs 2006). Thus, forest restoration acts can be implemented at the level of ecological restoration or can be broadly upgraded to the highly complex level of functional and landscape restorations (Stanturf et al. 2014). In addition, and while not sufficiently discussed, the topic of active *habitat restoration* (Miller and Hobbs 2007; Table 3.1) should also be considered.

THE PATH OF *ACTIVE* AND *PASSIVE* RESTORATION IN CORAL REEFS

Even following a vast literature interest in terrestrial ecosystems, the embracement of *active* and *passive* restoration notions and tools in the coral reef arena needs further investigation, due to the existing knowledge-based environmental complexities (Figure 3.1). The science of reef restoration is young compared to its foremost corresponding discipline of terrestrial restoration. Only two decades have passed since the first scientific triage for active reef restoration was suggested under the term *coral reef gardening* (Table 3.1), replacing the *semi-active* and less success reef restoration approach that relied on the transplantation of corals from a donor to the damaged site (Lirman and Schopmeyer 2016). This approach was the first to incorporate in reef restoration practices the principles, concepts, and theories used in silviculture (Epstein et al. 2003; Rinkevich 2005, 2006, 2014, 2015; Horoszowski-Fridman and Rinkevich 2017), while centered on a two-step restoration act, marked by the nursery phase and the transplantation phase. Predominant to this tenet was the repudiating of the stock material to the leniency of local reef conditions by adding to the practice, as an intermediate phase, coral mariculture in underwater nurseries, before their transplantation into denuded reef sites (Rinkevich 1995, 2005). Like terrestrial transplantation practices, the gardening concept entails testing a wide range of methodologies and approaches, with the aim of developing a restoration toolbox (Figure 3.1). As examples, studies focused on ramet survivorship and growth rates as measures for success (Epstein et al. 2001; Bongiorni et al. 2003; Forsman et al. 2006; Shafir and Rinkevich 2008; Bongiorni et al. 2011; dela Cruz et al. 2015), on the structural complexity of farmed corals (Rinkevich 2000; Epstein and Rinkevich 2001), the development of coral stocks from nubbins (Shafir et al. 2001) and from larvae (Linden and Rinkevich 2011, 2017, 2019), raising of corals in mid-water nursery (Shafir et al. 2006a, 2006b; Levi et al. 2010; Mbije et al. 2010), and on the development of transplantation acts (Shaish et al. 2010; Horoszowski-Fridman et al. 2011; Mbije et al. 2013).

The *gardening* tenet for active reef restoration was tested in a number of coral reefs worldwide with more than 86 coral species and several hundred thousand coral colonies that were successfully raised in various nursery prototypes and further supported by assorted novel transplantation procedures (Rinkevich 2014, 2015; Lirman and Schopmeyer 2016). As in silviculture, the literature shows that restoring any degraded reef area is intricate (Figure 3.1), primarily due to the various paths for reef dilapidation and the distinctly different manifestations of coral species abundances and ecosystem functions (Rinkevich 2005, 2014, 2015, 2020; Lirman and Schopmeyer 2016). While the concept of active reef restoration is currently well accepted (Rinkevich 2015, 2020), we still have a poor ability to accurately simulate restoration scenarios and trajectories that lead to restored sites, and therefore have no guarantee that specific restoration targets can be met.

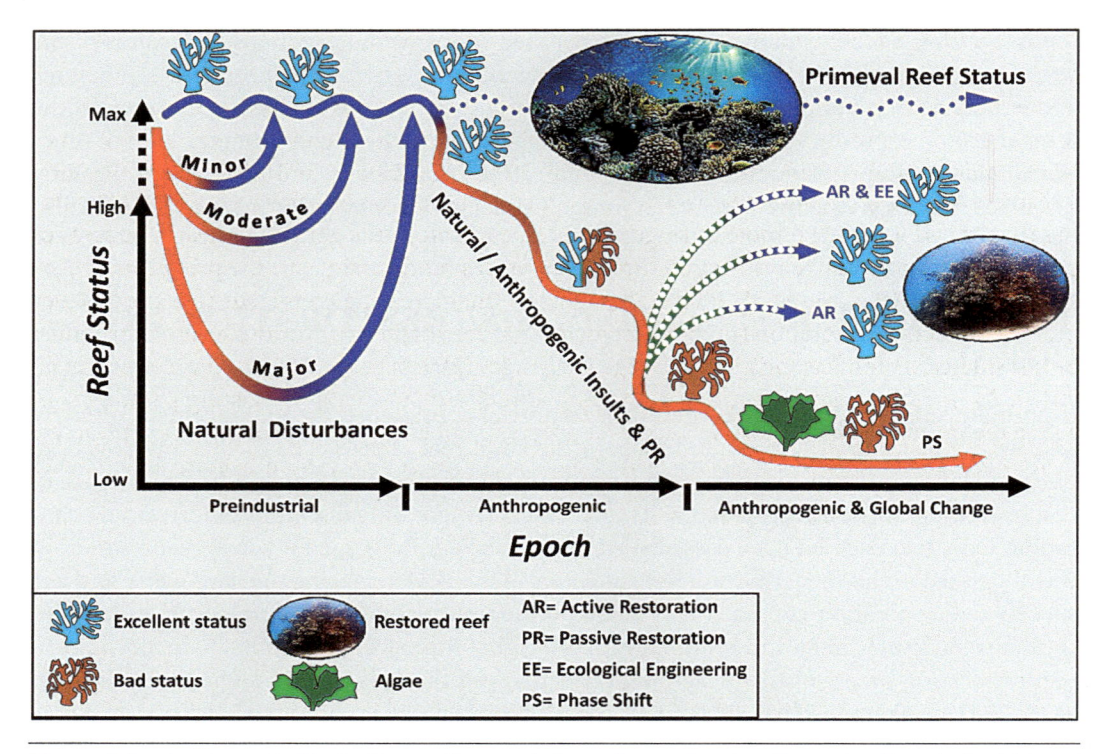

Figure 3.1 A schematic illustration on the needs for active reef restoration acts. At preindustrial and early anthropogenic eras, the magnitudes of environmental/human impacts (minor, moderate, and major) were within the scales that allow passive (natural) restoration, where no constructive actions were used and the only actions taken were to cease environmental stressors. This was enough for human-unassisted, natural recovery of damaged reef areas. Under current (and foreseen intensified global change) conditions, passive restoration is not enough (leading to complete reef destruction and phase shifts phenomena), and activities should be empowered by active restoration principles and methodologies. Various active restoration activities are culminating by various reef statuses, and the superior are those complemented by ecological engineering tools. Still, it is not expected to return reef ecosystems to primeval statuses because novel ecosystems that are adapted to the new environmental conditions emerge.

The progression of active reef restoration methodologies and principles in the last two decades has already overcome four major obstacles. Active reef restoration has already acquired credentials for (a) farming all types of coral species (massive, branching, and encrusting forms) in mid-water nurseries, (b) the creation of large stocks of coral colonies, (c) the successful transplantation of nursery-farmed coral colonies, and (d) ensuring the low cost of farming and transplanting coral colonies (Rinkevich 2014, 2015, 2019, 2020). Without yet delving into the functional or landscape types of restoration that are still circumventing the *reference site* obstacle, active reef restoration has paved its way directly into forward-looking ecological engineering approaches (Table 3.1). The recognition in the efficacy of ecological engineering approaches in reef restoration (Amar and Rinkevich 2007; Shafir et al. 2009; Levi et al. 2010; Shafir and Rinkevich 2010; Shaish et al. 2010; Horoszowski-Fridman et al. 2011, 2015; Rinkevich 2015; Lirman and Schopmeyer 2016; Horoszowski-Fridman and Rinkevich 2017; Linden and Rinkevich 2017, 2019; Rachmilovitz and Rinkevich 2017; Golomb et al. 2020) greatly overpasses the one it is attributed in silviculture (Mitsch 2012).

QUANDARY AND SOLUTION FOR ACTIVE REEF RESTORATION

The science of restoration ecology includes protocols developed for active restoration (both in terrestrial and aquatic ecosystems alike), and has swiftly advanced over the past three decades, already maturing (primarily when silviculture is considered) into a cohesive body of supporting theory and a practical toolbox (Figure 3.1). In contrast to the generally meager success of passive restoration, active restoration directly enhances biodiversity and the provision of ecosystem services (Benayas et al. 2009). This leads to the increasing consensus that the broader practices of active restoration (in different forms that are adapted for various ecosystems) must be considered in combatting global change challenges (Harris et al. 2006; Benito-Garzón et al. 2013). As in other quickly developing scientific disciplines, challenging existing paradigms in active reef restoration drives innovation and progress. Looking into the coral reef arena, active restoration powered by a strong scientific basis is starting to meaningfully contribute to reef and species recovery, offering alternate livelihoods to local stakeholders (Lirman and Schopmeyer 2016), despite the debates taking place about the developed practices (e.g., the creation of novel ecosystems; Hobbs et al. 2013; Miller and Bestelmeyer 2016).

The literature shows that global climate changes are intensifying and that anthropogenic and global change stressors, while affecting reefs differently according to which are prevalent in the specific region, are still instigating unprecedented global degradation of coral reefs (O'Neill et al. 2017; Eddy et al. 2018). Passive reef restoration (including all traditional conservation methodologies), while insufficient for averting the tide of reef degradation, failed to support biodiversity and reef services (Rinkevich 2008). The alternative approach of active reef restoration (Rinkevich 1995, 2005, 2019, 2020) focused, at its onset, on restoring sites as close as possible to the pre-degradation state. Yet, it is not enough. The increasing anthropogenic and global change impacts will push many ecosystems, including coral reefs (Rinkevich 2014, 2015), into altered states beyond their *natural* variability (including phase shift scenarios; McManus and Polsenberg 2004), thus it may not be realistic to restore them to their historical conditions. In these cases, *novel ecosystems* emerge (Hallett et al. 2013; Hobbs 2013; Miller and Bestelmeyer 2016)—ecosystems where the ecological characteristics include goods and services that diverge from the properties in earlier eras. This places active reef restoration in a position for wider theoretical and practical dimensions (Figure 3.1). Furthermore, active reef restoration includes additional restoration interventions, such as ecological engineering tools (Rinkevich 2015, 2020; Lirman and Schopmeyer 2016), thus representing a significant shift in the rationale and objectives of restoration as was set by the SER (2004).

The hidden costs (Zahawi et al. 2014) for passive reef restoration are not well acknowledged as of yet in the marine arena, primarily by opponents to active reef restoration. Nevertheless, active reef restoration as a concept (Figure 3.1) and the coral gardening approach as the applied tool (Rinkevich 1995, 2005) have emerged currently as the best practical instruments to mitigate global change impacts (Rinkevich 2014, 2015, 2020). During the elapsed short period from its inception, the toolbox for the coral gardening approach has been enriched not only with methodologies for farming coral colonies in underwater nurseries along with their transplantation, but is also empowered with ecological engineering tools, circumventing much of the ambiguity and debates being generated in forestation. It is moving into paradigms of novel ecosystems (Rinkevich 2015; Miller and Bestelmeyer 2016; Golomb et al. 2020) without delving at this stage into the functional and landscape restoration (Stanturf et al. 2014) issues, also freeing from both the consideration of a reference site (sensu SER 2004) and the costly approach for assisted migration.

Two emerging topics may further intensify the credibility of active reef restoration. The first deals with the inauguration of a large-scale transplantation act, the outplanting of up to one million coral colonies in a denuded reef area, in order to portray performance and ecological engineering impacts (Rinkevich 2014). The second involves cost–benefit analyses for active reef restoration that, in the past, did not include the high monetary value of the coral reefs' ecosystem services (Rinkevich 2017). This should be further highlighted since cost–benefit analyses for restoration projects are limited, full records for restoration costs that distinguish between *passive* and *active* restoration measures are sparse, the benefits to society are not evaluated in detail and the surplus benefits incurred from ecological engineering tactics are commonly unheeded (Rinkevich 2017, 2019, 2020). In any case, active reef restoration measures (Figure 3.1), specifically those based on the coral gardening tenet (Rinkevich 1995, 2005, 2014, 2015, 2019), underlie the foundation for the creation of coral populations that are best adapted to novel environmental impacts, like those presented by global climate change.

ACKNOWLEDGMENTS

This chapter was supported by the AID-MERC program (no M33-001), by the North American Friends of IOLR (NAF/IOLR), and by the Israeli-French High Council for Scientific & Technological Research Program (Maïmonide-Israel). Thanks are due to G. Paz for illustrating the figure.

REFERENCES

Alexander, S., J. Aronson, O. Whaley, and D. Lamb. 2016. "The relationship between ecological restoration and the ecosystem services concept." *Ecology and Society* 21(1):34.
Amar, K. O. and B. Rinkevich. 2007. "A floating mid-water coral nursery as larval dispersion hub: Testing an idea." *Mar. Biol.* 151, 713–718.
Benayas, J. M. R., A. C. Newton, A. Diaz, and J. M. Bullock. 2009. "Enhancement of biodiversity and ecosystem services by ecological restoration: A meta-analysis." *Science* 325(5944), 1121–1124.
Benito-Garzón, M., M. Ha-Duong, N. Frascaria-Lacoste, and J. Fernández-Manjarrés, 2013. "Habitat restoration and climate change: Dealing with climate variability, incomplete data, and management decisions with tree translocations." *Rest. Ecol.* 21(5), 530–536.
Bongiorni, L., D. Giovanelli, B. Rinkevich, A. Pusceddu, L. M. Chou, and R. Danovaro. 2011. "First step in the restoration of a highly degraded coral reef (Singapore) by in situ coral intensive farming." *Aquaculture* 322–323, 191–200.
Bongiorni, L., S. Shafir, D. Angel, and B. Rinkevich. 2003. "Survival, growth and gonadal development of two hermatypic corals subjected to in situ fish farm nutrient enrichment." *Mar. Ecol. Prog. Ser.* 253, 137–144.
Bradshaw, A. D. 1996. "Underlying principles of restoration." *Can. J. Fish. Aquat. Sci.* 53(Suppl. 1), 3–9.
Brancalion, P. H., D. Schweizer, U. Gaudare, J. R. Mangueira, F. Lamonato, F. T. Farah, A. G. Nave, and R. R. Rodrigues. 2016. "Balancing economic costs and ecological outcomes of passive and active restoration in agricultural landscapes: The case of Brazil." *Biotropica* 48(6), 856–867.
Bruno, J. F. and E. R. Selig. 2002. "Regional decline of coral cover in the Indo-Pacific: Timing, extent, and subregional comparisons." *PLoS ONE* 2, e711.
Carnevale, N. J. and F. Montagnini. 2002. "Facilitating regeneration of secondary forests with the use of mixed and pure plantations of indigenous tree species." *Forest Ecol. Manag.* 163, 217–227.
Clewell, A. F. and J. Aronson. 2006. "Motivations for the restoration of ecosystems." *Conserv. Biol.* 20(2), 420–428.

dela Cruz, D. W., B. Rinkevich, E. D. Gomez, and H. T. Yap. 2015. "Assessing an abridged nursery phase for slow growing corals used in coral restoration." *Ecol. Eng.* 84, 408–415.

Eddy, T. D., W. W. Cheung, and J. F. Bruno. 2018. "Historical baselines of coral cover on tropical reefs as estimated by expert opinion." *PeerJ* 6, e4308.

Epstein, N. and B. Rinkevich. 2001. "From isolated ramets to coral colonies: The significance of colony pattern formation in reef restoration practices." *Basic Appl. Ecol.* 2, 219–222.

Epstein, N., R. P. M. Bak, and B. Rinkevich. 2001. "Strategies for gardening denuded coral reef areas: The applicability of using different types of coral material for reef restoration." *Rest. Ecol.* 9, 532–442.

———. 2003. "Applying forest restoration principles to coral reef rehabilitation." *Aq. Conser.* 13, 387–395.

Forsman, Z. H., B. Rinkevich, and C. L. Hunter. 2006. "Investigating fragment size for culturing reef-building corals (*Porites lobata* and *P. compressa*) in ex situ nurseries." *Aquaculture* 261, 89–97.

Florentine, S. K. and M. E. Westbrooke. 2004. "Restoration on abandoned tropical pasturelands—do we know enough?" *J. Nature Conserv.* 12, 85–94.

Golomb, D., N. Shashar, and B. Rinkevich. 2020. "Coral carpets—a novel ecological engineering tool aimed at constructing coral communities on soft sand bottoms." *Ecol. Eng.* 145, 105743.

Hallett, L. M., S. Diver, M. V. Eitzel, J. J. Olson, B. S. Ramage, H. Sardinas, Z. Statman-Weil, and K. N. Suding. 2013. "Do we practice what we preach? Goal setting for ecological restoration." *Rest. Ecol.* 21(3), 312–319.

Harris, J. A., R. J. Hobbs, E. Higgs, and J. Aronson. 2006. "Ecological restoration and global climate change." *Rest. Ecol.* 14(2), 170–176.

Hewitt, N., N. Klenk, A. L. Smith, D. R. Bazely, N. Yan, S. Wood, J. I. MacLellan, C. Lipsig-Mumme, and I. Henriques. 2011. "Taking stock of the assisted migration debate." *Biol. Conserv.* 144, 2560–2572.

Hobbs, R. J. 2013. "Grieving for the past and hoping for the future: Balancing polarizing perspectives in conservation and restoration." *Rest. Ecol.* 21(2), 145–148.

Hobbs, R. J., E. S. Higgs, and C. M. Hall. 2013. "Defining novel ecosystems." In *Novel Ecosystems: Intervening in the New Ecological World Order*. Hobbs, R. J. et al. (eds). John Wiley & Sons, pp. 58–60.

Holl, K. D. and T. M. Aide. 2011. "When and where to actively restore ecosystems?" *Forest Ecol. Manag.* 261 (10), 1558–1563.

Horoszowski-Fridman, Y. B. and B. Rinkevich. 2017. "Restoring the animal forests: Harnessing silviculture biodiversity concepts for coral transplantation." In: *Marine Animal Forests: The ecology of benthic biodiversity hotspots*. Rossi, S., L. Bramanti, A. Gori, and C. Orejas. (eds.), pp. 1313–1335.

Horoszowski-Fridman, Y. B., I. Izhaki, and B. Rinkevich. 2011. "Engineering of coral reef larval supply through transplantation of nursery-farmed gravid colonies." *J. Exp. Mar. Biol. Ecol.* 399, 162–166.

Horoszowski-Fridman, Y. B., J-C. Brêthes, N. Rahmani, and B. Rinkevich. 2015. "Marine silviculture: incorporating ecosystem engineering properties into reef restoration acts." *Ecol. Eng.* 82, 201–213.

King, E. G. and R. J. Hobbs. 2006. "Identifying linkages among conceptual models of ecosystem degradation and restoration: Towards an integrative framework." *Rest. Ecol.* 14(3), 369–378.

Levi, G., L. Shaish, A. Haim, and B. Rinkevich. 2010. "Mid-water rope nursery—testing design and performance of a novel reef restoration instrument." *Ecol. Eng.* 36, 560–569.

Linden, B. and B. Rinkevich. 2011. "Creating stocks of young colonies from brooding-coral larvae, amenable to active reef restoration." *J. Exp. Mar. Biol. Ecol.* 398, 40–46.

———. 2017. "Elaborating of an eco-engineering approach for stock enhanced sexually derived coral colonies." *J. Exp. Mar. Biol. Ecol.* 486, 314–321.

Linden, B., M. J. A. Vermeij, and B. Rinkevich. 2019. "The coral settlement box: A simple device to produce coral stock from brooded coral larvae entirely in situ." *Eco. Eng.* 132, 115–119.

Lirman, D. and S. Schopmeyer. 2006. "Ecological solutions to reef degradation: optimizing coral reef restoration in the Caribbean and Western Atlantic." *PeerJ* 4:e2597. doi 10.7717/peerj.2597.

Maginnis, S. and W. Jackson. 2007. "What is FLR and how does it differ from current approaches?" In Rietbergen-McCracken, J., S. Maginnis, and A. Sarre (eds.). *The Forest Landscape Restoration Handbook*. London, UK, Earthscan. pp. 19–34.

Mbije, N. E. J., E. Spanier, and B. Rinkevich. 2010. "Testing the first phase of the 'gardening concept' as an applicable tool in restoring denuded reefs in Tanzania." *Ecol. Eng.* 36, 611–750.

Mbije, N. E. J., E. Spanier, and B. Rinkevich. 2013. "A first endeavour in restoring denuded, post-bleached reefs in Tanzania." *Estuar. Coastal Shelf Sci.* 128, 41–51.

McManus, J. W. and J. F. Polsenberg. 2004. "Coral–algal phase shifts on coral reefs: Ecological and environmental aspects." *Prog. Oceanog.* 60(2–4), 263–279.

Miller, J. R. and B. T. Bestelmeyer. 2016. "What's wrong with novel ecosystems, really?" *Rest. Ecol.* 24(5), 577–582.

Miller, J. R. and R. J. Hobbs. 2007. "Habitat restoration—do we know what we're doing?" *Rest. Ecol.* 15(3), 382–390.

Mitsch, W. J. 2012. "What is ecological engineering?" *Ecol. Eng.* 45, 5–12.

Morrison, E. B. and C. A. Lindell. 2011. "Active or passive forest restoration? Assessing restoration alternatives with avian foraging behavior." *Rest. Ecol.* 19(201), 170–177.

NRC, National Research Council. 1992. *Restoration of aquatic ecosystems: Science, technology, and public policy*. National Academies Press, Washington, D.C.

O'Neill, B. C., M. Oppenheimer, R. Warren, S. Hallegatte, R. E. Kopp, and H. O. Pörtner, et al. 2017. "IPCC reasons for concern regarding climate change risks." *Nature Climate Change* 7(1), 28–37.

Rachmilovitz, E. N. and B. Rinkevich. 2017. "Tiling the reef—exploring the first step of an ecological engineering tool that may promote phase-shift reversals in coral reefs." *Ecol. Eng.* 105, 150–161.

Rinkevich, B. 1995. "Restoration strategies for coral reefs damaged by recreational activities: The use of sexual and asexual recruits." *Rest. Ecol.* 3, 241–251.

———. 2000. "Steps towards the evaluation of coral reef restoration by using small branch fragments." *Mar. Biol.* 136, 807–812.

———. 2005. "Conservation of coral reefs through active restoration measures: Recent approaches and last decade progress." *Environ. Sci. Technol.* 39, 4333–4342.

———. 2006. "The coral gardening concept and the use of underwater nurseries; lesson learned from silvics and silviculture." In: *Coral Reef Restoration Handbook*. W. F. Precht (ed). Boca Raton, FL., CRC Press. pp. 291–301.

———. 2008. "Management of coral reefs: We have gone wrong when neglecting active reef restoration." *Mar. Pollut. Bull.* 56, 1821–1824.

———. 2014. "Rebuilding coral reefs: Does active reef restoration lead to sustainable reefs?" *Curr. Opinion Environ. Sustainability*. 7, 28–36.

———. 2015. "Climate change and active reef restoration—ways of constructing the 'reefs of tomorrow.'" *J. Mar. Sci. Eng.* 3, 111–127.

———. 2017. "Rebutting the inclined analyses on the cost-effectiveness and feasibility of coral reef restoration." *Ecol. Appl.* 27, 1970–1973.

———. 2019. "The active reef restoration toolbox is a vehicle for coral resilience and adaptation in a changing world." *J. Mar. Sci. Eng.* 7, 201.

———. 2020. "Ecological engineering approaches in coral reef restoration." *ICES J. Mar. Sci.* (in press). doi:10.1093/icesjms/fsaa022.

Scowcroft, P. G. and J. T. Yeh. 2013. "Passive restoration augments active restoration in deforested landscapes: The role of root suckering adjacent to planted stands of Acacia koa." *Forest Ecol. Manag.* 305, 138–145.

SER, Society for Ecological Restoration International Science & Policy Working Group. 2004. *The SER International Primer on Ecological Restoration*. www.ser.org & Tucson: *Society for Ecological Restoration International*. 13 pp.

Shafir, S. and B. Rinkevich. 2008. "The underwater silviculture approach for reef restoration: An emergent aquaculture theme." In: *Aquaculture Research Trends*. S. H. Schwartz (ed.). Nova Science Publications, New York, NY. pp. 279–295.

———. 2010. "Integrated long term mid-water coral nurseries: A management instrument evolving into a floating ecosystem." *Mauritius Res. J.* 16, 365–379.

Shafir, S., J. Van Rijn, and B. Rinkevich. 2001. "Nubbing of coral colonies: A novel approach for the development of island broodstocks." *Aquarium Sci. Conser.* 3, 183–190.

———. 2006a. "A mid-water coral nursery." *Proc. 10th Intern. Coral Reef Symp*, pp. 1674–1679.

———. 2006b. "Steps in the construction of underwater coral nursery, an essential component in reef restoration acts." *Mar. Biol.* 149, 679–687.

Shafir, S., S. Abady, and B. Rinkevich. 2009. "Improved sustainable maintenance for mid-water coral nursery by the application of an anti-fouling agent." *J. Exp. Mar. Biol. Ecol.* 368, 124–128.

Shaish, L., G. Levi, G. Katzir, and B. Rinkevich. 2010. "Employing a highly fragmented, weedy coral species in reef restoration." *Ecol. Eng.* 36, 1424–1432.

Stanturf, J. A., B. J. Palik, M. I. Williams, R. K. Dumroese, and P. Madsen. 2014. "Forest Restoration Paradigms." *J. Sustain. Forestry* 33(sup1), S161–S194.

Vyver, M. L., R. M. Cowling, E. E. Campbell, and M. Difford. 2012. "Active restoration of woody canopy dominants in degraded South African semi-arid thicket is neither ecologically nor economically feasible." *Appl. Vegetation Sci.* 15(1), 26–34.

Williams, M. I. and R. K. Dumroese. 2013. "Preparing for climate change: Forestry and assisted migration." *J. Forestry* 114, 287–297.

Zahawi, R. A., J. L. Reid, and K. D. Holl. 2014. "Hidden costs of passive restoration." *Rest. Ecol.* 22(3), 284–287.

4

LIVE ROCK FARMER TO LIVE CORAL FARMER

Ken Nedimyer

ABSTRACT

Much of the story of active coral reef restoration in the Florida Keys begins with Ken Nedimyer and an offshore live rock aquaculture farm off Key Largo. Ken's extensive time in the water collecting marine life gave him unique insight into the life histories and distribution patterns of hundreds of species of marine life, and it gave him an appreciation for the critical role that live coral plays in the lives of the marine life he was collecting. This chapter will follow Ken's passion for coral reefs—from his life as a tropical fish collector and live rock farmer to founding the Coral Restoration Foundation (CRF) and developing perhaps the biggest offshore coral nursery in the world.

INTRODUCTION

This is a story about my unconventional path from being a commercial marine life fisherman in the Florida Keys to a leader in the field of coral reef restoration. Although I have an undergrad degree in biology, I think of myself as more of an entrepreneur or a visionary than a scientist. My transition from a fisherman to a conservationist happened as a result of several major environmental catastrophes that I experienced in the 1980s and 1990s while working in the Florida Keys. By the turn of the millennium, I realized that I couldn't just continue fishing and ignore what I was seeing underwater. My journey from marine life fisherman to live rock farmer to coral farmer has a lot of history and side roads, but for the purposes of this chapter, I've tried to portray an abbreviated version of the story and show that people with all kinds of backgrounds are contributing to the effort to restore coral reefs.

EARLY HISTORY: THE PASSION FOR CORAL REEFS

My story begins in the 1960s, when I was a young boy in Titusville, Florida, spending my free time catching minnows in the local streams and seining for critters at the beach. Growing up as I did on the east coast of Florida, beaches, estuaries, streams, and lakes surrounded me, and I became obsessed with the mystery of what was under these waters. By the mid-to-late 1960s, television programs like the "Underwater World of Jacques Cousteau" were bringing these mysterious places into focus, capturing the diverse populations of fish and invertebrates on film for the public. Once I realized that these magical places were as close as the Florida Keys, I began campaigning for the Keys to be our family's next annual vacation spot.

The first of many family trips to the Keys was in late 1969. The weather was marginal that year and all we had was a rowboat, but we were able to go snorkeling. I managed to catch a few fish for my brand new saltwater aquarium—a budding hobby of mine that was full of challenges. In the early days of saltwater aquariums, keeping fish was a big challenge—to say nothing of invertebrates and corals—but I loved the adventure and trial-and-error troubleshooting.

Fast forward to 1978; I found myself graduating from college with a degree in biology and a passion to be a marine biologist. Job opportunities in this field were scarce, and the few that I did find required experience and a higher degree. I was quite done with the school thing, so after a summer job at Sea Camp on Big Pine Key, I moved to the Keys full time and reverted to doing what had paid for a lot of my college education: catching and selling lobsters and tropical fish. It was fun and profitable—until December when the water turned cold and the lobsters all disappeared. By this point, any job that didn't require me to dive every day sounded appealing. When I saw a job listing in the local paper by a company called Ocean Farming Systems, I was drawn in by the idea of *ocean farming*. As I soon found out, the position being offered was for a common laborer to clean shrimp tanks and do odd jobs. Although it wasn't what I had hoped, I accepted the job when it was offered to me. I sensed that there was potential to expand my knowledge base and gain experience.

During my two years working for Ocean Farming Systems, I learned a lot about breeding and raising fish. One of the most valuable things I learned was the ins and outs of the marine ornamentals business. I discovered that the company had started out as a pompano farming venture. In an attempt to provide a steady cash flow for the company, they had diversified into the marine ornamentals business as marine life wholesalers while the aquaculture side of their business matured. My interests in the company were in the aquaculture side of it, but along the way I learned every aspect of the marine ornamentals trade—from collecting to shipping the final product all over the world. Little did I know that this was the knowledge and experience that would eventually provide my income for the next 30 years.

CATASTROPHIC CHANGES

I left Ocean Farming Systems in 1980 and spent a year doing contract work for another marine life wholesaler before eventually starting my own marine life wholesale business in 1982. Up until that time, I had done a lot of diving up and down the Keys; but now, as a marine life collector, I found myself in the water three to five days a week, diving every imaginable habitat in the Keys. My appreciation for the beauty and diversity of the marine environment of the Florida Keys grew exponentially in those years. I was beginning to see this underwater world as my second home. This shift in perspective fostered in me a sense of responsibility and protectiveness of our reefs that, when paired with two major environmental events, helped redirect my focus in life.

The first of these significant events was the sudden decline in long-spined sea urchin populations in 1983. I have to admit that I was initially delighted they were gone because it made my life as a marine life collector a lot easier. As you can imagine, it is never a pleasant experience to reach under a rock and shake hands with these fellas' sharp spines. Before the die-off, the urchins were everywhere. I couldn't catch a fish or a lobster without first moving a bunch of urchins out of the way. My hands almost always had black spines in them somewhere, so when they were suddenly gone, catching everything was so much quicker and easier—and less painful. I didn't appreciate the role they played until a couple of years had passed, and in their absence, the bare hard bottom habitats throughout the Keys became overgrown with macro algae. In some areas, the macro algae quickly outcompeted the stony corals, and the transition from coral-dominated habitats to algal-dominated habitats happened in a year or two. The process was slower in other areas, but over time, every hard bottom community in the Keys was affected by their disappearance.

The second noteworthy environmental change was the bleaching event of 1998, frequently referred to as the first *Global Bleaching Event* because of the unprecedented expanse of areas affected. I found myself becoming more aware of and concerned about the transformations I was witnessing on the reef. Live coral is what makes up a coral reef, and as I watched these two-hundred-year-old corals dying, I realized that the entire future of the coral reefs was being called into question. It was immediately clear to me that action must be taken not only to stop the decline but to find a way to reverse it. I knew I wanted to be involved, but what could I do to help?

To understand my answer to that question, indulge me in the following flashbacks.

THE LIVE ROCK FARM

The year is 1994, and I had just started my first offshore live rock aquaculture farm in the Florida Keys. So what is a live rock? Why would anyone want to *farm* rocks? I asked these questions myself when, after about 16 years as a commercial marine life fisherman, live rock became a sought-after product in the trade. To put it plainly, live rock is basically dead coral rubble that was primarily harvested from the reef rubble zones behind many of the outer fringing reefs in the Florida Keys. It didn't really look much like coral because it had been tumbled and rolled around on the crest of the reef for possibly hundreds of years. People were buying it because the rocks were weathered inside and out, making them ideal media for aerobic and anaerobic bacteria to grow. Combining these bacterial communities with a highly soluble form of calcium carbonate (the dead coral rock) made them an indispensable part of the biological filtration for high-end *reef* aquariums.

Over time, the increasing amount of rock being harvested from the federal and state waters off the Florida Keys raised questions about sustainability and habitat protection. There seemed to be an abundance of rock out there, but the concern was that we were harvesting a product that possibly served an important role on the reef. Since this resource was not being replaced with new coral rubble in any realistic time frame, state and federal fishery managers moved to phase out the wild harvest of live rock, favoring instead the development of an offshore live rock aquaculture program as a replacement. I applied for permits in both jurisdictions and was the first person to receive a permit in federal waters of the Florida Keys and the second person to receive a state permit (Figure 4.1).

During the development of both aquaculture programs, we were able to insert language for an exemption that would permit the harvest of rocks that had live coral colonies on them. This was an important distinction for live rock farmers because all stony corals are protected under state and federal laws that ban the harvest and sale of live coral in the United States. The exemption was important to us in particular because of the prevalence of coral colonies that developed on our live rocks. During the two years' time it took for the seed rock (quarried limestone boulders) to become ready for harvest, many of the rocks would have visible coral recruits growing on them, making them illegal to harvest.

Figure 4.1 Live Rock Farm Lease.

My first live rock farm was permitted in the summer of 1994 in federal waters off Tavernier, a small town on the south end of the island of Key Largo. I immediately started adding rocks to the site, and by the end of the year had placed about 40,000 lbs of oolitic limestone imported from the Bahamas. By the summer of 1995, I had begun to add limestone that I hand-picked from quarries in South Florida. At the end of the first year of operations, we had over 100,000 lbs of rock on the site. After a year in the water, close examination of the rocks revealed small coral colonies, mostly either *Siderastrea siderea*, *Porites furcata*, or *Agaricia agaricites*.

By the summer of 1996, I had close to 200,000 lbs of limestone boulders at the site, and I was seeing visible coral colonies on hundreds of rocks. Experience taught me that producing marketable live rock involved more than just putting it in the ocean; it required regular maintenance, which usually involved either digging the rock out of the sand after storms or turning and restacking the rocks to make sure they were getting growth on all sides. Hunting for new coral settlers became an interesting distraction from the mundane job of maintaining the site. Over the years, I was able to identify at least 21 different species of stony corals on the rocks, some of which were common, while others were extremely rare.

Staghorn coral, *Acropora cervicornis*, was one of those rare corals that I identified on my rock site. I only found coral recruits from this particular species from late 1996 to early 1997. At the time, I figured if I saw recruits one year, they would appear every year. That turned out to be a false assumption for *A. cervicornis*, as well as for a couple other species that I found later on, including *Orbicella faveolata* (two recruits), *Diploria labyrinthiformis* (two recruits), and *Oculina diffusa* (five recruits). Fortunately, I had the presence of mind early on to start concentrating the rocks with the nicer corals onto one mound. This practice allowed me to keep track of how many different species of corals I was finding, as well as give them special attention after storms (Figure 4.2).

In the case of staghorn coral, I think I caught the tail end of the period of time when that species was effectively spawning and recruiting. By the end of 1998, after two consecutive years of severe bleaching and a Category 2 hurricane, the population was reduced to just remnant, fragmented colonies scattered about a wide area. I don't think the full effects of the 1997/1998 bleaching events sunk in for me until the summer of 1999 when I was able to revisit a lot of the areas that I regularly fished. What I found shocked me profoundly. I had witnessed previous bleaching events, but they were usually short-lived and didn't end up killing many corals. The 1998 bleaching event started in early June, and by early July, all corals throughout the entire Keys were bleached, and they stayed bleached until mid-October. This prolonged period of bleaching had a devastating effect on corals throughout the Keys, with some high value coral habitats experiencing massive losses, resulting in a rapid and complete phase shift to macro algae-dominated hard bottom communities. The various corals that I had carefully segregated onto one mound at my live rock site also bleached in 1998. Many of them died, but the staghorn corals somehow survived not only the bleaching but also the battering from hurricanes Georges and Mitch.

I spent the next year digging my live rock out of the sand and trying to eke out a living collecting tropical fish in the aftermath of each hurricane. Most offshore reefs had been scoured clean by the storms and had very few fish or invertebrates on them until the summer and fall of 1999. Just as things were looking better and the live rock farm was back in order, we had hurricane Irene pass through the Keys, stirring the water up, scouring the reefs, and damaging my live rock farm. Once again, the special mound of rock that harbored all of my staghorn corals held together, and the corals survived the storm.

In the next two years, I decided to completely rebuild the live rock farm by reinforcing the mounds of rock with large boulders and changing the whole design of the farm. I considered

Figure 4.2 First hard corals naturally recruited and growing attached to live rock.

fortifying my special *coral mound*, but since it had fared so well on its own and seemed to be held together by sponges, I decided to preserve its natural structure. Over those years, I continued to add other coral rocks to it as they developed on the rest of the live rock farm.

THE CORAL FARM

In November of 2001, I was invited to attend a conference in Orlando called Marine Ornamentals. As I shared in discussions with other members of the marine aquarium community, I realized that we all had similar concerns about the future of this delicate ecosystem. The energy and innovation that filled the conference center were inspiring, and my experience there sparked the idea that perhaps I could do something with the staghorn corals that were still growing at my live rock farm.

After the conference I shared my inspiration with my wife and daughters. Our family was involved in a 4-H club in the Upper Keys, and my second daughter, Kelly, took special interest in developing this idea as her 4-H project. Together, Kelly and I hatched out a plan to build a coral farm at the live rock site, thinking to eventually sell the harvested corals to the aquarium trade. Since she was only 14 and still had school obligations, I knew that a lot of the work would fall on me, so I set aside a chunk of time from collecting to dedicate to the development of our coral farm. Little did either of us know that this project would eventually lead to the development of a thriving multi-million-dollar nonprofit organization dedicated to replanting coral reefs.

Our first challenge was to come up with a plan for how we would set up our farm. I learned that other people were growing corals in aquariums all over the country, so I figured if they could grow them in an aquarium, then surely, we could use some of the same tools and techniques to do it in the open ocean. I had heard that people were growing corals in open ocean coral farms, but I didn't know anything about how or where they were doing it. Keep in mind this was 2001, and although the internet was in use, Google was a new idea. I still had dial-up internet at my house (high-speed, I might add, 56-Kbits/s), and my new cell phone was a flip phone with a 300 minute-per-month plan.

Our coral exemption at the time dictated that the corals must be attached to the rock while in my possession, so Kelly and I came up with a creative solution of pruning the end tips of the coral branches and attaching them to small rocks that we had glued onto bigger rocks. The thought was that when the corals were of a marketable size, we would detach the small rocks from the big rocks and sell the coral and small rock together. Because this idea was a little in the gray, I contacted people at the Florida Keys National Marine Sanctuary (FKNMS) and explained what I was planning to do. They had known about the corals since 1997, and their feeling was that they were my corals and I could do what I wanted with them. Accepting this sentiment as approval, we moved forward with our plans.

At first, we thought we could just cut pieces off the branches of the main colonies and wedge them into holes in the rocks, but this method failed more often than it succeeded. I then reached out to John Halas at the Upper Keys office of the FKNMS and asked if he had any ideas. John was involved in developing the mooring buoy system used all around the world, and I figured he might have some good ideas for underwater adhesives. He suggested using the two-part epoxy system that they use to fasten mooring pins to the bottom. So, I bought the special epoxy, the special caulk gun that dispensed it, and the special mixing tubes that went on the end of the epoxy tubes—and we went on our merry way to mount our corals (Figure 4.3).

Figure 4.3 Kelly Nedimyer using epoxy to attach fragments.

Our first day out was filled with many learning opportunities for us. First, we discovered that the epoxy was almost neutrally buoyant and tended to float around a bit as runny strands of sticky slime. The second issue was that it didn't readily stick to the rock or the coral but instead, preferred to stick to our hands. Finally, we discovered that the epoxy set up pretty fast, so if we stopped dispensing it for as little as five minutes, it would harden in the end of the mixing tube and we would have to replace it. Despite some of the frustrating setbacks of that first day, we not only successfully mounted our first 25 corals but also gained valuable insight that helped us to improve our methodology (Figure 4.4).

Something in me changed after cutting and mounting those first corals in May of 2002; from that day on, I spent a lot more time thinking about coral. I had certainly always appreciated coral before, but now it had a new value to me. What's more, I had the ability to do something good with it, and that realization awakened a new passion in me. I soon found myself going out of my way to check on my new coral babies, and because staghorn corals grow so fast, I was seeing changes in them every week.

Kelly shared my excitement and joined me as often as her school schedule would allow. As part of her 4-H project, we tried to track the growth of the individual corals by measuring the length of the different branches. The measuring was easy, but it became apparent that we needed to develop an effective system of labeling and tracking the individual corals. We started to rethink our nursery design. The initial design was working fine for the small farm, but we knew that if we wanted to scale up production and keep track of different batches of coral, we were going to need to try something different. We had also discovered that, in our small-rock-glued-to-a-big-rock model, the big rocks would either move or settle into the sand during storms. So, in February of 2003, we started gluing the small rocks to concrete blocks and standardized the process at ten rocks per block. The blocks were then organized in rows and partially buried in the sand to provide stability. This seemed to work pretty well, so we also decided to try growing finger coral (*Porites furcata*), another branching coral that was common on our live rock; thus, we designated a few blocks for growing these corals (Figure 4.5).

Figure 4.4 First staghorn corals cut and glued onto live rock.

Figure 4.5 Coral attached to concrete blocks.

CORAL REEF RESTORATION

By the summer of 2003, the corals we had mounted in May 2002 had grown well and were large enough for propagation. We made it a family day, and my wife and three of our four girls went out and propagated the old corals in order to make a new batch of corals. We had more coral available than we had places to mount the fragments, so some of the corals were left to continue growing. It was also in that summer of 2003 that we approached the FKNMS team about possibly planting some of our corals onto a reef in an attempt to re-establish a staghorn coral thicket at that reef. We took a couple of dead colonies in with us to show them the size we had available, and to discuss what we had in mind. When they saw the corals, their eyes lit up. As fate would have it, one of the people sitting in on our presentation was Harold Hudson, the head of the sanctuary's Damage and Restoration Program (DARP). Harold was able to see past the bureaucracy we were facing and understand the full potential of what we were proposing to do. He kindly let us know that there was not a definitive permitting process to do what we were asking, but he had an idea and would get back to us.

I'm not sure who he ever talked to, but Harold soon reached out to us with a proposal. He told us that if we planted the corals at a ship grounding site that he and the rest of the DARP team were attempting to restore, then the activities would be covered under his *manager's permit*, and we could proceed without any further permitting as long as he and some of the DARP team supervised us. Without any other options in sight, we agreed to the proposal and proceeded to set up a date and time to collect the corals and outplant them onto the grounding site.

October 29, 2003, was the first day when our schedules and the weather aligned properly. Harold and two of his team members met us at the local boat ramp, and we loaded up the boat and headed for the live rock farm/coral farm. We selected six staghorn coral clusters and two finger coral clusters, loaded them in the boat, and made our way to nearby Molasses Reef. The Wellwood restoration site at Molasses Reef is the site where the M/V *Wellwood* ran aground onto the reef on August 4, 1984, causing extensive damage to the reef. Harold had designed a restoration strategy that involved placing pre-made modules on the damaged portion of the reef and attaching them in place with concrete. This process was part of a major restoration project that had begun in 2001. The DARP team and other research groups were continuing to monitor the progress of the recovery. To keep from interfering with their work, Harold directed my coral restoration efforts to a lone module that was away from the primary restoration area (Figure 4.6).

Neither Kelly nor I had ever planted a coral on the reef, so we were following Harold's instructions and doing it according to his tried-and-true methods. Anyone who knows Harold knows he likes to work with cement—in fact, he is quite an artist with it—so we mounted the corals onto the restoration module using Harold's wonder-mix of Portland cement and modeling plaster. The whole thing could have been done in 20 minutes if it was just Harold doing the work, but Harold chose to invest the time to teach Kelly and me how to do it, so the process took close to an hour. We had no idea if any of the corals would live or how they would do over the next few years, but it was exciting to have done something that just might make a difference.

Figure 4.6 Kelly Nedimyer, outplanting corals at Wellwood site.

A CORAL FARM BECOMES A CORAL NURSERY

In early November 2003, Lauri MacLaughlin from the FKNMS contacted me and wanted to know if I would be interested in helping to collect and care for some corals that were being removed from a sea wall at the U.S. Navy base in Key West. The sea wall was being replaced. Everything on the wall was going to be destroyed, so they were looking for organizations that could use or care for the corals. The task of removing the corals was well underway, and many of the bigger and more important corals had already been removed. I was invited to take as many corals under 10 cm in diameter as I wanted, with the obvious understanding that they were not to be sold or introduced into the aquarium trade. I figured this would be a good opportunity to learn more about corals and to get involved with like-minded people, so I quickly got onboard and added a bunch of new species to my expanding coral nursery (Figure 4.7).

Because of my responsibilities as a fisherman, I wasn't able to get back out to the Molasses Reef restoration site until January 2004. I had received good reports from several different people, however, and I was thrilled to know that the corals were still alive. Those reports fueled my ever-growing interest in coral and the reef restoration initiative. Between the early opportunities with the Key West rescue corals and seeing our own corals growing on the reef, I knew our coral farm was going to have a different purpose than we had originally envisioned. I discussed this change of heart with Kelly, and she expressed her support. We hatched a new plan: instead of farming coral for profit, we would grow our corals and donate them to support the

Figure 4.7 Coral nursery with *corals of opportunity* from construction projects.

research and development of a coral restoration program for our local reefs. Even at the time, I realized that this change in direction would have financial repercussions for us. For one thing, had we stuck with our plan to produce and market these corals to the marine aquarium trade, we would have been the only people in the world offering that particular species of coral. The profits could have been significant. With our decision to donate them, we knew we would not only be missing out on the profits, but spending a lot of our own time and money to produce and maintain our coral populations. We had reached a crossroads, and the road that led to the potential of restoring the magnificence of local reefs had a stronger pull. So, we decided to go with what felt right and take a leap of faith into the unknown. Thus began the transformation of our coral *farm* into a coral *nursery*.

At some point in mid-2004, we were approached by Dr. Margaret Miller with the National Oceanic and Atmospheric Administration (NOAA) Fisheries about having our corals genotyped. I knew Margaret from work I had done with her in 2002 with long spine sea urchins. She had been using my live rock site for some manipulative experiments with sea urchins, so she was aware that I was developing a staghorn nursery for restoration and research. Apparently, a woman named Iliana Baums at the University of Miami was developing and perfecting a genotyping process that would allow them to determine whether two samples of the same species of coral were genetically the same—or different. To be honest, I didn't fully understand the significance of it at the time. I figured if she thought it was important, then it must be important; so I went ahead with the request. To prepare for the sampling and in order to take advantage of the results, I needed to first go out and label all of the corals that I was going to sample. I created some crude markers labeled *A* through *Z* and attached them next to each colony that I sampled (Figure 4.8). When the results came back, Kelly and I rearranged the corals into three groups corresponding to the three different genotypes and assigned them a name of K-1, K-2, or K-3—with K being an arbitrary letter chosen to stand for both Kelly and Ken.

Switching our efforts to producing corals for science and restoration meant that we could do away with mounting the corals on rocks and instead mount them on something that was easier to clean and that could be tagged and tracked. Up until that point in time, I was still unaware of what was being done elsewhere in commercial coral farms or in the fledgling field of coral reef restoration. I did know a little bit about what was being done in the marine aquarium industry, however, so I modified some of their ideas and came up with materials and processes that would work in the open ocean. For instance, we took their idea of a ceramic *frag plug* for mounting the corals, and we enlarged it and made it more suitable for our needs. We continued with our idea to use concrete blocks as our base, but we added concrete pedestals on top of the blocks to get the corals further away from the ocean floor. Each block had ten pedestals, and on top of each pedestal, we glued a cement disk that held the coral (Figures 4.9 and 4.10).

We also started to experiment with different underwater glues and epoxies. After trying at least a dozen different adhesives, I discovered an underwater epoxy called *All-Fix* that seemed to be exactly what we needed. Unlike the epoxy mix we had used on our very first outplants back in 2002, All-Fix had a long shelf life, could be mixed above or below water, had a long working time once it was mixed, and stuck to the desired substrate. When properly mixed, it hardened like a rock and the corals readily grew over it. It became the epoxy of choice for my work and has since become the epoxy of choice for most people attaching small corals underwater.

Figure 4.8 Tagging system for outplanted corals.

Figure 4.9 Coral on cement block plus extended pedestals.

Figure 4.10 Extended height off of the bottom using PVC piping.

In the fall of 2004, as part of Kelly's ongoing 4-H project, we decided to do a service project that would involve other students and 4-H members. David Makepeace, the local high school marine science teacher, offered to pay for a dive boat charter if we would include some of his marine science students. Thrilled to include the local high school, we took him up on his offer and prepared for our first service project. Preparations involved getting blocks out to the site and positioned properly, attaching the disks to the blocks in an organized fashion, and making sure there was enough space around each block for the teams of divers to work. On November 29, 2004, about 15 students and 6 adult supervisors gathered at the dive shop for a task overview and tutorial before we headed out to the nursery site. The service project proved to be a great success; the teams worked well together and were able to complete their tasks with focus and efficiency. This would be the first of many trips I would take with students, and the idea of training and involving recreational divers to help with the work would eventually evolve into a very important part of the business model for the nonprofit organization that I started a few years later (Figure 4.11).

Moving into 2005, everything seemed to be working great. The corals were growing, the nursery was expanding, and the other projects with the corals from Key West were doing great. We were on a roll. Then hurricane season started, and we had one of the most active and destructive hurricane seasons the Florida Keys had experienced in decades. The problems started in July when Hurricane Dennis passed south of the Keys, sparing us a direct hit but still giving us wind, rain, and big waves. Our method of half burying the concrete blocks had been effective

Figure 4.11 Students cleaning coral bottom modules.

for the average weather conditions we experienced during the year. It had even survived the active hurricane season of 2004, when four storms passed north of us. But we were hit by the sloppy side of Dennis, and the impacts to our nursery were significant. Most of our blocks were either toppled or partially buried by shifting sand, and we lost at least half of our corals. We had barely finished digging the nursery out of the sand when hurricane Katrina hit us, followed a few weeks later by hurricane Rita, then finally hurricane Wilma at the end of October. When the hurricanes finally subsided and the water cleared enough to assess the damages, the results were sobering. Of the 2,800 corals that were in the nursery in June, only 94 were left. The biggest lesson learned was that we needed to stabilize the blocks better and possibly get them up higher out of the sand (Figure 4.12).

The year 2006 was one of rebuilding at the nursery. We decided to stabilize every block by driving a long steel rebar rod next to each block and attaching it to the block with a long cable tie. One rod in the middle of the block proved to be sufficient, and later hurricanes and tropical storms had little to no effect on the nursery. We ended up putting a PVC pipe over the rod to make it easier to clean. Having the PVC pipe stick up over the top of the block also helped deflect turtle and shark traffic, which was becoming more of a problem (Figure 4.13).

This was also the year when we got involved with The Nature Conservancy (TNC) on a Florida Reef Resiliency Program (FRRP) funded project. The project actually started in late 2005, but because of late-season hurricanes and the disruption they caused, we didn't do much until the beginning of 2016. This project called for adding 20 new genotypes of staghorn coral to the nursery, then eventually outplanting them into different habitat types to see how the different genotypes would perform. This ended up being a pilot project for a much bigger project

Figure 4.12 Hurricane damage to field nursery modules.

Figure 4.13 Block nursery with pedestals.

that involved groups from the University of Miami, Nova Southeastern University, Florida Fish and Wildlife Commission, Mote Marine Lab, and Dry Tortugas National Park.

By spring 2007, our nursery inventory had expanded to 2,500 corals, not including the TNC/FRRP corals. Many of them were ready to be outplanted onto the reef. Although we had previously done this in 2003, and all of those corals were still alive, we had not yet *officially* applied for and received permits to outplant any nursery-grown corals onto the reef. After discussing our path forward with FKNMS staff, we decided that the logical next step would be to apply for a research permit to continue our work at the *Wellwood* restoration site on Molasses Reef.

We received our permit in early July 2007 to outplant 18 corals onto the reef adjacent to the *Wellwood* site on Molasses Reef. We once again teamed up with David Makepeace and some of his high school students. Since Kelly was now in college, we also recruited several of her college friends to help collect the corals and outplant them onto the reef. This was the first permit ever issued to allow aqua-cultured corals to be outplanted onto a reef in Florida—and it was noteworthy because the work was done by volunteer students. This was also the first time epoxy had been used to glue corals to the reef, a technique that would grow to become one of the most popular attachment choices for aqua-cultured corals in years to come.

Eighteen corals doesn't seem like a big deal now, but it certainly was a big deal for us at the time. That outplanting proved to be the spark that would ignite a large and growing effort to restore coral reefs in Florida and around the Caribbean. To be clear, there were other sparks igniting similar programs elsewhere, but this was certainly the beginning for Florida, and the press that would come as the program developed helped stimulate projects around the Caribbean.

I monitored the corals monthly for several months. By the fall of 2007, I was already working on a draft for my next application to plant even more corals. I was also regularly monitoring the six corals we had originally outplanted at the *Wellwood* site. Each time I visited, I found branches that had been broken off the original colonies. Thanks to the efficacy and convenience of my newly discovered epoxy putty, I was able to collect the fragments, mix up a small batch of epoxy, and attach them to the module on the same dive. Eventually, I ran out of space on the module and instead began to plant them around the module. When that area filled up, I moved a bit farther away from the module. I continued this way until there were hundreds, if not thousands, of small colonies planted in an area that covered several hundred square meters (Figure 4.14).

Figure 4.14 *Wellwood* site location after two years of growth.

STARTING THE CORAL RESTORATION FOUNDATION

By fall 2007, I realized I had a new life calling: to restore coral reefs. I began to think about how I would answer that call. I had job offers and letters of interest from a variety of organizations, but I knew that a salaried position would come with restrictions and obligations. After all of the freedom and flexibility I'd been enjoying as a marine life fisherman, I wasn't sure I was ready for that. I also knew that they wouldn't be able to match the income that I was still making; and, as a father of four girls entering their college years, I couldn't afford to take a pay cut just yet. I didn't like the idea of forming a for-profit company to restore the reefs because it would have gone against my whole motivation for doing the work. It wasn't about money or profit, it was about making a difference, and I knew I would be better able to rally others to this cause if it were disassociated from personal profit.

It was over a sandwich at Chad's Deli with my friend Lad Akins that I finally chose my path forward: I would form a nonprofit. I really didn't know exactly what that meant or how to go about it, but I knew it was the vehicle I needed to turn this vision into a reality. As fate would have it, I had joined the board of a local conservation nonprofit called Keys Marine Conservancy a year earlier. They were looking for a new vision, so I approached them with the idea of focusing on coral reef restoration and suggested some changes to accommodate the new vision. The proposed changes were well-received, so they called a special board meeting and voted on my proposal, which included renaming the company, installing new leadership, and adding two new board members. The vote was unanimous in favor of the changes, so out of the Keys Marine Conservancy, the CRF was formed in October 2007. As I was soon to discover, that transformation turned out to be the only easy thing about starting and running a nonprofit.

I had a seemingly simple and probably naïve vision for the organization: figure out how to grow and outplant enough staghorn corals to jump-start a natural recovery. Up until that time, almost every coral we had planted on the reef had survived and was doing well. It seemed logical to me that if we could just scale up our efforts, we could achieve that goal. By that time, I understood that genetic diversity was going to be a key component in any long-term population recovery, so I set out to get permits to increase the diversity we had in our nursery. I also applied for permits to establish coral nurseries at multiple locations up and down the Keys. The purpose for this was two-fold, allowing us to adequately distribute reproductive output as well as produce the corals close to the different geographical areas that needed to be restored.

Along with the new nursery and staghorn collecting permits, I received permits to collect elkhorn coral (*Acropora palmata*) and started working on developing nursery techniques for rearing this important reef-building coral. This was a really exciting step for me because elkhorn coral has always been my favorite coral and is possibly one of the most important reef-building corals in the Caribbean. Our first elkhorn nursery was located on the shallow crest of the reef, right where it likes to grow. We used the same disk-mounted techniques that we were using for staghorn coral, and we had solid success with most of the genotypes we collected (Figure 4.15).

In 2009, we once again teamed up with the same group we had worked with on the FRRP grant in 2006/2007 and were awarded a grant through the American Recovery and Reinvestment Act (ARRA). The secure, three-year funding from this grant allowed me to retire from marine life collecting at the end of 2009 and start drawing a regular salary as the president and general manager of the CRF. It also allowed me to hire two full-time employees and some part-time help, which took a lot of the day-to-day load off me and allowed me to think about how we could take the next step forward. Our nurseries were doing well, but they required

Figure 4.15 Snapper Ledge site location with elkhorn corals and nursery.

constant maintenance to keep the coral mounts clean and stay ahead of problems. I knew if we wanted to scale our program up to the point where it could reach the goals I had set for it, we were going to need to rethink how we were growing the corals. In early 2009, I had begun to experiment with the idea of growing the corals on horizontal lines hanging mid-water (Figure 4.16). I had seen some images of corals being grown on *line nurseries* in the Caribbean by Dr. Austin Bowden-Kerby and Andrew Ross, and I thought I'd give it a try. The early attempts were rudimentary at best, but the corals all lived, and actually grew really fast. I kept adding coral, and by the end of the year, I had about a hundred corals hanging from a multi-level line nursery located at our Tavernier nursery.

Figure 4.16 Line nursery, suspended mono-filament.

DEVELOPING THE CORAL TREE NURSERY DESIGN

It was timely and fortunate that I had begun to experiment with line nurseries when I did because in early January 2010 the Florida Keys were subjected to a prolonged cold front that ushered in some of the coldest air and water temperatures of the last hundred years—killing untold numbers of fish, invertebrates, and corals. We had temperature loggers at our nurseries at the time, and twice during that cold spell, the water temperature on the bottom dropped to 13.5 degrees centigrade (53 degrees Fahrenheit). We actually went out and were diving at the Tavernier nursery during one of those bone-chilling days, and the cold water was as stunning to us as it was to the corals and fish. Because cold water is denser than warm water, the coldest water was on the bottom, and we only had to get about two meters off the bottom to find warm, clear water. I could literally stand on the bottom and have my head in 72 degree water and the rest of my body be in 53 degree water.

During one of my dives in those frigid conditions, I noticed that most of the lines with corals on them were up above the cold lens of water. Only the bottom line dropped below this lens, and it only did so in the middle of the line, where the line drooped a bit from the weight of the corals. When I went back out to the nursery a few weeks later to assess the damages from the cold, all the corals on the line nursery were alive and well except for the corals in the middle of the bottom line, which were the ones that had dipped into the cold water. These were all dead.

The rest of the nursery sustained high losses as a result of the sustained cold, but the losses were not uniform and not complete. We found that some genotypes of staghorn coral experienced 100% losses, some experienced less than 10% loss, while most were somewhere in between. Our elkhorn nursery, which was located further offshore on the reef crest in shallow water, escaped any damage because cold water tends to hug the bottom and flow around the high spots on the reef on its way to deeper offshore waters. Fortunately, our Key West and North Key Largo nurseries were not yet stocked with corals, so we were spared cold-related losses at those sites.

The take-home lessons from this experience were that: (a) different genotypes react differently to cold and (b) getting the corals off the bottom and out of the cold could prevent losses from a future episode of cold water.

My first action was to install more line nurseries and get as many corals off the bottom and onto line nurseries as possible. I set up seven more line nursery structures at the nursery and set about moving a portion of every different genotype of coral onto one of the lines. We had to overcome some labeling and hanging challenges, but we soon became really fast and efficient at hanging staghorn coral fragments on lines. By late February, it was apparent that the corals on the lines were growing much faster than their cohorts mounted on disks, so I submitted a request to the sanctuary to add ten new line nurseries at each of our Key West and North Key Largo nurseries, as well as to the main nursery in Tavernier. In mid-March, I got a reply denying the request and citing concerns about the entanglement hazard they posed to endangered and protected sea turtles and marine mammals. It wasn't just the sanctuary pushing back, it was the U.S. Fish and Wildlife Service, NOAA Fisheries, and Florida Fish and Wildlife—so I knew this was going to be a dead end.

On the day we got the rejection email, it happened to be a cold and blustery day. Stuck on land because of the weather conditions, we had a few too many cups of coffee and started brainstorming a way to grow corals in the middle of the water column without creating an entanglement hazard. Our ideas went all over the place before we finally settled on one that entailed building a tree-like structure out of PVC pipe and hanging the corals from the branches with short pieces of wire. I happened to have a lot of spare PVC pipe and fittings laying around under the house, so we went downstairs and started building a prototype for this idea. By the end of the week we installed our first *coral tree nursery* model and hung some corals on it to see how it would do. Admittedly, we jumped the gun a little bit. I knew we needed approval for our new structure, but I was anxious to see if our idea would even work. After four weeks and quite a few nasty days, I was relieved to find that it was still intact and the corals looked fine.

I then went into the local FKNMS office and sat down with Bill Precht, the new head of the DARP program. We discussed our new coral tree idea and agreed that we should launch an experimental study to evaluate how a couple of different tree designs would perform in different weather conditions. We both believed that the entanglement issue had been alleviated, but we still had some concern about whether the structures could withstand adverse weather conditions. The testing lasted six months, and the results helped answer our questions about storm resistance, enabling us to further refine our design.

We intentionally did our experiments in a remote corner of our coral nursery work area because we felt we were onto something big and weren't ready for others to see it before we had finished testing the design. I had several people encouraging me to patent the idea; so, to keep my options open, I applied for a provisional patent. In the end, however, I felt that this idea was going to be a real game-changer for coral nursery and restoration programs, and I decided it was more important to get the idea out and let people use it freely rather than have it patented and used for personal gain. Once that decision had been made, I got together with my two coworkers, Kevin Gaines and Stephanie Roach, and we wrote and published a paper explaining the process in an open journal. The coral tree idea is now being used all over the world, and I have no regrets about the decision we made—it was the right one (Figure 4.17).

Figure 4.17 The original coral *tree* design.

TAKING IT TO THE NEXT LEVEL

At the CRF, once we realized how effective and efficient it was to grow corals on these midwater trees, we began the process of switching all of our nurseries over to the new method. During this transition process, we refined both the tree design and the process for hanging the corals in favor of developing a simple system that we could duplicate around the world (Figure 4.18). By the end of 2018, the CRF had scaled its Florida Keys nursery operation up to include four active, regional nurseries with over 600 tree structures between them, housing over 40,000 coral colonies from eight different species and hundreds of different genetic strains. Restoration output (the number of corals outplanted onto the reef) has grown to over 20,000 colonies per year with significant growth expected over the next few years as new species are added to the outplant mix and new techniques are developed (Figure 4.19).

Figure 4.18 Elkhorn corals growing on a coral tree.

Figure 4.19 Field nursery view of coral trees.

CONCLUSIONS

Developing and implementing strategies and programs for restoring coral reefs is going to require input from people who come from a wide variety of different backgrounds and who possess a wide variety of different skill sets. Scientists need to be involved in order to help answer some of the basic questions, but visionaries and entrepreneurs are needed to see the big picture, and businessmen are needed to create a successful business model to support the work. Coral reef restoration is moving from being an often criticized dream to a viable option for many areas—and the problem is not so much how to do it but how to pay for it.

I anticipate that active coral reef restoration is going to continue to become more sophisticated, efficient, and effective. There will always be skeptics who oppose the notion of trying to restore coral reefs, and their many objections do carry some legitimacy. It's true that the scale of the problem can seem to be overwhelming, that the threat posed by climate change is seemingly insurmountable, and that the money needed to make a difference could probably be allocated to solve a less challenging ecological problem. Those of us who are embarking on this crazy adventure are aware of the struggles lying ahead, but the difference is that we are not willing to give up and watch it all die. Our quest is not about money, fame, or power; it's about trying to save something we dearly love.

With the prospects of a rise in average global temperatures of 1.5 to 2.5 degrees centigrade over the next 100 years, coral reefs are expected to experience more frequent bleaching events; and unless global carbon emissions are reduced and active intervention is undertaken, reefs in many areas are not expected to survive. There are many different types of active intervention that can be applied to reefs around the world—from growing and outplanting key coral species to managing local activities and threats. If they are aggressive enough and if carbon emissions are tamed, I believe we have a chance to save many of the *at-risk* reefs around the world.

I've been saying for a long time that what we're doing in the reef restoration business is selling hope and buying time. What I mean is that if we can *sell* people on the idea that there is hope—in other words, that something can be done—then we can raise the financial support necessary to implement effective strategies that will buy time for coral reefs. The progress that has been made in the field and in the lab over the last ten years has given me more hope than ever that coral reefs can be saved. We have gotten really good at propagating corals asexually, we have gotten pretty good at producing corals by sexual reproduction, and we are now making great strides at selectively breeding corals to produce genetic strains that are more tolerant of the environmental conditions to be expected over the next 50 years. Despite the relative scarcity of funding to restore coral reefs, passionate people around the world are putting their heads and hearts together and developing real-world solutions to some of the challenges associated with our efforts to protect and restore coral reefs.

Oftentimes, our biggest challenge is convincing people that there is hope. We see the progress that is being made toward producing and outplanting corals on a scale that can make a difference, but we haven't done a very good job of getting the message out.

Buying time for coral reefs isn't just about growing and planting corals—it's also about reducing local stressors, such as local pollution, stormwater runoff, over-fishing, and physical impacts. It's about managing all activities that directly or indirectly impact the reefs. It's about stimulating awareness and motivating people to care about something they don't necessarily see without the aid of a mask and snorkel. Growing and planting corals is probably one of the cheapest and easiest ways to buy time, but it will be much more effective and will buy more time if it is paired with efforts to manage and reduce local stressors.

Can we buy enough time? I believe we can. I can't solve the worldwide climate change problem, but I can do my part in my own personal life—and I can do my part in my professional life by investing my time and energy into finding ways to save something that's important to me. If enough people make changes in their personal lives and invest their professional lives in saving something important to them, we can create a brighter future. In 2003, I could have decided to pursue money instead of pursuing my dream to save a few reefs in the Florida Keys. At the time, the money I could have made by selling my corals was a very attractive incentive for becoming a commercial coral farmer, but something more powerful was drawing me to choose a different path. I saw an opportunity to do something meaningful with my life, something that would have lasting value. The decision was surprisingly easy to make and is one I've never regretted.

The work I've done so far is just the beginning of a marathon effort to actively restore coral reefs. I and others who are contributing to this book have been working on developing some of the foundational technologies that will be the basis for new and exciting work that will be done by us and by those who follow in our footsteps. There will be failures along the way, but they will lead to successes. It's going to be a high stakes venture that I believe will involve people around the world, and one that will potentially affect the lives of billions of people. Count me in.

RECOMMENDED FUTURE RESEARCH

Advances in how we grow corals have transformed the challenge of restoring coral reefs. The big questions went from: *"How do we grow enough corals to make a difference?"* to *"How do we outplant all the corals we can grow?"* This is an important change because it now allows us to focus on other challenges that need to be solved if we want to restore reefs on an ecosystem scale instead of just small portions of a reef (see Figure 4.20).

Figure 4.20 Final tree design.

This new question will be answered in the next few years, and the new challenges will be to find the right corals for the right reefs. Over time, the role of offshore coral nurseries is going to change from being a place where large numbers of corals are produced for outplanting, to a place where corals are banked for genetic preservation, raised for selective breeding programs, and where sexually produced corals are field-tested and acclimated prior to being introduced into the wild.

Future research specifically needs to focus on how to produce corals that can not only live in warmer, more acidic water, but corals that will actually thrive in those conditions. Once those genetic strains of corals are being produced, we need to come up with ways to produce them in large quantities and outplant them onto the reef with minimal effort.

ACKNOWLEDGMENTS

I'd first like to acknowledge my wife, Denise, and our four girls, Kara, Kelly, Jennifer, and Julia. They have not only put up with me and my obsession to restore reefs, but they have gotten involved and given me strength and inspiration. Thanks to Mike Echevarria for believing in me and helping me find the right people to support this dream. Thanks to Tom and Jennifer Moore for their passion to see reef restoration work. Thanks to Kevin Gaines and Stephanie Roach for giving 110% in the early years of the CRF. I'd also like to thank John Hauk for all the time he's spent volunteering in order to help in whatever way he can. We need more John Hauks in this world.

SECTION II

Biological Considerations and Methodologies

5

LAND AND FIELD NURSERIES

David E. Vaughan

ABSTRACT

Typically, for all species of marine aquaculture production, there are three phases: the hatchery, the nursery, and the grow-out phases. In aquaculture for coral reef restoration, hatcheries are seldom utilized because corals can reproduce asexually, and at this point in time, gametes and resulting embryos are difficult to raise in a man-made hatchery setting. For the nursery phase in marine aquaculture as a whole, a land nursery or a field nursery may be used—and in many cases, both. In the first coral aquaculture operations, only field nurseries were utilized for outplanting into the field grow-out phase (final reef planting). As in most other marine aquaculture, once the species of interest has reached a certain size in the field nursery, it then would be harvested. In coral aquaculture, once corals reach a certain size in the field nursery, they are *outplanted* in a selected area where it is hoped that they will survive and grow into the reef system in that area. Now, coral aquaculture includes both land- and field-based nurseries and they are critical components in the production of corals for coral reef restoration. In this chapter, land and field nursery systems are discussed and strategies for the production of corals for restoration purposes are reviewed, compared, and forecasted for the future.

INTRODUCTION

Field nurseries for corals have historically been utilized for the branching type of corals, such as the staghorn coral (see Figure 5.1). It became evident that the branching type of corals naturally break or fracture during storms, or through contact with larger marine organisms, and could survive if these pieces landed and stuck in an appropriate hard bottom location. Scientists observed this in natural settings and enthusiastic aquarists also noticed this ability of broken pieces of coral to continue to grow under the right conditions. These combined observations helped set up a model on how to grow branching corals in field nurseries (see Chapter 6 regarding asexual reproduction: fragmentation and micro-fragmentation). *Acropora* sp. was the major species component in the Pacific, and the single staghorn species (*A. cervicornis*) was the first species in both the Atlantic and the Caribbean to be utilized in field nurseries. *Acropora* sp. was simply the first, the easiest, and the least expensive species to use. Presently other species are being added to the field nurseries since both the variations of equipment and processes are being improved and modified.

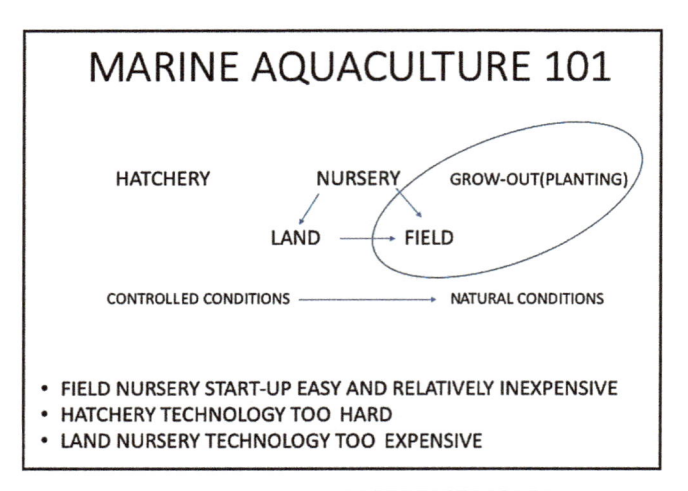

Figure 5.1 Diagram of typical marine aquaculture stages with three distinct phases. Notice that nurseries can be land-based, field-based, or both. Bullets reflect public perceptions. (Diagram by D. Vaughan.)

Land nurseries for aquaculture were first established for marine organisms such as clams, oysters, shrimp, and fish culture. Land nurseries for coral were established only very recently and initially were started for the marine aquarium trade. At the Harbor Branch Oceanographic Institution in the late 1990s, the Oceans, Reefs, and Aquariums (ORA) project added Pacific corals to their land-based production of clownfish and other marine ornamental organisms. Large tanks and raceways were used to produce hundreds of thousands of marine fish and over 100,000 branching corals, soft corals, and leather corals as marine ornamentals for sale for reef tanks (see Figure 5.2).

Figure 5.2 Picture of the author with Alexandra Cousteau and Philippe Cousteau at ORA land nursery, circa 1999 (photo by Jan Cousteau).

The actual process of coral fragmentation and micro-fragmentation will be covered as an asexual method for production of corals for restoration in Chapter 6. This chapter will cover the structures, supplies, materials, equipment, methods, and procedures needed to actually create land and field nurseries.

LOCATIONS FOR NURSERIES

Where to establish a land or field nursery is extremely important as the location can make a difference in: (1) the cost to permit, (2) the purchase/lease price, (3) the distance to travel to transport corals to the next stages, and (4) logistics for staffing and accessibility. For field nurseries accessibility, weather and wave conditions and storm hazards are paramount to the water quality conditions themselves. Location costs for land-based systems rival resorts and waterfront property values and possibly, a "not-in-front-of-my-summer-house" mentality. Both land and field nursery locations are possibly the most important decisions to be made for the new practitioner.

For land-based nurseries a primary consideration is where the salt water will come from to operate the nursery. Typically, land-based nurseries can use salt water from drilled ground wells or from adjacent water bodies such as canals, bays, and oceans. If there is no salt water naturally occurring, artificial salt in a recirculating system can be used, although this is not typically done for restoration work. For example, at Mote Marine Laboratory, salt water for the nursery comes from two sources: a saltwater well and the adjacent canal water.

How wastewater from land-based nurseries will be disposed of is another major consideration. Typically, this is either directly discharged to the adjacent water body or injected into a discharge well.

In general, the following considerations should be evaluated for each type of nursery.

Land-Based Nurseries

- Cost of waterfront property
- Availability of saltwater well and discharge well
- Availability of natural salt water to pump to nursery
- On- and off-loading equipment, corals, and gear from vessel or vehicles
- Security for both day and nighttime
- Storage for field gear
- Fuel storage for generators, vehicles, and vessels

Field-Based Nurseries

- Available nursery grounds or leases
- Water conditions good for growth and survival
- Wave and weather conditions good for access days to work safely
- Sheltered from storms and land-based runoff of sediments or pollutants
- Deep enough to be out of high surface temperatures (>3–5 Meters)
- Shallow enough to allow for unlimited bottom time (<10 Meters)
- Out of the way of other water users (skiers, fisherman, jet skis, boating channels)

AREA REQUIRED

The amount of area required for land or field nurseries can be fairly moderate. A one-acre land nursery is sufficient for a large-scale nursery production of 100,000 corals per year with room for parking, office, showers, laboratory, and housing. A small-scale facility with production of 12–25 thousand corals produced per year could be housed on a lot 60 ft × 100 ft or 20 m × 30 m (author personal experience).

The amount of bottom ground for a field nursery can also be fairly moderate. Permits for submerged land leases can be for one acre (220 ft × 220 ft) or less and be marked by anchored floats or buoys. Additional areas for the mooring or anchoring of working staff or visitors should be included in the design. A substantial corner buoy that is held down with a large mooring anchor can act as the nursery marker and mooring attachment, allowing for vessels to not have to anchor at all. The question of whether to mark the location or keep it stealth is dependent on the local population and favorite fishing hole. One suggestion is to stage a tour of the location with the local fisherman, divers, guides, and others who will benefit from the eventual outplanting to the reef in order to garner local support and protection from them. A no-anchoring lettering on the corner markers is highly recommended. Your permitting agency will most likely have their own regulations pertaining to marking and anchoring issues.

EQUIPMENT

The equipment utilized in nurseries has most likely been chosen for convenience, price, and existing materials at hand. Land-based nursery staff typically use leftover tanks from other types of aquaculture, and also make their own from materials such as plywood, fiberglass, or plastic. Many sizes and shapes of tanks, held up by platform bases, have been made that hold a limited amount of water in a condition that can be viewed, cleaned, and maintained easily while the corals grow. I sometimes refer to land nurseries as R&D, not for research and development, but for *refill and drain*. It is only the size and shape of the tanks that change—the methods of cleaning, monitoring, and changing tanks primarily stays the same (see Figure 5.3).

Figure 5.3 Example of land-based tanks or raceway with *O. faveolata*, grown from microfragments to 3 cm fragments at Mote Marine Lab, Florida Keys (photo by Dan Mele).

The shape and materials of field nursery equipment have more variations than land-based nursery equipment, but all rely on the same type of themes. They all include some sort of physical base, such as platforms, pipes, or lines that hold the corals securely in an area where: (1) they can be worked on, (2) they have a good chance of not getting buried in the sediments, and (3) they have the best conditions for growth and survival. Some of the classical types of physical bases are: tables, racks, modules, lines, floats, and trees.

- *Tables and racks*: some sort of fixed material to hold coral up off of the bottom sediments and in sufficient light conditions. These can have supportive legs that support the top surface material with some sort of screen or netting which support corals.
- *Modules*: usually weighted sections of materials such as concrete, pipe, and rebar to hold a base for corals to be attached to that is fixed on the bottom but supported off of the sediments. This could be as simple as a concrete block (see Figure 5.4) or as complex as concrete with extended PVC piping.
- *Line nurseries*: monofilament or polypropylene lines arranged vertically or in horizontal arrays or rows to support corals attached directly to or suspended from the lines. They can also support netting and become a three-dimensional floating nursery (see Figure 5.5).
- *Floating nurseries*: these are positioned at mid-water and provide endless opportunities for spaces and uses; they are usually healthier since they are subjected to enhanced water flow that supplies more nutrients while removing sediments. They can be positioned with lines at different depths and can be customized for allowing the gradual acclimatization to conditions of depth and radiation, and also for designated transplantation sites (Shafir and Rinkevich 2010).

Figure 5.4 Early field nursery equipment cement block supporting staghorn corals cemented on a concrete block (photo by Dave Gilliam).

- *Trees*: this is a term used for a suspended array of PVC or fiberglass pipes or rods with a vertical section supporting horizontal extensions or branches. Corals are either suspended from the extensions or attached in some form or fashion to look like a tree with hanging fruit. A bottom anchor and a top float support the *tree* in the water column. This method has been extensively used for staghorn corals and has now been extended with modification for some of the other species of corals (see Figure 5.6).

Figure 5.5 Field line and net nursery floating trays in the Red Sea (photo by B. Rinkevich).

Figure 5.6 Bottom modules and coral trees at Mote Marine Laboratory's (MML) field nursery (photo by E. Bartels/MML).

SUPPLIES AND MATERIALS

Land nurseries are basically an array of water holding tanks connected by pipes and valves to supply the salt water and air into the tanks, which allows for collection of excess water that drains from the tanks into the discharge or containment area (see Figure 5.7). These tanks are supplied by a water source in which the water has been filtered, treated, and stored prior to being pumped into the tanks that contain the growing coral (see Figure 5.8). A system of covers, shading cloth or devices, and tank support systems or legs are required but can be very simple in design (see Figure 5.9). The basic items are listed here:

- *Tanks*: these can be round or rectangular with sufficient water to cover the corals with at least a few inches (4–5 cm) of water to prevent excess sunlight penetration of ultraviolet (UV) light and higher temperature layers. Water is usually supplied from one side and drained from the opposite, hence the term *raceway* tank. Depth and total volume of tanks allow for stability of water quality from temperature swings during the daily or seasonal cycles and salinity variations from rain events. Materials such as fiberglass and epoxy coatings have been used by many industries and make an impervious surface that is easier to clean.

Figure 5.7 Land nursery tanks at Coral Vita, Grand Bahama (photo D. Vaughan).

- *Supports*: any materials that can physically support the weight of the tanks—such as concrete blocks, wooden racks and legs, or PVC piping and foam supports—have all been successfully used. Use a material that will last in outdoor conditions and is salt water tolerant.
- *Pumps*: there are many kinds of pumps from magnetic drives, centrifugal, and submersible types in all kinds of sizes, horsepower, materials, and performance. The costs to

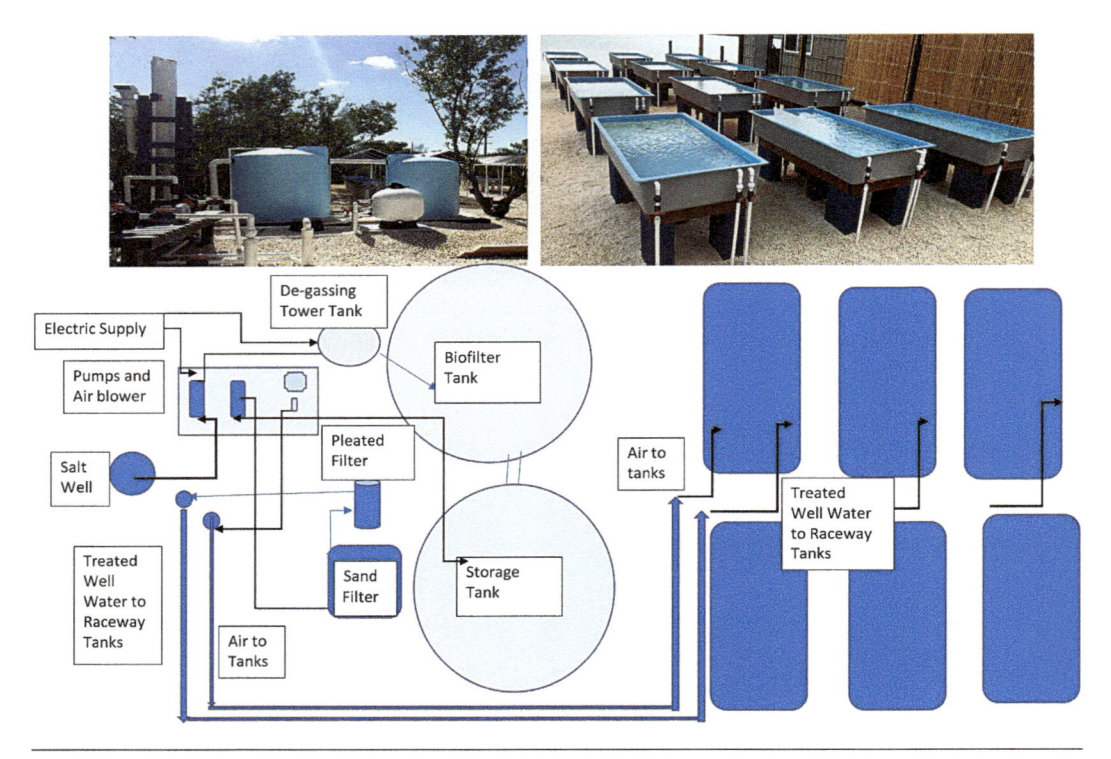

Figure 5.8 Land-based nursery designs and plans (Paul Hundley, HTH Aqua, and David Vaughan).

Figure 5.9 Scout S.T.E.M. training tanks for the Boy Scout High Adventure, SeaBase-Florida (photo D. Vaughan).

buy and the costs to run should be considered. The horsepower, volume pumped per minute, and the vertical head will all determine how much volume of water each tank will get. This is not a guessing game or an "any-pump-will-do" situation. Get with an experienced engineer or aquaculturist to determine what your real needs are. Add a little more for future expansion and then double the number of pumps purchased *to always have a backup.*

- *Pipes, valves, and fittings*: the design criteria for water flow through the tanks is very important to consider—it is not just a line from the pump to the tanks. The size of the pipe needs to be calculated by a professional or experienced party because both the supply lines to the tanks and the drain lines from the tanks need to match the flow volumes, rates, and pressures to provide the amount of water and flow rates needed. This is an engineering calculation based on tested flow rates and resistance to flow for pipes, plumbing fittings, size, and lengths of pipe—and professional or experienced help should be included. This is the case for air as well; if the piping is not properly sized, the pump will either burn out or not provide the flow. Proper valves that will direct flows, turn off flows, or moderate volumes need to be considered. Proper fittings for changing or adding sections along with the amount of friction loss can make a system efficient and expandable—or not.
- *Filtration equipment*: comes in all shapes and sizes, and the cost to install, operate, and maintain it will vary. This is an art unto itself. Just as there are so many kinds of filters in the aquarium aisle of a pet store, so are there plenty of choices for aquaculture. There are basically three types of filtration used to clean the water: (1) sediment or particle removal, (2) organic or biological removal, and (3) bacteriological removal or sterilization.
- *Sediment or particle removal*: this involves the separation of suspended particles such as sand and silt to clarify or clear the water. This is best done in one location for all water to all tanks rather than at each individual tank. It can be easily accomplished with sand filters, such as a pool type of filter or cartridge, or bag filters, at each tank location. If using more than just a few tanks, a general in-line filter such as a rapid sand filter can be used to filter the majority of materials with a simple back-flushing operation to maintain flows. Cartridge or bag filters are best used at the location and can be added if specific water quality at a point source is needed.
- *Organic or biological filtration*: is usually done with bio-filtration, which is the utilization of bacteria on a surface film or other material that can reduce items such as ammonia to nitrite, or nitrite to nitrate, which is a less toxic form of organic waste. This can be done with medium-to-large tanks with increased surface area materials such as *bio-rings*, etc., to provide the natural bacteria in large amounts that break down more toxic forms of nitrogen waste to less toxic forms and levels. As in any aquarium, these natural bacteria will develop on their own with time or you can purchase starter cultures to jump-start this process that are available through any aquarium store or aquaculture supplier.
- *Sterilization* to get rid of harmful organisms like algae, bacteria, and viruses can be done with systems such as UV light sterilizers where a specialized UV-emitting light bulb is used to sterilize micro-organisms before they get to your tanks. This process is done as a final sterilization step after filtration of larger particles. Care must be used with these systems in order to provide safe containment of the UV light and also to be aware of the use of electricity and water in the same location.

DESIGNS, PLANS, DRAWINGS, AND LAYOUTS

If you were any kind of a farmer, you would not just scatter seed haphazardly, you would plant in organized rows; if you were a plant nursery operator, you would place your greenhouse frames and racks in rows. As a land or field nursery operator, you need to first lay out and design your operation plan and drawings. You should start with a design concept and develop plans and a layout to proceed further. For most this would include an engineer or architect who is familiar with hydrology or aquaculture systems design. This should be done to assist with development of a budget, space configurations, and permitting needs. In some regions this is needed for local permitting and for any state, federal, or other requirements. Make sure to contact your local and regional agencies to learn what is required. Many agencies will not have experienced engineers in this field, so you may need to prove that you contacted an experienced professional to provide or review such plans. Next, you would develop an accurate list of the supplies required, create a budget, establish a plan for permitting from the appropriate agencies, and map out future management of your system.

A field-based nursery may require different equipment strategies—according to the different species, genotypes, and/or the age of the crop—that need to be organized, labeled, and operated effectively. Figure 5.6 shows organized rows of both bottom modules and coral trees. A certain amount of distance between nursery equipment is crucial for creating a working area that is easy to maintain and clean. It is also important to consider currents, waves, and storm conditions that may affect system spacing. As on land, good straight rows can be laid out with the help of stakes, pipes, and lines. Labeling of the rows, sections, and each separate piece of equipment is paramount for record keeping (see appendix) and tracking genotypes.

A land-based nursery system can be designed and planned as you would do for any aquaculture production facility. Remember, it is just not simply a bunch of tanks and some water. Planning the space, sizing the pumps, and calculating the water flows and pipe sizes are critical—and so is soliciting help from engineers and those with experience in culture production facilities to help in that planning. The pump locations, the layout of the tanks, and the piping on both a site plan (viewed from above) and a ground or elevation view (viewed from the side) will give the permitting agencies, contractors, and staff the details and directions necessary in order to purchase the right supplies and material, plus experienced installation advice (see Figure 5.8). These plans and diagrams can be provided by engineers, but they are also easy to prepare on your own by utilizing standard software programs that are affordable. I guarantee this will not be the only time you will use this tool in the planning stage. In addition, if modification and expansion of the facilities becomes a reality, this will enable that modification easily.

If at all possible, allow for sufficient room to work around tanks—usually 2 feet or 0.6 meters—and be able to utilize equipment (bins, buckets, hoses, etc.) and have staff members pass by. Keep in mind the amount of space needed for visitors and those who may have special needs to work, assist, volunteer, or observe. Figure 5.7 shows sufficient room for students, guests, and visitors at the Coral Vita nursery in the Bahamas. Figure 5.9 shows room around the tanks for S.T.E.M. education classes at the Boy Scout Sea Base facilities on Summerland Key, where high adventure experiences include coral restoration training. Shading for tanks is important in order to shield the tanks from excessive rains and harsh sunlight with various shading materials (see Figures 5.7 and 5.9).

FOULING—MAINTENANCE AND CLEANING

In addition to the initial set up, fragmenting, and harvesting, the majority of time in maintenance is the cleaning of fouling organisms. This is usually accomplished with small brushes or scrapers to remove algae and other encrusting fouling organisms. Each location may have its own fouling challenges and also may have varied differences seasonally. In some cases, cleaning is not required. Some cleaning can be encouraged by natural grazers such as in floating nurseries where grazing fish are congregated and allow for natural algal and fouling organisms to be removed from the nursery material and corals prior to outplanting (Frias-Torres and van de Geer 2015).

In land nurseries, natural grazers can be selected for use in the raceway tanks. Many grazing gastropod snails have been used to keep both the coral plugs as well as the tank, as clean as possible. Then only the snail grazer waste products need to be removed via siphoning rather than the whole tank surface. In some cases, siphoning and rotation of coral into clean tanks every week have worked to minimize the fouling organisms into later successional species (such as CCA, crustose coraline algae) that are harder to remove. A maintenance regime like this can be accomplished with one empty, clean tank in a group. So that each day, at least one tank full of corals is transferred to the clean tank; the fouled tank is then cleaned and allowed to dry overnight to become the clean tank for another transfer. In that way, a tank is no more colonized than what can grow in a week, thereby minimizing the labor, although there always seem to be volunteers ready to assist in this task. And if there is room for automation—robots and automation—this is what the volunteers would contribute as suggestions for getting to scaling.

LABEL EVERYTHING

In land or field nursery systems, the corals or groups of corals need to be identified and therefore labeled in some way. Since it is very hard to make any sort of marking directly onto the living coral itself, it is easier to mark the base, tray, tank, rack, or tree that they are located on. Coral plugs, whether ceramic or concrete, can be labeled using permanent ink markers or paints on the stem, side, or underside of the plug (see Figure 5.10). Permanent marker ink wears off over time due to fouling, so it is suggested that the marking be covered with clear super glue, or something similar, for protection. In Figure 5.10, the top plug on the left is labeled on the plug stem. The middle plug on the left is marked on the underside of the plug and super glue covers the right side for protection from elements and fouling. Labels should identify coral species, genotype, and fragment group if possible, along with any other valuable information. In Figure 5.10, the bottom plug on the left tells us it is AP or *Acropora palmata*, spawned in 2013, settlement genotype X, and fragmentation group 2. On the right side of the figure are corals that have been trimmed for *frag and fly* outplants, and these plugs are labeled on the bottom.

If the coral cannot be labeled sufficiently, the tray or tray section can be labeled instead. In Figure 5.10, on the right side, the tag faces up for easy reading and travels along with the coral fragments on the plastic rack from tank to tank. In this situation, the plug with the label on the top becomes the tag itself and can follow into a field nursery or field outplant. A simple system on land of a labeled plug or a labeled piece of PVC pipe can be a stable tagging system with the identification tags moving with the coral, rack of corals, or full tank of corals—so that accurate records can be kept on all of them (see appendix for record keeping).

Figure 5.10 Label of species, genotype, and cutting on plug stem or underside (left) and plug used as label and record of specific corals of the lower adjacent three corals (right).

Field nurseries and outplants may need more elaborate labels and tagging to survive more extreme fouling, grazing, and weather conditions. Figure 5.11 (bottom) shows a plastic cattle ear-tag that is sequentially numbered and attached with plastic tie wraps to both secure and move from field nursery tree or nursery structure to a field location. Field outplants can be labeled in this method and stamped aluminum tags nailed to the substrate can be used as well (Figure 5.11, upper left). The upper left of Figure 5.11 also includes a movable tile with the date that can be used for further size comparison measurements. Later photo monitoring of the same corals (upper right) shows the same tag, a new date tile, and numerous size reference tiles that can allow for more precise measurements after returning from the field.

Tagging can become a casualty of fouling. In Figure 5.12, we see a tile plate (left) with nine micro-fragments, and the tile is labeled by the species and the experiment ID# (6A) (plus a 2.5 cm^2 tile and a 1 cubic cm green plastic cube for size relationship). The same tile months later, (right photo) shows that the CCA, and other fouling organisms, have completely grown over the original label. Now a separate plug is labeled 6A and always travels on the plastic crate with the tile, as a tag and label.

Figure 5.11 An array of corals (top left) planted with aluminum tags and photo recorded with labeled tile for date and 2.5 cm² tiles for size reference; (top right) same array, five months later with aluminum tags still visible with stamped code, plus new tiles placed for dates and size references, also camera picture dated; (bottom) numbered plastic cattle tag for staghorn outplant site.

Figure 5.12 Land-based nursery labeled 6A on tile with a 2.5 cm^2 square with date and size reference and a 1 cubic cm green plastic cube for recording the size (left). Months later, the tile label is overgrown with CCA and a separate plug with a label of 6A accompanies the plastic rack for recording (right photo).

MEASURING THE GROWTH OF CORALS

Measurements to determine coral growth are very important for monitoring coral health and the ultimate success of any restoration project. Coral growth is determined by routinely taking size measurements of the coral and recoding the data. Many massive coral species in nurseries, as well as smaller sizes in the field, are measured with the dimensions of length and width—and can be easily done with a simple ruler or photo. The lateral extension measurements of both the length and width are used to determine growth for massive coral. Liner extension or expansion measurements are taken to determine growth in the branching corals. For staghorn corals, linear growth in all branches needs to be measured to get a full documentation of growth. As outplant sites get larger over time, future measurements will most likely become documentation of colony expansion and whole reef improvements, as restoration gets to scale.

For an example of measuring growth from photos, return to Figure 5.11. The top left of the figure shows outplanted coral and the top right side shows the coral five months later. To determine the growth, simple computer programs to measure size can be used. A mouse or cursor can be used to trace the size of the reference tile (here 2.5 cm × 2.5 cm), which allows the computer programs to calibrate and then accurately measure the circumference or outline of each coral in the before and after photos to determine the amount of growth. New methods of photogrammetry and photo mosaics are now used (Chapter 11) for large-scale recording of growth and expansion. Chapter 22 reviews new ways for photo mosaics and other health parameters using advanced technologies for monitoring and measurements.

PRODUCTION CAPACITY

Nurseries (land or field) are what allow for the more controlled care of the production of corals for the final outplanting to take place. Whether it is a land nursery or a field nursery, or better yet, a combination of both, this is where both the production at scale and the economic costs of production are lost or gained. Figure 5.13 shows the potential if one hatchery (discussed more in Chapter 8) provides genetic stocks to 10 land-based nurseries, which supply 100 field operations that each outplant 10,000 corals, resulting in one million corals. The land-based option, in comparison to the field-based option, may be more expensive in the initial setup if you have to purchase waterfront properties in order to construct the nursery. However, most land-based facilities can operate year-round and in almost all weather and wave conditions, without the limitations of possible dive time. No system is right or wrong since there are as many ways to culture organisms as there are culturists ready to try something new. And new techniques, materials, and equipment are being invented for the use of coral restoration at a rapidly increasing rate. More, faster, and cheaper is the direction that the industry is going as the scale of the need for restoration is as huge as the expanse of our tropical waters are wide.

So, what is the right capacity and what is the right cost-per-unit effort? It all depends on the need and the speed of restoration required for each area. Whether you need one large megafarm or hundreds of small farmer operations will depend on the location, the economics, and the social needs and involvement of the country or island nation. What was thought in the recent past to be a large expansion when a thousand corals had been grown and planted, soon will be a regular operational goal per day. What a few thousand corals can do in ten years of growth may be what gets accomplished with ten thousand corals in just one or two years. A small operation can be successful with just a few tanks or a few nursery tables or coral trees. With time, experience, volunteers, trained staff, and support, medium operations should be able to produce 25,000–50,000 corals per year. Large operations should be looking at 50,000–100,000 or more per year to be able to impact and restore a larger area. Five years ago, the largest future

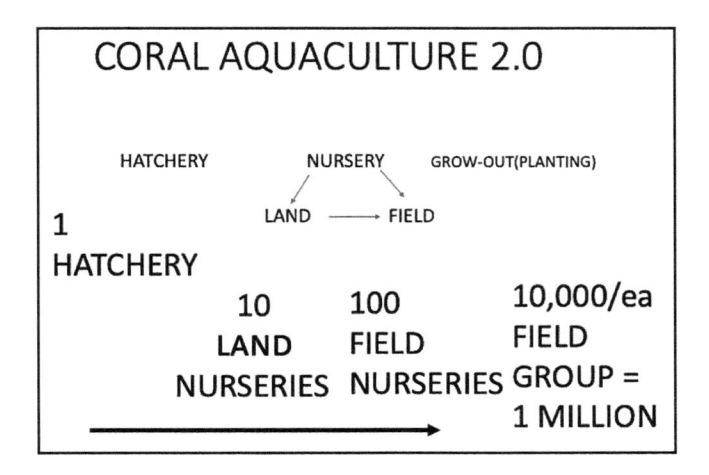

Figure 5.13 Coral aquaculture 2.0 shows the integration of hatchery, land, and field nurseries, and what they can produce in combinations—by using only one hatchery, you can supply 10 land nurseries, which can serve 100 field nurseries and result in one million corals (diagram by D. Vaughan).

goal would have been to plant a million corals; that will soon be accomplished by *numerous* organizations in the next five years. Improving the efficiency and productivity of the land and field nursery operations will be the key to this taking place.

VESSELS AND VEHICLES

Now I don't mean urns and cars, but transport vessels (boats and barges) and underwater vehicles (remotely operated underwater vehicles, autonomous underwater vehicles, drones, and robots). As this book is being written, there are already larval-dispersing robots, photo-monitoring drones, and crown-of-thorns killing machines—and soon, there will be underwater planting automation test vehicles. If you think the manual labor workforce in factories is becoming automated, expect the coral restoration processes in all areas to become more and more efficient with equipment, machines, and artificial-intelligence decision making.

Vessels will have to become more specialized in the transport of the types of equipment along with the amount of corals required from land to field and field to final outplantings. These may end up looking more like the aquaculture commercial boats to tend fish aquaculture with fingerlings, food, and harvested products. The use of recreational fishing boats to deliver thousands of corals—possibly in water—will look more like catamarans, barges, and moving platforms in the near future.

SAFETY CONCERNS

Any time you are working on, in, and around the water, there are safety concerns for all—including staff workers, bystanders, students, and volunteers. At land-based nurseries, any time you have electricity, pumps, and lights around salt water, there is the hazard of shocks and electrocution. Correctly grounded plugs, outlets, and extension cords, and correct operational protocols are a must. UV lights with water running around an electric bulb are notorious for stray voltage and also eye damage from improperly viewing if the UV light is on or not. Working in wet surface areas with *slip-and-fall* hazards, hoses, and extension cords can make a workplace unsafe.

Field nursery operations, outplanting, monitoring, and inspections at sea have all of the same hazards as commercial fisherman, boaters, and dive operators. As with any operation on the open water, proper boat handling and the safety of people swimming or scuba diving need to be encouraged, along with the avoidance of marine hazards from stings, bites, and overexposure to sun and temperatures. Water-based operations need to consider all of the boat safety rules, regulations, and good common sense put into practice by all water-dependent businesses and operations.

LEAST ECOLOGICAL IMPACT

Finally, it is important to keep in mind that restoration technologies and operations must also be aware of ecological impacts that the restoration process may have. Land-based system operators need to think about not only the water source for the coral nursery, but also the water discharge, location, and water quality measures. Many land systems that utilize saltwater wells for a pure source of water should also consider a saltwater well for discharge or disposing of water. Direct water discharge should consider the quality of the discharge and the point source of release to always be better than the water that it is going into. Also rinsing, cleaning, and sterilizing tanks should be done with discharges or containment in mind. Proper use of any chemicals, compounds such as bleach or acids, etc., should have clearance with the local permitting agencies. Some nurseries feed their corals brine shrimp (Artemia) that are native to the Great Salt Lakes, which may not be proper for discharge into other bodies of water.

Field operations should use only eco-friendly materials and supplies for cleaning and maintaining equipment, for the prevention of fouling, and for keeping pests or predators away. Coral restoration aquaculture cannot afford the stigma that land agriculture and aquaculture have sometimes been awarded, even if only caused by a few. Derelict equipment and materials should never be left behind as a monument to old technologies. The overuse of plastics is a global environmental problem and every effort should be made to look for alternative and reef-friendly materials that will not come back to haunt us. Remember, *first, do no harm* and leave only fin-prints—and many more corals than when you came.

DISCUSSION AND FUTURE WORK

It is imperative that aquaculture for coral restoration follows the lead of all of the other marine aquaculture species, and scale up! With technological development, improved equipment design, and an increase in dedicated and experienced people, we are in a position to scale up both land- and field-based nurseries for coral—and by using both, we can get to scale in the millions (Figure 5.13). Future economies of scale and exponential production levels will allow corals to be produced at a high speed and in appropriate numbers to successfully implement restoration programs around the world (Vaughan et al. 2019).

ACKNOWLEDGMENTS

I wish to acknowledge all of the hobbyists, aquaculture farmers, and scientists who have come together to share equipment, technologies, and experiences to make the propagation of corals at a scale that is sufficient enough to carry out the restoration of our coral reefs as a legitimate ecological process—now and in the future.

REFERENCES

Frias-Torres. S. and C. van de Geer. 2015. "Testing animal-assisted cleaning prior to transplantation in coral reef restoration." *PeerJ* 3:e1287.

Shafir, S. and B. Rinkevich. 2010. "Integrated long-term mid-water coral nurseries: A management instrument evolving into a floating ecosystem." *University of Mauritius Research Journal* 16:365–386.

Vaughan, D., S. Teicher, G. Halpern, and J. Oliver. 2019. "Building more resilient coral reefs through new marine technologies, science, and models." *Marine Technology Society Journal*. 53, 5:21–24.

6

ASEXUAL CORAL PROPAGATION—FRAGMENTATION AND MICRO-FRAGMENTATION

David E. Vaughan

ABSTRACT

Asexual reproduction is a type of reproduction by which offspring arise from a single organism and inherit the genes of that parent only; it does not involve the fusion of gametes and almost never changes the number of chromosomes. In coral colonies, asexual reproduction occurs when individual polyps divide through budding and in so doing, expand the colony size. This ability of corals to asexually reproduce is particularly helpful when corals break or fragment in nature and is an evolutionary adaptation, which allows for the growth and reattachment of broken fragments after storm conditions. People learned from nature and the first form of propagation of corals for reef restoration through the breakage or fragmentation of coral branches. Capitalizing first on the more fragile branching corals such as staghorn, made it simple, easy, and inexpensive. This technique was first adopted on a large scale by thousands of aquarists who took the broken tips of their own propagating colonies, grew them, and also shared them with others aquarists. This fragmentation method was also used for the first active coral restoration projects around the world. Using a relatively easy in-water field technology to simply break a fragment of coral from a branching coral, mount it nearby, and let it grow bigger, propagates more coral fragments for further restoration. The slow-growing, massive, reef-building corals do not branch, meaning that this manual fragmentation method could not be used; thus, they were ignored—until recently. Hope for the massive reef-building corals began when micro-fragmentation was discovered from a laboratory mistake (really a eureka moment!) (NY Times 2014) and provided a new way forward. Micro-fragmentation methods, used now on the reef-building corals, not only produced very small pieces that allow for large numbers of corals to be produced, but the resulting pieces are somehow stimulated into a rapid growth phenomenon that now equals both the production capacity and production scale regrowth that was so valued earlier by the branching coral restoration methods.

INTRODUCTION

Fragmentation

Fragmentation is essentially the process or state of breaking or being broken into small or separate parts. This general definition is a common phrase in both the reef restoration world and also the reef aquarium industry. Following mother nature's evolutionary adaptation by the fractional breaking of the fragile branching corals into pieces by storms or marine organism interactions and its reattachment is a proven successful form of asexual propagation and expansion of its territory. The natural occurrence of storms can break the more fragile branching corals species into pieces that can be physically transported modest distances from the parent colonies; and if they survive and continue to attach and to grow, it is an evolutionary advantage. Broken fragments rolling around in the sand or mud substrates are destined for unsuccessful re-establishment. But like the trees that send many new seeds into distant locations and only some take root and survive, so it is with natural coral fragmentation. Branching coral pieces that land or stick into crevasses, holes, or hard bottom locations, can continue to grow and reattach themselves with new tissue growth onto a hard bottom substrate. Many coral restoration practitioners have already found this to be true from their own field-based nursery stocks or outplanting areas after a storm event. Home reef aquarists have long known that a broken coral piece will reattach somewhere else in the aquarium tank and propagate a new colony. Exchanges of fragmented pieces between friends who are aquarists and other hobbyists have taken on an usual event of fragment trading, and the marine ornamental industry supplies coral tissue to the commercial reef-tank trade arena.

It is not surprising that for coral restoration, fragmentation of the branching corals became the first method of choice. The fragile branching corals evolved this way to take advantage of expanding their physical territory after breakage from storms or other events. There is also evidence of breakage caused by feeding animals such as turtles, sharks, and other large fish species trying to catch prey and causing collateral damage of the branches of corals. In the Atlantic and the Caribbean, this is emphasized with the staghorn-type of coral forms *Acropora cervicornis*—a classic, fragile, branching coral species with analogous forms in other parts of the ocean.

Fragmentation Background and the Staghorn (Acropora Species) Story

Jorge Cortes et al. (1984; republished 2010) showed that translocation of living branching corals from the surviving side of a storm ravaged island in the Pacific could be used for restoration at a large scale. Austin Bowen-Kerby expanded on this method of coral restoration in the 1980's with Acropora species as part of his graduate thesis in the Caribbean. Ken Nedimyer expanded on the methods in the Florida Keys, establishing the restoration process by using natural settled staghorn coral colonies that recruited to his live rock lease in the waters off of Key Largo (see Chapter 4). Ken clearly demonstrated the aquaculture potential of fragmentation in a Future Farmers of America project with his daughters; the technology expanded quickly as a restoration tool. Ken received funding support from The Nature Conservancy (TNC) and the National Oceanic and Atmospheric Administration (NOAA), and the underwater nursery materials, technologies, and methods evolved into a nonprofit restoration operation called the Coral Restoration Foundation. An NOAA stimulus grant expanded this program into all of South Florida using multiple partners—including universities, government agencies, and nonprofits—and was one of the first large-scale projects in the United States, located in south Florida and the Florida Keys. This coordinated project brought together reef restoration practitioners, researchers, and government agencies with the goal of demonstrating methods that are scalable and fundable, as well as job creators. This project provided larger than expected nursery production levels and the successful survival of outplantings. All of these used comparable materials that evolved over the grant period and produced even more efficient and effective equipment and methods, culminating in the *Acropora Restoration Guide: Best Practices for Propagation and Population Enhancement* produced by TNC (Johnson et al. 2011). Austin Bowden-Kerby (2014) supplemented this manual in Punta Cana, Dominican Republic, with the *Caribbean Acropora Restoration Guide: Best Practices for Propagation and Population Enhancement*. Approximately 30 or more staghorn coral field nurseries sprang up in Florida, Meso-America, and across the Caribbean, all taking advantage of the easy fragmentation methods of staghorn corals and the fast growth rates to show success. Methods were simple, inexpensive, relatively easy to permit in remote locations, and easy to teach to technicians and volunteers. This led to many photos, documentaries, video clips, and time sequences of growth rates being available to the public and expanded coral restoration outreach. However, this was primarily for only this one single species, *Acropora cervicornis* (staghorn coral).

Acropora corals were the first corals in the Atlantic and Caribbean to go on the U.S. Endangered Species Act. Both *Acropora palmata* and *Acropora cervicornis* were listed and are now classified as *critically endangered* according to the global International Union for Conservation of Nature Red List. It was recognized by many agencies that they should coordinate their management initiatives to address the multiple threats affecting these corals, including the need to protect the remaining populations and to rebuild, restore, and recover degraded populations. This book hopes to address a critical need that exists to develop and disseminate both a best practices manual for asexual and sexual propagation techniques, along with a strategy for managing health and genetic concerns for population restocking actions. The Smithsonian Institution and NOAA designed a workshop to take the first steps toward filling these gaps. Some of the Acropora Workshop recommendations are listed here (Johnson et al. 2011):

- Proper source population assessment and identification of donor coral colonies (e.g., high genotypic diversity, fast growing genotypes, and/or a range of environmental conditions or habitats to which the donors may be adapted)
- Suitable nursery site identification and assessment (including physical considerations such as protection from high wave action where appropriate, presence of intact trophic structures, and depth of nursery sites, as well as the presence of no-take marine protected areas, etc.)
- Determination of best collection methodologies (including considerations for size of fragments, disease prevalence, proximity, etc.)
- Use of best tracking methods (which may include the development of a number or lettering system to track genotypes from the original donor colony through successive generations of fragmentation to the outplanted colony/population)
- Determination of optimal transport and handling methods
- Determination, assessment, and use of best planting and propagation techniques
- Selection of best management protocols for predation, disease, and biofouling

- Determination and use of best long-term site monitoring protocols (including environmental conditions, survivorship, mortality, growth rates, predation, etc.) (Acropora Coral Conservation/Restoration Workshop Final Report November 12–13, 2009, Washington, D.C.)

Many if not all of the previously listed recommendations have been addressed or improved in multiple locations with slight or little divergence from the first staghorn nurseries established over the past 10 years. Details of these aforementioned publications are available to the public in the form of best practices, manuals, supplementary information, reports, and many videos that are available online.

Methods of Fragmentation

The general or overall process involves cutting or breaking of the coral tips, branches, or sections and allowing them to grow more tissue and increase in size and number of branches for further use as broodstock (grown or donor coral tissue that will be fragmented again). This can take place in either a field nursery based in local waters or at the site where restoration is to occur. Fragmentation can take place in either type of nursery (field- or land-based) as explained in Chapter 5. With fragmentation, one piece can be grown up to 10 times the original fragment size with an increased number of branches that can then be cut again to make more fragments (Figure 6.1). For staghorn corals, this can mean 5–10 pieces from every one original fragment in under one year and sometimes under six to nine months. This simple method can produce large numbers in short periods of time. However, they are all of the same genetic strains and technically clones of each other. Most practitioners have expanded their field nurseries to include as many genetic strains or genotypes as possible, in order to afford higher genetic diversity. Most practitioners will track and separate the field nursery structures by genetic types in order to track performance.

The equipment and materials for these field nursery operations have evolved quickly to take advantage of water flow conditions, light, and handling methods to optimize growth. Some of the first systems created were just simple concrete block bases where cement or epoxy were used as the adhesive to attach the fragments to each block. Many fragments were also attached to other types of bases such as plugs or pucks that were also made out of cement, allowing the practitioner to handle the fragment by the bottom of the base and not have to handle the coral itself. The size, shape, and thickness of these bases were usually dictated by the form or mold that was used to cast the concrete pieces. The bottoms of cups, egg cartons, and manufactured molds have been used to create bases. Commercial production of plug-shaped bases with stems have been made of ceramics, plastics, or cement and were available first for aquarists and now for restoration efforts. These are used in both land and field nurseries now and can be made on-site with Portland cement plus sand, using a rubber floor mat for a mold (Figure 6.2).

Field nursery equipment evolved from cinder blocks for concrete buildings to custom-poured base plates or bottom modules using cement and sand mixtures. Many learned that the increased height off of the bottom also increased the growth and survival of the coral with increased distance into the water column. Customization of bottom modules by using PVC pipe extensions also increased the distance that the plug and fragment could be positioned higher above the sediment and in better water flows. This trend continued by moving further up into the water column using various other designs, known as line nurseries, tables, and trees (see Chapter 5). Each of these have advantages and disadvantages—depending on costs, availability

Fragmentation—Growth by powers of 10: from 1 to 1,000

1 ten-inch piece of coral can be taken from a healthy colony and then cut into ten 1-inch pieces

10 1-inch pieces each grow ten inches (typically takes 6–12 months)
Then they are cut into ten sections each yielding a hundred fragments

100 1-inch fragments are then grown to ten inches (another 6–12 months), and cut yielding

1,000 new total fragments—possible in just 1–2 years total time.

Figure 6.1 Sequence of fragmentation to produce thousands.

of materials, durability, fouling, maintenance, environmental conditions, and permit restrictions (Figure 6.3).

Field nurseries of several different designs for the branching corals have been successful around the world (see the case studies in Chapters 11–21). The overall success is attributed to fast growth, ease of fragmentation under water, low costs of equipment and supplies, and the lack of need for a more expensive land-based nursery system. Initial stocks are usually from small field permitted collections of tissues from multiple colonies or genotypes or from *corals of opportunity* collections. Corals of opportunity is just the regulatory label for corals at risk, broken, or compromised in some way to allow for permitting agencies to categorize the corals for legal collection. The rapid growth of branching corals allows for many fragments to be produced from a single donor stock in less than a year. This allows for the logarithmic expansion of a field nursery and the ability to start field outplanting relatively early after the

Figure 6.2 The cement-based coral plugs in the four buckets were made using the individual spaces within a rubber floor mat as the molds (photo by D. Vaughan).

OLD and NEW TRICKS FOR CULTURING BRANCHING CORALS—STAGHORN

Figure 6.3 Variation of field nursery types of equipment: old style (upper left) on cement blocks on ocean bottom, and newer *coral trees* in water column anchored to the bottom.

initial start-up. The specifics of nominating nursery site locations, permitting requirements, maintenance, monitoring, outplanting sites, and best practices have been reviewed in detail in multiple publications (Johnson et al. 2011; Bowden-Kerby 2014).

MICRO-FRAGMENTATION

Fragmentation of corals, like vegetative plants, has been around for a long time, especially in the aquarium trade, but mostly with medium-to-large pieces and primarily using only the branching corals. The massive coral species were overlooked because of their large size, difficulty in cutting instead of manually breaking into fragments, and also their perceived slow growth rates and production capacity. The usual types of equipment to cut a massive coral with extensive skeletal mass were industrial tile saws which had to be done at a land-based facility. Cutting and growing fragments of the massive coral types was possible, but time-consuming and much slower than the faster growing branching corals.

The early development of fragmentation methods for the massive species was developed mainly for experimental research at universities and institutions (where they used similar sized replicates, such as 3 cm × 3 cm cut pieces) and not necessarily for restoration purposes. For this research, optimal sizes for fragmentation were published for branching corals (Rinkevich et al. 2005) and for massive species (Foresman et al. 2006). A pivotal discovery of how small a viable fragment can be occurred from the accidental breakage of a coral produced from sexual reproduction in the lab that yielded unexpected results ("Eureka Mistake" in NY Times 2014). Small sized, even single polyp pieces, from a three-year-old elkhorn coral (*A. palmata*), grown originally from the larval stage, were broken accidently on the bottom of an aquarium tank. These small fragments grew much faster than was considered *normal* from only a few broken pieces that were first thought unviable. This was the actual beginning of *micro-fragmentation* as a term and as a technology that has since been extended to many more of the massive species of hard corals with the same results of fast growth and big survival rates. Refinement and optimization of the materials, equipment, and procedures of micro-fragmentation led to the production of coral for outplanting at scale and affordability. From this method (Page et al. 2018), the restoration of diverse species of coral for the reef are possible. Micro-fragmentation is essential to create outplants of the massive coral species that were previously thought to be too slow growing for use in restoration, yet can now be grown in the numbers and growth rates of the branching corals (Vaughan et al. 2019).

Micro-fragmentation requires a more exact cutting instrument that will allow for the separation of a smaller-sized fragment, with only a minimal amount of skeletal material, and the ability to adhere it to a base plug or tile substrate for further growth (Figure 6.4). The large commercial tile saws for cutting ceramics work well for getting starter tissue material cut away from the field colony skeletons or off of the previously grown tissue on cement or ceramic bases or plugs. The next step is to make the finer cuts which can be done using a smaller band saw that was designed for cutting gems or coral rock into small stone-sized pieces for jewelry making. Commercial band saws outfitted with diamond-chipped blades work well (Gryphon) and need to be designed to also provide a saltwater supply to prevent the blade and coral from overheating. Thin pieces of the live tissue material with a minimal amount of dead skeletal material attached can be cut into slices and then cut again into cross sections to ultimately provide the size of pieces preferred. Figure 6.5 shows the pattern and sequence of the micro-fragmenting process. Basically, larger pieces can be reduced to a workable size (3–10 cm pieces) using a

Figure 6.4 Micro-fragmentation of massive corals into small pieces using a diamond blade band saw (Gryphon); this 2 cm piece of *O. faveolata* will be cut into ten or more micro-fragments (photo by D. Mele).

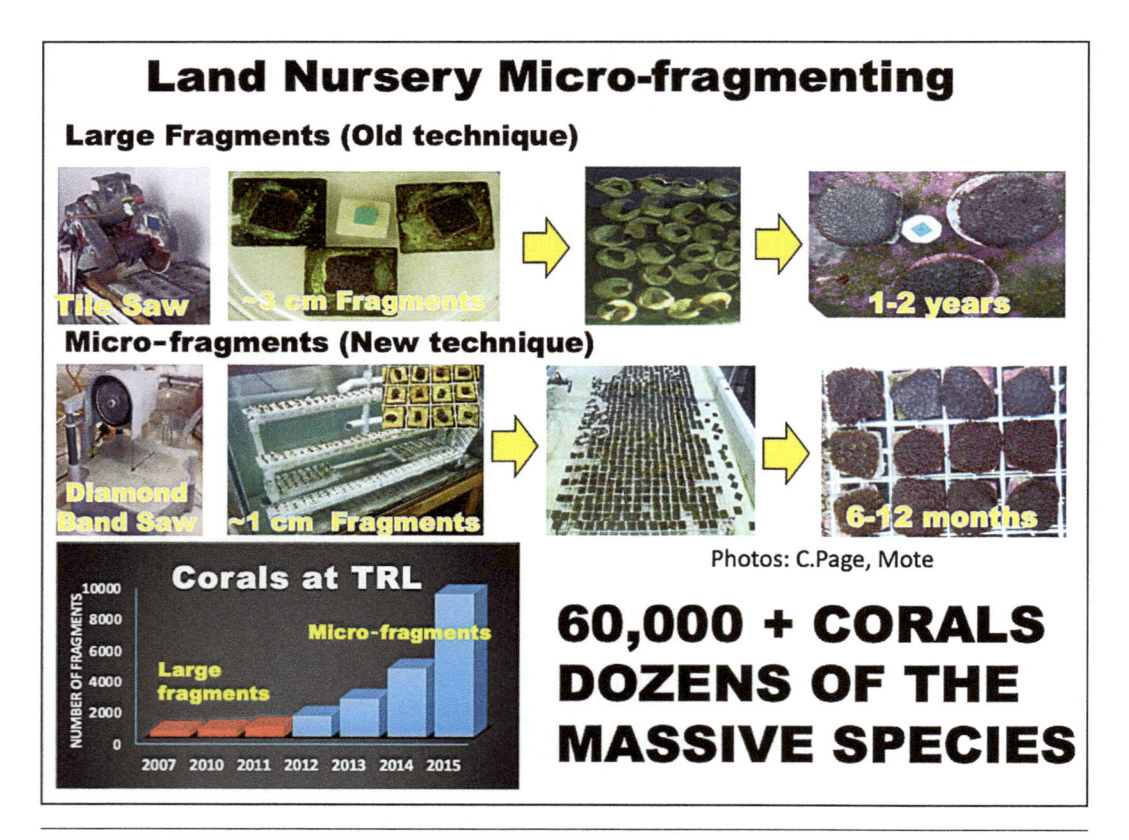

Figure 6.5 Comparison of common tile cutting saw fragmenting large pieces and diamond band saw (Gryphon) cutting micro-fragments (photo by C. Page).

standard tile saw. Next the band saw is used to cut them into 3–5 mm strips—or whatever size width is desired. Finally, the strips are cut into 3–5 mm lengths or the final sizes of micro-fragments desired. This process can be fairly rapid and with two or three experienced people put into a production line assembly to (1) cut, (2) wash off mucous, (3) clean and dry, and (4) attach with glue. Using this process, 500–1,000 micro-fragments can be produced in one day (Figure 6.6). When done in a land-based nursery, laboratory, or dock with electricity, it can easily be accomplished in any weather—rain, wind, or wave conditions—(if under cover) as opposed to field nursery operations where environmental variables come into play. Today these techniques, however, are being adapted for the field nursery and even final grow-out locations around the world.

Figure 6.5 shows the typical process flow, equipment, size, and number produced using regular fragmentation techniques for massive corals versus micro-fragmentation. The first major difference is the total number of new fragments produced from the same size colony or amount of tissue available. A regular colony size fragment of 3–4 cm may take one to two or even three years to grow enough to cut into just a few more fragments. Alternatively, this same size piece can be cut into 10–100 micro-fragments, dependent on the polyp size of that species. Each of these micro-fragments can be grown back to the original size in less than one year and sometimes in as little as six months; therefore generating a very large number of new colonies when micro-fragmenting, plus the added benefit of stimulating an increased growth rate back to size in just a portion of the time usually required.

Short-term accelerated growth was an unexpected but welcome benefit of this micro-fragmentation process. What is actually happening within the polyps to produce this accelerated growth effect is not certain at this point in time. It is theorized that this growth rate change is

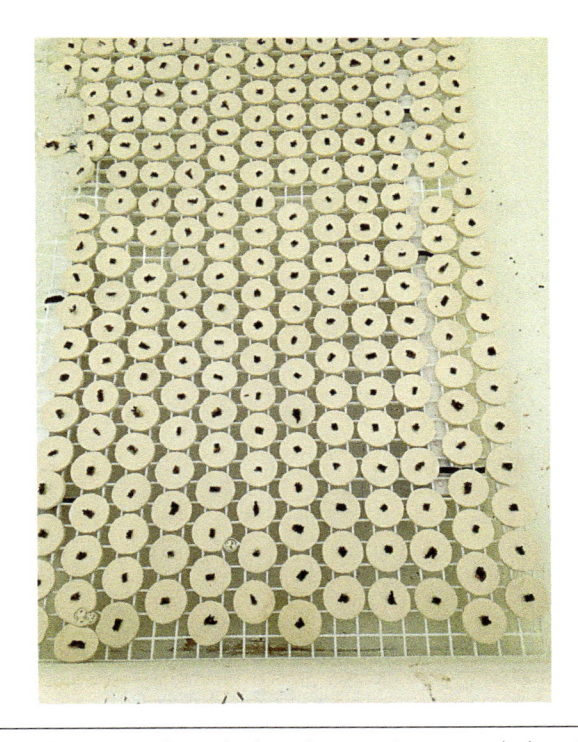

Figure 6.6 Production of large number of micro-fragments on coral plugs in a raceway tank.

a possible function of a *wound healing* response and is characterized by rapid lateral growth from the severed edge. This quick lateral extension is only for a limited period of time and may represent the process of healing over damaged tissue or re-establishing lost substrate area or re-colonizing surface material before a competing or fouling organism can. Whether the response is physiological: inducing a chemical or hormonal response, or induced physically: from the physical tearing of the tissues, or just evolutionarily: genetic advantages, remains for further research. This may have been a long-term reaction to healing after parrot fish bites. The resulting stimulated growth rate is many times the normal rate of lateral extension on a mature colony. This is an enormous advantage for the coral propagation process, where there is both the large number of fragments produced that grow more quickly to a size where they can be outplanted at the restoration site, or micro-fragmented again in the nursery.

The production capacity with micro-fragmentation can create in numbers that are exponential. The speed to cut and mount 500–1,000 micro-fragments per day makes large scale-up operations possible. The time for outplanting or re-fragmenting, for the massive corals that have been cut into micro-fragments, now rivals the faster-growing branching coral species. The growing space required to hold and grow 1,000 micro-fragments into fragment-size colonies (10 cm^2) is only one square meter.

Different species vary in the size of their polyps (small, medium, and large), and therefore, the number of polyps per centimeter of a micro-fragment piece also vary. In a plug or tile that is 10 square centimeters (3.2 cm × 3.2 cm), if the species are cut into just 2–3 polyps, depending on the size of the polyp, they can produce from 10–100 micro-fragments (Figure 6.7). Small stony coral polyps such as *Acropora palmata* have tiny polyps and can be cut into just 2–3 polyps that measure only a few millimeters in size. A fully grown plug of 3–4 cm in diameter can have over 200 polyps, and therefore, can be a donor of 40–100 fragments. This *Acropora* species (elkhorn) attains the thickness and size of massive reef-building species and therefore is conducive to micro-fragmentation as well.

Medium-sized coral polyps, such as in *Orbicella* sp., may only have 50 polyps possible on the same size diameter plug, so therefore 20 micro-fragments may be the average produced. Large-sized coral polyps, such as *Montaestrea* sp., with 5–6 mm polyps may only produce less than 10 fragments per cut from the parent colony. This is also the case with brain coral type species

Figure 6.7 Micro-fragments of just a few polyps of elkhorn corals *A. palmata*.

where the common polyps are arranged in grooved skeletons and have common mouths in the grooves along the ridges and, therefore, by including at least one mouth in the fragment, they may only produce a smaller amount of fragments from each donor colony plug or base. Usually, ten percent of the broodstock is kept to calculate production of more broodstock colonies for the growth to the next cutting cycle.

NEW WAYS OF FRAGMENTING

- *Frag-N-Fly*: the land-based cutting of micro-fragments using the usual land power equipment and saws, but then immediately (or limiting the land-nursery stage) moving into a field nursery or even final outplanting location (Figure 6.8).
- *Manual micro-fragmentation*: the use of manual clippers for either top-side cutting on a vessel or field cutting in a nursery. This can be accomplished with simple hand cutting tools and uses the outer growth area of a nursery overgrown plug edge or the thin new tissue from broodstock colonies. This can allow field nurseries to use micro-fragmentation technologies without the required land facilities. The field nursery can, therefore, cut the fragment in the vessel and drop it back under water at the field-nursery and place it back in the nursery equipment (Figure 6.9).
- *Multiple-cutting*: this is simply using the field outplanted colony as a repeatable nursery donor. Using fully grown outplants as the broodstock increases the potential for exponential production of nursery or field outplants. The field outplant, if used for a

Figure 6.8 Frag-N-Fly of micro-fragmentation and immediate outplanting to nursery by staff and students fragmenting colonies for the field (photo by Dan Mele at Mote, Florida Keys).

second cutting or continued cuttings as a donor, helps produce fragments in the same location from recent outplants. This reduces travel distances, reduces the earlier stages, and increases the total number produced from the original planting that could continue indefinitely. If every outplanted colony is used again in a year for a clipping of ten more fragments, and again after an appropriate amount of time to heal and grow back, you have a perpetual coral production machine. Theoretically, if 10 more fragments are possible every two to three months, in 10 years, that coral would provide 100 colonies. Each of these, in turn, could do the same in a few years and fill a reef in over an outplanting decade (Figure 6.10).

Figure 6.9 Manual use of cutters for micro-fragmenting on a vessel above the field nursery—another example of Frag-N-Fly but on a vessel (photos by D. Vaughan).

Figure 6.10 Multiple or second cutting of older outplant as secondary nursery in Cancun, Mexico, with J. Gonzales.

CONCLUSIONS

Asexual reproduction of corals is not only possible—but quick, easy, and inexpensive. The simple method for fragmentation of the branching corals is successful from aquaria hobbyists at home to staghorn type coral restoration projects in field nurseries. Micro-fragmentation is now a new and fast upcoming variation of that technology. It is similar in comparison to outdoor vegetative cuttings of plant materials to now common indoor laboratory-based tissue-culture production of plant material for agriculture. This is now being implemented in many locations around the world to increase both the coral restoration speed and also the scale of production that is now possible for the more massive species of corals that were once thought to be out of reach of restoration techniques. This practice is being done not only in land-based nurseries, but it is also being adapted to field-based nurseries and even used directly on the outplant site with greater success than ever before. This is a *game-changer* for coral restoration.

Discussion

Coral restoration technologies include the aquaculture propagation of coral colonies to outplant on the reef. Most restoration today utilizes the asexual production of corals through the breaking, cutting, or fragmenting of pieces of the colony in order to produce more growing pieces or *fragments* for planting. The addition of *micro-fragmentation* adds the additional massive coral species to the list of species that can be propagated and restored (Forsman, Page, Toonen, and Vaughan 2015). It also adds the advantage of increased growth to methods that can work at scale, while also lowering the price and the time from cultivation to outplantings. This can also be complementary to other methods such as *coral fusion* (Chapter 7) and relates to increasing the coral reef restoration potentials around the world.

RECOMMENDED FUTURE RESEARCH AND FUTURE TECHNIQUES

(See also: Chapter 21, Emerging Technologies)

- *How small can you go?* What is the smallest size that is possible to cut and still thrive? One single polyp is the most likely answer today—but in the future, who knows? This will also depend on more accurate cutting tools as is seen in other industries such as plant tissue culture and possibly by using automated cutting methods.
- *How fast can you grow the fragment?* The optimization of conditions that will make this process even faster may depend on understanding the mechanism that is producing faster growth and also on optimizing control of the water quality and all growing conditions.
- *How fast can you increase production at scale?* This may depend on how quickly fragments on the land-based or field-based nurseries can get outplanted to the field with successful survival. Decreasing the handling time or the distance from the final locations will help in the cost of labor. Automation may become a future player, as is seen in land nursery production of plants and animals in agriculture and aquaculture.

ACKNOWLEDGMENTS

I would like to acknowledge all of those who advanced the aquaculture production of corals—from the aquarists to the students, practitioners, and scientists who developed and progressed the technologies for the propagation of corals that are now used for reef restoration, were used in the past, and will be used in the future.

REFERENCES

Acropora Coral Conservation/Restoration Workshop Final Report, November 12–13, 2009. Washington, D.C.

Bowden-Kerby, A. 2001. "Low-tech coral reef restoration methods modeled after natural fragmentation processes." *Bulletin of Marine Science* 69:915–931.

———. 2008. "Restoration of threatened *Acropora cervicornis* corals: Intraspecific variation as a factor in mortality, growth, and self-attachment." In: Proc. 11th Int. Coral Reef, pp. 7–11.

Bowden-Kerby, A. et al. 2014. Best Practices Manual for Caribbean *Acropora* Restoration, Puntacana Ecological Foundation.

Cortés, J., C. Jiménez, A. Fonseca, and J. Alvarado. 2010. Status and conservation of coral reefs in Costa Rica. *Revista de Biología Tropical, 58*, (Suppl. 1), 33–50.

Forsman, Z. H., B. Rinkevich, and C. L. Hunter. 2006. "Investigating fragment size for culturing reef-building corals (*Porites lobata* and *P. compressa*) in ex situ nurseries." *Aquaculture* 261:89–97.

Forsman, Z. H., C. A. Page, R. J. Toonen, and D. Vaughan. 2015. "Growing coral larger and faster: Microcolony-fusion as a strategy for accelerating coral cover." *PeerJ* 3:e 1313.

Johnson, M. E., C. Lustic, E. Bartels, I. B. Baums, D. S. Gilliam, L. Larson, D. Lirman, M. W. Miller, K. Nedimyer, S. Schopmeyer. 2011. Caribbean *Acropora* Restoration Guide: Best Practices for Propagation and Population Enhancement. The Nature Conservancy, Arlington, VA.

NY Times. 2014. "A quest to regrow a coral reef." Vol CIXIV, No.66696.

Rinkevich, B. 2005. "Conservation of coral reefs through active restoration measures: Recent approaches and last decade progress." *Environmental Science & Technology* 39:43.

Vaughan, D., S. Teicher, G. Halpern, and J. Oliver. 2018. "Building more resilient coral reefs through new marine technologies, science and models." *Marine Technology Society Journal*, 53: 21–24.

7

CORAL FUSION: HARNESSING CORAL CLONALITY FOR REEF RESTORATION

Z. H. Forsman, C. Page, and David E. Vaughan

ABSTRACT

Fission and subsequent fusion of coral colonies is a natural process resulting from partial mortality caused by factors such as storm damage, vessel groundings, predation, bleaching, disease, and sedimentation. When any parts of the colony are separated or die, the surviving tissue can grow back together and fuse over a variety of substrates, including dead coral skeleton. When fragments from the same genotype grow back into proximity and come in contact, they will recognize each other as *self* and grow together or fuse again as a colony. On the other hand, if they are not the same genotype, an antagonistic reaction may be initiated. Fusion of the same genotypes (isogenic fusion) is an important life history strategy for clonal organisms to increase shared resources, to compete for space, and to recover from disturbance. For reef-building corals, fragmentation and colony fusion are key components of resilience to disturbance. Observations of small fragments that were rapidly spreading tissue and fusing over artificial substrates have led to the development and widespread adoption of the *micro-fragmentation and fusion method* for reef restoration applications. This includes things such as the creation of large artificial coral modules, the mass production of smaller *coral seedlings* that are designed to self-attach to the reef, or the use of micro-fragment plugs or tiles for *re-skinning* or *tiling* the dead coral rock or potentially turning artificial reefs and breakwaters from *gray* to *green or blue* infrastructure. Using rescued corals or *corals of opportunity* in combination with micro-fragmentation and fusion is an optimal approach. In this chapter, we review these new methods and discuss how this technology can become an important technique for coral restoration strategies—now and in the future.

INTRODUCTION

Fusion is the process of combining two or more distinct entities into a new whole. For corals, it means the combining or fusing of separated tissue and polyps into a new, larger colony. This happens in nature more often than might be expected when a colony suffers partial mortality and then subsequently grows back to reconnect living tissue (Hall and Hughes 1996; Gardner et al. 2005; Roff et al. 2014). For restoration purposes, harnessing the strategy of *micro-colony fusion* allows the practitioner to grow corals to a larger size at a faster rate. In this way small (~1–4 cm^2) fragments of a variety of coral species have been observed to spread over new substrate at a surprising rate—doubling or tripling the total tissue area coverage in as little as four months (Forsman et al. 2015; Page et al. 2018). This rapid spreading may be an innate quality in corals that are reduced in size or a wound-healing response to maximize tissue regeneration (Lirman et al. 2010; Page et al. 2018). If these small colonies are placed in an array within two to four centimeters of each other, they grow and fuse together producing a basketball-sized coral colony from a softball-sized piece of donor tissue in as little as five or six months (Figure 7.1).

Figure 7.1 Isogenic fusion (modified from Forsman et al. 2015). Top panel: *Orbicella faveolata* fusion experiments. (A) Initial fragments of *O. faveolata*; (B) the fragmented colonies after 90 days; (C) the fragmented colonies at 139 days, as colonies begin to fuse; Bottom panel: *Porites lobata* fragments placed on ceramic tiles and photographed after 205 and 368 days respectively.

One of the major benefits of the coral micro-fragmentation and fusion strategy is that for the first-time, massive corals—those species that are typically slow growers but resistant to bleaching stress (Loya et al. 2001; Lirman et al. 2011)—can be incorporated into restoration programs with a capacity and speed that is heretofore unprecedented (Page et al. 2018; Vaughan et al. 2019). Consequently, this method offers a new tool for reef restoration that builds resilience into restoration with considerable modular flexibility. Next, we will review a variety of applications and approaches that take advantage of micro-fragmentation and fusion.

CORAL RE-SKINNING

Coral micro-fragments that have grown to the edge of their substrates can be employed jointly to achieve rapid colony fusion in a process called *coral re-skinning* (Page 2013). In this strategy, micro-fragments are deployed in an array directly onto the reef. Fragments are mounted flush to continuous dead substrate so that tissue attaches and grows onto the existing framework. Each fragment will then grow independently of each other, allowing the practitioner to maximize the growing surface area within the array. If fragments originate from the same genotype of corals that come into contact with each other, they will fuse to form one large colony instead of many small ones (see Figure 7.2). This technique is not only extremely prolific, owing to the short generation time of micro-fragments (asexual reproduction was also discussed in Chapter 6), but also, array size is highly adaptable to the size and shape of existing dead reef structure. Reef structure that is successfully re-skinned is shielded from erosive wave action and reseeded with actively accreting coral tissue.

The coral re-skinning technique is effective when predation post outplant can be minimized. Page et al. (2018) suggested prior acclimation to site conditions to minimize initial predation since micro-fragments of *Orbicella faveolata* suffered substantial tissue loss up until two weeks post outplant. In stark contrast, the more visible, larger fragments acclimated to site conditions for two years prior to outplant incurred no apparent predation. Differences in predation may be due to differing symbiont density, nutrition, or chemical deterrents that are associated with captive colonies or a colony size threshold. Predation rates of micro-fragments were far higher in offshore outplants than nearshore outplants, indicating that selection of habitat is the key to successfully reducing mortality (Page et al. 2018).

Coral re-skinning utilizes the existing carbonate framework to restore living coral, primarily because this structure is difficult to replace, having taken decades to centuries to initially form. This structure with its complex rugosity and vertical profile forms the foundation of habitat for a diversity of marine invertebrates and reef fish, many of which are only found associated with

Figure 7.2 Example of the coral re-skinning technique (Page 2013, images from Forsman et al. 2015); (A) substrate cleaning and site preparation; (B) tiles are mounted with epoxy; (C) finished array; (D) a separate array two months after outplanting; (E) an example from a separate array of colonies fusing and self-attaching in the field after five months of growth.

live coral cover (Coker et al. 2012, 2014). Studies have shown that ecosystem diversity declines substantially when the reef structure erodes away (Graham et al. 2006). Covering this vacant substrate may help to decrease structural erosion due to wave action and acidification, as well as decrease its susceptibility to colonization by bioeroders or non-accreting organisms. Using this strategy also has the effect of orders of magnitude of increased growth rates compared to planting single fragments. Page et al. (2018) found that when using similar quantities of live tissue micro-fragments, arrays grew 2–10 times faster than single large fragments planted in the same location. This, combined with the fact that these arrays can be produced at least 3.5 times faster than larger fragments (Page et al. 2018), amounts to a substantially higher return on investment than the standard practice of using larger-sized fragments.

Finally, the size and sequence of colony fusion can be tailored by the spacing and number of established micro-fragments used to restore a plot of reef. This provides the practitioner with a great deal of flexibility as to the breadth and rate of restoration occurring on a particular reef. At Mote Marine Laboratory, arrays made up of 3, 5, 8, and 20 fragments were the most utilized initially to spread experimental effort across target reefs. This tactic is highly advised for new projects because successful establishment of fragments can vary considerably by location of each outplanted array. Once initial bottlenecks, such as predation, are successfully minimized, the rate of complete fusion is often proportional to the number of equally spaced colonies. In this way, the rate of vacant substrate coverage can dwarf rates exhibited by naturally occurring colonies. Using *O. faveolata* as an example, wild colonies have been documented to increase anywhere from 0.4–1.3 cm in diameter (Gladfelter et al. 1978; Hubbard and Scaturo 1985; Van Veghel and Bosscher 1995) taking approximately 25–75 years to grow into a colony 30 cm in diameter (705 cm^2). To achieve the same colony diameter, it would take twenty 2.5 cm *O. faveolata* micro-fragments (~120 cm^2) three to five years under field conditions (see Figure 7.3) expanding 8–15 times faster than wild colonies. Micro-fragments grow at rapid rates in the field, but they grow many times faster on land-based nurseries under optimal conditions. This phenomenon is most likely because arrays of micro-fragments have a high proportion of

Figure 7.3 Three 30 cm colonies, each started with twenty 2.5 cm fragments fusing into colonies that would have taken 25–75 years to grow, fused in 2–3 years (Cook Island, Florida Keys: photo by D. Vaughan).

growing perimeter from which to form sheets of tissue out across continuous surfaces rather than growing in roughly hemispherical fashion by vertical extension like larger colonies.

Because of this relationship, the capacity for the maximum size of a dead coral that can be covered is only limited by the surface area of the donor tissue. Figure 7.4. shows approximately 200 micro-fragments of *O. faveolata*. If this colony were grown from a recruit, it would be nearly 200 years old. These large colonies are crucial to ecosystem function because they provide habitat to an incredibly biodiverse community of organisms. Figure 7.4 also shows a larger, *bomby-sized* head with hundreds of attached clonal fragments. This, in reality, could bring a 500–1,000-year-old coral head back to life in only a few years. This method, therefore, has rapid results relative to the time, effort, and resources invested.

Figure 7.4 Coral head (1 m) with over 200 fragments attached (left) and 3–4 m coral heads with 800 fragments attached.

NATURAL OR ARTIFICIAL CORAL MODULES

Complex reef structure may take decades to centuries to achieve by natural means; however, deploying fully fused micro-colonies on an artificial structure may help to expedite this process with a coral head measuring less than ¼ meter across taking 25–75 years to grow depending on species and environmental conditions.

An alternative method to coral re-skinning is to grow an array of micro-fragments in controlled conditions over natural or artificial substrates in seawater tanks in an inland (ex situ) nursery or in a protected marine environment (in situ nursery). This method is being used by the State of Hawaii Department of Land and Natural Resources Division of Aquatic Resources (DLNR/DAR). The DAR Coral Restoration Nursery has been using this method since it opened in 2013, and it has produced hundreds of coral modules that are approximately 20 cm in diameter (Figure 7.5). Efforts are currently underway to produce modules that are up to one meter in diameter. Micro-fragmentation over coral modules results in a gain of approximately 40 times the area covered by coral in a period between three months and a year, depending on the tank conditions and the coral species. Initial field trials with artificial coral modules indicate a nearly 100% survivorship, and the DAR Coral Restoration Nursery is currently focused on scaling up capacity for larger scale production. Micro-fragmentation has been tested over

Figure 7.5 Artificial coral module produced by the State of Hawaii DAR Coral Restoration Nursery. The module is ~20 cm in diameter and was grown in approximately six months from ~5 cm of donor material. The module was attached to a degraded reef with epoxy and is currently thriving and growing.

a variety of substrates and rates of coral tissue spreading are fairly similar across coral and lava rock (Dubininkas 2017). The clear advantage of producing larger coral modules is that survivorship is likely higher in the field and ecological services (such as providing habitat and supporting biodiversity) are more immediately provided than numerous smaller units. A clear disadvantage of this approach is that transportation and attachment of modules to reef substrate is an engineering challenge that requires more work to become cost and time efficient.

TILING THE REEF

An alternative to large coral modules or an array of small pugs or tiles is to create fused arrays of small fragments in an ex situ or in situ nursery, which are then transported to the field site to be attached to the substrate. This method may be combined with artificial reefs or breakwaters to rapidly cover two-dimensional substrates. The attachment of flat panels directly to the reef is an engineering challenge that may require additional trials to perfect. Rachmilovitz and Rinkevich (2017) used the tiling method, naming the tiles Two-dimensional Coral Preparative tools (2D-CPs) in a floating coral nursery in the northern Gulf of Eilat. They proposed that mass production and deployment of these units could be an effective tool toward reversing a phase-shift from an algal dominated reef to a coral dominated one (Rachmilovitz and Rinkevich 2017). The State of Hawaii DAR Coral Restoration Nursery also used tiles during the initial production of coral modules before changing to growing fragments directly on concrete modules (Figure 7.6).

Figure 7.6 Coral micro-fragments spreading tissue over ceramic tiles in controlled aquaria at the State of Hawaii DAR Coral Restoration Nursery.

CORAL SEEDLINGS

Chamberland et al. (2017) developed a novel strategy of settling sexually propagated corals on tetrapod-shaped concrete substrates (~8 cm in diameter). This *coral seedling* approach is intended to reduce costs associated with manually attaching fragments to the reef substrate. Although the survivorship of these small, sexually derived coral recruits was very low (67% of tetrapods had at least one recruit and overall survival was only 9.6% after one year), the method resulted in an approximately 10-fold reduction in outplanting costs (Chamberland et al. 2017). These tetrapods rapidly wedge into reef cracks and crevices and become part of the reef as they were overgrown with crustose coralline algae and sponges, greatly reducing the costs and challenges associated with manual attachment to the substrate (Chamberland et al. 2017). Combining this approach with micro-fragmentation could result in much higher survivorship and faster mass production and outplanting, ultimately growing corals to a size that have a much higher chance of survival and self-attachment (Smith and Hughes 1999; Guest et al. 2011), while being able to compete with other reef organisms (Raymundo and Maypa 2004; Marshall et al. 2006). This method has yet to be tested under field conditions, although coral micro-fragments rapidly grow on these tetrapods in water tables at the DAR Coral Restoration Nursery (Figure 7.7). Future studies should focus on comparing natural and artificial

Figure 7.7 Coral micro-fragments on SECORE tetrapod seed modules. A 1 cm^2 micro-fragment of *Montipora patula* placed in the middle of each point resulted in complete coverage in six or seven months.

substrate *coral seedlings* when it comes to cost, rate of self-attachment, survival, and growth under various field conditions.

FUSION IN LAND NURSERIES

Land-based nurseries allow for the fusion or partial fusion of fragments to produce large colonies in a short period of time. By using fast-growing micro-fragments in an array of sizes with varied spacing, larger sizes of colonies can be formed in weeks or months. (see Figure 7.8, with *A. palmata*), This can be regulated to a size that is manageable from the land nursery to the field nursery or directly to the field.

This can also be done before full fusion is accomplished. Like any transfers from nurseries to outplanting sites, the size, age, and acclimation of the outplanting unit needs to be competent to survive the transfer, transport, outplanting, and survival to the new location and conditions. Will it be possible to transfer very large fused or partially fused colonies into the field locations? Most likely yes, but the handling and transport costs and equipment may make an optimal-sized unit something that can be easily handled and transported effectively and

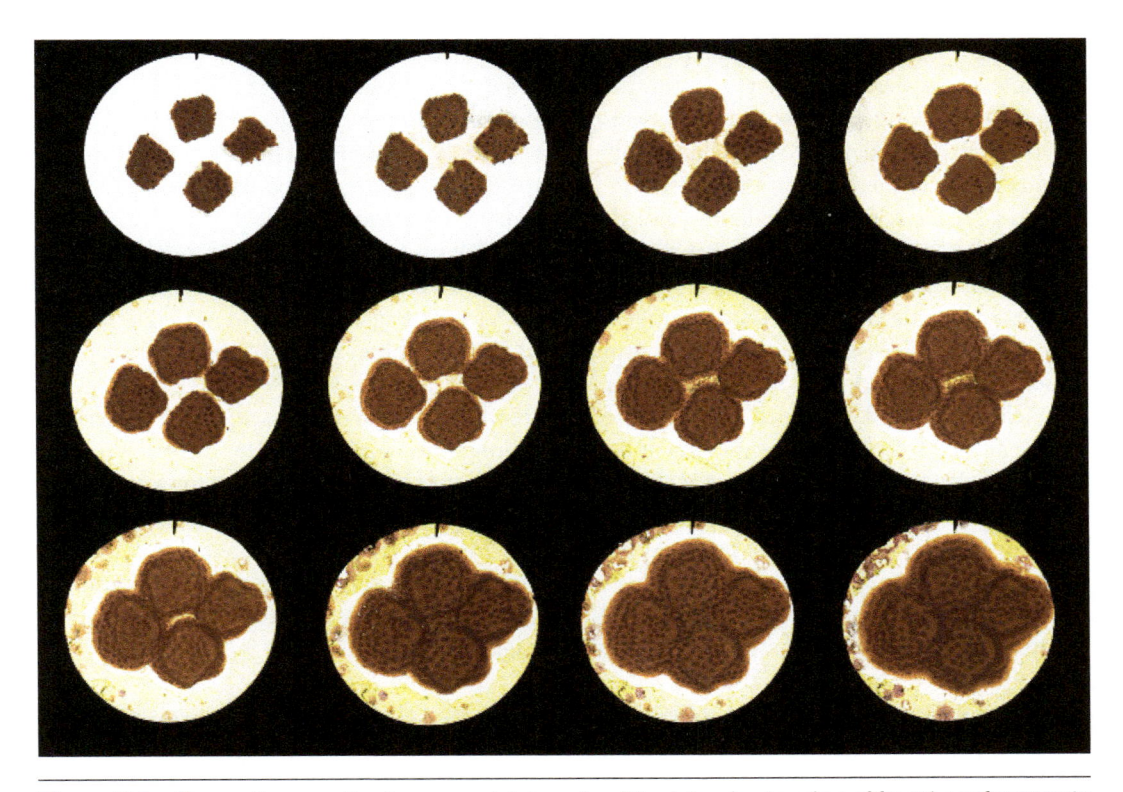

Figure 7.8 Shows the growth at one-week intervals of the lateral extension of four 1 cm fragments growing together in just 11 weeks (photo by Dan Mele Photography).

efficiently. A boulder-sized colony that cannot be lifted except with heavy machinery may be possible but not entirely practical. The amount of time in the nursery stage may also be limiting if the unit size is too large. Making and handling smaller units that can fit together into a larger unit may make more sense. The Hawaii DAR Coral Restoration Nursery routinely works with modules that are ~20 cm in diameter and work is currently underway to produce larger modules that can be joined to produce a colony that is a meter across. These modules provide more of a three-dimensional head start than 2D tiles or plugs; however, additional work is needed to overcome the engineering challenges of attachment to benthic substrates. Future work is needed to efficiently combine plugs, tiles, or modules with artificial or natural structures. Theoretically multiple modular units could be combined into larger interlocking units at a final outplanting location, combining the best aspects of artificial reefs with coral transplantation (Abelson 2006). Land-based nurseries may also be combined with field-based nurseries for intermediate-sized colonies.

FUSION IN FIELD NURSERIES

Field nurseries are integral components of restoration efforts proliferating around the world, providing the capacity to grow a large number of corals with minimal infrastructure. The integration of land-based and field-based nurseries in a multi-phased approach could take advantage of the strengths of each while minimizing weaknesses. Land-based nurseries allow for more control and delicate work on sexually derived recruits or micro-fragments, while field-based nurseries are cost effective above a certain size threshold. It is also possible to look at stand-alone field nurseries for coral fusion technologies. Field nurseries could allow for the extended growing time for full or partial fusion of the colony before it is transported to the final outplanting site. The only limitations so far include the convenience of the cutting and gluing or attachment out of the water and in more controlled conditions. Working with small fragments is only feasible on land—and glue or epoxy is challenging to work with underwater. Underwater epoxies or formulation of cement can work underwater, but with more labor and ease of handling when weather and water conditions and bottom time may be factors. Another factor to consider is that freshly fragmented corals have damaged tissue and are vulnerable to parasites and disease (Yap et al. 1998; Brandt et al. 2013), which can be better controlled in a land-based facility.

Field nursery grounds can take the place of extended land nursery space, requiring less expense and maintenance per unit area and allowing longer nursery residence times. Field nurseries can also provide conditions for acclimation to a particular restoration site for a cost that is affordable to most practitioners. Many branching coral field nurseries use similar genotypes in order to outplant in close proximity. Not necessarily for the formation of massive colonies but for the proliferation of branching coral *thickets* that allow similar genotypes to form multiple connection points in order to stabilize branching coral outplants and form dense and larger continuously covered areas, while minimizing antagonistic interactions.

THE FUSION PROCESS

The sequence of meeting a neighboring polyp likely starts with chemical or physical interactions. For many species, when new coral polyps are budding and growing on the lateral edge of the colony and are ready to divide and expand their territory, they are known to produce long-reaching tentacles that are occasionally many times the normal tentacle length and can extend out to explore new territory for expansion. These are called *sweeping tentacles* because they resemble an exploratory reaching motion to test the adjacent substrate availability (Ayre and Grosberg 2005). The resulting interactions are sensed by the two contacting corals that are able to recognize *self* from *non-self* through allorecognition and xenorecognition pathways. After first contact, there are four possible outcomes; (1) recognition of *self* and eventual fusing to form a larger colony, (2) recognition of *non-self* and initiating a clear tissue border without antagonistic behavior, (3) recognition of *non-self* and initiating antagonistic behavior (i.e., all-out war), or (4) the formation of a chimera of two genetically distinct organisms. The recognition of self vs non-self may depend on the size and developmental stage of the colony, whereby, below a certain size threshold, the allorecognition system is underdeveloped and the formation of chimeras is more likely (Barki et al. 2002; Wilson and Grosberg 2004). Chimerism has been implicated in a coral disease (Work et al. 2011) where genetically distinct individuals merged but the partnership may break down under some conditions. Chimeric colonies are also able to display a range of phenotypes and may therefore have greater adaptive potential (Rinkevich et al. 2016); but this is an area for future work and this path has not been well explored using micro-fragmentation.

When colonies with the same genotype fuse (isogenic fusion), the soft tissues first come in contact, followed by integration of the skeleton such that eventually the lines between fragments disappear; however, initially there can be lines of distinct tissue and the distinct patterns of the previous colonies still persist (Figure 7.9). This continues until new skeletal depositions

Coral Fusion: Harnessing Coral Clonality for Reef Restoration

Figure 7.9 Knobby brain coral head in the process of fusing together eight fragments into one large head—and the ridges and grooves and separate fragments are still apparent during the fusion (photo D. Vaughan).

are created (vertical skeletal extension as opposed to lateral tissue growth in a thin veneer with minimal skeletal deposition) and the growth patterns merge as one in as little as a few weeks or months after first contact, depending on the species. The speed of fusion and the ultimate size of the fused colony can be variable between species and environmental conditions. The relatively fast lateral extension of *A. palmata* (Figure 7.8) within 11 weeks can show the process in time lapse. This shows the new lateral growth of each of these micro-fragments with a white-halo ring at the outer edge showing some sort of preceding compound affecting the substrate (or attack by sweeping tentacles), algae, and even crustose coralline algae (CCA) disappear, thereby preparing a path for the new colony and the expansion of polyps. The contact points and eventual fusing of the tissue is producing at a rapid rate and each of the four micro-fragments are now touching and starting the fusing process within the first 6-week time period. By week 10, the area in between the colonies has fully grown together with normal-sized polyps connected. The growth rate of these four (1 cm micro-fragments) fusing into one large (6 cm) fused colony, shows the potential for growth and tissue coverage using this method (many times the volume in just 11 weeks).

The micro-fragmentation and fusion method works for a wide variety of Atlantic and Pacific corals (Forsman et al. 2015). The mountainous star coral (*Orbicella faveolata*), and other star, boulder, and mountainous corals show this rapid and potential scope for growth and fusion.

Figures 7.1, 7.2, 7.6, and 7.8 show the merging tissues of fragments growing back together with a filling in of new smaller polyps into the spaces between them. For the brain corals it takes a little longer to have the ridge and the groove sections appear connecting as usual. This is very apparent in Figure 7.9; this larger size colony head of Knobby Brain coral, *P. clivosa*, where the coordination of the ridge and groove sections is somehow being worked out as the fusion process continues and the original separate colonies are still discernible. In many of these cases, the soft tissue fuses before the skeletal tissue fuses together and is fully connected to the substrate. These fragments form a thin layer of tissue bridging separate fragments before populating the interface with new polyps suggesting that fragments have transitioned to function as one colony. A review of the speed to large head size is dependent not only on species and environmental conditions for scope for growth, but the number of fragments used and the distance apart they are positioned. This picture shows an attempt to produce a mature-sized colony using many smaller-sized micro-fragments but placing them closer together, so that they potentially can fuse in just a few months. This procedure was to test the theory that mature-sized colonies could be produced in just a small period of time (weeks instead of years).

FUSION OR CONFUSION: TO FUSE OR NOT TO FUSE?

Adjacent coral colonies of different genotypes recognize the threat of being overgrown by their proximal neighbor (Rinkevich 2004). And colonies of the same genotype recognize the ability to fuse back together again. The process of recognizing different antigenics, strains, or genotypes has allowed for the antagonistic behavior of not being overgrown by a competitor coral, or (non-self) neighbor. This entails recognition factors and potential adverse interactions of adjacent polyps and the eventual onslaught of coral *wars*. The survival of the fittest may be the biggest or just the best at fending off invading stinging tentacles or mesoderm ejections. These can be deadly interactions or at least the spoils of war by taking over more new ground for extended growth by the winner. In areas of mature reefs with a high percentage of coral cover, it is the usual competition for ground and light exposure that is the normal interaction because of growth limitations for both space and light. In many areas more recently, it is a competition by not just other genotypes of similar species, but competition by other species, families, orders, and even phyla, such as zoanthids, sponges—and by fleshy algae that can be overgrowing threats. On a coral reef or hard bottom, control of the available substrate space and the availability of access to grow and get sunlight is imperative.

Another interaction that has recently become more and more frequent is the loss of tissue in a coral colony and the resultant separation of the living polyps from each other. This occurs with increasing physical damage from vessels, anchors, or more frequent storms and also with increasing biological loss of tissue from thermal extremes, bleaching events, and diseases. This phenomenon is well documented in nature (see Figure 7.10), and has been repeated experimentally in several classic studies (Hildeman 1974; Jokiel et al. 1983; Neigel and Avise 1983; Buss et al. 1984; Willis and Ayre 1985; Hidaka et al. 1997). Florida's coral reef tract has suffered greatly in this respect, due to bleaching events as well as anomalous cold-water events, such as in January 2010 in Florida. During this period water temperatures dropped below 16°C for as long as six days with some areas dropping to as low as 10°C (Lirman et al. 2011) in just a few days. If this occurs and there is a partial loss of the coral colony and some of the living tissue survives but becomes disconnected, and if conditions allow for the regrowth of these similar tissues, they can fuse back together. Cold-spell surviving polyps are found in cracks and crevasses and can make a comeback faster than sexual recruitment. An ever-present example

Figure 7.10 A *Montastraea cavernosa* head with multiple polyps that survived the cold spell of 2010 and is starting to recover through re-skinning or fusion of the original colony (photo D. Vaughan).

of disease survivorship from circular losses caused by black-band and yellow-band diseases show partial tissue losses which can rebound and grow toward filling in the circular pattern again. Surviving colony sections from previous lost tissue caused by cold or high temperatures, bleaching events, or diseases, if resistant, could potentially grow back together again into a larger colony and be more resistant to similar events in the future.

SEXUAL OR ASEXUAL: TO CLONE OR NOT TO CLONE?

Harvesting coral larvae or producing larvae from slicks of gametes during mass spawning events is a highly sustainable and potentially inexhaustible source of donor material for reef restoration efforts. Progress toward this goal is rapidly increasing (e.g., Chamberland et al. 2015, 2017; Cruz and Harrison 2017); however, mortality rates for larvae and new recruits are astronomically high. Until coral larval husbandry is greatly improved, transplantation, fragmentation, and micro-fragmentation remain the most viable alternative options. There is no shortage of donor material for fragmentation—either from corals in nurseries that exhibit enhanced growth after fragmentation or *pruning vigor* (Lirman et al. 2014), or from corals that are in harm's way and in need of rescue. *Corals of opportunity* are corals that would otherwise have very slim chances of survival, including sources such as: recent fragmentation due to storms, ship groundings and anchor damage, growth on artificial substrates that needs to be removed (e.g., buoys, docks, and aquaculture pens), or in the path of construction or dredging projects (Monty 2006; Ng and Chou 2014; Feliciano et al. 2018).

A perceived potential risk of fragmentation or micro-fragmentation projects is the concern that *too much* clonal reproduction could result in genetic homogeneity and increased vulnerability to disease. In the case of corals of opportunity, this is not a major concern since these corals would otherwise be removed from the gene pool and rescuing them will actually increase the chance that they reproduce sexually and contribute to the gene pool. Furthermore, successful coral reproduction is density-dependent, requiring that enough adult colonies exchange eggs and sperm at the correct concentration, and natural reefs often consist of several monospecific stands or thickets composed of only a few genotypes. Corals are highly genetically heterogeneous (Shearer et al. 2009; Gorospe et al. 2015; Schweinsberg et al. 2016) such that randomly selecting an estimated 10 to 35 donor colonies will retain 50–90% of the genetic diversity of the original donor population (Shearer et al. 2009). Both sexual and asexual strategies are therefore important for reef restoration, although in either case, mismatch between environment and genotype is a far more important consideration. Arrays of coral micro-fragments can also serve as an assay to evaluate the performance of specific genotypes to a particular environment.

SPEEDING UP SEXUAL MATURITY WITH MICRO-FRAGMENTATION

Although the micro-fragmentation and fusion technique takes advantage of asexual reproduction (fragmentation), colonies that have undergone this process may reach the size of sexual maturity more rapidly than rates typically observed in nature. Although fragmentation typically results in lower fecundity under natural conditions, hypothetically, due to a decrease in the availability of shared resources (Sakai 1998; Okubo et al. 2007), fragments that fuse together and increase shared resources may have the opposite effect. Coral colonies that have undergone micro-fragmentation and fusion have been observed to spawn a few months after the procedure, e.g., several micro-fragmented colonies of *Montipora capitata* were observed to release large amounts of egg and sperm bundles (Forsman personal observation). In Florida, this was also seen (Vaughan and Page, personal observation), when multiple *Porites astaeroides* micro-fragments were attached to a rock substrate that was similar in size to the wild colonies that were collected for brood-stock spawning trials, they spawned. In the wild, similar-sized wild colonies start to mature and produce offspring starting at about 10–15 centimeters in size and about 10 years old or more. This fused colony was mature and successfully spawned—producing viable offspring at only 11 months old; yet it was the same size as a decade old colony. This phenomenon, if confirmed and tested at length on a variety of species, may provide a mechanism for producing mature colonies not only in size but in sexual competency. This means that fused colonies in the field may become sexually competent earlier, based on the size of the colony and not the relative age. This also means that researchers may be able to use large fused colonies to produce gametes and offspring over a faster generational *turn-around* time.

The rapid production of sexually mature-sized coral colonies is especially important for a rare or endangered population, in order to maintain the population densities that are necessary for successful reproduction (i.e., the Allee effect; specifically mate limitation). For captive breeding or *assisted evolution* projects, the rapid production of sexually mature-sized colonies is advantageous for the early formation and development of gametes for inducing controlled spawning from selected genotypes without having to wait decades for this to happen by a slow growth to larger mature sizes. A key question that micro-fragmentation can answer is: does size or age determine reproductive maturity? The potential for speeding up the time to sexual maturity using micro-fragmentation needs further work since enhanced reproductive capacity would provide many opportunities. All restoration practitioners hope to be able to assist nature and encourage natural processes to take over. To accomplish this, sexual reproduction must again be able to keep up with the loss of corals. In healthy coral reef ecosystems in the past, it may have sufficed to maintain populations even though the odds of survival of a coral larva to a reproductive adult was only one in a million because there were so many larvae. Corals often lived to be hundreds of years old, but now multiple stressors have resulted in plummeting life expectancy. The hope of reef restoration efforts is that by maintaining or increasing coral cover, natural processes and feedback cycles will begin to take over, making the scope for restoration success much more feasible. Increasingly, coral restoration studies are documenting these feedback cycles, where restoration projects result in increased juvenile fish recruitment, increased coral larval recruitment, and increased coral reef ecological function. Micro-fragmentation of corals of opportunity is an important restoration tool that can prevent loss, maximize output, and provide insight into positive ecological feedback cycles that maintain healthy coral reefs.

FUSION FOR GENETIC CROSSES

If micro-fragmentation and fusion can reduce the time to sexual maturity from a few decades to a few years, then it presents many exciting opportunities for breeding crosses and closing the life cycle in captivity. In much the same way as plant and animal breeding has led to the agricultural revolution, closing the life cycle for corals would provide many opportunities for reproductive crosses to understand the relationships between genotype and phenotype, and allow farming at a large scale. If many micro-fragments can be fused together into a mature-sized colony, this may be a new tool for crosses (see Figure 7.11). The topic of coral *assisted evolution*

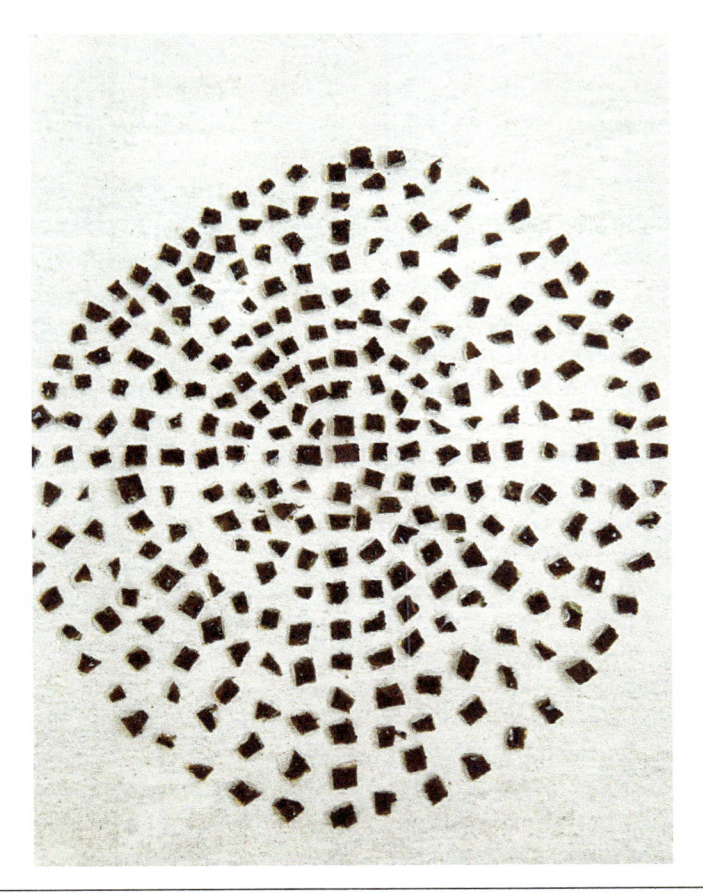

Figure 7.11 *Acropora palmata* elkhorn coral micro-fragmented into many pieces to test rapid fusion.

is very new and not without controversy (van Oppen et al. 2015, 2017; Camp et al. 2018); however, there is no question that breeding and manipulations of coral symbionts can bring about profound insights into coral biology (see Chapter 9 for more information). Humans have farmed and bred a wide variety of plants and animals on land for thousands of years and modern agriculture has completely transformed society and the land we live on, but in the oceans, we are primarily in the hunter and gatherer stage. Plant and animal research models—such as peas, corn, fruit flies, zebra fish, mice, and lab rats—have fundamentally transformed biology; likewise, improving cultivation methods for corals will allow the cultivation of habitat for the biodiversity that coral reefs support.

CONCLUSIONS

The phenomenon of coral fusion has many exciting potential applications for understanding coral organismal biology and ecology, as well as for reef restoration. Micro-fragmentation to produce a larger coral colony in reduced time is a game changer for reef restoration—producing coral colonies that would normally take tens or even a hundred years to develop in a fraction of that time. The method is flexible, allowing mass production of a variety of sizes and innovative formats, such as plugs, seedlings, tiles, modules, or seawall panels. The method can be used to bring coral colonies back from the dead, preventing further dissolution and erosion of habitat, or the method can be combined with artificial modules to create new complex habitat. The combination of land- and field-based nurseries will further improve efficiency, lower costs, and increase the scale of reef restoration. The micro-fragmentation method also has potential for reducing the time for corals to reach sexual maturity and provide additional insights in the biology of these clonal organisms.

Micro-fragmentation provides new opportunities for restoration and research, for example, growing corals on substrates that promote or encourage growth or prevent disease, 3D printed or engineered substrates that improve the ability to outplant, construction of coastal shoreline protection structures, artistic designs and sculptures to draw tourism away from natural reefs, and production of very large-scale coral heads or other modules ready for outplanting. The potential of producing sexually mature colonies for the production of gametes is also a topic of future work that could allow for a selection of resilient strains followed by fast-tracked maturation and reproductive crosses, moving corals closer to a model organism and improving the chances for survival in the face of changing conditions. The method also has important implications for the preservation of biodiversity and is already assisting populations that have been listed for protection under the U.S. Endangered Species Act or listed as threatened by international organizations such as the International Union for Conservation of Nature.

The source material for micro-fragmentation should be coral that would otherwise stand almost no chance of survival (e.g., *biofouling* on docks, pens, or mooring buoys, or storm-damaged fragments at risk of smothering in sand). Improving technology for reef restoration should always be used to provide a net positive result—but never as an excuse to destroy or move a pristine reef. Many natural wonders can never be replaced; just as the giant redwood forest should be protected, so should coral reefs. However, reefs that are in a degraded state from acute disturbance can be encouraged to recover more quickly, buying time to reduce the myriad of threats that corals face. Another very important use of micro-fragmentation is as a tool to test restoration sites *before* larger scale restoration work is scheduled in order to determine if the site is suitable for a particular species, genotype (selected for resilience to temperature extremes or disease resistance), or colony size . Micro-fragments can provide information on the trajectory of the reef in much the same way that juvenile coral colonies can (Kojis and Quinn 2001; Forsman et al. 2006). Ultimately, this information could identify the actionable tipping points that would change the trajectory of a reef from a downward spiral toward degradation and loss, to prolific and expansive growth. As we plant forests on land to provide habitat and prevent erosion, why can't we plant corals at similar scales in the ocean to do the same?

ACKNOWLEDGMENTS

The authors wish to thank the many salty hands that we have worked with over the years. Special thanks to Brian Neilson, David Gulko, Chelsea Wolke, Norton Chan, and Steven Ranson for their work at the State of Hawaii DAR Coral Restoration Nursery. We wish to thank Dirk Peterson and SECORE for providing us with coral seedling models for testing. Also, much appreciation goes out to the dedicated staff of Mote Marine Lab and the scientists, technicians, and student interns involved in the Coral Reef Restoration Program who paved the way and carried out the work that Dave Vaughan and Christopher Page initiated.

REFERENCES

Abelson, A. 2006. "Artificial reefs vs coral transplantation as restoration tools for mitigating coral reef deterioration: Benefits, concerns, and proposed guidelines." 78:151–159.

Ayre, D. J., and R. K. Grosberg. 2005. "Behind anemone lines: Factors affecting division of labour in the social cnidarian *Anthopleura elegantissima*." *Animal Behaviour* 70:97–110.

Barki, Y., D. Gateño, D. Graur, and B. Rinkevich. 2002. "Soft-coral natural chimerism: A window in ontogeny allows the creation of entities comprised of incongruous parts." *Mar. Ecol. Prog. Ser.* 231:91–99.

Brandt, M. E., T. B. Smith, A. M. S. Correa, and R. Vega-Thurber. 2013. "Disturbance driven colony fragmentation as a driver of a coral disease outbreak." *PLoS ONE* 8:e 57164.

Buss, L. W., C. S. McFadden, and D. R. Keene. 1984. "Biology of Hydractiniid Hydroids. 2. Histocompatibility effector system/competitive mechanism mediated by nematocyst discharge." *Biol. Bull.* 167:139–158.

Camp, E. F., V. Schoepf, and D. J. Suggett. 2018. "How can "Super Corals" facilitate global coral reef survival under rapid environmental and climatic change?" *Glob. Chang. Biol.* 24:2755–2757.

Chamberland, V. F., D. Petersen, J. R. Guest, U. Petersen, M. Brittsan, and M. J. A. Vermeij. 2017. "New seeding approach reduces costs and time to outplant sexually propagated corals for reef restoration." *Sci. Rep.* 7:18076.

Chamberland, V. F., M. J. A. Vermeij, M. Brittsan, M. Carl, M. Schick, S. Snowden, A. Schrier, and D. Petersen. 2015. "Restoration of critically endangered elkhorn coral (*Acropora palmata*) populations using larvae reared from wild-caught gametes." *Global Ecology and Conservation* 4:526–537.

Coker, D. J., N. A. J. Graham, and M. S. Pratchett. 2012. "Interactive effects of live coral and structural complexity on the recruitment of reef fishes." *Coral Reefs* 31:919–927.

Coker, D. J., S. K. Wilson, and M. S. Pratchett. 2014. "Importance of live coral habitat for reef fishes." *Reviews in Fish Biology and Fisheries* 24:89–126.

Cruz, D. W. D. and P. L. Harrison. 2017. "Enhanced larval supply and recruitment can replenish reef corals on degraded reefs." *Sci. Rep.* 7:13985.

Dubininkas, V. 2017. "Effects of substratum on the growth and survivorship of *Montipora capitata* and *Porites lobata* transplants." *Journal of Experimental Marine Biology and Ecology* 486:134–139.

Feliciano, G. N. R., T. P. I. Mostrales, A. K. M. Acosta, K. Luzon, J. C. A. Bangsal, and W. Y. Licuanan. 2018. "Is gardening corals of opportunity the appropriate response to reverse Philippine reef decline?" *Restor. Ecol.* 26:1091–1097.

Forsman, Z. H., C. A. Page, R. J. Toonen, and D. Vaughan. 2015. "Growing coral larger and faster: Microcolony-fusion as a strategy for accelerating coral cover." *PeerJ* 3:e 1313.

Forsman, Z. H., B. Rinkevich, and C. L. Hunter. 2006. "Investigating fragment size for culturing reef-building corals (*Porites lobata* and *P. compressa*) in ex situ nurseries." *Aquaculture* 261:89–97.

Gardner, T. A., I. M. Côté, J. A. Gill, A. Grant, and A. R. Watkinson. 2005. "Hurricanes and Caribbean coral reefs: Impacts, recovery patterns, and role in long-term decline." *Ecology* 86:174–184.

Gladfelter, E. H., R. K. Monahan, and W. B. Gladfelter. 1978. "Growth rates of five reef-building corals in the northeastern Caribbean." *Bulletin of Marine Science* 28:728–734.

Gorospe, K. D., M. J. Donahue, and S. A. Karl. 2015. "The importance of sampling design: Spatial patterns and clonality in estimating the genetic diversity of coral reefs." *Mar. Biol.* 162:917–928.

Graham, N. A. J., S. K. Wilson, S. Jennings, N. V. C. Polunin, J. P. Bijoux, and J. Robinson. 2006. "Dynamic fragility of oceanic coral reef ecosystems." *Proc Natl Acad Sci USA* 103:8425–8429.

Grosberg, R. K. 1988. "The evolution of allorecognition specificity in clonal invertebrates." *Q. Rev. Biol.* 63:377–412.

Grosberg, R. K. and J. F. Quinn. 1986. "The genetic control and consequences of kin recognition by the larvae of a colonial marine invertebrate." *Nature* 322:456–459.

Guest, J. R., R. M. Dizon, A. J. Edwards, C. Franco, and E. D. Gomez. 2011. "How quickly do fragments of coral "self-attach" after transplantation?" *Restoration Ecology* 19:234–242.

Hall, V. R. and T. P. Hughes. 1996. "Reproductive Strategies of Modular Organisms: Comparative Studies of Reef- Building Corals." *Ecology* 77:950–963.

Hidaka, M., K. Yurugi, S. Sunagawa, and R. A. Kinzie. 1997. "Contact reactions between young colonies of the coral *Pocillopora damicornis*." *Coral Reefs* 16:13–20.

Hildeman, W. H. 1974. "Phylogeny of immune responsiveness in invertebrates." *Life Sci.* 14:605–614.

Hubbard, D. K. and D. Scaturo. 1985. "Growth rates of seven species of scleractinean corals from Cane Bay and Salt River, St. Croix, USVI." *Bulletin of Marine Science* 36:325–338.

Jokiel, P. L., W. H. Hildemann, and C. H. Bigger. 1983. "Clonal population structure of two sympatric species of the reef coral Montipora." *Bulletin of Marine Science* 33:181–187.

Kojis, B. L. and N. J. Quinn. 2001. "The importance of regional differences in hard coral recruitment rates for determining the need for coral restoration." *Bulletin of Marine Science* 69:967–974.

Lirman, D., S. Schopmeyer, V. Galvan, C. Drury, A. C. Baker, and I. B. Baums. 2014. "Growth dynamics of the threatened Caribbean staghorn coral *Acropora cervicornis*: Influence of host genotype, symbiont identity, colony size, and environmental setting." *PLoS ONE* 9:e107253.

Lirman, D., S. Schopmeyer, D. Manzello, L. J. Gramer, W. F. Precht, F. Muller-Karger, K. Banks, et al. 2011. "Severe 2010 cold-water event caused unprecedented mortality to corals of the Florida reef tract and reversed previous survivorship patterns." *PLoS ONE* 6:e23047.

Lirman, D., T. Thyberg, J. Herlan, C. Hill, C. Young-Lahiff, S. Schopmeyer, B. Huntington, et al. 2010. "Propagation of the threatened staghorn coral *Acropora cervicornis*: Methods to minimize the impacts of fragment collection and maximize production." *Coral Reefs* 29:729–735.

Loya, Y., K. Sakai, K. Yamazato, Y. Nakano, H. Sambali, and R. van Woesik. 2001. "Coral bleaching: The winners and the losers." *Ecol. Lett.* 4:122–131.

Marshall, D. J., C. N. Cook, and R. B. Emlet. 2006. "Offspring size effects mediate competitive interactions in a colonial marine invertebrate." *Ecology* 87:214–225.

Monty, J. 2006. "Coral of opportunity survivorship and the use of coral nurseries in coral reef restoration." Proceedings of the 10th International Coral Reef Symposium 1665–1673.

Neigel, J. E. and J. C. Avise. 1983. "Clonal diversity and population structure in a reef-building coral, *Acropora cervicornis*: Self-recognition analysis and demographic interpretation." *Evolution* 37:437–453.

Ng, C. S. L. and L. M. Chou. 2014. "Rearing juvenile 'corals of opportunity' in in situ nurseries—A reef rehabilitation approach for sediment-impacted environments." *Marine Biology Research* 10:833–838.

Okubo, N., T. Motokawa, and M. Omori. 2007. "When fragmented coral spawn? Effect of size and timing on survivorship and fecundity of fragmentation in *Acropora formosa*." *Mar. Biol.* 151:353–363.

van Oppen, M. J. H., R. D. Gates, L. L. Blackall, N. Cantin, L. J. Chakravarti, W. Y. Chan, C. Cormick, et al. 2017. "Shifting paradigms in restoration of the world's coral reefs." *Glob. Chang. Biol.* 23:3437–3448.

van Oppen, M. J. H., J. K. Oliver, H. M. Putnam, and R. D. Gates. 2015. "Building coral reef resilience through assisted evolution." *Proc Natl Acad Sci USA* 112:2307–2313.

Page, C. 2013. "Reskinning a reef: Mote Marine Lab scientists explore a new approach to reef restoration." *Coral Magazine* 10:72–80.

Page, C. A., E. M. Muller, and D. E. Vaughan. 2018. "Microfragmenting for the successful restoration of slow growing massive corals." *Ecol. Eng.* 123:86–94.

Rachmilovitz, E. N. and B. Rinkevich. 2017. "Tiling the reef—exploring the first step of an ecological engineering tool that may promote phase-shift reversals in coral reefs." *Ecol. Eng.* 105:150–161.

Raymundo, L. J. and A. P. Maypa. 2004. "Getting bigger faster: Mediation of size-specific mortality via fusion in juvenile coral transplants." *Ecol. Appl.* 14:281–295.

Rinkevich, B. 2004. "Allorecognition and xenorecognition in reef corals: A decade of interactions." *Hydrobiologia* 530–531:443–450.

Rinkevich, B., L. Shaish, J. Douek, and R. Ben-Shlomo. 2016. "Venturing in coral larval chimerism: a compact functional domain with fostered genotypic diversity." *Sci. Rep.* 6:19493.

Roff, G., S. Bejarano, Y-M. Bozec, M. Nugues, R. S. Steneck, and P. J. Mumby. 2014. "Porites and the Phoenix effect: Unprecedented recovery after a mass coral bleaching event at Rangiroa Atoll, French Polynesia." *Mar. Biol.* 161:1385–1393.

Sakai, K. 1998. "Effect of colony size, polyp size, and budding mode on egg production in a colonial coral." *Biological Bulletin* 195:319–325.

Schweinsberg, M., R. Tollrian, and K. P. Lampert. 2016. "Genetic variation in the massive coral *Porites lobata*." *Mar. Biol.* 163.

Shearer, T. L., I. Porto, and A. L. Zubillaga. 2009. "Restoration of coral populations in light of genetic diversity estimates." *Coral Reefs* 28:727–733.

Smith, L. D. and T. P. Hughes. 1999. "An experimental assessment of survival, re-attachment and fecundity of coral fragments." *Journal of Experimental Marine Biology and Ecology* 235:147–164.

Van Veghel, M. L. and H. Bosscher. 1995. "Variation in linear growth and skeletal density within the polymorphic reef building coral *Montastrea annularis*." *Bulletin of Marine Science* 56:902–908.

Vaughan, D., S. Teicher, G. Halpern, and J. Oliver. 2019. "Building more resilient coral reefs through new marine technologies, science, and models." *Mar. Technol. Soc. J.* 53:21–24.

Willis, B. L. and D. J. Ayre. 1985. "Asexual reproduction and genetic determination of growth form in the coral Pavona cactus: Biochemical genetic and immunogenic evidence." *Oecologia* 65:516–525.

Wilson, A. C. C. and R. K. Grosberg. 2004. "Ontogenetic shifts in fusion—rejection thresholds in a colonial marine hydrozoan, Hydractinia symbiolongicarpus." *Behav Ecol Sociobiol* 57:40–49.

Work, T. M., Z. H. Forsman, Z. Szabó, T. D. Lewis, G. S. Aeby, and R. J. Toonen. 2011. "Inter-specific coral chimerism: Genetically distinct multicellular structures associated with tissue loss in Montipora capitata." *PLoS ONE* 6:e22869.

Yap, H. T., R. M. Alvarez, H. M. Custodio, and R. M. Dizon. 1998. "Physiological and ecological aspects of coral transplantation." *Journal of Experimental Marine Biology and Ecology* 229:69–84.

8

SEXUAL REPRODUCTION AND REARING CORALS FOR RESTORATION

Christopher Page, Nicole D. Fogarty, and David E. Vaughan

ABSTRACT

The sexual reproduction of corals has been observed only in recent times because it has taken scientific ingenuity to understand the timing and setting of these occurrences. Sexual reproduction, so common in the production of other organisms, escaped discovery among corals until the mid-1980s (Harrison et al. 1984). Even so, the use of this form of reproduction for purposes of restoring coral reefs has only just begun and efforts to enhance large-scale production of new offspring at a reasonable cost is ongoing (Chamberland et al. 2017; dela Cruz and Harrison 2017; Randall et al. 2020). This chapter covers the basic biological processes of sexual reproduction in corals and discusses the methods used to rear these corals in the laboratory to ensure genetic diversity in actively restored coral reefs.

INTRODUCTION

Dramatic improvements in coral reef restoration have occurred in the last decade; however, current sexual reproductive strategies are still inadequate to mitigate for the effects of global change (Bruno and Selig 2007; Graham et al. 2014; Rinkevich 2015). Worldwide mass-bleaching events, invasive coral diseases, and even cold anomalies (Lirman et al. 2010) continue unabated, resulting in stepwise declines in coral cover (Gardner et al. 2003; De'ath et al. 2012). This poor performance suggests that the current adaptation to changing conditions in corals is insufficient to ensure future persistence (Williams et al. 2014; Chan et al. 2019) and that it is necessary to build resilience on reefs rather than simply replacing what's been lost (Rinkevich 2015). Because of this, there is a desperate need to inject robust genetic diversity into coral populations, to promote selection of advantageous traits, and to facilitate adaptation through sexual recombination (Baums et al. 2019). However, restoration methodologies using sexual or asexual reproduction separately have severe limitations, so that each single strategy falls drastically short of meeting these requirements. It is therefore advantageous to implement a mixed approach that capitalizes on the strengths and minimizes the weaknesses of each approach in order to increase novel genetic combinations of corals on today's reefs. We are aware that corals have been dying around the world, but many scientists are unaware that the lack of new recruits from sexual reproduction contribute to the overall lack of resilience that is witnessed in reefs around the world. An example is the recruitment failure in the Florida Keys for *Acropora palmata*, a threatened Caribbean coral (Williams, Miller, and Kramer 2008; 2020). Coral populations change by the loss of existing corals and by the decrease in the number and survival of new coral recruits.

Asexual propagation through coral gardening (Bowden-Kerby 2001) and micro-fragmentation (Page et al. 2018) have allowed for the outplant of a wide range of stony coral species through intensive fragmentation and propagation (see Chapter 6). This practice is extremely prolific, allowing the practitioner a renewable supply of live coral for restoration and research. Outplants are typically larger than normal sexual recruits, are more robust to initial stress, and grow faster, while demonstrating high initial survival as well as substantial increases in coral cover (Quinn and Kojis 2006; Shaish et al. 2010; Page et al. 2018). Many efforts have even established persistent populations of restored corals that have grown to reproductive size (Young et al. 2012; Lirman and Schopmeyer 2016; Carne and Baums 2016). Experiments of nursery-grown stocks have yielded differences in growth rates (Drury et al. 2017; O'Donnel et al. 2017), susceptibility to bleaching (Lohr and Patterson 2017), and tolerance to disease (Muller et al. 2018). This accumulation of feedback has been instrumental to our continued success and allows the practitioner to devise adaptive strategies for use in future plantings. In addition to these efforts, genetic recombination through sexual reproduction must become a central focus in restoration; however, this process is rarely utilized in restoration efforts, thus precluding genetic selection in response to global change. The aforementioned asexual reproduction technologies can help to maintain ecosystem function in the short term; however, without further understanding of the sexual reproduction cycle (see Figure 8.1) and robust sexual reproduction in hatcheries, the future of restoration efforts will not be sufficient to fully restore coral reefs.

In most *branching* coral species, sexual reproduction occurs once or twice a year and is a rare occurrence compared to asexual fragmentation, which can occur several times a year. In synchronized events, broadcasting species cast eggs and sperm into the water column to fertilize and develop into swimming larvae, while brooding species fertilize internally in the maternal polyp (Richmond and Hunter 1990). On the reef substrate, swimming larvae settle, thereby forming the first polyp of a genetically distinct coral colony (recruit). However, this process is severely impaired on today's reefs where suitable quality substrate for settlement is hard to find. Fleshy algal species have overgrown many suitable habitats for coral larval attachment, thus reducing the survival of sexual recruits. Because of low naturally occurring sexual recruitment, many restoration practitioners seek to collect, fertilize, and rear coral larvae to enhance the survival of sexual recruits (see Figure 8.2).

Successful projects overcome fertilization and larval development bottlenecks to yield hundreds to tens of thousands of new larvae for settlement and immediate outplant in the field or for extended growout to increase survival after outplanting. Gametes or gamete bundles (spawned packets of eggs and sperm) are collected in the field during spawning events using nylon mesh collection nets similar to plankton nets (see Figure 8.3) and are subsequently fertilized in the laboratory. Once larvae are produced, they are either settled and released directly back on reefs (Chamberland et al. 2017) or are further grown in a nursery for a year or more and refragmented prior to outplant (Page and Vaughan, methodology at Mote 2013–2019).

Direct outplanting means placing newly settled recruits ranging in size from 300 u to 2.4 mm directly on the reef. This effort is attractive and frequently attempted because it requires less

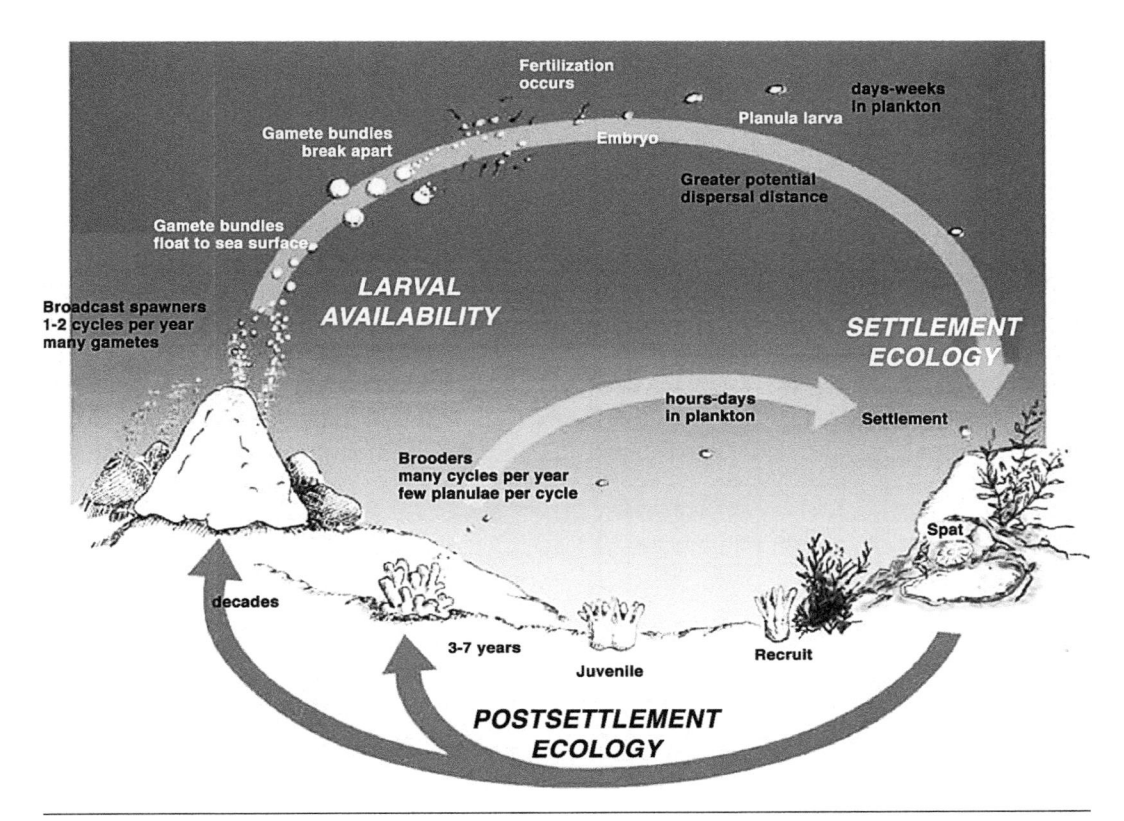

Figure 8.1 Diagram of sexual reproduction cycles for brooding and broadcast spawners (courtesy of Mark Vermeij).

effort and lower costs to scale. However, efforts to outplant recruits at these small sizes are rarely successful due to extensive early mortality (Edwards et al. 2015). This is because most size-dependent efficiencies consider 5 mm or 3–9 months old as the critical minimum size for survival (Babcock and Mumdy 1996). This was also highlighted by Doropoulus et al. (2012) for the chronic and acute impacts on coral recruits by the importance of size. Nonetheless, in the Philippines, dela Cruz and Harrison (2017) overcame early bottlenecks to establish a breeding population of 79 *Acropora tenuis* after supplying ~1.6 million larvae to artificial enclosures fastened to the reef for protection and targeted settlement on the reef. Similarly, in Curacao, Chamberland et al. (2015) established at least one *Acropora palmata* recruit on one out of three substrates after 2.5 years post deployment. Additionally, tetrapod substrates (ceramic kiln bases) that can be seeded with coral recruits and wedged into reef crevices have shown promise (Chamberland et al. 2017).

Alternatively, grow-out of recruits prior to outplant (intensive rearing) is attempted much less often because it is expensive and recruits are difficult to rear (Chamberland et al. 2015). In contrast to direct outplant of new recruits, these projects have achieved success most often (Iwao et al. 2010; Nakamura et al. 2011; Villanueva et al. 2012; Guest et al. 2013; Chamberland et al. 2016) due to recruits overcoming some of the first size-based survival bottlenecks prior to outplant (Vermeij and Sandin 2004; Guest et al. 2013). In the Philippines, after rearing *Acropora valida* recruits to six months, Villanueva et al. (2012) achieved 67% survival and a 37-fold increase in ecological volume (new coral cover) with an additional six months growth post

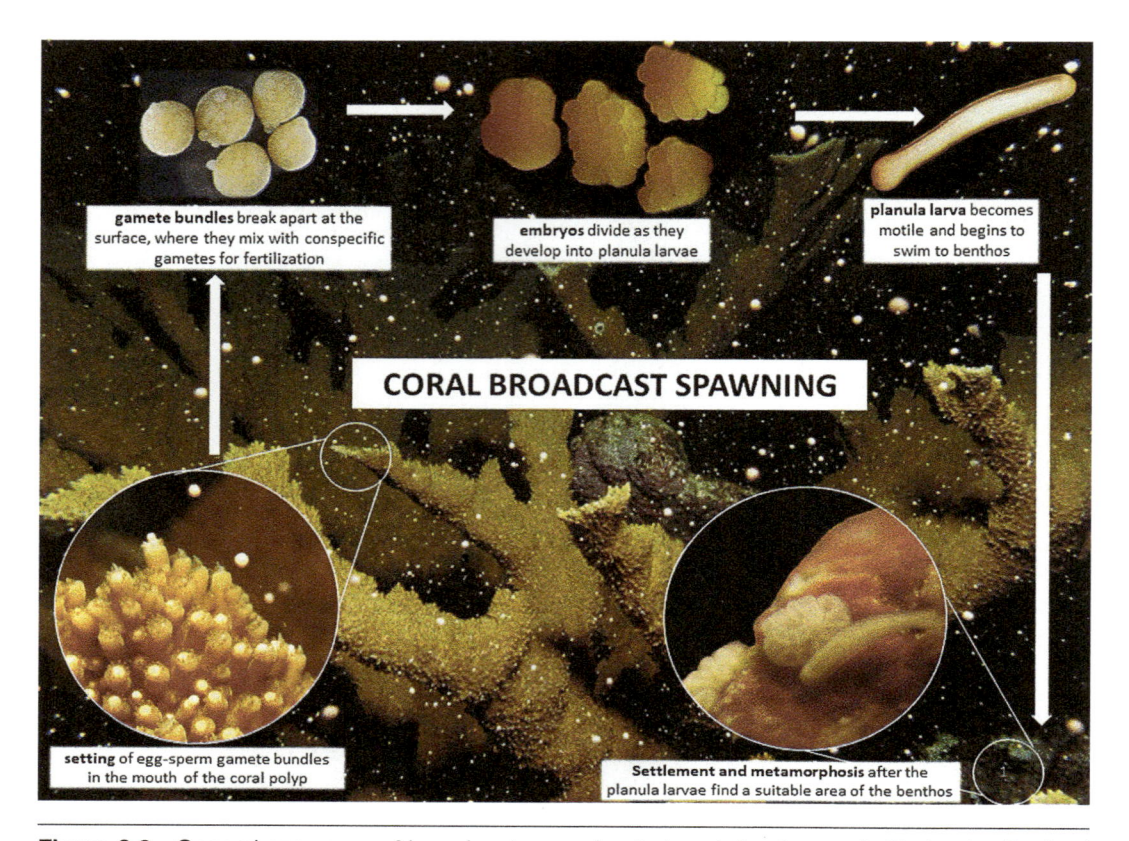

Figure 8.2 General sequence of broadcast spawning to larval development. Photos by Raphael Ritson-Williams (spawning, setting, gamete bundles) and Nicole Fogarty (embryos, planula, settlement, and metamorphosis).

Figure 8.3 A coral gamete collection net covers an *Acropora palmata* colony to optimize the collection of buoyant egg-sperm bundles that are released during spawning and float into the collection cup at the top of the net.

outplant. Similarly, after rearing *Acropora millepora* recruits to 19 months, Guest et al. 2013 demonstrated 47% survivorship after one-year post outplant. Some efforts have even resulted in the establishment of new reproductive colonies on target reefs (Iwao et al. 2010; Guest et al. 2013; Chamberland et al. 2016).

Though some efforts to raise larvae have resulted in new genotypes on the reef, these successes are rare and disregard the number of attempts and number of larvae that are necessary for success. In many cases thousands to hundreds-of-thousands of larvae are needed to establish a few new colonies on the reef (Miller 2014; dela Cruz and Harrison 2017). In addition, few species other than large recruits from brooders or acroporids have demonstrated viability with these techniques, leaving most species—including those more tolerant to bleaching (like many boulder corals)—without recourse. Indeed, strategies to maximize the utility of spawning events and then promote the mass proliferation of new genets are urgently needed.

The reality is that both asexual and sexual restoration techniques presently fall short of producing large quantities of genetically diverse corals for outplant. Despite this, techniques exhibit reciprocal strengths and weaknesses that may offset each other if methodologies are combined. Sexual recruits possess the new raw material to promote genetic adaptation, however, they are extremely fragile and prone to mass mortality at this size. This effect is most pronounced in direct outplant efforts, making it difficult to realize any survival six months or more post outplant (authors pers. observations, Miller et al. 2014). Indeed, prolonged survival in the Caribbean is so exceedingly rare that it begs the question: are the few surviving individuals from these efforts better adapted to site conditions and substrates or are they just inherently *lucky*. In addition, efforts to raise larvae is time-intensive and produces propagules that can be placed back in the ocean only once. This is particularly unfortunate, considering the resource expenditure for intensively reared recruits. These shortcomings stifle incremental progress in producing larger numbers of survivable offspring. Adding one or more asexual cycles through fragmentation or micro-fragmentation of grown recruits increases the utility of these precious new genetics allowing the renewable production of recruits for diverse outplantings.

Taking advantage of the sexual cycle of marine organisms to propagate more individuals in a hatchery setting is currently standard practice for almost all other animal aquaculture species (except for corals). In fact, the only method of propagation for clam, shrimp, and fish hatcheries is to capitalize on the sexual cycle exclusively, since they do not have the luxury of fragmenting their farmed animals into pieces to produce more. In contrast, the coral restoration community has the potential of both sexual and asexual methods of reproduction. Recently, more successful operations have been able to sexually produce coral larvae to surviving juvenile size in at least a few hundred or a few thousand in a hatchery, but millions are required to ensure a better survival rate. Many direct outplant projects have pointed toward this previously untapped sexual reproduction process as the answer to scale, speed, and economic sense (Chamberland et al. 2017; dela Cruz and Harrison 2017). However, projects as of yet have not resulted in consistent, large-scale survival in the field. Similarly, no other projects with other cultured invertebrate species have yet to be successful at scale by controlling only the fertilization and early settlement phases in the lab prior to outplant. The closest analogy would be the process of *remote-setting* with oysters. This is where the full larval stage is controlled in a hatchery and the stages of settlement through to juvenile occur in land and field nurseries. Though successful at scale, these methods are always in controlled environments for cleaning and protection from predators for as long as three to six months or even up to a year old (personal experience, D. Vaughan).

SEXUAL REPRODUCTION OF CORALS

To move forward in coral restoration, it is important to understand the biological processes of the sexual reproduction cycle within corals. Corals have two distinct strategies of sexual reproduction: as brooders or as broadcast spawners (Fadlallah 1983, Szmant 1986). Early research was focused on those corals that brood their embryos internally and release them as competent planulae larvae. Yet, most corals reproduce as broadcast spawners, releasing only gametes synchronously into the water column, where fertilization occurs externally (Szmant 1986). To make things more interesting and complex, they also can be either hermaphroditic (both sexes in one individual) or gonochoric (separate sexes), and there exist examples of coral species that possess each of these strategic alternatives. Historic conditions have most likely determined these strategies from natural selection processes—whether brooders or broadcast spawners were more successful in different conditions and during different time epics. Most larger species and acroporids are broadcast spawners and most of the smaller and *weedier* species are often brooders (Szmant 1986). The differences are becoming more pertinent today as survival, distribution, and genetic diversity become more important. For active restoration purposes, both of these strategies are important and can be utilized in hatchery operations to provide more individuals and more diverse genotypes.

For coral reefs to survive, successful reproduction, settlement, growth, and survival to reproductive age must outpace the losses from bleaching, disease, and predation—or suffer the trajectory that followed previous near extinction episodes caused by epic events such as volcanic activity and meteors. For this sexual growth cycle to occur on any given reef, larval survival and recruitment are dependent on a sequence of three phases: (1) larval availability, which integrates gamete production, fertilization success, and connectivity; (2) settlement, which relates to larval condition and substrate selection behavior; and (3) post-settlement survival, including substrate-specific survival and growth (Ritson-Williams et al. 2009).

Broadcast-spawning corals rely on environmental cues for physiological processes that lead to gametogenesis and spawning (Baird et al. 2009, Fogarty and Marhaver 2019). The use of a hierarchy of cues to synchronize the release of gametes is a highly adaptive strategy that is driven by high gamete densities that enhance fertilization (Levitan et al. 2004) and satiate predators (Babcock et al. 1986). Although most researchers discuss coral spawning synchronization on three temporal scales, specifically, month, day, and hour (Babcock et al. 1986), evidence suggests that cues exist for finer resolution synchrony, namely, minutes or tens of minutes (Levitan et al. 2011). The traditional view that high mean sea surface temperature (SST) triggers coral spawning at the level of *month* has been challenged, and evidence suggests the rapid increases in SST (Keith et al. 2016), the rate of change in solar radiation (van Woesik et al. 2006), tidal cycles and atmospheric pressure (Wolstenholme et al. 2018), periods of limited rainfall (Mendes and Woodley 2002), and regional wind patterns (van Woesik 2010) are stronger predictors of spawning at the level of month. The cues associated with spawning on the same day are signaled by lunar cycles, and the onset of darkness triggers the hour of spawning (however, some species spawn in daylight—see Chamberland et al. 2016). The precision of coral spawning at the level of *minute* is less studied, but evidence suggests that pheromones, individual coral genotypes (Levitan et al. 2011), and shifts in twilight color and intensity (Sweeny et al. 2011) may be involved.

Remarkably, recent progress recreating some of these cues by mimicking light, temperature, and lunar cycles in the laboratory has allowed for corals to spawn in captivity (Craggs et al.

2017). Furthermore, there has been interest in attempting *out-of-season* spawning of corals. The conditioning of captive broodstock and control of the hatchery environment to achieve maturation and induce spawning is a practice regularly used in nearly all other marine aquaculture hatcheries to culture large numbers of offspring using both in season and out of season spawning techniques. Current expectations are for these types of advancements to become a standard tool for modern coral hatcheries.

Sexual reproduction efforts have historically focused on the collection of naturally released gametes or gamete bundles that are collected in the ocean during calculated spawning seasonal events. A summary of when several Caribbean coral species spawn can be found in Jordan (2018). The timing of coral spawning in the Caribbean varies by species, the latitude at which they live, and the biological clock model that they follow (Lin et al. 2013; Lin and Nozawa 2017), making some coral species more predictable in their spawning times than others. For instance, acroporids tend to follow an hourglass biological clock model where changes in environmental conditions can influence spawning times. These corals tend to have high variability in spawning times (Lin and Nozawa 2017) and are therefore less predictable. The oscillation biological clock model, on the other hand, is endogenous, and species such as the Caribbean orbicellids are highly predictable (Levitan et al. 2011) and less likely to be influenced by environmental changes. In the Caribbean, the major spawning species (*Acropora* spp., *Orbicella* spp., *Colpophyllia natans*, *Pseudodiploria strigosa*, *Dendrogyra cylindrus*, *Montastraea cavernosa*, and *Stephanocoenia interspeta*) mostly spawn in August and September, three to nine days after the full moon, and 30–270 minutes after sunset. The northern latitudes tend to spawn earlier in the year, while the southern latitudes are shifted slightly later (Jordan 2018). *Diploria labyrinthiformis*, on the other hand, tends to spawn across a broader range of May through October for 10–13 days.

Like most other organisms, gamete production, fertilization, and development of a swimming larval form must be followed by successful settlement and metamorphosis and survival into a juvenile form. After many months as a single polyp, new recruits produce a multitude of new polyps being formed by asexual budding before eventually becoming noticeable to the naked eye. After many years, they grow to a size with reproductive potential. Figure 8.1 illustrates the classic reproductive spawning cycle for broadcast and brooding corals.

LARVAL CULTURE, SETTLEMENT, AND POST-METAMORPHOSIS

During natural spawning events investigators collect spawned bundles in nets that cover a coral colony to optimize the vertical collection of gamete bundles in an upper collection vial (Figure 8.3). Calculations of the timing of these events have been studied by location and by species. For those interested in how corals spawn synchronously, see publication by Fogarty and Marhaven (2019). Additionally, there are many hands-on workshops and demonstrations, including web-based information from experienced researchers on coral larval collection and settlement (i.e., Marhaven, Chamberland, and Fogarty 2017, CRC webinar).

The rest of this chapter will now focus on the larval culture, settlement, and post-metamorphic process from recruits through juvenile survival in land-based hatcheries and nurseries. The methods have been proven, the equipment is simple, and the supplies and materials are affordable. The most important factors are a *labor of love*, good water quality conditions, and attention to details.

From 2013 through 2018, Christopher Page and David Vaughan repeated the steps of larval production, recruit settlement, and grow-out, followed by the systematic micro-fragmentation of one-to-three-year-old juveniles, while at Mote Marine Laboratory in the Florida Keys. This led to the establishment of thousands of living, settled recruits that were grown and then further propagated in a land nursery—an asset that has greatly enhanced restoration efforts. Work by the authors at this facility has generated thousands of unique genotypes of various stony coral species and produced nearly 15,000 asexual replicates from this new genetic material for use in diverse planting projects. In doing so, this work has not only bolstered local genetic diversity in key species but has also helped to assist gene flow between unique subpopulations of a threatened elkhorn coral (Hagedorn et al. 2018). This excess of new genetic recombinations can be leveraged to produce robust replicates for diverse experimentation to increase the resilience on reefs.

Survival of any one new coral genotype that was produced by sexual reproduction in the ocean is rare; therefore, for restoration, culture systems that produce new genotypes readily should be created. The land-based hatchery stage must become more commonplace to achieve this, particularly if we hope to restore climate-adapted stony coral populations back to the reef. A significant problem to overcome is that rearing recruits in the lab to juveniles or adults is thought to be difficult. Furthermore, in the wild, settlement has been inconsistent year to year as algal turfs, sedimentation, disease, and predators can affect natural recruit survival. These setbacks can be more easily controlled and more successful in captive environments. The authors and others are continuing to refine protocols and increasing success from year to year and have demonstrated that these problems are not insurmountable. Overcoming the significant hurdles associated with early life history of coral recruits on a consistent and reliable basis, together with innovative successes like controlled spawning and micro-fragmentation, enhancing our understanding of resilient traits, as well as their selection for restoration are all within reach.

LARVAL DEVELOPMENT

Fertilization and larval development are crucial first steps and can be properly accomplished in simple plastic containers, bins, or buckets. Fertilization in broadcasting species can be accomplished in the field on the vessel staging collections or back at the land-based facilities if the travel time is not too long. Longevity of active sperm and viable eggs declines with time. Therefore, this process should take place within the first half hour to an hour if possible—noting that some species (i.e., *Orbicella spp*) do not fertilize well within the first 20 minutes. The removal of excess sperm is advisable to prevent *polyspermy* (more than one sperm trying to fertilize one egg), and because sperm quickly decompose and foul the water in the culture vessel. Separation of the fertilized eggs from sperm and other contaminants should be done as soon as possible and with care not to impact zygotes that are starting their fragile process of first cell division and development. Gravy separators work great for this (see Figure 8.4). Larvae can develop in any clean plastic container—petri dishes to five-gallon buckets—which can be easily purchased, cleaned, and re-used as larval development tanks and can hold thousands of swimming larvae (see Figure 8.4).

Larval care, though simple, is demanding and sometimes harder to accomplish, especially immediately after the obligatory all-night gamete collections. When everyone else is already extremely tired and pushed to the limit, that is when the second phase and the *real work* starts

Sexual Reproduction and Rearing Corals for Restoration

Figure 8.4 After gamete bundles have broken apart, gravy separators are used to pour off sperm and rinse eggs with sperm-free seawater (photo of Dr. Vaughan at Coral Vita, Bahamas).

with the larval care. Here, as in all other sections, water quality is paramount to making larval survival possible. It is the opinion of the authors that you cannot change water, clean or change containers, or skim off lipids too often or too much—as long as care is taken to avoid physically damaging the developing embryos. For the first few days beyond gastrulation, this water changing, cleaning of the container, and surface skimming should be done every three to six hours, around the clock. After the majority of lipids and the dead, dying, or undeveloped eggs are removed, then every six to ten hours is probably sufficient. Since the larvae are so full of stored lipids from the adult egg formation, many species do not sink, but float on the surface of the water early in development stages. The surface lipids and dead and dying eggs or larvae must be removed, either by sequential flushing with clean water or removal using lipophilic materials such as plastic wrap or plastic dishes that will adhere to the lipid but not the ciliated larvae. Multiple removals of the white-colored lipid or dead larvae can clean the container of contaminants very effectively. Next, both the container and culture water must be cleaned. This can be accomplished with inexpensive culture containers such as five-gallon buckets (see Figure 8.5). With the surface lipids removed, excess culture water can be removed by gently siphoning it through a properly sized sieve that excludes larvae (with drain holes that are approximately 50% of the size of the larvae). The healthy larvae can then be carefully decanted with minimal culture water into a new clean culture vessel with new clean water. This is done as often as you can and as often as you see the water quality in the vessel deteriorating. A cloudy water column means bacteria and eventually ciliates will gain dominance and the larvae will be in jeopardy. Do not try and save every larvae or egg and never keep what is on the bottom of the vessel until they are in the mode of behavior of searching on the bottom for a substrate to attach to. Larval culture can take from three days to three or more weeks, depending on species and water temperatures. Higher temperatures will develop the larvae quicker, but also the bacteria and ciliates. In any small vessel, watch for any of the larvae that might get stuck on the sides from surface tension. Use a squirt bottle to recover them before they dry out or use plastic containers that limit surface film. Also, when draining a container with larvae at the surface, use the squirt bottle generously to prevent larvae from becoming stranded on the sides.

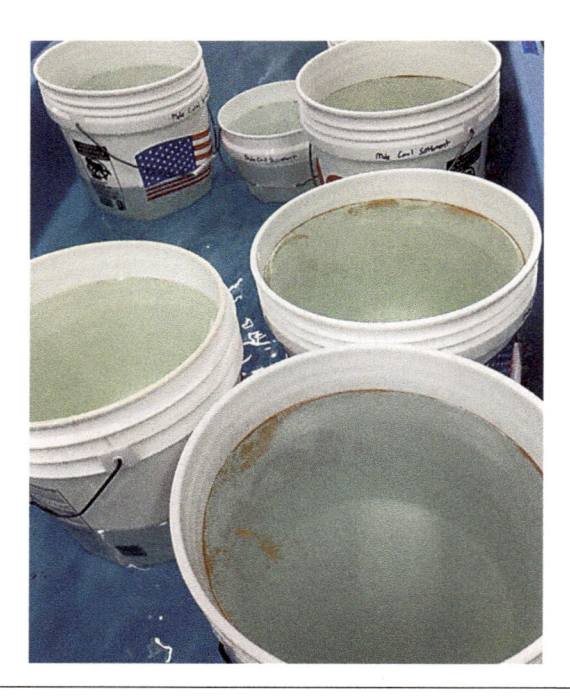

Figure 8.5 Pictures of *Acropora palmata* larvae in five-gallon buckets and swimming on the surface (photo D. Vaughan at Mote Marine Lab, Florida Keys).

SETTLEMENT AND METAMORPHOSIS

When the time comes for the larvae to initiate the *search for a substrate* behavior, they will spend more time in the water column than on the surface—and then more time on the bottom of the container. This is the time to separate these three water column positions (surface swimmers, water column swimmers, and bottom crawlers) from each other. Figure 8.6 shows some larvae on the surface and some starting to swim in the water column. This separation is easily done through water-column separations. Those larvae that are already searching the bottom should be moved to the settling tank, or container for this process. Properly seasoned substrates, plugs, or settlement tiles or clean tiles with an attractant should be used for the potential settlement of these larvae within the next 24–48 hours. We found that cleaned substrates dusted with small particles of live crustose coralline algae (CCA)—also called dusted substrates—stimulated the metamorphosis but did not overload the substrate with fouling organisms (see Figure 8.7). During growth in the nursery, this was highly beneficial because the number of fouling organisms that were competing with new recruits compared to field-seasoned substrates (organisms grown on the substrate in the ocean) is significantly less. On field-seasoned substrates, initial settlement was higher but survival was extremely low, as is similar in the wild.

Settlement and full metamorphoses can be rapid or drawn out. The search-for-substrate phase can take time if they are not yet fully competent and there is a lack of settlement cues to stimulate the attachment and final benthic adherence. Natural cues, colors, and chemical compounds, such as those given off by biofilms and CCA, are involved in stimulating

Sexual Reproduction and Rearing Corals for Restoration 133

Figure 8.6 Pictures of *Acropora palmata* larvae on surface and also swimming in the water column as they start the behavior of searching for a substrate to settle on.

Figure 8.7 Photo of ceramic coral settlement plugs; on left, clean plug *dusted* with CCA to attract coral larvae and on right, *seasoned* plugs with natural biofilm and CCA to attract coral larval settlement.

metamorphosis to a new recruit. Frequent water changes and additions of more cues or seasoned substrates seem to enhance the settlement behavior. If in doubt, small dish subsamples can be used to observe the process so that whole larval cultures are not disturbed during this critical stage (Figure 8.8).

Settlement size is not necessarily related to the size of the adult or the size of the adult polyp. In fact, most of the brooders and smaller polyp broadcasting spawners, like the acroporids, have very large-sized eggs, larvae, and resultant recruits. Once the recruit is sufficiently attached to the substrate (1–2 days), it can be easily and safely removed from the settlement tanks on that substrate to prevent further recruiting by more individuals, if desired. If moving at this size or stage to the wild, many recruits may be warranted as survival will be low. If in good controlled conditions of a nursery, only a few recruits are needed to produce the preferred survival of 1 recruit per substrate. Figure 8.9 has a large-sized settled recruit of a small polyp stony coral, *Acropora palmata,* that has flattened out as the primary polyp and firmly attached to the substrate.

The size and rate of settlement and growth after metamorphosis can be variable. Some recruits stay in the primary polyp stage for longer periods of time than others. Figure 8.10 shows a primary polyp on the left and multiple polyps on the right. This may be from nutritional storage left after swimming or the timing of infection by Symbiodinaceae (zooxanthellae) algal cells. Notice the size of the primary polyp is the same size as the multiple polyps. Also notice that the CCA around the outside of the picture is growing over the substrate and could grow over the coral recruits.

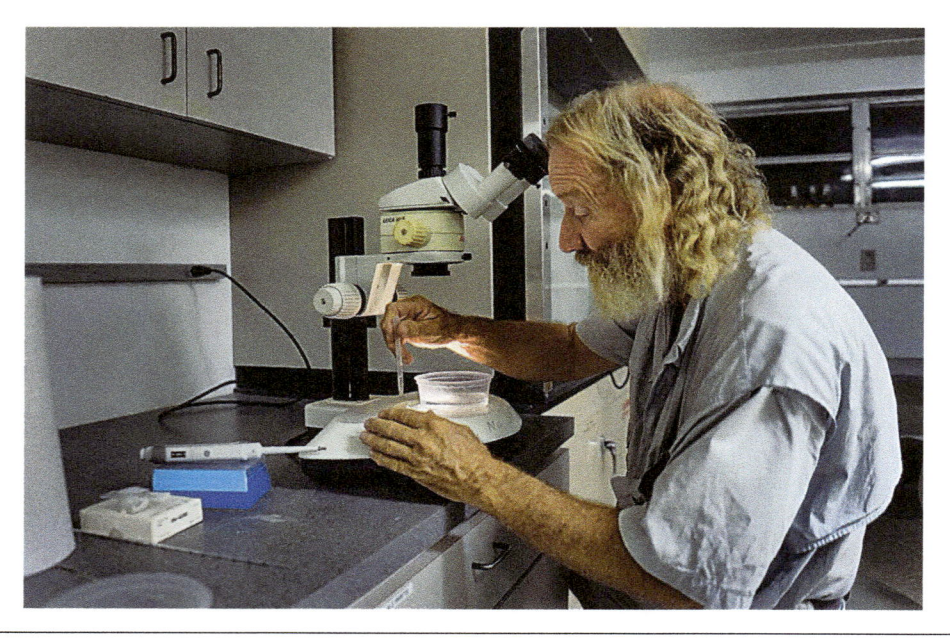

Figure 8.8 Small dish sub-samples can be used to observe the settlement process so that whole larval cultures are not disturbed during this critical stage; Dr. Vaughan using a dissecting scope with lighting above and below (photo by Dan Mele).

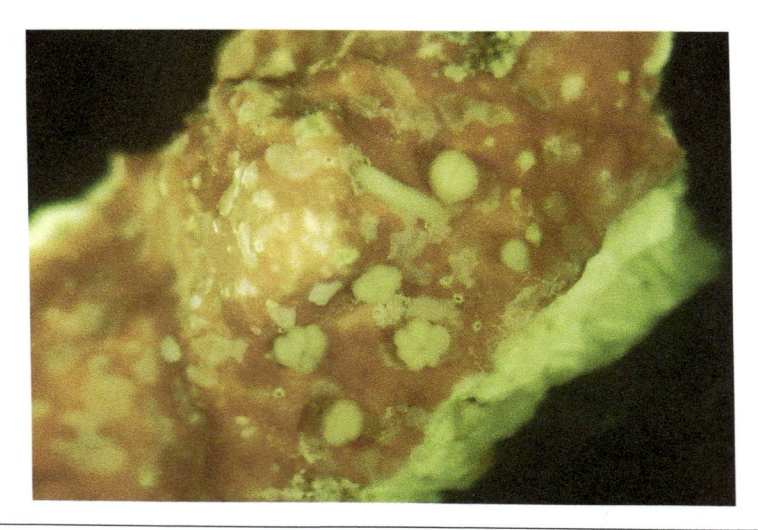

Figure 8.9 Microscopic photo of an *Acropora* sp. settled recruit that is metamorphosed and firmly attached.

Figure 8.10 Two similar-sized recruits of *Acropora palmata*—left, single polyp; right, recent budded multiple polyps (photo by Dan Mele).

MULTIPLE SETTLEMENT AND SURVIVAL

If multiple settlers survive to post-metamorphic sizes, there can also be an issue of tryin separate the individual colonies onto separate plugs or substrates as individual genotypes ure 8.11).

Multiple settlers surviving on a substrate can lead to compatible fusion if settlers mee in development or overtopping due to developed competitive responses. This occurs b settlers are genetically distinct individuals and not identical clones. Most often, fusion of ent genotypes can be successful at only the early stages of juvenile development. After a of time, they will establish their own genotypic behavior and fight with stinging tentacle using mesoderm material ejected on adjacent colonies that they do not detect as their

Figure 8.11 Multiple recruits on single settlement plugs with many colonies growing too close together and covered with CCA and other algae (photo C. Page).

POST-SETTLEMENT CARE

Post-settlement care for the first few weeks is similar to care of the larvae as far as water changes and tank cleaning, except easier because there are no free-swimming larvae to contend with. Tanks, trays, plugs, and tiles can all be moved to a new clean tank container or raceway tanks with ease. It's best to place settled substrates on trays, racks, or supports so that they can be moved in groups. Materials are best utilized in a modular fashion where possible so that they can easily be cleaned and replaced or moved en masse to different locations. For the authors and many others, plastic grading (eggcrate-lighting material) the size of a dinner plate is frequently used to hold nearly 70 to 100 substrates or 2.5 cm plugs (see Figure 8.12). Periodically, substrates are moved to a duplicate rack, so the old rack can be sanitized, dried, and stored. This is extremely effective at controlling the buildup of fouling biomass on rack surfaces preventing the subsequent spread elsewhere in the raceway. This is a critical stage in giving new coral recruit a head start above the other fouling organisms. Even with inside tank conditions, other algae, bacteria, and microorganisms can also settle and be in a race to colonize the substrate. Zooanthellae alga uptake or *infection* takes place at different times for different species. Brooders often settle with their symbionts already incorporated; spawners vary by species and algal availability as to onset of symbiosis. One strategy is to add sources to the tank as soon as possible so that the presence of symbionts is not limiting. Facilities culture their own strains, others rely on introducing adults of the same species to the culture vessel, and still others let mother nature go it alone. Those settled recruits that acquire algal symbionts early seem to have a better rate of growth past the primary polyp stage than those which don't (personal observations). At some point in time, it is better to move the recruits to an outside raceway with natural sunlight, rather than the indoor

Sexual Reproduction and Rearing Corals for Restoration

Figure 8.12 Dr. Vaughan and Zack Rago (Chasing Coral) holding an egg crate tray full of live coral on ceramic plugs, used to handle, clean, and transfer corals easily.

tanks with artificial LED lighting. However, this is best accomplished through trial and error with a few trays at a time.

GROW OUT TO JUVENILE SIZE

This stage is the *make it or break it* stage for all of the culturists' previous work. With the right methods and care, it can mean thousands of new juveniles that can then be processed through asexual propagation (see Figure 8.13). Production increases grew from just a few into the hundreds—and then thousands were realized. Proper experience and rigorous optimization of methods can lead to increasing success and progressively faster growth rates ranging from a few months to a few years. This will allow scientists to carry out asexual propagation in a routine and timely fashion for the rapid replication of valuable genetic seed stock.

What is success? It is the potential to produce new genotypes using sexual reproduction with gametes from existing resistant or resilient strains, then settling new recruits with new genetic recombinations to produce broodstock for asexual propagation. The authors have found that growing recruits to the size of a fully grown microfragment ready for outplant (2.5 cm) is a great size to propagate the individual into several new fragments. For some species, this could take as little as six to eight months or up to three years for slower growers (see Figure 8.14). This amount of time may shorten drastically as experience and optimization of growth conditions are achieved.

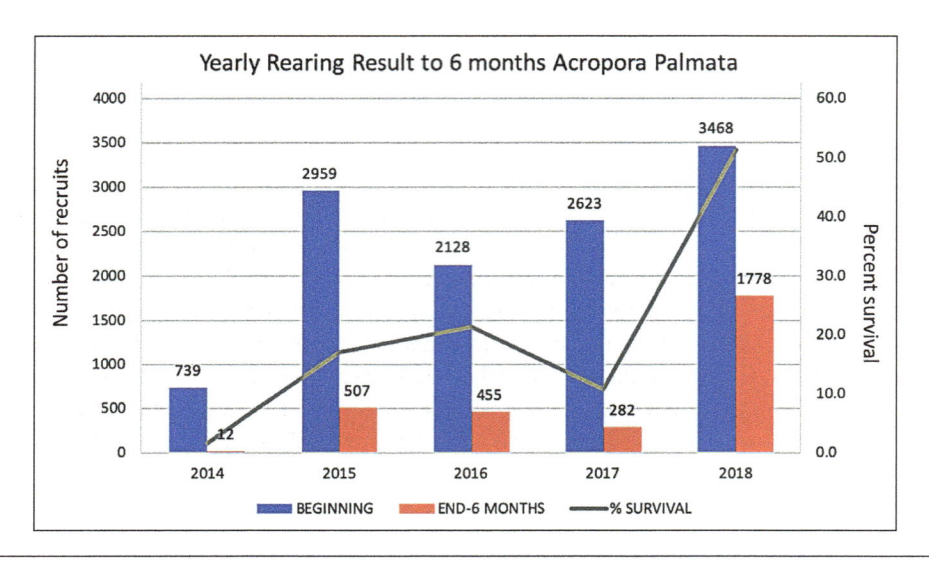

Figure 8.13 Graph of increasing production in number and the percent of survival for rearing recruits to over six months old for *Acropora palmata*. From 2014 to 2018, there were increasing numbers produced (starting with blue bar numbers in the beginning, to the red bar end numbers surviving until six months old). The percent of survival is shown to have increased to near 50% by the grey line (the exception to the increasing trend was in 2017 during hurricane Irma).

Figure 8.14 Typical size achieved for eight-month-old *Acropora palmata*, in three different years of growout. The left side picture is 2015, the middle is 2017, and the right is 2018. Notice the size difference and the fast-growing outer edge producing a white band that is eliminating the colored CCA covering (photo by C. Page).

NURSERY GROWTH TO A JUVENILE AND RACEWAY ECOLOGY

Perhaps the most overlooked aspect of recruit husbandry is the ecology of the culture vessel and how it affects survival and growth during long-term grow-out. Specifically, how the fouling organisms that raise up with recruits simultaneously compete with recruits for resources and space. This subject, though complex, traditionally receives little attention from the culturist, often being overlooked in favor of equally important but more easily monitored metrics like water quality, flow, and lighting. Raceway ecology encompasses more obvious direct competition such as algal overgrowth (see Figure 8.10), but also includes cryptic effects such as the production of allelochemicals (see Figure 8.14) and unfavorable microbial activity that interferes with the corals. The latter represents an understudied avenue of assault on captive recruits, but is suspected to be a major source of mortality. This, coupled with evidence from field work (Gross 2003, Kuntz et al. 2005, Kuffner et al. 2006), necessitates deeper consideration of this topic.

The raceway's ecology is not a fixed trait, rather it is an ever-changing landscape filled with a diverse assemblage of organisms as on the reef. Colonization of a new vessel is similar to that which occurs on new materials deployed in the field (see Wanders 1977 and Borowitska et al. 1978). The first to colonize are those organisms that take hold and reproduce quickly, such as bacteria and film algae. As time progresses, intermediate colonizers such as filamentous algae, CCA, and cyanobacteria are abundant—finally, fleshy macro-algae can come to dominate. This successional trend (henceforth referred to as raceway or tank succession) is highly predictable, but species makeup and time frame vary almost endlessly. Similarly, invertebrate fouling, which happens concurrently, is also extremely diverse but without recognizable patterning. The most common taxa include Polychaetes, cnidarians, poriferans, foraminiferas, and bivalves. This cornucopia of fouling organisms and the limitless amount of assemblages therein, represents one of the most variable components to rearing recruits and can easily lead to mortality since many fouling organisms are superior competitors to coral recruits.

There are diverse mechanisms by which coral recruits are outcompeted by the fouling community—all of which can vary in magnitude with changing constituents. The most immediate threat is direct overgrowth by invasive algae or invertebrates. This can happen at an exceptional rate via early colonizers like diatoms or CCA, or can be the result of recruits being slowly choked out by things like fleshy algae or stinging invertebrates. Controlling this overgrowth is of the utmost priority, but it is far from the only avenue in which recruits can be lost. Algae, cyanobacteria, and other microbial organisms are suspected to be disproportionately responsible for unexplained mortality, through the production of harmful allelochemicals. These aqueous secondary metabolites are potent disruptors of processes like enzyme activity and photosynthesis (Gross 2003) or may weaken defenses against microbes (Vermeij et al. 2009). However, identification of the active compound is rare in numerous pairings between invertebrates and primary producers.

Kuffner and Paul (2004) found that the presence of the cyanobacteria *Lyngbya majuscula* in coral settlement chambers significantly decreased survival of *Acropora surculosa* larvae, and recruitment on unoccupied substrate in *Pocillopora damicornis*. Miller et al. (2009) found that water that was briefly conditioned by diverse algal assemblages inhibited larval settlement in *Orbicella faveolata, Pseudodiploria strigosa*, and *Acropora palmata*. Paul et al. (2011) found that lipophilic extracts of *Dyctyota pulchella* and *D. pinnatifida* reduced larval survival in *Porites astreoides*. Due to the inevitability of algal growth alongside recruits, it is likely that similar phenomena will occur in the culture vessel. It is commonly observed that recruits will experience higher survival and growth when introduced into a clean raceway, rather than a raceway with an established fouling community. Consequently, the presence and buildup of fouling organisms in the culture vessel must now be considered, regardless of whether recruits are being directly overgrown.

Given the complexity of interactions that can occur in the culture vessel, it is not surprising that rearing recruits successfully is often considered a mystifying process. Therefore, developing methodology that minimizes the ecologic complexity of the culture vessel is a key component to success that has been previously overlooked. Considering this, the essential strategy is to start with a clean raceway and minimize the buildup of fouling organisms in the culture vessel, in addition to ensuring consistent water quality and physical conditions.

MANAGING RACEWAY ECOLOGY

If a raceway's or a tank's ecology is left unmanaged it will often develop into a community that is inhospitable to even the hardiest of recruits (simulating the wild environment). A culturist's first line of defense is to prevent the introduction of as many invasive organisms as possible. This is achieved, in part, by minimizing the number of incoming contaminates that are entering through the vessel's water source. A series of simple mechanical filters, such as a sand filter and a pleated filter, can serve to remove particulates, floating algae, and a portion of the algal spores or invertebrate larvae that are present. Ideally, these would be followed in line with a properly installed ultraviolet sterilizer to further minimize algae, invertebrates, and bacteria, allowing for a more standard culture medium to enter the vessel. Similarly, it is advisable to avoid use of items collected from the field or used in other existing raceways, in the new culture, wherever possible. This is because the organisms seeded on these items (be they microbial, algal, or invertebrate) will have bypassed your filtration and have a disproportionate chance of invading the culture vessel, thereby altering the raceway's succession in unpredictable ways. Organisms that can capitalize on quick reproduction such as microbes, hair algae, stinging cnidarians, or cyanobacteria, as well as mobile hitchhikers such as corallivorous crabs or gastropods are often introduced in this way and can go unnoticed until they reach plague proportions that resist eradication. This recommendation is in stark contrast to commonly practiced strategies, such as the use of *live* rock by aquarists or the field seasoning of substrates for coral settlement. Finally, minimizing the structural complexity of the culture vessel and selecting materials that are less favorable for fouler recruitment can also help prevent the establishment of invasive species. Highly porous or rugose materials should be avoided wherever possible since these surfaces are also difficult to clean thoroughly, thus leaving room for microbial buildup. The ideal material for use in the culture vessel is inert, flat, and smooth (having low porosity). For this reason, plastics are invaluable, food-grade plastics are best, however, PVC piping and plastic egg crate (sold as fluorescent light diffusers) are regularly used.

Once the fouling organism entering culture has been minimized, the raceway's succession must be actively managed. Introducing organisms that will graze algae but not prey on or irritate recruits can be an invaluable selection tool. However, this is not as straightforward as you would think because some grazers may consume or damage recruits while foraging. Some fish from the genus *Acanthurus* or invertebrates like the long-spined sea urchin (*Diadema antillarum*) will substitute consuming or harming coral tissue if preferential algae are not abundant. Similarly, benthic grazers can damage recruits by repeatedly abrading them with their shell or test. Because of this, small gastropod grazers in adequate but not overwhelming densities are preferred. Juvenile *L. tectum* (≥ 1 cm) work well for many species of recruits in Florida; however, the intertidal snail *Batillaria minima* is the grazer of choice by the authors. This is because they rarely grow larger than 1 cm, they are abundant on rocky shorelines in the Florida Keys, and they can be siphoned up and redistributed in the raceway to graze problematic areas.

Finally, CCA are considered the only harmless (or potentially beneficial) fouler that grow up in the raceway, provided they are raised up slowly alongside growing recruits and are not present in overwhelming proportions. This is because as CCAs occupy vacant space, other more invasive algae decrease in proportion.

CONCLUSIONS

Sexual reproduction of corals has been only recently discovered (1980s). Because, historically, the resilience of coral communities has relied on natural recruits, the scaling up of restoration efforts would benefit from greater use of producing restoration corals sexually (Randall et.al. 2020). Only more recently (2010–2020) have culturists aimed to assist this process through ex situ settlement efforts, despite this strategy being common practice for other cultured marine organisms. Work with other species, however, has always been in conjunction with a land-based hatchery and land and field nurseries for as much as a year, not with direct outplant of larvae. For years, experiments with corals with the intent to directly release swimming larvae or brand-new settled recruits directly back to the field environment have met with inadequate survival and therefore inadequate success. More recent work has shown that there is potential for this in the future (Chamberland et al. 2015, dela Cruz and Harrison 2017); however, we are not there yet. Today we have witnessed the successful larval settlement and survival to juvenile stages in the thousands by use of a land-based hatchery and nursery. This, in conjunction with efficient asexual propagation, can lead to the mass proliferation of new genets for outplant and study on coral reefs. It is our hope that this mixed approach of sexual plus asexual reproduction will help to greatly increase the number and success of practitioners who are working to plant new and novel genotypes in ongoing restoration efforts—and thereby, to help bolster genetic diversity and facilitate the discovery of mechanisms to promote resilience at scale on our imperiled reefs.

Our hope is that both scientists and restoration practitioners will use sexual reproduction as a way to produce new genotypes. It is possible that work with sexually reproduced coral larvae and recruits will become more feasible for those who are only using the asexual reproduction method at this time. Ideally, there will be a two-stage approach to coral restoration projects: a sexual reproduction cycle producing hundreds of new genotypes followed by an asexual reproduction cycle producing thousands of replicate individuals for these new genets via new techniques such as micro-fragmentation. This hybrid approach will produce more genetically diverse, and hopefully more resilient, corals—for all future active coral reef restoration efforts.

REFERENCES

Babcock, R. C. and A. J. Heyward. 1986. "Larval development of certain gamete-spawning scleractinian corals." *Coral Reefs* 5(3), 111–116.

Babcock, R. C., A. H. Baird, S. Piromvaragorn, D. P. Thomson, and B. L. Willis. 2003. "Identification of scleractinian coral recruits from Indo-Pacific reefs." *Zoological Studies-Taipei* 42(1), 211–226.

Babcock, R. C. and C. Mundy. 1996. "Coral recruitment: Consequences of settlement choice for early growth and survivorship in two scleractinians." *J. Ex.Biol Ecol* 206:179–201.

Baird, A. H., J. R. Guest, and B. L. Willis. 2009. "Systematic and biogeographical patterns in the reproductive biology of scleractinian corals." *Annual Review of Ecology, Evolution, and Systematics* 40, 551–571.

Baums, I. B., A. C. Baker, S. W. Davies, A. G. Grottoli, C. D. Kenkel, S. A. Kithen, I. B. Kuffner, et al. 2019. "Considerations for maximizing the adaptive potential of restored coral populations in the western Atlantic. Ecological Applications."

Borowitzka, M. A., A. W. Larkum, and L. J. Borowitzka. 1978. "A preliminary study of algal turf communities of a shallow coral reef lagoon using an artificial substratum." *Aquatic Botany* 5(2–3), 365–381.

Bowden-Kerby, A. 2001. "Low-tech coral reef restoration methods modelled after natural fragmentation processes." *Bulletin of Marine Science* 69:915–931.

Bruno, J. F. and E. R. Selig. 2007. "Regional decline of coral cover in the Indo-Pacific: Timing, extent, and subregional comparisons." *PLoS ONE* 2(8), e711.

Carne, L. and I. B. Baums. 2016. "Demonstrating effective Caribbean acroporid population enhancement: All three nursery-grown, outplanted taxa spawn August 2015 & 2016 in Belize." *Reef Encounter* 31(2), 42–43.

Chamberland, V. F., D. Petersen, J. R. Guest, U. Petersen, M. Brittsan, and M. J. Vermeij. 2017. "New seeding approach reduces costs and time to outplant sexually propagated corals for reef restoration." *Scientific Reports* 7(1), 1–12.

Chamberland, V. F., D. Petersen, K. R. W. Latijnhouwers, S. Snowden, B. Mueller, and M. J. A. Vermeij. 2016. "Four-year-old Caribbean Acropora colonies reared from field-collected gametes are sexually mature." *Bulletin of Marine Science* 92(2), 263–264.

Chamberland, V. F., S. Snowden, K. L. Marhaver, D. Petersen, and M. J. Vermeij. 2017. "The reproductive biology and early life ecology of a common Caribbean brain coral, Diploria labyrinthiformis (Scleractinia: Faviinae)." *Coral Reefs* 36(1), 83–94.

Chamberland, V. F., M. J. Vermeij, M. Brittsan, M. Carl, M. Schick, S. Snowden, and D. Petersen. 2015. "Restoration of critically endangered elkhorn coral (*Acropora palmata*) populations using larvae reared from wild-caught gametes." *Global Ecology and Conservation* 4, 526–537.

Chan, A. N., C. L. Lewis, K. L. Neely, and I. B. Baums. 2019. "Fallen pillars: The past, present, and future population dynamics of a rare, specialist coral-algal symbiosis." *Frontiers in Marine Science* 6, 218.

Craggs, J., J. R. Guest, M. Davis, J. Simmons, E. Dashti, and M. Sweet. 2017. "Inducing broadcast coral spawning ex situ: Closed system mesocosm design and husbandry protocol." *Ecology and evolution* 7(24), 11066–11078.

De'ath, G., K. E. Fabricius, H. Sweatman, and M. Puotinen. 2012. "The 27-year decline of coral cover on the Great Barrier Reef and its causes." *Proceedings of the National Academy of Sciences* 109(44), 17995–17999.

dela Cruz, D. W. and P. L. Harrison. 2017. "Enhanced larval supply and recruitment can replenish reef corals on degraded reefs." *Scientific Reports* 7(1), 1–13.

Dropoulus, C., S. Ward, A. Marshell, G. Diaz-Pulido, and P. J. Mumby. 2012. "Interactions among chronic and acute impacts on coral recruits: The importance of size-escape thresholds." *Ecology* 93:2131–2138.

Drury, C., D. Manzello, and D. Lirman. 2017. "Genotype and local environment dynamically influence growth, disturbance response and survivorship in the threatened coral, Acropora cervicornis." *PLoS ONE* 12(3).

Edwards, A. J., J. R. Guest, A. J. Heyward, R. D. Villanueva, M. V. Baria, I. S. Bollozos, and Y. Golbuu. 2015. "Direct seeding of mass-cultured coral larvae is not an effective option for reef rehabilitation." *Marine Ecology Progress Series* 525, 105–116.

Fadlallah, Y. H. 1983. "Sexual reproduction, development and larval biology in scleractinian corals." *Coral Reefs* 2(3), 129–150.

Fogarty, N. D. and K. L. Marhaven. 2019. "Coral spawning, unsynchronized." *Science* 365(6457), 987–988.

Gardner, T. A., I. M. Côté, J. A. Gill, A. Grant, and A. R. Watkinson. 2003. "Long-term region-wide declines in Caribbean corals." *Science* 301(5635), 958–960.

Graham, N. A., J. E. Cinner, A. V. Norström, and M. Nyström. 2014. "Coral reefs as novel ecosystems: Embracing new futures." *Current Opinion in Environmental Sustainability* 7, 9–14.

Gross, E. M. 2003. "Allelopathy of aquatic autotrophs." *Critical Reviews in Plant Sciences* 22(3–4), 313–339.

Guest, J. R., M. V. Baria, E. D. Gomez, A. J. Heyward, and A. J. Edwards. 2014. "Closing the circle: Is it feasible to rehabilitate reefs with sexually propagated corals?" *Coral Reefs* 33(1), 45–55.

Hagedorn, M., C. A. Page, K. ONeill, D. M. Flores, L. Tichy, V. F. Chamberland, and T. Vardi. 2018. "Successful demonstration of assisted gene flow in the threatened coral Acropora palmata across genetically-isolated Caribbean populations using cryopreserved sperm." *bioRxiv* 492447.

Iwao, K., M. Omori, H. Taniguchi, and M. Tamura. 2010. "Transplanted Acropora tenuis (Dana) spawned first in their life 4 years after culture from eggs." *Galaxea, Journal of Coral Reef Studies* 12(1), 47–47.

Jordan, A. C. 2018. "Patterns in caribbean coral spawning." https://nsuworks.nova.edu/occ_stuetd/468/.

Keith, S. A., J. A Maynard, A. J. Edwards, J. R. Guest, A. G. Bauman, R. Van Hooidonk, and C. Rahbek. 2016. "Coral mass spawning predicted by rapid seasonal rise in ocean temperature." *Proceedings of the Royal Society B: Biological Sciences* 283(1830), 20160011.

Kuffner, I. B. and V. J. Paul. 2004. "Effects of the benthic cyanobacterium Lyngbya majuscula on larval recruitment of the reef corals Acropora surculosa and Pocillopora damicornis." *Coral Reefs* 23(3), 455–458.

Kuffner, I. B., L. J. Walters, M. A. Becerro, V. J. Paul, R. Ritson-Williams, and K. S. Beach. 2006. "Inhibition of coral recruitment by macroalgae and cyanobacteria." *Marine Ecology Progress Series* 323, 107–117.

Kuntz, N. M., D. Kline, S. A. Sandin, and F. Rohwer. 2005. "Pathologies and mortality rates caused by organic carbon and nutrient stressors in three Caribbean coral species." *Marine Ecology Progress Series* 294, 173–180.

Levitan, D. R., N. D. Fogarty, J. Jara, K. E. Lotterhos, and N. Knowlton. 2011. "Genetic, spatial, and temporal components of precise spawning synchrony in reef building corals of the Montastraea annularis species complex." *Evolution: International Journal of Organic Evolution* 65(5), 1254–1270.

Levitan, D. R., H. Fukami, J. Jara, D. Kline, T. M. McGovern, K. E. McGhee, and N. Knowlton. 2004. "Mechanisms of reproductive isolation among sympatric broadcast-spawning corals of the Montastraea annularis species complex." *Evolution* 58(2), 308–323.

Lin, C. H. and Y. Nozawa. 2017. "Variability of spawning time (lunar day) in Acropora versus merulinid corals: A 7-yr record of in situ coral spawning in Taiwan." *Coral Reefs* 36(4), 1269–1278.

Lirman, D. and S. Schopmeyer. 2016. "Ecological solutions to reef degradation: Optimizing coral reef restoration in the Caribbean and Western Atlantic." *PeerJ*, 4, e2597.

Lirman, D., S. Schopmeyer, D. Manzello, L. J. Gramer, W. F. Precht, F. Muller-Karger, and J. Byrne. 2011. "Severe 2010 cold-water event caused unprecedented mortality to corals of the Florida reef tract and reversed previous survivorship patterns." *PLoS ONE* 6(8).

Lohr, K. E. and J. T. Patterson. 2017. "Intraspecific variation in phenotype among nursery-reared staghorn coral Acropora cervicornis (Lamarck 1816)." *Journal of Experimental Marine Biology and Ecology* 486, 87–92.

Marhaven, K., V. Chamberland, and N. Fogarty. 2017. "Coral spawning research and larval propagation webinar 2017." *Coral Restoration Consortium*.

Mendes, J. M. and J. D. Woodley. 2002. "Timing of reproduction in Montastraea annularis: Relationship to environmental variables." *Marine Ecology Progress Series* 227, 241–251.

Miller, M. W. 2014. "Post-settlement survivorship in two Caribbean broadcasting corals." *Coral Reefs* 33(4), 1041–1046.

Miller, M. W., A. Valdivia, K. L. Kramer, B. Mason, D. E. Williams, and L. Johnston. 2009. "Alternate benthic assemblages on reef restoration structures and cascading effects on coral settlement." *Marine Ecology Progress Series* 387, 147–156.

Muller, E. M., E. Bartels, and I. B. Baums. 2018. "Bleaching causes loss of disease resistance within the threatened coral species Acropora cervicornis." *Elife* 7, e35066.

Nakamura, R., W. Ando, H. Yamamoto, M. Kitano, A. Sato, M. Nakamura, and M. Omori. 2011. "Corals mass-cultured from eggs and transplanted as juveniles to their native, remote coral reef." *Marine Ecology Progress Series* 436, 161–168.

O'Donnell, K. E., K. E. Lohr, E. Bartels, and J. T. Patterson. 2017. "Evaluation of staghorn coral (Acropora cervicornis, Lamarck 1816) production techniques in an ocean-based nursery with consideration of coral genotype." *Journal of Experimental Marine Biology and Ecology* 487, 53–58.

Page, C. A., E. M. Muller, and D. E. Vaughan. 2018. "Microfragmenting for the successful restoration of slow growing massive corals." *Ecological Engineering* 123, 86–94.

Paul, V. J., I. B. Kuffner, L. J. Walters, R. Ritson-Williams, K. S. Beach, and M. A. Becerro. 2011. "Chemically mediated interactions between macroalgae Dictyota spp. and multiple life-history stages of the coral Porites astreoides." *Marine Ecology Progress Series* 426, 161–170.

Quinn, N. J. and B. L. Kojis. 2006. "Evaluating the potential of natural reproduction and artificial techniques to increase Acropora cervicornis populations at Discovery Bay, Jamaica." *Revista de Biología Tropical* 54, 105–116.

Randall, C. J., A. P. Negri, K. M. Quigley, T. Foster, G. F. Ricardo, N. S. Webster, and A. J. Heyward. 2020. "Sexual production of corals for reef restoration in the Anthropocene." *Marine Ecology Progress Series* 635, 203–232.

Richmond, R. H. and C. L. Hunter. 1990. "Reproduction and recruitment of corals: Comparisons among the Caribbean, the Tropical Pacific, and the Red Sea." Marine ecology progress series. *Oldendorf* 60(1), 185–203.

Rinkevich, B. 2015. "Climate change and active reef restoration—ways of constructing the 'Reefs of Tomorrow.'" *Journal of Marine Science and Engineering* 3(1), 111–127.

Ritson-Williams, R., S. N. Arnold, N. D. Fogarty, R. S. Steneck, M. Vermeij, and V. J. Paul. 2009. "New perspectives on ecological mechanisms affecting coral recruitment on reefs." *Smithsonian Institution publication.*

Shaish, L., G. Levy, G. Katzir, and B. Rinkevich. 2010. "Employing a highly fragmented, weedy coral species in reef restoration." *Ecological Engineering* 36(10), 1424–1432.

Sweeney, A. M., C. A. Boch, S. Johnsen, and D. E. Morse. 2011. "Twilight spectral dynamics and the coral reef invertebrate spawning response." *Journal of Experimental Biology* 214(5), 770–777.

Szmant, A. M. 1986. "Reproductive ecology of Caribbean reef corals." *Coral Reefs* 43:54.

Van Woesik, R. 2010. "Calm before the spawn: Global coral spawning patterns are explained by regional wind fields." Proceedings of the Royal Society B: *Biological Sciences* 277(1682), 715–722.

Van Woesik, R., F. Lacharmoise, and S. Köksal. 2006. "Annual cycles of solar insolation predict spawning times of Caribbean corals." *Ecology Letters* 9(4), 390–398.

Vermeij, M. J. A. and S. A. Sandin. 2008. "Density-dependent settlement and mortality structure the earliest life phases of a coral population." *Ecology* 89(7), 1994–2004.

Vermeij, M. J. A., J. E. Smith, C. M. Smith, R. V. Thurber, and S. A. Sandin. 2009. "Survival and settlement success of coral planulae: Independent and synergistic effects of macroalgae and microbes." *Oecologia*, 159(2), 325–336.

Villanueva, R. D., M. V. B. Baria, and D. W. dela Cruz. 2012. "Growth and survivorship of juvenile corals outplanted to degraded reef areas in Bolinao-Anda Reef Complex, Philippines." *Marine Biology Research* 8(9), 877–884.

Wanders, J. B. W. 1977. "The role of benthic algae in the shallow reef of Curacao (Netherlands Antilles) III: The significance of grazing." *Aquatic Botany* 3, 357–390.

Williams, D. E., K. Nedimyer, and M. Miller. 2020. Genotypic inventory of *Acropora palmata* (elkhorn coral) populations in south Florida. NOAA Southeast Fisheries Science Center, Protected Resources and Biodiversity Division Center Report, NOAA/SEFSC/PRBD-2020-01.

Williams, D. E., M. W. Miller, and I. B. Baums. 2014. "Cryptic changes in the genetic structure of a highly clonal coral population and the relationship with ecological performance." *Coral Reefs* 33(3), 595–606.

Williams, D. E., M. W. Miller, and K. L. Kramer. 2008. "Recruitment failure in Florida Keys Acropora palmata, a threatened Caribbean coral." *Coral Reefs* 27(3), 697–705.

Wolstenholme, J., Y. Nozawa, M. Byrne, and W. Burke. 2018. "Timing of mass spawning in corals: Potential influence of the coincidence of lunar factors and associated changes in atmospheric pressure from northern and southern hemisphere case studies." *Invertebrate Reproduction & Development* 62(2), 98–108.

Young, C. N., S. A. Schopmeyer, and D. Lirman. 2012. "A review of reef restoration and coral propagation using the threatened genus Acropora in the Caribbean and Western Atlantic." *Bulletin of Marine Science* 88(4), 1075–1098.

9

ASSISTED EVOLUTION AND CORAL REEF RESILIENCE

Hanna R. Koch

ABSTRACT

The marine environment is an essential component of the global life-support system. Oceans regulate the Earth's climate and harbor some of the largest reservoirs of biodiversity. From an ecological and evolutionary perspective, biodiversity is crucial to the maintenance of healthy ecosystems since it boosts ecosystem productivity and plays a pivotal role in ecosystem recovery after natural or anthropogenic disturbances. Coral reef ecosystems constitute a mere fraction of the marine environment (<1%) yet have profound importance and value on a global scale. They provide a wide range of economic, environmental, and ecosystem services including jobs, tourism, coastline protection, carbon and nitrogen fixation, oxygen production, and the delivery of essential nutrients to food chains. Coral reefs are biodiversity hubs themselves, supporting an estimated 25% of all marine life, and serve as valuable sources of raw resources like food, novel building materials, and medicines. Coral reefs are, however, facing a number of severe local and global threats, including rapid climate change. Crucial to the persistence of coral reefs in the face of climate change is the capacity of reef-building corals to acclimatize and adapt to environmental stressors. It is feared, however, that increased rates and complexity of environmental change are overwhelming the intrinsic ability of these foundation species to adapt and survive over the long term. In response to this dilemma, scientists are developing novel interventions and strategies for building more resilient coral reefs through human-assisted evolution. This new line of research harnesses and accelerates naturally occurring evolutionary processes to enhance the stress tolerance of corals and adaptive potential of coral populations to be used for ecological restoration. The five main approaches, which are based on physiological, genetic, and reproductive interventions, are acclimatization, experimental evolution of algal endosymbionts, manipulation of the host microbiome, interspecific hybridization, and intraspecific managed breeding. Coupled with advancements in sequencing technology, -*omic* analytical tools, and coral propagation techniques, these approaches serve as a powerful biological toolbox for enhancing resilience and mitigating the impacts of disturbance. Given the immediate need to stabilize, restore, and prepare coral reef ecosystems for future change, it is important that assisted evolution becomes embedded, thoughtfully and responsibly, within coral reef restoration initiatives.

INTRODUCTION

Why Corals Need Our Assistance

The extensive degradation and loss of coral reefs on a global scale have led to the realization that without human intervention, coral populations will not recover on their own (Pandolfi et al. 2011). Significant declines in coral abundance have been recorded for all major tropical basins since the 1980s, with an estimated 80% loss in the Caribbean, a 50% loss on the Great Barrier Reef, and a 50% loss worldwide (Gardner et al. 2003; Pandolfi et al. 2003; Burke et al. 2011; Hughes et al. 2017; Hughes et al. 2018). Given that coral reefs are some of the longest-living ecosystems, existing for hundreds of millions of years and changing and adapting as the Earth's climate has changed (Veron 2008), this relatively recent, rapid, and widespread loss is extremely alarming. Over time, the magnitude of human activities and their impacts on the environment have grown, resulting in an increasing number of local and global threats to coral reefs. Most notably, anthropogenic-induced climate change has led to serious consequences for the global marine environment, including rapid increases in sea-surface temperatures (SSTs), ocean acidification (OA), and disease prevalence (Kleypas et al. 1999; Barnett et al. 2001; Hughes et al. 2003; Pandolfi et al. 2003; Bellwood et al. 2004; Hoegh-Guldberg 2004; Graham et al. 2006; Hoegh-Guldberg et al. 2007; Pandolfi et al. 2011; Hoegh-Guldberg 2014). On a local scale, anthropogenic disturbances include destructive fishing, overharvesting, terrestrial run-off, ship groundings, pollution, anchor damage, and coastal development (SER 2004). As such, the number and severity of local and global stressors that coral reefs currently face, along with the continued decline in coral cover worldwide (Gardner et al. 2003; Bruno and Selig 2007), suggest that natural rates of evolution of stress tolerance are too slow to maintain functional coral reef ecosystems into a future characterized by rapid climate change (Csaszar et al. 2010; Hoegh-Guldberg and Bruno 2010; Pereira et al. 2010; Dawson et al. 2011; Hoegh-Guldberg 2012; Honisch et al. 2012; Logan et al. 2014; Pacifici et al. 2015; Urban 2015; van Oppen et al. 2017). Corals can tolerate a range of values for factors like temperature, salinity, sedimentation, light, and toxicant exposure, which demonstrates the ability of populations and species to adapt via natural selection (Carpenter et al. 2008; Palumbi et al. 2014; Rose et al. 2018). However, as the disparity between rates of environmental change and adaptation increases, the more difficult it becomes for organisms to effectively respond to such changes and for populations to recover naturally (Osborne et al. 2017).

Therefore, one of the major concerns regarding coral reefs is that natural populations cannot keep pace with unprecedented rates of environmental change (Donner et al. 2005; Donner et al. 2007; Hoegh-Guldberg et al. 2007; Veron et al. 2009; Bell 2013; IPCC 2014). As a consequence of increased greenhouse gas emissions (e.g., carbon dioxide, CO_2), the average global temperature of our planet has increased by approximately 0.8°C (1.4°F) since 1880, with two-thirds of the warming occurring since 1975, at a rate of approximately 0.15–0.20° per decade. Global warming has led to an increase in the number and severity of acute high-temperature events that coral reefs are exposed to each year (Figure 9.1). Exacerbated by increasing temperatures, emerging diseases over the last thirty years are attributed with causing approximately 30% of the worldwide coral mortality (Reshef et al. 2006). In the Caribbean especially, the rapid loss of corals from disease outbreaks is unprecedented in the geological records (Aronson and Precht 2001a; Gardner et al. 2003). Furthermore, ocean acidification has increased by 30% since preindustrial times, due to increases in CO_2 levels in the surface ocean as atmospheric CO_2 rises—and it is projected to rise by another 120% by 2100 if CO_2 emissions continue at

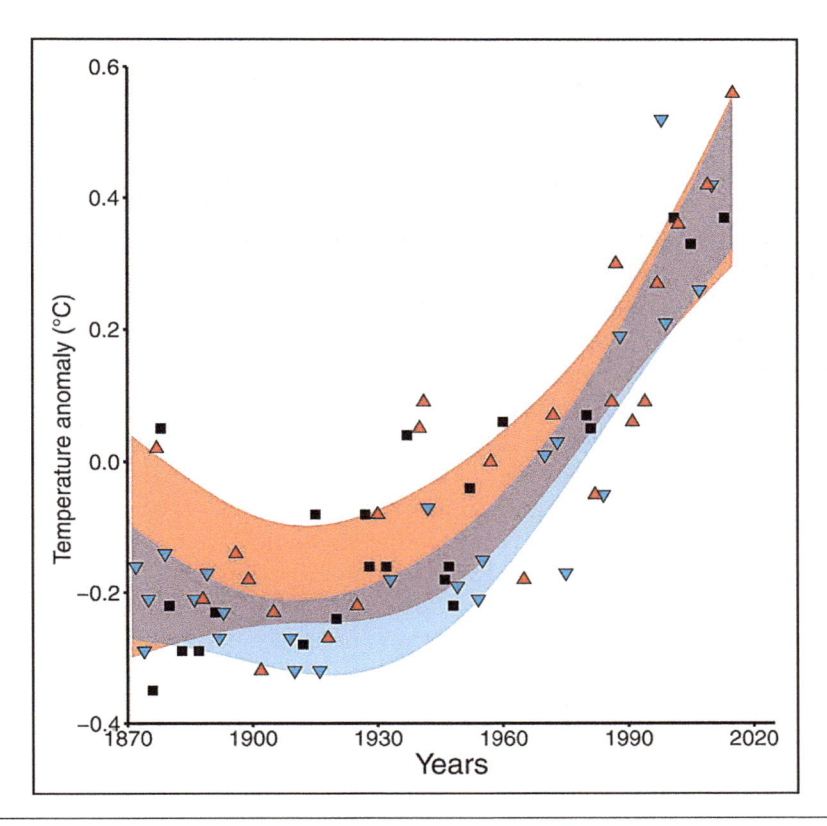

Figure 9.1 Dramatic increase in ocean temperatures since 1930. SST anomalies within 100 coral habitats compared to the 1961–1990 average. Data points differentiate El Niño (red triangles), La Niña (blue triangles), and ENSO (El Niño-Southern Oscillation) neutral periods (black squares). Ninety-five percent confidence intervals are shown for nonlinear regression fits for years with El Niño and La Niña conditions (orange and blue shading, respectively; overlap is shown in purple). (Source: Hughes et al. 2018.)

current rates (Hoegh-Guldberg et al. 2007; Doney et al. 2009; Pandolfi et al. 2011; Schnoor 2014; Clarkson et al. 2015; Jokiel et al. 2016; Kawahata et al. 2019). A 6% drop in reef calcification, owing to OA, was recently reported for southern sites along the Great Barrier Reef (Albright et al. 2016). Globally, coral reef calcification is predicted to decrease 20–60% by 2100, relative to pre-industrial times (Kleypas et al. 1999). Looking to the next 50 years, projected increases in CO_2 and temperature exceed the conditions under which coral reefs have flourished over the past half-million years (Hughes et al. 2003). If rates of environmental change outpace adaptation, populations become maladapted and are unable to restore positive growth rates (Bay et al. 2017). Ultimately, this leaves populations vulnerable to extinction.

While population responses and evolutionary trajectories are likely to be system-specific, the tipping point from adaptation to extinction will generally be shaped by a multitude of factors, including initial population size, population growth rates, genetic architecture, the strength of selection, gene flow, and rates of sexual/asexual reproduction (Bay et al. 2017). The appearance and fixation of new adaptive genetic mutations (via *de novo* mutation and positive selection) usually requires several generations, suggesting that only organisms with short generation times will be able to adapt at rates matching the pace of current environmental change

(Rice and Emery 2003; Torda et al. 2017). There is, however, a growing body of evidence that rapid genetic adaptation can occur over ecological timescales (i.e., within a few generations, *contemporary evolution*) in response to strong selection pressure(s) (Fussmann et al. 2007; Pelletier et al. 2009; Schoener 2011; Koch et al. 2014), though the best cases of contemporary evolution are for populations with high standing genetic variation and recombination rates (Turcotte et al. 2011; Barrick and Lenski 2013; Cameron et al. 2013; Messer and Petrov 2013), or for systems with strong eco-evolutionary feedback dynamics (Koch et al. 2014). Even though genetic diversity estimates are lacking for most coral species, coral populations are generally considered genetically diverse (Shearer et al. 2009). Reef-building (*hermatypic*) corals do not, however, possess some of the other traits that are typically found for species undergoing contemporary evolution (e.g., fast growth rates and short generations).

While the time frame over which corals are capable of adapting to environmental conditions associated with climate change is currently under debate (Lasker and Coffroth 1999; Baker 2001; Hoegh-Guldberg et al. 2002; Reshef et al. 2006), there are multiple life-history traits characteristic of reef-building corals that contribute to slower rates of adaptation in general. Reef-building corals, also referred to as stony or hard corals (order Scleractinia), create the framework of reefs by depositing hard calcareous material (calcium carbonate, $CaCO_3$) as their skeletons. This process is quite slow, however; massive or mounding coral species (e.g., the brain and boulder corals) only grow about 1.5–25 mm per year, whereas branching corals may grow up to 10–30 cm per year (Lough 2008; Lirman et al. 2014; Lough and Cantin 2014; Anderson et al. 2017; Neal et al. 2017; Weil et al. 2020). Because sexual maturity is a condition of size, not age, this results in long generation times (2–25 years depending on species) and strongly overlapping generations (Babcock 1991; Schopmeyer et al. 2017) (Figure 9.2). Also potentially exacerbating slow rates of adaptation are high levels of spawning asynchronicity and/or low recruitment rates for some populations/species (Wilson and Harrison 2003; Mangubhai and Harrison 2008; Williams et al. 2008; Albright et al. 2010; Miller et al. 2018; Hughes et al. 2019; Shlesinger and Loya 2019), in addition to reduced population sizes and connectivity stemming from chronic stress exposure and repeated acute disturbances. Persistent reproductive failure can lead to aging populations that are more vulnerable to local extinction (Schlesinger and Loya 2019). Small populations, for example, suffer a loss of allelic diversity at functional genes, which can compromise their ability to adapt to new or changing environments (Soule 1985; Blomqvist et al. 2010; Lundgren 2011) (Figure 9.3). As populations dwindle, so may connectivity between and among them. This can cause processes like gene flow and sexual reproduction to become less efficient in introducing novel adaptive alleles (Slatkin 1987). Collectively, these attributes may constrain the adaptive potential of declining coral populations, especially if they are subjected to concurrent extrinsic pressures (e.g., increasing SSTs, OA, and disease), and/or if traits under selection are negatively genetically correlated (e.g., trade-offs exist) (Antonovics 1976; Sgro and Hoffmann 2004). Adaptive potential is the ability of populations/species to respond to selection via phenotypic or molecular changes. Importantly, the effectiveness of conservation practices can be improved by considering the adaptive potential of species (Hoffmann and Sgro 2011; Becker et al. 2013; Munday et al. 2013; Eizaguirre and Baltazar-Soares 2014; Harrisson et al. 2014).

Acclimatization via phenotypic plasticity may buffer populations against rapid environmental change, allowing genetic adaptation to catch up over the longer term (Munday et al. 2013; Torda et al. 2017) (Figure 9.4). Acclimatization is phenotypic adaptation in response to variation in the natural environment. Phenotypic plasticity is the ability of one genotype to produce more than one phenotype when exposed to different environments, thereby allowing an individual organism to change its phenotypic state in response to variation in environmental

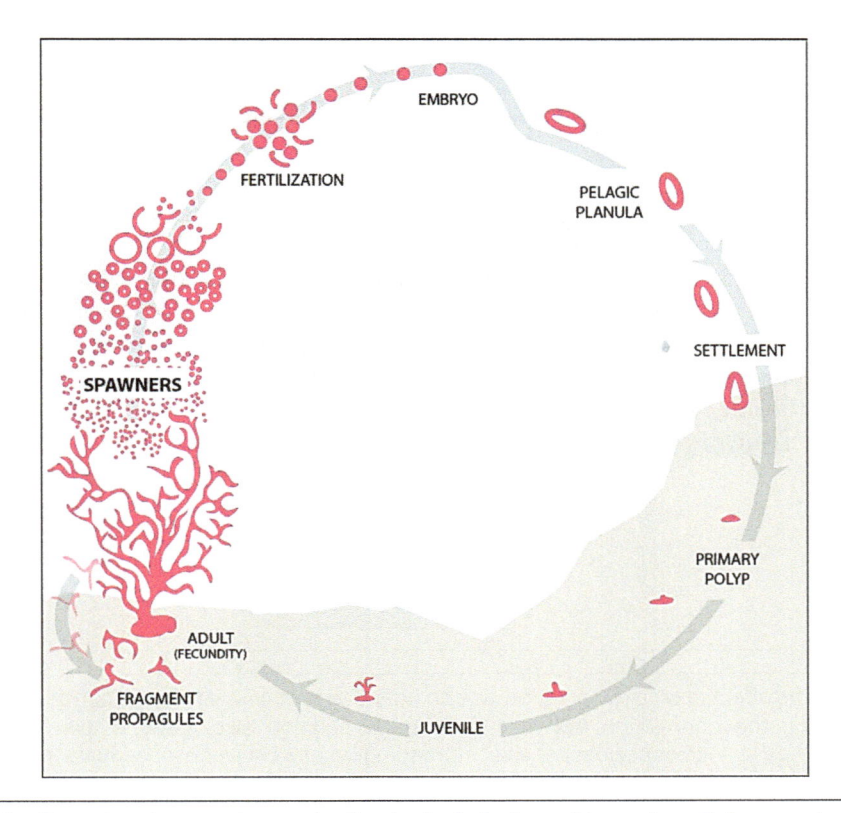

Figure 9.2 Sexual and asexual reproduction typical of a branching scleractinian species. Diagram of *Acropora* spp. life cycle showing the different stages, and relative time difference, of one sexual generation of a broadcast spawning coral (full loop) versus faster asexual propagation via fragmentation (fragment propagules). Stony corals possess multiple reproductive strategies, but most species are hermaphroditic broadcast spawners, releasing their eggs and sperm into the water column for external fertilization during annual synchronized mass spawning events. Rapid population growth can occur via repeated fragmentation. (Source: NOAA Fisheries.)

conditions. Alternatively, with genetic adaptation, the genetic information of an individual organism contains a blueprint for its response to a particular stimulus. Through natural selection, responses to the surrounding environment can cause the genetic composition of a population/species to change and shift over time. It has been suggested that the generation of a temporal buffer through phenotypic plasticity may be particularly important for organisms already persisting at the edge of their performance thresholds, like scleractinian corals (Reusch 2014).

Genomic analyses and ecological modeling used to predict evolutionary trajectories under different climate scenarios have found that rapid adaptation in coral populations may occur, but only under mild climate-change scenarios (i.e., representative concentration pathways, RCP2.6 and RCP4.5) (IPCC 2014; Bay et al. 2017). Furthermore, the high number of mortality events that have occurred across coral metapopulations in recent decades (e.g., from bleaching and disease) indicates that these populations have already undergone several strong selective events (Eakin et al. 2010; Smith et al. 2013; Precht et al. 2016; Walton et al. 2018). Therefore, ensuing adaptation may be considered rapid where survivors of high mortality events are particularly robust and may be expected to spawn a new generation of more stress-tolerant corals (Libro and Vollmer 2016; Muller et al. 2018; Baums et al. 2019). Nonetheless, if certain measures are

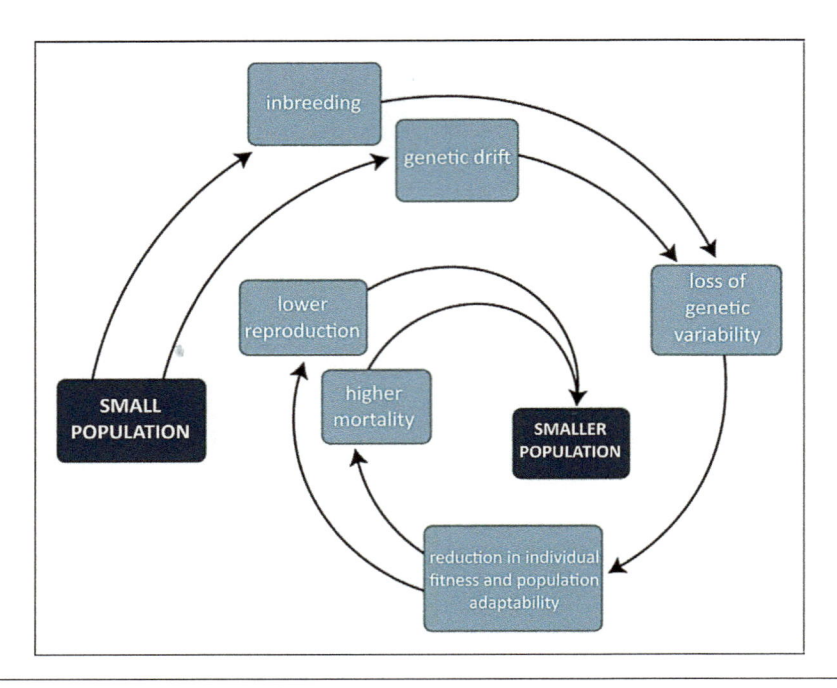

Figure 9.3 The effect of small population size on adaptive potential. An illustration of the extinction vortex showing the connection between reduced population size, genetic diversity, adaptive capacity, and further loss of population size. Inbreeding occurs between individuals that are closely related, and can lead to increased homozygosity, which can decrease offspring fitness through the unmasking of deleterious or recessive alleles. Genetic drift describes random fluctuations in allele frequencies in a population, and typically occurs in small populations where infrequently occurring alleles face a greater chance of being lost. (Sources: Lundgren 2011 and Blomqvist et al. 2010, © Commonwealth of Australia (GBRMPA).)

not taken immediately to reduce climate change and its impacts, and we therefore do not proceed under a *mild* scenario, a catastrophic collapse of coral reef ecosystems may be expected in the near future (Hoegh-Guldberg and Bruno 2010; Pereira et al. 2010; Dawson et al. 2011; IPCC 2014; Pacifici et al. 2015; Urban 2015). It is predicted that up to 90% of coral reefs will be gone by the year 2050, and perhaps all, if human intervention does not take place immediately (Burke et al. 2011b). To prevent this complete collapse, coral reef scientists, practitioners, and managers are actively seeking novel solutions and strategies for preserving what remains, as well as preparing corals for what is to come.

The overarching goal of most coral reef restoration initiatives has traditionally been to restore reefs to their historical, pre-disturbance state (Ruiz-Jaen and Aide 2005; Perring et al. 2015). This *pristine* condition is typically characterized by high levels of coral cover, fish biomass, recruitment, algal grazing, biodiversity, and three-dimensionality (Graham et al. 2013). However, reductions in these important factors have occurred repeatedly for contemporary reef systems worldwide (Pandolfi et al. 2003) from global climate change and local anthropogenic disturbances (SER 2004). As a result, pristine coral reefs no longer exist (Pandolfi et al. 2003). If coral reef ecosystems have changed so dramatically, and beyond levels of long-term natural variability, then it may not be practical or possible to restore them to their pre-disturbance state anymore (Hobbs et al. 2009; Graham et al. 2013; van Oppen et al. 2017).

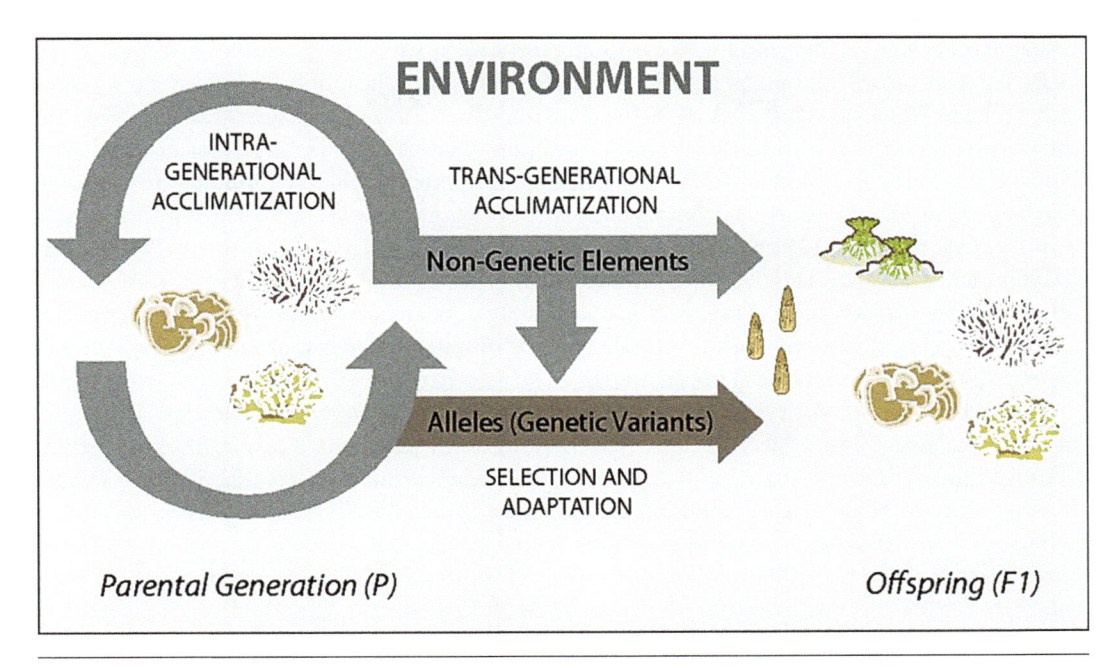

Figure 9.4 Acclimatization and adaptation. Diagram showing the response of corals to environmental change through genetic (i.e., adaptation) and nongenetic (i.e., acclimatization) processes. Acclimatization, through phenotypic plasticity, can occur over the course of an individual's lifespan (intragenerational) or across generations via transgenerational inheritance and may buffer populations against rapid environmental change, allowing genetic adaptation to catch up over the longer term. Genetic adaptation is defined as a change in the phenotype from one generation to the next through natural selection and involves a genetic change in the form of allele frequency changes between generations. (Source: van Oppen et al. 2015.)

Borne out of the need to address a similar issue for terrestrial ecosystems, the field of intervention ecology combines multiple subfields (e.g., restoration ecology and conservation biology) for considering a broader approach to managing ecosystems for future change (Hobbs et al. 2011). This advent has contributed to a paradigm shift in coral reef restoration science, where innovative management methods and intervention strategies are currently being developed and tested for enhancing the resilience of remaining natural coral populations (Mascarelli 2014; van Oppen et al. 2015; van Oppen et al. 2017) and for engineering novel ecosystems (Graham et al. 2014), as well as for restoring degraded reefs (Villanueva et al. 2012; Guest et al. 2014; dela Cruz and Harrison 2017). Of these innovative approaches, human-assisted evolution (hereafter referred to as assisted evolution) has emerged as one potential solution.

What Is Assisted Evolution?

Assisted evolution is a range of approaches involving active intervention to accelerate the rate of naturally occurring evolutionary processes to enhance certain traits of interest (Jones and Monaco 2009; van Oppen et al. 2015). Such processes include genetic adaptation, acclimatization, and shifts in the composition of associated microbial communities. The genetic enhancement of plants and animals for the benefit of human populations, for example, is a practice that has been around for centuries and has led to significant improvements in commercially valuable species (e.g., crop and livestock domestication). However, considering such manipulations for noncommercial purposes like restoration and conservation is relatively new (Jones and Monaco 2009; van Oppen et al. 2015). The first discussion of using assisted evolution for the purpose of ecological restoration was for designing native plant materials for domesticated landscapes (Jones and Monaco 2009). For such altered terrestrial ecosystems, it was proposed that evolution should be assisted by the inclusion of plants that (1) reflect general historical evolutionary patterns, (2) are particularly suited to the modified environment, (3) are able to adapt to contemporary selection pressures, and (4) contribute to the restoration of ecosystem structure and function (Jones and Monaco 2009). As any ecological restoration initiative should strive for, this framework is intended to maximize the representation and perpetuity of genetic diversity within natural populations.

Evolutionary response requires genetically based variation among individuals. Therefore, maintaining genetic diversity is crucial for the long-term persistence of natural populations because it promotes resilience by providing a buffer against novel environmental change and the flexibility to adapt (Reusch et al. 2005; Barrick and Lenski 2013). Conversely, the loss of genetic diversity translates into loss of adaptive capacity, population viability, and fitness (Reed and Frankham 2003). Resilience refers to the overall ability of individuals, populations, or communities to respond positively after a disturbance. In this context, genetic diversity is used to refer to population-level resilience, but mechanisms of resilience differ across organizational levels. For example, individuals may exhibit varying levels of physiological resilience based on intrinsic differences in growth, survival, and reproduction. Where communities can show resilience in ecosystem traits such as diversity, productivity, trophic linkages, or sustained biomass through shifts in species composition, the diversity within communities is important for functional redundancy, modularity, and strong feedback loops (Levin and Lubchenco 2008; NASEM 2018). Importantly though, assisted evolution can be used directly or indirectly to promote resilience at any organizational level.

Coral reef scientists have since adapted the concept of assisted evolution for building coral reef resilience within marine ecosystems that have been altered by climate change (van Oppen et al. 2015; van Oppen et al. 2017). It is widely acknowledged that the best approach to coral reef restoration will be one that incorporates both evolutionary and ecologically sound practices by linking basic research—for example, theory of adaptation (Eizaguirre and Baltazar-Soares 2014), microevolution (Stockwell et al. 2003; Harrisson et al. 2014), and restoration genetics (Baums 2008)—with applied practices in ecological restoration (McKay et al. 2005; Rogers et al. 2009; Munday et al. 2013; Rinkevich 2014; van Oppen et al. 2015). Therefore, an underlying premise of assisted evolution of corals is that with rigorous, well-designed experimentation and advanced tools, we may be able to enhance the environmental stress tolerance (and therefore adaptive potential) of coral populations/species to be used for outplanting onto degraded reefs—both now and in the future when environmental conditions are likely to be different. We may then be able to maintain or restore key ecosystem functions and attributes by utilizing these resilient stocks (van Oppen et al. 2015). The resilient traits identified as most relevant for adaptation to climate-change conditions—and which should serve as targets of assisted evolution—are increased tolerance to warmer, acidified waters with fluctuating salinity, as well as disease resistance, resilience to nutrient exposure/herbicides/other pollutants, and increased skeletal density to withstand intensifying natural disasters (van Oppen et al. 2017; Rippe et al. 2018).

Although scleractinian corals possess life-history traits that create challenges for evolution-based experimentation (e.g., slow growth rates and long generation times), they also exhibit a range of attributes which, conversely, promote evolvability and make them amenable to such experimental testing. These characteristics include: (1) the common occurrence of sexual and asexual reproduction within most species (Harrison and Wallace 1990; Harrison 2011) (Figure 9.5); (2) high fecundity in some species, especially broadcast spawners; (3) a lack of distinction between germ and somatic cell lines (meaning, any somatic point mutation that occurs over the life of an adult coral may be inherited by offspring) (van Oppen et al. 2011); (4) the occurrence of interspecific hybridization in some taxa (Wallace 1999; Chan et al. 2018; van Oppen et al. 2000); (5) naturally occurring high levels of genetic variation in some species (Hemond and Vollmer 2010); and (6) the existence of symbiosis with a range of potentially fast-evolving microbes (Chakravarti et al. 2017; Chakravarti and van Oppen 2018). These attributes, coupled with recent advancements in technology (e.g., next-generation sequencing and -*omics*) and methodology (e.g., ex situ coral propagation), open the doors for novel experimental investigation into building environmental stress tolerance of corals. These new lines of assisted evolution research are acclimatization, experimental evolution of algal endosymbionts, manipulation of the coral microbiome, interspecific (between species) hybridization, and intraspecific (within species) managed breeding (Figure 9.6). The methodology behind each approach varies, but the desired outcome is the same—to promote resilience on some level. Acclimatization and the manipulation of coral-associated microorganisms are physiological interventions that can influence the physiological responses of corals without changing their individual genomes and can compensate for the impacts of environmental stress in different ways and at different points

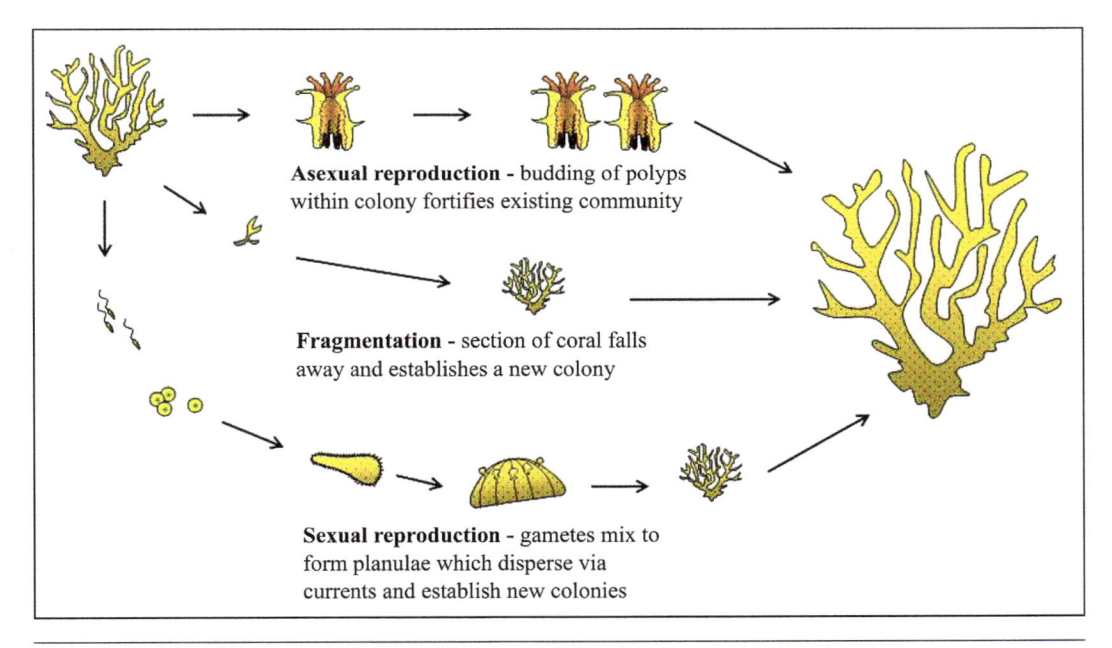

Figure 9.5 Common reproductive strategies of scleractinian species. Reef-building corals can reproduce both sexually and asexually. Asexual reproduction promotes rapid colonial growth (via budding) and population growth (via fragmentation). Asexually produced individuals (*fragments* or *clones*) are genetically identical to their donor colonies. Most species are simultaneous hermaphrodites (contain both sexes) and sexually reproduce via broadcast spawning which involves external fertilization and larval development. Sexually produced offspring are genetically distinct. Less common strategies include gonochorism, where colonies are either male or female (separate sexes), and brooding, where corals have internal fertilization and release larvae competent for settlement. (Source: NOAA's National Ocean Service.)

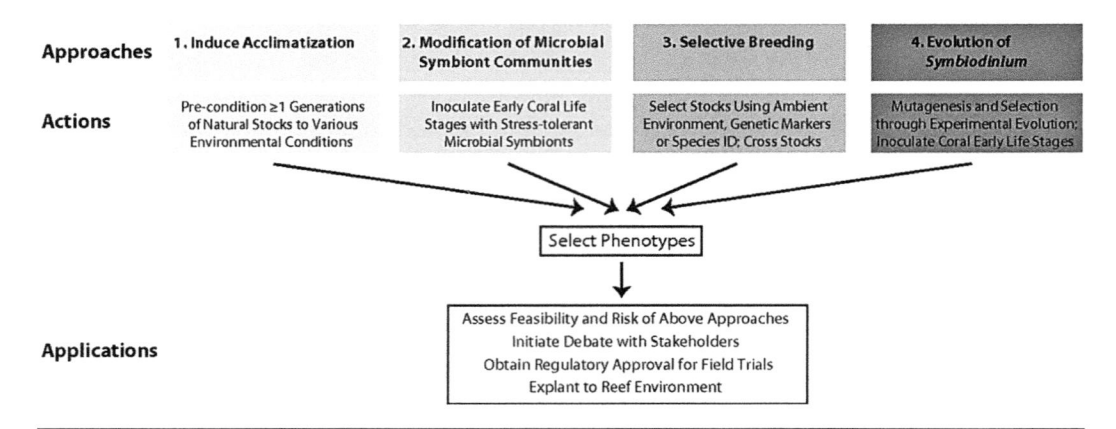

Figure 9.6 Diagram summarizing the various assisted evolution approaches proposed for enhancing coral reef resilience, excluding interspecific hybridization, which can be combined conceptually with managed breeding. Hybridization and managed breeding represent genetic and reproductive interventions, while acclimatization and manipulation of coral-associated microorganisms (e.g., Symbiodiniaceae) represent nongenetic, physiological interventions. (Source: modified from van Oppen et al. 2015.)

in the stress response. Alternatively, hybridization and managed breeding represent genetic and reproductive interventions for increasing genetic diversity within populations to allow them to adapt to a changing environment; or they permit selection of traits that may improve the resilience of coral populations and species (NASEM 2018).

ASSISTED EVOLUTION APPROACHES: ACCLIMATIZATION (NONGENETIC) PROCESSES

Generally, acclimatization refers to phenotypic adaptation in response to variation in the natural environment. It can alter performance and possibly enhance fitness, but it does not involve genetic change. This is contrary to genetic adaptation, which proceeds through adjustments in the frequency of genes over several generations that code for traits affecting fitness, and results in shifts in mean trait values (Figure 9.7). Acclimatization can occur within generations, across generations, and through a variety of mechanisms—for example, physiological/metabolic, epigenetic or gene expression changes, and parental effects. Previously, it was thought that acclimatization could only occur over an organism's lifespan, and without trait evolution from one generation to the next—for example, physiological responses via metabolic changes (Gates and Edmunds 1999). Now, it is well recognized that some environmentally induced nongenetic changes are heritable (*transgenerational inheritance*) (Daxinger and Whitelaw 2010; Donelson et al. 2012; Torda et al. 2017). This is attributable to the burgeoning field of epigenetics, which studies how heritable post-synthesis modification of DNA or DNA-associated proteins may serve as one such mechanism of phenotypic plasticity with the potential for facilitating rapid beneficial acclimatization (Huey et al. 1999; Wilson and Franklin 2002; Putnam et al. 2016).

Epigenetic mechanisms such as DNA methylation, histone modification, and chromatin remodeling do not involve a change in the DNA sequence itself (Feil and Fraga 2012), rather they

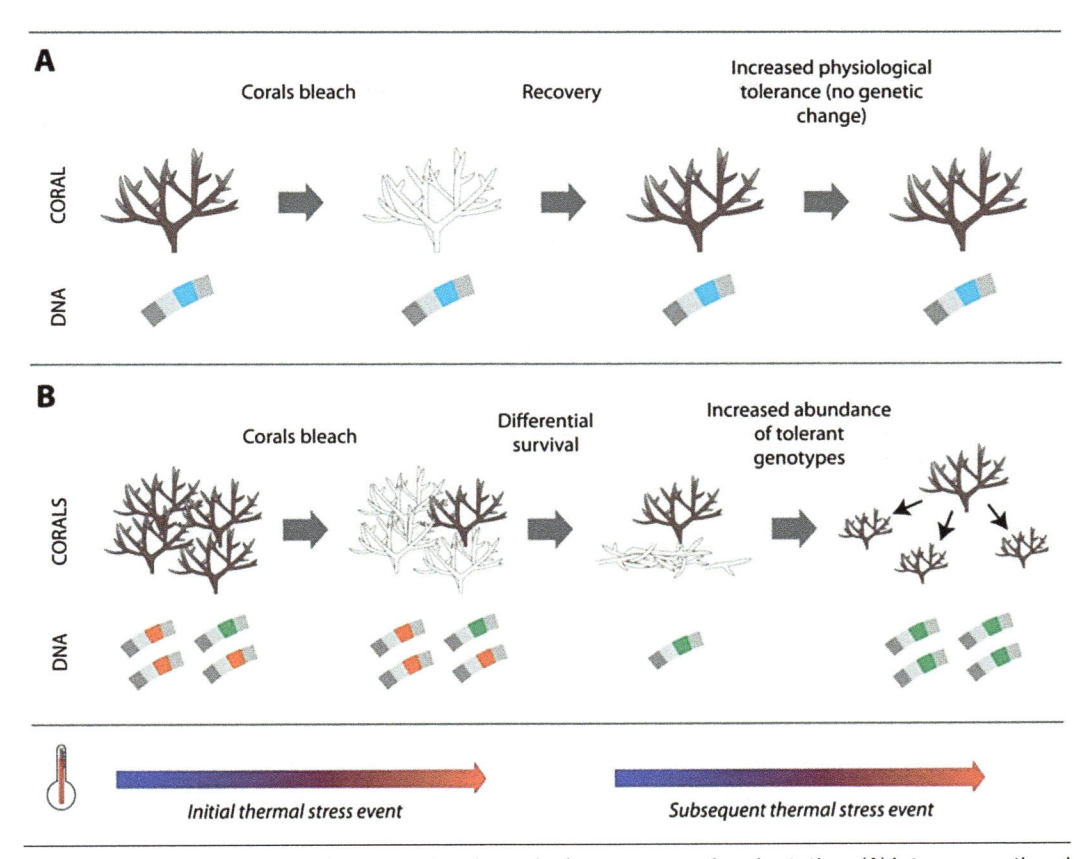

Figure 9.7 Acclimatization (nongenetic adaptation) versus genetic adaptation. (A) Intragenerational acclimatization occurs at the individual level where exposure to sublethal stress may result in physiological changes that increase tolerance to future stress events. It can alter performance and possibly enhance fitness, but it does not involve genetic change. (B) Genetic adaptation proceeds through DNA sequence changes that cause phenotypic changes, which allow the organism to be better suited to its environment; through differential fitness and survival, these changes are inherited by subsequent generations. (Source: Lundgren 2011, © Commonwealth of Australia GBRMPA).

provide the ability for the genome to produce different outcomes from the same genetic material via changes in gene expression (Bossdorf et al. 2008; Bondurianksy and Day 2009; Schlichting and Wund 2014). Cells can respond to environmental perturbations through changes in gene expression that are coordinated in magnitude and time. Stress-related gene expression programs can be hard-wired where the modulation of gene expression plays a central role in cellular adaptation to short- or long-term environmental changes, or they can be transient and include a wide range of plastic responses for coping with environmental change (Lopez-Maury et al. 2008). Hence, stress-related gene expression programs may offer a faster means of dealing with acute stress and contribute to acclimatization.

For the purpose of assisted evolution in corals, researchers are currently investigating the role of preconditioning acclimatization (*conditioning, stress-hardening, pre-exposure, intragenerational acclimatization, acclimation*, or *priming*) and transgenerational acclimatization (*transgenerational plasticity, transgenerational epigenetic inheritance*, or *epigenetic programming*) for promoting environmental stress tolerance (Putnam 2012; Palumbi et al. 2014; Putnam and Gates 2015). Generally, this involves exposing corals to sublethal levels of abiotic stress to induce physiological changes that increase individual tolerance to future stress events (i.e., intragenerational acclimatization) and/or to induce heritable increased stress tolerance and fitness in offspring (i.e., transgenerational acclimatization). The initial exposure can be either acute or chronic, include single or multiple stressors, and involve a single shock exposure or incremental increases over time (NASEM 2018).

Of these possibilities, there are three main approaches for inducing acclimatization (NASEM 2018). The first approach, *acute preconditioning*, involves short-term exposure (i.e., days to weeks) of corals (at the larval, recruit, or adult colony stage) to certain conditions at a specific time in order to trigger a response with long-lasting effects. The timing of exposure can be manipulated to achieve various outcomes: (1) adult colonies can be exposed during gametogenesis or larval development in an attempt to directly affect the next generation; (2) sexual recruits can be reared under stressful conditions within a land nursery system prior to outplanting in order to promote individual tolerance from an early age; or (3) in situ nursery corals can be bleached during early spring to allow them to recover during the warming summer months. The second approach, *chronic preconditioning*, involves long-term exposure (i.e., months to years) of adult colonies to a particular set of conditions with the expectation that a variety of mechanisms may be triggered leading to more robust corals. This could be achieved realistically—through the use of inshore coral nurseries or other similarly stressful environments—as a staging phase before outplanting onto reefs. With the third approach, *corals of opportunity* can be sourced from locations assumed to have already undergone an acute exposure event or chronic stressful conditions to be used for coral reef restoration programs. Ultimately, the value of acclimatization as an intervention strategy to increase the resilience of corals depends on how long the compensatory response lasts once the initial exposure has ended. It also depends on the mechanism(s) involved, e.g., epigenetic modification or changes in gene expression or symbiont composition (discussed herein).

Intragenerational Acclimatization

Intragenerational acclimatization studies in corals primarily focus on increasing tolerance to the abiotic stressors of low pH and/or high temperature. These stressful conditions can reduce coral calcification and growth rates (Albright et al. 2018) and are worsening as the ocean warms and acidifies (Hoegh-Guldberg et al. 2007; Fabry 2008; Doney et al. 2009). A preconditioning study on acclimatization to OA conditions in the cold-water coral, *Lophelia pertusa*, showed that while corals experienced a 26–29% reduction in calcification over a one-week exposure to acidified seawater, they were subsequently able to maintain calcification during six-month incubations with conditions that would normally cause dissolution (Form and Riebesell 2012). Corals have also been shown to acclimatize to temperature within a generation, through preconditioning, where corals with a history of bleaching ended up showing resistance to subsequent thermal stress events (Brown et al. 2002; Middlebrook et al. 2008; Armoza-Zvuloni et al. 2011; Carilli et al. 2012). Mechanistic underpinnings most likely include symbiont switching or shuffling (see *Acclimatization and Microbes* in this chapter) and/or epigenetic processes (Berkelmans and van Oppen 2006; Brown and Cossins 2011; Putnam et al. 2016). Acclimatization of corals to high irradiance could also help to protect them from bleaching through the production of photoprotective fluorescent proteins, which can reduce oxidative stress on corals (Salih et al. 2006). Additional research is necessary to test these ideas.

Transgenerational Acclimatization in Corals

With transgenerational acclimatization, the phenotype of a new generation is influenced by the environment experienced by the previous generation, and it can be adaptive when the exposure of parents to a particular environment leads to improved performance of offspring in the same environment. Parents can influence offspring phenotypes through various mechanisms, including the transmission of nutritional, cytoplasmic, somatic, or epigenetic material between generations (Bonduriansky and Day 2009; Marshall and Morgan 2011; Torda et al. 2017) (Figure 9.8). The importance of maternal effects (e.g., egg provisioning) for influencing offspring fitness is well-studied (Bernardo 1996; Mousseau and Fox 1998; McCormick 2003; Marshall and Keough 2006; McEdward and Miner 2006). Less understood, but increasing in number, are instances of epigenetic processes and microbial associations potentially facilitating transgenerational adaptive responses (Daxinger and Whitelaw 2010; Putnam and Gates 2015; Dimond and Roberts 2016; Dixon et al. 2016). However, to date, there is only one study linking environmental variation to epigenetic changes in corals (Putnam et al. 2016), highlighting the need for further investigation.

Importantly, epigenetic mechanisms provide a possible explanation for the substantial amount of heritable variation that cannot be explained by genomic DNA sequence variation alone (Holeski et al. 2012; Springer 2013). More specifically, transgenerational epigenetic inheritance via the gametes (i.e., transmission of epigenetic marks between generations) has the potential to explain many examples of transgenerational phenotypic effects that are not easily accounted for by inherited genetic variation (Holeski et al. 2012; Torda et al. 2017). However, causality for the association between epigenetic marks and overall phenotypes, as well as exact mechanisms and the extent to which they have an effect, remains to be determined (Ptashne 2013; Metzger and Schulte 2016; Torda et al. 2017).

Despite the potential benefits of transgenerational acclimatization for influencing host stress responses, this process is unlikely to be the primary driver of plasticity in most coral species since the vast majority are broadcast spawners (Baird et al. 2009), for which the parental environment is a relatively poor predictor of the offspring environment (Torda et al. 2017). Rather, it is more likely to be adaptive in brooding species where offspring often settle in a habitat similar to that of their parents (Putnam 2012; Torda et al. 2017). Testing a range of coral species with robust experimental designs is necessary to confirm this. Such studies might consider testing multiple environmental stressors, individually and synergistically, along with intra- and transgenerational exposure tests for evaluating the potential of acclimatization experiments for generating more resilient offspring (Chakravarti et al. 2016).

For example, Putnam and Gates (2015) provided evidence for parental effects in a cross-generational exposure experiment testing tolerance to temperature and OA in reef-building corals. They found that preconditioning coral larvae to high temperature and OA inside parental polyps during development resulted in parental effects that may contribute to transgenerational acclimatization in the newly released larvae (for the brooding species, *Pocillopora damicornis*). Specifically, they exposed adults to high or ambient temperature and OA treatments during the larval brooding period and found that even though exposure to high treatment negatively affected adult performance, their larvae displayed size differences and metabolic acclimation when subsequently re-exposed, unlike larvae from parents exposed to ambient conditions (Putnam and Gates 2015). Future studies should determine whether these beneficial parental effects last throughout the lifespan of the initial offspring generation and beyond.

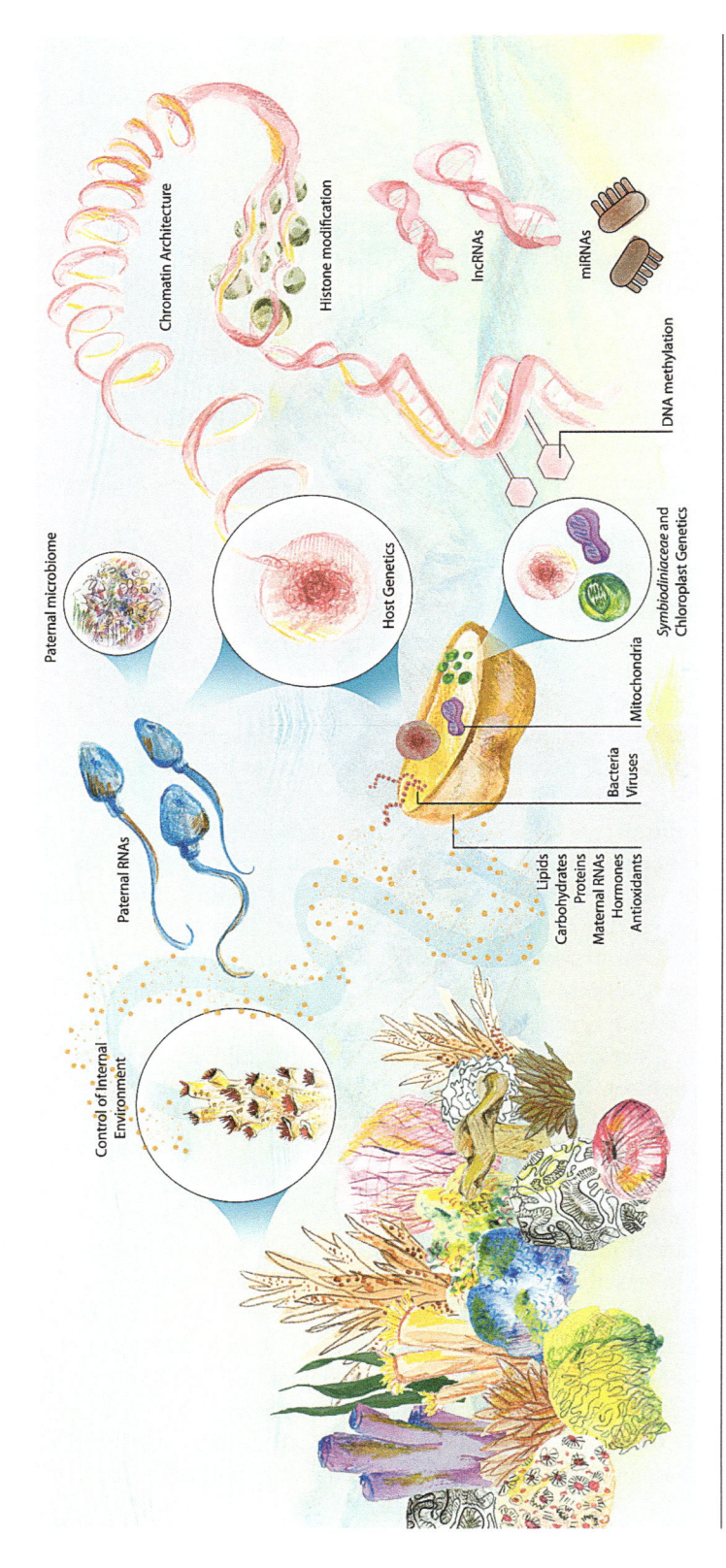

Figure 9.8 Potential mechanisms of transgenerational acclimatization. Illustration showing the various pathways that may enable transgenerational acclimatization in corals, including somatic and epigenetic factors of coral gametes, as well as their associated microbes transmitted vertically from one generation to the next. Epigenetics refers to mechanisms that potentially regulate gene expression, such as DNA methylation, histone modification, and noncoding and antisense RNAs. In addition to epigenetic mechanisms, parents can influence offspring fitness via a range of factors transmitted to the embryo through paternal and maternal germ cells. For example, nutritional factors passed through the oocyte's cytoplasm, such as lipids and carbohydrates, may directly influence the metabolic capacity of the early zygote and larva. For a more detailed discussion of these mechanisms, refer to Torda et al. 2017. (Source: Hillary Smith; adapted from Torda et al. 2017.)

Future work should also consider unintentional and/or indirect effects of preconditioning. One study found that laboratory preconditioning of the coral *Porites porites* with elevated partial pressure of CO$_2$ (pCO$_2$) resulted in slower calcification and feeding rates when subsequently exposed to experimental heat stress (Towle et al. 2016). Given the presence of concurrent environmental pressures, increasing the tolerance threshold of one trait at the expense of another is not a realistic solution. Using multiple, simultaneous stressors during preconditioning, as well as testing performance under alternative environmental stressors after preconditioning, will be important for evaluating the long-term efficacy of this approach.

Acclimatization and Microbes

Understanding multigenerational effects in corals is further complicated by the intimate relationship they form with diverse groups of microorganisms that may contribute to phenotypic plasticity (Boulotte et al. 2016; Torda et al. 2017; Webster and Reusch 2017). Corals live in close association with various eukaryotic/prokaryotic microorganisms that may adapt or acclimatize faster than their host, possibly lending additional adaptive capacity to the holobiont. A holobiont is an assemblage of different species that form a single ecological unit; in this case, the holobiont is the coral animal and its pro- and eukaryotic symbionts (Rohwer et al. 2002). Hence, some have extended the definition of epigenetics to include associated microbial symbionts (e.g., algal endosymbionts, bacteria, and viruses) since they play key roles in host stress tolerance and can influence host phenotypes (van Oppen et al. 2009b; Gates and Ainsworth 2011; Bourne and Webster 2013; Krediet et al. 2013; McFall-Ngai et al. 2013).

Much attention has been paid to the association between coral hosts and their photosynthetic algal endosymbionts (family Symbiodiniaceae; LaJeunesse et al. 2018) for understanding holobiont stress responses and acclimatization to environmental change (Blackall et al. 2015). Corals can undergo *symbiont shuffling* as a stress response by varying the taxonomic composition of associated algal endosymbiont communities, which can help to balance photosynthetic activity and stress tolerance (Baker 2001; Jones et al. 2008; Howells et al. 2016; Ziegler et al. 2016). If such shifts improve host health, they may also enhance the size and maternal provisioning of eggs or larvae. This could ultimately benefit offspring through maternal effects, which is a mechanism of phenotypic plasticity and acclimatization (Baker 2001; Jones et al. 2008; Howells et al. 2016; Quigley et al. 2016; Ziegler et al. 2016). Alternatively, a shift toward hosting a more heat-tolerant algal genotype (via *symbiont switching*) may lead to trade-offs in the physiology of the coral host, where hosts harboring thermally tolerant clades grow slower than those harboring thermally sensitive ones (Jones and Berkelmans 2010). This demonstrates the magnitude of trade-offs likely to be experienced by some coral species as they acclimatize to warming seas by switching to more thermally tolerant strains (Jones and Berkelmans 2011; Jones and Berkelmans 2012). Whether symbiont shuffling (or switching) is an adaptive response and can be harnessed or manipulated to promote host stress tolerance is a topic of active research (see *Experimental Evolution of Algal Endosymbionts (Symbiodiniaceae)* in this chapter).

Potentially contributing to the acclimatization/adaptive capacity of their hosts as well, are specific bacterial groups that are found within different microhabitats of the coral. These bacteria have a wide range of metabolic capabilities and are predicted to play a role in immunity, nitrogen fixation, nutrient cycling, osmoregulation, and oxidative stress response (McFall-Ngai et al. 2013; Bourne et al. 2016). Additionally, high phenotypic plasticity, rapid evolution (stemming from genetic and/or epigenetic processes), and compositional shifts can occur in bacteria (Casadesus and Low 2013). A study linking bacterial community dynamics with patterns of coral heat tolerance found that transplanting corals to a warmer environment resulted in shifts in the associated bacterial community that correlated with increased holobiont thermotolerance (Ziegler et al. 2017). Bacteria can also be vertically transmitted from parent to offspring, potentially transferring any beneficial effects of the host-microbe interaction to the next generation (Sharp et al. 2012). These observations illustrate the potential for bacteria to contribute to plastic responses of the holobiont and improve its function, but direct experimental evidence on the link between bacteria-coral symbiosis and acclimatization remains insufficient (Reshef et al. 2006; Torda et al. 2017; Webster and Reusch 2017).

Discussion and Future Directions

Thus far, results are equivocal, but the body of literature on the significance, or not, of acclimatization for promoting rapid adaptive responses to climate change is growing (Hughes et al. 2003; Hoegh-Guldberg 2004; Donner et al. 2007; Hoegh-Guldberg et al. 2007; Edmunds and Gates 2008; Maynard et al. 2008; Hoegh-Guldberg 2012; Putnam 2012; Munday et al. 2013; Hoegh-Guldberg et al. 2014; Putnam and Gates 2015; Torda et al. 2017; Coles et al. 2018). Preconditioning as part of intragenerational acclimatization may quickly build resilience at the individual level, but the long-term consequences of such manipulations for the conditioned and subsequent generations are still not well understood. The transmission of epigenetic marks or beneficial host-microbe associations from parents to offspring may facilitate transgenerational adaptive responses, but there are profound gaps in our current knowledge of these mechanisms, as well as the extent to which they successfully contribute to acclimatization in reef-building corals. Harnessing epigenetic modification serves as a strategy to generate multiple phenotypes from a single genotype, which may be prompted by preconditioning. As the field of epigenetics continues to advance, so do the tools and assays that can be used for assessing epigenetic modifications, lending greater insight into potential underlying mechanisms (DeAngelis et al. 2008; Bell and Spector 2011). Gene expression analysis can be a straightforward and cost-effective method for assaying the response of corals to environmental change. This approach is referred to as RNA-Seq, and methodologically, relies primarily on sequencing millions of cDNA fragments using the Illumina platform (Moya et al. 2012; Hou et al. 2018).

Future studies aiming to understand the mechanistic basis of transgenerational acclimatization in corals, while logistically challenging, will need to employ more complex experimental designs and span at least two to three generations (NASEM 2018). This may restrict such experiments, at least initially, to brooding species because larvae of brooding corals are available for a much longer time period compared to the annual mass spawning event of broadcast spawners, and they can be cultured in aquariums or laboratories over long periods of time where they will most likely continue to release larvae (Richmond and Jokiel 1984; Shlesinger et al. 1998; Vermeij et al. 2003). While preconditioning may only be relevant for brooders because larvae of broadcast spawners may disperse to habitats too dissimilar to that of the preconditioned parents, this idea needs further investigation. The degree of local adaptation (see Chapter 10), scale of environmental gradients, and larval dispersal dynamics (gene flow) will differ across tropical basins harboring coral reefs, so the feasibility of this approach for broadcast spawning species may differ across regions. Several years would be necessary to test multiple generations.

Also necessary in order to conduct acclimatization research is access to lab infrastructure, in situ and/or ex situ coral nurseries, and corals of different species and/or life stages. This type of work will most likely be limited by the ability to scale up in space and time. Scalability of this application will depend on the specific approach used (refer to NASEM 2018). For example, preconditioning gravid colonies has the potential for a greater impact compared to exposure targeted at the non-gravid adult stage because most colonies are fecund and release very large numbers of gametes or larvae. Preconditioning large batches of recruits or adult colonies can be carried out in a land nursery prior to outplanting for restoration, but numbers will depend on the capacity of the facility used. Settling larvae and rearing sexual recruits are not trivial matters either, so manipulating and testing the early life stages of corals will require someone with prior knowledge and experience. In conclusion, we still have a lot to learn about coral acclimatization, but, given that it may provide the temporal buffer needed to ensure ecological persistence in a rapidly changing environment, continued focus on this topic is important.

EXPERIMENTAL EVOLUTION OF ALGAL ENDOSYMBIONTS (SYMBIODINIACEAE)

Scleractinian corals have evolved an obligate, mutually beneficial symbiosis with dinoflagellates of the family Symbiodiniaceae (referred to as algal endosymbionts or zooxanthellae). Corals depend on these algal endosymbionts for much of their nutritional requirements (up to 90%) (Muscatine et al. 1981; Falkowski et al. 1984), and their relationship is fundamental to the productivity and high calcification rates that generate reef structures. A recent taxonomic revision has occurred (LaJeunesse et al. 2018), advancing our understanding from nine major groups (*clades*, A-I) of a single genus *Symbiodinium* (Pochon and Gates 2010) to a new family, Symbiodiniaceae. Symbiodiniaceae comprises genera corresponding to what were formerly the nine clades of the single *Symbiodinium* genus (a genus retained to refer to certain members of clade A) and members of the other genera (corresponding to former *Symbiodinium* clades A, B, C, D, F, G, H) (NASEM 2018). For example, the former *Symbiodinium* clades C and D are now the genera *Cladocopium* and *Durusdinium*, respectively.

Different symbiont types have different physiological optima and they can influence the stress phenotype of their host. For example, inoculation of genetically similar coral hosts with distinct Symbiodiniaceae types from different thermal environments leads to varying degrees of thermal tolerance of the holobiont (Mieog et al. 2009; Howells et al. 2012). Some coral species, and even different individuals within the same species, can (1) harbor multiple types within a single colony (Baker 2003; Mieog et al. 2007; van Oppen et al. 2009a), (2) shuffle the relative abundance of the different types, and/or (3) acquire new types from the environment in response to stress (Rowan et al. 1997; Baker 2003; Mieog et al. 2007; Jones et al. 2008; van Oppen et al. 2009a; DeSalvo et al. 2010; Cunning et al. 2015). Thus, shifting or switching the community composition of symbiont types to those that are better suited to the prevailing environmental condition(s) may serve as a swift mechanism for stony corals to cope with sudden or sustained environmental change (Baker et al. 2004; Boulotte et al. 2016). However, owing to conflicting reports of symbiont stability and change (Goulet 2006; Sampayo et al. 2008; Stat et al. 2009; LaJeunesse et al. 2010; Stat 2011), there is considerable debate whether such changes in symbiont composition are adaptive (Baker 2001; Kinzie et al. 2001) and how long these changes persist after the disturbance has ended (Thornhill et al. 2006b).

Symbiodiniaceae and Coral Bleaching

Rapid ocean warming, as a consequence of rising anthropogenic carbon emissions, is seriously threatening coral reefs and the coral-Symbiodiniaceae relationship. When temperatures become too high, the symbiosis breaks down, causing the stressed coral to expel its algal endosymbionts and appear white (*bleached*) since its tissues no longer retain the colored microalgae and its white skeleton is visible (Figure 9.9). In this condition, corals can survive only for a limited time; prolonged bleaching will cause them to starve and eventually die (Baird and Marshall 2002). The specific trigger(s) that induce coral cells to initiate symbiont ejection remain unknown, but fundamental cellular stress responses like apoptosis (programmed cell death), cell detachment, and protein folding have been implicated (Gates et al. 1992; Weis 2008; Ruiz-Jones and Palumbi 2017). Furthermore, coral bleaching research indicates that the cellular mechanism causing bleaching has different environmental thresholds for corals of different species and for corals hosting different species of algal endosymbionts (Berkelmans and van Oppen 2006; LaJeunesse et al. 2009; Stat et al. 2009). Substantial differences among three Symbiodiniaceae species were found through genomic and transcriptomic analyses, indicating a genomic basis to explain differential compatibilities to a variety of hosts and environments, and revealing the putative importance of gene duplications as an evolutionary mechanism in Symbiodiniaceae (Aranda et al. 2016).

Bleaching reactions are most commonly driven by temperature extremes corresponding to 1–2°C above the normal maximum summer temperatures and increase in likelihood under prolonged temperature extremes (NASEM 2018). Prolonged bleaching has led to widespread coral mortality over the last three decades, where mass bleaching events in 1998, 2010, and 2014–2017 are attributed with major losses (Heron et al. 2016; Hughes et al. 2017; Hughes et al. 2018). The Great Barrier Reef, for example, was recorded to have 50–80% coral mortality on several northern reefs following back-to-back high mortality mass bleaching events in 2016 and 2017 (Anthony et al. 2017). Alarmingly, the severity and frequency of mass bleaching events are expected to increase in the future (Hughes et al. 2017). To retain just less than 10% of the world's coral reefs, warming must be limited to below 1.5°C (Frieler et al. 2013), but climate models predict a less than 5% chance that the global temperature increase since pre-industrial times will be less than 2°C by 2050 (Raftery et al. 2017). While some marine species are able to migrate to cooler habitats in response to warming waters (Cheung et al. 2009), corals are sessile, already near their physiological thermal limits, and most coral reefs are forecasted to experience annual severe bleaching before the end of the century (Hoegh-Guldberg 1999; van Hooidonk et al. 2016).

Importantly, corals are capable of re-establishing a symbiosis when the acute stress event has ended (Cunning et al. 2015). However, recovery post bleaching can result in either positive or negative outcomes. For example, bleached corals have been documented to recover with symbiont communities dominated by *Durusdinium*, a genus comprised of several thermotolerant species (e.g., *D. trenchii* and *D. glynni*) that confer high bleaching tolerance to their coral hosts (Berkelmans and van Oppen 2006; Jones et al. 2008; LaJeunesse et al. 2009; Cunning et al. 2015). Not only has it been shown that switching to *Durusdinium* increases bleaching thresholds by roughly 1–2°C (Berkelmans and van Oppen 2006; Jones et al. 2008; LaJeunesse et al. 2009; Cunning et al. 2015), but corals with *D. trenchii* appear to also retain their symbionts during periods of cold stress even though the symbionts are impaired, suggesting that some *Durusdinium* may also be resistant to expulsion in general (Silverstein et al. 2017; NASEM 2018). For coral reefs in certain locations that have suffered mortality as a result of both high and low temperature stress, like Florida (Lirman et al. 2011), having tolerance to both extremes may be beneficial and necessary. However, negative outcomes of symbiont re-establishment are possible as well. Corals can either recover with the same symbiont community they had prior to bleaching (Goulet 2006; Thornhill et al. 2006a; Stat et al. 2009), be left susceptible to disease (Kushmaro et al. 1997; Kushmaro et al. 1998; Harvell et al. 1999; Miller et al. 2009; Merselis et al. 2018), show reduced growth, or be reproductively compromised (Baird and Marshall 2002).

Assisted Evolution and Coral Reef Resilience

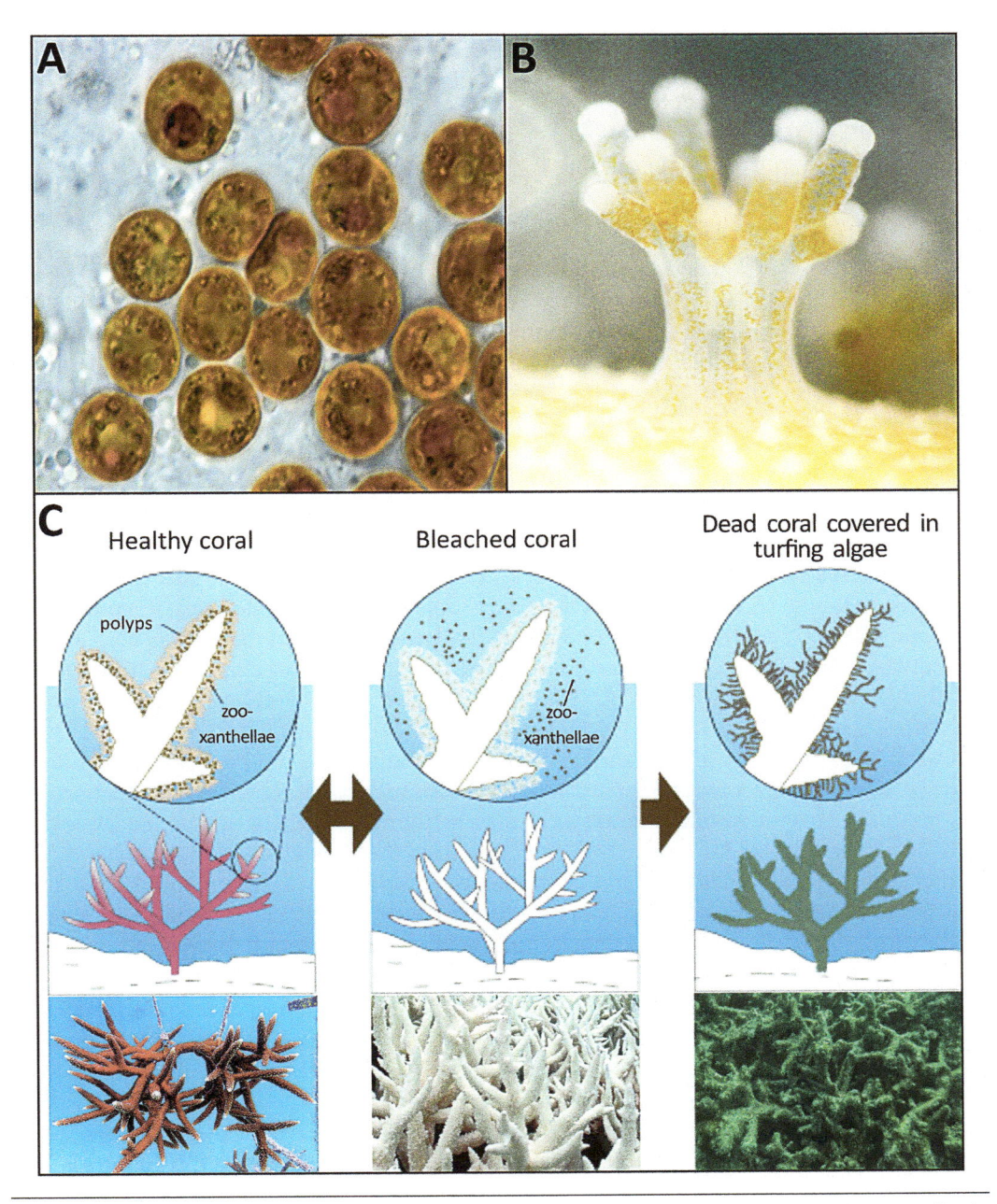

Figure 9.9 Coral-Symbiodiniaceae symbiosis. (A) Micrograph of golden-brown *S. fitti* cells, in hospite. (Source: Alison M. Lewis and Todd LaJeunesse.) (B) A coral polyp with *Symbiodinium* cells inhabiting host tissues. (Source: Chuya Shinzato, Okinawa Institute of Science and Technology Graduate University.) (C) The stages of coral bleaching, before (left), during (middle), and after (right). A healthy coral retains the algal endosymbionts (*zooxanthellae*) within its tissues, oftentimes giving the coral colony its color (left). As a stress response to acute thermal events, the coral will expel the zooxanthellae from its tissues, resulting in the characteristic bleached appearance as the white coral skeleton is exposed (middle). If the coral cannot recover via the uptake of new zooxanthellae, it will eventually starve, die, and be taken over by fouling organisms and turf algae (right). (Sources: Illustration and bottom middle coral image (Marshall and Schuttenberg 2006), © Commonwealth of Australia (GBRMPA); bottom left and right coral images, Hanna R. Koch.)

Ultimately, recovery from bleaching depends on the severity of the heat stress event, to include the degree and duration of the temperature increase, and the condition of the corals.

Manipulating Symbiodiniaceae

Owing to their vital contributions to the coral host and impact on holobiont stress tolerance, researchers are attempting to manipulate algal symbiont associations to favor partnerships that confer increased stress tolerance to the coral. Given that algal endosymbionts can evolve faster than the host itself (Chakravarti et al. 2017; Torda et al. 2017; Chakravarti and van Oppen 2018), manipulating them by introducing resistant strains that are absent in local populations may serve as a viable assisted evolution approach (van Oppen et al. 2015). Most phytoplankton groups have a great phenotypic plasticity for physiological acclimation to changes in their environmental conditions, which is supported by modifications of gene expression (Fogg 2001); but when these changes exceed physiological limits, species survival depends exclusively on adaptive evolution, which is in turn driven by the occurrence and selection of beneficial mutations that confer resistance (Sniegowski and Lenski 1995).

Generating and utilizing resistant algal strains can be achieved by experimentally evolving, in the lab, cultures of Symbiodiniaceae under elevated temperature and/or pCO_2 selection, and then inoculating coral hosts with the evolved algal cultures (van Oppen et al. 2017). Directed lab evolution (*experimental evolution*) in Symbiodiniaceae is possible due to asexual reproduction and comparatively short generation times. A single generation within the host (*in hospite*), may last between three and 74 days, depending on host conditions (Muscatine et al. 1984; Hoegh-Guldberg et al. 1987; Wilkerson et al. 1988)—whereas in culture, doubling times are often less than a few days (Fitt and Trench 1983b; Kinzie et al. 2001; Taguchi and Kinzie 2001). Previous work has shown that in a lab environment, Symbiodiniaceae can be cultured outside the host (*ex hospite*) under strong thermal selection conditions that promote large population sizes and minimize generation times, thereby maximizing the rate of genetic adaptation (Bromham 2009). Commonly used for directed lab evolution (e.g., thermal selection) is a ratchet experimental design in which temperatures are increased in stepwise increments and cells that are showing positive growth at each temperature are selected to seed cultures at the next elevated temperature (Figure 9.10). The coral hosts can then be inoculated with the evolved symbionts and assessed for growth and bleaching resistance under thermal stress.

Experimental results thus far from prolonged thermal selection in Symbiodiniaceae look promising. At elevated temperatures where previously there was no growth, the microalgae were able to continue asexual reproduction at 30°C after only 55 generations (Huertas et al. 2011) and at 31°C after 80 generations (~2.5 years; Chakravarti et al. 2017). Another study showed a stable adaptive change after a one-year exposure (~41–69 asexual generations) to increasing temperatures in three out of five tested Symbiodiniaceae strains (Chakravarti and van Oppen 2018) (Figure 9.10). Furthermore, selected cells exhibited superior photophysiological performance at elevated temperatures compared to wildtype cells (Chakravarti et al. 2017; Chakravarti and van Oppen 2018), and showed faster growth rates under short-term, acute heat stress (Chakravarti and van Oppen 2018). This indicates Symbiodiniaceae thermal tolerance itself can be enhanced. While coral bleaching is a natural stress response, utilizing resilient Symbiodiniaceae strains may help to prevent or reduce holobiont bleaching responses, which if become prolonged or recurrent, can lead to mortality.

Despite the successful experimental evolution of Symbiodiniaceae, recent findings also highlight the need for continued research on the broad-scale applicability of this approach

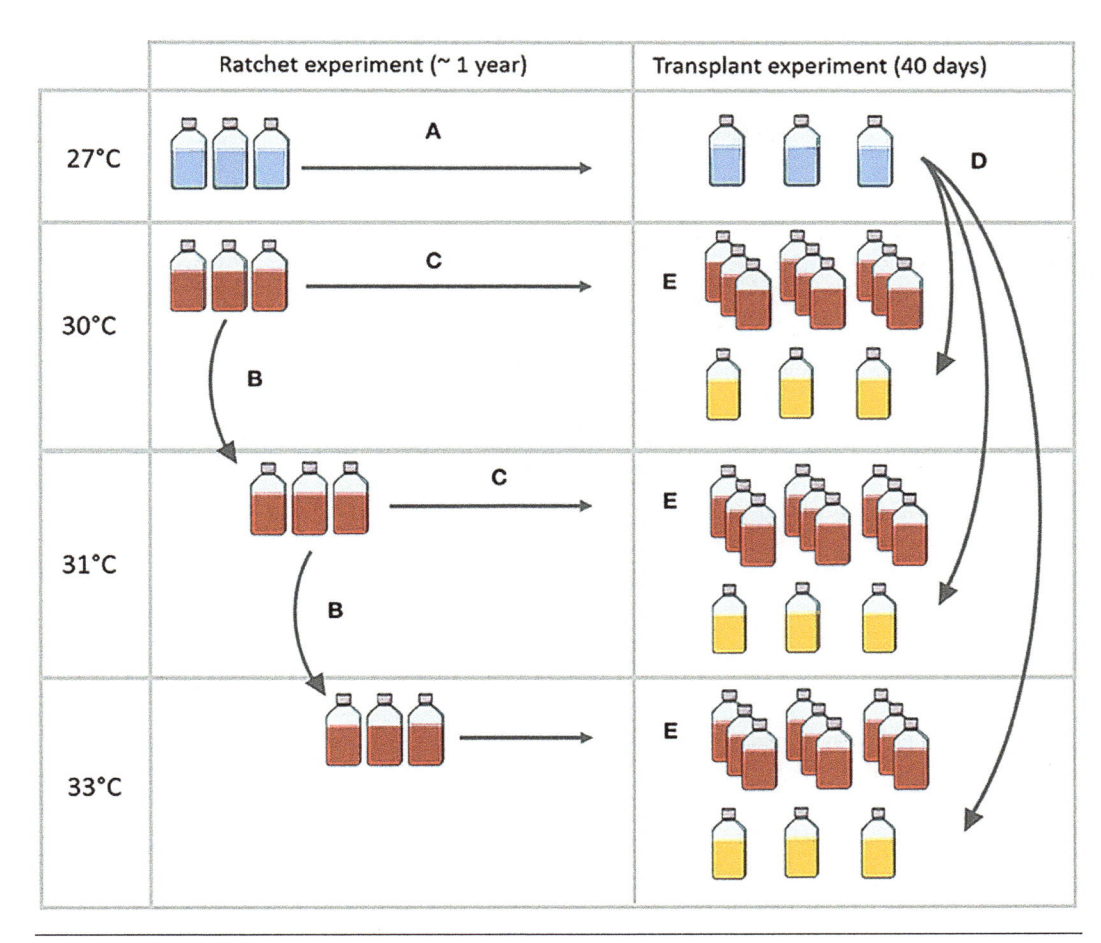

Figure 9.10 Directed lab evolution of Symbiodiniaceae. Schematic illustration of the experimental design used to conduct a ratchet experiment (for long-term thermal selection) followed by an acute heat-stress transplantation experiment. The ratchet method can be used to experimentally assess the maximum capacity of phytoplankton to adapt to a warming process by analyzing the growth of individual species subjected to increasing temperature (as the selecting agent) over many generations. This protocol permits selection and preservation of the occurrence of both pre-existing and *de novo* mutations that benefit the population and lead to thermal adaptation. (A) Replicate control cultures were maintained at 27°C for the duration of the long-term selection experiment. (B) If replicate populations exhibited positive growth after six weeks, they were transferred to the next elevated-temperature treatment. (C) For populations that were eligible to be transferred to the next temperature treatment, an aliquot was also maintained at the same temperature conditions during the experiment. (D) After one year, replicate control cultures were transferred to each of the elevated temperature treatments that the temperature-selected populations had achieved. (E) After one year of thermal selection, selected populations were divided into three replicate cultures and kept in their own temperature conditions, followed by a 40-day transplant experiment. (Source: Chakravarti and van Oppen 2018.)

for assisted evolution of corals. For example, even when selected symbionts showed increased thermotolerance (ex hospite), the effect was less apparent when they were in recruits (in hospite) (Chakravarti et al. 2017). And a lack of a difference in the rate and severity of bleaching between coral recruits harboring wildtype or selected cells suggests further work is necessary to determine why there is limited transference of enhanced symbiont thermotolerance to the coral holobiont (Chakravarti et al. 2017). For this type of work, it will be important to evaluate (1) whether selection for positive cell-growth rates necessarily translates to higher bleaching tolerance and (2) the longevity of the increased thermotolerance once the selective pressure is removed (NASEM 2018).

Another challenge moving forward will be to find a way for manipulated coral-Symbiodiniaceae associations to remain stable (van Oppen et al. 2015). Presently there is no compelling evidence that adult corals can establish a stable symbiosis with novel Symbiodiniaceae types (Coffroth et al. 2010). To date, deliberate manipulation of symbionts in adult corals has only been achieved by duplicating disturbances in the lab through controlled bleaching and recovery. While inducing bleaching in the lab is feasible, it is unlikely to be practical, in terms of effective scaling, given the need to manipulate large numbers of corals. It could also lead to unwanted stress and mortality if not conducted correctly. Therefore, this technique may currently be used for testing the effect of evolved symbionts on adult host tolerance, but an alternative method will need to be developed for successfully inoculating adult corals with symbionts without needing to bleach them beforehand.

Until this is resolved, scalable manipulations will likely be restricted to early life stages. Most scleractinian species, which are predominantly broadcast spawners, produce larvae without zooxanthellae (*aposymbiotic*). Zooxanthellae are subsequently taken up from the environment during larval development, or soon after settlement as early sexual recruits, through a process called horizontal transmission (Baird et al. 2009). Vertical transmission of zooxanthellae from mother to larvae is less common overall (~15% of species), but more common within brooding species (Thornhill et al. 2006a; Padilla-Gamino et al. 2012). Thus, it is presently possible to utilize aposymbiotic life stages (i.e., larval or early recruit) for inoculating with different stress-tolerant symbiont types to explore the phenotypic benefits of such novel symbioses (van Oppen et al. 2015). However, the application of methods utilizing coral larvae may not yet be feasible in areas where successful recruitment is limited, such as Florida and parts of the Caribbean (Williams et al. 2008; Albright et al. 2010; Miller et al. 2018; NASEM 2018). Nonetheless, the window during which symbionts may be readily acquired can last for several months, lending greater flexibility for such experimental manipulations (Abrego et al. 2009; Boulotte et al. 2016). Deliberate infection of coral juveniles with particular symbionts followed by outplanting to natural reef environments has already occurred as a small-scale experiment on the Great Barrier Reef (Little et al. 2004), which shows promise as a potential application for assisted evolution and large-scale restoration.

Discussion and Future Directions

Given that (1) different Symbiodiniaceae types can influence the host's stress phenotype, (2) that corals of the same species hosting different symbionts typically vary in their physiological capabilities (especially when it comes to bleaching), and (3) that the thermal tolerance of Symbiodiniaceae can be enhanced, attempts are currently underway to manipulate algal symbiont associations to favor partnerships that confer stress tolerance to the coral host. However, the degree to which corals can change their symbiont communities in favor of these stress-tolerant partnerships, the coral life stage at which it is most appropriate to attempt these changes, and the consequences of doing so, remain topics of active research (NASEM 2018). Moving forward, studies should investigate the infectivity of a wide taxonomic diversity of Symbiodiniaceae strains (experimentally evolved or not) under different temperature conditions, their stability in hospite, and their effect on holobiont bleaching tolerance and health across different coral life stages, as well as if and why thermal tolerance differs ex and in hospite (Chakravarti et al. 2017; Chakravarti and van Oppen 2018).

Taking into account the aposymbiotic condition and natural predisposition of most coral larvae or juveniles for acquiring algal symbionts from environmental sources, these early life stages are likely the most effective way of manipulating changes in symbiont communities because existing communities do not need to be displaced or outcompeted in order to become dominant, as is the case with adult corals (NASEM 2018). Furthermore, since absolute specificity in corals is rare (Silverstein et al. 2012; Quigley et al. 2014) and because the host environment and/or nutritional needs of corals may change throughout their life history (Abrego et al. 2008; Jones et al. 2008; Abrego et al. 2009; Quigley et al. 2016), infecting aposymbiotic corals with a cocktail of experimentally evolved Symbiodiniaceae types could serve as a boost to the holobiont's adaptive potential. Under thermal stress, the host could retain the most beneficial types via symbiont shuffling (Chen et al. 2005; Berkelmans and van Oppen 2006; Thornhill et al. 2006b; Mieog et al. 2007), potentially aiding in a flexible response to environmental change (Chakravarti and van Oppen 2018). As colonies containing manipulated symbionts are introduced to reefs, this could increase the local availability of these beneficial symbionts on reefs over time, including for new sexual recruits (NASEM 2018).

An understudied but potentially relevant area that merits consideration is cryptic sex in Symbiodiniaceae. It is hypothesized that Symbiodiniaceae can reproduce sexually (Fitt and Trench 1983a), but definitive evidence of sex (e.g., karyogamy and meiosis) remains lacking (LaJeunesse 2001). Sexual reproduction may have yet to be directly observed in Symbiodiniaceae because suppression of outcrossing when in the symbiotic state may be adaptive in that clonality is selected for (Heitman 2010). When in the symbiotic state, sex may also be inactive if the creation of new allelic combinations would affect the relationship between Symbiodiniaceae and its host, or if only one Symbiodiniaceae mating type is present because of strain selection by the host (Chi et al. 2014). Therefore, cryptic sex may be occurring in Symbiodiniaceae's seldom-seen free-living state while being inactive in the symbiotic state (Chi et al. 2014). Support for this comes from molecular population genetic patterns revealed in allozymes and the discovery of a number of meiosis-specific and meiosis-related genes (LaJeunesse 2001; Chi et al. 2014; Liu et al. 2018). The ability of Symbiodiniaceae to reproduce sexually offers increased efficiency of selection and adaptation (de Visser and Elena 2007), as well as another possible route for manipulating Symbiodiniaceae to enhance stress tolerance by inducing sex and genetic recombination in the free-living state. Crossing different strains of [facultatively sexual] Symbiodiniaceae could allow for beneficial mutations from different lineages to recombine, increased genetic variation, and reduced fitness trade-offs (e.g., Koch and Becks 2017). This process could be combined with directed lab evolution (e.g., thermal selection) of Symbiodiniaceae for promoting holobiont stress tolerance.

When working with traits under selection (e.g., thermal selection), it is imperative to consider fitness trade-offs, which can cause undesirable or unintentional effects and constrain adaptation. Trade-offs occur when increased selection of a trait(s) leads to the diminishment of another (Stearns 1989), and oftentimes as a consequence of limited energetic capabilities. Other mechanisms of (evolutionary) trade-offs include genetic constraints like antagonistic pleiotropy or multivariate selection (Hoffmann 2013). Broad-scale trade-offs are expected in the evolution of heat tolerance (Huey and Kingsolver 1989), where polymorphisms in a population that confer increased thermotolerance likely also confer some fitness disadvantage, otherwise they would be fixed by selection over time. For example, while some corals can shift the relative ratio of Symbiodiniaceae varieties within one coral colony—a response correlated with tolerance to extreme temperatures (Berkelmans and van Oppen 2006; Jones et al. 2008)—further investigation of these putatively more tolerant types reveals a physiological trade-off in terms of reduced growth and competitiveness (Little et al. 2004). Perhaps these more heat-tolerant types translocate less photosynthetically fixed carbon (Cantin et al. 2009). Furthermore, higher proportions of heat-tolerant symbionts may linearly increase bleaching resistance, but simultaneously reduce photochemical efficiency, suggesting that a change in the community structure may oppositely impact performance and stress tolerance (Cunning et al. 2015). Consequently, the benefit of increased survivorship relative to reduced growth, or other traits associated with thermotolerance like host reproductive output or disease susceptibility, likely depends on the temperature regime at the restoration site of interest (NASEM 2018). Regardless, selection experiments should include tests for fitness trade-offs with unselected traits since this will be important for evaluating the suitability of such manipulations for the purpose of assisted evolution.

Finally, other limitations to consider include genetic risks of field introduction of manipulated symbionts, host specificity and flexibility, and symbiont tolerance longevity and availability (refer to NASEM 2018). Hybridization of experimentally evolved symbionts with native ones as a consequence of sexual reproduction in the free-living state could lead to outbreeding depression—the crossing of too genetically dissimilar individuals that can result in fitness reductions (see Chapter 10). Coral-Symbiodiniaceae associations and the nature of those associations (i.e., the propensity for symbiont shuffling or switching) are more well-known for certain species (Rowan et al. 1997; Baker 2001; Berkelmans and van Oppen 2006; LaJeunesse et al. 2009; Cunning et al. 2015; Silverstein et al. 2017), but other species may be far less labile in their associations, potentially limiting the broad-scale utility of this intervention. In terms of symbiont longevity and availability, new symbionts may be lost over time (Thornhill et al. 2006a; Thornhill et al. 2006b; LaJeunesse et al. 2010) or experimentally evolved symbionts could lose their evolved thermotolerance if environmental conditions subsequent to thermal selection are very different and impose their own selective pressures post manipulation. The capacity for corals to undergo changes in symbionts likely depends on the availability of local alternative types, so successful switching or shuffling may also be region-specific. Nonetheless, the manipulation of Symbiodiniaceae for promoting holobiont stress tolerance represents a clear opportunity for intervention.

MANIPULATING THE HOST MICROBIOME

Corals harbor a diverse assemblage of microorganisms (collectively referred to as the coral microbiome) that inhabit the mucus layer, skeleton, and tissues of corals (Ritchie 2006; Sweet et al. 2011) (Figure 9.11). These microbes include symbiotic algae, bacteria, fungi, viruses, and archaea, which confer benefits to their host through mechanisms of photosynthesis, nitrogen fixation, nutritional provisioning, and disease resistance (Rosenberg et al. 2007; Blackall et al. 2015) (Figure 9.12). Photosynthesis, the process of producing fixed carbon from carbon dioxide and water using light-derived energy, is one of the most important contributions of endosymbiotic algae inhabiting the cells of the coral's gastrodermis. Endolithic algae may serve a purpose during bleaching events, where through basal photosynthetic activity, nutrients may be transferred from the skeleton to the coral tissue in order to keep the coral alive until recolonization of Symbiodiniaceae (Verbruggen and Tribollet 2011). The nitrogen provided by nitrogen-fixing bacteria is likely to support the host and its associated microbiota, including

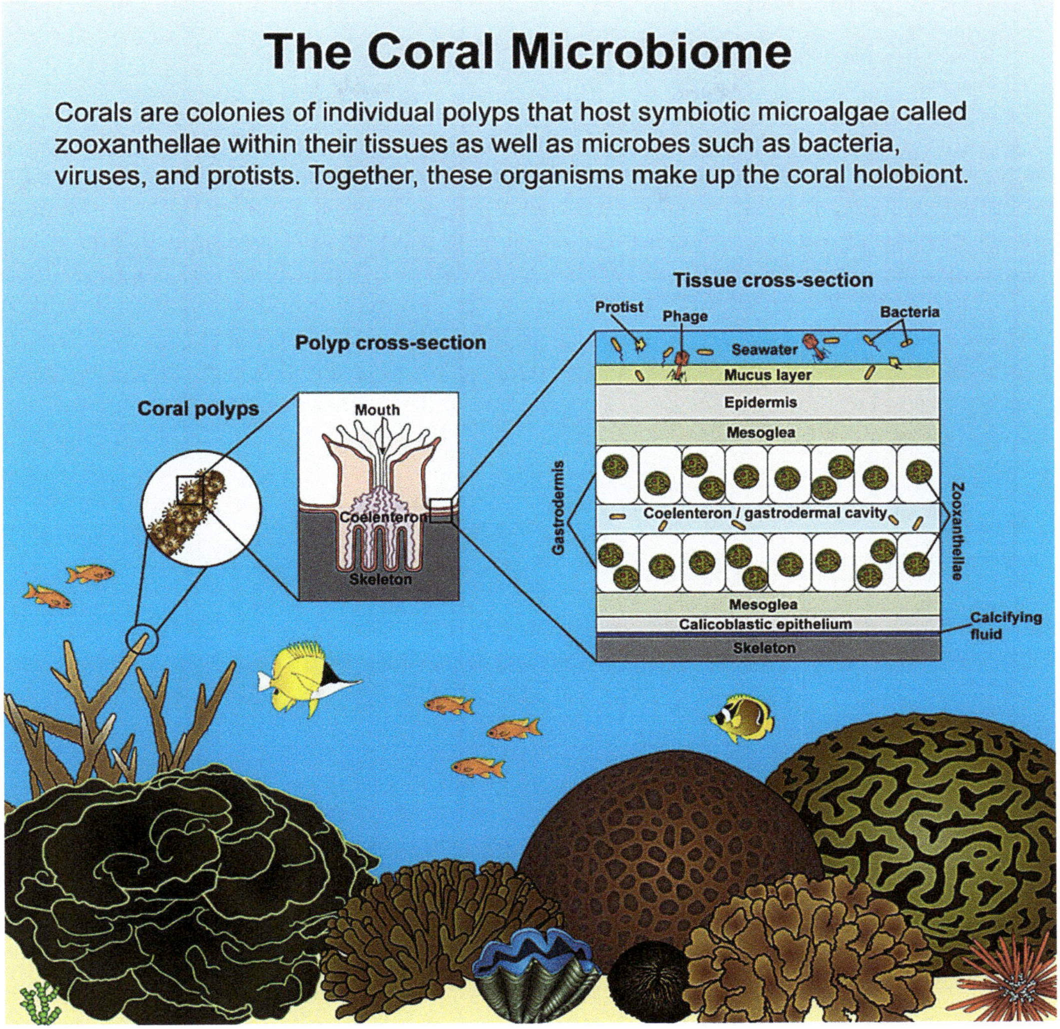

Figure 9.11 Digital illustration of the coral microbiome. Image shows magnified representation of coral polyps on a branch (left) with nested cross-sections of a coral polyp (middle) and its tissue layers (right), hosting various microorganisms within the different layers. Reef-building corals respond to changes in their environment through mechanisms that can originate either in the coral host or in its microbiome, so coral reef health and function depend on the responses of, and interactions between, all of these partners. (Source: Digital illustration by Adi Khen.)

Symbiodiniaceae (Santos et al. 2014). In terms of disease resistance, corals can protect themselves against pathogen infection, for example, using the mucus microbiome as a barrier (Glasl et al. 2016), where the production of antibiotics within the mucus serves as a protective agent (Ritchie 2006). These symbionts and their roles in promoting coral health represent examples of beneficial microorganisms for corals (BMCs), a term and concept proposed by Peixoto et al. (2017).

Alongside commensal and mutualistic relationships, coral-associated microorganisms can be pathogenic as well (Garren and Azam 2012). Certain microorganisms can disrupt

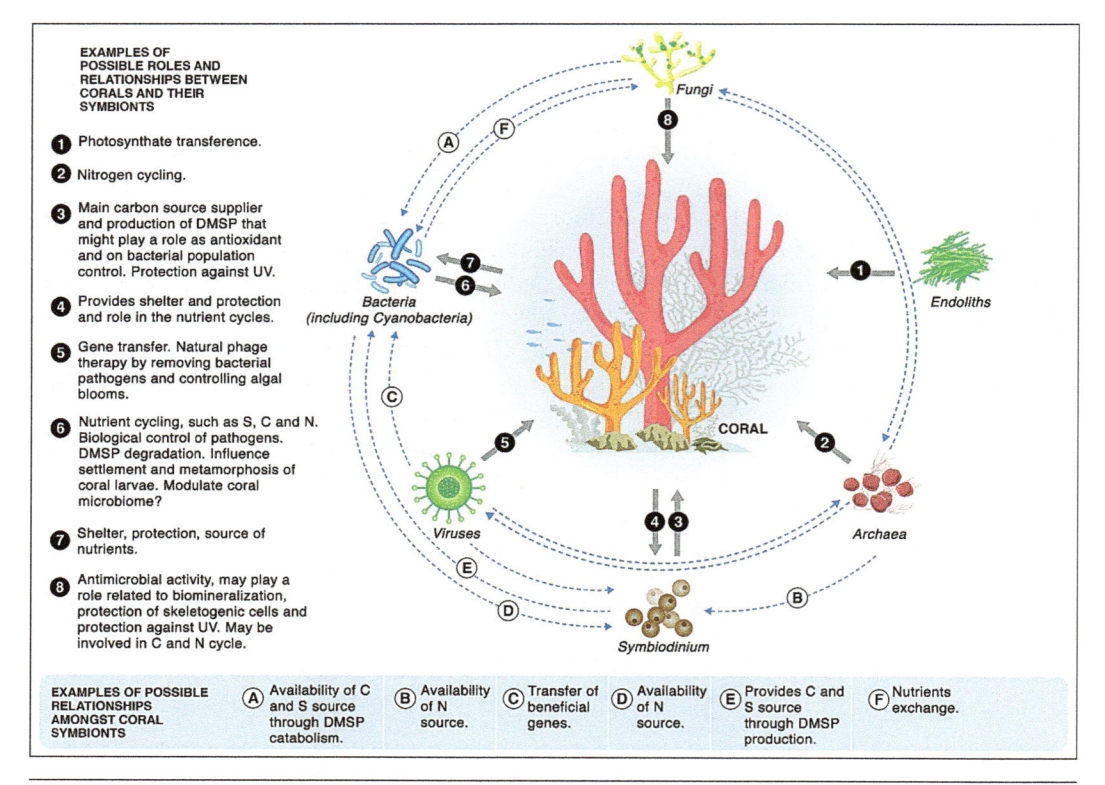

Figure 9.12 Beneficial microorganisms for corals (BMCs). Illustration of the potential roles and relationships between corals and their symbiotic microbial groups including phages, bacteria, protists, and archaea. These relationships highlight proposed mechanisms for enhancing coral health and resilience through the manipulation of BMCs; other relevant roles yet to be discovered are likely important targets in the future. DMSP refers to dimethylsulfoniopropionate; coral-associated bacterial groups are capable of metabolizing and consuming its products for their own metabolic processes. The catabolism of DMSP also potentially generates sulfur-based antimicrobial compounds, which at low concentrations can inhibit the growth of certain coral pathogens. Therefore, the production and metabolism of sulfur compounds represents a potential BMC mechanism. The manipulation of these key microbial groups, and other BMCs, may promote coral health through the regulation of key symbiotic populations, antimicrobial activity, and nutrient input. (Source: Peixoto et al. 2017.)

homeostasis, cause bleaching or disease under environmental stress, and lead to shifts in microbiome or virome composition in response (Sunagawa et al. 2009; Thurber et al. 2009; Sato et al. 2010; Zaneveld et al. 2016). Thus, coral-associated microorganisms are not only critical to host fitness and survival, but they are sensitive to environmental disturbances and the physiological status of their host as well. Consequently, the coral microbiome is considered one of the most complex microbial biospheres studied to date (Hernandez-Agreda et al. 2017). Even though the ability of microbes to metabolize nutrients that can be translocated to the host is likely a driver in the establishment of coral-associated microbial assemblages, we are still uncertain of how coral-microbe symbioses evolved.

The Coral Core Microbiome

While coral microbiome research is still in its infancy, a number of studies have already been published on the coral microbiome, its composition, spatio-temporal variability, and response to environmental change from different reef locations around the world and from corals in both healthy and diseased states (for a review, refer to Hernandez-Agreda et al. 2017). This work feeds into the present challenge of microbiome research which is to uncover general rules for the assembly of coral microbiomes (Pollock et al. 2018). Researchers are currently characterizing the 'core microbiome' and its constituents, which are a group of microbes commonly found within a host's microbiome. An assumption here is that the persistence of the association—within the host and within a niche across spatio-temporal boundaries—serves as a criterion for selecting microbes that are potentially providing critical function within the habitat in which they are found (Hernandez-Agreda et al. 2017).

Research into the core microbiome and the identity and functional contribution of core microbes was first applied to understanding bacterial communities associated with humans (Fierer et al. 2008; Turnbaugh et al. 2009; Qin et al. 2010). This concept has since been adopted across microbial systems, including those associated with corals (Ainsworth et al. 2015; Bourne et al. 2016; Hernandez-Agreda et al. 2017; Hernandez-Agreda et al. 2018), in order to identify central metabolic pathways associated with the core microbiome that may provide valuable information about how host-microbiome interactions are established and maintained (Ainsworth et al. 2015). Results thus far from microbiome research in other species indicate, however, that the functional core microbiome is potentially more important than a taxonomic core because functional redundancy is a common characteristic of complex microbial communities (Burke et al. 2011a). This finding may be relevant for corals where microbial community diversity may change in response to environmental conditions, but essential functions can be maintained by new taxonomic groups (Peixoto et al. 2017). Finally, microorganisms comprising the core microbiome may be less sensitive to the surrounding environment because they inhabit host-constructed niches (Hester et al. 2016), but they may also be capable of adapting to environmental change (McFall-Ngai et al. 2013; Santos et al. 2014), which is relevant for attempting to manipulate them for the purpose of assisted evolution.

Coral-Associated Bacteria

Excluding coral-Symbiodiniaceae research, a predominant portion of coral microbiome work focuses on coral-associated bacterial communities, as they are predicted to play crucial roles in organism function and ecosystem dynamics (Graham et al. 2011; Blackall et al. 2015). Moreover, the identity and diversity of coral-associated bacteria depends on the environmental habitat and surrounding conditions (Rohwer et al. 2002). For example, in a recent microbiome study, coral heat tolerance was causally linked with the associated bacterial community and corals exposed to different thermal regimes harbored different microbiomes (Ziegler et al. 2017). Advances in molecular technologies have helped to discover the richness and composition of bacterial communities of the coral host and next-generation sequencing is now widely used for evaluating bacterial diversity (Claesson et al. 2010; Wu et al. 2010). Such sequencing methods can reveal the identity of the bacterial community constituents, including rare or less abundant species, as well as unveil the level of conservation of bacterial types within microhabitats and between individual hosts (Pedros-Alio 2006; Sunagawa et al. 2010).

Research has yet to determine, however, the stability of most bacterial associations of corals, including the consistency of dominant associations between individuals, within and between coral species, and across spatio-temporal scales and depth gradients (Hernandez-Agreda et al. 2017). The need for further investigation into the stability of such associations stems from recent findings where deep sequencing of the microbiome revealed substantial variability between reef habitats, species, and perhaps most compelling, between individuals (Ainsworth et al. 2015; Hernandez-Agreda et al. 2016; Hester et al. 2016). While the variability between individuals may be attributable to coral colony age (Williams et al. 2015), it is still important to distinguish the individual's microbiome from that of species-specific microbial consortia for identifying symbiotic microbial roles and their contribution to host fitness and phenotype (Hernandez-Agreda et al. 2018). Ultimately, it is necessary to identify the key players comprising the dominant associations before it is possible to manipulate them for enhancing host fitness.

For example, *Vibrio shiloi* is a bacterial pathogen that causes the coral bleaching disease *Oculina patagonica* every summer in the eastern Mediterranean Sea when seawater temperatures rise (Rosenberg and Falkovitz 2004). Researchers have used this model system to show that these corals can rapidly adapt to changing environmental conditions by altering their population of symbiotic bacteria (Reshef et al. 2006). This has led to the Coral Probiotic Hypothesis, which posits that a dynamic relationship exists between symbiotic microorganisms and environmental conditions which brings about the selection of the most advantageous coral holobiont; changing their microbial partners would allow the corals to adapt to changing conditions more rapidly (i.e., days to weeks) than via mutation and selection (i.e., several years) (Reshef et al. 2006). By identifying the causative agent and manipulating the bacteria-host association, scientists suggest that the Probiotic Hypothesis could lead to the development of resistance of the coral holobiont to diseases (Reshef et al. 2006).

Coral-Associated Viruses

Even less understood than the coral-bacteria relationship, is how viruses modulate the adaptive capacity of their hosts (but see Torda et. al. 2017). In a seminal review of the role viruses play in influencing the phenotypic performance of the coral holobiont, Thurber and colleagues discuss both negative and potentially positive effects of the coral virome (Thurber et al. 2017). Because viruses are obligate symbionts and have been widely implicated in coral bleaching and disease, they are generally perceived as parasitic and harmful to their hosts. However, viruses of coral-associated microorganisms may have beneficial effects for their hosts by interacting with them through lysogeny, the process of integrating their genome into their host genome. Viruses and lysogenic infection are prevalent in the ocean, with an estimated average of 10^7 viruses per milliliter (Wigington et al. 2016). While little is known about the factors triggering lysogenic infections, lysogenization of microorganisms can protect them from other viruses and/or boost their metabolism and survival through the expression of auxiliary metabolic genes that are encoded in viral genomes (Thurber et al. 2017). Through a process called *piggyback the winner*, lysogenic conversion increases microbial abundance and growth in coral reefs (Knowles et al. 2016). However, whether lysogenic infections can be manipulated for the purpose of influencing coral host performance or resilience is currently unknown.

The Coral Microbiome and Microhabitats

Another piece to the puzzle that is the coral microbiome is the suite of microhabitats in which coral-associated microorganisms reside. Coral mucus, tissue, and skeleton microbiomes differ in microbial community composition, richness, and response to host versus environmental drivers (Ainsworth and Gates 2016; Apprill et al. 2016; Pollock et al. 2018). Diverse microbial communities inhabit the external nutrient-rich mucus layer and are likely influenced by both the external conditions surrounding the holobiont and coral secretions (*exudates*) (Bourne and Webster 2013). The microbiome within coral tissues is much less diverse and highly organized within bacteriocytes called coral-associated microbial aggregates (Work and Aeby 2014), which might respond to stress differently based on the bacterial taxon involved. The coral skeleton contains a diverse and distinct microbiome compared to other niches of the holobiont (Bourne et al. 2016), and while endolithic communities may vary depending on coral morphology (i.e., branching versus mounding), they typically comprise a mix of eu- and prokaryotic communities (Marcelino et al. 2017). Only recently have studies begun to document the taxonomy and functional attributes of associated endolithic communities, and it is currently unknown what effects they have on the holobiont (Yang et al. 2016). Lastly, the gastric vascular and coelenteron fluid connecting and running through the coral polyps harbor a unique and diverse microbial community that can be influenced by water flow and heterotrophic feeding of coral polyps (Bourne et al. 2016).

These microhabitats serve as separate realms for hypothesis testing, especially for patterns of phylosymbiosis, which are correlations between host phylogenetic relationships and microbial community composition (Brooks et al. 2016). Mechanisms for phylosymbiosis include co-diversification of multiple lineages, microbial habitat filtering by host traits, or the interaction of host and microbial biogeography (Douglas and Werren 2016). Evidence thus far indicates the presence of coral-microbe phylosymbiosis, in which coral microbiome composition and richness reflect coral phylogeny, and interestingly, the coral skeleton represents the most biodiverse coral microbiome with the strongest signal of phylosymbiosis (Pollock et al. 2018). These findings reveal that different anatomical regions of animal hosts may show distinct evolutionary patterns.

Coral Microbiome Manipulations

To date, only a handful of studies have conducted coral microbiome manipulations, serving as precursors to the establishment of scalable assisted evolution interventions. Damjanovic et al. (2017) exposed *Acropora tenuis* larvae to coral-derived microbial-laden mucus from four different species, reared them for four months and then assessed their microbial community compositions, which revealed differences across all initial mucus addition treatments. This work suggests that even just one addition of a mucus/microbial cocktail can shift the coral-associated microbiome during early ontogeny, but if or how those shifts impacted coral health or fitness remains unknown. In another study, the predatory bacterium *Halobacteriovorax*, isolated from the coral microbiome regulated the coral-associated microbial communities through top-down control of certain bacterial species (Yang et al. 2016). In related work, when the predatory bacterium was added to corals that had also been challenged with the coral pathogen *Vibrio coralliilyticus*, the predatory bacterium ameliorated changes in the coral microbiome and prevented secondary colonization of opportunistic bacterial groups identified as indicators in compromised coral health (Welsh et al. 2016; Welsh et al. 2017). Finally, preliminary work on BMCs by Peixoto and colleagues has resulted in the successful development of BMC cocktails by isolating a range of bacterial species displaying potential beneficial traits for corals (Peixoto et al. 2017). These include nitrogen fixation and/or denitrification, degradation of sulfur compounds (e.g., DMSP), and antagonistic activity against putative bacterial pathogens. In subsequent trials, a BMC cocktail was added to corals in aquariums that were subjected to heat stress to simulate a bleaching event, as well as a bacterial challenge with the coral pathogen *V. coralliilyticus* (NASEM 2018). Compared to control corals, BMC-inoculated corals exhibited improved health through lower bleaching metrics, suggesting that BMC cocktails can be used to minimize the impacts of environmental stressors (NASEM 2018). These studies serve as examples of feasible small-scale microbiome manipulations (e.g., initiating microbiome shifts and adding microbial isolates), and demonstrate the propensity for improving coral host conditions under stress. However, the way in which the microbiome is shifted at the cellular level and by which mechanisms these benefits are conferred to the host, remains unclear.

Discussion and Future Directions

The microbiome can rapidly respond to the surrounding environment through a variety of mechanisms, including rapid adaptive evolution (Elena and Lenski 2003), which demonstrates the potentially powerful influence it may have on coral acclimatization and/or adaptation to environmental disturbances and stress (Webster and Reusch 2017). The potential for coral-associated microbes to be drivers of adaptive coral host responses stems from their increased abundance, diversity, and growth rates. Therefore, by manipulating the coral microbiome, the resilience of corals to changing environments may be increased for existing coral populations and potentially passed on to future generations. This is possible, in part, because many marine invertebrates vertically transmit their microbial symbionts, potentially facilitating microbiome-mediated transgenerational acclimatization if it also confers lasting adaptive benefits to the coral host (van Oppen et al. 2015). Henceforth, there are a number of microbiome-orientated approaches for trying to build resilience of the coral host to environmental stress (NASEM 2018). They are as follows: (1) subjecting the coral holobiont to environmental stress to promote selection of microbiome members that may have adaptive traits to confer benefits to the coral host and its native microbes (related to preconditioning acclimatization, see *Acclimatization (Nongenetic) Processes* in this chapter); (2) shifting the abundance of existing coral microbiome populations through isolation and addition of these native communities to the coral holobiont (similar to algal symbiont manipulation, see *Experimental Evolution of Algal Endosymbionts (Symbiodiniaceae)* in this chapter); (3) inoculating corals with new (bacterial) populations that have functions beneficial to the coral holobiont (e.g., BMC cocktails).

Peixoto et al. (2017), have provided a general workflow outlining suggested steps for the selection, assembly, manipulation, and application of BMCs for promoting coral resilience, including extensions for assisted evolution (Figure 9.13). They suggest that the recovery and selection of such beneficial microbes can be developed through basic microbiology methods using tailored culture media and cultivation strategies, as well as screening for specific

---

Figure 9.13 (see facing page) Potential strategies for identifying and utilizing BMCs for increasing coral resilience. The process would start with randomly isolating microorganisms from the surrounding reef water and target coral species, followed by BMC identification, screening for beneficial interactions with the coral host through aquarium-based experiments, and evaluation of the mechanisms by which the microorganisms confer benefits to the coral host. Extensive screening of BMCs would be undertaken to ensure no pathogenic interactions occur and to investigate potential antagonistic interactions between consortia of selected BMCs. The process would conclude with the application of the developed strategy in large mesocosm systems under relevant environmental stress conditions and include bacterial challenges to assess effectiveness of treatments before any field trials could begin. (Source: Peixoto et al. 2017.)

Assisted Evolution and Coral Reef Resilience

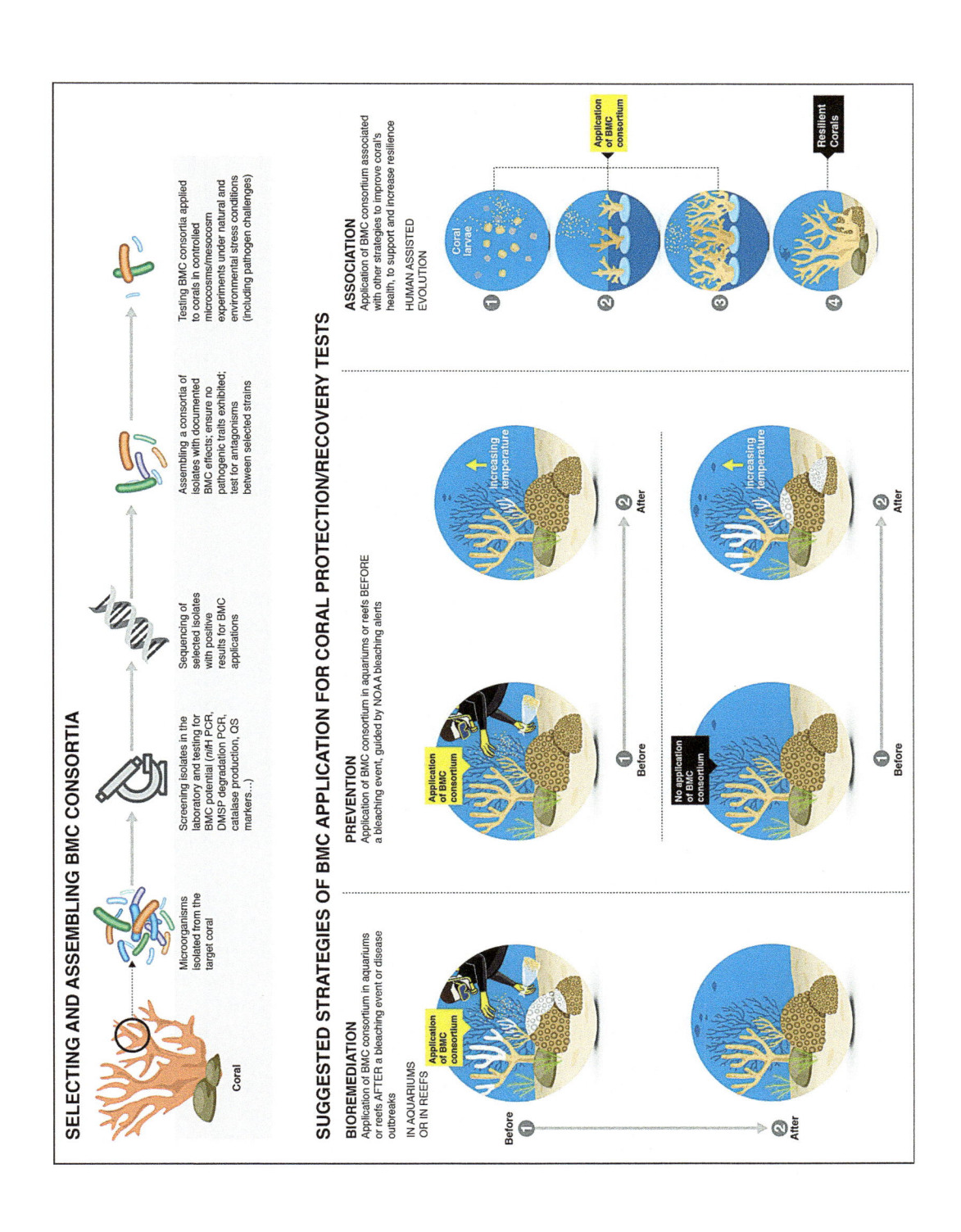

mechanisms (Peixoto et al. 2017). The selection of appropriate culture media can be based on current knowledge of the nutritional requirements of microbes. The inoculation of such microbes can occur with potentially novel applications at different coral life stages—either during the early life stages before zooxanthellae uptake or when they are adults. While it will be important to draw upon successful inoculation strategies that are used for other organisms in order to generate similar methods for corals, novel inoculation applications could include the use of microencapsulation and nanoparticles to heterotrophically feed adult corals and thereby transfer a BMC cocktail directly into the coral's gastrovascular cavity (Peixoto et al. 2017). Alginate, a widely used cost-effective and biodegradable substrate (Sivakumar et al. 2014), could serve as an eco-friendly, scalable method for the encapsulation and delivery of BMCs as heterotrophic feed particles (*coral food packets*) (Peixoto et al. 2017). Ultimately, these applications—and the use of specific BMC consortia inoculants—could be developed with assisted evolution goals in mind, such as the continual inoculation of BMCs during early stages of coral development for increasing coral resilience and survival rates. Additionally, the co-application of phage therapy and BMCs is worth investigating as BMCs could serve to improve coral fitness while phages act directly to control potential pathogens (Kellogg 2007; Cohen et al. 2013; Peixoto et al. 2017). It will be important, however, to establish whether manipulated microbiome components can be vertically transferred from one generation to the next, and prior to that, it will need to be understood that the identification and application of BMCs will be different based on coral life stage and species, as well as geographic region.

Moving forward with coral microbiome research, we still have many questions to consider (refer to Hernandez-Agreda et al. 2017). What are the functional contributions of host-microbe interaction for coral-associated microorganisms other than bacteria and Symbiodiniaceae? To answer this, we may need better tools for studying the activity, diversity, and ecological effects of viruses in hosts and habitats, as well as more sophisticated models for predicting how environmental conditions change the interactions between viruses and their hosts (Thurber et al. 2017). Can we differentiate between healthy (symbiotic) and unhealthy (dysbiotic) microbial states? What roles do factors such as feeding strategy (autotrophy and heterotrophy), feeding time, growth stage, patterns of microbial succession, or immune status play? Prokaryotes can play a role in immunity by disrupting pathogen virulence and producing antimicrobials (Krediet et al. 2013), suggesting potential avenues for manipulation. How stable are coral-microbe associations across different organizational levels, environments, seasons, and life stages? This will be important for determining the relevant timescales governing these interactions, as well as the biotic and abiotic factors that may disrupt symbioses. What is the functional role of ubiquitous bacteria in corals? The habitat in which ubiquitous bacteria reside will certainly influence its functional role in the host and once the spatio-temporal stability of resources available within those habitats is identified, the next step will be to develop methods for replicating those symbiotic conditions within the lab, thereby allowing experimental investigation into the functional characteristics of symbiotic bacteria (Hernandez-Agreda et al. 2017). Finally, what are the mechanisms promoting, maintaining, or disrupting bacterial symbioses in corals? Hernandez-Agreda et. al. (2017) point out that this question relates to the establishment, maintenance, and fidelity of the bacteria–coral symbiosis, and to answer it, it is necessary to determine: (1) the mechanisms of bacterial acquisition (horizontal or vertical uptake), (2) the host corals' role in bacterial species selection and/or the bacterias' abilities to overcome the host immune defense, and (3) the biotic or abiotic factors and the host's role in the disruption of the symbiosis. These questions serve as starting points for further investigation into the feasibility of manipulating the coral microbiome for enhancing holobiont stress tolerance.

Regardless of the numerous avenues down which coral microbiome research could go, either for assisted evolution of corals or basic science, it is imperative to follow strict ethical guidelines, as currently indicated for microbiome research and manipulation of other organisms in order to prevent undesirable side effects (Rhodes et al. 2013; NASEM 2018). Consistent with the current principles of assisted evolution for the natural enhancement of stress tolerance, manipulation of naturally occurring and nongenetically modified microbes is a start. Concurrently, microbiome manipulations/applications must be conducted in well-designed, controlled, experimental systems before field application for initiating reef recovery. A survey of the target reef should be done to determine what components are most appropriate for attempting to improve the health of the site (Peixoto et al. 2017). Furthermore, factors such as the stability of the host-microbial associated community, the microbiome transmission route (i.e., vertical versus horizontal), and the cross-species relationships (neutral, beneficial, or pathogenic) must first be established (Peixoto et al. 2017). There are also risks associated with propagating, incubating, and releasing microbial pathogens into open reef systems. Therefore, disease management and quarantine operating procedures need to be optimized to reduce risks of unintended spread of disease into native populations (NASEM 2018). Also, any added or manipulated members of the coral microbiome need to be extensively tested to prevent them from becoming disease agents for other organisms associated with coral reefs (NASEM 2018). Nevertheless, microorganisms are central to their host's physiology and the microbiome can respond rapidly to the surrounding environment, suggesting its potentially powerful role in influencing coral acclimatization and even adaptation to rapid anthropogenic-driven changes.

INTERSPECIFIC HYBRIDIZATION

Interspecific hybridization is the breeding of individuals from different species, usually within the same genus (*congenerics*). It can occur naturally or through controlled manipulation in the lab (Veron 1995; Willis et al. 1997). On reefs, numerous coral species coexist sympatrically, sexually reproducing in mass spawning events (Harrison et al. 1984; Babcock et al. 1986). Given (1) the apparent absence of temporal barriers to interspecific breeding provided by such mass spawning events, (2) the co-occurrence of high numbers of coral species on reefs where currents mix positively buoyant gametes in a thin layer at the sea surface, and (3) the reliance of the mate recognition system on interactions among gametes for assortative fertilization (Palumbi 1994), opportunities for natural hybridization should be high (Willis et al. 2006). Natural hybridization has in fact played a historic role in the evolution of several coral taxa (Willis et al. 2006; Budd and Pandolfi 2010; Combosch and Vollmer 2015; Arrigoni et al. 2016), which points to its potential significance for restoring fitness as part of a deliberate assisted evolution intervention (NASEM 2018). A consequence of outcrossing between species can be increased novel genetic variation within the hybrid taxon, providing additional materials for mutation, drift, and selection to act upon, and potentially leading to diversification and new adaptations over time (see Chapter 10). Thus, hybridization events are important on evolutionary timescales, generating the capacity for adaptive evolution by increasing genomic diversity and heterozygosity (Miller and van Oppen 2003).

Hybridization and Genetic Adaptation

Hybridization may play a role in enhancing the adaptive potential of a threatened or endangered species by increasing genetic variation, breaking correlations that constrain evolvability of parental lineages, and promoting the acquisition of adaptive traits (Hoffmann and Sgro

2011; Becker et al. 2013; Carlson et al. 2014; van Oppen et al. 2015; Hamilton and Miller 2016; Meier et al. 2017; Chan et al. 2018). For example, rapid hybrid speciation has contributed to the evolutionary success of Darwin's finches where hybridization provided genetic variance in morphology for adapting to changing environments (Grant and Grant 2010). Hybridization can be achieved by targeted crossing of individuals or species carrying desirable phenotypic traits (e.g., thermotolerance). It can also be done by crossing species with the objective of augmenting genetic diversity and novel variation for natural selection to act upon, and possibly generating hybrid vigor (*heterosis* or *outbreeding enhancement*) (e.g., Fogarty 2012) (see Chapter 10). Hybrid vigor is the superiority of hybrid progeny for some trait(s) compared to the parent species (Chan et al. 2018) and is attributed to the masking of deleterious alleles or to greater fitness in heterozygotes compared to homozygotes in diploid organisms (see Chapter 10). Generally though, the relative fitness of hybrids compared to parent species depends on the presence of additive, dominant, over-dominant, or under-dominant gene effects, and/or maternal effects (for explanations and review, refer to Lippman and Zamir 2007; Li et al. 2008; Chen 2013; Chan et al. 2018). These effects need to be accounted for when evaluating interspecific hybridization as potential conservation/restoration interventions.

Hybridization and Coral Reef Restoration

Within the context of restoration, there are many aspects of hybridization—positive and negative—to be considered. For example, hybrid vigor, resulting from dominance or over-dominance, may serve as a desirable outcome if hybrid offspring obtain some combination of beneficial traits from the parental species and prove to be more resilient. Whereas outbreeding depression, the reduction of offspring fitness as a result of crossing too genetically distant individuals or species, can produce inferior offspring (for a review, refer to Hamilton and Miller 2016). It is also important to establish whether prezygotic barriers exist, which can prevent hybridization (Willis et al. 1997). Asynchronous gamete release between related taxa and/or gametic incompatibility are considered the major prezygotic barriers to hybridization between externally fertilizing sympatric species like broadcast-spawning corals (Levitan et al. 2004). If reproductive barriers are not present, hybridization may have positive effects on rates of sexual maturity. Sexual maturity in corals is size-dependent (Soong and Lang 1992; Willis et al. 1997; Smith et al. 2005), and the higher survival and larger recruit size observed in some hybrids may reduce post-settlement mortality (Chan et al. 2018), thereby helping corals to reach a larger size faster and reproduce sooner. This could ultimately promote faster recovery of degraded reef systems.

Moreover, hybridization may conserve genetic diversity by protecting the parental genome from risk of extinction or increase it by combining two divergent genomes within a single individual (Garnett et al. 2011). A notable example is the Florida panther where hybridization successfully enhanced genetic diversity, increased population size, and ultimately rescued the highly inbred remnant population from extinction (Johnson et al. 2010). This is a case of genetic rescue, which can occur naturally or as a mitigation strategy for restoring genetic diversity and reducing extinction risks in small, isolated, and oftentimes inbred populations (Whiteley et al. 2015).

For corals, genetic rescue may serve as a viable mitigation strategy as well. A study investigating the genomic determinants of coral heat tolerance across latitudes found that heat-tolerant genes from corals close to the equator could provide a lifeline to corals suffering elsewhere from the effects of global warming (Dixon et al. 2015). Researchers collected *Acropora millepora* colonies from two locations, 500 km apart, off the Queensland coast in Australia, with the northern location experiencing summer water temperatures of up to 31°C but only up to 29°C at the southern location (Dixon et al. 2015). They used pools to crossbreed the corals and then subjected the larvae to heat stress (35.5°C); their chance of survival was 10 times greater when their parents came from a warmer location (Dixon et al. 2015). Furthermore, after conducting a genomic analysis, they found around 200 genes that were likely responsible for the increased heat tolerance in the offspring, indicating that corals can inherit such genes from their parents (Dixon et al. 2015). While it is already known that corals can gain heat tolerance by acclimatizing to the environment, these results suggest that corals can also rely on genetic rescue to adapt to climate change. Although this example involves distinct populations of the same species, this strategy could serve as an assisted evolution approach via hybridization, where crossbreeding heat-tolerant corals from warmer locations with less-tolerant corals from cooler locations—either from the same or related species—could provide a rapid mechanism for enhanced tolerance in more vulnerable coral populations (NASEM 2018). If indeed separate species are utilized, then a comprehensive assessment of the value of interspecific hybridization to coral reef restoration requires multigeneration fitness examinations of hybrids and backcrosses (Chan et al. 2018). Finally, for corals manipulated in this way, it needs to be understood that there will likely be additional environmental differences, other than just temperature, between distant transplant sites, so crossbred and enhanced populations may still suffer negative fitness effects from translocation (see Chapter 10). Therefore, a comprehensive understanding of the environmental stressors and differences between locations is important.

Hybridization Within the *Acropora* Genus

Most hybridization studies focus on the genus *Acropora* because of its ecological dominance, limited pre- and post-zygotic isolating mechanisms among species (Willis et al. 1997; Fogarty 2012; Fogarty et al. 2012; Baird et al. 2013), and apparent evolutionary success (van Oppen et al. 2001; Willis et al. 2006). There are more than 100 species present in the Indo-Pacific, 70 of which exist in sympatry and many of those which are cross-fertile *in vitro* (Figure 9.14A). Whereas in the Caribbean, there are only three endemic species, *A. cervicornis*, *A. palmata*, and *A. prolifera*, with the latter being a hybrid of the first two (Wallace 1999), based on its intermediate morphology and geographic and allelic distributions (van Oppen et al. 2000) (Figure 9.14B). Rapid environmental degradation and massive population declines in Caribbean populations of *A. cervicornis* and *A. palmata* have resulted in increased natural hybridization and expansion of *A. prolifera* (Fogarty 2012; Japaud et al. 2014; Aguilar-Perera and Hernandez-Landa 2018). Alternative to introgression (i.e., transmission of genetic information from one species to another via hybridization and repeated backcrossing), hybridization may be one such mechanism for producing long-lived asexual hybrid morphotypes that have little evolutionary potential but may occupy nonparental niches, owing to intermediate morphology, like *A. prolifera*, which are F_1 hybrids thought to propagate only asexually (Miller and van Oppen 2003). Indeed, *A. prolifera* has expanded to marginal environments where parent species are absent (Fogarty 2012), but molecular evidence of Caribbean *Acropora* spp. has shown unidirectional gene flow from *A. palmata* into *A. cervicornis*, suggesting that their hybrid, *A. prolifera*, may be fertile and able to backcross with at least one parental species (Vollmer and Palumbi 2002, 2007). Further testing of *A. prolifera* F_1 hybrid fertility is needed to confirm this and to be able to assess if directed hybridization is a viable strategy for Caribbean populations.

Figure 9.14 Comparison of acroporid assemblages on Indo-Pacific reefs (A), where the *Acropora* genus has the greatest diversity of all extant corals (>100 species) and typically dominates coral communities (nearly all corals in the assemblage are acroporids), and on Caribbean reefs (B) where there are only three extant species: *A. cervicornis* (left), *A. palmata* (middle), and their F_1 hybrid, *A. prolifera* (right). (Sources: (top) Zoe Richards; (bottom) Robert Brewer.)

Perhaps more compelling than the Caribbean complex are the numerous Indo-Pacific acroporids that can be used for evaluating interspecific hybridization as a tool for developing coral stock with enhanced climate resilience. A recent study crossed two *Acropora* species pairs from the Great Barrier Reef and examined multiple phenotypic traits over 28 weeks of exposure to ambient and elevated temperature and pCO_2 (Chan et al. 2018) (Figure 9.15). Even though experimental conditions negatively affected size and survival of both purebreds and hybrids, higher survival and larger recruit size were observed in some of the hybrid offspring groups

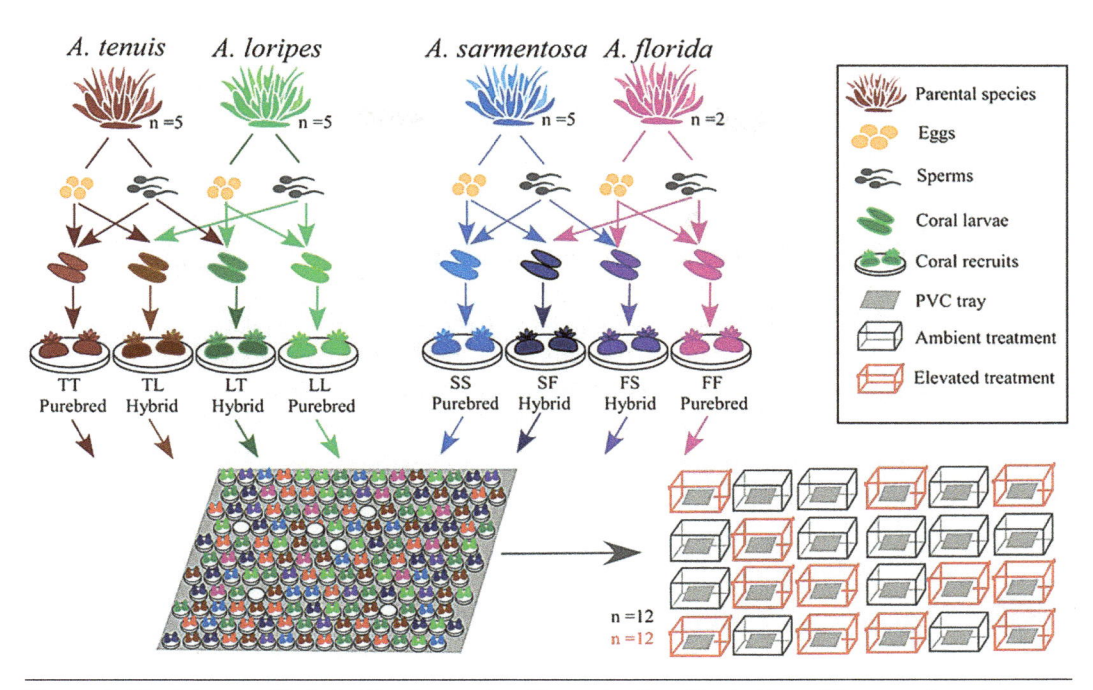

Figure 9.15 Interspecific hybridization and resiliency testing. Illustration of the experimental setup used for conducting interspecific hybridization of multiple *Acropora* spp. pairs. Crosses included *A. tenuis* (T) × *A. loripes* (L) and *A. sarmentosa* (S) × *A. florida* (F), with the four resultant offspring groups from each cross being TT, TL, LT, LL; and SS, SF, FS, FF, respectively (the first letter of the cross denotes the egg donor and the second letter denotes the sperm donor). Comparisons across crosses included larval settlement as well as hybrid and purebred fitness under ambient and elevated conditions. The different colors used for the offspring groups in the figure reflect differently colored settlement plugs used for each offspring group. Ambient and elevated conditions were 27°C, 415 ppm pCO_2 and 28°C, 685 ppm pCO_2, respectively, with the elevated treatment including a ramping-up phase where abiotic stress levels were increased to the target temperature and pCO_2 from ambient at a rate of +0.2°C and + ~50 ppm per day. (Source: Chan et al. 2018.)

under both ambient and elevated conditions (Chan et al. 2018). Hybrids also had high fertilization rates, normal embryonic development, and Symbiodiniaceae uptake and photochemical efficiency similar to purebred offspring (Chan et al. 2018). Yet to be investigated is the fitness of these hybrids in the field, as well as their reproductive and backcrossing potential.

In a follow-up study on interspecific gamete compatibility and hybrid larval fitness, researchers investigated whether the high hybrid fitness of *Acropora* recruits and juvenile colonies was also observable at the larval stage (Chan et al. 2019). Their results showed that while temporal isolation in gamete release between the *Acropora* spp. was limited, gametic incompatibility was present, varied in strength between species pairs, and depended on the direction of the hybrid cross (Chan et al. 2019). Also, after examining the fitness of hybrid and purebred larvae under heat stress, they found that the fitness of the majority of hybrid larvae was similar to that of the purebred larvae of both parental species, and in some cases, it was higher than that of the purebred larvae of one of the parental species (Chan et al. 2019). Collectively, these findings demonstrate that there may be circumstances under which F_1 hybrid *Acropora* might perform better in some environments, and that increased hybrid fitness can be achieved after overcoming partial prezygotic barriers, suggesting that interspecific hybridization may be a tool to enhance coral recruitment and climate resilience.

Discussion and Future Directions

The use of hybrids in coral reef recovery may vary, but a potential benefit of human-mediated hybridization between species would be the development of new forms that have higher fitness than the progenitor species (see Chapter 10). If the goal is to increase coral cover and the long-term fitness of a community using individuals with novel genotypes, then fertile hybrids may be preferred (NASEM 2018). Whereas sterile hybrids may be preferred if the goal is to increase coral cover while reducing impacts on local species diversity (NASEM 2018). Either way, successful hybridization in this context relies on candidate species that can produce viable hybrids following reproduction, fitness comparisons to the progenitor species, and field testing of hybrid performance in different target environments for evaluating their utility.

Furthermore, testing for hybrid fertility (or lack thereof) is essential for determining the long-term consequences of hybridization over several generations because, in some cases, fitness benefits in first generation hybrids dissipate or disappear altogether in future generations (Burton 1990). Testing hybrid fertility is also important during risk assessments because a potential negative outcome is outbreeding depression. This may include the production of a wide range of novel genotypes that include less-fit individuals or the loss of genetic diversity as a result of bottlenecks and using too few individuals in initial crosses (see Chapter 10). Moreover, interactions between hybrids and parental or native species could lead to demographic losses of the latter, through competition or through reproduction with parental species if hybrids are fertile (NASEM 2018). However, competition between hybrids and parental species may be nominal if the reef and parental populations are already severely degraded (NASEM 2018). Natural hybridization between native and invasive species has been shown to cause diversity declines within and among populations (Rhymer and Simberloff 1996; Mooney and Cleland 2001; Neira et al. 2006), and should therefore be avoided as a directed application unless appropriate ecological and genetic risk assessments suggest otherwise. Regardless of application, ecological and genetic risks of hybrids and their fertility should be evaluated with the development of genetic management plans that include clear performance indicators and monitoring plans (NASEM 2018).

In addition to testing F_1 hybrid fertility among targeted crosses, future studies should also investigate hybridization capabilities of coral genera other than *Acropora*. Thus far, experimental crosses that resulted in successfully hybridized species include corals within the *Montipora* and *Platygyra* genera (Willis et al. 1997), whereas failed hybridization was reported for species within the *Ctenactis* genus (Baird et al. 2013)—suggesting the need for such testing in additional coral genera to determine the broad applicability of this approach. Also worth considering is combining interspecific hybridization with methods being developed for deploying coral larvae/recruits onto degraded reefs, an intervention referred to as larval seeding (Amar and Rinkevich 2007; Omori 2010; Nakamura et al. 2011; Villanueva et al. 2012; Guest et al. 2014; dela Cruz and Harrison 2017). Larval seeding is considered a low-tech, affordable, scalable method for enhancing coral settlement and promoting faster recovery of degraded reefs. It can be achieved either by the mass settlement of coral larvae on specially designed, conditioned substrates, which are then affixed to or wedged in degraded reefs (e.g., Chamberland et al. 2017), or via direct seeding of mass-cultured or harvested coral larvae across reef areas (e.g., dela Cruz and Harrison 2017). The efficacy of this latter approach is currently under debate (Heyward et al. 2002; Edwards et al. 2015).

If morphology is a targeted trait (e.g., for promoting resilience against intensifying natural disasters), considering which species donates which gamete (egg or sperm) may be important for predicting hybrid morphology. *A. prolifera* morphology is, for example, dictated by the species that provides the egg (Vollmer and Palumbi 2002). A study conducted in *A. prolifera* in Puerto Rico sampled two distinct morphotypes—bushy and palmate (of which all individuals are F_1 hybrids)—and found that they differed in which species donated its egg and mitochondrion to the hybridization event; all *bushy* hybrids had a *palmata* maternal and mitochondrial background, whereas all of the *palmate* hybrids had a *cervicornis* background (Vollmer and Palumbi 2002) (Figure 9.16). This suggests that maternal and/or cytoplasmic effects account for the marked differences in these two hybrid morphotypes. Thus, coral morphology appears sensitive to not only nuclear genetic effects, but also to nuclear-cytoplasmic interactions within a hybrid nuclear genome (Vollmer and Palumbi 2002). Understanding the interplay of these factors for different target species will help to inform directed hybridization experiments with morphology-based objectives linked to ecological restoration. For example, if certain morphotypes appear to have greater structural integrity or robustness, they may be preferred over morphotypes that are more easily fragmented in regions where severe natural disturbances, like hurricanes, are common.

Finally, Chan et al. (2018) have highlighted key considerations and questions in moving forward with interspecific hybridization as a tool for assisted evolution. When selecting

Figure 9.16 Caribbean acroporids and their different hybrid morphotypes in Puerto Rico. Parental species, (A) *A. cervicornis* and (B) *A. palmata*. F_1 hybrids, *A. prolifera*, as (C) bushy and (D) palmate morphs. (Source: Vollmer and Palumbi 2002.)

species pairs for hybridization to facilitate reef restoration, both targeted crossing with species/individuals that carry phenotypic traits of value under climate change (e.g., high thermotolerance) and nontargeted crossing between species could be considered. Species with high climate resilience, for example, *Acropora loripes* (Chan et al. 2018), may be useful for targeted hybridization efforts, whereas nontargeted crossing among related species could be used to generate hybrid vigor and increase genetic diversity for future adaptation (NASEM 2018). Key questions include: (1) what are the fitness differences of hybrids versus purebreds in the field, which can be tested by outplanting both sets in the field and monitoring their relative fitness over time; (2) what is the reproductive and backcrossing potential of F_1 hybrids, which will help to identify potentially beneficial effects from introgression (i.e., gene flow between species); and (3) what is the fitness of advanced generation hybrids and backcrosses, which will be important for estimating the long-term persistence of such hybrids (Chan et al. 2018). Ideally, F_1 hybrids would reproduce sexually, via hybridization, with other F_1 hybrids and/or backcross with parental species to generate novel genotypes that are climate resilient and to maintain high fitness in advanced generation hybrids and backcrosses (Chan et al. 2019). However, before hybrids can be safely used as stock for restoration, it must be demonstrated that the risk of this strategy is low by showing that the fitness of later generations remains equal or superior to that of the parental species in nature (Chan et al. 2018). Nonetheless, there are increasing calls for the use of interspecific hybridization in the face of rapidly changing environments (Hamilton and Miller 2016) because they may provide adaptive potential beyond that of the phenotypic range of the parental species, along with a means of preserving genomes at the risk of extinction (see Chapter 10) (NASEM 2018).

INTRASPECIFIC MANAGED BREEDING AND GENETIC ADAPTATION

The Importance of Sexual Reproduction for Population Persistence and Coral Reef Restoration

One of the most common methods of coral restoration is population enhancement and reef rehabilitation via coral gardening, where large numbers of asexually propagated coral fragments are raised in land- or field-based nurseries and then outplanted to a degraded reef site to increase live coral cover. This process is well established for multiple species and locations (Rinkevich 2005; Edwards 2010; Johnson et al. 2011; Young et al. 2012). However, since coral fragments are genetically identical to their donor colonies (i.e., they are clones), there is the concern that restored populations will have less genetic diversity than the original population due to repopulation with a large number of fragments from a few donor colonies (Rinkevich 1995, 2000; Baums 2008; Shearer et al. 2009). A genetically depauperate population is more vulnerable to local extinction under environmental stress, especially if variation in traits conferring disease and bleaching resistance is low (Nei et al. 1975; Altizer et al. 2003; McKay et al. 2005).

Importantly, scleractinian species also reproduce sexually and possess multiple reproductive strategies (Harrison 2011) that can be harnessed or manipulated for the purpose of genetic and reproductive interventions. For most species, sexual maturity is size-dependent (Soong and Lang 1992), so extensive fragmentation can reduce the sexual reproductive output and adaptive potential of a population (Zakai et al. 2000; Okubo et al. 2007). This is important because sexual reproduction can promote population persistence in the face of environmental change and facilitate recovery post disturbance where new genotypes are created via recombination, leading to the production of variable offspring—some of which may be better suited to prevailing environmental conditions (Baums 2008; Chamberland et al. 2015). Therefore, prolonged absence of sexual reproduction can lead to reduced genotypic diversity via stochastic loss of genotypes that are not replaced. Evolutionary response requires genetically based variation among individuals, so the preservation of genetic diversity is essential not only for the maintenance of stable productivity in ecosystems, but also for the long-term persistence of natural populations because it promotes resilience by providing a buffer against novel environmental change and the flexibility to adapt (see Chapter 10) (Tilman et al. 1994; Reed and Frankam 2003; Rice and Emery 2003; Baums 2008; Johnson et al. 2011; Baums et al. 2019).

Thus, including coral sexual propagation (also referred to as *assisted sexual reproduction*) within restoration strategies will help to promote the adaptive potential and persistence of restored populations (see Chapter 10) (McKay et al. 2005; Baums 2008; Guest et al. 2014; Baums et al. 2019). For example, genetic and reproductive interventions involving sexually reproducing corals can provide an opportunity to increase genetic diversity within populations to allow them to adapt to changing environmental conditions, or permit selection of traits that may enhance the resilience of degraded coral populations and species at risk (NASEM 2018). Importantly, because corals are highly fecund, sexual reproduction can provide access to millions of propagules, thereby increasing the number of individuals that can be reared for restoration while maintaining genetic diversity (Guest et al. 2014; Chamberland et al. 2015).

As reports of rapid climate change impairing coral recruitment dynamics increase (e.g., Hughes and Tanner 2000; Williams et al. 2008; Albright et al. 2010; Hughes et al. 2019), so does the need for appropriate genetic and reproductive interventions that can address deficits associated with natural recruitment. Recruitment is the process by which sexually produced planulae undergo larval settlement and become part of the adult population. In marine systems, including reef-building corals, larval production and recruitment are fundamental to the self-sustainment of natural populations, replenishment of depleted adult populations, maintenance of population-level resilience, and promotion of faster recovery post disturbance (Underwood et al. 2009; Kleypas et al. 2016; Holbrook et al. 2018). Therefore, the importance of conserving, restoring, and utilizing sexually reproducing corals as part of restoration strategies cannot be understated.

Intraspecific Managed Breeding Regimes

There have been increased investments in developing methods and guidelines for conducting managed breeding in corals (i.e., crossing individuals to generate genotypes exhibiting certain desirable phenotypes and/or to increase genetic variation within offspring populations to be used for restoration) (NASEM 2018; Baums et al. 2019; Randall et al. 2020). Humans have been improving natural plant and animal species for centuries by selecting superior phenotypes stemming from managed breeding regimes (Lind et al. 2012; Morrell et al. 2012; Springer 2013). By extension, the ability of coral reefs to tolerate stressful conditions and recover more quickly after acute events may be enhanced by using genetically resilient or modified coral stocks (Jones and Monaco 2009; van Oppen et al. 2015).

For managed breeding to work though, traits under selection need to be heritable—meaning phenotypic variation in the trait needs to have a genetic basis (i.e., the basis for genetic adaptation). However, trait heritabilities are largely unknown for the majority of coral species. Only a handful of studies thus far have investigated genotype-dependent responses to thermal stress in corals (Meyer et al. 2009; Csaszar et al. 2010; Baums et al. 2013; Kenkel et al. 2013; Polato et al.

2013; Dixon et al. 2015; Kenkel et al. 2015; Dziedzic et al. 2019), the mechanisms underlying pH tolerance (McCulloch et al. 2012a; McCulloch et al. 2012b; Barkley et al. 2017), and the genetic susceptibility of certain genotypes to particular diseases (Muller and van Woesik 2014; Libro and Vollmer 2016; Muller et al. 2018; Miller et al. 2019). However, if desirable traits are heritable, crossing individuals with different resilient traits (e.g., thermotolerance and disease resistance) may generate more robust offspring with beneficial traits inherited from both parents, thereby enhancing the fitness and adaptive potential of offspring populations to be used for restoration. This approach harnesses the power of sexual reproduction for generating novel genotypes and increasing genetic variation while simultaneously increasing resilience within the offspring population.

An important side note, the process of sexual reproduction and recombination shuffling genes, creating new beneficial combinations, and generating genetic variation, already occurs in nature. It becomes inefficient or ineffective, however, when populations are small, patchy, genetically depauperate, have asynchronous spawning, or have reduced connectivity (gene flow) or natural recruitment—which is the case for many contemporary coral populations under rapid degradation and decline (Hughes and Tanner 2000; Hughes et al. 2019; Shlesinger and Loya 2019; Williams et al. 2020). Sexual cycles are also disrupted by chronic stress (e.g., disease) and acute disturbances (e.g., hurricanes and bleaching events) (Richmond 1987; Szmant and Gassman 1990; Rinkevich 1996; Sakai 1998; Lirman 2000; Zakai et al. 2000; Omori et al. 2001). A stressed, diseased, or fragmented coral will likely shift its limited energy resources from sexual reproduction to survival and/or growth if an energy trade-off exists and there is a reproductive cost on colony growth or regeneration during ontogeny (Harrison 2011). Utilizing reproductive interventions may therefore greatly benefit populations/species that are experiencing persistent reproductive failure.

While enhancing coral stress tolerance and population resilience are typically the primary goals, breeding regimes may have different sub-objectives depending on the source of parental colonies to be crossed (NASEM 2018). For example, intraspecific breeding can occur within or between populations of the same species, with slightly different outcomes. Managed breeding within populations supports recovery goals that aim to increase population sizes, and therefore coral cover, while maintaining or increasing local genetic diversity. This strategy may help to promote the long-term persistence of such populations since selection is more efficient in larger populations with increased genetic variation and ability to adapt to changing conditions (see Chapter 10) (Kimura 1983). Alternatively, outcrossing between populations aims to increase fitness within populations by introducing novel genetic variation from other populations through gene flow and sexual reproduction. This approach can be referred to as *assisted gene flow* and may be a viable strategy to help buffer coral populations against global climate change (see Chapter 10) (Aitken and Whitlock 2013). The transmission of novel adaptive alleles into a small, degraded population could save it and lead to increased population fitness through a process called genetic rescue (Hedrick et al. 2011). Similarly, this strategy can also be used to increase population sizes and coral cover, but the potential for outbreeding depression is also higher because it involves crossing individuals that are more genetically dissimilar (see Chapter 10) (Baums 2008). Therefore, characterization of the extent of local adaptation and population structure across target populations, as well as prior knowledge of the fitness of individuals resulting from such crosses within the environment of the reef to be restored, will be necessary (NASEM 2018).

In any case, the process of harvesting coral gametes, performing crosses, settling larvae, and rearing recruits will depend on the target species and its mode of sexual reproduction.

Techniques based on sexual reproductive mode (i.e., broadcasters versus brooders) for mass producing larvae are reasonably well-established (see Chapter 8) (Guest et al. 2010; Omori and Iwao 2016; Randall et al. 2020). Broadcast spawning corals are simultaneous hermaphrodites, producing sperm and eggs at the same time, which are released into the water column during synchronized mass spawning events. Eggs are externally fertilized, followed by development into planktonic larvae (planulae), dispersal, settlement back down to the seafloor, and metamorphosis into a singular polyp that grows and divides to form a new coral colony. Gametes can be harvested in various ways, including in situ gamete collection during mass spawning events (Figure 9.17) or ex situ collection from colonies brought in temporarily to the lab. A collection of sexually mature colonies can be held within an in situ spawning nursery, providing easier and more reliable access to spawning corals (*broodstock*). Techniques for inducing coral spawning ex situ in the lab have also been developed (Craggs et al. 2017; Craggs et al. 2018). With asynchronous spawning between individuals potentially leading to reduced fertilization success or underrepresentation of specific crosses (e.g., Miller et al. 2018; Shlesinger and Loya 2019), inducing corals to spawn may be necessary to achieve such crosses (Craggs et al. 2017).

Figure 9.17 Mass coral spawning. Most scleractinian species are hermaphroditic broadcast spawners that release gamete bundles of sperm and eggs during annual synchronized mass spawning events. (A) Synchronous spawning of outplanted *Acropora tenuis* coral colonies in Japan. (Source: Zayasu and Shinzato 2016.) (B) Close-up of *A. cervicornis* releasing gamete bundles. (Source: Hanna R. Koch.) (C) Close-up of a spawning mountainous star coral (*Orbicella faveolata*). (Source: Olivia Williamson.)

Two-parent crosses can be performed by collecting gamete bundles from different parental genotypes, separating the eggs from sperm to create two gamete stocks for each parent, and then combining them in replicate pairwise fertilization batches (e.g., Baums et al. 2013; Marhaver et al. 2017; Chan et al. 2018). Direct and reciprocal crosses can be conducted where the eggs from one parent are fertilized by the sperm of another parent and vice versa, which can help to identify maternal versus paternal effects. All gametes from multiple parents can be mixed in batch cultures as well (Baums et al. 2013; Pollock et al. 2017). This may lead to greater fertilization success, but the parental identities of resulting offspring will not be readily known unless a parentage analysis is done (Baums et al. 2013), which may not be necessary unless estimation of the heritability of targeted traits is a specific objective (Davies et al. 2015).

Conversely, brooding corals have internal fertilization and embryogenesis before releasing more developed larvae competent for settlement. Most brooding species release larvae in a temporally cyclic mode (Harrison and Wallace 1990), oftentimes triggered by the lunar cycle (Richmond and Hunter 1990). There are species known to release larvae continuously, which allows greater access to brooded larvae that could be used for restoration (Golbuu and Richmond 2007; Nietzer et al. 2018). Certain brooding species, like *Porites astreoides*, have mixed sexuality, where some colonies are hermaphrodites and others are female (Chornesky and Peters 1987). In this case, male gametes (sperm) could be collected from hermaphroditic colonies during monthly spawning events, but not eggs. Rare parthenogenetic reproduction has been documented in some brooding species as well (e.g., *Porites astreoides* and *Pocillopora damicornis*) and involves the development of embryos without sperm/fertilization but leads to larvae genetically identical to the mother (Harrison 2011; Combosch and Vollmer 2013). Consequently, managed breeding may be more difficult in brooding corals if the identity of egg and sperm contributors (i.e., the parents) or whether larvae were produced sexually or parthenogenetically is not readily discernible. Starting with colonies that are sexually immature, virgin females or those that have been held long enough in captivity without exposure to sperm may be necessary to conduct controlled crosses with known parental identity.

Still in the experimental stage are ex situ methods for larval settlement and recruit rearing (Petersen and Tollrian 2001; Nakamura et al. 2011; Okamoto et al. 2012; Ferse et al. 2013; Cooper et al. 2014; Guest et al. 2014). Larval settlement can be carried out using a variety of settlement substrates, which may or may not be preconditioned (Guest et al. 2014; Chamberland et al. 2017; Ricardo et al. 2017), as well as using a variety of settlement cues (e.g., crustose coralline algae (CCA) or bacterial biofilms) (for a review, refer to Dobretsov and Rittschof 2020). Optimal methods will depend on species and available resources (see Chapter 6) (Harrington et al. 2004; Ritson-Williams et al. 2010; Tebben et al. 2015; Whalan et al. 2015; Kegler et al. 2017). Land-based nurseries or similar lab facilities that are equipped with seawater systems and mesocosms are necessary for rearing sexual recruits (Figure 9.18) (see Chapter 5). The utility of in situ larval rearing pools is also being investigated. Resources for learning how to carry out gamete collection, fertilization, larval settlement, and recruit rearing are available through online webinars, coral reef restoration manuals, and published scientific or grey literature (see Chapter 6) (Edwards and Gomez 2007; Hagedorn et al. 2009; Edwards 2010; Chamberland et al. 2015).

Finally, release strategies are also an important component of an effective managed breeding program. Different release strategies of captively reared individuals have been attempted with varying levels of success, but most have included small-scale single generation releases utilizing locally derived broodstock (Nakamura et al. 2011; Villanueva et al. 2012; Guest et al. 2014; dela Cruz and Harrison 2017).

Figure 9.18 Land-based coral nursery. (A) Mote Marine Laboratory's Elizabeth Moore International Center for Coral Reef Research and Restoration in the Florida Keys has a large land-based nursery for growing tens of thousands of coral fragments of a number of endemic scleractinian species within large flow-through mesocosms (*raceways*) with running seawater, air supply, and shading. (B and C) This nursery setup is also used for rearing and propagating hundreds to thousands of sexual recruits that require daily husbandry. A major advantage of land-based nurseries is the practitioner's ability to manipulate environmental conditions and promote optimal coral survivorship and growth year-round. (Sources: (A) Dan Mele; (B and C) Hanna R. Koch.)

Releasing offspring early reduces the time and resources needed for captive rearing, but mortality rates may be higher due to predation and/or competition (Miller 2001; Williams et al. 2014). Examples include larval seeding (e.g., dela Cruz and Harrison 2017) and outplanting early sexual recruits. Alternatively, outplanting or transplanting juveniles may increase survivorship (e.g., Nakamura et al. 2011), but it also requires more time, effort, space, and funds for ex situ rearing. Ultimately, effective reintroduction or release strategies will require risk assessments, appropriate permits, and consideration of larval release versus outplanting juveniles (refer to NASEM 2018). Also necessary is a monitoring strategy for tracking settlement and/or post-settlement survival for evaluating recruitment success and persistence at the target site. Thus, tracking the performance and reproductive success of outplants is essential for determining overall project success.

Broodstock Selection

Establishing a diverse set of broodstock is important and there are a number of ways to identify the best candidates (NASEM 2018). Observation of responses in the natural environment is one way to identify them since natural selection has already acted upon wild populations to generate concentrations of adaptive alleles in habitats with increased exposure to stressful conditions. As a result of the long history of population adaptation across the environmental mosaic of reefs, genetically adapted corals exist and can serve as the raw material for subsequent use (refer to Baums et al. 2019). Therefore, potential broodstock candidates are those found in areas with known levels of elevated stress. For example, areas to look for thermotolerant corals include (1) shallow back reef pools, reef flats, and patch reefs that heat up during daytime low tides, (2) lower latitude locations along latitudinally elongated reefs such as the Great Barrier Reef or the Meso-American Reef, and (3) equatorial locations with high summer temperatures (NASEM 2018). Corals with high thermotolerance can also be identified following acute bleaching events where some corals within a wild population or field-based nursery do not bleach or are able to recover (e.g., Muller et al. 2018). Alternatively, locations to look for corals with increased resistance include (1) harbors where corals may be locally adapted to increased levels of heavy metals, (2) offshore areas where corals may exhibit pesticide resistance as a result of exposure to agricultural runoff, and (3) areas nearby sewer outfalls where corals may experience elevated levels of pharmaceuticals and nutrients, but low oxygen levels (NASEM 2018).

Although there are both genetic and acclimatization components to differential tolerances of corals exposed to environmental stressors, there are a number of ways to disentangle them in the lab to identify genetically adapted corals for breeding. Common garden experiments are frequently used to test for variation in genetically based stress tolerance (Lohr and Patterson 2017; Muller et al. 2018; Suzuki et al. 2018; Morikawa and Palumbi 2019). Such experiments are used to control for phenotypic plasticity and genotype-by-environment interactions by growing individuals from different populations in a common environment to look for inter- or intrapopulation genetic variation. Stress-testing and phenotyping of corals is possible using climate simulator systems where conditions like temperature and pH can be manipulated to test corals under current and/or future environmental conditions (Figure 9.19). Diagnostic biomarkers such as PAM fluorometry can be used as a proxy for photosynthetic function (Warner et al. 2010). Furthermore, molecular tools permit differentiation between evolutionary adaptations to a particular environment as opposed to those that are temporarily acclimatized to change (e.g., Palumbi et al. 2014). These molecular tools include (1) genomics, which can be used to identify genotypic diversity associated with certain habitats and novel genotypes (e.g., Dixon et al. 2015); (2) genome-wide association studies (GWAS), which can help to identify individuals that have a high genomic breeding value for a particular adaptive trait (Crossa et al. 2017); (3) proteomics, which can be used in a diagnostic manner to identify key stressors at certain locations and the genotypes able to effectively respond through protein expression (Downs et al. 2012); and (4) transcriptomics, which can be used to identify gene expression patterns

Figure 9.19 Mote Marine Laboratory's climate simulator system (Climate and Acidification Ocean Simulator). Temperature and pCO_2 conditions can be manipulated for running experiments mimicking future ocean-acidification and climate-change scenarios (left), or held constant to provide optimal, controlled conditions for staging corals brought in from the field for spawning (right). (Sources: (left) Mote Marine Laboratory; (right) Hanna R. Koch.)

linked to particular genotypes that up- or down-regulate responses to specific stressors (e.g., DeSalvo et al. 2010). These tools can be used individually or in concert for evaluating broodstock candidates.

Examples of Candidate Species for Managed Breeding

Species that would greatly benefit from managed-breeding efforts include those that are foundational (i.e., reef-builders) and are experiencing reproductive failure and declines in abundance (Baums et al. 2019). Two exemplary candidates are *A. cervicornis* (staghorn coral) and *A. palmata* (elkhorn coral), which are found throughout the western Atlantic, the Bahamas, and the Caribbean. Once among the most prevalent corals within shallow reefs of the western Atlantic and the Caribbean (Jackson et al. 2001; Pandolfi and Jackson 2001; Pandolfi 2002), these species are now listed as threatened under the U.S. Endangered Species Act due to declines in abundance (coverage and colony numbers) estimated at greater than 97% (for areas where quantified, e.g., Florida Keys, Dry Tortugas, Belize, Jamaica, and the U.S. Virgin Islands) (Acropora Biological Review Team 2005). Losses, predominantly occurring over the last 40 years, are attributed to infectious disease outbreaks, high SSTs, overfishing, habitat degradation, and hurricanes (Precht et al. 2002; Acropora Biological Review Team 2005; Gardner et al. 2005; NMFS 2015; NCCOS 2018; Goergen et al. 2019).

Despite dramatic declines in abundance, *A. cervicornis* presently exhibits relatively high levels of genetic diversity (Drury et al. 2016; Drury et al. 2017) but limited gene flow (Vollmer and Palumbi 2007). Moreover, there is the potential for a future genetic bottleneck within Florida populations, via reduced population connectivity, which could impact the evolutionary potential of this species even further (Hemond and Vollmer 2010). For *A. palmata*, the loss of genotypic diversity is worsening over time, with the rate of decline in Florida accelerating even more since 2014 (Williams et al. 2014; 2020). Scientists have already presumed *A. palmata* to be functionally extinct in Florida (Williams et al. 2020).

Outbreaks of white band disease in the late 1970s and early 1980s are responsible for significant losses within both species (Figure 9.20) (Aronson and Precht 2001b). Despite widespread outbreaks beginning fifty years ago, this disease continues to cause high rates of mortality (Aronson and Precht 2001b; Miller et al. 2014), especially in Florida (Precht et al. 2016). Further, anomalously high SSTs are increasing the probability of disease throughout the region

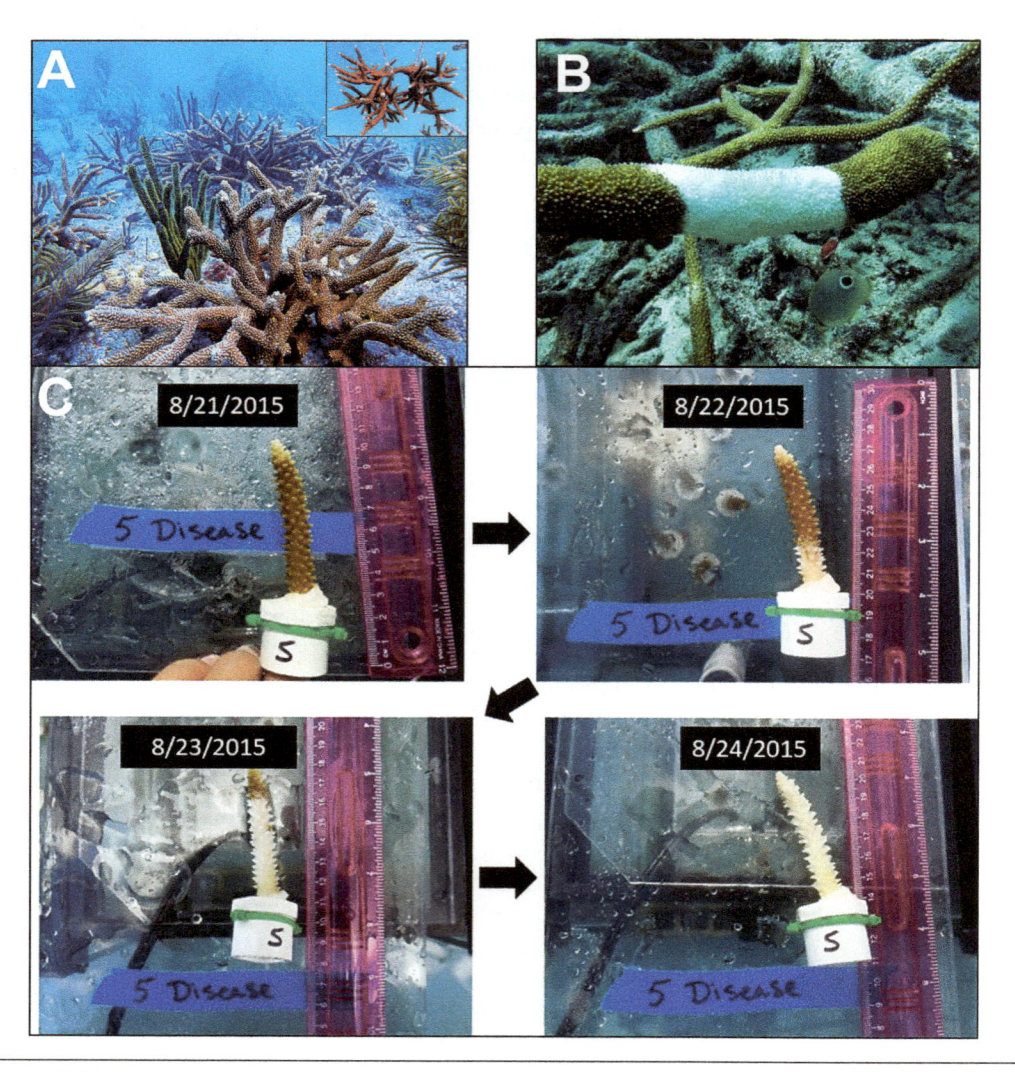

Figure 9.20 *Acropora cervicornis* (staghorn coral) and white band disease. (A) Healthy staghorn coral, a fast-growing branching species that can form large thickets of adult colonies. (Source: Hanna R. Koch.) (B) Staghorn coral infected with white band disease off the coast of Belize. (Source: Lauren Piro.) (C) Digital photograph of an *A. cervicornis* fragment showing typical signs of white band disease spreading from the base of the skeleton to the branch tip over three days. (Source: Muller et al. 2018.)

(Muller et al. 2008; Miller et al. 2009; Edwards et al. 2015; Manzello 2015; Randall and van Woesik 2015).

While our understanding of coral epidemiology is still in its infancy, variation in disease susceptibility of *Acropora* spp. has been documented. For example, 6% of the *A. cervicornis* tested in Panama were resistant to white band disease (Vollmer and Kline 2008), indicating disease resistant variants exist in some locations, albeit in low numbers. A more recent field study found significant genotypic variation in disease susceptibility across 12 genotypes of *A. palmata* and 31 genotypes of *A. cervicornis* within an in situ nursery used for coral reef restoration (Miller et al. 2019). Moreover, while field monitoring suggests that bleached corals are more susceptible to disease (Muller et al. 2008), alternative field observations indicate a negative association between heat tolerance and disease susceptibility in *A. cervicornis* (Merselis et al. 2018).

To further explore the potential relationship between disease resistance and susceptibility to high temperatures, Muller et al. (2018) studied the interaction between these major stressors by conducting two experiments exposing *A. cervicornis* genotypes to white band diseased tissue before and during a coral bleaching event. While 27% of the coral genotypes exhibited disease resistance prior to a thermal anomaly, twice as many died when exposed to white band disease during bleaching (Muller et al. 2018). The loss of disease resistance during the bleaching event was largely attributed to compromised coral hosts or increased pathogenic dose/virulence. Interestingly though, 13% (2 out of 15) of the coral genotypes tested were resistant to the disease even when bleached, and there was no trade-off between disease resistance and temperature tolerance (Baums et al. 2010; Muller et al. 2018; Parkinson et al. 2018). Disease susceptibility was independent of *Symbiodinium* strain, indicating that these traits are driven by host genotype rather than strain variation in *Symbiodinium fitti*, the dominant symbiont in these coral colonies (Baums et al. 2010; Muller et al. 2018; Parkinson et al. 2018). While these findings confirm the notion that susceptibility to temperature stress creates an increased risk of disease-associated mortality, they also show that *A. cervicornis* populations in the lower Florida Keys harbor a few existing genotypes that are resistant to both warming and disease, and that disease resistance and temperature tolerance appear to evolve independently. These last two points are crucial for considering *A. cervicornis* as a candidate for managed breeding of stress-resistant host genotypes; variation in thermotolerance and disease resistance exists, and the two traits do not appear to correlate negatively, suggesting that there is no trade-off between them (Muller et al. 2018).

Design of effective breeding strategies requires an understanding of how genotypes respond to interacting stressors, not just singular selective pressures since multiple traits under selection can lead to trade-offs. At least for some species and traits, this may not be a problem. For example, Muller et al. (2018) discovered that while a particular genotype would not have been chosen as a candidate for managed breeding based on its disease resistance or bleaching susceptibility alone, the observation that this same genotype became disease tolerant when bleached makes it a potentially valuable genotype. Thoughtfully incorporating these traits, along with the potential for fitness trade-offs, into managed breeding and restoration initiatives may increase the likelihood of population-based recovery.

Furthermore, managed breeding has the potential to help mitigate the effects of persistent recruitment failure that has been documented for these species (Williams et al. 2008; Kuffner and Toth 2016). Asexual reproduction dominates many Caribbean reefs (Miller et al. 2018), especially for branching corals like *A. cervicornis* and *A. palmata* (Tunnicliffe 1981; Lirman 2000; Kuffner and Toth 2016). These species rely heavily on physical disturbance and fragmentation for propagation and population growth (Tunnicliffe 1981; Highsmith 1982; Fong and Lirman 1995), but still engage in sexual reproduction, usually once a year, to produce larvae for dispersal and recruitment (Szmant 1986). However, with reports of declining coral cover (Gardner et al. 2003), spawning asynchronicity (Miller et al. 2016), genotype incompatibilities (Baums et al. 2013; Miller et al. 2018), and persistent recruitment failure (Dustan 1977; Baums et al. 2005; Williams et al. 2008; Albright et al. 2010; Williams et al. 2014), the current supply of coral larvae appears insufficient to maintain and replenish adult populations (Vermeij 2006; Gleason and Hofmann 2011). Moreover, if adult populations are low in density and patchy, the Allee effect—the decrease in gamete density and subsequent fertilization of eggs—may be more pronounced and contribute further to failed recruitment and population recovery (Doropoulos et al. 2017). In fact, in a Florida elkhorn population that was monitored over a 15-year period, no new larval recruits were observed (Williams et al. 2008; Williams et al. 2014). Therefore, the establishment of breeding initiatives that start with large collections of gametes and end with releases of large numbers of resilient larvae, recruits, or juveniles, could significantly help to achieve increased population sizes and genetic variation (NASEM 2018). In this way, outplanting hundreds or thousands of sexually produced offspring, which are all genetically unique, bolsters restored populations by accelerating the process of genetic restoration by a single generation. Finally, *Acropora* outplants have been shown to reach sexual maturity within two years (Schopmeyer et al. 2017), indicating that managed breeding and active restoration have the propensity to drive restored populations to a sexually mature, self-sustaining state relatively quickly.

Discussion and Future Directions

Genetic and reproductive interventions offer a scalable means for promoting population resilience and coral reef persistence. The controlled and careful outcrossing of genetically distinct individuals in a managed setting can be done to create a captive population with substantial genetic diversity, and individuals from those captive propagation efforts can then be released into the wild to increase the genetic diversity of native populations and introduce new, resilient genotypes (NASEM 2018). Scalability of proven breeding practices will depend on a number of factors, including available resources and program-specific objectives, and relevant regulatory frameworks. Ultimately the development of an effective breeding program relies on the maintenance of diverse populations, clear program objectives, and clearly outlined broodstock management and release protocols, as well as long-term monitoring and performance tracking strategies (NASEM 2018).

Risks

Breeding initiatives need to consider the risks that are associated with crossing and reintroduction. For example, managing the risks of managed breeding within populations will depend on (1) the ability of the rearing program to sample sufficient diversity from natural populations, (2) the preservation of that genetic diversity throughout the captive rearing program, (3) the prevention of adaptation to culture conditions, (4) the maintenance of an optimal effective population size of the reintroduced individuals, and (5) the assurance of high reintroduction success (NASEM 2018). Even though coral species are fecund, they can display variation in reproductive success, including genotype incompatibilities (Baums et al. 2013; Miller et al. 2018)—meaning captive rearing could result in the release of many individuals representing a few families. If too few captive-reared families are used to generate offspring populations for restoration, they may end up dominating and eventually supplanting the natural population, leading to a genetic bottleneck (i.e., the loss of genetic diversity and further limited capability to respond to environmental change and stress) (see Chapter 10). Generally though, utilizing a diverse broodstock, adding new genotypes over time, rearing numerous different families, and moderating release sizes will help to mitigate the genetic effects of captive rearing and prevent negative outcomes like founder effects (i.e., the loss of genetic variation that occurs when a new population is established by a very small number of individuals from a larger population) (see Chapter 10). Another possible negative outcome of outcrossing is a reduction in offspring fitness as a result of outbreeding depression where recombination between different parental genomes disrupts interacting co-adapted loci that are inherited together (see Chapter 10). The breakdown of co-adapted gene complexes, and its effects on offspring fitness, may be observable in the first or subsequent generations (refer to NASEM 2018). Nonetheless, trials can be carried out using colonies from distinct habitats on the same reef, colonies from nearby reefs, or from more distant reefs to access a larger window of genetic diversity (see Chapter 10) (refer to Baums et al. 2019).

Finally, selection acting upon a trait(s) can lead to trade-offs with other traits, whether through limited energy allocation or genetic constraints. An experiment imposing a selection regime or focused on enhancing the resilience of a particular trait needs to consider the potential for fitness trade-offs. Trade-offs may occur regardless, but selectively bred corals may have offspring populations with enough variation in phenotypic responses to reveal that some offspring have reduced trade-offs and are still good candidates for restoration.

Timelines
Timelines associated with breeding regimes will depend on the target species (i.e., fast-growing branching versus slow-growing massive corals), but will most likely require multiple years for identifying broodstock candidates, collecting gametes, performing controlled crosses in the lab, settling larvae, rearing recruits, evaluating offspring performance, carrying out release strategies, and monitoring. Some species only spawn once a year, greatly reducing the number of opportunities for collecting gametes and increasing the time necessary to make progress. However, methods for ex situ induction of coral spawning have been developed, which should help to reduce the timelines that are associated with managed breeding (Craggs et al. 2017; Craggs et al. 2018). Advances in molecular tools (e.g., *-omics*) can also help to more swiftly identify the mechanisms and responses through which stony corals survive stress, which will aid in the appropriate selection of candidate colonies or genotypes for managed breeding trials (refer to NASEM 2018).

Ecosystem-Based Restoration
As the establishment of breeding initiatives grows, researchers should explore breeding capabilities across different coral species, functional types, and reproductive modes, which can then be used in concert within restoration initiatives for promoting coral reef resilience at the community and ecosystem levels as well. A diversity of corals, and hence reef structure, better supports coral-associated assemblages (Graham et al. 2006; Wilson et al. 2006), as well as ecosystem functions and services (Bellwood et al. 2004). Moreover, having a diversity of robust genotypes and species should help to promote reef persistence when multiple stressors (e.g., disease, pollution, sedimentation, temperature, or acidification) and/or trade-offs in tolerance to different stressors are present. Corals with genotypes that are already resistant to multiple stressors may already exist and be used for managed breeding (NASEM 2018). For example,

corals occurring near watershed discharge points, where conditions typically involve multiple selective pressures like high levels of sediments and toxicants but low levels of light and salinity, most likely have already undergone natural selection in order for them to persist there. Ultimately, the decision to focus on increasing the cover of resilient genotypes or species and/or to focus on maintaining diversity will be driven by reef management goals and values at the local level (NASEM 2018).

That said, coral genotypes/species targeted for managed breeding should be chosen to reflect the conservation needs of a particular habitat or region. Within the Caribbean, there are five to seven main reef-building species (Gladfelter et al. 1978), but there are many more within the Indo-Pacific (DeVantier et al. 2006). Along the Florida Reef Tract, for example, reef-building species are under intense stress due to rising temperatures and disease prevalence (Kuffner et al. 2015; Manzello 2015; Precht et al. 2016), as well as intensifying natural disasters like hurricanes (Gardner et al. 2005; NCCOS 2018). The Florida Keys from Key West to Key Biscayne face a 16% chance of hurricane impacts in any given year (NOAA Hurricane Research Division). Across the Caribbean, coral cover is reduced by 17%, on average, in the year following a hurricane impact, and the magnitude of immediate loss increases with hurricane intensity and frequency (Gardner et al. 2005). With research showing a long-term reduction in skeletal density of certain corals along the Florida Reef Tract (Rippe et al. 2018), the impacts of intensifying hurricanes on individual corals and reef structures may be exacerbated even more. Thus, corals displaying increased skeletal density, in addition to increased thermotolerance and disease resistance, would be ideal candidates for managed breeding (as long as traits are heritable).

Cryopreservation
Breeding regimes should consider the use of cryopreservation as a tool for increasing genetic variation in critically endangered species, as well as for more successfully sexually propagating species/populations with high spawning asynchronicity or that are not well-connected (NASEM 2018). Declining environmental conditions and populations may result in less synchronized spawning events (Shlesinger and Loya 2019), which will preclude the cross-fertilization of corals spawning on different nights because coral gametes are only viable for a limited number of hours post release. Furthermore, if clonal colonies spawn at the same time but no other genotypes do, selfing may be the only outcome, which is generally undesirable (see Chapter 10). By cryopreserving coral sperm, a process which freezes cells in a way that they remain viable after being thawed, scientists can essentially preserve this genetic material for later use. The preserved sperm can be used for crossing with fresh eggs released from a different colony at a different time or location. While much of the effort for corals has focused on gamete preservation, particularly sperm, there have been some efforts to test methods to cryopreserve embryonic material, larvae, and adult tissues (Hagedorn et al. 2013; Hagedorn and Carter 2016; NASEM 2018). The use of cryopreservation has already led to the successful implementation of assisted gene flow among distant populations of an endangered species in the Caribbean and western Atlantic (Hagedorn et al. 2017; Hagedorn et al. 2019) and therefore shows promise for similar conservation and assisted evolution objectives. Furthermore, cryopreservation is a powerful tool for maintaining diverse genetic repositories of existing species that are endangered in the wild and preventing further loss of genetic variation as populations decline (i.e., a *coral gene bank*) (Hagedorn and Carter 2016).

Integrating Growth and Reproductive Interventions to Maximize Sexual Reproductive Success

It is important that restored populations become self-sustaining through natural sexual cycles as quickly as possible (Baums et al. 2019), but with sexual maturity being size-dependent (Harvell and Grosberg 1988; Babcock 1991; Soong and Lang 1992; Hall and Hughes 1996), it could take several years, or even decades, to reach that point because corals grow so slowly, especially under stressful conditions (De'ath et al. 2009). Thus, the benefit of combining growth and reproductive interventions may be two-fold: (1) it can help to get outplants and restored populations to a sexually mature state sooner so that populations are self-sustaining, but also so that sexually mature outplants can be used as gamete sources for managed breeding efforts, and (2) it can serve as a means to create sexually mature colonies more quickly in the lab that can also be used as broodstock for ex situ spawning and breeding (Figure 9.21).

Such growth interventions include micro-fragmentation and reskinning (Figure 9.21) (Forsman et al. 2015; Page et al. 2018). With micro-fragmentation, corals are cut into small uniform pieces, with optimal fragment size (e.g., one to five polyps) depending on the polyp size and colony morphology of the species. Without knowing the exact mechanism, but probably related to processes responsible for rapid wound healing (Palmer et al. 2011; Traylor-Knowles 2016), this fragmentation process stimulates the coral tissue to grow up to 50 times faster (Mote *unpublished data*). The fragments are then grown in a land- or field-based nursery before being outplanted onto degraded reefs in arrays of 7–20 fragments of the same genotype, with different arrays based on different genotypes and numerous genotypes outplanted at any given site. Because the fragments within an array are clones, they do not compete, and instead fuse to form a larger colony faster (Figure 9.21). Decades-old sized colonies can thus be created in a matter of two to three years, significantly cutting down the time necessary to reach the onset of puberty. Clonal fragments can also be dispersed across the surface of a deceased coral's skeleton, a process called reskinning, to promote faster recolonization of a dead coral head (Figure 9.21) (Page 2015). Ultimately, this strategy will help to (1) restore large reef areas in a shorter amount of time, (2) ensure that there is sufficient genetic and phenotypic variation to support population resilience in the face of environmental change, (3) drive outplants to a larger, sexually mature state sooner, and (4) ensure that there is sufficient genotypic diversity to support successful sexual reproduction when the corals becomes sexually mature. The outplants can then be used as gamete sources for managed breeding efforts. Similarly, micro-fragmentation and reskinning can be used to create sexually mature colonies in the lab, which are then used as broodstock within ex situ spawning systems.

The offspring generated from such efforts can be directly outplanted or used for further research. For example, the offspring can be screened for variation in stress tolerance by exposing them to contemporary and/or future projected conditions, based on temperature and pH, using a climate simulator system (Figure 9.19). Genotypes particularly resilient to current conditions can be moved into propagation pipelines for resilience-based restoration. If the genes underlying resilience can be identified, then such offspring could be candidates for selective breeding. Alternatively, offspring showing resilience to future conditions can be *banked* in a land nursery. Since climate change conditions are expected to worsen (IPCC 2018), creating and maintaining a gene bank of corals that are resilient to future conditions will be invaluable because they can be used as broodstock/nursery stock for future managed breeding and restoration schemes.

A candidate for this type of work is *Orbicella faveolata* (mountainous star coral), one of the most important reef-building species in the Caribbean and the western Atlantic (Rippe et al.

2017). Recent epizootics of virulent coral diseases and bleaching events have led to high mortality rates, compromised reproductive output, persistent recruitment failure, and thus, drastically reduced population sizes (Knowlton et al. 1992; Hughes and Tanner 2000; Bruckner and Bruckner 2006; Miller et al. 2006; Bruckner and Hill 2009; Weil et al. 2009; van Woesik et al. 2014; Edmunds 2015; Meyer et al. 2019; Muller et al. 2020). Traits like slow growth and long-life span inhibit rapid recovery following mortality events (Gladfelter et al. 1978). As such, the *Orbicella* spp. complex was listed as threatened under the U.S. Endangered Species Act in 2014 (NMFS 2014). Owing, however, to its historical significance to Caribbean reef structures (Jackson 1992), concerted restoration efforts across the western Atlantic and the Caribbean are currently underway.

For example, as part of the Coral Reef Restoration Program at Mote Marine Laboratory's Elizabeth Moore International Center for Coral Reef Research and Restoration in the Florida Keys, scientists are studying, screening, stress-testing, propagating, and outplanting several endemic species, including *O. faveolata*. In addition, species that are susceptible to the stony coral tissue loss disease, including *O. faveolata* (Aeby et al. 2019; Meyer et al. 2019; Muller et al. 2020), are the focus of Mote's Florida Keys Coral Disease Response & Restoration Initiative, which specifically aims to identify and outplant disease resistant or resilient genotypes. As part of this process, scientists use the micro-fragmentation-reskinning methodology to accelerate the growth of outplanted brain, boulder, and star corals in order to rapidly reskin dead coral heads and increase and promote the faster onset of puberty and sexual reproduction (Figure 9.21) (see Chapters 6 and 7) (Forsman et al. 2015; Page et al. 2018).

Figure 9.21 (see facing page) Photographic outline of a resilience-based coral reef restoration strategy incorporating growth and reproductive interventions, including micro-fragmentation, re-skinning, and managed breeding, with *Orbicella faveolata* as an example. Resilient genotypes (A) are identified via stress-test experiments or by locating survivors of acute/chronic stress events in nature; traits of interest may include increased skeletal density, bleaching and disease resistance or resilience, rapid wound healing, increased reproductive output, and tolerance to nutrient exposure, herbicides, and other pollutants. The wild colony (B) or captive coral (C) is cut into micro-fragments of similar size and then (D) grown out in a land- or field-based nursery for several months. Replicate clonal fragments (e.g., 7–20) are outplanted as arrays so that when they are fully fused, they are roughly the puberty size of that species (e.g., 15–30 cm diameter). The arrays can be affixed to various types of substrates, such as a ceramic or cement dome (E) for rapid growth and fusion ex situ—or outplanted onto a degraded reef or dead coral skeleton for in situ growth and fusion (F–G). Upon fusion, the sexual maturity of outplants can be assessed by taking a small (~1 cm^3) core sample to check for the presence of gametes developing within the colony (H) or core (I). A core sample revealing a string of mature pink-orange eggs to the right of a ribbon of sperm (J). Gametes are harvested (K) ex situ or (L) in situ, with (M) gamete bundle *setting* serving as a visual cue of imminent spawning because the bundles are moved into position for release and visible by eye. Following fertilization and larval settlement (N–U), sexual recruits are reared under optimal conditions in the lab. (N) Four-week-old sexual recruit in the early stages of zooxanthellae uptake, followed by (O) full zooxanthellae acquisition and new tentacular growth two weeks later. Blue light technology and natural coral fluorescence can be used to identify/quantify microscopic recruits (P). The primary polyp (Q) continues to grow, eventually (R) budding to form new polyps within days or months, depending on the species (nine-month-old recruit shown here). Within one (S–T) to two years (U) for slow-growing species (or ~six months for fast-growing species), the genetically diverse, stress-tolerant juvenile corals can be directly outplanted, micro-fragmented, and put through the pipeline again, and/or used for research experiments and new rounds of stress testing. (Sources: (A) Mote Marine Laboratory (MML); (B, D–G, I–J, L–M, S–T) Hanna R. Koch/MML; (C, K) Dan Mele; (H) Sarah Hamlyn/MML; (N–O, U) Lydia Wasmer/MML; (P–R) Cody Engelsma/MML.)

Assisted Evolution and Coral Reef Resilience 199

Recent results from this seminal work in Florida have demonstrated the power of this approach where outplanted arrays of mountainous star coral were documented to be fully fused within two to three years—depending on the number and spacing of fragments—and reproductively viable within five years (Mote *unpublished data*). Replicate outplants, ranging in size from 15 to 30 cm in diameter, spawned in 2020 with high synchrony during the peak spawning window predicted for this species (i.e., six to eight nights after the August full moon) (Figure 9.21). These are the first corals of any slow-growing massive or mounding species documented to reach sexual maturity and spawn after being restored in Florida or Caribbean waters (Mote *unpublished data*). What this means for coral reef restoration worldwide is that this approach can be used to successfully create reproductively viable corals in a fraction of the time, which ultimately supports faster population and reef recovery.

These results also showcase how a restoration approach is further bolstered by the use of resistant or stress-tolerant corals (i.e., *resilience-based restoration*). Indeed, within the five years since being outplanted (in 2015), Mote's restored mountainous star corals survived multiple bleaching events, a Category-4 hurricane in 2017, and the stony coral tissue loss disease outbreak that occurred at this site in 2019 (Mote *unpublished data*). By extension, this approach can be applied to any other species and used to create sexually mature colonies in the lab as well. Such corals can then be placed into ex situ spawning systems for induced spawning and breeding (e.g., Craggs et al. 2017). Thus, combining growth and reproductive interventions in both the field and the lab can support multiple overlapping objectives related to asexual and sexual restoration.

CONCLUSIONS

Already 50% of the world's tropical corals have been lost in the last 50 years (Pandolfi et al. 2003; Burke et al. 2011; Hughes et al. 2017; Hughes et al. 2018), and up to 90% could disappear by 2050 (Donner et al. 2005; Frieler et al. 2013; van Hooidonk et al. 2016). As such, there have been increased investments in developing, refining, and upscaling science-based interventions to increase the resilience of coral reefs. Assisted evolution serves as a biological toolbox for enhancing resilience and mitigating the impacts of disturbance, with the overarching goal to sustain or restore essential ecosystem services and biodiversity in the face of rapid climate change (van Oppen et al. 2015, 2017). Assisted evolution approaches vary in methodology, genetic underpinnings, timeline, and level of intervention and risk. Strategies may also differ depending on target species and region. Before these strategies are embedded within restoration initiatives, they should be developed in such a way that they are guided by historical information, contribute to the restoration of ecological function and structure, and include modified stocks with genetic diversity that is sufficient for adaptation to contemporary (and possibly future) selection pressures (van Oppen et al. 2017). Because coral species represent different functional groups, enhanced coral stock should be developed for species representing branching, massive, and encrusting forms so that coral reef functionality and dimensionality are not lost. Furthermore, for those interested in harnessing these strategies, it is suggested to begin with those requiring the lowest level of intervention and move up (Jones 2003; Hobbs et al. 2014; van Oppen et al. 2017). To help guide such efforts, van Oppen et al. (2017) created a decision tree for coral reef restoration, which includes assisted evolution strategies. Also imperative to the process is the inclusion of risk/benefit analyses, ecologically and evolutionary sound practices (see Chapter 10), socioeconomic considerations, ethical perspectives, and active discussions with experts in the field. These factors will help to ensure that the social and experimental feasibility of assisted evolution develops in step and that appropriate solutions can be administered without major delays or public controversy (van Oppen et al. 2017). In conclusion, given the profound importance of coral reefs to both humans and the natural world, concerted efforts to conserve, restore, and prepare these vital ecosystems for the future should continue with haste.

ACKNOWLEDGMENTS

I would genuinely like to thank Dr. Abigail Clark and Michele Mason for providing valuable feedback on this work, and Nils Ehmke for unconditional support. This work was carried out under a Postdoctoral Research Fellowship awarded to HK by the German Research Foundation (DFG, #394448490).

REFERENCES

Abrego, D., K. E. Ulstrup, B. L. Willis, and M. J. H. van Oppen. 2008. "Species-specific interactions between algal endosymbionts and coral hosts define their bleaching response to heat and light stress." *P Roy Soc B-Biol Sci*, 275, 2273–2282.

Abrego, D., M. Van Oppen, and B. Willis. 2009. "Onset of algal endosymbiont specificity varies among closely related species of *Acropora* corals during early ontogeny." *Mol Ecol*, 18, 3532–3543.

Acropora Biological Review Team. 2005. "Atlantic Acropora status review." In: *Report to National Marine Fisheries Service*.

Aguilar-Perera, A. and R. C. Hernandez-Landa. 2018. "Occurrence of large thickets of *Acropora prolifera* (Scleractinia: Acroporidae) in the southern Gulf of Mexico." *Mar Biodivers* 48, 2203–2205.

Ainsworth, T. D. and R. D. Gates. 2016. "Corals' microbial sentinels: The coral microbiome will be key to future reef health." *Science* 352, 1518–1519.

Ainsworth, T. D., L. Krause, T. Bridge, G. Torda, J. B. Raina, M. Zakrzewski, et al. 2015. "The coral core microbiome identifies rare bacterial taxa as ubiquitous endosymbionts." *Isme J* 9, 2261–2274.

Aitken, S. N. and M. C. Whitlock. 2013. "Assisted gene flow to facilitate local adaptation to climate change." *Ann Rev Ecol Evol Syst*, 44, 367–374.

Albright, R., L. Caldeira, J. Hosfelt, L. Kwiatkowski, J. K. Maclaren, B. M. Mason, et al. 2016. "Reversal of ocean acidification enhances net coral reef calcification." *Nature* 531, 362–368.

Albright, R., B. Mason, M. Miller, and C. Langdon. 2010. "Ocean acidification compromises recruitment success of the threatened Caribbean coral *Acropora palmata*." *P Natl Acad Sci USA* 107, 20400–20404.

Albright, R., Y. Takeshita, D. A. Koweek, A. Ninokawa, K. Wolfe, T. Rivlin, et al. 2018. "Carbon dioxide addition to coral reef waters suppresses net community calcification." *Nature* 555, 516–19.

Amar, K.O. and B. Rinkevich. 2007. "A floating mid-water coral nursery as larval dispersion hub: Testing an idea." *Mar Biol* 151, 713–718.

Anderson, K. D., N. E. Cantin, S. F. Heron, C. Pisapia, and M. S. Pratchett. 2017. "Variation in growth rates of branching corals along Australia's Great Barrier Reef." *Sci Rep-Uk* 7.

Anthony, K., L. K. Bay, R. Costanza, J. Firn, J. Gunn, P. Harrison, et al. 2017. "New interventions are needed to save coral reefs." *Nat Ecol Evol* 1, 1420–1422.

Antonovics, J. 1976. "Nature of limits to natural selection." *Ann Mo Bot Gard* 63, 224–247.

Apprill, A., L. G. Weber, and A. E. Santoro. 2016. "Distinguishing between microbial habitats unravels ecological complexity in coral microbiomes." *Msystems* 1.

Aranda, M., Y. Li, Y. J. Liew, S. Baumgarten, O. Simakov, M. C. Wilson, et al. 2016. "Genomes of coral dinoflagellate symbionts highlight evolutionary adaptations conducive to a symbiotic lifestyle." *Sci Rep-Uk* 6.

Armoza-Zvuloni, R., R. Segal, E. Kramarsky-Winter, and Y. Loya. 2011. "Repeated bleaching events may result in high tolerance and notable gametogenesis in stony corals: *Oculina patagonica* as a model." *Mar Ecol Prog Ser* 426, 149–159.

Aronson, R. B. and W. F. Precht. 2001a. "Applied paleoecology and the crisis on Caribbean coral reefs." *Palaios* 16, 195–196.

———. 2001b. "White-band disease and the changing face of Caribbean coral reefs." *Hydrobiologia* 460, 25–38.

Arrigoni, R., F. Benzoni, T. I. Terraneo, A. Caragnano, and M. L. Berumen. 2016. "Recent origin and semi-permeable species boundaries in the scleractinian coral genus *Stylophora* from the Red Sea." *Sci Rep-Uk* 6.

Babcock, R. C. 1991. "Comparative demography of 3 species of scleractinian corals using age-dependent and size-dependent classifications." *Ecol Monogr* 61, 225–244.

Babcock, R. C., G. Bull, P. Harrison, A. Heyward, J. Oliver, C. Wallace, et al. 1986. "Synchronous spawnings of 105 scleractinian coral species on the Great Barrier Reef." *Mar Biol* 90, 379–394.

Baird, A. H., V. R. Cumbo, J. Figueiredo, and S. Harii. 2013. "A pre-zygotic barrier to hybridization in two con-generic species of scleractinian corals." *F1000Res* 2.

Baird, A. H., J. R. Guest, and B. L. Willis. 2009. "Systematic and biogeographical patterns in the reproductive biology of scleractinian corals." *Annu Rev Ecol Evol S* 40, 551–571.

Baird, A. H. and P. A. Marshall. 2002. "Mortality, growth and reproduction in scleractinian corals following bleaching on the Great Barrier Reef." *Mar Ecol Prog Ser* 237, 133–141.

Baker, A. C. 2001. "Ecosystems—Reef corals bleach to survive change." *Nature* 411, 765–766.

———. 2003. "Flexibility and specificity in coral-algal symbiosis: Diversity, ecology, and biogeography of Symbiodinium." *Annu Rev Ecol Evol S* 34, 661–689.

Baker, A. C., C. J. Starger, T. R. McClanahan, and P. W. Glynn. 2004. "Corals' adaptive response to climate change." *Nature* 430, 741.

Barkley, H. C., A. L. Cohen, D. C. McCorkle, and Y. Golbuu. 2017. "Mechanisms and thresholds for pH tolerance in Palau corals." *J Exp Mar Biol Ecol* 489, 7–14.

Barnett, T. P., D. W. Pierce, and R. Schnur. 2001. "Detection of anthropogenic climate change in the world's oceans." *Science* 292, 270–274.

Barrick, J. E. and R. E. Lenski. 2013. "Genome dynamics during experimental evolution." *Nat Rev Genet* 14, 827–839.

Baums, I. B. 2008. "A restoration genetics guide for coral reef conservation." *Mol Ecol* 17, 2796–2811.

Baums, I. B., A. C. Baker, S. W. Davies, A. G. Grottoli, C. D. Kenkel, S. A. Kitchen, et al. 2019. "Considerations for maximizing the adaptive potential of restored coral populations in the western Atlantic." *Ecol Appl* 29.

Baums, I. B., M. K. Devlin-Durante, N. R. Polato, D. Xu, S. Giri, N. S. Altman, et al. 2013. "Genotypic variation influences reproductive success and thermal stress tolerance in the reef building coral, *Acropora palmata*." *Coral Reefs* 32, 703–717.

Baums, I. B., M. E. Johnson, M. K. Devlin-Durante, and M. W. Miller. 2010. "Host population genetic structure and zooxanthellae diversity of two reef-building coral species along the Florida Reef Tract and wider Caribbean." *Coral Reefs* 29, 835–842.

Baums, I. B., M. W. Miller, and M.E. Hellberg. 2005. "Regionally isolated populations of an imperiled Caribbean coral, *Acropora palmata*." *Mol Ecol* 14, 1377–1390.

Bay, R. A., N. H. Rose, C. A. Logan, and S. R. Palumbi. 2017. "Genomic models predict successful coral adaptation if future ocean warming rates are reduced." *Sci Adv* 3.

Becker, M., N. Gruenheit, M. Steel, C. Voelckel, O. Deusch, P. B. Heenan, et al. 2013. "Hybridization may facilitate in situ survival of endemic species through periods of climate change." *Nat Clim Change* 3, 1039–1043.

Bell, G. 2013. "Evolutionary rescue and the limits of adaptation." *Philos T R Soc B* 368.

Bell, J. T. and T. D. Spector. 2011. "A twin approach to unraveling epigenetics." *Trends Genet* 27, 116–125.

Bellwood, D., T. Hughes, C. Folke, and M. Nystrom. 2004. "Confronting the coral reef crisis." *Nature* 429, 827–833.

Berkelmans, R. and M. van Oppen. 2006. "The role of zooxanthellae in the thermal tolerance of corals: A 'nugget of hope' for coral reefs in an era of climate change." *P Roy Soc B-Biol Sci* 273, 2305–2312.

Bernardo, J. 1996. "The particular maternal effect of propagule size, especially egg size: Patterns, models, quality of evidence and interpretations." *Am Zool* 36, 216–236.

Blackall, L. L., B. Wilson, and M. J. H. van Oppen. 2015. "Coral—the world's most diverse symbiotic ecosystem." *Mol Ecol* 24, 5330–5347.

Blomqvist, D., A. Pauliny, M. Larsson, and L. A. Flodin. 2010. "Trapped in the extinction vortex? Strong genetic effects in a declining vertebrate population." *BMC Evol Biol* 10.

Bonduriansky, R. and T. Day. 2009. "Nongenetic inheritance and its evolutionary implications." *Annu Rev Ecol Evol S* 40, 103–125.

Bossdorf, O., C. L. Richards, and M. Pigliucci. 2008. "Epigenetics for ecologists." *Ecol Lett* 11, 106–115.

Boulotte, N., S. Dalton, A. Carroll, P. Harrison, H. Putnam, L. Peplow, et al. 2016. "Exploring the Symbiodinium rare biosphere provides evidence for symbiont switching in reef-building corals." *Isme J* 10, 2693–2701.

Bourne, D. G., K. M. Morrow, and N. S. Webster. 2016. "Insights into the coral microbiome: Underpinning the health and resilience of reef ecosystems." *Annu Rev Microbiol* 70, 317–324.

Bourne, D. G. and N. S. Webster. 2013. "Coral reef bacterial communities." Springer, Berlin, Heidelberg.

Bromham, L. 2009. "Why do species vary in their rate of molecular evolution?" *Biol Letters* 5, 401–404.

Brooks, A., K. Kohl, R. Brucker, E. van Opstal, and S. Bordenstein. 2016. "Phylosymbiosis: Relationships and functional effects of microbial communities across host evolutionary history." *PLoS Biol* 14.

Brown, B. E. and A. R. Cossins. 2011. "The potential for temperature acclimatisation of reef corals in the face of climate change." *Coral Reefs: An Ecosystem in Transition* 421–433.

Brown, B. E., R. P. Dunne, M. S. Goodson, and A. E. Douglas. 2002. "Experience shapes the susceptibility of a reef coral to bleaching." *Coral Reefs* 21, 119–126.

Bruckner, A. W. and R. J. Bruckner. 2006. "The recent decline of *Montastraea annularis* (complex) coral populations in western Curaçao: A cause for concern?" *Revista de Biología Tropical* 54, 45–58.

Bruckner, A. W. and R. L. Hill. 2009. "Ten years of change to coral communities off Mona and Desecheo Islands, Puerto Rico, from disease and bleaching." *Dis Aquat Organ* 87, 19–31.

Bruno, J. F. and E. R. Selig. 2007. "Regional decline of coral cover in the Indo-Pacific: Timing, extent, and subregional comparisons." *PLoS ONE* 2.

Budd, A. F. and J. M. Pandolfi. 2010. "Evolutionary novelty is concentrated at the edge of coral species distributions." *Science* 328, 1558–1561.

Burke, C., P. Steinberg, D. Rusch, S. Kjelleberg, and T. Thomas. 2011a. "Bacterial community assembly based on functional genes rather than species." *P Natl Acad Sci USA* 108, 14288–14293.

Burke, L., K. Reytar, M. Spalding, and A. Perry. 2011b. *Reefs at Risk Revisited*. World Resources Institute, Washington, D.C.

Burton, R. S. 1990. "Hybrid breakdown in physiological response—a mechanistic approach." *Evolution* 44, 1806–1813.

Cameron, T. C., D. O'Sullivan, A. Reynolds, S. B. Piertney, and T. G. Benton. 2013. "Eco-evolutionary dynamics in response to selection on life-history." *Ecol Lett* 16, 754–763.

Cantin, N. E., M. J. H. van Oppen, B. L. Willis, J. C. Mieog, and A. P. Negri. 2009. "Juvenile corals can acquire more carbon from high-performance algal symbionts." *Coral Reefs* 28, 405–414.

Carilli, J., S. D. Donner, and A. C. Hartmann. 2012. "Historical temperature variability affects coral response to heat stress." *PLoS ONE* 7.

Carlson, S. M., C. J. Cunningham, and P. A. H. Westley. 2014. "Evolutionary rescue in a changing world." *Trends Ecol Evol* 29, 521–530.

Carpenter, K., M. Abrar, G. Aeby, R. Aronson, S. Banks, A. Bruckner, et al. 2008. "One-third of reef-building corals face elevated extinction risk from climate change and local impacts." *Science* 321, 560–563.

Casadesus, J. and D. A. Low. 2013. "Programmed heterogeneity: Epigenetic mechanisms in bacteria." *J Biol Chem* 288, 13929–13935.

Chakravarti, L. J., V. H. Beltran, and M. J. H. van Oppen. 2017. "Rapid thermal adaptation in photosymbionts of reef-building corals." *Global Change Biol* 23, 4675–4688.

Chakravarti, L. J., M. D. Jarrold, E. M. Gibbin, F. Christen, G. Massamba-N'Siala, P. U. Blier, et al. 2016. "Can trans-generational experiments be used to enhance species resilience to ocean warming and acidification?" *Evol Appl* 9, 1133–1146.

Chakravarti, L. J. and M. J. H. van Oppen. 2018. "Experimental evolution in coral photosymbionts as a tool to increase thermal tolerance." *Front Mar Sci* 5, 1–15.

Chamberland, V. F., D. Petersen, J. R. Guest, U. Petersen, M. Brittsan, and M. J. A. Vermeij. 2017. "New seeding approach reduces costs and time to outplant sexually propagated corals for reef restoration." *Sci Rep-Uk* 7.

Chamberland, V. F., M. J. A. Vermeij, M. Brittsan, M. Carl, M. Schick, S. Snowden, et al. 2015. "Restoration of critically endangered elkhorn coral (*Acropora palmata*) populations using larvae reared from wild-caught gametes." *Glob Ecol Conserv* 4, 526–537.

Chan, W., L. Peplow, P. Menéndez, A. Hoffmann, and M. van Oppen. 2018. "Interspecific hybridization may provide novel opportunities for coral reef restoration." *FronT Mar Sci* 5.

Chan, W., L. Peplow, and M. J. H. van Oppen. 2019. "Interspecific gamete compatibility and hybrid larval fitness in reef-building corals: Implications for coral reef restoration." *Sci Rep-Uk* 9.

Chen, C. A., A. T. Wang, L. S. Fang, and Y. W. Yang. 2005. "Fluctuating algal symbiont communities in *Acropora palifera* (Scleractinia: Acroporidae) from Taiwan." *Mar Ecol Prog Ser* 295, 113–121.

Cheung, W. W. L., V. W. Y. Lam, J. L. Sarmiento, K. Kearney, R. Watson, and D. Pauly. 2009. "Projecting global marine biodiversity impacts under climate change scenarios." *Fish Fish* 10, 235–251.

Chi, J. Y., M. W. Parrow, and M. Dunthorn. 2014. "Cryptic sex in *Symbiodinium* (Alveolata, Dinoflagellata) is supported by an inventory of meiotic genes." *J Eukaryot Microbiol* 61, 322–327.

Claesson, M. J., Q. O. Wang, O. O'Sullivan, R. Greene-Diniz, J. R. Cole, R. P. Ross, et al. 2010. "Comparison of two next-generation sequencing technologies for resolving highly complex microbiota composition using tandem variable 16S rRNA gene regions." *Nucleic Acids Res* 38.

Clarkson, M. O., S. A. Kasemann, R. A. Wood, T. M. Lenton, S. J. Daines, S. Richoz, et al. 2015. "Ocean acidification and the Permo-Triassic mass extinction." *Science* 348, 229–232.

Coffroth, M., D. Poland, D. Petrou, D. Brazeau, and J. Holmberg. 2010. "Environmental symbiont acquisition may not be the solution to warming seas for reef-building corals." *PLoS ONE* 5.

Cohen, Y., F. J. Pollock, E. Rosenberg, and D. G. Bourne. 2013. "Phage therapy treatment of the coral pathogen *Vibrio coralliilyticus*." *Microbiologyopen* 2, 64–74.

Coles, S. L., K. D. Bahr, K. S. Rodgers, S. L. May, A. E. McGowan, A. Tsang, et al. 2018. "Evidence of acclimatization or adaptation in Hawaiian corals to higher ocean temperatures." *Peerj*, 6.

Combosch, D. and S. Vollmer. 2013. "Mixed asexual and sexual reproduction in the Indo-Pacific reef coral *Pocillopora damicornis*." *Ecol Evol* 3, 3379–3387.

Combosch, D. and S. Vollmer. 2015. "Trans-Pacific RAD-Seq population genomics confirms introgressive hybridization in Eastern Pacific *Pocillopora* corals." *Mol Phylogenet Evol* 88, 154–162.

Cooper, W. T., D. Lirman, M. P. VanGroningen, J. E. Parkinson, J. Herlan, and J. W. McManus. 2014. "Assessing techniques to enhance early post-settlement survival of corals in situ for reef restoration." *B Mar Sci* 90, 651–664.

Craggs, J., J. Guest, A. Brett, M. Davis, and M. Sweet. 2018. "Maintaining natural spawning timing in *Acropora* corals following long distance inter-continental transportation." *J Zoo Aquar Res* 6, 30–36.

Craggs, J., J. Guest, M. Davis, J. Simmons, E. Dashti, and M. Sweet. 2017. "Inducing broadcast coral spawning ex situ: Closed system mesocosm design and husbandry protocol." *Ecol Evol* 7, 11066–11078.

Crossa, J., P. Perez-Rodriguez, J. Cuevas, O. Montesinos-Lopez, D. Jarquin, G. de los Campos, et al. 2017. "Genomic selection in plant breeding: Methods, models, and perspectives." *Trends Plant Sci* 22, 961–975.

Csaszar, N. B. M., P. J. Ralph, R. Frankham, R. Berkelmans, and M. J. H. van Oppen. 2010. "Estimating the potential for adaptation of corals to climate warming." *PLoS ONE* 5.

Cunning, R., D. M. Yost, M. L. Guarinello, H. M. Putnam, and R. D. Gates. 2015. "Variability of *Symbiodinium* communities in waters, sediments, and corals of thermally distinct reef pools in American Samoa." *PLoS ONE* 10.

Davies, S. W., S. V. Scarpino, T. Pongwarin, J. Scott, and M. V. Matz. 2015. "Estimating trait heritability in highly fecund species." *G3-Genes Genom Genet* 5, 2639–2645.

Dawson, T. P., S. T. Jackson, J. I. House, I. C. Prentice, and G. M. Mace. 2011. "Beyond predictions: Biodiversity conservation in a changing climate." *Science*, 332, 53–58.

Daxinger, L. and E. Whitelaw. 2010. "Transgenerational epigenetic inheritance: More questions than answers." *Genome Res* 20, 1623–1628.

De'ath, G., J. M. Lough, and K. E. Fabricius. 2009. "Declining coral calcification on the Great Barrier Reef." *Science* 323, 116–119.

de Visser, J. A. G. M. and S. F. Elena. 2007. "The evolution of sex: Empirical insights into the roles of epistasis and drift." *Nat Rev Genet* 8, 139–149.

DeAngelis, J. T., W. J. Farrington, and T. O. Tollefsbol. 2008. "An overview of epigenetic assays." *Mol Biotechnol* 38, 179–183.

dela Cruz, D. W. and P. L. Harrison. 2017. "Enhanced larval supply and recruitment can replenish reef corals on degraded reefs." *Sci Rep-Uk* 7.

DeSalvo, M. K., S. Sunagawa, C. R. Voolstra, and M. Medina. 2010. "Transcriptomic responses to heat stress and bleaching in the elkhorn coral *Acropora palmata*." *Mar Ecol Prog Ser* 402, 97–113.

DeVantier, L., G. De'ath, E. Turak, T. J. Done, and K. E. Fabricius. 2006. "Species richness and community structure of reef-building corals on the nearshore Great Barrier Reef." *Coral Reefs* 25, 329–340.

Dimond, J. L. and S. B. Roberts. 2016. "Germline DNA methylation in reef corals: Patterns and potential roles in response to environmental change." *Mol Ecol* 25, 1895–1904.

Dixon, G. B., L. K. Bay, and M. V. Matz. 2016. "Evolutionary consequences of DNA methylation in a basal metazoan." *Mol Biol Evol* 33, 2285–2293.

Dixon, G. B., S. W. Davies, G. A. Aglyamova, E. Meyer, L. K. Bay, and M. V. Matz. 2015. "Genomic determinants of coral heat tolerance across latitudes." *Science* 348, 1460–1462.

Donelson, J. M., P. L. Munday, M. I. McCormick, and C. R. Pitcher. 2012. "Rapid transgenerational acclimation of a tropical reef fish to climate change." *Nat Clim Change* 2, 30–32.

Doney, S. C., V. J. Fabry, R. A. Feely, and J. A. Kleypas. 2009. "Ocean Acidification: The other CO_2 problem." *Annu Rev Mar Sci* 1, 169–192.

Donner, S. D., T. R. Knutson, and M. Oppenheimer. 2007. "Model-based assessment of the role of human-induced climate change in the 2005 Caribbean coral bleaching event." *P Natl Acad Sci USA* 104, 5483–5488.

Donner, S. D., W. J. Skirving, C. M. Little, M. Oppenheimer, and O. Hoegh-Guldberg. 2005. "Global assessment of coral bleaching and required rates of adaptation under climate change." *Global Change Biol* 11, 2251–2265.

Doropoulos, C., N. Evensen, L. Gomez-Lemos, and R. Babcock. 2017. "Density-dependent coral recruitment displays divergent responses during distinct early life-history stages." *Roy Soc Open Sci* 4.

Douglas, A. E. and J. H. Werren. 2016. "Holes in the hologenome: Why Host-microbe symbioses are not holobionts." *Mbio* 7.

Downs, C. A., G. K. Ostrander, L. Rougee, T. Rongo, S. Knutson, D. E. Williams, et al. 2012. "The use of cellular diagnostics for identifying sub-lethal stress in reef corals." *Ecotoxicology* 21, 768–782.

Drury, C., K. E. Dale, J. M. Panlilio, S. V. Miller, D. Lirman, E. A. Larson, et al. 2016. "Genomic variation among populations of threatened coral *Acropora cervicornis*." *BMC Genomics* 17.

Drury, C., S. Schopmeyer, E. Goergen, E. Bartels, K. Nedimyer, M. Johnson, et al. 2017. "Genomic patterns in *Acropora cervicornis* show extensive population structure and variable genetic diversity." *Ecol Evol* 7, 6188–6200.

Dustan, P. 1977. "Vitality of reef coral populations off Key Largo, Florida—Recruitment and mortality." *Environ Geol* 2, 51–58.

Dziedzic, K., H. Elder, H. F. Tavalire, and E. Meyer. 2019. "Heritable variation in bleaching responses and its functional genomic basis in reef-building corals (*Orbicella faveolata*)." *bioRxiv* 185595.

Eakin, C. M., J. A. Morgan, S. F. Heron, T. B. Smith, G. Liu, L. Alvarez-Filip, et al. 2010. "Caribbean corals in crisis: Record thermal stress, bleaching, and mortality in 2005." *PLoS ONE* 5.

Edmunds, P. J. 2015. "A quarter-century demographic analysis of the Caribbean coral, *Orbicella annularis*, and projections of population size over the next century." *Limnol Oceanogr* 60, 840–855.

Edmunds, P. and R. Gates. 2008. "Acclimatization in tropical reef corals." *Mar Ecol Prog Ser* 361, 307–310.

Edwards, A. J. 2010. *Reef Rehabilitation Manual*. The Coral Reef Targeted Research and Capacity Building for Management Program. St. Lucia, Australia.

Edwards A. J., J. Guest, A. Heyward, R. Villanueva, M. Baria, I. Bollozos, et al. 2015. "Direct seeding of mass-cultured coral larvae is not an effective option for reef rehabilitation." *Mar Ecol Prog Ser* 525, 105–116.

Edwards, A. J. and E. Gomez. 2007. *Reef Restoration Concepts and Guidelines: Making sensible management choices in the face of uncertainty*. The Coral Reef Targeted Research and Capacity Building for Management Program, St. Lucia, Australia.

Eizaguirre, C. and M. Baltazar-Soares. 2014. "Evolutionary conservation-evaluating the adaptive potential of species." *Evol Appl* 7, 963–967.

Elena, S. F. and R. E. Lenski. 2003. "Evolution experiments with microorganisms: The dynamics and genetic bases of adaptation." *Nat Rev Genet* 4, 457–469.

Fabry, V. J. 2008. "Ocean science—marine calcifiers in a high CO_2 ocean." *Science*, 320, 1020–1022.

Falkowski, P. G., Z. Dubinsky, L. Muscatine, and J. W. Porter. 1984. "Light and the bioenergetics of a symbiotic coral." *Bioscience* 34, 705–709.

FDEP, Florida Department of Environmental Protection. 2016. "Threats to Southeast Florida coral reefs." http://www.dep.state.fl.us/coastal/programs/coral/threats.htm.

Feil, R. and M. F. Fraga. 2012. "Epigenetics and the environment: Emerging patterns and implications." *Nat Rev Genet* 13, 97–109.

Ferse, S. C. A., M. M. Nugues, S. B. C. Romatzki, and A. Kunzmann. 2013. "Examining the use of mass transplantation of brooding and spawning corals to support natural coral recruitment in Sulawesi/Indonesia." *Restor Ecol* 21, 745–754.

Fierer, N., M. Hamady, C. L. Lauber, and R. Knight. 2008. "The influence of sex, handedness, and washing on the diversity of hand surface bacteria." *P Natl Acad Sci USA* 105, 17994–17999.

50 Reefs. 2017. Available at: https://www.50reefs.org/.

Fitt, W. K. and R. K. Trench. 1983a. "Endocytosis of the symbiotic dinoflagellate *Symbiodinium-Microadriaticum Freudenthal* by endodermal cells of the scyphistomae of *Cassiopeia-Xamachana* and resistance of the algae to host digestion." *J Cell Sci* 64, 195–212.

———. 1983b. "The relation of diel patters of cell division to diel patterns of motility in the symbiotic dinoflagellate *Symbiodinium microadriaticum freudenthal* in culture." *New Phytol* 94, 421–432.

Fogarty, N. D. 2012. "Caribbean Acroporid coral hybrids are viable across life history stages." *Mar Ecol Prog Ser* 446, 145–159.

Fogarty, N. D., S. V. Vollmer, and D. R. Levitan. 2012. "Weak prezygotic isolating mechanisms in threatened caribbean *Acropora* corals." *PLoS ONE* 7.

Fogg, G. E. 2001. "Algal adaptation to stress." In: *Algal adaptation to environmental stresses: Physiological, biochemical and molecular mechanisms*. L. C. Rai and J. P. Gaur (eds). Springer Berlin, Germany, pp. 1–20.

Fong, P. and D. Lirman. 1995. "Hurricanes cause population expansion of the branching coral *Acropora palmata*: Wound healing and growth patterns of asexual recruits." *Mar Ecol-P S Z N* 16, 317–335.

Form, A. U. and U. Riebesell. 2012. "Acclimation to ocean acidification during long-term CO_2 exposure in the cold-water coral *Lophelia pertusa*." *Global Change Biol* 18, 843–853.

Forsman, Z. H., C. A. Page, R. J. Toonen, and D. Vaughan. 2015. "Growing coral larger and faster: Micro-colony-fusion as a strategy for accelerating coral cover." *Peerj* 3.

Frieler, K., M. Meinshausen, A. Golly, M. Mengel, K. Lebek, S. D. Donner, et al. 2013. "Limiting global warming to 2 degrees C is unlikely to save most coral reefs." *Nat Clim Change* 3, 165–170.

Fussmann, G. F., M. Loreau, and P. A. Abrams. 2007. "Eco-evolutionary dynamics of communities and ecosystems." *Funct Ecol* 21, 465–477.

Gardner, T. A., I. M. Cote, J. A. Gill, A. Grant, and A. R. Watkinson. 2003. "Long-term region-wide declines in Caribbean corals." *Science* 301, 958–960.

———. 2005. "Hurricanes and Caribbean coral reefs: Impacts, recovery patterns, and role in long-term decline." *Ecology* 86, 174–184.

Garnett, S. T., P. Olsen, S. H. M. Butchart, and A. A. Hoffmann. 2011. "Did hybridization save the Norfolk Island boobook owl *Ninox novaeseelandiae undulata*?" *Oryx* 45, 500–504.

Garren, M. and F. Azam. 2012. "New directions in coral reef microbial ecology." *Environ Microbiol* 14, 833–844.

Gates, R. D. and T. D. Ainsworth. 2011. "The nature and taxonomic composition of coral symbiomes as drivers of performance limits in scleractinian corals." *J Exp Mar Biol Ecol* 408, 94–101.

Gates, R. D., G. Baghdasarian, and L. Muscatine. 1992. "Temperature stress causes host-cell detachment in symbiotic cnidarians—implications for coral bleaching." *Biol Bull* 182, 324–332.

Gates, R. D. and P. J. Edmunds. 1999. "The physiological mechanisms of acclimatization in tropical reef corals." *Am Zool* 39, 30–43.

Gladfelter, E. H., R. K. Monahan, and W. B. Gladfelter. 1978. "Growth-rates of 5 reef-building corals in the northeastern Caribbean." *B Mar Sci* 28, 728–734.

Glasl, B., G. J. Herndl, and P. R. Frade. 2016. "The microbiome of coral surface mucus has a key role in mediating holobiont health and survival upon disturbance." *Isme J* 10, 2280–2292.

Gleason, D. F. and D. K. Hofmann. 2011. "Coral larvae: From gametes to recruits." *J Exp Mar Biol Ecol* 408, 42–57.

Goergen, E., A. Moulding, B. Walker, and D. Gilliam. 2019. "Identifying causes of temporal changes in *Acropora cervicornis* populations and the potential for recovery." *Front Mar Sci* 6.

Golbuu, Y. and R. H. Richmond. 2007. "Substratum preferences in planula larvae of two species of scleractinian corals, *Goniastrea retiformis* and *Stylaraea punctata*." *Mar Biol* 152, 639–644.

Goulet, T. L. 2006. "Most corals may not change their symbionts." *Mar Ecol Prog Ser* 321, 1–7.

Graham, N. A. J., T. Ainsworth, A. Baird, N. Ban, L. Bay, J. Cinner, et al. 2011. "From microbes to people: Tractable benefits of no-take areas for coral reefs." *Oceanogr Mar Biol* 49, 105–135.

Graham, N. A. J., D. R. Bellwood, J. E. Cinner, T. P. Hughes, A. V. Norstrom, and M. Nystrom. 2013. "Managing resilience to reverse phase shifts in coral reefs." *Front Ecol Environ* 11, 541–548.

Graham, N. A. J., J. E. Cinner, A. V. Norstrom, and M. Nystrom. 2014. "Coral reefs as novel ecosystems: Embracing new futures." *Curr Opin Env Sust* 7, 9–14.

Graham, N. A. J., S. K. Wilson, S. Jennings, N. V. C. Polunin, J. P. Bijoux, and J. Robinson. 2006. "Dynamic fragility of oceanic coral reef ecosystems." *P Natl Acad Sci USA* 103, 8425–8429.

Grant, P. R. and B. R. Grant. 2010. "Conspecific versus heterospecific gene exchange between populations of Darwin's finches." *Philos T R Soc B* 365, 1065–1076.

Guest, J. R., M. V. Baria, E. D. Gomez, A. J. Heyward, and A. J. Edwards. 2014. "Closing the circle: Is it feasible to rehabilitate reefs with sexually propagated corals?" *Coral Reefs* 33, 45–55.

Hagedorn, M. and V. L. Carter. 2016. "Cryobiology: Principles, species conservation and benefits for coral reefs." *Reprod Fert Develop* 28, 1049–1060.

Hagedorn, M., V. L. Carter, E. Henley, M. van Oppen, R. Hobbs, and R. Spindler. 2017. "Producing coral offspring with cryopreserved sperm: A tool for coral reef restoration." *sci rep-uk* 7.

Hagedorn, M., V. L. Carter, L. Hollingsworth, J. C. Leong, R. Kanno, E. H. Borneman, et al. 2009. "Ex situ culture of Caribbean and Pacific coral larvae comparing various flow-through chambers." *Smithson Contrib Mar Sci* 38, 259–267.

Hagedorn, M., A. Farrell, and V. Carter. 2013. "Cryobiology of coral fragments." *Cryobiology* 66, 17–23.

Hagedorn, M., C. Page, K. O'Neil, D. Flores, L. Tichy, V. F. Chamberland, et al. 2019. "Successful demonstration of assisted gene flow in the threatened coral *Acropora palmata* across genetically-isolated Caribbean populations using cryopreserved sperm." *bioRxiv*.

Hall, V. R. and T. P. Hughes. 1996. "Reproductive strategies of modular organisms: Comparative studies of reef-building corals." *Ecology* 77, 950–963.

Hamilton, J. A. and J. M. Miller. 2016. "Adaptive introgression as a resource for management and genetic conservation in a changing climate." *Conserv Biol* 30, 33–41.

Harrington, L., K. Fabricius, G. De'Ath, and A. Negri. 2004. "Recognition and selection of settlement substrata determine post-settlement survival in corals." *Ecology* 85, 3428–3437.

Harrison, P. L. 2011. "Sexual reproduction of scleractinian corals." *Coral Reefs: An Ecosystem in Transition* 59–85.

Harrison, P. L., R. C. Babcock, G. D. Bull, J. K. Oliver, C. C. Wallace, and B. L. Willis. 1984. "Mass spawning in tropical reef corals." *Science* 223, 1186–1189.

Harrison, P. L. and C. C. Wallace. 1990. *Reproduction, dispersal and recruitment of scleractinian corals*. Elsevier, Amsterdam, The Netherlands.

Harrisson, K. A., A. Pavlova, M. Telonis-Scott, and P. Sunnucks. 2014. "Using genomics to characterize evolutionary potential for conservation of wild populations." *Evol Appl* 7, 1008–1025.

Harvell, C. D. and R. K. Grosberg. 1988. "The timing of sexual maturity in clonal animals." *Ecology* 69, 1855–1864.

Harvell, C. D., K. Kim, J. M. Burkholder, R. R. Colwell, P. R. Epstein, D. J. Grimes, et al. 1999. "Review: Marine ecology—emerging marine diseases—climate links and anthropogenic factors." *Science* 285, 1505–1510.

Hedrick, P. W., J. R. Adams, and J. A. Vucetich. 2011. "Reevaluating and broadening the definition of genetic rescue." *Conserv Biol* 25, 1069–1070.

Heitman, J. 2010. "Evolution of eukaryotic microbial pathogens via covert sexual reproduction." *Cell Host Microbe* 8, 86–99.

Hemond, E. M. and S. V. Vollmer. 2010. "Genetic diversity and connectivity in the threatened staghorn coral (*Acropora cervicornis*) in Florida." *PLoS ONE* 5.

Hennige, S. J., C. L. Morrison, A. U. Form, J. Buscher, N. A. Kamenos, and J. M. Roberts. 2014. "Self-recognition in corals facilitates deep-sea habitat engineering." *Sci Rep-Uk* 4.

Hernandez-Agreda, A., R. D. Gates, and T. D. Ainsworth. 2017. "Defining the core microbiome in corals' microbial soup." *Trends Microbiol* 25, 125–140.

Hernandez-Agreda, A., W. Leggat, P. Bongaerts, and T. D. Ainsworth. 2016. "The microbial signature provides insight into the mechanistic basis of coral success across reef habitats." *Mbio* 7.

Hernandez-Agreda, A., W. Leggat, P. Bongaerts, C. Herrera, and T. D. Ainsworth. 2018. "Rethinking the coral microbiome: Simplicity exists within a diverse microbial biosphere." *Mbio* 9.

Heron, S. F., J. A. Maynard, R. van Hooidonk, and C. M. Eakin. 2016. "Warming trends and bleaching stress of the world's coral reefs 1985–2012." *Sci Rep-Uk* 6.

Hester, E. R., K. L. Barott, J. Nulton, M. J. A. Vermeij, and F. L. Rohwer. 2016. "Stable and sporadic symbiotic communities of coral and algal holobionts." *Isme J* 10, 1157–1169.

Heyward, A. J., L. D. Smith, M. Rees, and S. N. Field. 2002. "Enhancement of coral recruitment by in situ mass culture of coral larvae." *Mar Ecol Prog Ser* 230, 113–118.

Highsmith, R. C. 1982. "Reproduction by fragmentation in corals." *Mar Ecol Prog Ser* 7, 207–226.

Hobbs, R. J., L. M. Hallett, P. R. Ehrlich, and H. A. Mooney. 2011. "Intervention ecology: Applying ecological science in the twenty-first century." *Bioscience* 61, 442–450.

Hobbs, R. J., E. Higgs, C. M. Hall, P. Bridgewater, F. S. Chapin, E. C. Ellis, et al. 2014. "Managing the whole landscape: Historical, hybrid, and novel ecosystems." *Front Ecol Environ* 12, 557–564.

Hobbs, R. J., E. Higgs, and J. A. Harris. 2009. "Novel ecosystems: Implications for conservation and restoration." *Trends Ecol Evol* 24, 599–605.

Hoegh-Guldberg, O. 1999. "Climate change, coral bleaching and the future of the world's coral reefs." *Mar Freshwater Res* 50, 839–866.

———. 2004. "Coral reefs and projections of future change." *Coral Health and Disease* 463–484.

———. 2012. "The adaptation of coral reefs to climate change: Is the Red Queen being outpaced?" *Sci Mar* 76, 403–408.

———. 2014. "Coral reefs in the Anthropocene: Persistence or the end of the line?" *Geol Soc Spec Publ* 395, 167–183.

Hoegh-Guldberg, O. and J. F. Bruno. 2010. "The impact of climate change on the world's marine ecosystems." *Science* 328, 1523–1528.

Hoegh-Guldberg, O., R. S. Cai, E. S. Poloczanska, P. G. Brewer, S. Sundby, K. Hilmi, et al. 2014. "The Ocean." *Climate Change 2014: Impacts, Adaptation, and Vulnerability, Pt B: Regional Aspects* 1655–1731.

Hoegh-Guldberg, O., R. J. Jones, S. Ward, and W. K. Loh. 2002. "Ecology—Is coral bleaching really adaptive?" *Nature* 415, 601–602.

Hoegh-Guldberg, O., L. R. McCloskey, and L. Muscatine. 1987. "Expulsion of zooxanthellae by symbiotic cnidarians from the Red Sea." *Coral Reefs* 5, 201–204.

Hoegh-Guldberg, O., P. J. Mumby, A. J. Hooten, R. S. Steneck, P. Greenfield, E. Gomez, et al. 2007. "Coral reefs under rapid climate change and ocean acidification." *Science* 318, 1737–1742.

Hoffmann, A. 2013. "Evolutionary limits and constraints." In: *The Princeton Guide to Evolution*. Princeton University Press.

Hoffmann, A. and C. Sgro. 2011. "Climate change and evolutionary adaptation." *Nature* 470, 479–485.
Holbrook, S. J., T. C. Adam, P. J. Edmunds, R. J. Schmitt, R. C. Carpenter, A. J. Brooks, et al. 2018. "Recruitment drives spatial variation in recovery rates of resilient coral reefs." *Sci Rep-Uk* 8.
Holeski, L. M., G. Jander, and A. A. Agrawal. 2012. "Transgenerational defense induction and epigenetic inheritance in plants." *Trends Ecol Evol* 27, 618–626.
Honisch, B., A. Ridgwell, D. N. Schmidt, E. Thomas, S. J. Gibbs, A. Sluijs, et al. 2012. "The Geological record of ocean acidification." *Science* 335, 1058–1063.
Howells, E. J., D. Abrego, E. Meyer, N. L. Kirk, and J. A. Burt. 2016. "Host adaptation and unexpected symbiont partners enable reef-building corals to tolerate extreme temperatures." *Global Change Biol* 22, 2702–2714.
Howells, E. J., V. H. Beltran, N. W. Larsen, L. K. Bay, B. L. Willis, and M. J. H. van Oppen. 2012. "Coral thermal tolerance shaped by local adaptation of photosymbionts." *Nat Clim Change* 2, 116–120.
Huertas, I. E., M. Rouco, V. Lopez-Rodas, and E. Costas. 2011. "Warming will affect phytoplankton differently: Evidence through a mechanistic approach." *P Roy Soc B-Biol Sci* 278, 3534–3543.
Huey, R. B., D. Berrigan, G. W. Gilchrist, and J. C. Herron. 1999. "Testing the adaptive significance of acclimation: A strong inference approach." *Am Zool* 39, 323–336.
Huey, R. B. and J. G. Kingsolver. 1989. "Evolution of thermal sensitivity of ectotherm performance." *Trends Ecol Evol* 4, 131–135.
Hughes, T. P., K. D. Anderson, S. R. Connolly, S. F. Heron, J. T. Kerry, J. M. Lough, et al. 2018. "Spatial and temporal patterns of mass bleaching of corals in the Anthropocene." *Science* 359, 80–84.
Hughes, T. P., A. H. Baird, D. R. Bellwood, M. Card, S. R. Connolly, C. Folke, et al. 2003. "Climate change, human impacts, and the resilience of coral reefs." *Science* 301, 929–933.
Hughes, T. P., J. T. Kerry, M. Alvarez-Noriega, J. G. Alvarez-Romero, K. D. Anderson, A. H. Baird, et al. 2017. "Global warming and recurrent mass bleaching of corals." *Nature* 543, 373–381.
Hughes, T. P., J. T. Kerry, A. H. Baird, S. R. Connolly, T. J. Chase, A. Dietzel, et al. 2019. "Global warming impairs stock-recruitment dynamics of corals." *Nature* 568, 387–392.
Hughes, T. P. and J. E. Tanner. 2000. "Recruitment failure, life histories, and long-term decline of Caribbean corals." *Ecology* 81, 2250–2263.
IPCC. 2014. "Climate Change 2014: Synthesis Report. Contribution of Working Groups I, II and III to the Fifth Assessment Report of the Intergovernmental Panel on Climate Change." Geneva, Switzerland, pp. 1–151.
IPCC. 2018. "Global Warming of 1.5°C: An IPCC Special Report on the impacts of global warming of 1.5°C above pre-industrial levels, related global greenhouse gas emission pathways, in the context of strengthening the global response to the threat of climate change, sustainable development, and efforts to eradicate poverty." V. Masson-Delmotte, P. Zhai, H-O. Pörtner, D. Roberts, J. Skea, P. Shukla, et al. (eds). World Meteorological Organization Geneva, Switzerland, p. 32.
Jackson, J. B. C. 1992. "Pleistocene perspectives on coral-reef community structure." *Am Zool* 32, 719–731.
Jackson, J. B. C., M. X. Kirby, W. H. Berger, K. A. Bjorndal, L. W. Botsford, B. J. Bourque, et al. 2001. "Historical overfishing and the recent collapse of coastal ecosystems." *Science* 293, 629–638.
Japaud, A., C. Fauvelot, and C. Bouchon. 2014. "Unexpected high densities of the hybrid coral *Acropora prolifera* (Lamarck 1816) in Guadeloupe Island, Lesser Antilles." *Coral Reefs* 33, 593–593.
Johnson, M., C. Lustic, E. Bartels, I. Baums, D. Gilliam, L. Larson, et al. 2011. "Caribbean *Acropora* restoration guide: Best practices for propagation and population enhancement." NOAA, TNC.
Johnson, W. E., D. P. Onorato, M. E. Roelke, E. D. Land, M. Cunningham, R. C. Belden, et al. 2010. "Genetic restoration of the Florida panther." *Science* 329, 1641–1645.
Jokiel, P. L., C. P. Jury, and I. B. Kuffner. 2016. "Coral calcification and ocean acidification." *Coral Reefs World* 6, 7–45.
Jones, A. M. and R. Berkelmans. 2010. "Potential costs of acclimatization to a warmer climate: Growth of a reef coral with heat tolerant vs. sensitive symbiont types." *PLoS ONE* 5.
———. 2011. "Tradeoffs to thermal acclimation: Energetics and reproduction of a reef coral with heat tolerant *Symbiodinium* type-D." *J Mar Bio* doi:10.1155/2011/185890.
———. 2012. "The photokinetics of thermo-tolerance in *Symbiodinium*." *Mar Ecol-Evol Persp* 33, 490–498.

Jones, A. M., R. Berkelmans, M. J. H. van Oppen, J. C. Mieog, and W. Sinclair. 2008. "A community change in the algal endosymbionts of a scleractinian coral following a natural bleaching event: Field evidence of acclimatization." *P Roy Soc B-Biol Sci* 275, 1359–1365.

Jones, T. A. 2003. "The restoration gene pool concept: Beyond the native versus non-native debate." *Restor Ecol* 11, 281–290.

Jones, T. A. and T. A. Monaco. 2009. "A role for assisted evolution in designing native plant materials for domesticated landscapes." *Front Ecol Environ* 7, 541–547.

Kawahata, H., K. Fujita, A. Iguchi, M. Inoue, S. Iwasaki, A. Kuroyanagi, et al. 2019. "Perspective on the response of marine calcifiers to global warming and ocean acidification: Behavior of corals and foraminifera in a high CO_2 world "hot house."" *Prog Earth Planet Sc* 6.

Kegler, P., H. F. Kegler, A. Gardes, S. C. A. Ferse, M. Lukman, Y. R. Alfiansah, et al. 2017. "Bacterial biofilm communities and coral larvae settlement at different levels of anthropogenic impact in the Spermonde Archipelago, Indonesia." *Front Mar Sci* 4.

Kellogg, C. A. 2007. "Phage therapy for Florida corals?" USGS and Mote Marine Laboratory. https://pubs.usgs.gov/fs/2007/3065/pdf/fs2007-3065.pdf.

Kenkel, C. D., G. Goodbody-Gringley, D. Caillaud, S. W. Davies, E. Bartels, and M. V. Matz. 2013. "Evidence for a host role in thermotolerance divergence between populations of the mustard hill coral (*Porites astreoides*) from different reef environments." *Mol Ecol* 22, 4335–4348.

Kenkel, C. D., S. P. Setta, and M. V. Matz. 2015. "Heritable differences in fitness-related traits among populations of the mustard hill coral, *Porites astreoides*." *Heredity* 115, 509–516.

Kimura, M. 1983. *The Neutral Theory of Molecular Evolution*. Cambridge University Press, Cambridge, UK.

Kinzie, R. A., M. Takayama, S. R. Santos, and M. A. Coffroth. 2001. "The adaptive bleaching hypothesis: Experimental tests of critical assumptions." *Biol Bull* 200, 51–58.

Kleypas, J., R. Buddemeier, D. Archer, J. Gattuso, C. Langdon, and B. Opdyke. 1999. "Geochemical consequences of increased atmospheric carbon dioxide on coral reefs." *Science* 284, 118–120.

Kleypas, J., D. M. Thompson, F. S. Castruccio, E. N. Curchitser, M. Pinsky, and J. R. Watson. 2016. "Larval connectivity across temperature gradients and its potential effect on heat tolerance in coral populations." *Global Change Biol* 22, 3539–3549.

Kline, D. I. and S. V. Vollmer. 2011. "White band disease (type I) of endangered Caribbean acroporid corals is caused by pathogenic bacteria." *Sci Rep-Uk* 1.

Knowles, B., C. B. Silveira, B. A. Bailey, K. Barott, V. A. Cantu, A. G. Cobian-Guemes, et al. 2016. "Lytic to temperate switching of viral communities." *Nature* 531, 466–469.

Knowlton, N., E. Weil, L. A. Weigt, and H. M. Guzman. 1992. "Sibling species in *Montastraea annularis*, coral bleaching, and the coral climate record." *Science* 255, 330–333.

Koch, H. R. and L. Becks. 2017. "The consequences of facultative sex in a prey adapting to predation." *J Evol Biol* 30, 210–220.

Koch, H. R., J. Frickel, M. Valiadi, and L. Becks. 2014. "Why rapid, adaptive evolution matters for community dynamics." *Front Ecol Evol* 2.

Krediet, C. J., K. B. Ritchie, V. J. Paul, and M. Teplitski. 2013. "Coral-associated microorganisms and their roles in promoting coral health and thwarting diseases." *P Roy Soc B-Biol Sci* 280.

Kuffner, I. B., B. H. Lidz, J. H. Hudson, and J. S. Anderson. 2015. "A century of ocean warming on Florida Keys coral reefs: Historic in situ observations." *Estuar Coast* 38, 1085–1096.

Kuffner, I. B. and L. T. Toth. 2016. "A geological perspective on the degradation and conservation of western Atlantic coral reefs." *Conserv Biol* 30, 706–715.

Kushmaro, A., E. Rosenberg, M. Fine, Y. Ben Haim, and Y. Loya. 1998. "Effect of temperature on bleaching of the coral *Oculina patagonica* by *Vibrio AK-1*." *Mar Ecol Prog Ser* 171, 131–137.

Kushmaro, A., E. Rosenberg, M. Fine, and Y. Loya. 1997. "Bleaching of the coral *Oculina patagonica* by *Vibrio AK-1*." *Mar Ecol Prog Ser* 147, 159–165.

LaJeunesse, T. C. 2001. "Investigating the biodiversity, ecology, and phylogeny of endosymbiotic dinoflagellates in the genus *Symbiodinium* using the its region: In search of a "species" level marker." *J Phycol* 37, 866–880.

LaJeunesse, T. C., J. E. Parkinson, P. W. Gabrielson, H. J. Jeong, J. D. Reimer, C. R. Voolstra, et al. 2018. "Systematic revision of Symbiodiniaceae highlights the antiquity and diversity of coral endosymbionts." *Curr Biol* 28, 2570–2582.

LaJeunesse, T. C., R. Smith, M. Walther, J. Pinzon, D. T. Pettay, M. McGinley, et al. 2010. "Host-symbiont recombination versus natural selection in the response of coral-dinoflagellate symbioses to environmental disturbance." *P Roy Soc B-Biol Sci* 277, 2925–2934.

LaJeunesse, T. C., R. Smith, J. Finney, and H. Oxenford. 2009. "Outbreak and persistence of opportunistic symbiotic dinoflagellates during the 2005 Caribbean mass coral 'bleaching' event." *P Roy Soc B-Biol Sci* 276, 4139–4148.

Lasker, H. R. and M. A. Coffroth. 1999. "Responses of clonal reef taxa to environmental change." *Am Zool* 39, 92–103.

Levin, S. A. and J. Lubchenco. 2008. "Resilience, robustness, and marine ecosystem-based management." *Bioscience* 58, 27–32.

Levitan, D. R., H. Fukami, J. Jara, D. Kline, T. M. McGovern, K. E. McGhee, et al. 2004. "Mechanisms of reproductive isolation among sympatric broadcast-spawning corals of the *Montastraea annularis* species complex." *Evolution* 58, 308–323.

Libro, S. and S. V. Vollmer. 2016. "Genetic signature of resistance to white band disease in the Caribbean staghorn coral *Acropora cervicornis*." *PLoS ONE* 11.

Lind, C. E., R. W. Ponzoni, N. H. Nguyen, and H. L. Khaw. 2012. "Selective breeding in fish and conservation of genetic resources for aquaculture." *Reprod Domest Anim* 47, 255–263.

Lirman, D. 2000. "Fragmentation in the branching coral *Acropora palmata* (Lamarck): Growth, survivorship, and reproduction of colonies and fragments." *J Exp Mar Biol Ecol* 251, 41–57.

Lirman, D., S. Schopmeyer, V. Galvan, C. Drury, A. C. Baker, and I. B. Baums. 2014. "Growth dynamics of the threatened Caribbean staghorn coral *Acropora cervicornis*: Influence of host genotype, symbiont identity, colony size, and environmental setting." *PLoS ONE* 9.

Lirman, D., S. Schopmeyer, D. Manzello, L. J. Gramer, W. F. Precht, F. Muller-Karger, et al. 2011. "Severe 2010 cold-water event caused unprecedented mortality to corals of the Florida Reef Tract and reversed previous survivorship patterns." *PLoS ONE* 6.

Little, A. F., M. J. H. van Oppen, and B. L. Willis. 2004. "Flexibility in algal endosymbioses shapes growth in reef corals." *Science* 304, 1492–1494.

Liu, H. L., T. G. Stephens, R. A. Gonzalez-Pech, V. H. Beltran, B. Lapeyre, P. Bongaerts, et al. 2018. "*Symbiodinium* genomes reveal adaptive evolution of functions related to coral-dinoflagellate symbiosis." *Commun Biol* 1.

Logan, C. A., J. P. Dunne, C. M. Eakin, and S. D. Donner. 2014. "Incorporating adaptive responses into future projections of coral bleaching." *Global Change Biol* 20, 125–139.

Lohr, K. E. and J. T. Patterson. 2017. "Intraspecific variation in phenotype among nursery-reared staghorn coral *Acropora cervicornis* (Lamarck, 1816)." *J Exp Mar Biol Ecol* 486, 87–92.

Lopez-Maury, L., S. Marguerat, and J. Bahler. 2008. "Tuning gene expression to changing environments: From rapid responses to evolutionary adaptation." *Nat Rev Genet* 9, 583–593.

Lough, J. M. 2008. "Coral calcification from skeletal records revisited." *Mar Ecol Prog Ser* 373, 257–264.

Lough, J. M. and N. E. Cantin. 2014. "Perspectives on massive coral growth rates in a changing ocean." *Biol Bull* 226, 187–202.

Lundgren, P. 2011. "Genetics and genetic tools in coral reef management." GBRMPA.

Mangubhai, S. and P. L. Harrison. 2008. "Asynchronous coral spawning patterns on equatorial reefs in Kenya." *Mar Ecol Prog Ser* 360, 85–96.

Manzello, D. P. 2015. "Rapid recent warming of coral reefs in the Florida Keys." *Sci Rep-Uk* 5.

Marcelino, V., K. Morrow, M. van Oppen, D. Bourne, and H. Verbruggen. 2017. "Diversity and stability of coral endolithic microbial communities at a naturally high pCO_2 reef." *Mol Ecol* 26, 5344–5357.

Marhaver, K., V. Chamberland, and N. Fogarty. 2017. "Coral spawning research and larval propagation webinar. Coral restoration consortium and reef resilience network." https://crc.reefresilience.org/coral-spawning-research-larval-propagation/.

Marshall, D. J. and M. J. Keough. 2006. "Complex life cycles and offspring provisioning in marine invertebrates." *Integr Comp Biol* 46, 643–651.

Marshall, D. J. and S. G. Morgan. 2011. "Ecological and evolutionary consequences of linked life-history stages in the sea." *Curr Biol* 21, R718-R725.

Marshall, P. and H. Schuttenberg. 2006. *A Reef Manager's Guide to Coral Bleaching*. Great Barrier Reef Marine Park Authority, Townsville, Australia.

Mascarelli, A. 2014. "Designer reefs." *Nature*, 508, 444-446.

Maynard, J. A., K. R. N. Anthony, P. A. Marshall, and I. Masiri. 2008. "Major bleaching events can lead to increased thermal tolerance in corals." *Mar Biol* 155, 173-182.

McCormick, M. I. 2003. "Consumption of coral propagules after mass spawning enhances larval quality of damselfish through maternal effects." *Oecologia* 136, 37-45.

McCulloch, M., J. Falter, J. Trotter, and P. Montagna. 2012a. "Coral resilience to ocean acidification and global warming through pH up-regulation." *Nat Clim Change* 2, 623-633.

McCulloch, M., J. Trotter, P. Montagna, J. Falter, R. Dunbar, A. Freiwald, et al. 2012b. "Resilience of cold-water scleractinian corals to ocean acidification: Boron isotopic systematics of pH and saturation state up-regulation." *Geochim Cosmochim Ac* 87, 21-34.

McEdward, L. R. and B. G. Miner. 2006. "Estimation and interpretation of egg provisioning in marine invertebrates." *Integr Comp Biol* 46, 224-232.

McFall-Ngai, M., M. G. Hadfield, T. C. G. Bosch, H. V. Carey, T. Domazet-Loso, A. E. Douglas, et al. 2013. "Animals in a bacterial world, a new imperative for the life sciences." *P Natl Acad Sci USA* 110, 3229-3236.

McKay, J. K., C. E. Christian, S. Harrison, and K. J. Rice. 2005. "How local is local?"—A review of practical and conceptual issues in the genetics of restoration." *Restor Ecol* 13, 432-440.

Meier, J. I., D. A. Marques, S. Mwaiko, C. E. Wagner, L. Excoffier, and O. Seehausen. 2017. "Ancient hybridization fuels rapid cichlid fish adaptive radiations." *Nat Commun* 8.

Merselis, D. G., D. Lirman, and M. Rodriguez-Lanetty. 2018. "Symbiotic immuno-suppression: Is disease susceptibility the price of bleaching resistance?" *Peerj* 6.

Messer, P. W. and D. A. Petrov. 2013. "Population genomics of rapid adaptation by soft selective sweeps." *Trends Ecol Evol* 28, 659-669.

Metzger, D. C. H. and P. M. Schulte. 2016. "Epigenomics in marine fishes." *Mar Genom* 30, 43-54.

Meyer, E., S. Davies, S. Wang, B. L. Willis, D. Abrego, T. E. Juenger, et al. 2009. "Genetic variation in responses to a settlement cue and elevated temperature in the reef-building coral *Acropora millepora*." *Mar Ecol Prog Ser* 392, 81-92.

Middlebrook, R., O. Hoegh-Guldberg, and W. Leggat. 2008. "The effect of thermal history on the susceptibility of reef-building corals to thermal stress." *J Exp Biol* 211, 1050-1056.

Mieog, J. C., J. L. Olsen, R. Berkelmans, S. A. Bleuler-Martinez, B. L. Willis, and M. J. H. van Oppen. 2009. "The roles and interactions of symbiont, host and environment in defining coral fitness." *PLoS ONE* 4.

Mieog, J. C., M. J. H. van Oppen, N. E. Cantin, W. T. Stam, and J. L. Olsen. 2007. "Real-time PCR reveals a high incidence of *Symbiodinium* clade D at low levels in four scleractinian corals across the Great Barrier Reef: Implications for symbiont shuffling." *Coral Reefs* 26, 449-457.

Miller, D. J. and M. J. H. van Oppen. 2003. "A 'fair go' for coral hybridization." *Mol Ecol* 12, 805-807.

Miller, J., E. Muller, C. Rogers, R. Waara, A. Atkinson, K. R. T. Whelan, et al. 2009. "Coral disease following massive bleaching in 2005 causes 60% decline in coral cover on reefs in the US Virgin Islands." *Coral Reefs* 28, 925-937.

Miller, J., R. Waara, E. Muller, and C. Rogers. 2006. "Coral bleaching and disease combine to cause extensive mortality on reefs in US Virgin Islands." *Coral Reefs* 25, 418.

Miller, M. W. 2001. "Corallivorous snail removal: Evaluation of impact on *Acropora palmata*." *Coral Reefs* 19, 293-295.

Miller, M. W., K. E. Lohr, C. M. Cameron, D. E. Williams, and E. C. Peters. 2014. "Disease dynamics and potential mitigation among restored and wild staghorn coral, *Acropora cervicornis*." *Peerj* 2.

Miller, M. W., D. E. Williams, and J. Fisch. 2016. "Genet-specific spawning patterns in *Acropora palmata*." *Coral Reefs* 35, 1393-1398.

Miller, M. W., I. Baums, R. Pausch, A. Bright, C. Cameron, D. Williams, et al. 2018. "Clonal structure and variable fertilization success in Florida Keys broadcast spawning corals." *Coral Reefs* 37, 239-249.

Miller, M. W., P. J. Colburn, E. Pontes, D. E. Williams, A. J. Bright, X. M. Serrano, et al. 2019. "Genotypic variation in disease susceptibility among cultured stocks of elkhorn and staghorn corals." *Peerj* 7.

Mooney, H. A. and E. E. Cleland. 2001. "The evolutionary impact of invasive species." *P Natl Acad Sci USA* 98, 5446–5451.

Morikawa, M. and S. Palumbi. 2019. "Using naturally occurring climate resilient corals to construct bleaching-resistant nurseries." *Proc Nat Acad Sci* 116, 10586–10591.

Morrell, P. L., E. S. Buckler, and J. Ross-Ibarra. 2012. "Crop genomics: Advances and applications." *Nat Rev Genet* 13, 85–96.

Mousseau, T. A. and C. W. Fox. 1998. "The adaptive significance of maternal effects." *Trends Ecol Evol* 13, 403–407.

Muller, E. M., E. Bartels, and I. B. Baums. 2018. "Bleaching causes loss of disease resistance within the threatened coral species *Acropora cervicornis*." *Elife* 7.

Muller, E. M., C. Rogers, A. Spitzack, and R. van Woesik. 2008. "Bleaching increases likelihood of disease on *Acropora palmata* in Hawksnest Bay, St John, US Virgin Islands." *Coral Reefs* 27, 191–195.

Muller, E. M. and R. van Woesik. 2014. "Genetic susceptibility, colony size, and water temperature drive white-pox disease on the coral *Acropora palmata*." *PLoS ONE* 9.

Munday, P. L., R. R.Warner, K. Monro, J. M. Pandolfi, and D. J. Marshall. 2013. "Predicting evolutionary responses to climate change in the sea." *Ecol Lett* 16, 1488–1500.

Muscatine, L., P. G. Falkowski, J. W. Porter, and Z. Dubinsky. 1984. "Fate of photosynthetic fixed carbon in light-adapted and shade-adapted colonies of the symbiotic coral *Stylophora pistillata*." *Proc R Soc Ser B-Bio* 222, 181–202.

Muscatine, L., L. R. Mccloskey, and R. E. Marian. 1981. "Estimating the daily contribution of carbon from zooxanthellae to coral animal respiration." *Limnol Oceanogr* 26, 601–611.

Nakamura, R., W. Ando, H. Yamamoto, M. Kitano, A. Sato, M. Nakamura, et al. 2011. "Corals mass-cultured from eggs and transplanted as juveniles to their native, remote coral reef." *Mar Ecol Prog Ser* 436, 161–168.

NASEM, National Academies of Sciences, Engineering, Medicine. 2018. "A research review of interventions to increase the persistence and resilience of coral reefs." Washington, DC.

NCCOS, National Centers for Coastal Ocean Science. 2018. "Assessment of hurricane impacts to coral reefs in Florida and Puerto Rico." https://coastalscience.noaa.gov/project/assessment-of-hurricane-impacts-to-coral-reefs-in-florida-and-puerto-rico/.

Neal, B. P., A. Khen, T. Treibitz, O. Beijbom, G. O'Connor, M. A. Coffroth, et al. 2017. "Caribbean massive corals not recovering from repeated thermal stress events during 2005–2013." *Ecol Evol* 7, 1339–1353.

Neira, C., E. D. Grosholz, L. A. Levin, and R. Blake. 2006. "Mechanisms generating modification of benthos following tidal flat invasion by a Spartina hybrid." *Ecol Appl* 16, 1391–1404.

Nietzer, S., M. Moeller, M. Kitamura, and P. J. Schupp. 2018. "Coral larvae every day: *Leptastrea purpurea*, a brooding species that could accelerate coral research." *Front Mar Sci* 5, Article 466.

NMFS, National Marine Fisheries Service. 2014. "Final listing determinations on proposal to list 66 reef-building coral species and to reclassify elkhorn and staghorn corals." 0648-XT12 C.F.R.

———. 2015. "Recovery plan for elkhorn (*Acropora palmata*) and staghorn (*A. cervicornis*) corals." Silver Spring, MD, p. 167.

Okamoto, M., K. Roeroe, M. Yap, L. Lalamentic, S. Fujiwara, and K. Oyamada. 2012. "Experimental transplantation of corals using sexual reproduction in Manado, Indonesia." In: *12th International Coral Reef Symposium* Cairns, Australia.

Okubo, N., T. Motokawa, and M. Omori. 2007. "When fragmented coral spawn? Effect of size and timing on survivorship and fecundity of fragmentation in *Acropora formosa*." *Mar Biol*, 151, 353–363.

Omori, M. 2010. "Degradation and restoration of coral reefs: Experience in Okinawa, Japan." *Mar Biol Res* 7, 3–12.

Omori, M., H. Fukami, H. Kobinata, and M. Hatta. 2001. "Significant drop of fertilization of *Acropora* corals in 1999. An after-effect of heavy coral bleaching?" *Limnol Oceanogr* 46, 704–706.

Omori, M. and K. Iwao. 2016. "Methods of farming sexually propagated corals and outplanting for coral reef rehabilitation." A.M.S. Lab.

Osborne, K., A. A. Thompson, A. J. Cheal, M. J. Emslie, K. A. Johns, M. J. Jonker, et al. 2017. "Delayed coral recovery in a warming ocean." *Global Change Biol* 23, 3869–3881.

Pacifici, M., W. B. Foden, P. Visconti, J. E. M. Watson, S. H. M. Butchart, K. M. Kovacs, et al. 2015. "Assessing species vulnerability to climate change." *Nat Clim Change* 5, 215–225.

Padilla-Gamino, J. L., X. Pochon, C. Bird, G. T. Concepcion, and R. D. Gates. 2012. "From parent to gamete: Vertical transmission of *Symbiodinium* (Dinophyceae) ITS2 sequence assemblages in the reef building coral *Montipora capitata*." *PLoS ONE* 7.

Page, C. 2015. "Reskinning a reef: Mote Marine Lab scientists explore a new approach to reef restoration." In: *Coral Magazine* pp. 72–80.

Page, C. A., E. M. Muller, and D. E. Vaughan. 2018. "Microfragmenting for the successful restoration of slow growing massive corals." *Ecol Eng* 123, 86–94.

Palmer, C. V., N. G. Traylor-Knowles, B. L. Willis, and J. C. Bythell. 2011. "Corals use similar immune cells and wound-healing processes as those of higher organisms." *PLoS ONE* 6.

Palumbi, S. R. 1994. "Genetic-divergence, reproductive isolation, and marine speciation." *Annu Rev Ecol Syst* 25, 547–572.

Palumbi, S. R., D. J. Barshis, N. Traylor-Knowles, and R. A. Bay. 2014. "Mechanisms of reef coral resistance to future climate change." *Science* 344, 895–898.

Pandolfi, J. M. 2002. "Coral community dynamics at multiple scales." *Coral Reefs* 21, 13–23.

Pandolfi, J. M., R. H. Bradbury, E. Sala, T. P. Hughes, K. A. Bjorndal, R. G. Cooke, et al. 2003. "Global trajectories of the long-term decline of coral reef ecosystems." *Science* 301, 955–958.

Pandolfi, J. M., S. R. Connolly, D. J. Marshall, and A. L. Cohen. 2011. "Projecting coral reef futures under global warming and ocean acidification." *Science* 333, 418–422.

Pandolfi, J. M. and J. B. C. Jackson. 2001. "Community structure of Pleistocene coral reefs of Curacao, Netherlands Antilles." *Ecol Monogr* 71, 49–67.

Parkinson, J. E., E. Bartels, M. K. Devlin-Durante, C. Lustic, K. Nedimyer, S. Schopmeyer, et al. 2018. "Extensive transcriptional variation poses a challenge to thermal stress biomarker development for endangered corals." *Mol Ecol* 27, 1103–1119.

Pedros-Alio, C. 2006. "Marine microbial diversity: Can it be determined?" *Trends Microbiol* 14, 257–263.

Peixoto, R. S., P. M. Rosado, D. C. D. Leite, A. S. Rosado, and D. G. Bourne. 2017. "Beneficial microorganisms for corals (BMC): Proposed mechanisms for coral health and resilience." *Front Microbiol* 8.

Pelletier, F., D. Garant, and A. P. Hendry. 2009. "Eco-evolutionary dynamics." *Philos T R Soc B* 364, 1483–1489.

Pereira, H. M., P. W. Leadley, V. Proenca, R. Alkemade, J. P. W. Scharlemann, J. F. Fernandez-Manjarres, et al. 2010. "Scenarios for global biodiversity in the 21st century." *Science* 330, 1496–1501.

Perring, M. P., R. J. Standish, J. N. Price, M. D. Craig, T. E. Erickson, K. X. Ruthrof, et al. 2015. "Advances in restoration ecology: Rising to the challenges of the coming decades." *Ecosphere* 6.

Peters, E. C. 1984. "A survey of cellular reactions to environmental-stress and disease in Caribbean scleractinian corals." *Helgolander Meeresun* 37, 113–137.

Petersen, D. and R. Tollrian. 2001. "Methods to enhance sexual recruitment for restoration of damaged reefs." *B Mar Sci* 69, 989–1000.

Pochon, X. and R. D. Gates. 2010. "A new *Symbiodinium* clade (Dinophyceae) from soritid foraminifera in Hawai'i." *Mol Phylogenet Evol* 56, 492–497.

Polato, N. R., N. S. Altman, and I. B. Baums. 2013. "Variation in the transcriptional response of threatened coral larvae to elevated temperatures." *Mol Ecol* 22, 1366–1382.

Pollock, F. J., S. M. Katz, J. A. J. M. van de Water, S. W. Davies, M. Hein, G. Torda, et al. 2017. "Coral larvae for restoration and research: A large-scale method for rearing *Acropora millepora* larvae, inducing settlement, and establishing symbiosis." *Peerj* 5.

Pollock, F. J., R. McMinds, S. Smith, D. G. Bourne, B. L. Willis, M. Medina, et al. 2018. "Coral-associated bacteria demonstrate phylosymbiosis and cophylogeny." *Nat Commun* 9.

Precht, W. F., A. W. Bruckner, R. B. Aronson, and R. J. Bruckner. 2002. "Endangered acroporid corals of the Caribbean." *Coral Reefs* 21, 41–42.

Precht, W. F., B. E. Gintert, M. L. Robbart, R. Fura, and R. van Woesik. 2016. "Unprecedented disease-related coral mortality in southeastern Florida." *Sci Rep-Uk* 6.

Ptashne, M. 2013. "Epigenetics: Core misconcept." *P Natl Acad Sci USA* 110, 7101–7103.

Putnam, H. M. 2012. "Resilience and acclimatization potential of reef corals under predicted climate change stressors." University of Hawai'i at Manoa.

Putnam, H. M., J. Davidson, and R. D. Gates. 2016. "Ocean acidification influences DNA methylation and phenotypic plasticity in environmentally susceptible corals." *Integr Comp Biol* 56, E177-E177.

Putnam, H. M. and R. D. Gates. 2015. "Preconditioning in the reef-building coral *Pocillopora damicornis* and the potential for trans-generational acclimatization in coral larvae under future climate change conditions." *J Exp Biol* 218, 2365-2372.

Qin, J. J., R. Q. Li, J. Raes, M. Arumugam, K. S. Burgdorf, C. Manichanh, et al. 2010. "A human gut microbial gene catalogue established by metagenomic sequencing." *Nature* 464, 59-U70.

Quigley, K. M., S. W. Davies, C. D. Kenkel, B. L. Willis, M. V. Matz, and L. K. Bay. 2014. "Deep-sequencing method for quantifying background abundances of *Symbiodinium* types: Exploring the rare *Symbiodinium* biosphere in reef-building corals." *PLoS ONE* 9.

Quigley, K. M., B. L. Willis, and L. K. Bay. 2016. "Maternal effects and *Symbiodinium* community composition drive differential patterns in juvenile survival in the coral *Acropora tenuis*." *Roy Soc Open Sci* 3.

Raftery, A. E., A. Zimmer, D. M. W. Frierson, R. Startz, and P. R. Liu. 2017. "Less than 2 degrees C warming by 2100 unlikely." *Nat Clim Change* 7, 637-642.

Randall, C. J., A. P. Negri, K. M. Quigley, T. Foster, G. F. Ricardo, N. S. Webster, et al. 2020. "Sexual production of corals for reef restoration in the Anthropocene." *Mar Ecol Prog Ser* 635, 203-232.

Randall, C. J. and R. van Woesik. 2015. "Contemporary white-band disease in Caribbean corals driven by climate change." *Nat Clim Change* 5, 375-379.

Raymundo, L. J. and A. P. Maypa. 2004. "Getting bigger faster: Mediation of size-specific mortality via fusion in juvenile coral transplants." *Ecol Appl* 14, 281-295.

Reed, D. H. and R. Frankham. 2003. "Correlation between fitness and genetic diversity." *Conserv Biol* 17, 230-237.

Reshef, L., O. Koren, Y. Loya, I. Zilber-Rosenberg, and E. Rosenberg. 2006. "The coral probiotic hypothesis." *Environ Microbiol* 8, 2068-2073.

Reusch, T. B. H. 2014. "Climate change in the oceans: Evolutionary versus phenotypically plastic responses of marine animals and plants." *Evol Appl* 7, 104-122.

Reusch, T. B. H., A. Ehlers, A. Hammerli, and B. Worm. 2005. "Ecosystem recovery after climatic extremes enhanced by genotypic diversity." *P Natl Acad Sci USA* 102, 2826-2831.

Rhodes, R., N. Gligorov, and A. B. Schwab. 2013. *The Human Microbiome: Ethical, Legal and Social Concerns*. Oxford University Press, New York, NY.

Rhymer, J. M. and D. Simberloff. 1996. "Extinction by hybridization and introgression." *Annu Rev Ecol Syst* 27, 83-109.

Ricardo, G. F., R. J. Jones, M. Nordborg, A. P. Negri. 2017. "Settlement patterns of the coral *Acropora millepora* on sediment-laden surfaces." *Sci Total Environ* 609, 277-288.

Rice, K. J. and N. C. Emery. 2003. "Managing microevolution: Restoration in the face of global change." *Front Ecol Environ* 1, 469-478.

Richmond, R. H. 1987. "Energetic relationships and biogeographical differences among fecundity, growth and reproduction in the reef coral *Pocillopora damicornis*." *B Mar Sci* 41, 594-604.

Richmond, R. H. and C. L. Hunter. 1990. "Reproduction and recruitment of corals—Comparisons among the Caribbean, the tropical Pacific, and the Red-Sea." *Mar Ecol Prog Ser* 60, 185-203.

Rinkevich, B. 1995. "Restoration strategies for coral reefs damaged by recreational activities: The use of sexual and asexual recruits." *Restor Ecol* 3, 241-251.

———. 1996. "Do reproduction and regeneration in damaged corals compete for energy allocation?" *Mar Ecol Prog Ser* 143, 297-302.

———. 2000. "Steps towards the evaluation of coral reef restoration by using small branch fragments." *Mar Biol* 136, 807-812.

———. 2005. "Conservation of coral reefs through active restoration measures: Recent approaches and last decade progress." *Environ Sci Technol* 39, 4333-4342.

———. 2014. "Rebuilding coral reefs: Does active reef restoration lead to sustainable reefs?" *Curr Opin Env Sust* 7, 28-36.

Rippe, J. P., J. H. Baumann, D. N. De Leener, H. E. Aichelman, E. B. Friedlander, S. W. Davies, et al. 2018. "Corals sustain growth but not skeletal density across the Florida Keys Reef Tract despite ongoing warming." *Global Change Biol* 24, 5205-5217.

Ritchie, K. B. 2006. "Regulation of microbial populations by coral surface mucus and mucus-associated bacteria." *Mar Ecol Prog Ser* 322, 1–14.

Ritson-Williams, R., V. J. Paul, S. N. Arnold, and R. S. Steneck. 2010. "Larval settlement preferences and post-settlement survival of the threatened Caribbean corals *Acropora palmata* and *A. cervicornis*." *Coral Reefs* 29, 71–81.

Rogers, C. S., E. Muller, T. Spitzack, and J. Miller. 2009. "Extensive coral mortality in the US Virgin Islands in 2005/2006: A review of the evidence for synergy among thermal stress, coral bleaching and disease." *Caribb J Sci* 45, 204–214.

Rohwer, F., V. Seguritan, F. Azam, and N. Knowlton. 2002. "Diversity and distribution of coral-associated bacteria." *Mar Ecol Prog Ser* 243, 1–10.

Rose, N. H., R. A. Bay, M. K. Morikawa, and S. R. Palumbi. 2018. "Polygenic evolution drives species divergence and climate adaptation in corals." *Evolution* 72, 82–94.

Rosenberg, E. and L. Falkovitz. 2004. "The *Vibrio shiloi/Oculina patagonica* model system of coral bleaching." *Annual Review of Microbiology* 58, 143–159.

Rosenberg, E., O. Koren, L. Reshef, R. Efrony, and I. Zilber-Rosenberg. 2007. "The role of microorganisms in coral health, disease and evolution." *Nat Rev Microbio*, 5, 355–362.

Rowan, R., N. Knowlton, A. Baker, and J. Jara. 1997. "Landscape ecology of algal symbionts creates variation in episodes of coral bleaching." *Nature* 388, 265–269.

Ruiz-Jaen, M. C. and T. M. Aide. 2005. "Restoration success: How is it being measured?" *Restor Ecol* 13, 569–577.

Ruiz-Jones, L. J. and S. R. Palumbi. 2017. "Tidal heat pulses on a reef trigger a fine-tuned transcriptional response in corals to maintain homeostasis." *Sci Adv* 3.

Rylaarsdam, K. W. 1983. "Life histories and abundance patterns of colonial corals on Jamaican reefs." *Mar Ecol Prog Ser* 13, 249–260.

Sakai, K. 1998. "Delayed maturation in the colonial coral *Goniastrea aspera* (Scleractinia): Whole-colony mortality, colony growth and polyp egg production." *Res Popul Ecol* 40, 287–292.

Salih, A., G. Cox, R. Szymczak, S. Coles, A. Baird, A. Dunstan, et al. 2006. "The role of host-based color and fluorescent pigments in photoprotection and in reducing bleaching stress in corals." In: *10th International Coral Reef Symposium* Okinawa, Japan.

Sampayo, E. M., T. Ridgway, P. Bongaerts, and O. Hoegh-Guldberg. 2008. "Bleaching susceptibility and mortality of corals are determined by fine-scale differences in symbiont type." *P Natl Acad Sci USA* 105, 10444–10449.

Santos, H. F., F. L. Carmo, G. Duarte, F. Dini-Andreote, C. B. Castro, A. S. Rosado, et al. 2014. "Climate change affects key nitrogen-fixing bacterial populations on coral reefs." *Isme J* 8, 2272–2279.

Sato, Y., B. L. Willis, and D. G. Bourne. 2010. "Successional changes in bacterial communities during the development of black band disease on the reef coral, *Montipora hispida*." *Isme J* 4, 203–214.

Schlichting, C. D. and M. A. Wund. 2014. "Phenotypic plasticity and epigenetic marking: An assessment of evidence for genetic accommodation." *Evolution* 68, 656–672.

Schnoor, J. L. 2014. "Ocean acidification: The other problem with CO_2." *Environ Sci Technol* 48, 10529–10530.

Schoener, T. W. 2011. "The Newest Synthesis: Understanding the interplay of evolutionary and ecological dynamics." *Science* 331, 426–429.

Schopmeyer, S. A., D. Lirman, E. Bartels, D. S. Gilliam, E. A. Goergen, S. P. Griffin, et al. 2017. "Regional restoration benchmarks for *Acropora cervicornis*." *Coral Reefs* 36, 1047–1057.

SER, Society for Ecological Restoration. 2004. "International science and policy working group." In: *The SER International Primer on Ecological Restoration*. Tucson, Arizona.

Sgro, C. M. and A. A. Hoffmann. 2004. "Genetic correlations, tradeoffs and environmental variation." *Heredity* 93, 241–248.

Sharp, K. H., D. Distel, and V. J. Paul. 2012. "Diversity and dynamics of bacterial communities in early life stages of the Caribbean coral *Porites astreoides*." *Isme J* 6, 790–801.

Shearer, T. L., I. Porto, and A. L. Zubillaga. 2009. "Restoration of coral populations in light of genetic diversity estimates." *Coral Reefs* 28, 727–733.

Shlesinger, T. and Y. Loya. 2019. "Breakdown in spawning synchrony: A silent threat to coral persistence." *Science* 365, 1002–1007.
Silverstein, R. N., A. M. S. Correa, and A. C. Baker. 2012. "Specificity is rarely absolute in coral-algal symbiosis: Implications for coral response to climate change." *P Roy Soc B-Biol Sci* 279, 2609–2618.
Silverstein, R., R. Cunning, and A. Baker. 2017. "Tenacious D: *Symbiodinium* in clade D remain in reef corals at both high and low temperature extremes despite impairment." *J Exp Biol* 220, 1192–1196.
Sivakumar, P., R. Parthasarthi, and V. Lakshmipriya. 2014. "Encapsulation of plant growth promoting inoculant in bacterial alginate beads enriched with humic acid." *Int J Curr Microbiol Appl Sci* 3, 415–422.
Slatkin, M. 1987. "Gene flow and the geographic structure of natural populations." *Science*, 236, 787–792.
Smith, L. D., M. Devlin, D. Haynes, and J. P. Gilmour. 2005. "A demographic approach to monitoring the health of coral reefs." *Mar Pollut Bull* 51, 399–407.
Smith, T. B., M. E. Brandt, J. M. Calnan, R. S. Nemeth, J. Blondeau, E. Kadison, et al. 2013. "Convergent mortality responses of Caribbean coral species to seawater warming." *Ecosphere* 4.
Sniegowski, P. D. and R. E. Lenski. 1995. "Mutation and adaptation—the directed mutation controversy in evolutionary perspective." *Annu Rev Ecol Syst* 26, 553–578.
Soong, K. Y. and J. C. Lang. 1992. "Reproductive integration in reef corals." *Biol Bull* 183, 418–431.
Soule, M. E. 1985. "What is conservation biology." *Bioscience* 35, 727–734.
Springer, N. M. 2013. "Epigenetics and crop improvement." *Trends Genet* 29, 241–247.
Stat, M. and R. D. Gates. 2011. "Clade D *Symbiodinium* in scleractinian corals: A "nugget" of hope, a selfish opportunist, an ominous sign, or all of the above?" *J. Mar. Biol.* 1–9.
Stat, M., W. K. W. Loh, T. C. LaJeunesse, O. Hoegh-Guldberg, and D. A. Carter. 2009. "Stability of coral-endosymbiont associations during and after a thermal stress event in the southern Great Barrier Reef." *Coral Reefs* 28, 709–713.
Stearns, S. C. 1989. "Trade-offs in life-history evolution." *Funct Ecol* 3, 259–268.
Stockwell, C. A., A. P. Hendry, and M. T. Kinnison. 2003. "Contemporary evolution meets conservation biology." *Trends Ecol Evol* 18, 94–101.
Sunagawa, S., T. Z. DeSantis, Y. M. Piceno, E. L. Brodie, M. K. DeSalvo, C. R. Voolstra, et al. 2009. "Bacterial diversity and White Plague Disease-associated community changes in the Caribbean coral *Montastraea faveolata*." *Isme J* 3, 512–521.
Sunagawa, S., C. M. Woodley, and M. Medina. 2010. "Threatened corals provide underexplored microbial habitats." *PLoS ONE* 5.
Suzuki, G., W. Okada, Y. Yasutake, S. Kai, Y. Fujikura, I. Tanita, et al. 2018. "Interspecific differences in the post-settlement survival of *Acropora* corals under a common garden experiment." *Fisheries Sci* 84, 849–856.
Sweet, M. J., A. Croquer, and J. C. Bythell. 2011. "Bacterial assemblages differ between compartments within the coral holobiont." *Coral Reefs* 30, 39–52.
———. 2014. "Experimental antibiotic treatment identifies potential pathogens of white band disease in the endangered Caribbean coral *Acropora cervicornis*." *P Roy Soc B-Biol Sci* 281.
Szmant, A. M. 1986. "Reproductive ecology of caribbean reef corals." *Coral Reefs* 5, 43–53.
Szmant, A. M. and N. J. Gassman. 1990. "The effects of prolonged bleaching on the tissue biomass and reproduction of the reef coral *Montastrea annularis*." *Coral Reefs* 8, 217–224.
Taguchi, S. and R. A. Kinzie. 2001. "Growth of zooxanthellae in culture with two nitrogen sources." *Mar Biol*, 138, 149–155.
Tebben, J., C. A. Motti, N. Siboni, D. M. Tapiolas, A. P. Negri, P. J. Schupp, et al. 2015. "Chemical mediation of coral larval settlement by crustose coralline algae." *Sci Rep-Uk* 5.
Thornhill, D. J., W. K. Fitt, and G. W. Schmidt. 2006a. "Highly stable symbioses among western Atlantic brooding corals." *Coral Reefs* 25, 515–519.
Thornhill, D. J., T. C. LaJeunesse, D. W. Kemp, W. K. Fitt, and G. W. Schmidt. 2006b. "Multi-year, seasonal genotypic surveys of coral-algal symbioses reveal prevalent stability or post-bleaching reversion." *Mar Biol* 148, 711–722.
Thurber, R. V., J. P. Payet, A. R. Thurber, and A. M. S. Correa. 2017. "Virus-host interactions and their roles in coral reef health and disease." *Nat Rev Microbiol* 15.

Thurber, R. V., D. Willner-Hall, B. Rodriguez-Mueller, C. Desnues, R. A. Edwards, F. Angly, et al. 2009. "Metagenomic analysis of stressed coral holobionts." *Environ Microbiol* 11, 2148–2163.

Tilman, D., J. Downing, and D. Wedin. 1994. "Does diversity beget stability-Reply." *Nature* 371, 114.

Torda, G., J. M. Donelson, M. Aranda, D. J. Barshis, L. Bay, M. L. Berumen, et al. 2017. "Rapid adaptive responses to climate change in corals." *Nat Clim Change* 7, 627–636.

Towle, E. K., A. C. Baker, and C. Langdon. 2016. "Preconditioning to high CO_2 exacerbates the response of the Caribbean branching coral *Porites porites* to high temperature stress." *Mar Ecol Prog Ser* 546, 75–84.

Traylor-Knowles, N. 2016. "Distinctive wound-healing characteristics in the corals *Pocillopora damicornis* and *Acropora hyacinthus* found in two different temperature regimes." *Mar Biol* 163.

Tunnicliffe, V. 1981. "Breakage and propagation of the stony coral *Acropora cervicornis*." *P Natl Acad Sci-Biol* 78, 2427–2431.

Turcotte, M. M., D. N. Reznick, and J. D. Hare. 2011. "Experimental assessment of the impact of rapid evolution on population dynamics." *Evol Ecol Res* 13, 113–131.

Turnbaugh, P. J., M. Hamady, T. Yatsunenko, B. L. Cantarel, A. Duncan, R. E. Ley, et al. 2009. "A core gut microbiome in obese and lean twins." *Nature* 457, 480-U487.

Underwood, J. N., L. D. Smith, M. J. H. van Oppen, and J. P. Gilmour. 2009. "Ecologically relevant dispersal of corals on isolated reefs: Implications for managing resilience." *Ecol Appl* 19, 18–29.

Urban, M. C. 2015. "Accelerating extinction risk from climate change." *Science* 348, 571–573.

van Hooidonk, R., J. Maynard, J. Tamelander, J. Gove, G. Ahmadia, L. Raymundo, et al. 2016. "Local-scale projections of coral reef futures and implications of the Paris Agreement." *Sci Rep-Uk* 6.

van Oppen, M. J. H., A. C. Baker, M. A. Coffroth, and B. L. Willis. 2009a. *Bleaching resistance and the role of algal endosymbionts*. Springer-Verlag, Berlin, Heidelberg.

van Oppen, M. J. H., R. D. Gates, L. L. Blackall, N. Cantin, L. J. Chakravarti, W. Y. Chan, et al. 2017. "Shifting paradigms in restoration of the world's coral reefs." *Global Change Biol* 23, 3437–3448.

van Oppen, M. J. H., J. A. Leong, and R. D. Gates. 2009b. "Coral-virus interactions: A double-edged sword?" *Symbiosis*, 47, 1–8.

van Oppen, M. J. H., B. J. McDonald, B. Willis, and D. J. Miller. 2001. "The evolutionary history of the coral genus *Acropora* (Scleractinia, Cnidaria) based on a mitochondrial and a nuclear marker: Reticulation, incomplete lineage sorting, or morphological convergence?" *Mol Biol Evol* 18, 1315–1329.

van Oppen, M. J. H., J. K. Oliver, H. M. Putnam, and R. D. Gates. 2015. "Building coral reef resilience through assisted evolution." *P Natl Acad Sci USA*, 112, 2307–2313.

van Oppen, M. J. H., P. Souter, E. J. Howells, A. Heyward, and R. Berkelmans. 2011. "Novel genetic diversity through somatic mutations: Fuel for adaptation of reef corals?" *Diversity* 3, 405–423.

van Oppen, M. J. H., B. L. Willis, H. W. J. A. Van Vugt, and D. J. Miller. 2000. "Examination of species boundaries in the *Acropora cervicornis* group (Scleractinia, Cnidaria) using nuclear DNA sequence analyses." *Mol Ecol* 9, 1363–1373.

van Woesik, R., W. J. Scott, and R. B. Aronson. 2014. "Lost opportunities: Coral recruitment does not translate to reef recovery in the Florida Keys." *Mar Pollut Bull*, 88, 110–117.

Verbruggen, H. and A. Tribollet. 2011. "Boring algae." *Curr Biol* 21, R876–R877.

Vermeij, M. 2006. "Early life-history dynamics of Caribbean coral species on artificial substratum: The importance of competition, growth and variation in life-history strategy." *Coral Reefs* 25, 59–71.

Veron, J. E. N. 1995. *Corals in Space and Time: The Biogeography and Evolution of the Scleractinia*. UNSW Press, Sydney NSW, Australia.

———. "Mass extinctions and ocean acidification: Biological constraints on geological dilemmas." *Coral Reefs* 27, 459–472.

Veron, J. E. N., O. Hoegh-Guldberg, T. M. Lenton, J. M. Lough, D. O. Obura, P. Pearce-Kelly, et al. 2009. "The coral reef crisis: The critical importance of <350 ppm CO_2." *Mar Pollut Bull* 58, 1428–1436.

Villanueva, R., M. Baria, and D. dela Cruz. 2012. "Growth and survivorship of juvenile corals outplanted to degraded reef areas in Bolinao-Anda Reef Complex, Philippines." *Mar Biol Res* 8, 877–884.

Vollmer, S. and D. Kline. 2008. "Natural disease resistance in threatened staghorn corals." *PLoS ONE*, 3.

Vollmer, S. V. and S. R. Palumbi. 2002. "Hybridization and the evolution of reef coral diversity." *Science* 296, 2023–2025.

———. 2007. "Restricted gene flow in the Caribbean staghorn coral *Acropora cervicornis*: Implications for the recovery of endangered reefs." *J Hered*, 98, 40–50.

Wallace, C. C. 1999. *Staghorn corals of the world: A revision of the genus Acropora*. CSIRO Publishing, Collingwood, Victoria.

Walton, C. J., N. K. Hayes, and D. S. Gilliam. 2018. "Impacts of a regional, multi-year, multi-species coral disease outbreak in southeast Florida." *Frontiers in Marine Science* 5.

Webster, N. S. and T. B. H. Reusch. 2017. "Microbial contributions to the persistence of coral reefs." *Isme J*, 11, 2167–2174.

Weil, E., A. Croquer, and I. Urreiztieta. 2009. "Yellow band disease compromises the reproductive output of the Caribbean reef-building coral *Montastraea faveolata* (Anthozoa, Scleractinia)." *Dis Aquat Organ* 87, 45–55.

Weil, E., N. M. Hammerman, R. L. Becicka, and J. J. Cruz-Motta. 2020. "Growth dynamics in *Acropora cervicornis* and *A. prolifera* in southwest Puerto Rico." *Peerj* 8.

Weis, V. M. 2008. "Cellular mechanisms of cnidarian bleaching: Stress causes the collapse of symbiosis." *J Exp Biol*, 211, 3059–3066.

Welsh, R. M., S. M. Rosales, J. R. Zaneveld, J. P. Payet, R. McMinds, S. L. Hubbs, et al. 2017. "Alien vs. predator: Bacterial challenge alters coral microbiomes unless controlled by Halobacteriovorax predators." *Peerj* 5.

Welsh, R. M., J. R. Zaneveld, S. M. Rosales, J. P. Payet, D. E. Burkepile, and R. V. Thurber. 2016. "Bacterial predation in a marine host-associated microbiome." *Isme J* 10, 1540–1544.

Whalan, S., M. A. A. Wahab, S. Sprungala, A. J. Poole, and R. de Nys. 2015. "Larval settlement: The role of surface topography for sessile coral reef invertebrates." *PLoS ONE* 10.

Whiteley, A. R., S. W. Fitzpatrick, W. C. Funk, and D. A. Tallmon. 2015. "Genetic rescue to the rescue." *Trends Ecol Evol* 30, 42–49.

Wigington, C., D. Sonderegger, C. Brussaard, A. Buchan, J. Finke, J. Fuhrman, et al. 2016. "Re-examination of the relationship between marine virus and microbial cell abundances." *Nat Microbiol*, 1.

Wilkerson, F. P., D. Kobayashi, and L. Muscatine. 1988. "Mitotic index and size of symbiotic algae in Caribbean reef corals." *Coral Reefs* 7, 29–36.

Williams, A. D., B. E. Brown, L. Putchim, and M. J. Sweet. 2015. "Age-related shifts in bacterial diversity in a reef coral." *PLoS ONE* 10.

Williams, D. E., M. W. Miller, and I. B. Baums. 2014. "Cryptic changes in the genetic structure of a highly clonal coral population and the relationship with ecological performance." *Coral Reefs* 33, 595–606 10.1007/s00338-014-1157-y.

Williams, D. E., M. W. Miller, and K. L. Kramer. 2008. "Recruitment failure in Florida Keys *Acropora palmata*, a threatened Caribbean coral." *Coral Reefs* 27, 697–705.

Williams, D. E., K. Nedimyer, and M. W. Miller. 2020. "Genotypic inventory of *Acropora palmata* (elkhorn coral) populations in south Florida." In: *NOAA/SEFSC/PRBD-2020-01*. U.S. Department of Commerce.

Willis, B. L., R. C. Babcock, P. L. Harrison, and C. C. Wallace. 1997. "Experimental hybridization and breeding incompatibilities within the mating systems of mass spawning reef corals." *Coral Reefs* 16, S53–S65.

Willis, B. L., M. J. H. van Oppen, D. J. Miller, S. V. Vollmer, and D. J. Ayre. 2006. "The role of hybridization in the evolution of reef corals." *Annu Rev Ecol Evol S* 37, 489–517.

Wilson, J. R. and P. L. Harrison. 2003. "Spawning patterns of scleractinian corals at the Solitary Islands—a high latitude coral community in eastern Australia." *Mar Ecol Prog Ser* 260, 115–123.

Wilson, R. S. and C. E. Franklin. 2002. "Testing the beneficial acclimation hypothesis." *Trends Ecol Evol* 17, 66–70.

Wilson, S. K., N. A. J. Graham, M. S. Pratchett, G. P. Jones, and N. V. C. Polunin. 2006. "Multiple disturbances and the global degradation of coral reefs: Are reef fishes at risk or resilient?" *Global Change Biol* 12, 2220–2234.

Work, T. M. and G. S. Aeby. 2014. "Microbial aggregates within tissues infect a diversity of corals throughout the Indo-Pacific." *Mar Ecol Prog Ser* 500, 1–9.

Wu, G. D., J. D. Lewis, C. Hoffmann, Y. Y. Chen, R. Knight, K. Bittinger, et al. 2010. "Sampling and pyrosequencing methods for characterizing bacterial communities in the human gut using 16S sequence tags." *BMC Microbiol* 10.

Yang, S. H., S. T. M. Lee, C. R. Huang, C. H. Tseng, P. W. Chiang, C. P. Chen, et al. 2016. "Prevalence of potential nitrogen-fixing, green sulfur bacteria in the skeleton of reef-building coral *Isopora palifera*." *Limnol Oceanogr* 61, 1078–1086.

Young, C., S. Schopmeyer, and D. Lirman. 2012. "A review of reef restoration and coral propagation using the threatened genus *Acropora* in the Caribbean and western Atlantic." *B Mar Sci* 88, 1075–1098.

Zakai, D., O. Levy, and N. E. Chadwick-Furman. 2000. "Experimental fragmentation reduces sexual reproductive output by the reef-building coral *Pocillopora damicornis*." *Coral Reefs* 19, 185–188.

Zaneveld, J. R., D. E. Burkepile, A. A. Shantz, C. E. Pritchard, R. McMinds, J. P. Payet, et al. 2016. "Overfishing and nutrient pollution interact with temperature to disrupt coral reefs down to microbial scales." *Nat Commun* 7.

Zayasu, Y. and C. Shinzato. 2016. "Hope for coral reef rehabilitation: Massive synchronous spawning by outplanted corals in Okinawa, Japan." *Coral Reefs* 35, 1295.

Ziegler, M., A. Roik, A. Porter, K. Zubier, M. S. Mudarris, R. Ormond, et al. 2016. "Coral microbial community dynamics in response to anthropogenic impacts near a major city in the central Red Sea." *Mar Pollut Bull* 105, 629–640.

Ziegler, M., F. O. Seneca, L. K. Yum, S. R. Palumbi, and C. R. Voolstra. 2017. "Bacterial community dynamics are linked to patterns of coral heat tolerance." *Nat Commun* 8.

10

GENETIC CONSIDERATIONS FOR CORAL REEF RESTORATION

Hanna R. Koch

ABSTRACT

The widespread degradation of coral reef ecosystems and the rapid decline in coral abundance have led to an increased interest in active coral reef restoration. When practitioners restore corals to an area from which they have been nearly or completely lost, they determine the genetic properties, and thus evolutionary trajectory of the restored population. Genetic considerations played a minor role in early coral reef restoration projects, but more recent investments in developing comprehensive restoration strategies highlight the need for incorporating genetic and evolutionary thinking. The genetic information of an individual organism contains a blueprint for its response to a particular stimulus; through natural selection, responses to changes in the surrounding environment can cause the genetic composition of a population or species to change over time. Therefore, the ability to effectively respond to environmental change—and persist in the face thereof—hinges upon the presence of genetically based variation within a population. Thus, maintaining genetic diversity is fundamental to the conservation of a species. Restoration geneticists emphasize that having a more complete understanding of the role of evolution in shaping coral species and populations will help restoration practitioners make coral reef management decisions that facilitate the persistence of diversity in the face of rapid climate change. More specifically, they will know how to effectively manipulate the genetic structure of source populations to maximize the adaptive potential of restored populations, which is a primary goal—to get restored populations to a sexually mature, self-sustaining state with sufficient genetic and phenotypic variation to effectively respond to environmental change. The aim is that by implementing sound ecological and evolutionary strategies, coral populations will have the means to cope with rapid climate change more effectively, while efforts to reduce carbon emissions and improve water quality continue. Increasing the resilience of coral reef populations should help to recover essential ecosystem services and functions. The purpose of this chapter is to (1) synthesize relevant genetic and evolutionary concepts that should be considered when designing and implementing coral reef restoration projects, (2) highlight potential risks associated with various interventions, (3) outline recommended strategies for maximizing the adaptive potential of restored coral populations, and (4) discuss a number of molecular tools that can help guide restoration efforts.

INTRODUCTION

Coral reefs are facing unparalleled levels of environmental change and stress. Global stressors linked to anthropogenic induced climate change and local stressors, such as destructive fishing and pollution, have caused precipitous declines in coral cover and health on a widespread scale (IPCC 2014a, b). Up to 50% of the world's tropical corals have been lost in the last 50 years (Pandolfi et al. 2003; Burke et al. 2011; Hughes et al. 2017; Hughes et al. 2018a). The foundation of these vital ecosystems, reef-building corals (order Scleractinia), are especially under threat (Gardner et al. 2003; Goldberg and Wilkinson 2004; De'ath et al. 2012), with over one-third of scleractinian species at increased risk of extinction (Carpenter et al. 2008). Looking forward, an estimated 70–90% of the world's corals could disappear by 2050 (Donner et al. 2005; Frieler et al. 2013; van Hooidonk et al. 2016). Although stony corals inhabit a wide range of environments and tolerate a wide variety of conditions—demonstrating their ability to adapt via natural selection—there are concerns as to whether or not they can keep pace with unprecedented rates of environmental change (Hoegh-Guldberg et al. 2007; Hoegh-Guldberg et al. 2008b; Maynard et al. 2008; Baird et al. 2009a; Torda et al. 2017; Catullo et al. 2019). Pervasive patterns of population decline and degradation have led to shifts in many coral reef management strategies from basic conservation to active restoration (Luttinger 1997; Goreau et al. 2000; McClanahan et al. 2002; van Oppen et al. 2017; Boström-Einarsson et al. 2020). As such, large investments have been made to upscale restoration efforts and develop novel interventions to jump-start critical population recovery and restore essential ecosystem functions (van Oppen et al. 2017; Ladd et al. 2018; Baums et al. 2019; NOAA 2019; ONMS 2019; Boström-Einarsson et al. 2020).

As these initiatives are designed and implemented, it is important that restoration practitioners incorporate genetic and evolutionary considerations. A more complete understanding of the role of evolution in shaping stony coral populations and species will help practitioners make management decisions that promote genetic diversity and population persistence in the face of rapid climate change (Rice and Emery 2003; Stockwell et al. 2003; Lankau et al. 2011). The growing number of species that require management has spurred rapid developments in conservation science (Petit et al. 1998; Hedrick 2001; Stockwell et al. 2003; Frankham 2005a, b; van Oppen and Gates 2006; Mumby and Steneck 2008), with emerging fields like evolutionary conservation (Eizaguirre and Baltazar-Soares 2014) and restoration genetics (Baums 2008; Williams et al. 2014a) providing the guiding principles to support population recovery and persistence as part of restoration projects.

Restoration Genetics and Coral Reefs

Applied practices of restoration genetics incorporate ecological genetics and microevolutionary theory. Microevolution (i.e., changes in the genome or frequency of a gene in a population) is influenced by mutation, selection, gene flow, and genetic drift (for a review, refer to Rice and Emery 2003). Restoration geneticists point out the importance of addressing scales of local adaptation, the effects of gene flow on adaptation, and the importance of genetic variation in promoting adaptive responses (Rice and Emery 2003). Local adaptation occurs when a population of organisms evolves to be better suited to its local environment compared to other individuals of the same species (Kawecki and Ebert 2004). It is shaped by evolutionary forces such as natural selection and gene flow. Studies have shown that adaptive differentiation occurs in numerous marine invertebrate populations in response to selection imposed by strong gradients, and more complex mosaics of abiotic and biotic conditions (Sanford and Kelly 2011). Gene flow represents the transfer of genetic variation from one population to another via migration or dispersal and can promote or inhibit local adaptation under different conditions (Lenormand 2002). Since corals are sessile, they rely on larval dispersal as a mechanism of gene flow. Adaptive divergence among populations has been observed over a range of spatial scales, including fine-grained ones (i.e., m to km), indicating an ongoing balancing act between selection and gene flow (Sanford and Kelly 2011). Interestingly, a high proportion of the marine invertebrates known or suspected of exhibiting local adaptation are species with planktonic dispersal (Sanford and Kelly 2011).

Gene flow is also a key process determining population and genetic connectivity, metapopulation dynamics, and community structure in benthic marine ecosystems, including coral reefs. Metapopulations are networks of discrete populations distributed across fragmented landscapes, connected through dispersal (e.g., the movement of planktonic coral propagules by currents over varying spatial scales). Understanding the forces that influence marine population connectivity is a significant theme within marine environment conservation, especially regarding the creation of marine protected areas (MPAs) (Palumbi 2003; Jenkins and Stevens 2018; Balbar and Metaxas 2019). In fact, one of the most common applications of genetic studies in coral reef management is the use of population genetic data to design MPAs (Lundgren 2011). Knowledge of population and genetic connectivity via larval dispersal helps to identify source and sink populations, as well as the potential for population recovery after disturbances (Bode et al. 2006; Taninaka et al. 2019; Frys et al. 2020; Harrington and Lewis 2020). Collectively, these topics are of critical importance to understanding how human manipulation of microevolution may facilitate or inhibit the capacity of organisms to evolve and adapt to rapid climate change (Rice and Emery 2003).

Despite the fact that genetic considerations have played a larger role in certain areas of marine conservation (e.g., MPA design), other fields like coral reef restoration have only begun to incorporate them more recently. This is largely because marine populations and coral reef ecosystems were previously viewed as *open* over ecological timescales (Roughgarden et al. 1985; Sale 1991; Artzy-Randrup et al. 2007), well connected via long-distance dispersal of larval stages (Thorson 1950; Scheltema 1986), homogeneous over large spatial scales (Rosenblatt and Waples 1986; Doherty et al. 1995; Ayre and Hughes 2004), and temporarily stable on the scale of millennia (Jackson 1992; Jones et al. 2009). The lack of population structure in mitochondrial DNA found within surveys of coral populations reinforced the notion that these systems were large and well-mixed (Hellberg 2006; Baums 2008). Finally, limited opportunities for small-scale adaptation (Warner 1997) and the observation of phenotypic plasticity of several coral species over small spatial scales (Bruno and Edmunds 1997) further contributed to the view that coral reef populations were open, spatially uniform, and stable (Baums 2008). It was therefore assumed by early coral reef restoration projects that the risk of complications arising from site-adaptation was low (Baums 2008).

Over time, advances in biophysical modeling tools and genetic/genomic analyses have improved our understanding of connectivity in marine systems, the structuring of coral populations, and the potential for local adaptation. Now, coral reef systems are viewed as heterogeneous, potentially closed over smaller spatial and temporal scales, and more fragile than previously thought (Mumby and Steneck 2008). Evidence from population genetic studies and computer simulations reveals extensive variability in larval dispersal distances (and therefore connectivity), ranging from a few meters to hundreds of kilometers (Schultz and Cowen 1994; Jones et al. 1999; Swearer et al. 1999; Palumbi 2003; Cowen et al. 2006; Lo-Yat et al. 2006;

Shanks 2009). Broad connectivity is clearly present (Nakajima et al. 2010; Goodbody-Gringley et al. 2012; Hock et al. 2017; Rippe et al. 2017; Hammerman et al. 2018; Studivan and Voss 2018) as larvae have the potential for long-distance dispersal (Thorson 1950; Scheltema 1986), but cases of no or highly restricted gene flow have also been found, suggesting dispersal may be more limited and local retention more common than previously regarded (Cowen et al. 2000; Thorrold et al. 2001; Taylor and Hellberg 2003; Paris and Cowen 2004; Baums et al. 2005; Jones et al. 2005; Vollmer and Palumbi 2007; Goodbody-Gringley et al. 2010; Markey et al. 2016; Quigley et al. 2019). Thus, in these latter cases, there appears to be a large degree of coupling between local production and recruitment (Meekan et al. 1993). Research suggests many reefs around the globe will experience strong increases in local retention of larvae as a consequence of ocean warming (Figueiredo et al. 2014). Nevertheless, the diversity of patterns and rates of gene flow is attributed to the complex nature of larval dispersal dynamics and population connectivity, which are influenced by a number of abiotic and biotic factors including species identity, reproductive mode, oceanographic conditions (e.g., water temperature, speed and direction of currents), geographic location, and bathymetry (depth) (Baums et al. 2012; Thomas et al. 2014; Schill et al. 2015; Lukoschek et al. 2016; Serrano et al. 2016; Bongaerts et al. 2017; Romero-Torres et al. 2018).

Our understanding of coral populations has also been reshaped by mounting evidence of phenotypic/genetic differentiation along environmental gradients (or across contrasting habitat types) and local adaptation (Sanford and Kelly 2011; Howells et al. 2012; Pratlong et al. 2015; Thomas et al. 2017; Wang et al. 2019). We know scleractinian species exist across a range of environmental gradients, and increasingly more studies are demonstrating the ability of corals to genetically adapt to their local conditions, especially with regard to temperature and depth (Howells et al. 2012; Kenkel et al. 2012; Barshis et al. 2013; Kenkel et al. 2013a; Polato et al. 2013; Bay and Palumbi 2014; Dixon et al. 2015; Baums et al. 2019; Selmoni et al. 2020). For example, a study that combined population genomics, biophysical modeling, and evolutionary simulations to investigate the adaptive potential of a common reef-building coral along the latitudinal range of the Great Barrier Reef found evidence of local thermal adaptation across the heterogeneous environment despite high dispersal rates (Matz et al. 2018) This demonstrates that scleractinian species may be more accurately characterized as systems of subpopulations adapted to diverse environments and connected via varying degrees of larval dispersal (Baums et al. 2019).

Finally, in situ observations over recent decades have altered our perception of the stability of coral reef ecosystems. For example, the 1980s marked a significant change in our understanding of the vulnerability of such systems when a pathogen-induced mass mortality event occurred in a dominant herbivore on Caribbean reefs, *Diadema antillarum*, leading to a *phase-shift* from coral to algal dominance (Hughes 1994). No one predicted that the mortality of a single species could drive such a rapid and radical change across an entire region (Mumby and Steneck 2008). Outbreaks of infectious diseases (notably, white band disease and stony coral tissue loss disease) have contributed to unprecedented levels of rapid coral loss across the Caribbean and the western Atlantic as well (Aronson and Precht 2001; Precht et al. 2016; Alvarez-Filip et al. 2019; Muller et al. 2020). Devastating changes have also occurred on the world's largest coral reef system, the Great Barrier Reef (GBR, ~2,300 km), as a result of crown-of-thorns starfish (*Acanthaster planci*) predation and recurrent mass mortality events driven by warming waters and coral bleaching (Burke et al. 2011; Hughes et al. 2018a). For example, following the 2016 mass bleaching event, 50.3% of the coral cover on reef crests along the northern one-third of the GBR (~700 km) was lost within eight months—an unprecedented level of loss over a very short time frame (Hughes et al. 2018b). These are just a few, of many, examples that underline the point that coral reefs are indeed more vulnerable to stress and disturbance than previously regarded.

With a more complete picture of coral reef ecosystems and the processes that shape coral reef populations across their ranges, restoration practitioners should be better able to incorporate ecologically and evolutionary based metrics of success (e.g., increased live coral cover and increased adaptive genetic diversity, respectively). Coral reef restoration initiatives should strive to get restored populations to a sexually mature self-sustaining state, and with sufficient genetic and phenotypic variation to effectively respond to environmental change and stress (Baums et al. 2019). In addition, the advent of the coral reef crisis has given rise to rapid developments in molecular and genetic tools that can, and should, be utilized as part of coral restoration activities. Therefore, the objective of this chapter is to synthesize the evolutionary concepts and genetic tools that can help guide such efforts.

THE NEED FOR AN EVOLUTIONARY PERSPECTIVE WITHIN CORAL REEF RESTORATION

For the effective conservation and restoration of a species, it is paramount to incorporate evolutionary thinking into management strategies (Stockwell et al. 2003; Munday et al. 2013; Eizaguirre and Baltazar-Soares 2014; Baums et al. 2019). This requires an understanding of the life-history characteristics of the species targeted for restoration, as well as the genetic and demographic properties that influence the ability of populations to adapt to rapidly changing selective pressures (i.e., microevolutionary forces) (Rice and Emery 2003; Baums 2008). Although stony coral species exist across a range of environmental gradients, which demonstrates their ability to adapt via natural selection, it is currently debated whether they can keep pace with rapid climate change (Hoegh-Guldberg 1999; Ayre and Hughes 2004; Hoegh-Guldberg et al. 2007; Hoegh-Guldberg et al. 2008b; Maynard et al. 2008; Baird et al. 2009a; Torda et al. 2017; Catullo et al. 2019). Nonetheless, evolutionary change can occur more rapidly than previously thought (i.e., rapid adaptation and contemporary evolution over ecological timescales) (Thompson 1998; Hendry and Kinnison 1999; Hairston et al. 2005), and may be an important means by which species escape extinction in the face of rapid climate change (Skelly et al. 2007; Hoffmann and Sgro 2011; Anderson et al. 2012; Torda et al. 2017; Catullo et al. 2019). In fact, most cases of rapid evolutionary change documented in natural populations involve responses to anthropogenic induced pressures (Palumbi 2001; Reznick and Ghalambor 2001; Ashley et al. 2003).

To understand the role of evolution in restoration, we must first understand some fundamental concepts of evolutionary biology. As the blueprint of life, DNA contains the genetic instructions for the development and function of all living things. It is the code that defines the boundaries of what an organism can become and is the basis for evolutionary adaptation—adjustment of organisms to their environment in order to improve their chances of survival that environment. Environmental stress can be characterized as a selective pressure—a force that is shaping adaptation and evolution in changing environments. It is a property of both the stressor and the stressed (Bijlsma and Loeschcke 2005). From an evolutionary perspective environmental stress can imply a reduction in fitness of the organism or population caused the environmental factor (Bijlsma and Loeschcke 2005). *Fitness* refers to how well an organism is able to survive and reproduce in its environment. To overcome such fitness reduc organisms and populations can respond phenotypically or genetically, and evolve adaptive mechanisms to reduce the detrimental impact of the stressor (Bijlsma and Loeschcke 2005). Such adaptations may involve changes in morphology, physiology, or behavior that improves their survival and reproductive success in the particular environment.

Adaptation via the expression of phenotypic plasticity refers to the ability of one genotype to express varying phenotypes when exposed to different environmental conditions. Research has shown that rates of phenotypic change influenced by phenotypic plasticity can be greater in anthropogenic contexts (i.e., human disturbance) than in natural ones (Hendry et al. 2008). Alternatively, genetic (or evolutionary) adaptation occurs via selection of particular phenotypes, resulting in the modification of genetic variation in the population (Ghalambor et al. 2007; Fox et al. 2019b).

In the simplest case, evolutionary response of a population to a changing or stressful environment is a function of heritable variation in the population and the strength of selection. Thus, evolutionary response hinges upon the presence of genetically based variation among individuals (intraspecific genetic variation). The presence of substantial heritable genetic variation plays a critical role in the adaptive potential of a population (see Box 10.1), which is the ability of populations/species to respond to selection via phenotypic or molecular changes (Eizaguirre and Baltazar-Soares 2014). While the traditional view of adaptive evolution was that it is very slow, we now know that it can occur rapidly over ecological timescales (Hendry and Kinnison 1999; Reznick and Ghalambor 2001; Hairston et al. 2005; Schoener 2011). Where there is existing genetic variation (i.e., *standing genetic variation*) for a trait within a population and that trait comes under strong selection, the trait can change substantially across just a few generations (Barrett and Schluter 2008; Schlotterer et al. 2016). The process can be accelerated even further by sexual reproduction where shuffling of the genetic diversity initially present in population may generate fitter genotypes faster than waiting for new beneficial mutations to rise (Figure 10.1) (Barrick and Lenski 2013). Other important factors influencing the adaptive tential of a population are population size and gene flow.

BOX 10.1

Standing Genetic Variation and Adaptation

onary response relies largely on available heritable variation. Understanding the source tic variation and how it affects adaptation are important for predicting how populations respond to changing environments (Hoffmann and Sgrò 2011). Populations adapt to hanging conditions primarily through selection on preexisting genetic variation and utations, which represent alternative sources of beneficial alleles that can result in olutionary dynamics and distinct genetic outcomes (Barret and Schluter 2008). netic variation (SGV) is the presence of alternative forms of a gene (alleles) at a a population and is influenced by several factors: biological characteristics of g., dispersal propensity, distribution, mating system, and generation time), human (e.g., habitat fragmentation, pollution, and fishing), and evolutionary forces stochastic (e.g., genetic drift), deterministic (e.g., mutation), and adaptive ction) processes (Amos and Harwood 1998).

h *de novo* mutations, adaptation from SGV is likely to lead to faster evolu- ficial alleles are immediately available, usually start at higher frequencies, ady had multiple advantageous genetic changes because they are older than new mutations and, thus, have already passed through a *selective filter* where they were pretested by selection in past environments, in another part of the species' range, or even in another species with which the population has exchanged genes (Rieseberg et al. 2003; Schluter et al. 2004; Liti et al. 2006; Barrett and Schluter 2008). Gene flow from populations experiencing different environmental conditions is one of the mechanisms that can preserve relatively high levels of SGV (Barret and Schluter 2008). As such, the mechanisms that influence the generation and maintenance of variation strongly shape the evolutionary trajectories of populations (Mitchell-Olds et al. 2007; O'Donnell et al. 2014).

Natural rates of adaptation of corals may not be able to keep pace with rapid climate change (Hoegh-Guldberg 2012; van Oppen et al. 2015; Bay et al. 2017). However, in linked sets of metapopulations, global change could be rapidly matched by the recombination of preexisting adaptive genetic variants (Baums 2008; Whiteley et al. 2015; Matz et al. 2018; Baums et al. 2019). Importantly, SGV is typically high in corals and has been demonstrated in resilient populations from highly variable environments or in bleaching survivors (Palumbi et al. 2014; Dixon et al. 2015; Drury et al. 2016; Quigley et al. 2019). Such findings underpin the exploration of various assisted evolution interventions to *fast-track* thermal adaptation by capitalizing on the presence of putatively adaptive loci (PAL) correlated with thermotolerance (Kenkel et al. 2014; Dixon et al. 2015; Dziedzic et al. 2019; Quigley et al. 2019). Such interventions include assisted gene flow (AGF), hybridization, and selective breeding (see Chapter 9 and *General Guidelines for Coral Gardening* herein). The translocation of warm-adapted adults, or their offspring, through AGF efforts may facilitate adaptation to new or anticipated local conditions by directly introducing PAL into populations with an absence or low prevalence of such genetic variants (Aitken and Whitlock 2013; Quigley et al. 2019). Through intraspecific hybridization or selective breeding, warm-adapted corals harboring PAL may be crossbred with conspecifics from cooler reefs (e.g., Dixon et al. 2015) to produce offspring that are used for restoration at cooler, but warming, sites. This intervention aims to facilitate the introgression of heat tolerance alleles into the genomic background of cooler-environment corals to support more rapid adaptation to ocean warming, while maintaining fitness under local conditions (Hagedorn et al. 2019; Quigley et al. 2019).

The presence of SGV in climate-related traits (e.g., Bay et al. 2017) and the identification of PAL in corals provide hope that human interventions that are focused on assisting the spread of putatively adaptive alleles can accelerate adaptation to rapid climate change (Bay and Palumbi 2014). In addition, there are several factors that can increase the efficacy of assisted PAL spread in corals, including soft sweeps, SGV, connectivity, naturally high levels of genetic diversity, and large donor population sizes. For a more detailed discussion of these factors and how they can increase the likelihood of achieving positive fitness benefits for corals through the application of AGF and selective breeding interventions, refer to Quigley et al. (2019). Nonetheless, further research is needed to ground truth putatively adaptive loci correlated with thermotolerance in corals, as well to identify candidate adaptive loci correlated with other climate-related traits (Parkinson et al. 2020).

While scleractinian species do not possess some of the attributes that are more commonly found to facilitate rapid evolution (e.g., short generation times and fast growth rates, as found in microbes), they do possess a number of characteristics that promote evolvability (van Oppen et al. 2015). These include (1) the common occurrence of sexual and asexual reproduction within most species (Harrison and Wallace 1990; Harrison 2011); (2) high fecundity in some species, especially broadcast spawners (Szmant 1986); (3) the occurrence of interspecific hybridization in some taxa (Willis et al. 1995; Vollmer and Palumbi 2002; Chan et al. 2018); (4) naturally occurring high levels of genetic variation in some species (Hemond and Vollmer 2010); and (5) the existence of symbiosis with a range of potentially fast-evolving microbes

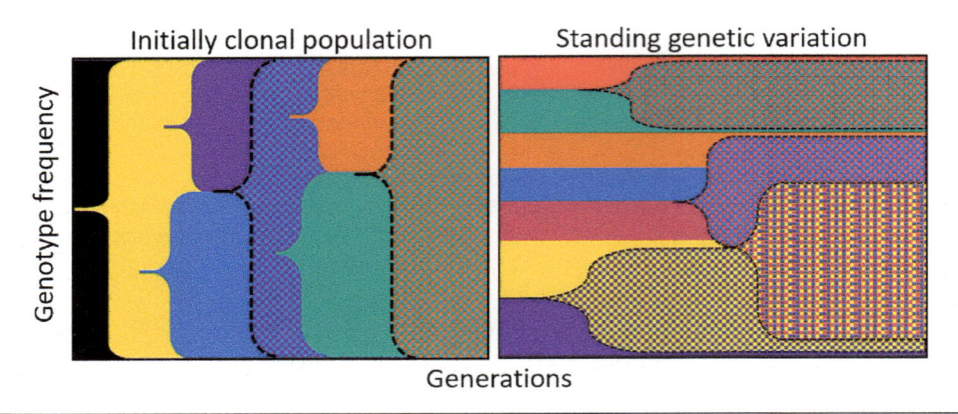

Figure 10.1 Schematic example of how sexual reproduction can generate fitter genotypes faster in a population that has standing genetic variation compared to a population that is initially clonal. The plots represent experimental populations and frequencies of different genotypes (different colors) over time. As new beneficial mutations arise, they are linked with those that arose previously in their predecessors and within an initially clonal population (left), sexual reproduction can recombine them into the same genetic background (new genotypes, mixed colors with black dashed borders). This process can be even more efficient in a population with standing genetic variation (right) because sexual reproduction shuffles genetic diversity that is already present within the population, thereby generating fitter genotypes faster than waiting for new beneficial mutations to occur. (Source: Illustration adapted from Barrick and Lenski 2013.)

(Chakravarti et al. 2017; Chakravarti and van Oppen 2018). Furthermore, the high number of mortality events that have occurred across coral metapopulations in recent decades (e.g., from bleaching and disease) indicates that these populations have already undergone several strong selective events (Eakin et al. 2010; Smith et al. 2013; Precht et al. 2016; Walton et al. 2018). Therefore, ensuing adaptation is likely to be rapid where survivors of high mortality events are particularly robust and may be expected to spawn a new generation of more stress-tolerant corals (Libro and Vollmer 2016; Muller et al. 2018; Baums et al. 2019).

Despite these attributes contributing to the evolvability of scleractinian species, coral health and abundance continue to decline under the cumulative effects of concurrent stressors and rapid environmental change. Such changes have serious implications for the evolutionary potential of degraded populations, especially if they are characterized as small, patchy, and experiencing persistent reproductive failure (Knowlton 2001; Ortiz et al. 2018). Small populations are more vulnerable to genetic drift (i.e., the stochastic loss of allelic diversity at functional genes), which can compromise their ability to adapt to new or changing environments (Soule 1985; Blomqvist et al. 2010; Lundgren 2011). As populations dwindle so will larval connectivity. This can cause processes like gene flow and sexual reproduction to become less efficient in introducing novel adaptive alleles (Slatkin 1987). Rapid environmental degradation can compromise fertilization (Gilmour 1999; Omori et al. 2001) or lead to a breakdown in the environmental cues broadcast spawners rely on for synchronizing mass spawning events, resulting in failed or asynchronous spawning (Shlesinger and Loya 2019). Gamete viability decreases with time, so fertilization failure is more likely to occur for colonies spawning in temporal or spatial isolation (Oliver and Babcock 1992; Levitan et al. 2011). Thus, sparsely populated coral reefs are also at a greater risk of reproductive failure because low population densities, asynchronous spawning, and/or low reproductive output per individual will likely lead to failed fertilization (Levitan and

Petersen 1995; Courchamp et al. 1999; Gascoigne and Lipcius 2004; Doropoulos et al. 2017; Hartmann et al. 2018). With failed fertilization, stressful environmental conditions, and phase-shifts from coral to algal-dominated reefs, natural recruitment is negatively affected, which in turn dampens the potential for population recovery (Hughes 1994; Hughes and Tanner 2000; Williams et al. 2008; Albright et al. 2010; Hughes et al. 2019).

Most alarming, there are increasing reports of persistent recruitment failure (Hughes and Tanner 2000; Williams et al. 2008; van Woesik et al. 2014; Kuffner and Toth 2016; Hughes et al. 2019), loss of genotypic diversity and abundance (Williams et al. 2014c; Williams et al. 2020), limited gene flow (Baums et al. 2005; Vollmer and Palumbi 2007; Thomas et al. 2017), the potential for genetic bottlenecks (Hemond and Vollmer 2010), spawning asynchronicity (Miller et al. 2018; Fogarty and Marhaver 2019; Shlesinger and Loya 2019), delayed sexual maturation (Koch *unpublished data*), and failed spawning altogether (Levitan et al. 2014; Miller et al. 2016). As a result, species may face functional extinction if populations are so small that they can hardly provide essential ecosystem services like reef structure and habitat and/or can no longer effectively produce the next generation to support population persistence. A viable solution to combat these issues is to combine refined coral reef restoration methods (see Chapters 6 and 7) with novel interventions (see Chapter 9) and advanced molecular tools, while efforts continue to reduce greenhouse gas emissions and improve water quality. With that said, restoration goals and metrics of success should be both ecologically and evolutionary oriented.

FACTORS THAT COULD DRIVE REDUCTIONS IN FITNESS DURING RESTORATION ACTIVITIES

Coral reef restoration efforts are increasing, and methods may differ depending on a number of factors including: species being restored, scale of project, source of disturbance, established legal and regulatory frameworks, level of investment by relevant stakeholders, or availability of resources such as infrastructure, equipment, funds, and experienced personnel (Rinkevich 2005). Some of the first restoration techniques developed were reattaching coral fragments (Bowden-Kerby 2001; Bruckner and Bruckner 2001; Boström-Einarsson et al. 2020), coral gardening and outplanting (Amar and Rinkevich 2007; Lirman and Schopmeyer 2016), colony translocation (or *transplantation*) (Hoegh-Guldberg et al. 2008a; Coles and Riegl 2013), and larval seeding (Heyward et al. 2002; dela Cruz and Harrison 2017). All of these techniques had varying levels of initial success and might or might not have incorporated genetics (Edwards and Clark 1998; Muko and Iwasa 2011; Suding 2011; Edwards et al. 2015; Fox et al. 2019a).

Many of these initial efforts were in response to the loss of live coral cover from local disturbances such as dynamite fishing, ship groundings (Lirman and Miller 2003), and anchor damage (Jameson et al. 1999). Other restorative techniques were carried out in an attempt to salvage corals from pending construction activities that would otherwise destroy or disturb them (Gayle et al. 2005; Ferse et al. 2013; Kotb 2016; Rodgers et al. 2017; Boström-Einarsson et al. 2020). It is unlikely that corals will adapt to acute human disturbances, but some of the aforementioned methods could negatively impact the adaptive potential of restored or transplanted populations if, for example, the genetic diversity of coral stocks is low, translocated colonies are maladapted to their new surroundings, or reproductive success is compromised by the presence of genotype incompatibilities (Baums 2008; Baums et al. 2013). In addition, translocating corals can lead to the unintentional movement of other non-native or harmful organisms (for a more detailed discussion of the risks associated with translocating corals, refer to NASEM 2018).

Over time, many restoration efforts have shifted in response to the decline in coral abundance that is driven by rapid climate change, which represents the greatest threat to reef ecosystems worldwide (Hoegh-Guldberg et al. 2007; Hoegh-Guldberg and Bruno 2010). As such, restoration projects have been upscaled, new and more refined methods have been developed, and our understanding of the genetic consequences of manipulating corals for restoration has improved. When practitioners restore a population to an area from which it has been nearly or completely extirpated, they determine the genetic properties, and thus, the evolutionary trajectory of that population (Rice and Emery 2003). Moreover, the finding that local adaptation is more widespread than previously thought may influence restoration projects with regard to the physical and evolutionary distance from the source that wild and/or captive bred propagules can be moved without causing a loss of fitness in the restored population (Baums 2008). In these next subsections, the importance of genetic and genotypic diversity, as well as sexual reproduction will be discussed, followed by an outline of the potential drivers of fitness reductions in restored coral populations (see Box 10.2).

BOX 10.2

Summary of Genetic Risks to Consider During Coral Reef Restoration

The following is a list of factors that could lead to fitness reductions in corals or coral populations, along with the anticipated level of concern or risk that should be considered when designing and implementing coral reef restoration projects. To prevent or reduce these risks, recommended guidelines should be followed (see *Recommendations* herein).

1. *Founder effects*—high risk within coral gardening and captive breeding programs if a limited number of individuals/genotypes are propagated.
2. *Genetic swamping*—via natural hybridization and introgression (low risk); via translocation (low risk in general, but higher for species that frequently propagate asexually via fragmentation).
3. *Inbreeding depression*—low risk for most species that are self-incompatible and genetically diverse, but higher for species/populations that are highly outbred (compared to those that have been inbred from some time) because of purging. Also a higher risk for small and/or genetically depauperate populations and captive breeding programs that use F_1 or subsequent generations as broodstock. The potential for inbreeding and inbreeding depression in corals requires further research.
4. *Outbreeding depression*—low risk in general, but warrants further research, especially within the context of AGF projects.
5. *Reproductive failure*—high risk for restored populations, especially those composed of acroporids or gonochores, if limited genotypes are outplanted together.
6. *Unintended selection in nursery settings*—medium risk.

Genetic and Genotypic Diversity

Quantifying and maintaining genetic diversity are fundamental tenets of conservation science (Haig 1998; Petit et al. 1998; Reed and Frankham 2003; Van Oppen and Gates 2006; DiBattista 2008; Shearer et al. 2009). Genetic diversity refers to the amount of variation on the level of individual genes within a population; it can be expressed as heterozygosity or allelic richness and can differ among the genomes within a cell (Baums 2008). Unlike mitochondrial genomes within coral species, which are characterized by low genetic diversity (Hellberg 2006), nuclear genomes appear to have high levels of observed and expected heterozygosity (Solecava and Thorpe 1991; Hellberg 2006; Baums 2008).

A genotype refers to the genetic makeup of an organism, and genotypic diversity is defined as the number of unique multilocus genotypes (MLGs)—which varies on the level of whole organisms. Oftentimes for corals, genotypes are referred to as *genets* and clonal colonies as *ramets*, with individuals produced via sexual and asexual reproduction, respectively (Figure 10.2). Genet and ramet are terms that are characteristic of long-lived clonal animals (e.g., redwoods, seagrasses, and corals) (Devlin-Durante et al. 2016). Estimates of genotypic diversity are a function of both the number of genotypes observed in a sample (genotypic richness) and the evenness of the distribution of genotypes within the sample. Thus, the number and relative abundance of ramets from different genets determine the genotypic richness and evenness, respectively (Arnaud-Haond et al. 2007; Baums 2008). The genotype of an individual can be

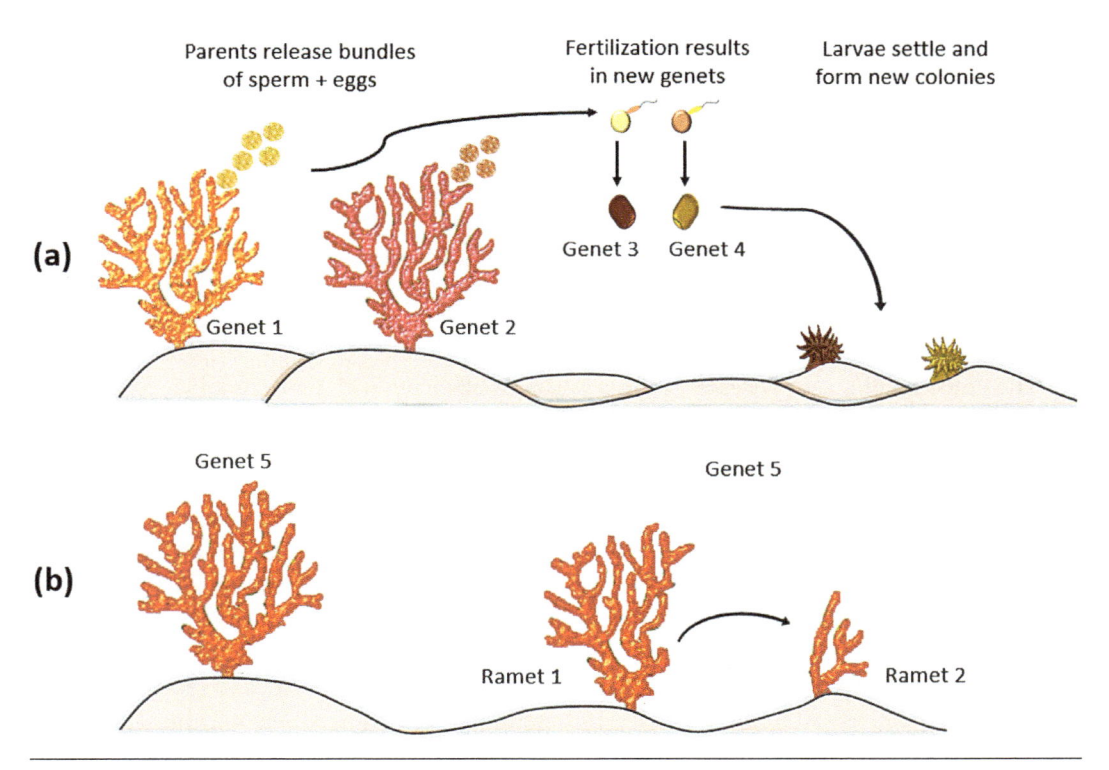

Figure 10.2 Coral reproduction. (a) Most reef-building species in the Caribbean and western Atlantic are self-incompatible hermaphroditic broadcast spawners. Adult colonies sexually reproduce by releasing bundles of sperm and eggs into the water column for external fertilization between conspecifics and pelagic larval development. Larvae settle onto the reef, undergo metamorphosis, form a primary polyp, and then grow and divide to form more polyps and a new colony. Sexually produced offspring (also referred to as sexual recruits) are genetically unique so they have different genotypes (*genets*). (b) Colonies may fragment, producing clones (*ramets*) that are genetically identical to their donor colony (i.e., they have the same genotype). The fragments can reattach, grow, and sexually reproduce when they reach puberty size. (Source: Illustration adapted from Baums et al. 2019 and Devlin-Durante et al. 2016.)

identified using a variety of genetic tools, and routine genotyping of propagated coral stock is highly recommended (see *Genotyping* herein).

Restoration geneticists point out that genetic and genotypic diversity describe processes that need to be managed separately (refer to Baums et al. 2008; see *Recommendations* herein). Usually, the loss of genetic diversity in non-domesticated species is associated with a reduction in population size. Small populations are more vulnerable to genetic drift, genetic bottlenecks, and inbreeding. Loss of genetic diversity can reduce a population's ability to adapt to changing environmental conditions. Using recommended sampling methods to source nursery stocks can help to ensure that collections have sufficient levels of adaptive genetic diversity, whereas sexually propagating corals for restoration (via *assisted sexual reproduction*) is one way to quickly increase the number of genotypes that can be outplanted (see *Recommendations* herein).

Genetic Variation and Sexual Reproduction

Genetic variation is a prerequisite for evolution because it allows natural selection to increase or decrease the frequency of alleles present in a population. Sources of genetic variation include mutation, gene flow, and sexual reproduction. Genetically, the most obvious feature of sexual reproduction is that it causes alleles to be shuffled into different combinations (Agrawal 2006; Roze 2012). An allele is one of two or more alternative forms of a gene that arise by mutation and are found at the same place (locus) on a chromosome. During meiosis, genetic shuffling (*recombination*) occurs when segments of DNA are exchanged between homologous chromosomes (*crossing-over*), resulting in new gene combinations. The new combinations can be beneficial, neutral, or deleterious. Independent assortment describes the process by which allele pairs separate independently during gamete formation, leading to differences in the combinations of chromosomes inherited from parents. Fertilization produces embryos from random combinations of genetically diverse sperm and eggs.

The outcome of these processes is the creation of offspring with new combinations of traits that differ from those found in the parents. Certain combinations may be more beneficial than others (i.e., there is variation in offspring fitness). However, sexual reproduction does not always increase genetic variation and because it is a random process that indiscriminately alters associations among alleles, the consequences for offspring fitness can be positive or negative (Otto and Lenormand 2002). For example, sexual reproduction can combine multiple beneficial alleles into a single individual, thereby creating offspring with fitter genotypes (Figure 10.1), but it can also lead to a loss of fitness if associations between beneficial combinations of interacting alleles are broken up during recombination (*recombination load*) (Charlesworth and Charlesworth 1975). Genotypes that are able to survive to adulthood and reproduce prove that they are relatively fit in their own environment; reproducing sexually may disrupt beneficial genetic combinations and lower the mean fitness of offspring (Roze 2012). The following subsections discuss how the interplay of factors like genetic diversity, gene flow, and reproduction impacts fitness under different scenarios.

Founder Effects

A founder effect is the loss of genetic diversity that occurs when a new population is established by a limited number of individuals. It can happen in natural populations when a few individuals colonize a new site (Barres et al. 2008), or within captive breeding programs if breeding is carried out with individuals that capture only a small portion of the natural diversity of the source population (Ralls and Ballou 1986; Baums 2008; Fraser 2008; Jamieson 2011). Potential consequences of founder effects include reduced adaptive potential and increased risks associated with inbreeding and genetic drift—especially if the initial population size is small. Genetic bottlenecks may also occur, which can lead to inbreeding, but it takes considerable time at the low population size for inbreeding to become an issue (Kirkpatrick and Jarne 2000; Kristensen and Sorensen 2005). Nevertheless, the severity of a bottleneck depends on a number of factors including population growth rates, mating systems, degree of gene flow from other populations, and initial genetic diversity (Hedrick 2001; Williams 2001).

Founder effects can also arise during coral reef restoration activities. A primary objective of many restoration projects is to increase live coral cover as quickly as possible. This is usually done via coral gardening by asexually propagating and outplanting replicate (clonal) fragments of a certain number of genotypes, which can be problematic if a limited number of genotypes are used. The concern is that restored populations will have less genetic diversity than the original population due to repopulation with a large number of fragments from a few donor colonies (Rinkevich 1995, 2000; Shearer et al. 2009). A genetically depauperate population is more vulnerable to local extinction under environmental stress, especially if variation in traits conferring disease and/or bleaching resistance is low (Nei et al. 1975; Altizer et al. 2003; McKay et al. 2005). Moreover, sampling from a few random donor colonies of a gonochoric species (i.e., colonies with separate sexes) could result in a restored population of a single gender or a skewed sex ratio that limits reproductive success. Strategies for avoiding founder effects during restoration are discussed in *Recommendations* herein.

Genetic Swamping

Genetic swamping is a process that is influenced by gene flow and reproduction. Non-native species can bring about a form of extinction of native flora and fauna by hybridization and introgression, either through intentional introduction by humans or habitat modification, bringing previously isolated species into contact (Rhymer and Simberloff 1996). Introgression describes the movement of a gene from one species into the gene pool of another by the repeated backcrossing of an interspecific hybrid with one of its parent species. In addition, gene flow from common species can put rare species at increased risk of extinction by genetic swamping if local genotypes are replaced by hybrids (or by demographic swamping) and population growth rates are reduced due to outbreeding depression (Ellstrand and Rieseberg 2016). The swamping effect comes from an increase in the frequency of introduced/common genotypes or alleles relative to native/rare ones, either because they outnumber them or have a fitness advantage (Baums 2008).

For threatened scleractinian species, genetic swamping may stem from human interventions involving the translocation of individuals into remnant natural populations or directed hybridization efforts. However, if the numerical advantage of the introduced variant is large enough, swamping may occur without hybridization of introduced and native individuals (Baums 2008). This is possible because of the frequent occurrence of asexual reproduction in many species. Asexual reproduction in stony corals includes fragmentation (Highsmith 1982; Lirman 2000), budding (Gilmour 2002, 2004), parthenogenesis (i.e., production of asexual larvae) (Lively and Johnson 1994; Combosch and Vollmer 2013), and polyp bailout (i.e., when a single coral polyp splits from an adult polyp before drifting off and settling elsewhere) (Sammarco 1982; Serrano et al. 2018). For species more susceptible to physical disturbance, like acroporids, propagation and population growth resulting from fragmentation are more common (Tunnicliffe 1981;

Highsmith 1982; Fong and Lirman 1995). Larger fragments have a higher chance of survival (Lirman 2000), so dispersal may be limited by the size of fragments, but the outcome can be the occurrence of genotypes extended over tens of meters (Neigel and Avise 1983; Baums et al. 2006; Baums 2008). Similar to the propagation of asexual fragments, several brooding species produce asexual larvae that are predicted to have the same dispersal potential as sexual counterparts, so they could in fact be transported further than fragments (Stoddart 1983; Baums 2008). The outcome of these processes can have considerable variability in genotypic evenness and richness on small spatial scales within and across species (Hunter 1993; Ayre and Hughes 2000; Baums et al. 2006; Baums 2008; Miller et al. 2018; Williams et al. 2020). As such, sites may have minimal clonal replication or reefs may be dominated by a single genotype.

It has been suggested that while genetic swamping of local genotypes by translocated colonies is possible in corals, for genetic swamping to occur, local adaptation of genotypes must be small (Baums 2008). Since local adaptation in corals may be more common than previously thought, genetic swamping may be less of a concern (Baums 2008). Even so, the propensity for corals to reproduce asexually must be considered within restoration projects (Baums 2008). Local dominance of a small number of genotypes can have similar consequences as previously described for populations experiencing founder effects (e.g., reduced genetic diversity and reproductive success) (Gascoigne and Lipcius 2004; Baums et al. 2013; Teo and Todd 2018).

Inbreeding and Selfing

Inbreeding depression is the reduction in fitness due to the mating of closely related individuals. It is more likely to occur in small, threatened, isolated populations in the wild or within captive breeding programs using limited broodstock (Carlon 1999; Frankham 2005b). It has the potential to drive small populations to extinction (Saccheri et al. 2005). In diploid organisms, deleterious or lethal alleles can persist in a population if they are recessive and carried at low frequency in heterozygotes. The harmful or lethal effects of these alleles are exposed when both copies are present in homozygotes. Mating among relatives decreases genetic variation and increases homozygosity in offspring genomes (Wang et al. 1999). Combining multiple deleterious alleles into a single individual is a mechanism by which the efficacy of selection can be increased through sexual reproduction because it generates less fit individuals that are more effectively purged from the population (Kondrashov 1988).

Self-fertilization (or *selfing*) is an extreme case of inbreeding but is widespread, especially among plants and hermaphroditic invertebrates (Barrett 2002; Jarne and Auld 2006). It involves the fusion of male and female gametes from a single genetic individual and represents an evolutionary and reproductive mechanism for isolated individuals to create local populations (Jarne and Charlesworth 1993). However, a negative consequence of this can be reduced genetic variation and, thus, limited potential for adaptation to environmental change. Another theoretical explanation for the benefit of selfing is that it may in fact reduce the magnitude of inbreeding depression as deleterious recessive alleles are expressed and purged through selection (Husband and Schemske 1996). If selection acts differently across life-history stages and deleterious effects are uncorrelated among stages, then the timing of inbreeding depression may also evolve with inbreeding (Husband and Schemske 1996). Evidence for this comes from theoretical and empirical studies (Lande and Schemske 1985; Schemske and Lande 1985; Charlesworth and Charlesworth 1990; Cohen 1996; Hardner and Potts 1997; Swindell and Bouzat 2006) and supports the hypothesis that most early-acting inbreeding depression is due to lethal recessive alleles that can be purged by selection via inbreeding, whereas much of the late-acting inbreeding depression is due to slightly deleterious alleles that are much more difficult to purge, even with strong inbreeding (Husband and Schemske 1996).

Most scleractinian species are hermaphrodites, so individuals produce both male and female gametes (Richmond and Hunter 1990; Harrison 2011). Of those displaying simultaneous hermaphroditism, most are broadcast spawners that release eggs and sperm into the water column for external fertilization and pelagic larval development (Baird et al. 2009b). Brooding species release sperm but retain eggs for internal fertilization and development (Richmond 1997). Brooded larvae are released in various states of advanced development (e.g., larger in size and already containing endosymbiotic algae acquired via vertical transmission from the maternal colony) (Harrison and Wallace 1990; Baird et al. 2009b). As such, they may be competent to settle more quickly after release, which has prompted expectations of shorter dispersal distances compared to broadcasting species (Ayre and Hughes 2000; Harrison 2011). Of the two sexual reproductive modes in scleractinian species (broadcast spawning and brooding), brooding is less common overall but there is a higher proportion of brooding species in the western Atlantic compared to other regions of the world (Szmant 1986). Regardless, the distance over which reproduction occurs defines the local population (Waples and Gaggiotti 2006; Warner et al. 2016). Thus, the spatial extent of gamete and offspring dispersal influences the degree of inbreeding within—and genetic structure among—populations of a species (Jain 1976; Dick et al. 2008; Warner et al. 2016).

Selfing may be a viable reproductive strategy for some scleractinian species (Kojis and Quinn 1981; Heyward and Babcock 1986; Stoddart et al. 1988; Brazeau et al. 1998; Goffredo et al. 2004; Miller and Mundy 2005; Sherman 2008), but most, including the major Caribbean reef builders, are partially or entirely reproductively self-incompatible (Heyward and Babcock 1986; Wallace and Willis 1994; Szmant et al. 1997; Willis et al. 1997). It was previously suggested that hermaphroditic species with broad dispersal potential (i.e., broadcasters) are either completely, or almost completely, self-incompatible, whereas species with limited dispersal potential (i.e., brooders) have high, but variable, rates of self-fertilization (Carlon 1999). More recent discussions of this topic suggest however, that this pattern may not hold true in a general sense (refer to Baums et al. 2008).

Regardless, Warner et al. (2016) argue that the most accepted advantage to self-fertilization is reproductive assurance (Jarne and Auld 2006), with selfing being an effective strategy for persistence following colonization of a new area (Baker 1955) or if sperm limitation exists (Yund 2000). A mixed mating strategy of selfing and outcrossing is common in plants and has been suggested for coral species that are colonizing new areas (Warner et al. 2016). However, higher frequencies of selfing during founder events or following population bottlenecks will increase homozygosity (Wright 1921). These may be relevant considerations for restoration of species with higher selfing rates and methods involving captive breeding, translocation, or coral gardening if a limited number of genotypes are used. As the population size and density increases, outcrossing may be increasingly favored to reduce potential inbreeding depression and facilitate the success of long-distance dispersal (Charlesworth and Charlesworth 1987; Warner et al. 2016). However, this has yet to be demonstrated within coral restoration studies.

Variability in mating strategies within and across scleractinian species makes it difficult to develop a uniform restoration strategy based on factors like the potential for inbreeding depression (Gleason et al. 2001). Even so, because most major reef-building species are broadcast spawners that are highly outbred and genetically diverse (Baums 2008; Baird et al. 2009b), it may not be necessary to determine their relatedness to avoid inbreeding because the likelihood of picking two parents in natural populations that are closely related as a result of sexual reproduction is vanishingly low (Baums et al. 2019). With that said, some populations of Caribbean/western Atlantic species are known to be highly clonal with genetically identical neighboring colonies due to asexual fragmentation (Baums et al. 2006; Foster et al. 2007; Williams et al. 2020), so restoration strategies may need to be modified in these cases (see *Recommendations* herein).

Finally, since current restoration methods associated with sexual propagation only raise first-generation offspring, inbreeding depression in this context is not a major concern (Baums et al. 2019). In theory, inbreeding depression could occur after repeated rounds of sexual reproduction among closely related genotypes in a nursery setting, but Baums et al. (2019) deem this a far-off risk given the challenges of long-term coral culture and breeding, combined with relatively long generation times. The same authors suggest, though, that since inbreeding and outbreeding depression have yet to be tested experimentally in corals, these topics should be the focus of future research.

Outbreeding

Outbreeding (or *outcrossing*) refers to the mating of individuals that are not closely related, whether they come from differentiated populations of the same species (*intraspecific hybridization*) or from different species (*interspecific hybridization*). Either way, there can be both positive and negative effects of outbreeding. A positive effect includes outbreeding enhancement, also known as *heterosis* or *hybrid vigor,* which describes the increased fitness of crossbred organisms compared to their purebred parents (Shull 1948). While mechanistic underpinnings are still debated, genetic explanations include increased heterozygosity, the masking of deleterious recessive alleles (*dominance*) (Jones 1917; Li et al. 2008), the superior fitness of heterozygous genotypes over homozygous genotypes at a single locus (*overdominance*) (Pujolar et al. 2005; Lariepe et al. 2012), and the production of novel allele combinations that result in new favorable multilocus genotypes (*epistasis*) (Schnell and Cockerham 1992; Melchinger et al. 2007; Jiang et al. 2017).

Studies across animal and plant species have demonstrated the positive effects of outbreeding on traits that influence growth, fertility, and survival (Sheridan 1986; Hedgecock et al. 1995; Johansen-Morris and Latta 2006; Birchler 2016; Lembeye et al. 2016; Bunning et al. 2019). As such, heterosis has been exploited in many agricultural and livestock production systems because of its immense economic value (Lippman and Zamir 2007). In addition, hybrid vigor has been documented in soft corals (Slattery et al. 2008) and Caribbean acroporids (Fogarty 2012) (see *Interspecific Hybridization* herein). For genetically depauperate populations (e.g., *A. palmata*) (Williams et al. 2020), outcrossing conspecifics from distant populations may be a targeted restoration strategy (see *Assisted Gene Flow* herein) (Hagedorn et al. 2019).

Conversely, outbreeding depression is the reduction in fitness resulting from mating populations or species that are too genetically distinct. Mechanisms include the loss of locally adapted alleles (Templeton, 1986) or disruption of co-adapted genes at different loci (epistasis). In the former (*extrinsic outbreeding depression*), individuals created as a result of outcrossing or hybridization receive only half the allelic combinations present in either parent population and may be unsuited to one or both of the parental environments (i.e., they are maladapted) (Edmands 2007). In the latter (*intrinsic outbreeding depression*), recombination between different parental genomes may lead to a breakdown of interactions between co-adapted loci that are inherited together and influence a fitness-related trait (Edmands 2007). Fitness reductions resulting from recombination and the dilution of locally adapted genotypes may be observed within

F_1 generations or later, whereas reductions stemming from epistatic interactions may not be seen until after the second generation (F_2) (for a more detailed discussion, refer to Baums et al. 2008 and Willis et al. 2006). Gene flow is an important force in these scenarios because the introduction of new individuals from nonlocal source populations can introduce maladapted alleles or cause the breakup of co-adapted gene complexes via reproduction and recombination.

As previously mentioned, since outbreeding (and inbreeding) depression have yet to be tested experimentally in corals, empirical support for the potential effects that these processes may have on the long-term success of coral restoration projects is lacking. Typically, detection of these phenomena include careful experimentation including breeding studies, common garden experiments, and reciprocal transplants of hybrid individuals (Hufford and Mazer 2003; Baums 2008). Improvements in coral sexual propagation methods, including assisted fertilization, larval settlement, and recruit rearing should increase the feasibility of such experiments (see Chapter 8). Other potential avenues include using model organisms and long-term field studies (Hufford and Mazer 2003; Baums 2008). Although outbreeding depression has never been directly tested in corals, associated risks are predicted to be low (Baums et al. 2019), especially in rapidly declining local populations (Ralls et al. 2018). Despite this, outbreeding depression could still occur if the number of outplanted genotypes approaches the number of genotypes surviving in nature, which could cause resources to be wasted by outplanting maladapted genotypes or cause rapid local adaptation to be inhibited when non-native genotypes reproduce with native ones (Baums et al. 2019).

RECOMMENDATIONS

There is no *one-size-fits-all* strategy for coral reef restoration because species selection for restoration will depend on what the overall goal of the project is (e.g., shoreline protection, fisheries habitat provisioning, tourism, species conservation, and/or ecosystem recovery) (Baums et al. 2019). Regardless, rapid climate change is a serious threat to coral reef ecosystems worldwide, so irrespective of the motivation behind a specific project, practitioners should understand the genetic consequences of their manipulations because they will impact the adaptive potential of restored populations. For example, if the motivation is to increase live coral cover as quickly as possible to support tourism, but only a handful of *fast-growing* genotypes are used to do so, then negative genetic consequences may include reduced genetic diversity and trade-offs, which in turn may lead to reductions in fitness, population resilience, and reproductive success. As another example, a selective breeding project may aim to cross corals with desirable traits to create robust offspring for restoring degraded reefs. Without knowing the heritability of targeted traits though, the project may prove futile because, for traits to be inherited across generations, they must be genetically based. Moreover, there is limited knowledge regarding the genetic basis of traits that will be relevant in the future when conditions are likely different (Baums et al. 2019), as well as the potential for interactions among traits leading to fitness trade-offs (Muller et al. 2018)—indicating that further research is necessary in order to understand how such factors may influence the adaptive potential of restored populations now and in the future.

For many coral reef restoration practitioners, the goal is to enhance coral reef resilience so that essential ecosystem services and functions are restored. Therefore, the recommended strategy, through directed restoration interventions, is to harness and promote the adaptive genetic diversity that is already present within natural populations (Baums et al. 2019). Discussions with experts, including experienced practitioners and restoration geneticists, prior to the design and implementation of projects will likely improve the probability of project success. Furthermore, restoration genetics is a rapidly growing field. New developments, refined methods, and more comprehensive guidelines are continuously being published, so practitioners should constantly monitor these updates, examine scientific/grey literature, and optimize strategies accordingly (refer to NASEM 2018). The remainder of this section outlines general recommendations for population enhancement via coral gardening, as well as specific recommendations for restoring populations of threatened reef-building species in the western Atlantic (e.g., along Florida's Coral Reef).

General Guidelines for Coral Gardening

One of the most common active restoration methods is population enhancement via coral gardening, especially across the Caribbean and western Atlantic (Young et al. 2012; Rinkevich 2014; Barton et al. 2017). Coral gardening activities should always take into account the genetic component of restoration because population enhancement methods take advantage of asexual fragmentation by producing large numbers of clonal fragments that are genetically identical (RRN 2020). Selection of a limited number of genotypes to propagate and outplant can lead to reduced genetic diversity of restored populations, reproductive failure if genotype incompatibilities exist, and reduced phenotypic variation or trade-offs if selections are based on a single trait (e.g., *fast-growing*). Thus, selecting a few genotypes that are considered *top-performers* can be subjective and lead to failed efforts if, for example, environmental conditions change or outbreaks of novel diseases occur.

The use of coral nurseries may also pose a risk for genetic diversity by exposing corals to conditions that are not optimal for all genotypes maintained within the nursery (O'Neil 2015; RRN 2020). This can lead to unintended selection of phenotypes/genotypes that are better suited to the conditions under which the corals are raised but may not experience on the reef (Christie et al. 2012; Christie et al. 2016; Morvezen et al. 2016; Horreo et al. 2018; O'Donnell et al. 2018). These considerations are especially important for species that are threatened or low in abundance because they have likely already undergone genetic bottlenecks where dramatic losses of coral colonies coincided with reductions in standing genetic variation (Baums 2008).

General guidelines for population enhancement of scleractinian species via coral gardening are as follows (Baums 2008; Johnson et al. 2011; RRN 2020):

1. Aim to cultivate and outplant as many genotypes as possible. Initial collections for the purpose of creating nursery stocks should capture as much of the local genetic diversity of the species as possible. Fragments should be collected from as many physically separated reef areas as possible to increase the likelihood of obtaining unique genotypes for propagation efforts. A number of genetic tools are available for genotyping corals (e.g., molecular markers based on microsatellites or single nucleotide polymorphisms (SNPs)) (see *Genotyping* herein). The ideal scenario would be to determine genotypes for every coral brought into the nursery and keep detailed records of all corals during fragmentation, grow-out, and outplanting. If this is not feasible, it is recommended to collect corals from a wide range of sites and habitats and determine the genotypes for a subset of corals.
2. If limited colonies are available to establish a nursery, it is not recommended to use genetically depauperate coral fragments, which can lead to further reduced genetic diversity due to high selectivity in nurseries. Alternative to moving colonies from more distant coral reef sites, gametes can be moved across large distances and larvae reared

in captivity. Sexual recruits can be directly outplanted or micro-fragmented and then outplanted (see Chapters 6 and 8).
3. A wide range of genotypes should be propagated regardless of whether a genotype displays high or low productivity within nurseries. Performance within nurseries (land- or field-based) does not always predict performance when outplanted because genotypes may have widely different growth rates depending on environmental conditions (Lirman et al. 2014b; Drury et al. 2017; O'Donnell et al. 2018). Corals that grow more slowly may have other, untested, traits that affect their fitness under different conditions (e.g., if trade-offs exist). For these reasons, characterizing the phenotypes of different genotypes is important (see *Phenotypic Traits of Propagated Corals* herein), as is tracking the performance of genotypes over time in the different environments and after outplanting.
4. Outplanting design is also a crucial component of an effective restoration strategy. Species should be outplanted within native habitat types to prevent maladaptation (e.g., *A. palmata* prefers shallow habitats with high wave energy). How coral fragments and genotypes are spatially arranged across a restoration site can influence survival, reproduction, and the pace of recovery. For example, one approach is to outplant replicate (clonal) fragments in an array so that they fuse and form a larger colony faster, thereby reducing the time to sexual maturity and reproduction (see Chapter 9). If fragments within an array come from different genotypes, intraspecific competition and mortality may occur. To ensure high genetic diversity site-wide and successful sexual reproduction of different (and compatible) genotypes, different arrays should be composed of different genotypes. For gonochoric species, restored populations should maintain appropriate sex ratios. For example, *Montastraea cavernosa*, typically has a 1:1 sex ratio of male to female colonies in nature (Acosta and Zea 1997). Knowing or identifying the gender of outplanted corals will be important for ensuring reproductive success and preventing restored populations that are comprised of a single gender or skewed sex ratios.

Restoration of Threatened Scleractinian Species in the Western Atlantic

Coral reefs across the Caribbean and western Atlantic have been hard hit by warming waters, hurricanes, a mass die-off of a key herbivore, destructive human activities, ocean acidification (OA), and outbreaks of deadly diseases. Large-scale bleaching events have increased in frequency and intensity over the last 40 years, with six mass bleaching events causing widespread mortality (Gardner et al. 2003; Manzello et al. 2007; Eakin et al. 2010; Kuffner et al. 2015; Manzello 2015). Some species benefit from physical disturbance associated with natural weather events (e.g., hurricanes) because it can support asexual propagation and population expansion (Fong and Lirman 1995). But as tropical storms intensify, so does the magnitude of immediate loss following such events (Lugo et al. 2000; Gardner et al. 2005; Cheal et al. 2017; NCCOS 2018). The rapid mass die-off of a keystone species, the long-spined sea urchin (*Diadema antillarum*), changed the face of coral reefs in this region, resulting in a phase-shift from coral to algal-dominance (Lessios et al. 1984; Hughes 1994; Lessios 2016). Apex predators are important for maintaining healthy ecosystems (Ripple et al. 2014), but destructive human activities, like overfishing, have caused the decline of countless large marine predator species (Estes et al. 2011; McCauley et al. 2015; Valdivia et al. 2017). The negative impact of OA on the calcification of adult coral reefs is well documented, but research on a Caribbean coral species indicates OA also has the potential to impact multiple, sequential early life history stages, thereby severely compromising sexual recruitment and the ability of coral reefs to recover from disturbance

(Albright et al. 2010). Finally, the rapid loss of corals from disease outbreaks occurring in this region is unprecedented in the geological records (Aronson and Precht 2001a; Gardner et al. 2003), with mass mortalities strongly attributed to outbreaks of white band disease (Aronson and Precht 2001; Precht et al. 2016) and stony coral tissue loss disease (FDEP 2020; Muller et al. 2020). The net effect? A massive region-wide decline in coral abundance, with the average hard coral cover on reefs reduced by 80% (Gardner et al. 2003). Some species have experienced declines in abundance estimated at greater than 97% (NMFS 2015), while others have been recently classified as functionally extinct and/or very near to local extinction (Chan et al. 2019a; Williams et al. 2020).

Investments in active restoration of corals across the Caribbean and the western Atlantic have increased over the last 20 years (Lirman and Schopmeyer 2016), especially with regard to acroporids (Young et al. 2012; Chamberland et al. 2015). Once among the most abundant and important reef-building species in this area, widespread population declines have led numerous publications to outline species recovery plans, including comprehensive strategies for rebuilding and assuring the long-term viability of elkhorn and staghorn populations in the wild. For detailed guidelines, which include genetic considerations, refer to *Recovery Plan: Elkhorn Coral (Acropora palmata) and Staghorn Coral (A. cervicornis)* (NMFS 2015), and the following publications (Acropora Biological Review Team 2005; Lirman et al. 2010; Johnson et al. 2011; Young et al. 2012; Chamberland et al. 2015; O'Neil 2015; Schopmeyer et al. 2017).

Even apart from the acroporids, the number of reef-building species that warrant active restoration is increasing in this region, and the loss of dominant reef-builders is resulting in the loss of ecological and structural functions. For example, declines in coral health and abundance, along with long-term recruitment failure, have also been documented for another key reef-builder, *Orbicella faveolata* (Hughes and Tanner 2000; Edmunds and Elahi 2007; Levitan et al. 2014; Aeby et al. 2019; Fisch et al. 2019). Because there is no ecological redundancy in this region to make up for deficits associated with the reef-accretion function of foundational species, many reefs have shifted from net accretional to net erosional states (Kuffner and Toth 2016; Yates et al. 2017), leaving coastal communities and shorelines more vulnerable to waves, storms, and floods. In addition to having limited functional redundancy, the Caribbean/western Atlantic region is characterized by a lower number of reef-building species, lower overall species diversity, a lack of sexual recruitment, and shifts in recruitment from long-lived broadcast spawning species to more weedy brooding species (Rogers et al. 1984; Hughes and Tanner 2000; Bellwood et al. 2004; Edmunds and Elahi 2007; Williams et al. 2008). As such, multi-species restoration strategies are imperative.

In response to this, an expert team of coral reef scientists and restoration geneticists (as part of the Coral Restoration Consortium's Genetics Working Group) has recently published a comprehensive plan with restoration guidelines for maximizing the adaptive potential of reef-building corals across the western Atlantic (Baums et al. 2019) (Figure 10.3). These guidelines are meant to aid practitioners in their efforts to re-establish populations that are capable of sexual recruitment and genetic exchange under changing environmental conditions. The

Figure 10.3 (see facing page) Diagram of the Coral Restoration Consortium (CRC) Genetics Working Group's basic restoration guidelines to maximize the adaptive potential of restored populations of reef-building species under rapid environmental change. New genotypes (genets) are the product of sexual reproduction, whereas clones (ramets) arise from asexual reproduction (e.g., via fragmentation), and are genetically identical to their donor colonies. (Source: Adopted from Baums et al. 2019.)

Genetic Considerations for Coral Reef Restoration

Acquire genets for propagation

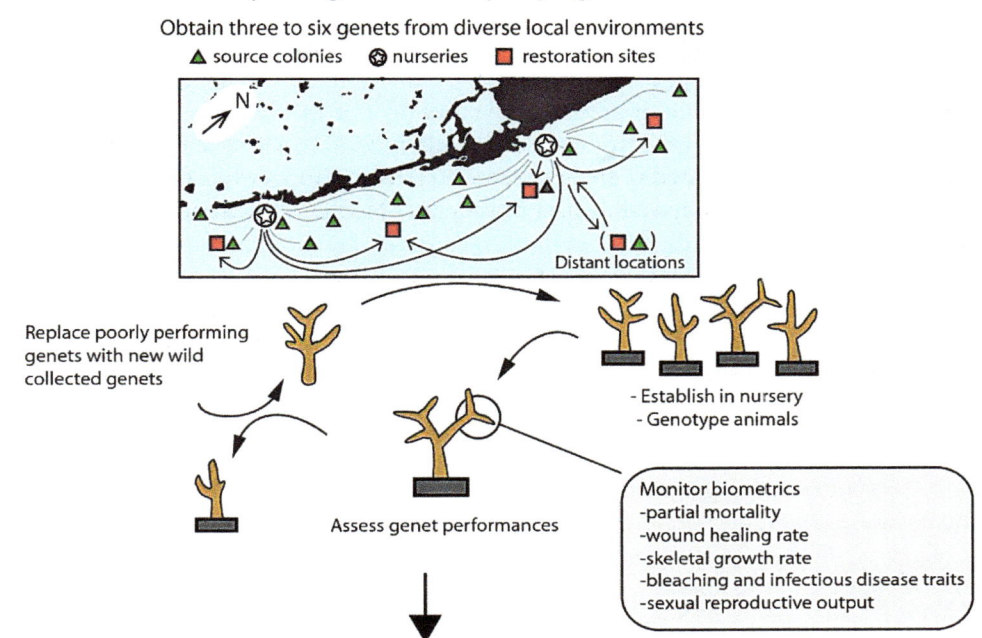

Obtain three to six genets from diverse local environments
▲ source colonies ◉ nurseries ■ restoration sites

Replace poorly performing genets with new wild collected genets

- Establish in nursery
- Genotype animals

Assess genet performances

Monitor biometrics
- partial mortality
- wound healing rate
- skeletal growth rate
- bleaching and infectious disease traits
- sexual reproductive output

Outplanting and community restoration

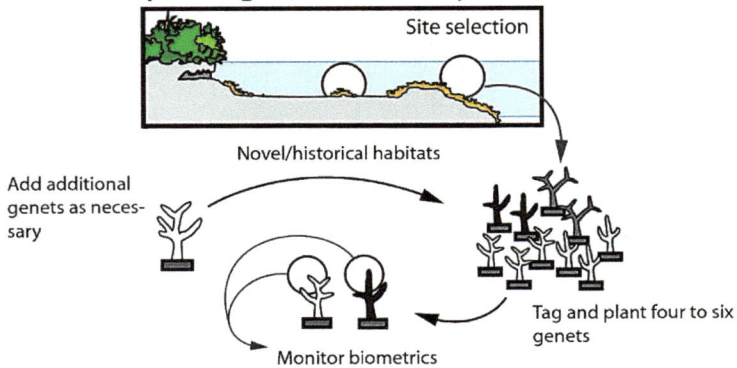

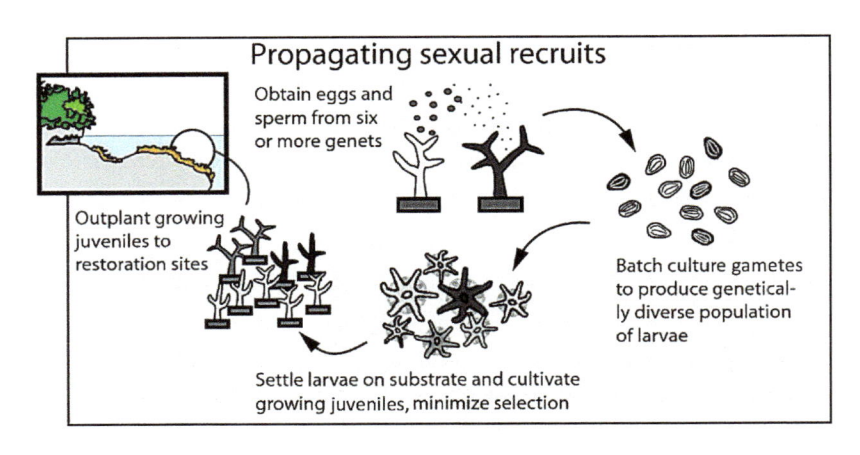

Site selection

Add additional genets as necessary

Novel/historical habitats

Tag and plant four to six genets

Monitor biometrics

Propagating sexual recruits

Obtain eggs and sperm from six or more genets

Outplant growing juveniles to restoration sites

Batch culture gametes to produce genetically diverse population of larvae

Settle larvae on substrate and cultivate growing juveniles, minimize selection following subsections outline specific recommendations for how to (1) strategically sample different reef habitats to capture as much of the adaptive genetic variation remaining in natural populations, (2) outplant different genotypes, and (3) evaluate long-term restoration success via monitoring, as well as suggestions for possible enhancements to restoration practices including (a) routine genotyping of propagated stock, (b) trait-based assessments of genotype performance, (c) sexual propagation of species with failing sexual cycles in the wild, and (d) management of endosymbiont diversity in restored populations (Baums et al. 2019). Alternative or complementary strategies proposed by the National Academies of Sciences are also included throughout, which represent different options to consider if additional funds and/or resources are available to practitioners (NASEM 2018).

Target Species

For ecosystem-based restoration, species selection should be based on those that are (1) foundational (i.e., reef-builders), (2) experiencing severe declines in cover, and (3) are consistently failing to sexually recruit (Baums et al. 2019). Four species meeting all of these requirements include *A. cervicornis*, *A. palmata*, *O. faveolata*, and *O. annularis* (van Woesik et al. 2014). Other candidate species include *Dendrogyra cylindrus* (which faces local extinction in the Florida Keys (Chan et al. 2019a)), *Pseudodiploria* spp., *Siderastrea siderea*, *Stephanocoenia intersepta*, *M. cavernosa*, *Colpophyllia natans*, *Diploria labyrinthiformis*, and *O. franksii*. These species are candidates because they can build reef structure and/or successfully produce sexual recruits. Genetic banking, in addition to active restoration, is recommended for species that are rare or are not main reef-builders, including *Dendrogyra*, *Porites*, *Agaricia*, *Dichocoenia*, and *Favia* (Hagedorn et al. 2012). Banking of genetic material (e.g., cryopreservation of gametes) and live animals in aquaria (ex situ gene banking) are means of safeguarding species/community diversity for future action (Hagedorn and Carter 2016; Hagedorn et al. 2017). Finally, prioritization of species should follow an adaptive management strategy under which demographic monitoring of wild and restored populations is evaluated every five to ten years to determine changes in population growth rates and sexual recruitment rates (refer to Baums et al. 2019).

Sourcing Corals as Part of a Mixed Provenance Strategy

Prior assumptions about potential genetic risks, especially gene swamping and outbreeding depression (Edmands 2007), led to the *local-is-best* provenance strategy, which placed strict limits on the geographic range of sourcing corals (refer to McKay et al. 2005). However, the CRC's Genetics Working Group argues that poor performance of most local populations in recent years indicates that whatever local adaptation is present in these populations, it may be insufficient to ensure persistence as environments continue to change (Williams et al. 2008; Williams et al. 2014a; Baums et al. 2019; Chan et al. 2019a). In other words, populations are so degraded, and these genetic risks are so low, that a more flexible strategy—one that promotes assisted gene flow across more distant populations, for example—may be more appropriate for this region. This idea represents a *climate-adjusted* provenance strategy (Prober et al. 2005), which incorporates representation of both locally sourced genotypes and ones from across an environmental gradient skewed toward those coming from populations already experiencing predicted future environmental conditions (Baums et al. 2019). This strategy is recommended over the more simple approach of making selections based only on single traits (e.g., thermotolerant genotypes) because, in this context, the propensity for trade-offs (e.g., with growth or disease resistance) is either unknown or untested (Baums et al. 2019).

Assisted Gene Flow

The mixed provenance strategy is especially recommended when designing assisted gene flow (AGF) projects across the western Atlantic (Baums et al. 2019). Source material from locally adapted populations can be used to improve the fitness of distant depauperate populations by facilitating gene flow—and the spread of adaptive alleles—between them. For example, because corals can adapt to local temperature conditions, genetic variants conferring heat tolerance should already be present in high frequencies in warm-adapted populations (Polato et al. 2010; Bay and Palumbi 2014; Palumbi et al. 2014; Dixon et al. 2015). In some cases, natural gene flow via larval dispersal is predicted to be successful in exchanging adaptive genetic variants among varying thermal environments (e.g., on the Great Barrier Reef) (Matz et al. 2018). However, this prediction may not hold true for other regions, and because ongoing ocean warming is predicted to alter dispersal patterns by shortening planktonic periods and altering the speed and direction of currents, AGF may be necessary to ensure the exchange of such variants (Heyward and Negri 2010; Baums et al. 2013; Figueiredo et al. 2014; Wood et al. 2016; Baums et al. 2019).

Source materials may include translocated colonies that will spawn and sexually reproduce with resident colonies, propagules (gametes) that are used in assisted fertilization interventions to cross different populations, or genes. Potential negative consequences of AGF to keep in mind include (1) outbreeding depression for hybrids between translocated and native colonies (van Oppen et al. 2014), (2) the disruption of local adaptation to nonclimatic factors such as mismatches in spawning times that could reduce fitness, fertilization success, or the likelihood of introgression of stress-tolerant genes into local populations (Baird et al. 2009b), and (3) gene swamping where the input of translocated maladapted genes may dominate over existing, better-adapted genes and cause a decline in total genetic variation across locations (NASEM 2018). While negative consequences of introducing maladapted alleles are predicted to be nominal for coral populations with very large sizes (e.g., on the GBR) (Matz et al. 2018), they may be more likely in coral populations that are small or experiencing severe declines (e.g., in the Florida Keys) (Baums et al. 2019). Candidate species for this type of work are those that are foundational with wide geographic ranges and large population sizes (Aitken and Whitlock 2013; Hagedorn et al. 2019).

Nursery and Broodstock Selection

Selection of coral stocks for asexual and/or sexual propagation is important (*nursery stock* and *broodstock*, respectively). Propagation in nurseries can be done in situ (field-based) or ex situ (land-based). Baums et al. (2019) suggest that nurseries should strive to establish stocks with a good representation of adaptive alleles that are beneficial in various contemporary reef environments and that capture a significant portion of the adaptive genetic diversity existing within the species. However, because the availability of biomarkers is limited (see *Biomarkers*) and the identities of potentially adaptive alleles largely remain unknown, most practitioners rely on a narrow set of traits to identify resilient corals (see *Phenotypic traits of propagated corals*). Nonetheless, practitioners may still be able to ensure sufficient adaptive genetic diversity within stocks by using specific collection methods.

Suggested methods for maximizing the chance that collections will capture alleles that help scleractinian species adapt to various environments across the western Atlantic (Baums et al. 2019), are as follows:

1. *Identify environmentally diverse source reef patches to attempt a climate-adjusted provenance strategy.* Across the largest practical area, identify reef sites that differ in their environmental conditions. Some of these sites may feature projected future environmental

conditions (e.g., elevated temperature), more variable temperature regimes, and/or a lower aragonite saturation state (Baums et al. 2019). The strongest evidence for local adaptation of corals is associated with depth (e.g., Bongaerts et al. 2011; Brazeau et al. 2013) and temperature (e.g., Dixon et al. 2015), but pH (Comeau et al. 2014; Schoepf et al. 2017), turbidity (Anthony and Fabricius 2000), the level of inorganic nutrients, and reef habitat type may be relevant factors influencing local adaptation as well (Baums et al. 2019). When sourcing corals, it is important to sample as widely as possible along environmental gradients, but in the same depth range as the target restoration site. Corals inhabiting greater depths (>15–20 m) may be reproductively isolated from shallower populations of the same species and/or unsuitable for shallow-water nurseries or restoration sites (Prada and Hellberg 2013; Serrano et al. 2016; Bongaerts et al. 2017, but see Prasetia et al. 2017).

2. *Select the best candidates for asexual and sexual propagation.* Collect three to six genotypes per patch, colonies that are growing more than 5 m apart to prevent sampling clones (Baums et al. 2006; Foster et al. 2007), and healthy colonies with visible variation in morphology and/or size (Baums et al. 2019). Sexual maturity is size-dependent, with reproductive size varying considerably among species (Soong and Lang 1992), so predetermine the necessary minimum colony size for corals that will be used for sexual propagation. Because genotype compatibilities may exist, it is recommended to select more genotypes for sexual propagation of most species (i.e., 5–10). More genotypes (~10) may need to be collected for *Acropora* spp. that have less synchrony in spawning and higher variability in fertility among genotypes (Fogarty et al. 2012; Baums et al. 2013; Miller et al. 2016), as well as for gonochoric species to increase chances of sampling both genders, which are necessary for successful sexual reproduction. Sampling three to four genotypes from a population is sufficient to capture many (>50%) of the common alleles (frequency >5%) that are locally adaptive, whereas sampling 12 genotypes will capture the majority (>90%) of allelic diversity (Shearer et al. 2009; Baums et al. 2019). The resulting minimum number of genotypes for each species propagated within a nursery should be on the order of 20–25 and include representatives from reef sites spanning the full range of environmental conditions experienced by the species (Baums et al. 2019).

3. *Continuously monitor genotype performance and replace genotypes, as necessary.* Propagate selected corals in land- or field-based nurseries and monitor their performance. Genotypes that are poorly performing in a nursery setting can be exchanged. However, keep in mind that the nursery environment may be different from that of the reef where the colony was sourced, and that nursery performance is not always indicative of performance at an outplant site (i.e., genotypes can respond differently across environments, *genotype x environment interactions*) (O'Donnell et al. 2018). Differences in performance across environments could also be the result of symbiont switching or artificial selection. Some species are capable of switching algal endosymbionts; switching to a more heat-tolerant strain may lead to trade-offs in the physiology of the coral host and slower growth (Jones and Berkelmans 2010). It has also been observed that corals propagated in a land nursery harbored a different Symbiodiniaceae strain compared to those propagated in a field nursery, even though they were the same host genotype (Mote *unpublished data*). Holding corals in nurseries for extended periods of time can also lead to selection of genotypes particularly suited to nursery conditions, which may differ from the outplant site. Nonetheless, poorly performing genotypes can be *banked* where they are maintained in a nursery but not propagated; they may be useful in the future if conditions change.

4. *Alternative Strategy Proposed by the National Academies of Sciences: Managed Selection* (NASEM 2018). Managed selection refers to the detection of corals with above average stress tolerance and their use in subsequent interventions (see Chapter 9). Similar to #1 in this list, managed selection builds on the fact that coral reefs exist along a range of environmental gradients, reflecting the ability of individuals to acclimatize, of populations to adapt via selection of resilient phenotypes, and of species to adapt to one or multiple environmental pressures. It also takes advantage of the high levels of genetic diversity found in many coral species, and the potential for natural selection to generate concentrations of adaptive alleles in habitats with increased exposure to stressful conditions (NASEM 2018). Such corals can be identified experimentally, using common garden or reciprocal transplant experiments (Muller et al. 2018; O'Donnell et al. 2018), by their presence in chronic extreme conditions (e.g., during disease outbreaks), or by their survival after acute stress events (e.g., bleaching). Sources can also include environments with multiple ongoing stressors to identify corals with genotypes that are resistant to multiple stressors that often co-occur (e.g., sites with increased levels of sediments and toxicants, or reduced light levels and salinities) (NASEM 2018). Multiple *omic* approaches (genomics, transcriptomics, proteomics, and metabolomics) can help identify if phenotypic differences in corals that were collected from different reefs are due to fixed features, but such approaches require additional time, funds, skill sets, and equipment (see *Other Tools* herein). For a more detailed discussion of managed selection, refer to NASEM 2018.

Sexual Propagation

As previously discussed, sexual reproduction is vital to the survival and long-term persistence of coral populations/species. Random fertilization and recombination can increase genetic variation within offspring and generate novel or fitter genotypes. Sexual reproduction produces larvae that can disperse to establish new populations or promote genetic exchange among existing populations, thereby facilitating the spread of adaptive alleles. Sexual recruits can replenish depleted adult populations and promote population recovery post-disturbance. Ultimately, these processes can enhance the adaptive potential and resilience of populations under environmental change. Therefore, ensuring that restored populations reach a sexually mature self-sustaining state is critical to the long-term success of restoration projects.

More recently, there have been increased investments in developing new—or improving already established—methods for sexually propagating various threatened scleractinian species for the specific purpose of coral reef restoration (also referred to as *assisted sexual reproduction*). This has led to significant progress regarding spawning (in situ and ex situ), fertilization, larval settlement, and recruit rearing (see Chapter 8) (Abe et al. 2008; Craggs et al. 2017; Pollock et al. 2017; Calle-Trivino et al. 2018; Chan et al. 2018; Brainard 2019; Chan et al. 2019b; Randall et al. 2020). Harnessing the sexual cycle of corals provides access to hundreds of thousands of propagules that can be used for research and restoration. Outplanting hundreds or thousands of lab-reared sexual recruits, which are all genetically unique, bolsters restored populations by accelerating the process of genetic restoration by a single generation (Baums et al. 2019). With increased genetic and phenotypic variation, restored populations can more effectively respond to environmental change. Outplanting sexually produced offspring can be done instead of, or in addition to, outplanting asexually propagated fragments, and may in fact be especially valuable for species experiencing persistent recruitment failure (e.g., Caribbean acroporids and orbicellids) (Baums et al. 2019).

Alternative Forms of Sexual Propagation

Coral sexual propagation may also be referred to as *managed, captive,* or *selective breeding*—with different uses likely pertaining to different methods and/or goals. For example, sexual propagation or assisted sexual reproduction may describe a more general, opportunistic approach of crossing whatever genotypes spawn synchronously and using resulting offspring for population enhancement of degraded reefs (i.e., restoration) (Figure 10.4). Selective breeding is more explicit in that specific genotypes are crossed to test specific research questions or to breed individuals with desirable traits, such as increased thermotolerance, which may already exist in bleaching survivors and populations from naturally extreme or marginal environments

Figure 10.4 (see facing page) Example of coral sexual propagation for research and restoration. Photographic outline depicting the process of propagating *A. cervicornis* over 2½ years (from setting up a spawning nursery to outplanting and monitoring), in the Florida Keys (Koch *unpublished data*). (1) *A. cervicornis* spawning nursery. (2) In the weeks prior to the species' predicted spawning window, gravid colonies are identified by sampling a branch to look for developing gametes within (strings of eggs seen here). (3) Corals are brought into the lab a few days before their predicted spawning window to acclimate. (4) Depending on the project objectives, corals/genotypes can be kept together (e.g., for batch crossing) or isolated during spawning (e.g., for conducting 2-parent crosses and evaluating broodstock compatibility). (5) During spawning, gamete bundles are collected as they float to the surface. (6) Gamete bundles. (7) Micrograph of a freshly released, tightly packed gamete bundle. (8, 9) Gamete bundle dissolution revealing sperm packets surrounded by pink eggs. (10) For 2-parent crosses or specific research questions, separate sperm and egg stocks are created for each genotype. (11) Micrograph of eggs. (12) Micrograph of sperm. (13) Micrograph of sperm cloud (right) moving towards an egg (left) during fertilization. (14) Fertilization culture. (15) Twelve-hour-old embryo culture; here, fertilization rates are quantified by enumerating fertilized eggs (*cornflake stage*, irregular in shape) versus unfertilized eggs (round). (16) When the embryos develop into motile larvae (*planulae*), they are competent for settlement. (17–18) Settlement setups may vary; examples here include a (17) small settlement bin and a (18) larger 5-gallon tank with ceramic settlement substrates (*plugs*) and crushed up crustose coralline algae (CCA) used as the settlement cue. (19) Larva attaching to the substrate (*settling*). (20) Metamorphosis. (21) The primary polyp with a ring of tentacles surrounding a central mouth. (22) The sexual recruit begins to grow by *sheeting out* new tissue. (23) The primary polyp begins to secrete its calcium carbonate skeleton and (24) divide to produce new polyps. (25–26) Blue light technology and natural coral fluorescence are used to identify/quantify microscopic recruits. (27–32) Zooxanthellae acquisition occurring over several days. (33–34) The sexual recruits are reared in a land-based nursery for several months with optimal growth conditions, biological control (i.e., grazers), feeding and careful husbandry. (35) Once the sexual recruits are full-plug-sized (~six months for staghorn corals), the juveniles can be directly outplanted as singles (not shown here); (36a) micro-fragmented to produce clones that are grown out again and then (36b) outplanted as tagged arrays with (36c) many different arrays at a site representing many different genotypes, followed by monitoring over time to track (36d–e) their growth, health, fusion, sexual maturation, time to first sexual reproduction and next generation recruitment (thriving eight-month-old outplants shown here); or the juvenile corals can be (37a–b) placed on trees in an underwater nursery to illicit (37c–d) rapid branching where the (37e) ~5 cm branches are snipped off and hung to create whole new trees with new genotypes that are (37f) repeatedly and rapidly propagated asexually via in situ fragmentation and outplanted as arrays. In both cases (36–37), the rapid growth and fusion of clonal fragments in an array will produce larger, sexually mature colonies sooner, and the inclusion of numerous different genotypes at a restoration site promotes population resilience and more successful sexual reproduction when the corals become sexually mature and spawn. (Sources: (1) Sarah Hamlyn; (2–6, 10, 14, 16–18, 33, 35, 36d–e, 37a–b) Hanna R. Koch; (7–9, 11–13, 15, 19–32, 34, 36a) Cody Engelsma; (36b–c, 37c–f) Erich Bartels, Mote Marine Laboratory.)

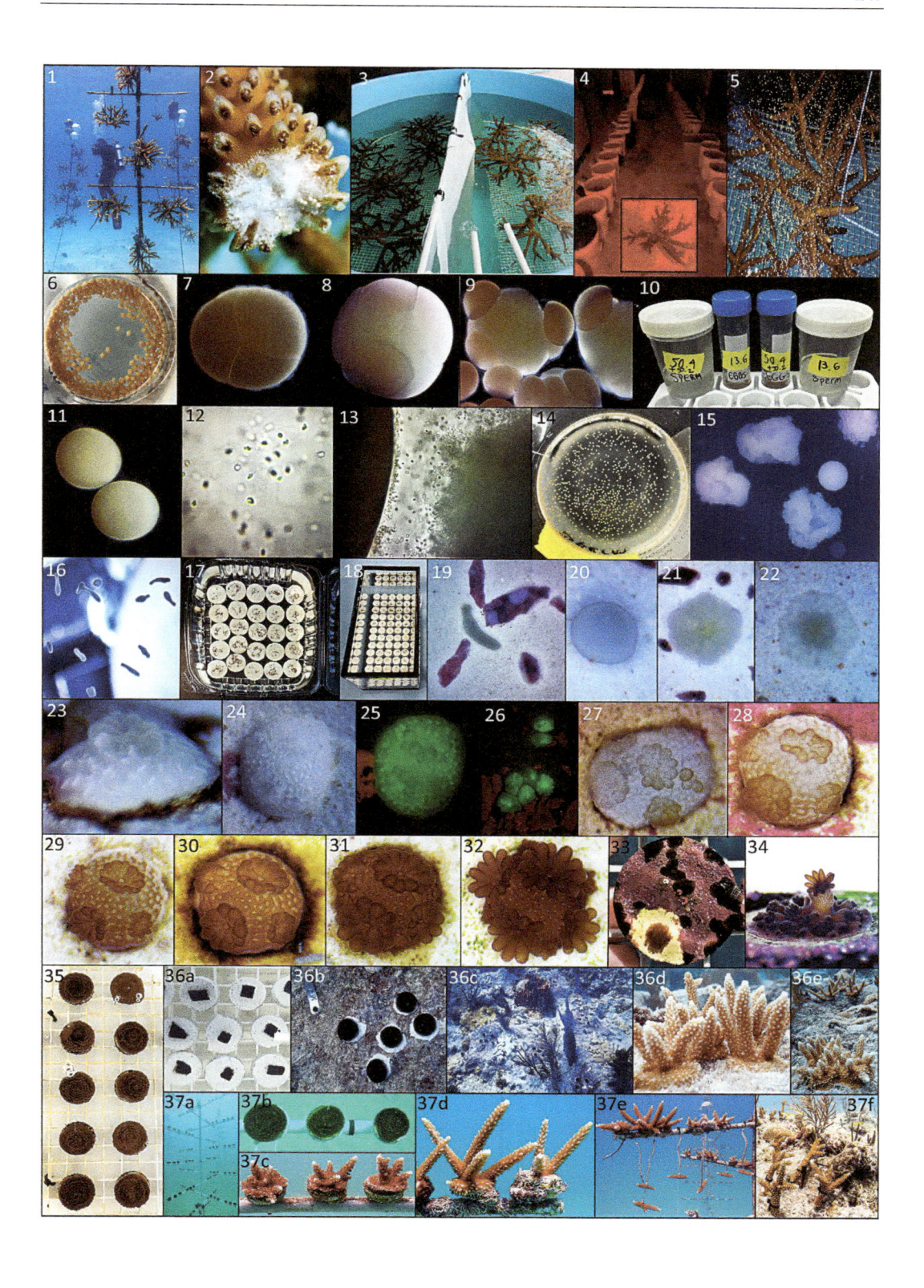

Genetic Considerations for Coral Reef Restoration

247

(see Chapter 9) (Barshis et al. 2013; van Oppen et al. 2015; Howells et al. 2016; van Oppen et al. 2017; Randall et al. 2020). Managed (or captive) breeding may fall somewhere in the middle and also be directed toward more general restoration goals (see below). Selective breeding as a coral reef restoration intervention remains largely experimental. Thus far, most cases have been tests of interspecific hybridization or heat tolerance heritability (Chan et al. 2018; Chan et al. 2019b; Quigley et al. 2019; Quigley et al. 2020), but results look promising. Alternatively, sexual propagation and managed breeding have been under investigation for a bit longer (Guest et al. 2010; Guest et al. 2014; Omori and Iwao 2016; Barton et al. 2017; Chamberland et al. 2017; Ligson et al. 2020; Randall et al. 2020).

Regarding managed breeding, different strategies may involve (1) supportive breeding, which seeks to enhance population sizes by sampling a subset of individuals from a population for captive rearing and then releasing the captively reared offspring back into their native habitat (Ryman and Laikre 1991), (2) outcrossing between populations, which aims to introduce novel genetic variation within a species range, following reproduction between individuals from different populations (e.g., Hagedorn et al. 2019), and (3) hybridization between species, which uses sexual reproduction to create individuals with novel genotypes that are more fit than the parental species (e.g., Chan et al. 2018). For details on how to carry out these different strategies, refer to NASEM 2018.

Potential Risks Associated with Sexual Propagation

Managing the genetic risks that are associated with the aforementioned strategies will also differ. For supportive breeding within populations, managing risks depends on the ability of the rearing program to sample sufficient diversity from natural populations, retain that genetic diversity throughout the entire process, prevent adaptation to culture conditions, maintain an optimal effective population size for reintroduced individuals, and ensure a high reintroduction success rate (NASEM 2018). Programs should prevent the release of too many captive-reared individuals from just a few families and keep in mind founder effects. Negative consequences of captive rearing and release can also occur through inadvertent selection where high variance in reproductive success and large nonrandom mortalities in larvae or juveniles result in fitness losses (NASEM 2018). For outcrossing between populations, success will depend on knowledge of the extent of population structure and local adaptation, along with the fitness outcomes of hybridization beyond the first generation (NASEM 2018). Frankham et al. (2000) have developed guidelines for predicting the risk of outbreeding depression in the absence of species-specific information. For coral populations/species that are experiencing reproductive failure (Kuffner and Toth 2016), the benefits of outcrossing may outweigh the potential genetic risks. For interspecific hybridization, risks include hybrid sterility, outbreeding depression, genetic bottlenecks, and demographic losses of either parent species through reproduction with fertile hybrids or competition (see *Interspecific Hybridization* herein) (NASEM 2018). Ecological effects such as competition may, however, be small in situations where there is substantial degradation of the coral reef (NASEM 2018). Finally, for selective breeding, the potential for genetic constraints and trade-offs need to be considered (e.g., Muller et al. 2018). Fitness trade-offs that are associated with local adaptation have been documented in corals and may impact their ability to acclimatize (Barshis et al. 2010; Howells et al. 2013; Kenkel et al. 2015; Bay and Palumbi 2017).

Harvesting Gametes

There are several techniques for harvesting coral gametes, including (1) in situ collections from wild colonies (or captive colonies in field-based spawning nurseries) during natural spawning events, (2) ex situ collections from corals of opportunity (or captive colonies from a spawning nursery) that are brought into the lab just before the predicted spawning window, and (3) from induced spawning of wild (or captive) colonies in ex situ spawning systems (Craggs et al. 2017). Following fertilization, offspring are returned to the field in various stages of development: mass-cultured larvae can be directly introduced to reefs via larval seeding (e.g., dela Cruz and Harrison 2017), larvae can be settled on a variety of substrates that are later affixed to reefs (e.g., Chamberland et al. 2017), or sexual recruits can be directly outplanted or grown out, micro-fragmented to produce replicates, and then outplanted in arrays (see Figure 10.4).

Spawning Nurseries

In situ spawning nurseries can provide easier access to reliably spawning corals for research and/or restoration (Figure 10.4). Replicated, sexually mature colonies of different genotypes can be maintained in a single location that is more readily accessible than a reef site. If nighttime field operations or inclement weather pose severe challenges, the corals can be brought into the lab for spawning and returned afterward. As they are maintained in the field throughout the year, the corals will receive the necessary environmental cues to induce gametogenesis and spawning. For branching corals that can hang from monofilament lines, coral *trees* should be modified to hold larger, heavier corals, whereas massive species may need to be held on blocks attached to substratum to minimize sedimentation and/or predation. Nursery redundancy is advisable in regions that are particularly susceptible to hurricanes (i.e., Atlantic and Caribbean), with replicate spawning nurseries set up in different locations. Genotypes can be added or replaced over time to maintain high genetic diversity, but keep in mind the potential for inbreeding if offspring genotypes are eventually included as new broodstock.

Suggested Methods for Coral Sexual Propagation

Suggested methods for broodstock selection and sexually propagating corals in the western Atlantic (Baums et al. 2019) are as follows:

1. *Maximize fertilization success.* For breeding purposes, it is typically not necessary to determine relatedness to avoid inbreeding because most major reef-building species are broadcast spawners that are highly outbred and genetically diverse (Baums 2008; Baird et al. 2009b). Therefore, the likelihood of picking two parents from natural populations that are closely related as a result of sexual reproduction (i.e., are siblings) is very low (Baums et al. 2019). However, for some Caribbean/western Atlantic species, populations are highly clonal with genetically identical neighboring colonies due to asexual fragmentation (e.g., *Acropora* spp., *Orbicella* spp., *D. cylindrus*) (Baums et al. 2006; Foster et al. 2007; Miller et al. 2018). Although these species are hermaphroditic, research suggests they are practically self-incompatible and require gametes from two different parents to successfully produce offspring (Fogarty et al. 2012; Baums et al. 2013; Williams et al. 2020). To minimize sampling from clones, select colonies that are relatively far apart (>5 m) (Baums et al. 2006; Foster et al. 2013). Alternatively, this issue can be resolved by genotyping every sampled or collected coral, which is highly recommended (see *Genotyping* herein). Other factors to consider during in vitro fertilization include (1) the potential for incompatibilities among conspecifics, (2) appropriate gamete concentrations, (3) duration of fertilization, and (4) cleanliness of cultures. Genotype incompatibilities may exist and lead to failed fertilization (Fogarty et al. 2012; Baums et al. 2013; Miller et al. 2018). Crossing gametes from a mix of different parents (5–10 genotypes recommended) *en masse* can increase fertilization success (Iwao et al. 2014; Miller et al. 2018). However, parental identity of offspring crossed in batch cultures will

be unknown unless genotyping is done (e.g., Baums et al. 2013). Furthermore, offspring from batch cultures may show varying degrees of genetic diversity depending on the relative contribution of each parent (Baums et al. 2019). Alternatively, offspring stemming from two-parent crosses are *full-sibs* (r = 0.5). Fertilization success is highly dependent on sperm concentration, with the optimum being ~10^6 cells/mL (Oliver and Babcock 1992; Nozawa et al. 2015). Gamete viability decreases over time, so it is recommended to use those that are as fresh as possible (Oliver and Babcock 1992; Fogarty et al. 2012; dela Cruz and Harrison 2020). If cultures are left for too long, polyspermy may occur (i.e., multiple sperm fertilize an egg), leading to failed embryogenesis. The recommended duration of fertilization is anywhere from 45 to 90 minutes (Oliver and Babcock 1992; Fogarty et al. 2012; Baums et al. 2013; Pollock et al. 2017; Chan et al. 2018; Chan et al. 2019b). Finally, cultures should be continuously monitored and cleaned since the presence of unfertilized eggs can lead to significant overall mortality of cultures (Pollock et al. 2017).

2. *Use larval crosses to increase local genetic diversity or numbers of sexual recruits.* Additional methods for fertilization will depend on specific project goals (Baums et al. 2019). For example, if the goal is to maximize fertilization success and the genetic diversity of offspring, then crosses should be carried out in batch cultures with equal contribution from each parent. If the goal is to maximize fertilization success and create the largest number of larvae regardless of their genetic diversity, then all gametes from all parents should be mixed in a batch culture. For restoration, it is recommended to use 5–10 different parents for batch fertilization (Iwao et al. 2014). For establishing captive breeding programs, it may be useful to identify potential genotype incompatibilities among broodstock. This can be achieved by carrying out two-parent crosses, with replicate direct and reciprocal crosses, and quantifying fertilization and settlement rates (e.g., Baums et al. 2013; Marhaver et al. 2017) (Figure 10.4).

3. *Maximize settlement and post-settlement survival.* Reducing post-settlement mortality rates and maintaining a high number of sexual recruits throughout the rearing process represent significant ongoing challenges in sexual propagation research. Large differences in settlement preferences, settlement rates, and post-settlement survival rates have been observed across species, suggesting there is no universal strategy for settling and rearing coral sexual recruits (Ritson-Williams et al. 2010; Strader et al. 2015; Whalan et al. 2015; Ritson-Williams et al. 2016; Marhaver et al. 2017; Elmer et al. 2018; Gomez-Lemos et al. 2018). Nonetheless, there are examples of sexual recruits surviving into adulthood and reaching sexual maturity (Guest et al. 2014; Chamberland et al. 2016; dela Cruz and Harrison 2017). Additionally, the Coral Reef Restoration Program at Mote Marine Laboratory's Elizabeth Moore International Center for Coral Reef Research and Restoration in the Florida Keys consistently propagates (sexually and asexually) and outplants resilient strains of a number of endemic, yet threatened, scleractinian species (MML 2020) (Figure 10.4). Finally, careful site selection for outplanting sexual recruits is critical because survival can be reduced by predation (e.g., corallivorous snails) and/or competition with turf algae (Miller 2001; Williams et al. 2014b).

4. *Enhance adaption potential via assisted gene flow.* Outcrossing colonies that are sourced from widely separated and environmentally divergent reefs could lead to the production of offspring with increased phenotypic variation, some of which may be especially fit in either parental habitat (Baums et al. 2019). Since maternal effects are known to influence offspring fitness (Dixon et al. 2015; Kenkel et al. 2015), this feature could be

exploited to further enhance the survival of first-generation sexual recruits by ensuring that mothers (i.e., egg donors) come from the habitat that the first-generation offspring will be outplanted to (Baums et al. 2019). Negative effects from outbreeding depression are expected to be low, especially in rapidly declining populations—a feature of many of the western Atlantic coral species (see *Outbreeding* herein). To cross gametes that are collected from distantly located populations or from different timepoints, cryopreservation techniques will be necessary (e.g., Hagedorn et al. 2019). However, such techniques can also lead to unintentional selection.

5. *Interspecific hybridization*. Interspecific hybridization has played an important evolutionary role in several coral lineages (Veron 1995; Vollmer and Palumbi 2002; Willis et al. 2006). Hybridization can serve as a mechanism for exchanging adaptive genetic variation among constituent species if hybrids can successfully reproduce with purebreds (i.e., *backcross*). In the Caribbean, recent environmental degradation and massive population decline in *A. cervicornis* and *A. palmata* have favored hybridization and expansion of their F_1 hybrid, *A. prolifera* (Fogarty 2012). In addition, these hybrids had equivalent or higher fitness relative to the parent species in multiple life history stages that were examined and expanded to marginal environments where either parent species is absent (Fogarty 2012). *A. prolifera* hybrids are also known to have extensive morphological variation (Vollmer and Palumbi 2007). Thus, hybridization can also serve as a source of novel morphological diversity as a restoration target to enhance reef habitat structure in very shallow, high-light environments where these hybrids are usually found (Vollmer and Palumbi 2007; Baums et al. 2019). There is little concern about genetic swamping of parental species with hybrid alleles because later generation genotypes remain rare in the population and both parental species have very low rates of successful natural sexual reproduction (Hughes and Tanner 2000; Miller et al. 2016; Baums et al. 2019). Additionally, there is the potential to combine selective breeding and interspecific hybridization to produce *A. prolifera* from stress-tolerant *A. cervicornis* and *A. palmata* genotypes (e.g., Chan et al. 2018; Chan et al. 2019). These offspring would serve as restoration targets for resilient outplant stocks and morphological variation. While the evolutionary potential of this hybrid may be limited, there are potential benefits associated with having more diverse morphological restoration of degraded, shallow offshore reefs with subtidal depths of up to 30 m. More important though, interspecific hybridization is unlikely to be a viable strategy to create broodstock for restoration because the continued existence of both parents as separate species indicates that hybrids are inferior on some level; even if F_1 hybrids show increased fitness, subsequent generations (F_2 and beyond) may reveal genetic incompatibilities (e.g., Dobzhansky-Muller model of hybrid incompatibility) (Dobzhansky 1937; Muller 1942; Wu and Ting 2004). Finally, hybrids have also been documented within the *Orbicella* species complex, which occur at different frequencies across the Caribbean (Fukami et al. 2004). For either species complex, outplanting strategies of hybrids should follow the same recommendations as for purebreds (Baums et al. 2019).

Phenotypic Traits of Propagated Corals

Maintaining phenotypic diversity in outplants is critical to maximizing the adaptive potential of restored populations (Baums et al. 2019). Phenotypic variation results from both genetic and environmental factors; the particular source determines whether a trait has the ability to respond to natural selection (i.e., whether the trait has evolutionary potential), as well as whether the trait can respond to environmental changes. Selection acts on phenotypes, and maintaining a diversity of phenotypes increases the capacity of a population to respond to environmental stress or change through phenotypic changes. However, as previously discussed, performance of corals that are propagated within nurseries does not always predict performance when outplanted to a reef site. Genotypes may have widely different growth rates depending on environmental conditions (Lirman et al. 2014; Drury et al. 2017; O'Donnell et al. 2018). Performance may be further modulated by trade-offs between beneficial traits (e.g., growth and thermal tolerance), which can be attributable to the endosymbiont (Symbiodiniaceae) strain being harbored (Ladd et al. 2018). Tracking the key traits in nursery stocks will help practitioners optimize stocks, as well as ensure that a diverse set of potentially important traits is included within restored populations (Baums et al. 2019).

Identifying and quantifying fitness-related traits can be challenging, time-consuming, and expensive. It is therefore recommended that to optimally manage nurseries, restoration programs establish consistent practical guidelines for collecting the most informative data (Baums et al. 2019). Regardless of whether or not corals are asexually or sexually propagated, there are often limits to the number of corals and different genotypes that can be reasonably managed (e.g., limited nursery space). When this is the case, Baums et al. (2019) recommend that the key traits that can help guide which genotypes to propagate include (1) partial mortality (Lirman et al. 2014a), (2) wound healing rate (Palmer et al. 2011b), (3) skeletal growth rate (Kuffner et al. 2017), (4) bleaching and disease resistance or resilience (Palmer et al. 2011a; Muller et al. 2018), and (5) reproductive output (e.g., fecundity or sperm motility) (Hall and Hughes 1996; Hagedorn et al. 2006) (for a review of these traits and quantification methods, refer to Baums et al. 2019).

Finally, given the paucity of available trait data for a large number of scleractinian species, a trait-based approach has been proposed to guide research efforts that, in the end, could benefit restoration (Madin et al. 2016). Madin et al. (2016) recommend that to fill remaining gaps, scientists should (1) prioritize traits that are easy to measure, (2) estimate key traits for species with missing data, and (3) identify super-traits that capture a large amount of variation for a range of biological and ecological processes (refer to Madin et al. 2016 for further discussion).

Outplanting

The survivorship of outplants and restored populations is highly contingent upon optimal site selection. High variation in survivorship observed across outplant sites that was not attributed to specific ecological factors indicates other factors may influence outplant survivorship (Lirman et al. 2014b; Drury et al. 2017). These may include protection status, the frequency of human visitation, intact trophic structure of the reef (e.g., levels of herbivory and corallivory), water quality, historical occurrence of the species, and alleviation of the stressors that caused the original coral decline (Baums et al. 2019). Generally, though, individual species should be outplanted within their general habitat niches—historical and fossil records can be used to guide such efforts (Goreau 1959; Dollar 1982; Rosen 1988; Toth et al. 2018).

Suggested methods for outplanting and monitoring (Baums et al. 2019), are as follows:

1. *Site selection for fragments*—it is generally recommended to adopt a climate-adapted provenance strategy and outplant genotypes across individual sites, with proportional representation of all genotypes from available stocks outplanted across sites (Baums et al. 2019).

2. *Site selection for sexual recruits*—since sexually produced offspring are genetically unique, the number of genotypes outplanted to a site will be significantly higher than what can be achieved via asexual propagation. Sexual recruits can be outplanted at various stages during development. Outplant survivorship may be increased, and predation risk decreased, if larger recruits are outplanted (Raymundo and Maypa 2004; Penin et al. 2011; Guest et al. 2014), but this can require significantly more time, effort, and nursery space during the ex situ rearing process. If such resources exist, sexual recruits can be reared in a land- or field-based nursery and micro-fragmented to produce replicates (i.e., clones). Those replicates can then be outplanted in arrays of varying numbers to promote fusion and the creation of a larger, sexually mature colony sooner (Forsman et al. 2015; Page et al. 2018). Genotypes should not be mixed within arrays, but different arrays based on genotype should be outplanted across a site, as is done with asexually propagated genotypes (see Chapter 6). It is generally recommended to mix and match as many genotypes as possible to promote adaptive potential and support more successful sexual reproduction in the future (Rice and Emery 2003; Baums 2008; Eizaguirre and Baltazar-Soares 2014; Whiteley et al. 2015; Baums et al. 2019).

3. *Maximizing the potential for sexual reproduction*—to promote successful sexual reproduction within restored populations of broadcast spawning species, more than one genotype is necessary. Two genotypes may only provide marginal fertilization success, especially if the potential for incompatibility between them is unknown. Mixtures of four to six genotypes showed high fertilization success during experiments (Baums et al. 2013; Iwao et al. 2014), and even more genotypes (~10) are likely necessary for acroporids and gonochores (Baums et al. 2019). If more genotypes are available within nursery stocks, they can be outplanted in different combinations across sites. If phenotypic information on stress-resistant genotypes is unavailable, they can be stratified among sites to ensure that some resistant phenotypes are outplanted to each site (Baums et al. 2019). If certain genotypes exhibit multiple beneficial traits (e.g., low partial mortality and rapid wound healing), these fitter genotypes should be distributed across as many outplant sites as possible, keeping in mind that nursery performance of exceptionally fit genotypes may not translate directly when outplanted. Optimal distance between outplants has not been directly studied, so 2–3 m is currently the general recommendation (Baums et al. 2019). Being too close may instigate intraspecific competition and being too far away may reduce fertilization success. Finally, practitioners should maintain accurate records of all outplanting activities, and tag/track outplants when possible (Figure 10.4).

4. *Monitoring*—monitoring strategies will depend on project goals, availability of resources, and the nature of the outplants (i.e., early settlers, juveniles, individual fragments, or arrays). However, tracking the success of different genotypes across sites, and over time, will provide valuable insight into their performances and help optimize future outplanting strategies. The phenotype/genotype data that is collected can also be submitted to reputable online databases to be used as shared resources among practitioners and scientists (refer to Baums et al. 2019). If collecting such data is not feasible, genotypes that are lost over time should be replaced with different ones from nursery stocks that were not originally included at that site. Finally, a targeted outcome is to get restored populations to a sexually mature state so that they become self-sustaining (Baums et al. 2019). However, for most restoration projects, this objective has rarely been explicitly stated or proven via sufficient monitoring over the long term (i.e., more than one year)

(Boström-Einarsson et al. 2020). Given that sexual maturity is size-dependent, and varies considerably across species (Soong and Lang 1992), it can take years or decades for corals to produce the next generation (Harrison and Wallace 1990; Soong 1993; Hall and Hughes 1996; Chamberland et al. 2016; St. Gelais et al. 2016; Schopmeyer et al. 2017). Ceasing monitoring after one year will likely not provide the longevity required to evaluate sexual maturity or long-term success of restoration efforts. Assessing the sexual maturity of restored populations may be more straightforward for fast-growing corals (i.e., the acroporids), where outplanted staghorn (Schopmeyer et al. 2017) and elkhorn (Chamberland et al. 2016) corals were documented to be sexually mature within two to four years, respectively, and where branches can be easily sampled from the center (and oldest part) of the colony to look for developing gametes inside. However, a recent restoration breakthrough in Florida showed that outplants of the slow-growing mountainous star coral (*O. faveolata*) were sexually mature within just five years of being restored, which was first documented through the identification of mature gametes inside small core samples and then later confirmed via direct spawning observations (Mote *unpublished data*). Documenting spawning and recruitment is especially valuable for species experiencing long-term recruitment failure in this region (i.e., the acroporids and orbicellids) (Hughes and Tanner 2000; Williams et al. 2008). Data collected from spawning observations can also be submitted to online databases that track region-wide spawning patterns for a number of species every year (e.g., the CRC's Larval Propagation Working Group) (Marhaver et al. 2017; Jordan 2018; CRC 2020).

Coral Reef Restoration in Other Regions of the World

Restoration case studies have been reported across 56 countries, with the majority of projects occurring in the United States (Florida and Hawaii) (for a systematic review of coral reef restoration projects globally, refer to Boström-Einarsson et al. 2020). Furthermore, while specific recommendations for restoration discussed herein are aimed at projects occurring throughout the western Atlantic, the genetic risks associated with founder effects, genetic swamping, and inbreeding/outbreeding depression are universal. Strategies for other regions will differ because species and species complexes differ—as do levels of species diversity, functional redundancy, natural recruitment, and coral cover/abundance, for example.

The National Environmental Science Program, as part of the Australian Government's Department of Agriculture, Water, and Environment, has established an initiative called the Best Practice Coral Restoration for the Great Barrier Reef. Under this new initiative, a working group of experts will conduct a global review of the restoration practices that have been successful in other regions of the world (based on published scientific and grey literature), followed by an information filtering process to set and publish guidelines for suggested, local-scale restoration methods on the GBR.

Additionally, *resilience-based management* (RBM) of coral reef ecosystems has been suggested as a general strategy (Mcleod et al. 2019). RBM is defined as "using knowledge of current and future drivers influencing ecosystem function (e.g., coral disease outbreaks; changes in land-use, trade, or fishing practices) to prioritize, implement, and adapt management actions that sustain ecosystems and human well-being" (Mcleod et al. 2019). It provides a comprehensive framework of suggested research priorities focused on natural processes that promote resistance and recovery. While RBM has a much larger scope in that it considers the entire socio-ecological system, several key components of RBM are based on actions that will need to consider the genetic and evolutionary principles discussed herein. For example, one of the suggested research priorities is to invest in experimental approaches to support resilience. Such approaches will need to take into account the genetic and demographic properties influencing population resilience to rapid environmental change.

THE CORAL HOLOBIONT AND ROLE OF ALGAL SYMBIONTS

Corals are indeed animals, but they live in close association with a suite of eukaryotic and prokaryotic microorganisms including bacteria, archaea, fungi, viruses, and protists. Collectively, they make up the coral holobiont (Rohwer et al. 2002). Endosymbiotic algae of the family Symbiodiniaceae (LaJeunesse et al. 2018), or *zooxanthellae*, live within the coral host's tissues, photosynthesize, and provide the coral with the nutrients necessary for growth and survival in nutrient poor environments, as well as the energy required to deposit calcium carbonate skeletons that form the basis of reefs (Muscatine and Porter 1977). Bacteria play a role in host defenses and have been found to contribute to the nitrogen fixation capacity of corals (Rohwer et al. 2002; Rosenberg et al. 2007), while viruses are hypothesized to have an indirect effect on reef ecosystem function by triggering the release and movement of nutrients (Sweet and Bythell 2017; Thurber et al. 2017). The role of certain microbes is more well-understood than others though.

The holobiont is the unit of ecological selection, so understanding the role that microorganisms play in the structure and function of the holobiont is essential for understanding how corals maintain homeostasis and acclimate to changing environmental conditions (Thompson et al. 2015; van Oppen and Blackall 2019). Research has already shown that coral-associated microbes play key roles in host stress tolerance and can influence host phenotypes (van Oppen et al. 2009; Gates and Ainsworth 2011; Bourne and Webster 2013; Krediet et al. 2013; McFall-Ngai et al. 2013). For example, corals may respond to changing environmental conditions over the short term, by changing the bacterial communities that are inhabiting their mucus layers (Reshef et al. 2006) or by altering the composition of algal endosymbiont communities (Baker 2001; Boulotte et al. 2016).

A key factor modulating the adaptive response of coral holobionts to thermal stress is their symbiotic association with various genera of zooxanthellae that have different physiological optima (Chang et al. 1983; Mieog et al. 2009; Kenkel et al. 2012; Kenkel et al. 2013a; Parkinson and Baums 2014; Howells et al. 2016). Patterns of host-symbiont association include variation across depth gradients (Rowan et al. 1997; LaJeunesse 2002; Warner et al. 2006; Frade et al. 2008), differences in host specificity where some hosts harbor more than one type of Symbiodiniaceae strain (either simultaneously or by switching) while others are exclusive (Baker 2003), and differences in bleaching thresholds (Lasker et al. 1984; Rowan et al. 1997; Glynn et al. 2001). Baums et al. (2008) point out that selection by higher water temperatures on the coral-microalgae symbiosis could have multiple effects by favoring (1) already resistant strains of zooxanthellae, (2) corals that harbor resistant strains, (3) corals that can associate with new types of zooxanthellae, and/or (4) coral colonies that are thermally tolerant themselves. It is thus difficult to disentangle the adult coral host's response from that of the holobiont's.

Evaluating the performance of host genotypes can be achieved, however, using aposymbiotic life stages (i.e., symbiont-free larvae or early recruits). Broadcast spawning species typically acquire their zooxanthellae each generation—as larvae or early sexual recruits—from their environment (i.e., horizontal transmission). The onset of symbiosis in these species can be as early as two to six days after fertilization (Edmunds et al. 2005; Harii et al. 2009), but the period of acquisition can last up to months as well (McIllroy and Coffroth 2017). The period before symbionts are acquired represents a window of opportunity to test for genotypic differences attributable to the coral host. Indeed, research results indicate the potential for adaptive variation attributable to the coral host alone (Meyer et al. 2009; Polato et al. 2010; Meyer et al. 2011; Polato et al. 2013). Nonetheless, both factors—host genotype and symbiont strain—contribute to the holobiont's response to thermal stress.

Considering the Role of Algal Symbionts in Restoration Programs

Conclusive evidence for the specific impacts that algal symbionts may have in nurseries or outplant sites is lacking (Lirman et al. 2014b; Parkinson and Baums 2014; O'Donnell et al. 2018; Parkinson et al. 2018). Nonetheless, there is evidence that symbionts can influence host stress responses and phenotypes so it is reasonable to assume that algal symbionts can affect restoration outcomes. Many species propagated for restoration are capable of hosting multiple strains of Symbiodiniaceae, whether concomitantly or by switching, so it is possible that algal symbiont diversity may influence phenotypic and genotypic differences among restoration units that are not attributable to the coral host (Parkinson and Baums 2014; Baums et al. 2019). However, unlike host genetic differences, symbiont genetic differences may not be fixed over a coral's lifespan because the symbiont community can potentially change over time in response to disturbances and/or prevailing environmental conditions (Baums et al. 2019). Unless direct collaboration with scientists is possible for identifying and monitoring changes in symbiont community using genetic methods (see *Genotyping* herein), Baums et al. (2019) suggest that it may not be practical for most restoration practitioners to take explicit account of Symbiodiniaceae diversity at this time.

The manipulation of coral-associated microorganisms to enhance host stress tolerance is an area of active research (see Chapter 9). Research observations thus far suggest coral-associated microbes may adapt or acclimatize faster than their host, possibly lending additional adaptive capacity to the holobiont (Peixoto et al. 2017; Chakravarti and van Oppen 2018). If and when such interventions become widely available to restoration practitioners, they could potentially be integrated into routine propagation and outplanting activities. Nevertheless, restoration practitioners should realize the potential for confounding effects of symbiont strain, symbiont change, and/or trade-offs on the performance of coral hosts across different settings (i.e., land nursery, field nursery, or outplant site). A climate-adapted provenance strategy may also be a pragmatic approach here, where warmer local environments are expected to have higher abundances of both thermally tolerant coral host genotypes and symbionts, which could serve as ideal sources for coral stocks (Baums et al. 2019).

Consideration of algal symbionts may also be relevant for restoration programs that are sexually propagating corals. For species that acquire their symbionts via horizontal transmission, it is suggested that the effects of breeding design on the population structure and diversity of these symbionts are not a major concern (Baums et al. 2019). Typical Symbiodiniaceae sources from which larvae or early sexual recruits may acquire them in nature include the water column, sediments, and co-cultured adult corals (Coffroth et al. 2006; Nitschke et al. 2016; Quigley et al. 2018; Ali et al. 2019; Randall et al. 2020). In a land-based nursery setting with flow-through systems, symbionts may be acquired naturally from the seawater that the corals are maintained in (Koch *unpublished data*). In the lab, it is also possible to provision juvenile corals with mixtures of cultivated micro-algae when they are kept in small aquaria, but only a subset of Symbiodiniaceae is currently cultured (Baums et al. 2019). Also, little is known about how to provision specific symbionts in situ, but one particular strategy to be used during restoration is to outplant sexual recruits before they uptake their symbionts from a land- or field-based nursery, in order to ensure acquisition of strains that are present in their outplant environment (LaJeunesse et al. 2004; LaJeunesse et al. 2010; Abrego et al. 2012; Howells et al. 2012). However, studies have shown that it can take up to four years for a symbiont community to stabilize as the colony grows and matures (Coffroth et al. 2010; Poland and Coffroth 2017). Thus, an alternative [hybrid] approach may be to stage sexual recruits at the outplant site for a few weeks for symbiont acquisition, and then return them to the lab for continued grow-out before finally outplanting them (Baums et al. 2019).

MOLECULAR TOOLS

Molecular tools can be valuable resources for coral reef restoration practitioners. They can be used to guide the selection of optimal sources for coral stocks, assess and manage levels of genetic diversity, determine appropriate spatial arrangements of out-transplants, and evaluate the success of projects by tracking the performance of restored corals (Baums 2008; Lundgren 2011). Molecular tools can also be used to help identify the mechanisms and responses through which resilient corals survive stress (NASEM 2018). For example, they can be used to differentiate between evolutionary adaptations to a particular environment, as opposed to those individuals that are temporarily acclimatized to change, which can influence how corals are manipulated for restoration.

Molecular Markers

Since the genetic code of every individual is unique, DNA variations and patterns can be used to discover a wealth of information about individuals, populations, and species, including the identity of any sampled individual (e.g., via genotyping), signatures of selection in a population (e.g., as in genomic studies), differences within and between populations (population genetics), evolutionary history and relationships among individuals or groups of organisms (phylogenetics), evolutionary relatedness (taxonomy), and patterns of trait inheritance (e.g., pedigrees), to name a few. *Molecular markers* (or *genetic markers*) are fragments of DNA associated with a particular region of the genome. They can be useful tools for assessing important ecological and evolutionary issues such as connectivity (gene flow), local adaptation, range shifts, genetic diversity estimates, inbreeding, biodiversity depletion, speciation, and invasion.

Molecular markers are also referred to as *neutral genetic markers* because they typically do not reflect patterns of selection (Reed and Frankham 2001; McKay and Latta 2002). Instead, they take advantage of neutral genetic variation (i.e., the gene variants detected do not have any direct effect on fitness) to investigate processes such as gene flow, migration, or dispersal. They cannot tell us anything about the adaptive or evolutionary potential of a population or species (Holderegger et al. 2006); to investigate these processes, quantitative genetic or genomic approaches are necessary (McKay and Latta 2002; Santure and Garant 2018).

A common application of molecular markers is for *genotyping*, which determines differences in the genetic makeup of an individual by examining the individual's DNA sequence by using biological assays and then comparing it with another individual's sequence or a reference sequence. Within conservation science, the use of molecular markers is also integral to quantifying genetic diversity, which can be done by estimating levels of heterozygosity or allelic richness. Allelic richness of scleractinian coral populations can be estimated using markers, such as *microsatellites*, and may be a more appropriate estimate of genetic diversity than expected heterozygosity for coral populations whose population sizes have dramatically decreased over the past several decades (Shearer et al. 2009). As previously discussed, genetic and genotypic diversity describe processes that need to be managed separately within coral restoration activities; genotypic diversity is the total number of genetically distinct individuals (genotypes) within a population, whereas genetic diversity is the amount of variation between genotypes on the level of individual genes.

Genotyping

Within coral reef conservation and restoration, genotyping is used to identify genetically unique individuals (produced via sexual reproduction) and distinguish them from clones (produced via asexual reproduction) (Figure 10.2). Over time, coral genotypes can extend over tens of meters and consist of tens to hundreds of colonies (Neigel and Avise 1983; Baums et al. 2006; Foster et al. 2007), resulting in substantial variability in genotypic evenness and richness on small spatial scales (e.g., ranging from minimal clonal replication to reefs dominated by a single genotype) (Ayre and Hughes 2000; Baums et al. 2006). Within coral reef restoration, because so many of the decisions surrounding nursery stock/broodstock selection, performance tracking, propagation, outplanting, and monitoring are structured around genotypes—and because very large numbers of sexual recruits and/or clonal fragments are typically cultivated within restoration programs—being able to reliably identify and track individuals over time and in an organized fashion is essential to maximizing project success. To track the genotypic diversity of corals and their symbionts, it is necessary to determine their unique multilocus genotypes (MLGs) via genetic analysis (refer to Baums et al. 2019).

Different genotyping methods are available for a number of Caribbean/western Atlantic coral species, which are based on allozymes, amplified fragment length polymorphisms (AFLPs), microsatellites, or SNPs. Microsatellites and SNPs are used more routinely in conservation genetic/genomic studies (Puckett 2017), and provide higher allelic variation that can be used to discriminate colonies that share an MLG because they were generated via asexual fragmentation versus those that share an MLG because they are closely related (e.g., siblings) (Baums et al. 2019). Microsatellite (or *simple sequence repeat*) markers are based on short, tandem, repeat sequences (2–6 bp in length) interspersed in the genome. The sequences flanking the repeats are conserved, but the length of the repeat itself varies, so these markers can be detected by polymerase chain reaction (PCR) using a pair of primers flanking the microsatellite. They are used to analyze the numbers of repeat base pairs in an allele, are considered neutral markers, and are ideal because of their abundance in genomes, high degree of variability in the repeat sequence, and reproducibility. For application within coral reef restoration (Baums et al. 2009; Davies et al. 2013; Nakajima et al. 2017; Rippe et al. 2017), additional benefits include flexibility in the number of samples that can be run, small data files, and straightforward genetic analysis.

SNPs are sites at which more than one nucleotide is found in a population (i.e., a single basepair change via mutation). SNPs are the most common type of genetic variation and can occur within a gene (the gene is thus described as having more than one allele) or in noncoding regions. They are commonly used as biological markers and can be detected through a variety of sequencing techniques including Restriction-site Associated DNA Sequencing (RADseq) (Combosch and Vollmer 2015; Everett et al. 2016; Iguchi et al. 2019) or Genotype-By-Sequencing

(GBS) (Puebla et al. 2014; Berthouly-Salazar et al. 2016; Drury et al. 2016), both of which represent *reduced representation sequencing* methods and are ideal for assaying a large number of SNP loci in any organism at a reasonable cost (Altshuler et al. 2000; Kitchen et al. 2018). They also represent applications of next-generation sequencing (NGS), a powerful technology that offers simultaneous sequencing of thousands to millions of nucleic acid sequences in a massively parallel way (i.e., high-throughput). RADseq (or RAD-tag sequencing) can identify and score thousands of genetic markers that are randomly distributed across the target genome from a group of individuals using Illumina technology and is ideal for population genetic studies on species with no, or limited, existing sequence data (e.g., nonmodel organisms) (Davey and Blaxter 2010; Toonen et al. 2013). It is similar to analyses using AFLPs in that it reduces the complexity of the genome by sub-sampling only at specific sites defined by restriction enzymes, but is much more robust in identifying, verifying, and scoring markers simultaneously (Davey and Blaxter 2010; but see Kitchen et al. 2018). However, when used by restoration practitioners, potential drawbacks include large data files and analyses that require programming and bioinformatics expertise (see Kitchen et al. 2018).

For coral reef restoration practitioners, it is important to keep in mind that testing and running a large number of samples for genotyping can become expensive, time-consuming, and challenging very quickly. As such, current genotyping methods are restricted to a few labs, thereby creating a bottleneck to conservation projects. In response, a team of scientists has developed the first high-resolution hybridization-based genotype array (SNPchip) for corals that, in conjunction with a more straightforward analysis pipeline, offers a standardized approach to genotyping at a comparable cost (Kitchen et al. 2018). The tool is called Standard Tools for Acroporid Genotyping (STAG) because this application is developed for use with acroporids and their algal symbionts. The array was designed to co-analyze hosts and symbionts based on bi-allelic SNP markers that were identified from genomic data of the two Caribbean *Acropora* species, as well as their dominant algal symbiont, *Symbiodinium 'fitti'* (Kitchen et al. 2018). SNPs were selected to resolve MLGs of host genotypes and symbiont strains, distinguish host populations, and determine ancestry of the coral hybrids in Caribbean acroporids. However, Pacific acroporids can also be genotyped using a subset of the SNP loci, and additional markers enable the detection of symbionts belonging to the genera *Breviolum*, *Cladocopium*, and *Durusdinium*. This tool is valuable to restoration practitioners for defining management units, designing strategies for outplanting, and assessing diversity of coral stocks (Kitchen et al. 2018).

Finally, tracking symbiont community diversity is also recommended for coral fragments and sexual recruits. However, unless one is able to use STAG because they are working with acroporids, the resolution of Symbiodiniaceae diversity will be limited due to current genetic tools. Nonetheless, a discussion of the different methods that are currently available for assessing symbiont communities can be found in Baums et al. (2019).

Biomarkers

Biomarkers are naturally occurring molecules, genes, or characteristics in a biological system that are used as indicators of exposure, effect, susceptibility, or disease. They can be diagnostic (i.e., they provide some information with respect to an ongoing condition) or predictive (i.e., they provide some information that can be used to make a decision about a potential future outcome) (NIH Biomarkers Definitions Working Group 2001). Within coral reef science and management, existing diagnostic biomarkers include pulse amplitude modulated (PAM) fluorometry (a proxy for photosynthetic function) (Warner et al. 2010) and the CoralWatch Coral

Health Chart (a bleaching indicator) (Siebeck et al. 2006), whereas the National Oceanic and Atmospheric Administration's (NOAA) degree heating weeks—an indicator of the likelihood of observing mass coral bleaching—is used as a predictive biomarker (Liu et al. 2003). In these cases, biomarkers represent easily assayable substitutes exhibiting strong correlations with meaningful biological phenotypes (Parkinson et al. 2020).

The idea to use biomarkers within coral reef restoration is quickly gaining traction. In addition to maximizing genetic diversity of restored coral populations, there is a growing desire to identify and outplant the most resilient corals, especially regarding disease and bleaching resistance (van Oppen et al. 2015; Muller et al. 2018; Parkinson et al. 2020). However, determining which readily quantifiable phenotypes are most indicative of resilience has been challenging (see *Phenotypic Traits of Propagated Corals* herein). Recent advances in biotechnology, genomics, and computational power have increased our ability to identify putative biomarkers (Sgro et al. 2011; Traylor-Knowles and Palumbi 2014), but an ideal scenario would be to have simple yet robust bioassays that restoration practitioners can use to facilitate rapid identification of resilient corals to be used as nursery/broodstock, diagnose stress events, and provide predictive information to optimize outplanting strategies (Baums et al. 2019; Parkinson et al. 2020).

Such biomarkers are still far from being available to coral reef restoration practitioners, however. Also, it is likely that multiple biomarkers will be needed, depending on the type of information sought after, and/or used in conjunction with other tools and approaches for managing diverse populations and ensuring sufficient adaptive potential (Baums et al. 2019; Parkinson et al. 2020). In addition, there are several steps between identifying a potential biomarker and using it in the field (refer to Parkinson et al. 2020). Nonetheless, as a consequence of the *omics* revolution, several different types of molecular biomarkers are currently being developed and evaluated in a high-throughput, cost-effective manner. These include (1) genetic/genomic biomarkers of coral hosts based on associations between DNA variation (among or within individuals, populations, or species) that can be used as predictive assays, (2) genetic/genomic biomarkers of holobiont community composition used as metrics of coral host performance and to reveal potential phenotypes of interest to restoration practitioners, (3) epigenetic/genomic biomarkers based on associations between phenotypes and different chemical modifications of the genome, (4) gene expression biomarkers based on associations between phenotypes of interest and changes in messenger RNA levels (which currently may be the most developed and usable within both diagnostic and predictive contexts), (5) protein-based biomarkers that relate levels of specific proteins to phenotypes of interest (which have also progressed in terms of overall development), and (6) metabolomic-based biomarkers that focus on associations between levels of metabolites and traits of interest. For a more detailed discussion of these examples and their associated advantages/disadvantages, refer to Parkinson et al. 2020. Given the profound usefulness that biomarkers could have for coral reef restoration (e.g., for predicting/diagnosing health, resilience, and other key performance traits), continued development should be a priority (Baums et al. 2019; Parkinson et al. 2020).

Other Tools

'Omics'

The reduced cost and more streamlined application of NGS methods for nonmodel organisms have allowed this powerful technology to be increasingly utilized within coral reef conservation and restoration. Now, fully or partially sequenced genomes and transcriptomes are available for a number of scleractinian species (Shinzato et al. 2011; Moya et al. 2012; Kenkel et al. 2013b;

Libro et al. 2013; Bhattacharya et al. 2016; Voolstra et al. 2017; Cunning et al. 2018; Ying et al. 2018; Kitchen et al. 2019; Shumaker et al. 2019; Ying et al. 2019). *Omic* technologies are primarily aimed at the detection of genes (genomics), mRNA (transcriptomics), proteins (proteomics) and metabolites (metabolomics) in a specific biological sample. Generally, *-omics* can help identify if phenotypic differences in corals collected from different reefs are due to fixed features.

Population genomic studies typically sample several individuals, genotype many loci (SNPs), identify the outliers among those loci, and then remove the outliers to estimate demographic parameters, such as population structure and expansion (Baums 2008). The dataset with outliers is used to investigate the cause of outlier behavior (e.g., selection) and resulting patterns observed at outlier loci are then correlated with evolutionary, phenotypic, ecological, or environmental observations (Luikart et al. 2003; Baums 2008). Marine invertebrate conservation genomics uses modern analyses like genomic monitoring and profiling to preserve the viability of populations and the biodiversity of living organisms (Lopez et al. 2019). Seascape genomics is a research field that studies how spatial dependence and environmental features in the ocean influence the geographic structure of genomic patterns in marine organisms and has been used to study the adaptive potential of *Acropora digitifera* populations by associating genotype frequencies with descriptors of historical environmental conditions (Selmoni et al. 2020).

Genomic approaches to studying adaptation can be useful for coral reef restoration as well (Baums 2008). They can help to identify rare adaptations that warrant protection, match populations with similar adaptations (Hufford and Mazer 2003), avoid transplantation of maladapted genotypes (McKay et al. 2005; Edmands 2007), and reduce the risk of inbreeding and outbreeding depression (Marshall and Spalton 2000; Lofflin and Kephart 2005). Genomics can also be used to identify novel genotypes and/or genotypic diversity associated with particular habitats, providing targets for restoration outcomes (NASEM 2018). Relevant to all coral species that are currently suffering from ocean warming, genomic analyses have demonstrated that variation in coral thermal tolerance across latitudes has a strong genetic basis and could serve as raw material for natural selection (Dixon et al. 2015; Dziedzic et al. 2019). Finally, genomics can also be used to identify individuals with high genomic breeding values for a trait using genomic predictions that are based on test populations (Crossa et al. 2017). Such information would be useful to those who are interested in carrying out managed breeding and assisted gene flow interventions (Flanagan et al. 2018).

Additional *omic* applications that are useful to coral reef restoration include proteomics to identify major stressors at specific locations and the genotypes able to effectively respond through protein expression (Downs et al. 2012), and transcriptomics to investigate patterns in gene expression, which ties back to the genotypes exhibiting resistance and the effectiveness of the proteins being up- or down-regulated in response to specific stressors (NASEM 2018). However, there are potential risks to consider when performing *-omic* analyses. These include causing further damage to corals that survive bleaching events (via sampling), collecting pressure on corals in stress-tolerant populations, and mis-assignment of phenotypic variation in common garden experiments as genetic rather than epigenetic (NASEM 2018). Regardless, *omic* analyses are powerful research tools that have many applications within coral reef conservation.

CONCLUSIONS

With increasing interest in active coral reef restoration, it is critical to project success that restoration strategies are ecologically and evolutionary sound. The methods with which practitioners select, propagate, rear, manipulate, and outplant corals for restoring degraded reefs will have consequences for the survivorship of outplants and resilience of populations. Through the act of restoration, practitioners can influence the adaptive potential and evolutionary trajectory of restored populations. Understanding the genetic and demographic properties that influence the ability of populations to adapt to rapidly changing selective pressures will help practitioners design and implement optimal strategies.

For example, cultivating corals in nurseries can lead to unintended selection by propagating genotypes better suited to nursery conditions, which can result in fitness reductions in outplants. Possible strategies for minimizing unintended selection include diversified provenancing (over different spatial and temporal scales), rearing/propagating as many genotypes as possible, assisting gene flow, identifying resilient or resistant genotypes through experiments/analyses, and matching the nursery and reef environments as closely as possible (Baums et al. 2019). Furthermore, while recommendations for maximizing the genetic diversity and adaptive potential of restored populations discussed herein were aimed at projects occurring in the western Atlantic, the genetic risks associated with founder effects, genetic swamping, and inbreeding/outbreeding depression are universal.

When moving corals or propagules across distances, the potential for unintentionally spreading other organisms needs to be considered as well—especially given the susceptibility to outbreaks of infectious diseases in the Caribbean and the western Atlantic (Precht et al. 2016; Walton et al. 2018; Alvarez-Filip et al. 2019). For example, an outbreak of a novel disease (stony coral tissue loss disease) that began in 2014 has already caused extensive mortality of corals across Florida's Coral Reef, and is now present throughout the Caribbean (Aeby et al. 2019; Alvarez-Filip et al. 2019; Muller et al. 2020). It is highly virulent and affects as many as 22 of the 45 coral species found on Florida's Coral Reef (Aeby et al. 2019; Meyer et al. 2019). While the causative agent(s) remains unknown, mounting evidence suggests it is bacterial in nature and has the potential for direct and waterborne transmission (Aeby et al. 2019; Meyer et al. 2019; Muller et al. 2020). Consultation with relevant legal and regulatory bodies should take place prior to moving corals within or across different zones of a disease outbreak. Following established biosecurity protocols is also highly recommended (e.g., quarantine protocols). It has been suggested, however, that translocating cryopreserved coral gametes or larvae as part of assisted gene flow interventions may help to minimize the risk (Hagedorn et al. 2012; Hagedorn and Carter 2016; Hagedorn et al. 2017; Baums et al. 2019).

Finally, regardless of whether or not restoration strategies are designed to promote the persistence of coral reef populations in the face of rapid climate change, efforts may be futile if greenhouse gas emissions continue unabated, water quality is not improved, other anthropogenic threats to coral reefs are not mitigated, and marine habitats remain unprotected (Possingham et al. 2015; Baums et al. 2019). While many coral reef management strategies may shift from more conventional approaches (e.g., passive habitat protection) to novel interventions associated with active restoration (Anthony et al. 2017; van Oppen et al. 2017), this does not imply that habitat protection is not important. In fact, studies have shown that optimal conservation outcomes include both habitat protection and restoration (Possingham et al. 2015). A project that aims to restore a reef that remains vulnerable to anthropogenic disturbances because there is a lack of established or enforced protective measures will likely fail and lead to wasted efforts and resources. A recent study that used a biophysical model to simulate fine-scale coral connectivity pathways across Florida's Coral Reef identified not only major connectivity pathways that warrant focused protection, but also reef sites that are best suited for directed restoration efforts (Frys et al. 2020). This is a great example of how advanced computational tools can be used to support knowledge-based decisions regarding allocation of resources for combined conservation and restoration efforts.

In closing, coral reef scientists argue that despite the daunting task of restoring reefs in the face of rapid climate change, the heterogeneity in response to stress is what provides the hope that such efforts are worth it, and that if novel interventions can leverage this natural heterogeneity in a way that accelerates natural selection, coral species and reef ecosystems may indeed be able to persist (Baums et al. 2019).

ACKNOWLEDGMENTS

I would like to thank Michele Mason and the CRC Genetics Working Group, especially Dr. Misha Matz, for constructive feedback on this work. This work was conducted under a Postdoctoral Research Fellowship awarded to HK by Mote Marine Laboratory.

REFERENCES

Abe, M., T. Watanabe, H. Hayakawa, and M. Hidaka. 2008. "Breeding experiments of hermatypic coral *Galaxea fascicularis*: Partial reproductive isolation between colonies of different nematocyst types and enhancement of fertilization success by presence of parental colonies." *Fisheries Sci* 74, 1342–1344.
Abrego, D., B. L. Willis, and M. J. H. van Oppen. 2012. "Impact of light and temperature on the uptake of algal symbionts by coral juveniles." *PLoS ONE*, 7.
Acosta, A. and S. Zea. 1997. "Sexual reproduction of the reef coral *Montastrea cavernosa* (Scleractinia: Faviidae) in the Santa Marta area, Caribbean coast of Colombia." *Mar Biol* 128, 141–148.
Acropora Biological Review Team. 2005. "Atlantic Acropora status review." In: *Report to National Marine Fisheries Service*.
Aeby, G., B. Ushijima, J. Campbell, S. Jones, G. Williams, J. Meyer, et al. 2019. "Pathogenesis of a tissue loss disease affecting multiple species of corals along the Florida Reef Tract." *Front Mar Sci* 6.
Agrawal, A. F. 2006. "Evolution of sex: Why do organisms shuffle their genotypes?" *Curr Biol* 16, R696–R704.
Aitken, S. N. and M. C. Whitlock. 2013. "Assisted gene flow to facilitate local adaptation to climate change." *Ann Rev Ecol Evol Sys* 44, 367–384.
Albright, R., B. Mason, M. Miller, and C. Langdon. 2010. "Ocean acidification compromises recruitment success of the threatened Caribbean coral *Acropora palmata*." *P Natl Acad Sci USA* 107, 20400–20404.
Ali, A., N. Kriefall, L. Emery, C. Kenkel, M. Matz, and S. Davies. 2019. "Recruit symbiosis establishment and Symbiodiniaceae composition influenced by adult corals and reef sediment." *Coral Reefs* 38, 405–415.
Altizer, S., D. Harvell, and E. Friedle. 2003. "Rapid evolutionary dynamics and disease threats to biodiversity." *Trends Ecol Evol* 18, 589–596.
Altshuler, D., V. Pollara, C. R. Cowles, W. J. Van Etten, J. Baldwin, L. Linton, et al. 2000. "SNP map of the human genome generated by reduced representation shotgun sequencing." *Nature* 407, 513–516.
Alvarez-Filip, L., N. Estrada-Saldivar, E. Perez-Cervantes, A. Molina-Hernandez, and F. Gonzalez-Barrios. 2019. "A rapid spread of the stony coral tissue loss disease outbreak in the Mexican Caribbean *Peerj* 7.
Amar, K. and B. Rinkevich. 2007. "A floating mid-water coral nursery as larval dispersion hub." *Mar Biol* 151, 713–718.
Amos, W. and J. Harwood. 1998. "Factors affecting levels of genetic diversity in natural populations." *Philos T Roy Soc B* 353, 177–186.
Anderson, J. T., A. M. Panetta, and T. Mitchell-Olds. 2012. "Evolutionary and ecological responses to anthropogenic climate change." *Plant Physiol* 160, 1728–1740.
Anthony, K., L. K. Bay, R. Costanza, J. Firn, J. Gunn, P. Harrison, et al. 2017. "New interventions are needed to save coral reefs." *Nat Ecol Evol* 1, 1420–1422.

Anthony, K. R. N. and K. E. Fabricius. 2000. "Shifting roles of heterotrophy and autotrophy in coral energetics under varying turbidity." *J Exp Mar Biol Ecol* 252, 221–253.

Arnaud-Haond, S., C. M. Duarte, F. Alberto, and E. A. Serrao. 2007. "Standardizing methods to address clonality in population studies." *Mol Ecol* 16, 5115–5139.

Aronson, R. B. and W. F. Precht. 2001. "White-band disease and the changing face of Caribbean coral reefs." *Hydrobiologia* 460, 25–38.

Artzy-Randrup, Y., R. Olinky, and L. Stone. 2007. "Size-structured demographic models of coral populations." *J Theor Biol* 245, 482–497.

Ashley, M. V., M. F. Willson, O. R. W. Pergams, D. J. O'Dowd, S. M. Gende, and J. S. Brown. 2003. "Evolutionarily enlightened management." *Biol Conserv* 111, 115–123.

Ayre, D. J. and T. P. Hughes. 2000. "Genotypic diversity and gene flow in brooding and spawning corals along the Great Barrier Reef, Australia." *Evolution* 54, 1590–1605.

———. 2004. "Climate change, genotypic diversity and gene flow in reef-building corals." *Ecol Lett* 7, 273–278.

Baird, A. H., R. Bhagooli, P. J. Ralph, and S. Takahashi. 2009a. "Coral bleaching: The role of the host." *Trends Ecol Evol* 24, 16–20.

Baird, A. H., J. R. Guest, and B. L. Willis. 2009b. "Systematic and biogeographical patterns in the reproductive biology of scleractinian corals." *Annu Rev Ecol Evol Sys* 40, 551–571.

Baker, A. C. 2001. "Ecosystems—Reef corals bleach to survive change." *Nature* 411, 765–766.

———. "Flexibility and specificity in coral-algal symbiosis: Diversity, ecology, and biogeography of Symbiodinium." *Annu Rev Ecol Evol Sys* 34, 661–689.

Baker, H. G. 1955. "Self compatibility and establishment after long distance dispersal." *Evolution* 9, 347–349.

Balbar, A. C. and A. Metaxas. 2019. "The current application of ecological connectivity in the design of marine protected areas." *Glob Ecol Conserv* 17.

Barres, B., F. Halkett, C. Dutech, A. Andrieux, J. Pinon, and P. Frey. 2008." Genetic structure of the poplar rust fungus *Melampsora larici-populina*: Evidence for isolation by distance in Europe and recent founder effects overseas." *Infect Genet Evol* 8, 577–587.

Barrett, R. D. H. and D. Schluter. 2008. "Adaptation from standing genetic variation." *Trends Ecol Evol* 23, 38–44.

Barrett, S. C. H. 2002. "The evolution of plant sexual diversity." *Nat Rev Genet* 3, 274–284.

Barrick, J. and R. Lenski. 2013. "Genome dynamics during experimental evolution." *Nat Rev Genet* 14, 827–839.

Barshis, D. J., J. T. Ladner, T. A. Oliver, F. O. Seneca, N. Traylor-Knowles, and S. R. Palumbi. 2013. "Genomic basis for coral resilience to climate change." *P Natl Acad Sci USA* 110, 1387–1392.

Barshis, D. J., J. H. Stillman, R. D. Gates, R. J. Toonen, L. W. Smith, and C. Birkeland. 2010. "Protein expression and genetic structure of the coral *Porites lobata* in an environmentally extreme Samoan back reef: Does host genotype limit phenotypic plasticity?" *Mol Ecol* 19, 1705–1720.

Barton, J. A., B. L. Willis, and K. S. Hutson. 2017. "Coral propagation: A review of techniques for ornamental trade and reef restoration." *Rev Aquacult* 9, 238–256.

Baums, I. B. 2008. "A restoration genetics guide for coral reef conservation." *Mol Ecol* 17, 2796–2811.

Baums, I. B., A. Baker, S. Davies, A. Grottoli, C. Kenkel, S. Kitchen, et al. 2019. "Considerations for maximizing the adaptive potential of restored coral populations in the western Atlantic." *Ecol Appl* 29.

Baums, I. B., J. N. Boulay, N. R. Polato, and M. E. Hellberg. 2012. "No gene flow across the Eastern Pacific Barrier in the reef-building coral *Porites lobata*." *Mol Ecol*,21, 5418–5433.

Baums, I. B., M. K. Devlin-Durante, L. Brown, and J. H. Pinzon. 2009. Nine novel, polymorphic microsatellite markers for the study of threatened Caribbean acroporid corals. *Mol Ecol Resour*, 9, 1155–1158.

Baums, I. B., M. K. Devlin-Durante, N. R. Polato, D. Xu, S. Giri, N. S. Altman, et al. 2013. "Genotypic variation influences reproductive success and thermal stress tolerance in the reef building coral, *Acropora palmata*." *Coral Reefs* 32, 703–717.

Baums, I. B., M. W. Miller, and M. E. Hellberg 2005. "Regionally isolated populations of an imperiled Caribbean coral, *Acropora palmata*." *Mol Ecol* 14, 1377–1390.

———. 2006. "Geographic variation in clonal structure in a reef-building Caribbean coral, *Acropora palmata*." *Ecol Monogr* 76, 503–519.

Bay, R. A. and S. R. Palumbi. 2014. "Multilocus adaptation associated with heat resistance in reef-building corals." *Curr Biol* 24.
———. 2017. "Transcriptome predictors of coral survival and growth in a highly variable environment." *Ecol Evol* 7, 4794–4803.
Bellwood, D., T. Hughes, C. Folke, and M. Nystrom. 2004. "Confronting the coral reef crisis." *Nature* 429, 827–833.
Berthouly-Salazar, C., C. Mariac, M. Couderc, J. Pouzadoux, J. B. Floc'h, and Y. Vigouroux. 2016. Genotyping-by-Sequencing SNP identification for crops without a reference genome: Using transcriptome based mapping as an alternative strategy." *Front Plant Sci* 7.
Bhattacharya, D., S. Agrawal, M. Aranda, S. Baumgarten, M. Belcaid, J. L. Drake, et al. 2016. "Comparative genomics explains the evolutionary success of reef-forming corals." *Elife* 5.
Bijlsma, R. and V. Loeschcke. 2005. "Environmental stress, adaptation and evolution: An overview." *J Evol Biol* 18, 744–749.
Birchler, J. A. 2016. "Plant science: Hybrid vigour characterized." *Nature* 537, 620–621.
Birky, C. W., P. Fuerst, and T. Maruyama. 1989. "Organelle gene diversity under migration, mutation, and drift—equilibrium expectations, approach to equilibrium, effects of heteroplasmic cells, and comparison to nuclear genes." *Genetics* 121, 613–627.
Blomqvist, D., A. Pauliny, M. Larsson, and L. A. Flodin. 2010. "Trapped in the extinction vortex? Strong genetic effects in a declining vertebrate population." *BMC Evol Biol* 10.
Bode, M., L. Bode, and P. R. Armsworth. 2006. "Larval dispersal reveals regional sources and sinks in the Great Barrier Reef." *Mar Ecol Prog Ser* 308, 17–25.
Bongaerts, P., C. Riginos, R. Brunner, N. Englebert, S. R. Smith, and O. Hoegh-Guldberg. 2017. "Deep reefs are not universal refuges: Reseeding potential varies among coral species." *Sci Adv* 3.
Bongaerts, P., C. Riginos, K. B. Hay, M. J. H. van Oppen, O. Hoegh-Guldberg, and S. Dove. 2011. "Adaptive divergence in a scleractinian coral: Physiological adaptation of *Seriatopora hystrix* to shallow and deep reef habitats." *BMC Evol Biol* 11.
Boström-Einarsson, L., R. C. Babcock, E. Bayraktarov, D. Ceccarelli, N. Cook, S. C. A. Ferse, et al. 2020. Coral restoration—a systematic review of current methods, successes, failures and future directions." *PLoS ONE* 15, e0226631.
Boulotte, N., S. Dalton, A. Carroll, P. Harrison, H. Putnam, L. Peplow, et al. 2016. "Exploring the *Symbiodinium* rare biosphere provides evidence for symbiont switching in reef-building corals." *Isme J* 10, 2693–2701.
Bourne, D. G. and N. S. Webster. 2013. *Coral Reef Bacterial Communities*. Springer, Berlin, Heidelberg.
Bowden-Kerby, A. 2001. Low-tech coral reef restoration methods modeled after natural fragmentation processes." *B Mar Sci* 69, 915–931.
Brainard, J. 2019. "Caribbean coral bred in lab." *Science* 365, 845.
Brazeau, D. A., D. F. Gleason, and M. E. Morgan. 1998. "Self-fertilization in brooding hermaphroditic Caribbean corals: Evidence from molecular markers." *J Exp Mar Biol Ecol* 231, 225–238.
Brazeau, D. A., M. P. Lesser, and M. Slattery. 2013. "Genetic structure in the coral, *Montastraea cavernosa*: Assessing genetic differentiation among and within mesophotic reefs." *PLoS ONE* 8.
Bruckner, A. W. and R. J. Bruckner. 2001. "Condition of restored *Acropora palmata* fragments off Mona Island, Puerto Rico, 2 years after the Fortuna Reefer ship grounding." *Coral Reefs* 20, 235–243.
Bruno, J. F. and P. J. Edmunds. 1997. "Clonal variation for phenotypic plasticity in the coral *Madracis mirabilis*." *Ecology* 78, 2177–2190.
Bunning, H., E. Wall, M. G. G. Chagunda, G. Banos, and G. Simm. 2019. "Heterosis in cattle crossbreeding schemes in tropical regions: Meta-analysis of effects of breed combination, trait type, and climate on level of heterosis." *J Anim Sci* 97, 29–34.
Burke, L., K. Reytar, M. Spalding, and A. Perry. 2011. "Reefs at risk revisited." World Resources Institute Washington, D.C.
Buroker, N. E. 1983. "Population-genetics of the American oyster *Crassostrea virginica* along the Atlantic coast and the Gulf of Mexico." *Mar Biol* 75, 99–112.
Calle-Trivino, J., C. Cortes-Useche, R. I. Sellares-Blasco, and J. E. Arias-Gonzalez. 2018. "Assisted fertilization of threatened Staghorn coral to complement the restoration of nurseries in Southeastern Dominican Republic." *Reg Stud Mar Sci* 18, 129–134.

Carlon, D. 1999. "Evolution of mating systems in tropical reef corals." *Trends Ecol Evol* 14, 491–495.
Carne, L., L. Kaufman, and K. S. Lord. 2016. "Measuring success for Caribbean acroporid restoration: Key results from ten years of work in southern Belize." In: *Proc 13th Int Coral Reef Sym*.
Carpenter, K., M. Abrar, G. Aeby, R. Aronson, S. Banks, A. Bruckner, et al. 2008. "One-third of reef-building corals face elevated extinction risk from climate change and local impacts." *Science* 321, 560–563.
Catullo, R. A., J. Llewelyn, B. Phillips, and C. C. Moritz. 2019. "The potential for rapid evolution under anthropogenic climate change." *Curr Biol* 29, R996–R1007.
Chakravarti, L. J., V. H. Beltran, and M. J. H. van Oppen. 2017. "Rapid thermal adaptation in photosymbionts of reef-building corals." *Global Change Biol* 23, 4675–4688.
Chakravarti, L. J. and M. J. H. van Oppen. 2018. "Experimental evolution in coral photosymbionts as a tool to increase thermal tolerance." *Front Mar Sci* 5, 1–15.
Chamberland, V. F., D. Petersen, J. Guest, U. Petersen, M. Brittsan, and M. Vermeij. 2017. "New seeding approach reduces costs and time to outplant sexually propagated corals for reef restoration." *Sci Rep-Uk* 7.
Chamberland, V. F., D. Petersen, K. R. W. Latijnhouwers, S. Snowden, B. Mueller, and M. J. A. Vermeij. 2016. "Four-year-old Caribbean *Acropora* colonies reared from field-collected gametes are sexually mature." *B Mar Sci* 92, 263–264.
Chamberland, V. F., M. J. A. Vermeij, M. Brittsan, M. Carl, M. Schick, S. Snowden, et al. 2015. "Restoration of critically endangered elkhorn coral (*Acropora palmata*) populations using larvae reared from wild-caught gametes." *Glob Ecol Conserv* 4, 526–537.
Chan, A. N., C. L. Lewis, K. L. Neely, and I. B. Baums. 2019a. "Fallen pillars: The past, present, and future population dynamics of a rare, specialist coral-algal symbiosis." *Front Mar Sci* 6.
Chan, W. Y., L. M. Peplow, P. Menéndez, A. A. Hoffmann, and M. J. H. van Oppen. 2018. "Interspecific hybridization may provide novel opportunities for coral reef restoration." *Front Mar Sci* 5.
Chan, W. Y., L. M. Peplow, and M. J. H. van Oppen. 2019b. "Interspecific gamete compatibility and hybrid larval fitness in reef-building corals: Implications for coral reef restoration." *Sci Rep-Uk* 9.
Chang, S. S., B. B. Prezelin, and R. K. Trench. 1983. "Mechanisms of photoadaptation in 3 strains of the symbiotic dinoflagellate *Symbiodinium microadriaticum*." *Mar Biol* 76, 219–229.
Charlesworth, B. and D. Charlesworth. 1975. "Experiment on recombination load in *Drosophila melanogaster*." *Genet Res* 25, 267–274.
Charlesworth, D. and B. Charlesworth. 1987. "Inbreeding depression and its evolutionary consequences." *Annu Rev Ecol Syst* 18, 237–268.
———. 1990. "Inbreeding depression with heterozygote advantage and its effect on selection for modifiers changing the outcrossing rate." *Evolution* 44, 870–888.
Cheal, A. J., M. A. Macneil, M. J. Emslie, and H. Sweatman. 2017. "The threat to coral reefs from more intense cyclones under climate change." *Global Change Biol* 23, 1511–1524.
Christie, M. R., M. L. Marine, S. E. Fox, R. A. French, and M. S. Blouin. 2016. "A single generation of domestication heritably alters the expression of hundreds of genes." *Nat Commun* 7.
Christie, M. R., M. L. Marine, R. A. French, and M. S. Blouin. 2012. "Genetic adaptation to captivity can occur in a single generation." *P Natl Acad Sci USA* 109, 238–242.
Coffroth, M. A., C. Lewis, S. Santos, and J. Weaver, J. 2006. "Environmental populations of symbiotic dinoflagellates in *Symbiodinium* can initiate symbioses with reef cnidarians." *Curr Biol* 16, R985–R987.
Coffroth, M. A., D. M. Poland, E. L. Petrou, D. A. Brazeau, and J. C. Holmberg. 2010. "Environmental symbiont acquisition may not be the solution to warming seas for reef-building corals." *PLoS ONE* 5.
Cohen, C. S. 1996. "The effects of contrasting modes of fertilization on levels of inbreeding in the marine invertebrate genus *Corella*." *Evolution* 50, 1896–1907.
Coles, S. L. and B. M. Riegl. 2013. "Thermal tolerances of reef corals in the Gulf: A review of the potential for increasing coral survival and adaptation to climate change through assisted translocation." *Mar Pollut Bull* 72, 323–332.
Combosch, D. J. and S. V. Vollmer. 2013. Mixed asexual and sexual reproduction in the Indo-Pacific reef coral *Pocillopora damicornis*. *Ecol Evol*, 3, 3379–3387.
———. 2015. "Trans-Pacific RAD-Seq population genomics confirms introgressive hybridization in Eastern Pacific *Pocillopora* corals." *Mol Phylogenet Evol* 88, 154–162.

Comeau, S., P. J. Edmunds, N. B. Spindel, and R. C. Carpenter. 2014. "Diel pCO^2 oscillations modulate the response of the coral *Acropora hyacinthus* to ocean acidification." *Mar Ecol Prog Ser* 501, 99–111.

Courchamp, F., T. Clutton-Brock, and B. Grenfell. 1999. "Inverse density dependence and the Allee effect." *Trends Ecol Evol* 14, 405–410.

Cowen, R., K. M. M. Lwiza, S. Sponaugle, C. B. Paris, and D. B. Olson. 2000. "Connectivity of marine populations: Open or closed?" *Science* 287, 857–859.

Cowen, R., C. Paris, and A. Srinivasan. 2006. "Scaling of connectivity in marine populations." *Science* 311, 522–527.

Craggs, J., J. R. Guest, M. Davis, J. Simmons, E. Dashti, and M. Sweet. 2017. "Inducing broadcast coral spawning ex situ: Closed system mesocosm design and husbandry protocol." *Ecol Evol* 7, 11066–11078.

CRC, Coral Restoration Consortium. 2020. Larval Propagation Working Group. http://crc.reefresilience.org/working-groups/scaling-up-larval-propagation/.

Crossa, J., P. Perez-Rodriguez, J. Cuevas, O. Montesinos-Lopez, D. Jarquin, G. de los Campos, et al. 2017. "Genomic selection in plant breeding: Methods, models, and perspectives." *Trends Plant Sci* 22, 961–975.

Cunning, R., R. Bay, P. Gillette, A. Baker, and N. Traylor-Knowles. 2018. "Comparative analysis of the *Pocillopora damicornis* genome highlights role of immune system in coral evolution." *Sci Rep-Uk* 8.

Davey, J. and M. Blaxter. 2010. "RADSeq: Next-generation population genetics." *Brief Funct Genomics* 9, 416–423.

Davies, S. W., M. Rahman, E. Meyer, E. Green, E. Buschiazzo, M. Medina, et al. 2013. "Novel polymorphic microsatellite markers for population genetics of the endangered Caribbean star coral, *Montastraea faveolata*." *Mar Biodivers* 43, 167–172.

De'ath, G., K. E. Fabricius, H. Sweatman, and M. Puotinen. 2012. "The 27-year decline of coral cover on the Great Barrier Reef and its causes." *P Natl Acad Sci USA* 109, 17995–17999.

dela Cruz, D. W. and P. L. Harrison. 2017. "Enhanced larval supply and recruitment can replenish reef corals on degraded reefs." *Sci Rep-Uk* 7.

———. 2020. "Optimising conditions for in vitro fertilization success of *Acropora tenuis*, *A. millepora* and *Favites colemani* corals in northwestern Philippines." *J Exp Mar Biol Ecol* 524.

Devlin-Durante, M. K., M. W. Miller, W. F. Precht, I. B. Baums, and C. A. R. Grp. 2016. "How old are you? Genet age estimates in a clonal animal." *Mol Ecol* 25, 5628–5646.

DiBattista, J. D. 2008. "Patterns of genetic variation in anthropogenically impacted populations." *Conserv Genet* 9, 141–156.

Dick, C., O. Hardy, F. A. Jones, and R. J. Petit. 2008. "Spatial scales of pollen and seed-mediated gene flow in tropical rain forest trees." *Tropical Plant Biology* 1, 20–33.

Dixon, G. B., S. W. Davies, G. A. Aglyamova, E. Meyer, L. K. Bay, and M. V. Matz. 2015. "Genomic determinants of coral heat tolerance across latitudes." *Science* 348, 1460–1462.

Dobzhansky, T. 1937. *Genetics and the Origin of Species.* Columbia University Press, New York, NY.

Doherty, P. J., S. Planes, and P. Mather. 1995. "Gene flow and larval duration in 7 species of fish from the Great-Barrier-Reef." *Ecology* 76, 2373–2391.

Dollar, S. 1982. "Wave stress and coral community structure in Hawaii." *Coral Reefs* 1, 71–81.

Donner, S. D., W. J. Skirving, C. M. Little, M. Oppenheimer, and O. Hoegh-Guldberg. 2005. "Global assessment of coral bleaching and required rates of adaptation under climate change." *Global Change Biol* 11, 2251–2265.

Doropoulos, C., N. R. Evensen, L. A. Gomez-Lemos, and R. C. Babcock. 2017. "Density-dependent coral recruitment displays divergent responses during distinct early life-history stages." *Roy Soc Open Sci* 4.

Downs, C. A., G. K. Ostrander, L. Rougee, T. Rongo, S. Knutson, D. E. Williams, et al. 2012. "The use of cellular diagnostics for identifying sub-lethal stress in reef corals." *Ecotoxicology* 21, 768–782.

Drury, C., K. E. Dale, J. M. Panlilio, S. V. Miller, D. Lirman, E. A. Larson, et al. 2016. "Genomic variation among populations of threatened coral: *Acropora cervicornis*." *BMC Genomics* 17.

Drury, C., D. Manzello, and D. Lirman. 2017. "Genotype and local environment dynamically influence growth, disturbance response and survivorship in the threatened coral, *Acropora cervicornis*." *PLoS ONE* 12.

Dziedzic, K. E., H. Elder, H. Tavalire, and E. Meyer. 2019b. "Heritable variation in bleaching responses and its functional genomic basis in reef-building corals (*Orbicella faveolata*)." *Mol Ecol* 28, 2238–2253.

Eakin, C. M., J. A. Morgan, S. F. Heron, T. B. Smith, G. Liu, L. Alvarez-Filip, et al. 2010. "Caribbean corals in crisis: Record thermal stress, bleaching, and mortality in 2005." *PLoS ONE* 5.

Edmands, S. 2007. "Between a rock and a hard place: Evaluating the relative risks of inbreeding and outbreeding for conservation and management." *Mol Ecol* 16, 463–475.

Edmunds, P. J. and R. Elahi. 2007. "The demographics of a 15-year decline in cover of the Caribbean reef coral *Montastraea annularis*." *Ecol Monogr* 77, 3–18.

Edmunds, P. J., R. D. Gates, W. Leggat, O. Hoegh-Guldberg, and L. Allen-Requa. 2005. "The effect of temperature on the size and population density of dinoflagellates in larvae of the reef coral *Porites astreoides*." *Invertebr Biol* 124, 185–193.

Edwards, A., J. Guest, A. Heyward, R. Villanueva, M. Baria, I. Bollozos, et al. 2015. "Direct seeding of mass-cultured coral larvae is not an effective option for reef rehabilitation." *Mar Ecol Prog Ser* 525, 105–116.

Edwards, A. and S. Clark. 1998. "Coral transplantation: A useful management tool or misguided meddling?" *Mar Pollut Bull* 37, 474–487.

Eizaguirre, C. and M. Baltazar-Soares. 2014. "Evolutionary conservation-evaluating the adaptive potential of species." *Evol Appl* 7, 963–967.

Ellstrand, N. C. and L. H. Rieseberg. 2016. "When gene flow really matters: Gene flow in applied evolutionary biology." *Evol Appl* 9, 833–836.

Elmer, F., J. J. Bell, and J. P. A. Gardner. 2018. "Coral larvae change their settlement preference for crustose coralline algae dependent on availability of bare space." *Coral Reefs* 37, 397–407.

Estes, J. A., J. Terborgh, J. S. Brashares, M. E. Power, J. Berger, W. J. Bond, et al. 2011. "Trophic downgrading of planet earth." *Science* 333, 301–306.

Everett, M. V., L. K. Park, E. A. Berntson, A. E. Elz, C. E. Whitmire, A. A. Keller, et al. 2016. "Large-Scale Genotyping-by-Sequencing indicates high levels of gene flow in the deep-sea octocoral *Swiftia simplex* (Nutting 1909) on the west coast of the United States." *PLoS ONE* 11.

FDEP, Florida Department of Environmental Protection. 2020. "Stony coral tissue loss disease response." https://floridadep.gov/rcp/coral/content/stony-coral-tissue-loss-disease-response2020.

Ferse, S., M. Nugues, S. Romatzki, and A. Kunzmann. 2013. "Examining the use of mass transplantation of brooding and spawning corals to support natural coral recruitment in Sulawesi/Indonesia." *Restor Ecol* 21, 745–754.

Figueiredo, J., A. H. Baird, S. Harii, and S. R. Connolly. 2014. "Increased local retention of reef coral larvae as a result of ocean warming." *Nat Clim Change* 4, 498–502.

Fisch, J., C. Drury, E. Towle, R. Winter, and M. Miller. 2019. "Physiological and reproductive repercussions of consecutive summer bleaching events of the threatened Caribbean coral *Orbicella faveolata*." *Coral Reefs* 38, 863–876.

Flanagan, S., B. Forester, E. Latch, S. Aitken, and S. Hoban. 2018. "Guidelines for planning genomic assessment and monitoring of locally adaptive variation to inform species conservation." *Evol Appl* 11, 1035–1052.

Fogarty, N. D. 2012. "Caribbean acroporid coral hybrids are viable across life history stages." *Mar Ecol Prog Ser* 446, 145–159.

Fogarty, N. D. and K. L. Marhaver. 2019. "Coral spawning, unsynchronized." *Science* 365, 987–988.

Fogarty, N. D., S. V. Vollmer, and D. R. Levitan. 2012. "Weak prezygotic isolating mechanisms in threatened Caribbean *Acropora* corals." *PLoS ONE* 7.

Fong, P. and D. Lirman. 1995. "Hurricanes cause population expansion of the branching coral *Acropora palmata*: Wound healing and growth patterns of asexual recruits." *Mar Ecol-P S Z N I* 16, 317–335.

Forsman, Z. H., C. A. Page, R. J. Toonen, and D. Vaughan. 2015. "Growing coral larger and faster: Micro-colony-fusion as a strategy for accelerating coral cover." *Peerj* 3.

Foster, N. L., I. B. Baums, and P. J. Mumby. 2007. "Sexual vs. asexual reproduction in an ecosystem engineer: The massive coral *Montastraea annularis*." *J Anim Ecol* 76, 384–391.

Foster, N. L., I. B. Baums, J. A. Sanchez, C. B. Paris, I. Chollett, C. L. Agudelo, et al. 2013. "Hurricane-driven patterns of clonality in an ecosystem engineer: The Caribbean coral *Montastraea annularis*." *PLoS ONE* 8.

Fox, H. E., J. L. Harris, E. S. Darling, G. N. Ahmadia, Estradivari, and T. B. Razak. 2019a. "Rebuilding coral reefs: Success (and failure) 16 years after low-cost, low-tech restoration." *Restor Ecol* 27, 862–869.

Fox, R. J., J. M. Donelson, C. Schunter, T. Ravasi, and J. D. Gaitan-Espitia. 2019b. "Beyond buying time: The role of plasticity in phenotypic adaptation to rapid environmental change." *Philos T R Soc B* 374.

Frade, P. R., F. De Jongh, F. Vermeulen, J. Van Bleijswijk, and R. P. M. Bak. 2008. "Variation in symbiont distribution between closely related coral species over large depth ranges." *Mol Ecol* 17, 691–703.

Frankham, R. 2005a. "Conservation biology—ecosystem recovery enhanced by genotypic diversity." *Heredity* 95, 183–183.

———. 2005b. "Stress and adaptation in conservation genetics." *J Evolution Biol* 18, 750–755.

Fraser, D. J. 2008. "How well can captive breeding programs conserve biodiversity? A review of salmonids." *Evol Appl* 1, 535–586.

Frieler, K., M. Meinshausen, A. Golly, M. Mengel, K. Lebek, S. D. Donner, et al. 2013. "Limiting global warming to 2 degrees C is unlikely to save most coral reefs." *Nat Clim Change* 3, 165–170.

Frys, C., A. Saint-Amand, M. Le Hénaff, J. Figueiredo, A. Kuba, B. Walker, et al. 2020. "Fine-scale coral connectivity pathways in the Florida Reef Tract: Implications for conservation and restoration." *Front Mar Sci*, 7.

Fukami, H., A. F. Budd, D. R. Levitan, J. Jara, R. Kersanach, and N. Knowlton. 2004. "Geographic differences in species boundaries among members of the *Montastraea annularis* complex based on molecular and morphological markers." *Evolution* 58, 324–337.

Gardner, T. A., I. M. Cote, J. A. Gill, A. Grant, and A. R. Watkinson. 2003. "Long-term region-wide declines in Caribbean corals." *Science* 301, 958–960.

———. 2005. "Hurricanes and Caribbean coral reefs: Impacts, recovery patterns, and role in long-term decline." *Ecology* 86, 174–184.

Gascoigne, J. and R. N. Lipcius. 2004. "Allee effects in marine systems." *Mar Ecol Prog Ser* 269, 49–59.

Gates, R. D. and T. D. Ainsworth. 2011. "The nature and taxonomic composition of coral symbiomes as drivers of performance limits in scleractinian corals." *J Exp Mar Biol Ecol* 408, 94–101.

Gayle, P. M. H., P. Wilson-Kelly, and S. Green. 2005. "Transplantation of benthic species to mitigate impacts of coastal development in Jamaica." *Revista De Biologia Tropical* 53, 105–115.

Ghalambor, C., J. McKay, S. Carroll, and D. Reznick. 2007. "Adaptive versus non-adaptive phenotypic plasticity and the potential for contemporary adaptation in new environments." *Funct Ecol* 21, 394–407.

Gilmour, J. 1999. "Experimental investigation into the effects of suspended sediment on fertilisation, larval survival and settlement in a scleractinian coral." *Mar Biol* 135, 451–462.

Gilmour, J. 2002. "Acute sedimentation causes size-specific mortality and asexual budding in the mushroom coral, *Fungia fungites*." *Mar Freshwater Res* 53, 805–812.

———. 2004. "Asexual budding in Fungiid corals." *Coral Reefs* 23, 595.

Gleason, D. F., D. A. Brazeau, and D. Munfus. 2001. "Can self-fertilizing coral species be used to enhance restoration of Caribbean reefs?" *B Mar Sci* 69, 933–943.

Glynn, P. W., J. L. Mate, A. C. Baker, and M. O. Calderon. 2001. "Coral bleaching and mortality in Panama and Ecuador during the 1997–1998 El Nino-Southern oscillation event: Spatial/temporal patterns and comparisons with the 1982–1983 event." *B Mar Sci* 69, 79–109.

Goffredo, S., L. Mezzomonaco, and F. Zaccanti. 2004. "Genetic differentiation among populations of the Mediterranean hermaphroditic brooding coral *Balanophyllia europaea*." *Mar Biol* 145, 1075–1083.

Goldberg, J. and C. Wilkinson. 2004. "Global threats to coral reefs: Coral bleaching, global climate change, disease, predator plagues and invasive species." In: *Status of Coral Reefs of the World*, pp. 67–92.

Gomez-Lemos, L., C. Doropoulos, E. Bayraktarov, and G. Diaz-Pulido. 2018. "Coralline algal metabolites induce settlement and mediate the inductive effect of epiphytic microbes on coral larvae." *Sci Rep-Uk* 8.

Goodbody-Gringley, G., S. V. Vollmer, R. M. Woollacott, and G. Giribet. 2010. "Limited gene flow in the brooding coral *Favia fragum* (Esper, 1797)." *Mar Biol* 157, 2591–2602.

Goodbody-Gringley, G., R. M. Woollacott, and G. Giribet. 2012. "Population structure and connectivity in the Atlantic scleractinian coral *Montastraea cavernosa* (Linnaeus, 1767)." *Mar Ecol-Evol Persp* 33, 32–48.

Goreau, T. 1959. "The Ecology of Jamaican coral reefs. 1. Species composition and zonation." *Ecology* 40, 67–90.

Goreau, T., T. McClanahan, R. Hayes, and A. Strong. 2000. "Conservation of coral reefs after the 1998 global bleaching event." *Conserv Biol* 14, 5–15.

Guest, J., A. Heyward, M. Omori, K. Iwao, A. Morse, and C. Boch. 2010. "Rearing coral larvae for reef rehabilitation." In: *Reef Rehabilitation Manual*, St. Lucia, Australia.

Guest, J., M. V. Baria, E. D. Gomez, A. J. Heyward, and A. J. Edwards. 2014. "Closing the circle: Is it feasible to rehabilitate reefs with sexually propagated corals?" *Coral Reefs* 33, 45–55.

Hagedorn, M. and V. Carter. 2016. "Cryobiology: Principles, species conservation and benefits for coral reefs." *Reprod Fert Develop* 28, 1049–1060.

Hagedorn, M., V. Carter, E. Henley, M. J. H. van Oppen, R. Hobbs, and R. E. Spindler. 2017. "Producing coral offspring with cryopreserved sperm: A tool for coral reef restoration." *Sci Rep-Uk* 7.

Hagedorn, M., V. Carter, K. Martorana, M. K. Paresa, J. Acker, I. B. Baums, et al. 2012. "Preserving and using germplasm and dissociated embryonic cells for conserving Caribbean and Pacific coral." *PLoS ONE* 7.

Hagedorn, M., V. Carter, R. A. Steyn, D. Krupp, J. C. Leong, R. P. Lang, et al. 2006. "Preliminary studies of sperm cryopreservation in the mushroom coral, *Fungia scutaria*." *Cryobiology* 52, 454–458.

Hagedorn, M., C. Page, K. O'Neil, D. Flores, L. Tichy, V. F. Chamberland, et al. 2019. "Successful demonstration of assisted gene flow in the threatened coral *Acropora palmata* across genetically-isolated Caribbean populations using cryopreserved sperm." *bioRxiv*.

Haig, S. M. 1998. "Molecular contributions to conservation." *Ecology* 79, 413–425.

Hairston, N. G., S. P. Ellner, M. A. Geber, T. Yoshida, and J. A. Fox. 2005. "Rapid evolution and the convergence of ecological and evolutionary time." *Ecol Lett* 8, 1114–1127.

Hall, V. R. and T. P. Hughes. 1996. "Reproductive strategies of modular organisms: Comparative studies of reef-building corals." *Ecology* 77, 950–963.

Hammerman, N., R. E. Rivera-Vicens, M. P. Galaska, E. Weil, R. S. Appledoorn, M. Alfaro, et al. 2018. Population connectivity of the plating coral *Agaricia lamarcki* from southwest Puerto Rico." *Coral Reefs* 37, 183–191.

Hardner, C. M. and B. M. Potts. 1997. "Postdispersal selection following mixed mating in *Eucalyptus regnans*." *Evolution* 51, 103–111.

Harii, S., N. Yasuda, M. Rodriguez-Lanetty, T. Irie, and M. Hidaka. 2009. "Onset of symbiosis and distribution patterns of symbiotic dinoflagellates in the larvae of scleractinian corals." *Mar Biol* 156, 1203–1212.

Harrington, P. D. and M. A. Lewis. 2020. "A next-generation approach to calculate source-sink dynamics in marine metapopulations." *B Math Biol* 82.

Harrison, P. L. 2011. "Sexual reproduction of scleractinian corals." *Coral Reefs: An Ecosystem in Transition* 59–85.

Harrison, P. L. and C. C. Wallace. 1990. *Reproduction, dispersal and recruitment of scleractinian corals*. Elsevier, Amsterdam, The Netherlands.

Hartmann, A. C., K. L. Marhaver, and M. J. A. Vermeij. 2018. "Corals in healthy populations produce more larvae per unit cover." *Conserv Lett* 11.

Hedgecock, D., D. J. McGoldrick, and B. L. Bayne. 1995. "Hybrid vigor in Pacific oysters: An experimental approach using crosses among inbred lines." *Aquaculture* 137, 285–298.

Hedrick, P. W. 2001. "Conservation genetics: Where are we now?" *Trends Ecol Evol* 16, 629–636.

Hellberg, M. E. 2006. "No variation and low synonymous substitution rates in coral mtDNA despite high nuclear variation." *BMC Evol Biol* 6.

———. 2007. "Footprints on water: The genetic wake of dispersal among reefs." *Coral Reefs* 26, 463–473.

Hemond, E. M. and S. V. Vollmer. 2010. "Genetic diversity and connectivity in the threatened staghorn coral (*Acropora cervicornis*) in Florida." *PLoS ONE* 5.

Hendry, A. P., T. J. Farrugia, and M. T. Kinnison. 2008. "Human influences on rates of phenotypic change in wild animal populations." *Mol Ecol* 17, 20–29.

Hendry, A. P. and M. T. Kinnison. 1999. "Perspective: The pace of modern life: Measuring rates of contemporary microevolution." *Evolution* 53, 1637–1653.

Heyward, A. J. and R. C. Babcock. 1986. "Self-fertilization and cross-fertilization in scleractinian corals." *Mar Biol* 90, 191–195.

Heyward, A. J. and A. P. Negri. 2010. "Plasticity of larval pre-competency in response to temperature: Observations on multiple broadcast spawning coral species." *Coral Reefs* 29, 631–636.

Heyward, A. J., L. D. Smith, M. Rees, and S. N. Field. 2002. "Enhancement of coral recruitment by in situ mass culture of coral larvae." *Mar Ecol Prog Ser* 230, 113–118.

Highsmith, R. C. 1982. "Reproduction by fragmentation in corals." *Mar Ecol Prog Ser* 7, 207–226.

Hock, K., N. Wolff, J. Ortiz, S. Condie, K. Anthony, P. Blackwell, et al. 2017. "Connectivity and systemic resilience of the Great Barrier Reef." *PLoS Biol* 15, e2003355. https://doi.org/10.1371/journal.pbio.2003355.

Hoegh-Guldberg, O. 1999. "Climate change, coral bleaching and the future of the world's coral reefs." *Mar Freshwater Res* 50, 839–866.

———. 2012. "The adaptation of coral reefs to climate change: Is the Red Queen being outpaced?" *Sci Mar* 76, 403–408.

Hoegh-Guldberg, O. and J. F. Bruno. 2010. "The impact of climate change on the world's marine ecosystems." *Science* 328, 1523–1528.

Hoegh-Guldberg, O., L. Hughes, S. McIntyre, D. B. Lindenmayer, C. Parmesan, H. P. Possingham, et al. 2008a. "Assisted colonization and rapid climate change." *Science* 321, 345–346.

Hoegh-Guldberg, O., P. J. Mumby, A. J. Hooten, R. S. Steneck, P. Greenfield, E. Gomez, et al. 2007. "Coral reefs under rapid climate change and ocean acidification." *Science* 318, 1737–1742.

———., et al. 2008b. "Coral adaptation in the face of climate change—Response." *Science* 320, 315–316.

Hoffmann, A. and C. Sgro. 2011. "Climate change and evolutionary adaptation." *Nature* 470, 479–485.

Holderegger, R., U. Kamm, and F. Gugerli. 2006. "Adaptive vs. neutral genetic diversity: Implications for landscape genetics." *Landscape Ecol* 21, 797–807.

Horreo, J. L., A. G. Valiente, A. Ardura, A. Blanco, C. Garcia-Gonzalez, and E. Garcia-Vazquez. 2018. "Nature versus nurture? Consequences of short captivity in early stages." *Ecol Evol* 8, 521–529.

Howells, E. J., D. Abrego, E. Meyer, N. L. Kirk, and J. A. Burt. 2016. "Host adaptation and unexpected symbiont partners enable reef-building corals to tolerate extreme temperatures." *Global Change Biol* 22, 2702–2714.

Howells, E. J., V. H. Beltran, N. W. Larsen, L. K. Bay, B. L. Willis, and M. J. H. van Oppen. 2012. "Coral thermal tolerance shaped by local adaptation of photosymbionts." *Nat Clim Change* 2, 116–120.

Howells, E. J., R. Berkelmans, M. J. H. van Oppen, B. L. Willis, and L. K. Bay. 2013. "Historical thermal regimes define limits to coral acclimatization." *Ecology* 94, 1078–1088.

Hufford, K. M. and S. J. Mazer. 2003. "Plant ecotypes: Genetic differentiation in the age of ecological restoration." *Trends Ecol Evol* 18, 147–155.

Hughes, T. P. 1994. "Catastrophes, phase-shifts, and large-scale degradation of a Caribbean coral-reef." *Science* 265, 1547–1551.

Hughes, T. P., K. D. Anderson, S. R. Connolly, S. F. Heron, J. T. Kerry, J. M. Lough, et al. 2018a. "Spatial and temporal patterns of mass bleaching of corals in the Anthropocene." *Science* 359, 80–94.

Hughes, T. P., M. L. Barnes, D. R. Bellwood, J. E. Cinner, G. S. Cumming, J. B. C. Jackson, et al. 2017. "Coral reefs in the Anthropocene." *Nature*, 546, 82–90.

Hughes, T. P., J. T. Kerry, A. H. Baird, S. R. Connolly, T. J. Chase, A. Dietzel, et al. 2019. "Global warming impairs stock-recruitment dynamics of corals." *Nature* 568, 387–92.

Hughes, T. P., J. T. Kerry, A. H. Baird, S. R. Connolly, A. Dietzel, C. M. Eakin, et al. 2018b. "Global warming transforms coral reef assemblages." *Nature* 556, 492–499.

Hughes, T. P. and J. E. Tanner. 2000. "Recruitment failure, life histories, and long-term decline of Caribbean corals." *Ecology* 81, 2250–2263.

Hunter, C. L. 1993. "Genotypic variation and clonal structure in coral populations with different disturbance histories." *Evolution* 47, 1213–1228.

Husband, B. C. and D. W. Schemske. 1996. "Evolution of the magnitude and timing of inbreeding depression in plants." *Evolution* 50, 54–70.

Iguchi, A., Y. Yoshioka, Z. Forsman, I. Knapp, R. Toonen, Y. Hongo. et al. 2019. "RADseq population genomics confirms divergence across closely related species in blue coral (*Heliopora coerulea*)." *BMC Evol Biol* 19.

IPCC, Intergovernmental Panel on Climate Change. 2014a. "Climate Change 2014: Impacts, Adaptation, and Vulnerability." Cambridge Univ., Cambridge.

———. "Climate Change 2014: Synthesis Report. Contribution of Working Groups I, II and III to the Fifth Assessment Report of the Intergovernmental Panel on Climate Change." Geneva, Switzerland, pp. 1–151.

Iwao, K., N. Wada, A. H. Ohdera, and M. Omori. 2014. "How many donor colonies should be cross-fertilized for nursery farming of sexually propagated corals?" *Natural Resources* 521–526.

Jackson, J. 1992. "Pleistocene perspectives on coral-reef community structure." *Am Zool* 32, 719–731.

Jain, S. K. 1976. "The evolution of inbreeding in plants." *Annu Rev Ecol Syst* 7, 469–495.

Jameson, S. C., M. S. A. Ammar, E. Saadalla, H. M. Mostafa, and B. Riegl. 1999. "A coral damage index and its application to diving sites in the Egyptian Red Sea." *Coral Reefs* 18, 333–339.

Jamieson, I. G. 2011. "Founder effects, inbreeding, and loss of genetic diversity in four avian reintroduction programs." *Conserv Biol* 25, 115–123.

Jarne, P. and J. R. Auld. 2006. "Animals mix it up too: The distribution of self-fertilization among hermaphroditic animals." *Evolution* 60, 1816–1824.

Jarne, P. and D. Charlesworth. 1993. "The evolution of the selfing rate in functionally hermaphrodite plants and animals." *Annu Rev Ecol Syst* 24, 441–466.

Jenkins, T. L. and J. R. Stevens. 2018. "Assessing connectivity between MPAs: Selecting taxa and translating genetic data to inform policy." *Mar Policy* 94, 165–173.

Jiang, Y., R. H. Schmidt, Y. S. Zhao, and J. C. Reif. 2017. "A quantitative genetic framework highlights the role of epistatic effects for grain-yield heterosis in bread wheat." *Nat Genet* 49, 1741–1749.

Johansen-Morris, A. D. and R. G. Latta. 2006. "Fitness consequences of hybridization between ecotypes of *Avena barbata*: Hybrid breakdown, hybrid vigor, and transgressive segregation." *Evolution* 60, 1585–1595.

Johnson, M., C. Lustic, E. Bartels, I. Baums, D. Gilliam, L. Larson, et al. 2011. "Caribbean Acropora Restoration Guide: Best Practices for Propagation and Population Enhancement." NOAA, TNC.

Jones, D. F. 1917. "Dominance of linked factors as a means of accounting for heterosis." *P Natl Acad Sci USA* 3, 310–312.

Jones, G., G. Almany, G. Russ, P. Sale, R. Steneck, M. van Oppen, et al. 2009. "Larval retention and connectivity among populations of corals and reef fishes: History, advances and challenges." *Coral Reefs* 28, 307–325.

Jones, G., M. J. Milicich, M. J. Emslie, and C. Lunow. 1999. "Self-recruitment in a coral reef fish population." *Nature* 402, 802–804.

Jones, G., S. Planes, and S. Thorrold. 2005. "Coral reef fish larvae settle close to home." *Curr Biol* 15, 1314–1318.

Jordan, A. 2018. "Patterns in Caribbean coral spawning." Nova Southeastern University, NSUWorks.

Karl, S. A. and J. C. Avise. 1992. "Balancing selection at allozyme loci in oysters—Implications from nuclear RFLPs." *Science* 256, 100–102.

Kawecki, T. J. and D. Ebert. 2004. "Conceptual issues in local adaptation." *Ecol Lett* 7, 1225–1241.

Kenkel, C. D., G. Goodbody-Gringley, E. Bartels, S. W. Davies, A. L. Percy, and M. V. Matz. 2012. "Evidence of local thermal adaptation in a Caribbean coral." *Integr Comp Biol* 52, E92.

Kenkel, C. D., G. Goodbody-Gringley, D. Caillaud, S. W. Davies, E. Bartels, and M. V. Matz. 2013a. "Evidence for a host role in thermotolerance divergence between populations of the mustard hill coral (*Porites astreoides*) from different reef environments." *Mol Ecol* 22, 4335–4348.

Kenkel, C. D., E. Meyer, and M. V. Matz. 2013b. "Gene expression under chronic heat stress in populations of the mustard hill coral (*Porites astreoides*) from different thermal environments." *Mol Ecol* 22, 4322–4334.

Kenkel, C. D., S. P. Setta, and M. V. Matz. 2015. "Heritable differences in fitness-related traits among populations of the mustard hill coral, *Porites astreoides*." *Heredity* 115, 509–516.

Kenkel, C. D., C. Sheridan, M. C. Leal, R. Bhagooli, K. D. Castillo, N. Kurata, et al. 2014. "Diagnostic gene expression biomarkers of coral thermal stress." *Mol Ecol Resour* 14, 667–678.

Kirkpatrick, M. and P. Jarne. 2000. "The effects of a bottleneck on inbreeding depression and the genetic load." *Am Nat* 155, 154–167.

Kitchen, S. A., A. Ratan, O. C. Bedoya-Reina, R. Burhans, N. D. Fogarty, W. Miller, et al. 2019. "Genomic variants among threatened *Acropora* corals." *G3-Genes Genom Genet* 9, 1633–1646.

Kitchen, S. A., K. G. Von, W. Miller, and I. B. Baums. 2018. "STAG: Standard Tools for Acroporid Genotyping." *Integr Comp Biol* 58, E353.

Knowlton, N. 2001. "The future of coral reefs." *P Natl Acad Sci USA* 98, 5419–5425.

Kojis, B. L. and N. J. Quinn. 1981. "Aspects of sexual reproduction and larval development in the shallow-water hermatypic coral, *Goniastrea australensis* (Edwards and Haime, 1857)." *B Mar Sci* 31, 558–573.

Kondrashov, A. S. 1988. "Deleterious mutations and the evolution of sexual reproduction." *Nature* 336, 435–440.

Kotb, M. M. A. 2016. "Coral translocation and farming as mitigation and conservation measures for coastal development in the Red Sea: Aqaba case study, Jordan." *Environ Earth Sci* 75.

Krediet, C. J., K. B. Ritchie, V. J. Paul, and M. Teplitski. 2013. "Coral-associated micro-organisms and their roles in promoting coral health and thwarting diseases." *P Roy Soc B-Biol Sci* 280.

Kristensen, T. N. and A. C. Sorensen. 2005. "Inbreeding—lessons from animal breeding, evolutionary biology and conservation genetics." *Anim Sci* 80, 121–133.

Kuffner, I. B., E. Bartels, A. Stathakopoulos, I. C. Enochs, G. Kolodziej, L. T. Toth, et al. 2017. "Plasticity in skeletal characteristics of nursery-raised staghorn coral, *Acropora cervicornis*." *Coral Reefs* 36, 679–684.

Kuffner, I. B., B. H. Lidz, J. H. Hudson, and J. S. Anderson. 2015. "A century of ocean warming on Florida Keys Coral Reefs: Historic in situ observations." *Estuar Coast* 38, 1085–1096.

Kuffner, I. B. and L. T. Toth. 2016. "A geological perspective on the degradation and conservation of western Atlantic coral reefs." *Conserv Biol* 30, 706–715.

Ladd, M. C., M. W. Miller, J. H. Hunt, W. C. Sharp, and D. E. Burkepile. 2018. "Harnessing ecological processes to facilitate coral restoration." *Front Ecol Environ* 16, 239–247.

LaJeunesse, T. C. 2002. "Diversity and community structure of symbiotic dinoflagellates from Caribbean coral reefs." *Mar Biol* 141, 387–400.

LaJeunesse, T. C., R. Bhagooli, M. Hidaka, L. DeVantier, T. Done, G. W. Schmidt, et al. 2004. "Closely related *Symbiodinium* spp. differ in relative dominance in coral reef host communities across environmental, latitudinal and biogeographic gradients." *Mar Ecol Prog Ser* 284, 147–161.

LaJeunesse, T. C., J. Parkinson, P. Gabrielson, H. Jeong, J. Reimer, C. Voolstra, et al. 2018. "Systematic revision of Symbiodiniaceae highlights the antiquity and diversity of coral endosymbionts." *Curr Biol* 28, 2570–2582.

LaJeunesse, T. C., R. Smith, M. Walther, J. Pinzon, D. T. Pettay, M. McGinley, et al. 2010. "Host-symbiont recombination versus natural selection in the response of coral-dinoflagellate symbioses to environmental disturbance." *P Roy Soc B-Biol Sci* 277, 2925–2934.

Lande, R. and D. W. Schemske. 1985. "The evolution of self-fertilization and inbreeding depression in plants. 1. Genetic Models." *Evolution* 39, 24–40.

Lankau, R., P. S. Jorgensen, D. J. Harris, and A. Sih. 2011. "Incorporating evolutionary principles into environmental management and policy." *Evol Appl* 4, 315–325.

Lariepe, A., B. Mangin, S. Jasson, V. Combes, F. Dumas, P. Jamin, et al. 2012. "The genetic basis of heterosis: Multiparental quantitative trait loci mapping reveals contrasted levels of apparent overdominance among traits of agronomical interest in maize (*Zea mays*)." *Genetics* 190, 795–U835.

Lasker, H. R., E. C. Peters, and M. A. Coffroth. 1984. "Bleaching of reef coelenterates in the San-Blas Islands, Panama." *Coral Reefs* 3, 183–190.

Lembeye, F., N. Lopez-Villalobos, J. L. Burke, and S. R. Davis. 2016. "Breed and heterosis effects for milk yield traits at different production levels, lactation number and milking frequencies." *New Zeal J Agr Res* 59, 156–164.

Lenormand, T. 2002. "Gene flow and the limits to natural selection." *Trends Ecol Evol* 17, 183–189.

Lessios, H. A. 2016. "The great *Diadema antillarum* die-off: 30 years later." *Ann Rev Mar Sci* 8, 267–283.

Lessios, H. A., D. R. Robertson, and J. D. Cubit. 1984. "Spread of *Diadema* mass mortality through the Caribbean." *Science* 226, 335–337.

Levitan, D. R., W. Boudreau, J. Jara, and N. Knowlton. 2014. "Long-term reduced spawning in *Orbicella* coral species due to temperature stress." *Mar Ecol Prog Ser* 515, 1–10.

Levitan, D. R., N. D. Fogarty, J. Jara, K. E. Lotterhos, and N. Knowlton. 2011. "Genetic, spatial, and temporal components of precise spawning synchrony in reef building corals of the *Montastraea annularis* species complex." *Evolution* 65, 1254–1270.

Levitan, D. R. and C. Petersen. 1995. "Sperm limitation in the sea." *Trends Ecol Evol* 10, 228–231.

Li, L. Z., K. Y. Lu, Z. M. Chen, T. M. Mu, Z. L. Hu, and X. Q. Li. 2008. "Dominance, overdominance and epistasis condition the heterosis in two heterotic rice hybrids." *Genetics* 180, 1725–1742.

Libro, S., S. T. Kaluziak, and S. V. Vollmer. 2013. "RNA-seq profiles of immune related genes in the staghorn coral *Acropora cervicornis* infected with white band disease." *PLoS ONE* 8.

Libro, S. and S. V. Vollmer. 2016. "Genetic signature of resistance to white band disease in the Caribbean staghorn coral *Acropora cervicornis*." *PLoS ONE* 11.

Ligson, C., T. Tabalanza, R. Villanueva, and P. Cabaitan. 2020. "Feasibility of early outplanting of sexually propagated *Acropora verweyi* for coral reef restoration demonstrated in the Philippines." *Restor Ecol* 28, 244–251.

Lippman, Z. B. and D. Zamir. 2007. "Heterosis: Revisiting the magic." *Trends Genet* 23, 60–66.

Lirman, D. 2000. "Fragmentation in the branching coral *Acropora palmata* (Lamarck): Growth, survivorship, and reproduction of colonies and fragments." *J Exp Mar Biol Ecol* 251, 41–57.

Lirman, D., N. Formel, S. Schopmeyer, J. S. Ault, S. G. Smith, D. Gilliam, et al. 2014a. "Percent recent mortality (PRM) of stony corals as an ecological indicator of coral reef condition." *Ecol Indic* 44, 120–127.

Lirman, D. and M. W. Miller. 2003. "Modeling and monitoring tools to assess recovery status and convergence rates between restored and undisturbed coral reef habitats." *Restor Ecol* 11, 448–456.

Lirman, D. and S. Schopmeyer. 2016. "Ecological solutions to reef degradation: Optimizing coral reef restoration in the Caribbean and western Atlantic." *Peerj* 4.

Lirman, D., S. Schopmeyer, V. Galvan, C. Drury, A. C. Baker, and I. B. Baums. 2014b. "Growth dynamics of the threatened Caribbean staghorn coral *Acropora cervicornis*: Influence of host genotype, symbiont identity, colony size, and environmental setting." *PLoS ONE* 9.

Lirman, D., T. Thyberg, J. Herlan, C. Hill, C. Young-Lahiff, S. Schopmeyer, et al. 2010. "Propagation of the threatened staghorn coral *Acropora cervicornis*: Methods to minimize the impacts of fragment collection and maximize production." *Coral Reefs* 29, 729–735.

Liti, G., D. B. H. Barton, and E. J. Louis. 2006. "Sequence diversity, reproductive isolation and species concepts in Saccharomyces." *Genetics* 174, 839–850.

Liu, G., W. Skirving, and A. E. Strong. 2003. "Potential for expansion of coral reefs into higher latitudes due to climate change." *Oceans 2003: Celebrating the Past, Teaming toward the Future* 2745–2747.

Lively, C. M. and S. G. Johnson. 1994. "Brooding and the evolution of parthenogenesis—Strategy models and evidence from aquatic invertebrates." *P Roy Soc B-Biol Sci* 256, 89–95.

Lofflin, D. L. and S. R. Kephart. 2005. "Outbreeding, seedling establishment, and maladaptation in natural and reintroduced populations of rare and common *Silene douglasii* (Caryophyllaceae)." *Am J Bot* 92, 1691–1700.

Lopez, J. V., B. Kamel, M. Medina, T. Collins, and I. B. Baums. 2019. "Multiple facets of marine invertebrate conservation genomics." *Annu Rev Anim Biosci* 7, 473–482.

Lo-Yat, A., M. G. Meekan, J. H. Carleton, and R. Galzin. 2006. "Large-scale dispersal of the larvae of nearshore and pelagic fishes in the tropical oceanic waters of French Polynesia." *Mar Ecol Prog Ser* 325, 195–203.

Lugo, A. E., C. Rogers, and S. Nixon. 2000. "Hurricanes, coral reefs and rainforests: Resistance, ruin and recovery in the Caribbean." *Ambio* 29, 106–114.

Luikart, G., P. R. England, D. Tallmon, S. Jordan, and P. Taberlet. 2003. "The power and promise of population genomics: From genotyping to genome typing." *Nat Rev Genet* 4, 981–994.

Lukoschek, V., C. Riginos, and M. J. H. van Oppen. 2016. "Congruent patterns of connectivity can inform management for broadcast spawning corals on the Great Barrier Reef." *Mol Ecol* 25, 3065–3080.

Lundgren, P. 2011. "Genetics and genetic tools in coral reef management." GBRMPA.

Luttinger, N. 1997. "Community-based coral reef conservation in the Bay Islands of Honduras." *Ocean Coast Manage* 36, 11–22.

Madin, J. S., M. O. Hoogenboom, S. R. Connolly, E. S. Darling, D. S. Falster, D. W. Huang, et al. 2016. "A trait-based approach to advance coral reef science." *Trends Ecol Evol* 31, 419–428.

Manzello, D. P. 2015. "Rapid recent warming of coral reefs in the Florida Keys." *Sci Rep-Uk* 5.

Manzello, D. P., R. Berkelmans, and J. C. Hendee. 2007. "Coral bleaching indices and thresholds for the Florida Reef Tract, Bahamas, and St. Croix, US Virgin Islands." *Mar Pollut Bull* 54, 1923–1931.

Marhaver, K., V. Chamberland, and N. Fogarty. 2017b. "Coral spawning research and larval propagation. Coral Restoration Consortium." https://crc.reefresilience.org/coral-spawning-research-larval-propagation/.

Markey, K. L., D. A. Abdo, S. N. Evans, and C. Bosserelle. 2016. "Keeping it local: Dispersal limitations of coral larvae to the high latitude coral reefs of the Houtman Abrolhos Islands." *PLoS ONE*, 11.

Marshall, T. C. and J. A. Spalton. 2000. "Simultaneous inbreeding and outbreeding depression in reintroduced *Arabian oryx*." *Anim Conserv* 3, 241–248.

Matz, M. V., E. A. Treml, G. V. Aglyamova, and L. K. Bay. 2018. "Potential and limits for rapid genetic adaptation to warming in a Great Barrier Reef coral." *PLoS Genet*, 14.

Maynard, J. A., K. R. N. Anthony, P. A. Marshall, and I. Masiri. 2008. "Major bleaching events can lead to increased thermal tolerance in corals." *Mar Biol* 155, 173–182.

McCauley, D. J., M. L. Pinsky, S. R. Palumbi, J. A. Estes, F. H. Joyce, and R. R. Warner. 2015. "Marine defaunation: Animal loss in the global ocean." *Science* 347.

McClanahan, T., N. Polunin, and T. Done. 2002. "Ecological states and the resilience of coral reefs." *Conserv Ecol* 6.

McFall-Ngai, M., M. Hadfield, T. Bosch, H. Carey, T. Domazet-Loso, A. Douglas, et al. 2013. "Animals in a bacterial world, a new imperative for the life sciences." *P Natl Acad Sci USA* 110, 3229–3236.

McIllroy, S. E. and M. A. Coffroth. 2017. "Coral ontogeny affects early symbiont acquisition in laboratory reared recruits." *Coral Reefs* 36, 927–932.

McKay, J. K., C. E. Christian, S. Harrison, and K. J. Rice. 2005. "'How local is local?'—A review of practical and conceptual issues in the genetics of restoration." *Restor Ecol* 13, 432–440.

McKay, J. K. and R. G. Latta. 2002. "Adaptive population divergence: Markers, QTL and traits." *Trends Ecol Evol* 17, 285–291.

Mcleod, E., K. R. N. Anthony, P. J. Mumby, J. Maynard, R. Beeden, N. A. J. Graham, et al. 2019. "The future of resilience-based management in coral reef ecosystems." *J Environ Manage* 233, 291–301.

Meekan, M. G., M. J. Milicich, and P. J. Doherty. 1993. "Larval production drives temporal patterns of larval supply and recruitment of a coral-reef damselfish." *Mar Ecol Prog Ser* 93, 217–225.

Melchinger, A. E., H. F. Utz, H. P. Piepho, Z. B. Zeng, and C. C. Schon. 2007. "The role of epistasis in the manifestation of heterosis: A systems-oriented approach." *Genetics* 177, 1815–1825.

Meyer, E., G. V. Aglyamova, and M. V. Matz. 2011. "Profiling gene expression responses of coral larvae (*Acropora millepora*) to elevated temperature and settlement inducers using a novel RNA-seq procedure." *Mol Ecol*, 20, 3599–3616.

Meyer, E., S. Davies, S. Wang, B. L. Willis, D. Abrego, T. E. Juenger, et al. 2009. "Genetic variation in responses to a settlement cue and elevated temperature in the reef-building coral *Acropora millepora*." *Mar Ecol Prog Ser* 392, 81–92.

Meyer, J. L., J. Castellanos-Gell, G. S. Aeby, C. C. Hase, B. Ushijima, and V. J. Paul. 2019. "Microbial community shifts associated with the ongoing stony coral tissue loss disease outbreak on the Florida Reef Tract." *Front Microbiol* 10.

Mieog, J. C., J. L. Olsen, R. Berkelmans, S. A. Bleuler-Martinez, B. L. Willis, and M. J. H. van Oppen. 2009. "The roles and interactions of symbiont, host and environment in defining coral fitness." *PLoS ONE* 4.

Miller, K. J. and C. N. Mundy. 2005. "In situ fertilisation success in the scleractinian coral *Goniastrea favulus*." *Coral Reefs* 24, 313–317.

Miller, M. W. 2001. "Corallivorous snail removal: Evaluation of impact on *Acropora palmata*." *Coral Reefs* 19, 293–295.

Miller, M. W., I. Baums, R. Pausch, A. Bright, C. Cameron, D. Williams, et al. 2018. "Clonal structure and variable fertilization success in Florida Keys broadcast-spawning corals." *Coral Reefs* 37, 239–249.

Miller, M. W., D. E. Williams, and J. Fisch. 2016. "Genet-specific spawning patterns in *Acropora palmata*." *Coral Reefs* 35, 1393–1398.

Mitchell-Olds, T., J. H. Willis, and D. B. Goldstein. 2007. "Which evolutionary processes influence natural genetic variation for phenotypic traits?" *Nat Rev Genet* 8, 845–856.

MML, Mote Marine Laboratory. 2020. https://mote.org/research/program/coral-reef-restoration.

Morvezen, R., P. Boudry, J. Laroche, and G. Charrier. 2016. "Stock enhancement or sea ranching? Insights from monitoring the genetic diversity, relatedness and effective population size in a seeded great scallop population (*Pecten maximus*)." *Heredity* 117, 142–148.

Moya, A., L. Huisman, E. E. Ball, D. C. Hayward, L. C. Grasso, C. M. Chua, et al. 2012. "Whole transcriptome analysis of the coral *Acropora millepora* reveals complex responses to CO_2-driven acidification during the initiation of calcification." *Mol Ecol* 21, 2440–2454.

Muko, S. and Y. Iwoasa. 2011. "Long-term effect of coral transplantation: Restoration goals and the choice of species." *J Theor Biol* 280, 127–138.

Muller, H. J. 1942. "Isolating mechanisms, evolution, and temperature." *Biology Symposium* 6, 71–125.

Muller, E. M., E. Bartels, and I. B. Baums. 2018. "Bleaching causes loss of disease resistance within the threatened coral species *Acropora cervicornis*." *Elife* 7.

Muller, E. M., C. Sartor, N. I. Alcaraz, and R. van Woesik. 2020. "Spatial epidemiology of the stony-coral-tissue-loss disease in Florida." *Front Mar Sci* 7.

Mumby, P. J. and R. S. Steneck. 2008. "Coral reef management and conservation in light of rapidly evolving ecological paradigms." *Trends Ecol Evol* 23, 555–563.

Munday, P. L., R. R. Warner, K. Monro, J. M. Pandolfi, and D. J. Marshall. 2013. "Predicting evolutionary responses to climate change in the sea." *Ecol Lett* 16, 1488–1500.

Muscatine, L. and J. W. Porter. 1977. "Reef Corals—Mutualistic symbioses adapted to nutrient-poor environments." *Bioscience* 27, 454–460.

Nakajima, Y., A. Nishikawa, A. Iguchi, and K. Sakai. 2010. "Gene flow and genetic diversity of a broadcast-spawning coral in northern peripheral populations." *PLoS ONE* 5.

Nakajima, Y., P. Wepfer, S. Suzuki, Y. Zayasu, C. Shinzato, N. Satoh, et al. 2017. "Microsatellite markers for multiple *Pocillopora* genetic lineages offer new insights about coral populations." *Sci Rep-Uk* 7.

NASEM, National Academies of Sciences, Engineering, Mathematics. 2018. *A Research Review of Interventions to Increase the Persistence and Resilience of Coral Reefs*. Washington, DC.

NCCOS, National Centers for Coastal Ocean Sciences. 2018. "Assessment of hurricane impacts to coral reefs in Florida and Puerto Rico." https://coastalscience.noaa.gov/project/assessment-of-hurricane-impacts-to-coral-reefs-in-florida-and-puerto-rico/.

Nei, M., T. Maruyama, and R. Chakraborty. 1975. "Bottleneck effect and genetic-variability in populations." *Evolution* 29, 1–10.

Neigel, J. and J. Avise. 1983. "Clonal diversity and population structure in a reef-building coral, *Acropora cervicornis*—self-recognition analysis and demographic interpretation." *Evolution* 37, 437–453.

Nishida, M. and J. S. Lucas. 1988. "Genetic differences between geographic populations of the crown-of-thorns starfish throughout the Pacific region." *Mar Biol* 98, 359–368.

Nitschke, M. R., S. K. Davy, and S. Ward. 2016. "Horizontal transmission of *Symbiodinium* cells between adult and juvenile corals is aided by benthic sediment." *Coral Reefs* 35, 335–344.

NMFS, National Marine Fisheries Service. 2015. "Recovery plan for elkhorn (*Acropora palmata*) and staghorn (*A. cervicornis*) corals." Silver Spring, MD, p. 167.

NOAA. 2019. "Restoring seven iconic reefs: A mission to recover the coral reefs of the Florida Keys." https://www.fisheries.noaa.gov/southeast/habitat-conservation/restoring-seven-iconic-reefs-mission-recover-coral-reefs-florida-keys.

Nozawa, Y., N. Isomura, and H. Fukami. 2015. "Influence of sperm dilution and gamete contact time on the fertilization rate of scleractinian corals." *Coral Reefs* 34, 1199–1206.

O'Donnell, D. R., A. Parigi, J. A. Fish, I. Dworkin, and A. P. Wagner. 2014. "The roles of standing genetic variation and evolutionary history in determining the evolvability of anti-predator strategies." *PLoS ONE* 9.

O'Donnell, K. E., K. E. Lohr, E. Bartels, I. B. Baums, and J. T. Patterson. 2018. "*Acropora cervicornis* genet performance and symbiont identity throughout the restoration process." *Coral Reefs* 37, 1109–1118.

Oliver, J. and R. Babcock. 1992. "Aspects of the fertilization ecology of broadcast spawning corals—Sperm dilution effects and in situ measurements of fertilization." *Biol Bull*, 183, 409–417.

O'Neil, K. 2015. "Land-based coral nurseries: A valuable tool for production and transplantation of *Acropora cervicornis*." Nova Southeastern University, NSUWorks.

Omori, M., H. Fukami, H. Kobinata, and M. Hatta. 2001. "Significant drop of fertilization of *Acropora* corals in 1999. An after-effect of heavy coral bleaching?" *Limnol Oceanogr* 46, 704–706.

Omori, M. and K. Iwao. 2016. "Methods of farming sexually propagated corals and outplanting for coral reef rehabilitation." A.M.S. Lab.

ONMS. Office of National Marine Sanctuaries. 2019. "Draft environmental impact statement for Florida Keys National Marine Sanctuary: A Restoration Blueprint." U.S. Department of Commerce, National Oceanic and Atmospheric Administration. Silver Spring, MD.

Ortiz, J. C., N. H. Wolff, K. R. N. Anthony, M. Devlin, S. Lewis, and P. J. Mumby. 2018. "Impaired recovery of the Great Barrier Reef under cumulative stress." *Sci Adv* 4.

Otto, S. P. and T. Lenormand. 2002. "Resolving the paradox of sex and recombination." *Nat Rev Genet* 3, 252–261.

Page, C. A., E. M. Muller, and D. E. Vaughan. 2018. "Microfragmenting for the successful restoration of slow growing massive corals." *Ecol Eng* 123, 86–94.

Palmer, C. V., E. S. McGinty, D. J. Cummings, S. M. Smith, E. Bartels, and L. D. Mydlarz. 2011a. "Patterns of coral ecological immunology: Variation in the responses of Caribbean corals to elevated temperature and a pathogen elicitor." *J Exp Biol* 214, 4240–4249.

Palmer, C. V., N. G. Traylor-Knowles, B. L. Willis, and J. C. Bythell. 2011b. "Corals use similar immune cells and wound-healing processes as those of higher organisms." *PLoS ONE* 6.

Palumbi, S. R. 2001. "Evolution—Humans as the world's greatest evolutionary force." *Science* 293, 1786–1790.

———. 2003. "Population genetics, demographic connectivity, and the design of marine reserves." *Ecol Appl* 13, S146–S158.

Palumbi, S. R., D. J. Barshis, N. Traylor-Knowles, and R. A. Bay. 2014. "Mechanisms of reef coral resistance to future climate change." *Science* 344, 895–898.

Pandolfi, J. M., R. H. Bradbury, E. Sala, T. P. Hughes, K. A. Bjorndal, R. G. Cooke, et al. 2003. "Global trajectories of the long-term decline of coral reef ecosystems." *Science* 301, 955–958.

Paris, C. B. and R. K. Cowen. 2004. "Direct evidence of a biophysical retention mechanism for coral reef fish larvae." *Limnol Oceanogr* 49, 1964–1979.

Parkinson, J. E., A. C. Baker, I. B. Baums, S. W. Davies, A. G. Grottoli, S. A. Kitchen, et al. 2020. "Molecular tools for coral reef restoration: Beyond biomarker discovery." *Conserv Lett* 13.

Parkinson, J. E., E. Bartels, M. K. Devlin-Durante, C. Lustic, K. Nedimyer, S. Schopmeyer, et al. 2018. "Extensive transcriptional variation poses a challenge to thermal stress biomarker development for endangered corals." *Mol Ecol* 27, 1103–1119.

Parkinson, J. E. and I. B. Baums. 2014. "The extended phenotypes of marine symbioses: Ecological and evolutionary consequences of intraspecific genetic diversity in coral-algal associations." *Front Microbiol* 5.

Peixoto, R. S., P. M. Rosado, D. C. D. Leite, A. S. Rosado, and D. G. Bourne. 2017. "Beneficial microorganisms for corals (BMC): Proposed mechanisms for coral health and resilience." *Front Microbiol* 8.

Penin, L., F. Michonneau, A. Carroll, and M. Adjeroud. 2011. "Effects of predators and grazers exclusion on early post-settlement coral mortality." *Hydrobiologia* 663, 259–264.

Petit, R. J., A. El Mousadik, and O. Pons. 1998. "Identifying populations for conservation on the basis of genetic markers." *Conserv Biol* 12, 844–855.

Poland, D. M. and M. A. Coffroth. 2017. "Trans-generational specificity within a cnidarian-algal symbiosis." *Coral Reefs* 36, 119–129.

Polato, N. R., N. S. Altman, and I. B. Baums. 2013. "Variation in the transcriptional response of threatened coral larvae to elevated temperatures." *Mol Ecol* 22, 1366–1382.

Polato, N. R., C. R. Voolstra, J. Schnetzer, M. K. DeSalvo, C. J. Randall, A. M. Szmant, et al. 2010. "Location-specific responses to thermal stress in larvae of the reef-building coral *Montastraea faveolata*." *PLoS ONE* 5.

Pollock, F. J., S. M. Katz, J. A. J. M. van de Water, S. W. Davies, M. Hein, G. Torda, et al. 2017. "Coral larvae for restoration and research: A large-scale method for rearing *Acropora millepora* larvae, inducing settlement, and establishing symbiosis." *Peerj* 5.

Possingham, H. P., M. Bode, and C. J. Klein. 2015. "Optimal conservation outcomes require both restoration and protection." *PLoS Biol* 13.

Prada, C. and M. E. Hellberg. 2013. "Long prereproductive selection and divergence by depth in a Caribbean candelabrum coral." *P Natl Acad Sci USA* 110, 3961–3966.

Prasetia, R., F. Sinniger, K. Hashizume, and S. Harii. 2017. "Reproductive biology of the deep brooding coral *Seriatopora hystrix*: Implications for shallow reef recovery." *PLoS ONE* 12.

Pratlong, M., A. Haguenauer, O. Chabrol, C. Klopp, P. Pontarotti, and D. Aurelle. 2015. "The red coral (*Corallium rubrum*) transcriptome: A new resource for population genetics and local adaptation studies." *Mol Ecol Resour* 15, 1205–1215.

Precht, W. F., B. E. Gintert, M. L. Robbart, R. Fura, and R. van Woesik. 2016. "Unprecedented disease-related coral mortality in southeastern Florida." *Sci Rep-Uk* 6.

Prober, S. M., K. R. Thiele, I. D. Lunt, and T. B. Koen. 2005. "Restoring ecological function in temperate grassy woodlands: Manipulating soil nutrients, exotic annuals and native perennial grasses through carbon supplements and spring burns." *J Appl Ecol* 42, 1073–1085.

Puckett, E. 2017. "Variability in total project and per sample genotyping costs under varying study designs including with microsatellites or SNPs to answer conservation genetic questions." *Conserv Genet Res* 9, 289–304.

Puebla, O., E. Bermingham, and W. O. McMillan. 2014. "Genomic atolls of differentiation in coral reef fishes (*Hypoplectrus* spp., Serranidae)." *Mol Ecol* 23, 5291–5303.

Pujolar, J. M., G. E. Maes, C. Vancoillie, and F. A. M. Volckaert. 2005. "Growth rate correlates to individual heterozygosity in the european eel, *Anguilla anguilla*." *Evolution* 59, 189–199.

Quigley, K. M., L. K. Bay, and M. J. H. van Oppen. 2019. "The active spread of adaptive variation for reef resilience." *Ecol Evol* 9, 11122–11135.

Quigley, K. M., L. K. Bay, and B. L. Willis. 2018. "Leveraging new knowledge of *Symbiodinium* community regulation in corals for conservation and reef restoration." *Mar Ecol Prog Ser* 600, 245–253.

Quigley, K. M., C. J. Randall, M. J. H. van Oppen, and L. K. Bay. 2020. "Assessing the role of historical temperature regime and algal symbionts on the heat tolerance of coral juveniles." *Biology Open* 9.

Ralls, K. and J. Ballou. 1986. "Captive breeding programs for populations with a small number of founders." *Trends Ecol Evol* 1, 19–22.

Ralls, K., J. Ballou, M. R. Dudash, M. D. E. Eldridge, C. B. Fenster, R. C. Lacy, et al. 2018. "Call for a paradigm shift in the genetic management of fragmented populations." *Conserv Lett* 11.

Randall, C. J., A. P. Negri, K. M. Quigley, T. Foster, G. F. Ricardo, N. S. Webster, et al. 2020. "Sexual production of corals for reef restoration in the Anthropocene." *Mar Ecol Prog Ser* 635, 203–232.

Raymundo, L. J. and A. P. Maypa. 2004. "Getting bigger faster: Mediation of size-specific mortality via fusion in juvenile coral transplants." *Ecol Appl* 14, 281–295.

Reeb, C. A. and J. C. Avise. 1990. "A genetic discontinuity in a continuously distributed species—Mitochondrial-DNA in the American oyster, *Crassostrea virginica*." *Genetics* 124, 397–406.

Reed, D. H. and R. Frankham. 2001. "How closely correlated are molecular and quantitative measures of genetic variation? A meta-analysis." *Evolution* 55, 1095–1103.

———. 2003. "Correlation between fitness and genetic diversity." *Conserv Biol* 17, 230–237.

Reshef, L., O. Koren, Y. Loya, I. Zilber-Rosenberg, and E. Rosenberg. 2006. "The coral probiotic hypothesis." *Environ Microbiol* 8, 2068–2073.

Reznick, D. and C. Ghalambor. 2001. "The population ecology of contemporary adaptations: What empirical studies reveal about the conditions that promote adaptive evolution." *Genetica* 112, 183–198.

Rhymer, J. and D. Simberloff. 1996. "Extinction by hybridization and introgression." *Annu Rev Ecol Syst* 27, 83–109.

Rice, K. J. and N. C. Emery. 2003. "Managing microevolution: Restoration in the face of global change." *Front Ecol Environ* 1, 469–478.

Richmond, R. H. 1997. "Reproduction and recruitment in corals: Critical links in the persistence of reefs. In: *Life and Death of Coral Reefs*." C. Birkeland (ed). Chapmand and Hall, New York, NY, pp. 175–197.

Richmond, R. H. and C. L. Hunter. 1990. "Reproduction and recruitment of corals—Comparisons among the Caribbean, the tropical Pacific, and the Red Sea." *Mar Ecol Prog Ser* 60, 185–203.

Ridgway, T. 2005. "Allozyme electrophoresis still represents a powerful technique in the management of coral reefs." *Biodivers Conserv* 14, 135–149.

Rieseberg, L., O. Raymond, D. Rosenthal, Z. Lai, K. Livingstone, T. Nakazato, et al. 2003. "Major ecological transitions in wild sunflowers facilitated by hybridization." *Science* 301, 1211–1216.

Rinkevich, B. 1995. "Restoration strategies for coral reefs damaged by recreational activities: The use of sexual and asexual recruits." *Restor Ecol* 3, 241–251.

———. 2000. "Steps towards the evaluation of coral reef restoration by using small branch fragments." *Mar Biol* 136, 807–812.

———. 2005. "Conservation of coral reefs through active restoration measures: Recent approaches and last decade progress." *Environ Sci Technol* 39, 4333–4342.

———. 2014. "Rebuilding coral reefs: Does active reef restoration lead to sustainable reefs?" *Curr Opin Env Sust* 7, 28–36.

Rippe, J. P., M. V. Matz, E. A. Green, M. Medina, N. Z. Khawaja, T. Pongwarin, et al. 2017. "Population structure and connectivity of the mountainous star coral, *Orbicella faveolata*, throughout the wider Caribbean region." *Ecol Evol* 7, 9234–9246.

Ripple, W. J., J. A. Estes, R. L. Beschta, C. C. Wilmers, E. G. Ritchie, M. Hebblewhite, et al. 2014. "Status and ecological effects of the world's largest carnivores." *Science* 343, 151–159.

Ritson-Williams, R., S. N. Arnold, and V. J. Paul. 2016. "Patterns of larval settlement preferences and post-settlement survival for seven Caribbean corals." *Mar Ecol Prog Ser* 548, 127–138.

Ritson-Williams, R., V. Paul, S. Arnold, and R. Steneck. 2010. "Larval settlement preferences and post-settlement survival of the threatened Caribbean corals *Acropora palmata* and *A. cervicornis*." *Coral Reefs* 29, 71–81.

Roberts, C. M. 1997. "Connectivity and management of Caribbean coral reefs." *Science* 278, 1454–1457.

Rodgers, K. S., K. Lorance, A. R. Dona, Y. Stender, C. Lager, and P. L. Jokiel. 2017. "Effectiveness of coral relocation as a mitigation strategy in Kane'ohe Bay, Hawai'i." *Peerj* 5.

Rogers, C. S., H. C. Fitz, M. Gilnack, J. Beets, and J. Hardin. 1984. "Scleractinian coral recruitment patterns at Salt River submarine canyon, St. Croix, US Virgin Islands." *Coral Reefs* 3, 69–76.

Rohwer, F., V. Seguritan, F. Azam, and N. Knowlton. 2002. "Diversity and distribution of coral-associated bacteria." *Mar Ecol Prog Ser* 243, 1–10.

Romero-Torres, M., E. A. Treml, A. Acosta, and D. A. Paz-Garcia. 2018. "The Eastern Tropical Pacific coral population connectivity and the role of the Eastern Pacific Barrier." *Sci Rep-Uk* 8.

Rosen, B. R. 1988. "Progress, problems and patterns in the biogeography of reef corals and other tropical marine organisms." *Helgolander Meeresun* 42, 269–301.

Rosenberg, E., O. Koren, L. Reshef, R. Efrony, and I. Zilber-Rosenberg. 2007. "The role of microorganisms in coral health, disease and evolution." *Nat Rev Microbiol* 5, 355–362.

Rosenblatt, R. H. and R. S. Waples. 1986. "A genetic comparison of allopatric populations of shore fish species from the eastern and central Pacific Ocean—Dispersal or Vicariance." *Copeia* 275–284.

Roughgarden, J., Y. Iwasa, and C. Baxter. 1985. "Demographic theory for an open marine population with space-limited recruitment." *Ecology* 66, 54–67.

Rowan, R., N. Knowlton, A. Baker, and J. Jara. 1997. "Landscape ecology of algal symbionts creates variation in episodes of coral bleaching." *Nature* 388, 265–269.

Roze, D. 2012. "Disentangling the benefits of sex." *PLoS Biol* 10.

RRN. Reef Resilience Network. 2020. https://reefresilience.org/restoration/coral-populations/coral-gardening/genetic-considerations/.

Ryman, N. and L. Laikre. 1991. "Effects of supportive breeding on the genetically effective population-size." *Conserv Biol* 5, 325–329.

Saccheri, I. J., H. D. Lloyd, S. J. Helyar, and P. M. Brakefield. 2005. "Inbreeding uncovers fundamental differences in the genetic load affecting male and female fertility in a butterfly." *P Roy Soc B-Biol Sci* 272, 39–46.

Sale, P. F. 1991. "Reef fish communities: Open nonequilibrial systems." In: *The Ecology of Fishes on Coral Reefs*. P. F. Sale (ed). Academic Press, New York, NY, pp. 564–598.

Sammarco, P. W. 1982. "Polyp bail-out—An escape response to environmental stress and a new means of reproduction in corals." *Mar Ecol Prog Ser* 10, 57–65.

Sanford, E. and M. W. Kelly. 2011. "Local adaptation in marine invertebrates." *Ann Rev Mar Gen* 3, 509–535.

Santure, A. W. and D. Garant. 2018. "Wild GWAS-association mapping in natural populations." *Mol Ecol Resour* 18, 729–738.

Scheltema, R. S. 1986. "On dispersal and planktonic larvae of benthic invertebrates—An eclectic overview and summary of problems." *B Mar Sci* 39, 290–322.

Schemske, D. W. and R. Lande. 1985. "The evolution of self-fertilization and inbreeding depression in plants. 2. Empirical observations." *Evolution* 39, 41–52.

Schill, S., G. Raber, J. Roberts, E. Treml, J. Brenner, and P. Halpin. 2015. "No reef is an island: Integrating coral reef connectivity data into the design of regional-scale marine protected area networks." *PLoS ONE* 10.

Schlotterer, C., R. Kofler, E. Versace, R. Tobler, and S. U. Franssen. 2016. "Combining experimental evolution with next-generation sequencing: A powerful tool to study adaptation from standing genetic variation." *Heredity* 116, 248–248.

Schnell, F. and Cockerham, C. 1992. "Multiplicative vs. arbitrary gene-action in heterosis." *Genetics*, 131, 461–469.

Schoener, T. W. 2011. "The newest synthesis: Understanding the interplay of evolutionary and ecological dynamics." *Science* 331, 426–429.

Schoepf, V., C. P. Jury, R. J. Toonen, and M. T. McCulloch. 2017. "Coral calcification mechanisms facilitate adaptive responses to ocean acidification." *P Roy Soc B-Biol Sci* 284.

Schopmeyer, S. A., D. Lirman, E. Bartels, D. S. Gilliam, E. A. Goergen, S. P. Griffin, et al. 2017. "Regional restoration benchmarks for *Acropora cervicornis*." *Coral Reefs* 36, 1047–1057.

Schultz, E. T. and R. K. Cowen. 1994. "Recruitment of coral reef fishes to Bermuda—Local retention or long-distance transport." *Mar Ecol Prog Ser* 109, 15–28.

Selmoni, O., E. Rochat, G. Lecellier, V. Berteaux-Lecellier, and S. Joost. 2020. "Seascape genomics as a new tool to empower coral reef conservation strategies: An example on north-western Pacific *Acropora digitifera*." *Evol Appl*.

Serrano, E., R. Coma, K. Inostroza, and O. Serrano. 2018. "Polyp bail-out by the coral *Astroides calycularis* (Scleractinia, Dendrophylliidae)." *Mar Biodivers* 48, 1661–1665.

Serrano, X. M., I. B. Baums, T. B. Smith, R. J. Jones, T. L. Shearer, and A. C. Baker. 2016. "Long distance dispersal and vertical gene flow in the Caribbean brooding coral *Porites astreoides*." *Sci Rep-Uk* 6.

Sgro, C. M., A. J. Lowe, and A. A. Hoffmann. 2011. "Building evolutionary resilience for conserving biodiversity under climate change." *Evol Appl* 4, 326–337.

Shanks, A. L. 2009. "Pelagic larval duration and dispersal distance revisited." *Biol Bull* 216, 373–385.

Shearer, T. L., I. Porto, and A. L. Zubillaga. 2009. "Restoration of coral populations in light of genetic diversity estimates." *Coral Reefs* 28, 727–733.

Shearer, T. L., M. J. H. van Oppen, S. L. Romano, and G. Worheide. 2002. "Slow mitochondrial DNA sequence evolution in the Anthozoa (Cnidaria)." *Mol Ecol* 11, 2475–2487.

Sheridan, A. K. 1986. "Selection for heterosis from crossbred populations—Estimation of the F1 heterosis and its mode of inheritance." *Brit Poultry Sci* 27, 541–550.

Sherman, C. D. H. 2008. "Mating system variation in the hermaphroditic brooding coral, *Seriatopora hystrix*." *Heredity* 100, 296–303.

Shinzato, C., E. Shoguchi, T. Kawashima, M. Hamada, K. Hisata, M. Tanaka, et al. 2011. "Using the *Acropora digitifera* genome to understand coral responses to environmental change." *Nature* 476, 320–U382.

Shlesinger, T. and Y. Loya. 2019. "Breakdown in spawning synchrony: A silent threat to coral persistence." *Science* 365, 1002–1009.

Shull, G. H. 1948. "What is heterosis." *Genetics* 33, 439–446.

Shumaker, A., H. M. Putnam, H. Qiu, D. C. Price, E. Zelzion, A. Harel, et al. 2019. "Genome analysis of the rice coral *Montipora capitata*." *Sci Rep-Uk* 9.

Siebeck, U. E., N. J. Marshall, A. Kluter, and O. Hoegh-Guldberg. 2006. "Monitoring coral bleaching using a colour reference card." *Coral Reefs* 25, 453–460.

Skelly, D. K., L. N. Joseph, H. P. Possingham, L. K. Freidenburg, T. J. Farrugia, M. T. Kinnison, et al. 2007. "Evolutionary responses to climate change." *Conserv Biol* 21, 1353–1355.

Slatkin, M. 1987. "Gene flow and the geographic structure of natural populations." *Science* 236, 787–792.

Slattery, M., H. N. Kamel, S. Ankisetty, D. J. Gochfeld, C. A. Hoover, and R. W. Thacker. 2008. "Hybrid vigor in a tropical Pacific soft-coral community." *Ecol Monogr* 78, 423–443.

Smith, T. B., M. E. Brandt, J. M. Calnan, R. S. Nemeth, J. Blondeau, E. Kadison, et al. 2013. "Convergent mortality responses of Caribbean coral species to seawater warming." *Ecosphere* 4.

Solecava, A. M. and J. P. Thorpe. 1991. "High levels of genetic variation in natural populations of marine lower invertebrates." *Biol J Linn Soc* 44, 65–80.

Soong, K. 1993. "Colony size as a species character in massive reef corals." *Coral Reefs* 12, 77–83.

Soong, K. and J. C. Lang. 1992. "Reproductive integration in reef corals." *Biol Bull* 183, 418–431.

Soule, M. E. 1985. "What is conservation biology." *Bioscience* 35, 727–734.

St. Gelais, A., A. Chaves-Fonnegra, A. Brownlee, V. Kosmynin, A. Moulding, and D. Gilliam. 2016. "Fecundity and sexual maturity of the coral *Siderastrea siderea* at high latitude along the FRT, USA." *Invertebr Biol* 135, 46–57.

Stockwell, C. A., A. P. Hendry, and M. T. Kinnison. 2003. "Contemporary evolution meets conservation biology." *Trends Ecol Evol* 18, 94–101.

Stoddart, J. 1983. "Asexual production of planulae in the coral *Pocillopora damicornis*." *Mar Biol* 76, 279–284.

Stoddart, J., R. C. Babcock, and A. J. Heyward. 1988. "Self-fertilization and maternal enzymes in the planulae of the coral *Goniastrea favulus*." *Mar Biol* 99, 489–494.

Strader, M. E., S. W. Davies, and M. V. Matz. 2015. "Differential responses of coral larvae to the colour of ambient light guide them to suitable settlement microhabitat." *Roy Soc Open Sci* 2.

Studivan, M. S. and J. D. Voss. 2018. "Population connectivity among shallow and mesophotic *Montastraea cavernosa* corals in the Gulf of Mexico identifies potential for refugia." *Coral Reefs* 37, 1183–1196.

Suding, K. N. 2011. "Toward an era of restoration in ecology: Successes, failures, and opportunities ahead." *Ann Rev Eco Evol Syst* 42, 465–487.

Swearer, S. E., J. E. Caselle, D. W. Lea, and R. R. Warner. 1999. "Larval retention and recruitment in an island population of a coral-reef fish." *Nature* 402, 799–802.

Sweet, M. and J. Bythell. 2017. "The role of viruses in coral health and disease." *J Invertebr Pathol* 147, 136–144.

Swindell, W. R. and J. L. Bouzat. 2006. "Ancestral inbreeding reduces the magnitude of inbreeding depression in *Drosophila melanogaster*." *Evolution* 60, 762–767.

Szmant, A. M. 1986. "Reproductive ecology of caribbean reef corals." *Coral Reefs* 5, 43–53.

Szmant, A. M., E. Weil, M. W. Miller, and D. E. Colon. 1997. "Hybridization within the species complex of the scleractinan coral *Montastraea annularis*." *Mar Biol* 129, 561–572.

Taninaka, H., L. P. C. Bernardo, Y. Saito, S. Nagai, M. Ueno, Y. F. Kitano, et al. 2019. "Limited fine-scale larval dispersal of the threatened brooding corals *Heliopora* spp. as evidenced by population genetics and numerical simulation." *Conserv Genet* 20, 1449–1463.

Taylor, M. S. and M. E. Hellberg. 2003. "Genetic evidence for local retention of pelagic larvae in a Caribbean reef fish." *Science* 299, 107–109.

Teo, A. and P. A. Todd. 2018. "Simulating the effects of colony density and intercolonial distance on fertilisation success in broadcast spawning scleractinian corals." *Coral Reefs* 37, 891–900.

Thomas, C., J. Lambrechts, E. Wolanski, V. Traag, V. Blondel, E. Deleersnijder, et al. 2014. "Numerical modelling and graph theory tools to study ecological connectivity in the Great Barrier Reef." *Ecol Model* 272, 160–174.

Thomas, L., W. J. Kennington, R. D. Evans, G. A. Kendrick, and M. Stat. 2017. "Restricted gene flow and local adaptation highlight the vulnerability of high-latitude reefs to rapid environmental change." *Global Change Biol* 23, 2197–2205.

Thompson, J. N. 1998. "Rapid evolution as an ecological process." *Trends Ecol Evol* 13, 329–332.

Thompson, J. R., H. E. Rivera, C. J. Closek, and M. Medina. 2015. "Microbes in the coral holobiont: Partners through evolution, development, and ecological interactions." *Front Cell Infect Mi* 4.

Thorrold, S. R., C. Latkoczy, P. K. Swart, and C. M. Jones. 2001. "Natal homing in a marine fish metapopulation." *Science* 291, 297–299.

Thorson, G. 1950. "Reproductive and larval ecology of marine bottom invertebrates." *Biol Rev* 25, 1–45.

Thurber, R. V., J. P. Payet, A. R. Thurber, and A. M. S. Correa. 2017. "Virus-host interactions and their roles in coral reef health and disease." *Nat Rev Microbiol* 15.

Torda, G., J. M. Donelson, M. Aranda, D. J. Barshis, L. Bay, M. L. Berumen, et al. 2017. "Rapid adaptive responses to climate change in corals." *Nat Clim Change* 7, 627–636.

Toth, L. T., I. B. Kuffner, A. Stathakopoulos, and E. A. Shinn. 2018. "A 3,000-year lag between the geological and ecological shutdown of Florida's coral reefs." *Global Change Biol* 24, 5471–5483.

Toonen, R. J., J. B. Puritz, Z. H. Forsman, J. L. Whitney, I. Fernandez-Silva, K. R. Andrews, et al. 2013. "ezRAD: a simplified method for genomic genotyping in non-model organisms." *Peerj* 1.

Traylor-Knowles, N. and S. R. Palumbi. 2014. "Translational environmental biology: Cell biology informing conservation." *Trends Cell Biol* 24, 265–267.

Tunnicliffe, V. 1981. "Breakage and propagation of the stony coral *Acropora cervicornis*." *P Natl Acad Sci-Biol* 78, 2427–2431.

Valdivia, A., C. Cox, and J. Bruno. 2017. "Predatory fish depletion and recovery potential on Caribbean reefs." *Sci Adv* 3.
van Hooidonk, R., J. Maynard, J. Tamelander, J. Gove, G. Ahmadia, L. Raymundo, et al. 2016. "Local-scale projections of coral reef futures and implications of the Paris Agreement." *Sci Rep-Uk* 6.
van Oppen, M. J. H. and L. L. Blackall. 2019. "Coral microbiome dynamics, functions and design in a changing world." *Nat Rev Microbiol* 17, 557–567.
van Oppen, M. J. H. and R. D. Gates. 2006. "Conservation genetics and the resilience of reef-building corals." *Mol Ecol* 15, 3863–3883.
van Oppen, M. J. H., R. D. Gates, L. L. Blackall, N. Cantin, L. J. Chakravarti, W. Y. Chan, et al. 2017. "Shifting paradigms in restoration of the world's coral reefs." *Global Change Biol* 23, 3437–3448.
van Oppen, M. J. H., J. A. Leong, and R. D. Gates. 2009. "Coral-virus interactions: A double-edged sword?" *Symbiosis* 47, 1–8.
van Oppen, M. J. H., J. K. Oliver, H. M. Putnam, and R. D. Gates. 2015. "Building coral reef resilience through assisted evolution." *P Natl Acad Sci USA* 112, 2307–2313.
van Oppen, M. J. H., E. Puill-Stephan, P. Lundgren, G. De'ath, and L. K. Bay. 2014. "First-generation fitness consequences of interpopulational hybridisation in a Great Barrier Reef coral and its implications for assisted migration management." *Coral Reefs* 33, 607–611.
van Oppen, M. J. H., P. Souter, E. J. Howells, A. Heyward, and R. Berkelmans. 2011. "Novel genetic diversity through somatic mutations: Fuel for adaptation of reef corals?" *Diversity* 3, 405–423.
van Woesik, R., W. Scott IV, and R. Aronson. 2014. "Lost opportunities: Coral recruitment does not translate to reef recovery in the Florida Keys." *Mar Pollut Bull* 88, 110–117.
Veron, J. E. N. 1995. *Corals in Space and Time: The Biogeography and Evolution of the Scleractinia*. UNSW Press, Sydney NSW, Australia.
Vollmer, S. V. and S. R. Palumbi. 2002. "Hybridization and the evolution of reef coral diversity." *Science* 296, 2023–2025.
———. 2007. "Restricted gene flow in the Caribbean staghorn coral *Acropora cervicornis*: Implications for the recovery of endangered reefs." *J Hered* 98, 40–50.
Voolstra, C. R., Y. Li, Y. J. Liew, S. Baumgarten, D. Zoccola, J. F. Flot, et al. 2017. "Comparative analysis of the genomes of *Stylophora pistillata* and *Acropora digitifera* provides evidence for extensive differences between species of corals." *Sci Rep-Uk* 7.
Wallace, C. C. and B. L. Willis. 1994. "Systematics of the coral genus *Acropora*—Implications of new biological findings for species concepts." *Annu Rev Ecol Syst* 25, 237–262.
Walton, C. J., N. K. Hayes, and D. S. Gilliam. 2018. "Impacts of a regional, multi-year, multi-species coral disease outbreak in southeast Florida." *Front Mar Sci* 5.
Wang, J., W. G. Hill, D. Charlesworth, and B. Charlesworth. 1999. "Dynamics of inbreeding depression due to deleterious mutations in small populations: Mutation parameters and inbreeding rate." *Gen Res* 74, 165–178.
Wang, J., Y. Wang, S. Keshavmurthy, P. Meng, and C. Chen. 2019. "The coral *Platygyra verweyi* exhibits local adaptation to long-term thermal stress through host-specific physiological and enzymatic response." *Sci Rep-Uk* 9.
Waples, R. S. and O. Gaggiotti. 2006. "What is a population? An empirical evaluation of some genetic methods for identifying the number of gene pools and their degree of connectivity." *Mol Ecol* 15, 1419–1439.
Warner, M. E., T. C. LaJeunesse, J. D. Robison, and R. M. Thur. 2006. "The ecological distribution and comparative photobiology of symbiotic dinoflagellates from reef corals in Belize: Potential implications for coral bleaching." *Limnol Oceanogr* 51, 1887–1897.
Warner, M. E., M. P. Lesser, and P. J. Ralph. 2010. "Chlorophyll fluorescence in reef building corals." *Devel Appl Phycol* 4, 209–222.
Warner, P. A., B. L. Willis, and M. J. H. van Oppen. 2016. "Sperm dispersal distances estimated by parentage analysis in a brooding scleractinian coral." *Mol Ecol* 25, 1398–1415.
Warner, R. R. 1997. "Evolutionary ecology: How to reconcile pelagic dispersal with local adaptation." *Coral Reefs* 16, S115–S120.
Whalan, S., M. A. Abdul Wahab, S. Sprungala, A. J. Poole, and R. de Nys. 2015. "Larval Settlement: The role of surface topography for sessile coral reef invertebrates." *PLoS ONE* 10.

Whiteley, A. R., S. W. Fitzpatrick, W. C. Funk, and D. A. Tallmon. 2015. "Genetic rescue to the rescue." *Trends Ecol Evol* 30, 42–49.

Williams, A. V., P. G. Nevill, and S. L. Krauss. 2014a. "Next generation restoration genetics: Applications and opportunities." *Trends Plant Sci* 19, 529–537.

Williams, D. E., M. W. Miller, A. J. Bright, and C. M. Cameron. 2014b. "Removal of corallivorous snails as a proactive tool for the conservation of acroporid corals." *Peerj* 2.

Williams, D. E., M. W. Miller, and I. B. Baums. 2014c. "Cryptic changes in the genetic structure of a highly clonal coral population and the relationship with ecological performance." *Coral Reefs* 33, 595–606.

Williams, D. E., M. W. Miller, and K. L. Kramer. 2008. "Recruitment failure in Florida Keys *Acropora palmata*, a threatened Caribbean coral." *Coral Reefs* 27, 697–705.

Williams, D. E., K. Nedimyer, and M. W. Miller. 2020. "Genotypic inventory of *Acropora palmata* (elkhorn coral) populations in south Florida." In: *NOAA/SEFSC/PRBD-2020-01*. U.S. Department of Commerce.

Williams, S. L. 2001. "Reduced genetic diversity in eelgrass transplantations affects both population growth and individual fitness." *Ecol Appl* 11, 1472–1488.

Willis, B. L., R. C. Babcock, P. L. Harrison, and C. C. Wallace. 1997. "Experimental hybridization and breeding incompatibilities within the mating systems of mass spawning reef corals." *Coral Reefs* 16, S53–S65.

Willis, B. L., M. J. H. van Oppen, D. J. Miller, S. V. Vollmer, and D. J. Ayre. 2006. "The role of hybridization in the evolution of reef corals." *Annu Rev Ecol Evol Syst* 37, 489–517.

Willis, B. L., C. C. Wallace, and D. J. Ayre. 1995. "Natural hybridization within the coral genus *Acropora*?" *J Cell Biochem Suppl* 19B.

Wood, S., I. B. Baums, C. B. Paris, A. Ridgwell, W. S. Kessler, and E. J. Hendy. 2016. "El Nino and coral larval dispersal across the eastern Pacific marine barrier." *Nat Commun* 7.

Worheide, G. 2006. "Low variation in partial cytochrome oxidase subunit I (COI) mitochondrial sequences in the coralline demosponge *Astrosclera willeyana* across the Indo-Pacific." *Mar Biol* 148, 907–912.

Wright, S. 1921. "Systems of mating. II. The effects of inbreeding on the genetic composition of a population." *Genetics* 6, 124–143.

Wu, C. I. and C. T. Ting. 2004. "Genes and speciation." *Nat Rev Genet* 5, 114–122.

Yates, K. K., D. G. Zawada, N. A. Smiley, and G. Tiling-Range. 2017. "Divergence of seafloor elevation and sea level rise in coral reef ecosystems." *Biogeosciences* 14, 1739–1772.

Ying, H., I. Cooke, S. Sprungala, W. W. Wang, D. C. Hayward, Y. R. Tang, et al. 2018. "Comparative genomics reveals the distinct evolutionary trajectories of the robust and complex coral lineages." *Genome Biol* 19.

Ying, H., D. C. Hayward, I. Cooke, W. Wang, A. Moya, K. R. Siemering, et al. 2019. "The whole-genome sequence of the coral *Acropora millepora*." *Genome Biol Evol* 11, 1374–1379.

Young, C. N., S. A. Schopmeyer, and D. Lirman. 2012. "A review of reef restoration and coral propagation using the threatened genus *Acropora* in the Caribbean and western Atlantic." *B Mar Sci* 88, 1075–1098.

Yund, P. O. 2000. "How severe is sperm limitation in natural populations of marine free-spawners?" *Trends Ecol Evol* 15, 10–13.

SECTION III

Case Studies from Around the World

11

BELIZE: FRAGMENTS OF HOPE

Lisa Carne and Maya A. Trotz

ABSTRACT

Fragments of Hope (FoH) is a nonprofit, community-based organization in Placencia, Belize, that focuses on the challenge of coral reef restoration. Their work started in 2006 in Laughing Bird Caye National Park (LBCNP), a United Nations World Heritage Site that was directly hit by Category 4 Hurricane Iris in 2001. Most of the shallow reefs there were degraded to 6% or less live coral cover. Their strategy includes mapping extant acroporids during the hottest time of the year, restoring shallow sites, identifying host and symbiont genetics, outplanting multiple genets in close proximity to each other, and documenting spawning, along with long-term monitoring of growth, survival, thermal tolerance, and disease resistance. FoH began mass outplanting of nursery-grown acroporid corals (*A. palmanta*, *A. cervicornis*, and *A. prolifera*) in 2010 and since March 2017 has used *micro-fragmentation* to outplant directly to the reefs. The original coral transplants have 14 years of survivorship, and sexual reproduction has been documented in nursery-grown outplanted corals spawning in consecutive years including 2014–2017.[1] As of now, there has been a 35% increase in live coral at LBCNP in recent years. To date, over a hectare of shallow reef has been replenished at LBCNP with more than 82K corals outplanted. Using Geographic Information System (GIS) calculations from a drone ortho-mosaic project that was conducted in July 2019, this translates to 21% live, solid acroporid cover of ~1 hectare available substrate in the shallow (1–3 m) fringing reef. FoH has also expanded in Belize to more than 10 sites in and near four marine protected areas (MPAs) with 23 nursery sites, including *Dendrogyra cylindrus*, *Montastrea cavernosa*, *Orbicella annularis*, *O. favelota*, *Pseudodiploria strigosa*, and *Diploria clivosa*. In situ temperature data, diver-based photomosaics, fish and benthic surveys, bleaching surveys, coral growth, and other observations are routinely collected for analysis of restoration efforts. A training program that was vetted and endorsed by the Belize Fisheries Department—complete with a manual that is available for download from the website www.fragmentsofhope.org, including a four-day, hands-on curricula targeting Belizean coastal community members like fishers, tour guides, and non-governmental organizations and government staff—transfers the knowledge regarding the methods to rapidly grow the Caribbean acroporid corals and place them on shallow degraded reefs in MPAs. To date, FoH has trained more than 70 Belizeans, and it is the involvement of the local community, ownership of the restoration work, and the inclusion of youth and women in education and training programs that ensures long-term appreciation of the importance of healthy coral reef ecosystems for shoreline protection, nursery habitat, food security, and tourism value. Collaboration with researchers from around the world, expansion of the training program to regional partners, and hands-on exchange programs are building a strong network to contribute to the coral restoration community of practice.

---

[1] The only years that spawning monitoring occurred.

INTRODUCTION

Once a fishing village, Placencia is now a rapidly developing tourism destination where more than one in four residents rely on marine tourism or fishing (pre-COVID-19). It is one of two villages on the Placencia Peninsula in Southern Belize. The FoH organization that is located there focuses on restoration of coral reefs and advocacy for the sustainable management of associated habitats. Registered in 2013, FoH trains fishers and tour guides for coral restoration and has, to date, certified 70 Belizeans in coral reef replenishment through its program that has been approved by the Belize Fisheries Department. Their work really began in 2006 at LBCNP and is considered today as one of the best examples of coral restoration success in the world. Over the years, FoH has expanded coral restoration work in Belize to 13 different cayes (Figure 11.1), using one or more of three different methods (cementing, planting ropes onto substrate, and micro-fragmenting) and a combination of seven different coral species (*Acropora palmata*, *Dendrogyra cylindrus*, *Acropora cerviconis*, *Montastraea cavernosa*, *Acropora prolifera*, *Orbicellus annularis* and *O. favelotata*). The Belizean government protected the parrotfish, the surgeon fishes, and the grazers in 2009, and MPAs include no-take zones for any marine species. FoH works in cayes within and outside of MPAs or national parks. The non-protected cayes in Figure 11.1 are False Caye, French Louie Caye, Moho Caye, and Whipray Caye.

This chapter tells the history of FoH's work, first showing results from coral restoration work at LBCNP between 2006 and 2018, and then describes current activities, methodologies, and lessons learned over the years.

LAUGHING BIRD CAYE NATIONAL PARK EXPERIENCE

Laughing Bird Caye, a unique faro atoll formation in the Caribbean, was declared a National Park in 1994. It is one of seven MPAs making up the Belize Barrier Reef World Heritage Site. LBCNP provides significant social and economic benefits to the local society. It is an important tourism resource with up to 10,000 visitors per year due to its proximity to Placencia Village since it provides sheltered snorkeling sites. It is co-managed by the Southern Environmental Association (SEA) and the Belize Forestry Department with a ranger station, and tourists are charged $10 USD for entry. With no fishing allowed, the site harbors good populations of conch, lobster, and finfish, which then spill into local fishing areas. Category 4 Hurricane Iris hit Belize in 2001, degrading most of the shallow reefs around LBCNP to 6% or less live coral cover. While large, live strands of *A. palmata* corals were still inside the Gladden Spit and the Silk Cayes Marine Reserve (GSSCMR), it was observations of live, broken *A. palmata* corals near San Pedro, another Belizean caye, that inspired Lisa Carne, FoH's founder, to think of *replanting*. In 2006 the Caribbean acroporids were listed by the United States as an endangered species (they made the International Union for Conservation of Nature Red List in 2008), and it was then that Belize's Protected Area Conservation Trust (PACT) funded the first restoration work in Belize—19 *A. palmata* fragments of opportunity were transferred from GSSCMR to shallow reef sites at LBCNP.

Figure 11.2 shows the survivorship of those initial *A. palmata*. In 10 years the number of discrete corals increased from 17 to 48, two of the original transplants died in 2007, and one died in 2019. This translates to 82% survival for 13 years, but does not account for increased coverage from natural asexual/reproduction/fragmentation.

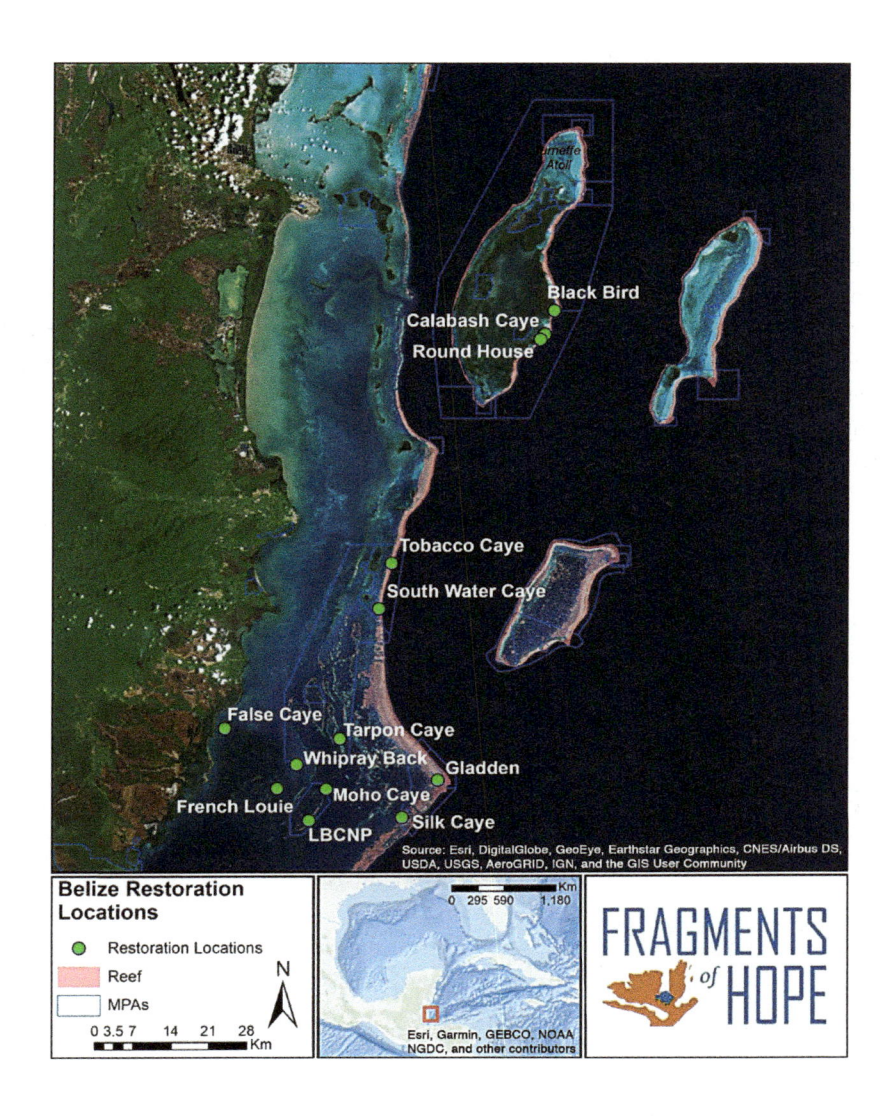

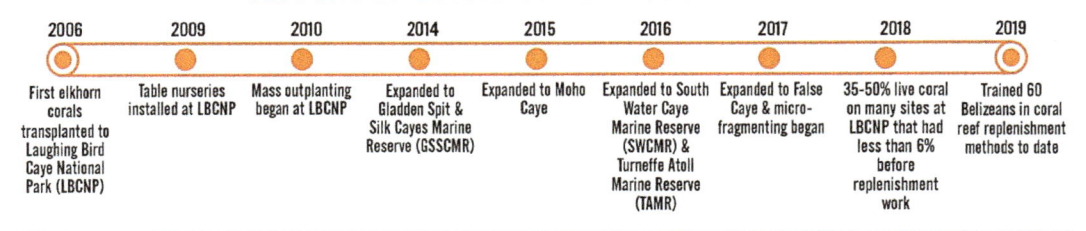

Figure 11.1 Timeline of FoH work in Belize between 2006 and 2019 with map of coral restoration sites.

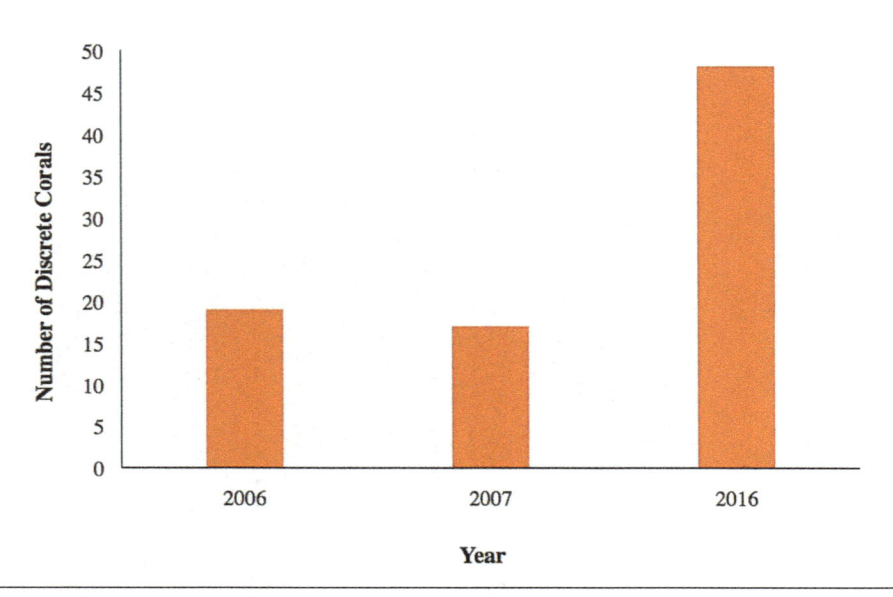

Figure 11.2 Survivorship of 19 *A. palmata* corals transplanted from GSSCMR to LBCNP in 2006.

In 2009 one in situ nursery table and one A-frame were established at LBCNP using culture methods from Dr. Austin Bowden-Kerby. Another table and five additional A-frames were established in four nearby cayes with the same corals/replicates. Corals that were harvested from shallow sites in neighboring cayes were either grown on ropes (*A. cervicornis* and *A. prolifera*) or attached to cement cookies (*A. palmata* and eight other species), as shown in Figure 11.3. After 11–18 months in the nursery, the corals were outplanted to various sites around LBCNP, as shown in Figure 11.4. Between 2010 and 2016, 187 *A. palmata* coral were outplanted at 16 sub-sites around LBCNP, with the number of discrete corals increasing to 234 over the six years. Figures 11.5 and 11.6 show the growth of outplanted *A. palmata* and *A. cervicornis* coral from the same sites over six and 10 years respectively.

Annual photomosaics of six reciprocal sub-sites at LBCNP, three on the leeward (9, 21, 24) and three on the windward (13, 20, 23) side (see Figure 11.4) have been used to quantify coral cover since 2014. Table 11.1 summarizes these sites in terms of size of sub-site, date of outplant, and combination of acroporid corals (*A. cervicornis*, *A. palmata*, and *A. prolifera*) outplanted. Once outplanted, no additional corals are added, so any increases in coral cover are due to natural sexual spreading and growth of these corals.

All of the completed LBCNP mosaics are processed by Dr. Arthur Gleason at the University of Miami and can be viewed online at:

http://web2.physics.miami.edu/~agleason/mosaic_results/belize_acropora/.

Figure 11.3 A coral nursery table at Whipray Caye shown at Day 0 (March 2009, top left), six months (August 2009, top right) and 11 months (March 2010, bottom). Tables are at 2–5 m depth, and measure 10 ft by 10 ft.

Figure 11.4 Map of FoH outplanting sub-sites at LBCNP, Belize, from 2010–2018. Sites 23 and 24 were unplanted (UP) in 2014 when photomosaics were first done.

Figure 11.5 Time series of nursery grown *A. palmata* coral outplanted in 2014–2020, at sub-site 22 at LBCNP.

Figure 11.6 Time series photographs of nursery-grown *A. cervicornis* coral outplanted in 2010 as two harvested ropes with 36 *A. cervicornis* and four *A. prolifera* fragments that were nailed to a degraded reef.

Table 11.1 Six sites were monitored for coral cover using photomosaics. All sites had zero acroporids at the start of outplanting, and sites were outplanted with a combination of *A. cervicornis* (ACER), *A. palmata* (APAL), and *A. prolifera* (APRO)

Site/Plot Name	Area (m²)	Outplant Date (status)	Species	% Coverage: Acroporid of Total Coral (year of assessment)
13	182	12/10	633 ACER, 3 APAL, 100 APRO	34% of 41% (2016)
9	110	4/10	209 ACER	36% of 39% (2018)
20	144	2/14	885 ACER, 19 APAL	28% of 32% (2018)
21	109	2/14	906 ACER, 11 APAL, 21 APRO	32% of 34% (2018)
23	112	11/14	461 ACER, 7 APAL	NA
24	40	11/14	1138 ACER, 12 APAL	25% of 29% (2018)

Figure 11.7 captures the results of coral restoration efforts at sub-site 9 at LBCNP over a four-year time period with live coral cover increasing by ~10% based on results from photomosaics, rebounding naturally (no new corals added) after Category 1 Hurricane Earl in 2016 (see Figure 11.8(a), yellow bars). LBCNP now has 33 sub-sites with over 80,000 coral outplants, counted as they are placed on the reef.

Figure 11.8(a) shows the results of LBCNP mosaics analyzed to date (2014–2018) reflecting 27 of the 30 total LBCNP mosaics. Processing of the remaining two plots remain present challenges because of their shallow depth, the time of day (glare) when media was collected, and ironically, the high coral cover that makes it difficult to match/distinguish from each other during the processing.

Figure 11.7 Photomosaics of sub-site 9 at LBCNP from 2014 (left) and 2018 (right). These were produced by Dr. Arthur Gleason, University of Miami.

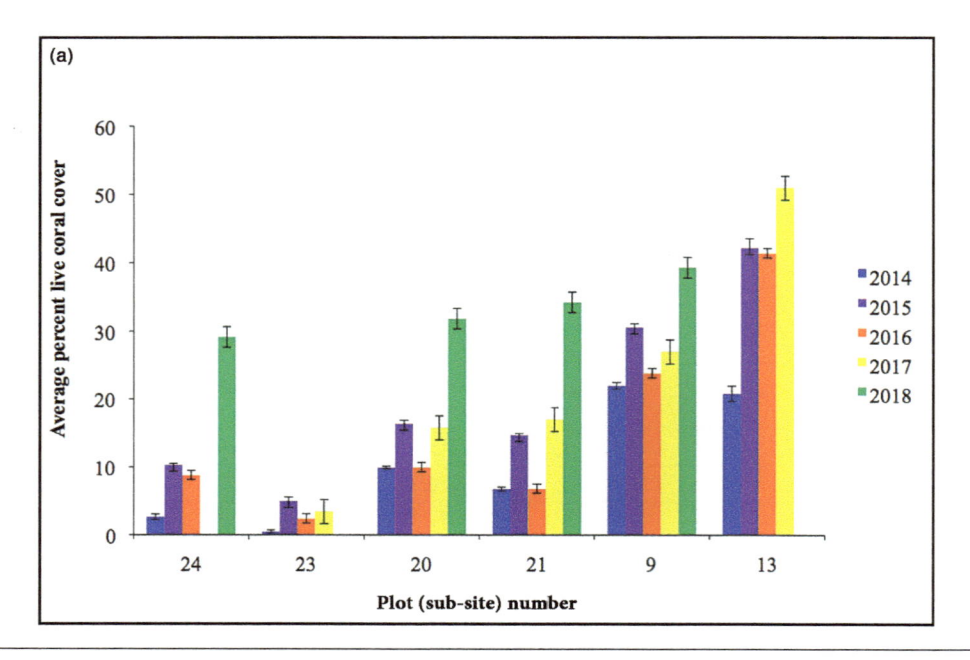

Figure 11.8(a) Comparison of live coral cover at six sub-sites at LBCNP, three on the leeward (9, 21, 24) and three on the windward (13, 20, 23) side, between 2014 and 2018. Sites 9 and 13 were outplanted in 2010, sites 20 and 21 were outplanted in February 2014, and sites 23 and 24 were outplanted in November 2014. Only sub-sites 23 and 24 were unplanted when mosaicked in 2014. Error bars are standard deviations of four × 100 random points on the photomosaic processed using CPCe.

Because of the challenges described previously and the limitations described in Figure 11.2 regarding survivorship and natural spreading coral coverage from asexual reproduction, and because diver-based mosaics are only small (1–200 m² each) snapshots of the total coral coverage at LBCNP, FoH began exploring the use of drone orthomosaics to map shallow corals to the species level. In their first draft product with Dr. Steve Schill, Lead Scientist at the Nature Conservancy, Caribbean Division (Figure 11.8(b)), imagery was acquired on July 31, 2019, using a Phantom 4 Pro flying at 300 ft AGL. The photos were captured in the early morning (7 a.m.–9 a.m. local time) to avoid sun glint. The 467 photos were processed into an orthophoto mosaic (2 cm RGB) using Pix4D 4.5.2 and segmented using eCognition 9.5. Segments were then manually classified using image interpretation techniques. For simplicity, all three acroporids are highlighted in orange on the map and taxa coverage was calculated as follows based on the July 31, 2019 flight (m²): *A. cervicornis* (1,938), *A. palmata* (250), *A. prolifera* (53). The red color represents a combination of live star corals (*Siderastrea siderea, Orbicella annualris, O. faveolata*) and dead coral including dead coral with encrusting sponge (*Cliona caribbaea*) or zooanthids (*Palythoa caribaeorum*). These other areas of live and dead coral (not including rubble) were estimated to cover just over one hectare. These results allow FoH to finally quantify their work at LBCNP and demonstrate that 21% of a hectare of the existing shallow fringing reef has been replenished with live acroporids. FoH will continue to work with Dr. Schill and others to refine this process and repeat the flights at all their sites on an annual basis.

The photomosaic data is a useful tool for quantifying the impact of the restoration efforts and serves as a permanent record over time that others can access; however, time series

Figure 11.8(b) Object-based classification of coral features at LBCNP based on an orthophoto mosaic (2 cm RGB) acquired with a DJI Phantom 4 Pro flying at 300 ft on July 31, 2019. The orange class represents all three replenished acroporid taxa (combined 2,190 m^2) and the red class represents star corals and dead coral structure, but not rubble (10,273 m^2).

photographs like those shown in Figure 11.9 are often more impactful for driving home the significance of FoH's work at LBCNP.

Using the photomosaic data, the changes in benthic community over time were averaged and compared across sites that were already outplanted in 2014 at LBCNP (Figure 11.10). As expected, with time there is less dead coral, sand, pavement, and rubble. A less obvious trend is the increase in crustose coralline algae (CCA) over time, as coral cover increases. While CCA is

Figure 11.9 Time series photographs showing coral cover increased from under 6% (day of outplanting in December 2010) to more than 50% (taken in October 2017) in less than seven years, with nursery-grown, outplanted corals at LBCNP, sub-site 13.

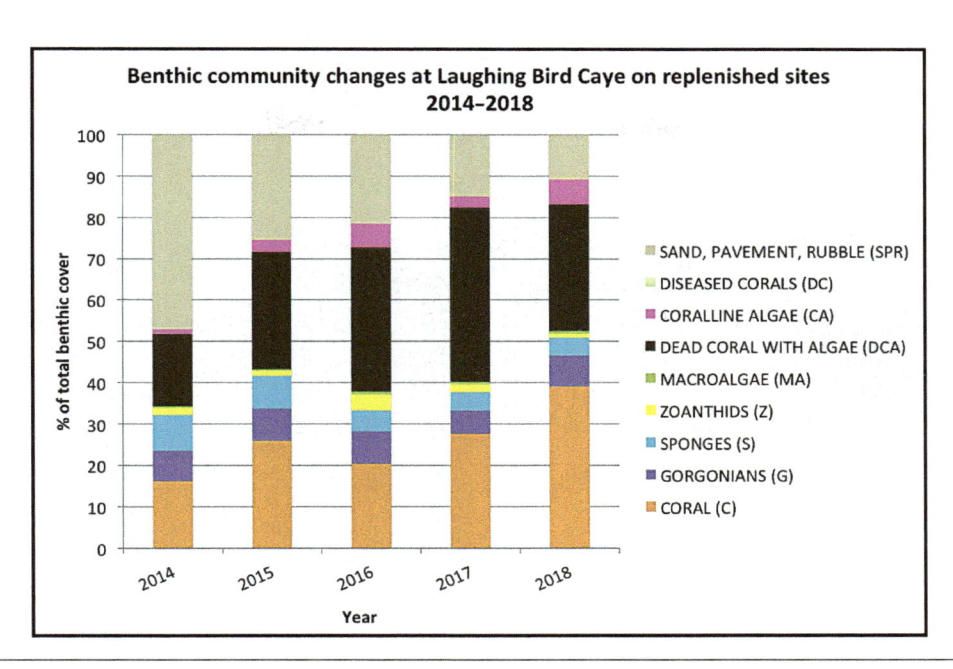

Figure 11.10 Benthic community changes at LBCNP on sites that were already outplanted in 2014 (but no additional corals were added).

part of FoH's site selection criteria because it is known to facilitate more natural (sexual) coral recruits, it is unclear yet what is driving the increase; although considered a positive change, further research is needed on these results.

Dr. Janie Wulff from Florida State University has conducted sponge surveys around LBCNP and, more recently, worked with FoH to transplant several different sponge species including *Aplysina fulva* and *Verongula rigida* to coral outplants that show the presence of reef eroding *Cliona caribbaea* (Figure 11.11).

Fish assemblages are assessed every 12 months by visual census using two methods: (1) a 30 m linear belt transect crossing a study plot at about the midpoint of the plot and (2) a count of fishes in the study plot (developed by Dr. Les Kaufman, Boston University in 2014). Figure 11.12 presents belt survey results of total fish biomass averaged over the plot area from 2015–2018 for six plots in LBCNP, three plots at Moho Caye where restoration began five years after LBCNP, and three plots at control sites (Lazy, Saddle Caye, and Dale's Reef) that all have natural *A. cervicornis* coral stands. While LBCNP is a reasonably well-enforced, protected National Park, Moho Caye and the control plots are unprotected from fishing pressure. The original data were taken as numbers of individuals of each fish species observed within 5 cm size class increments; length-weight coefficients of Klomp et al. (2003) were used to convert to biomass.

The fish biomass values that were observed at LBCNP and on naturally regenerated reef patches (>100 g/m^2) were higher than the 62 g/m^2 average for the *southern barrier complex* observed by the 2018 Healthy Reefs Initiative (Healthy Reefs Initiative, 2018) report card. LBCNP and the control sites are most similar in average fish biomass, which is likely because they have the higher/denser acroporid coverage than Moho Caye. With the exception of Moho Caye, there is an overall decrease in fish biomass in 2018, which may be real or may be a function of different data collectors.

Figure 11.11 "Good" sponge species (*Aplysina fulva* on the left, *Verongula rigida* on the right) transplanted with Dr. Janie Wulff at LBCNP in hopes of inhibiting the "bad" encrusting sponge, *Cliona caribbaea,* at LBCNP. Transplants were made April 29, 2019; photos from July 11, 2019.

Total fish biomass from the plot surveys decreased from 2015 to 2018. Changes in fish data collectors and the fact that the plots are surveyed at the same time the photo mosaics are being collected could reduce the number of fish on the small plots (50–200 m^2) due to human activity.

Figure 11.13 compares the proportion of fish biomass accounted for by various fish functional groups across LBCNP. Six functional groups are indicated, including herbivores (parrotfishes, surgeonfishes, and chubs), migratory invertebrate feeders (grunts and drums), resident invertebrate feeders (most wrasses), micro-omnivores (butterflyfishes, angelfishes, most damselfishes, and blennies), piscivores (groupers and snappers), and zooplanktivores (sergeant major and damselfishes, creole and social wrasses, tomtate grunt, and striped grunt).

The acroporids are foundation and keystone species that, like trees in a forest, attract other marine life such as lobster and crab back to the reef (Figure 11.14). Whenever the corals are moved from the nurseries, the small crabs are also moved. These are really important when it comes to the management of macro algae (Spadaro 2019).

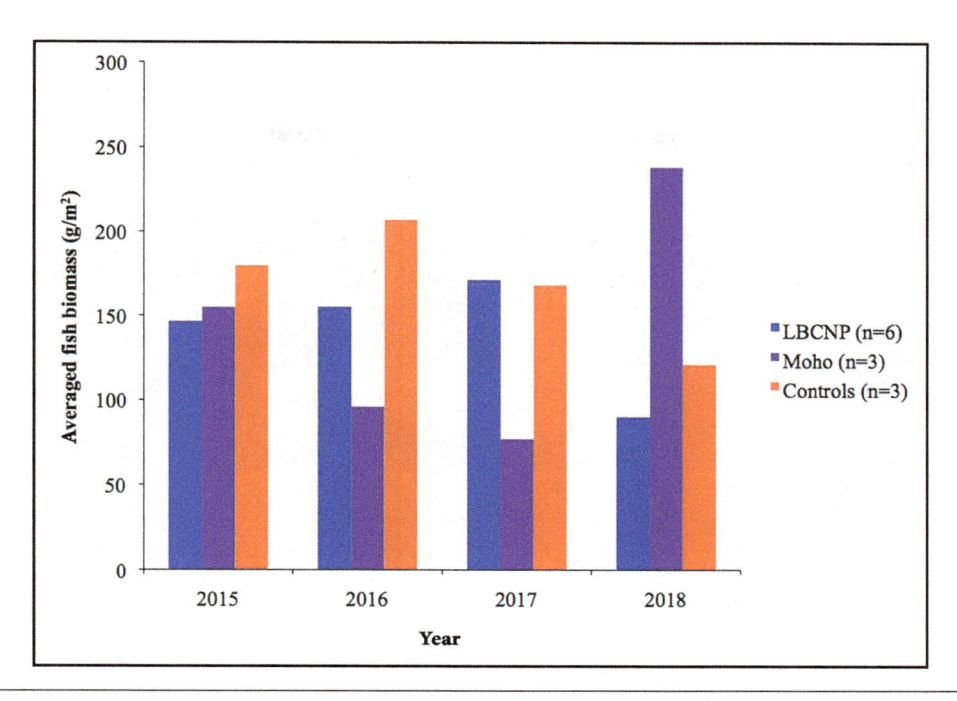

Figure 11.12 Average fish biomass (g/m²) calculated from belt transects only: LBCNP (a no-take zone), Moho Caye (unprotected), and control sites (unprotected) 2015–2018. These are averages of six plots at LBCNP and three plots at Moho Caye and one plot at each of the three control reefs.

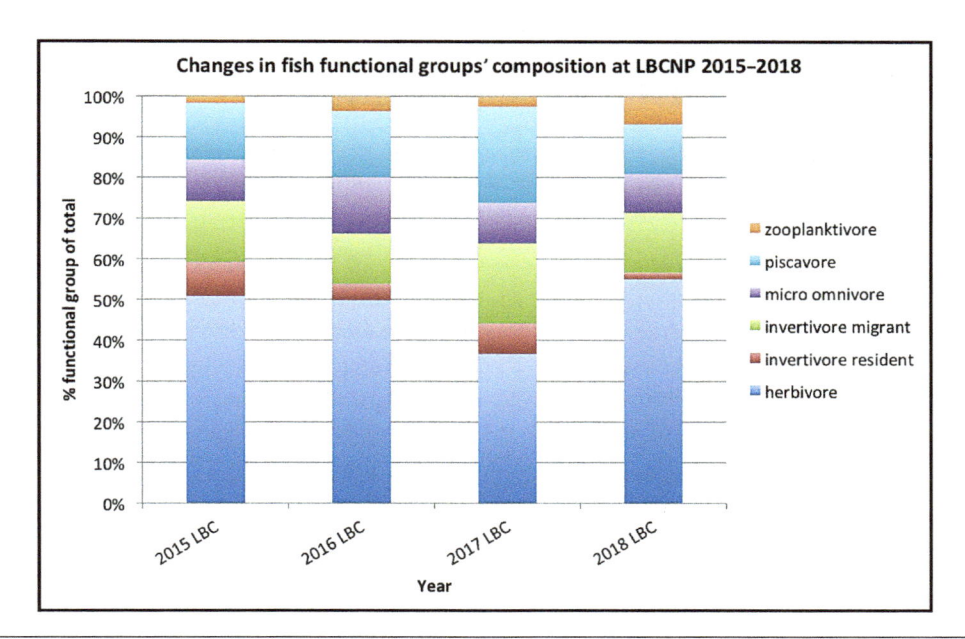

Figure 11.13 Comparing changes in fish functional groups at the six sites (averaged) at LBCNP, fully protected (with some verified and suspected poaching) across years, 2015–2018.

Figure 11.14 Acroporid-loving invertebrates, (a) the spotted lobster (*Panulirus guttatus*) and (b) the channel clinging crab (*Maguimithrax spinosissimus*), under *A. palmata* outplanted at LBCNP.

Chaetomorpha linum, a green algae species indicative of high nutrients, has been observed at LBCNP. In 2015 it was observed closer to sites 10 and the washroom facilities. Through partnership with the SEA and Ecofriendly Solutions Ltd., the facility was moved to the most southern part of the caye in 2017. Its capacity and treatment capability was also enhanced; however, the algae returned in 2019 (Figure 11.15). This ongoing challenge has opened opportunities for research with environmental engineers at the University of South Florida, and highlights FoH's approach to foster interdisciplinary collaborations that are needed to solve problems that impact the reefs.

Coral spawning observations were conducted around LBCNP in 2014–2017 and all three acropora taxa spawned. Dr. Nicole Fogerty's research group at Nova Southeastern University[2] confirmed that the gametes were viable. More recently, Dr. Claire Paris at the University of Miami has taken the coral mapping and spawning data from LBCNP and elsewhere and completed computer simulations of larval spawn (Figure 11.16). The generated larval dispersal

---

[2] Dr. Nicole Fogerty is now at the University of North Carolina.

Belize: Fragments of Hope

Figure 11.15 *Chaetomorpha linum*, a green algae species indicative of high nutrients, at LBCNP, photo from July 11, 2019.

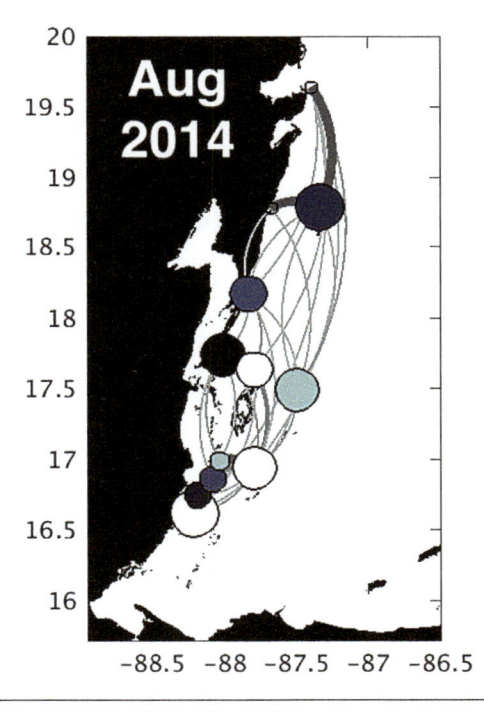

Figure 11.16 An example of connectivity of coral larvae spawn simulation models, specific for August 2014. The horizontal (Y-axis) and vertical (X-axis) are latitude and longitude, respectively, and the size and darkness of color in the circles represent higher connectivity importance. This work was done by Dr. Claire Paris.

maps will help to guide future site selection to ensure restoration occurs in areas that support natural reef regeneration.

CURRENT TECHNIQUES AND METHODS

The work presented on LBCNP captures the main methods for coral restoration and monitoring done by FoH. Lessons learned from that site, as well as other sites not discussed here, have helped to develop a coral restoration training manual for Belize. This information is summarized next to provide the latest approaches that FoH uses for coral restoration. A general rule of thumb is to only outplant during the period of December through May, which is outside of the hurricane season and in the cooler months.

First of all, especially during the hottest months, FoH maps corals in Belize to identify the stronger genets or genotypes in terms of those not impacted by bleaching and/or disease. These are ideal for coral restoration efforts, and putting multiple genets in close proximity to each other increases the chances of cross fertilization when they spawn. Genetics on both the host and the symbionts are being done, and then coupled with their temporal incidence of bleaching and disease as well.

Second, FoH uses a set of selection criteria for nursery sites. These include accessibility given the cost of fuel to get to sites, depth, water quality and flow, presence of healthy coral, protection from high surge, nonliving coral substrate and low seagrass density, permanent residents nearby, MPA status, permission from relevant authorities, stakeholder support, and *proximity to outplant sites, which should be identified before the nursery sites*. Coral nursery tables are built from steel (rebar) materials easily sourced in Placencia that can be readily constructed by two persons (Figure 11.3). It should be noted that FoH has seven dome structures at two sites with limited hard coral substrate (rubble).

Third, for outplanting site selection, similar parameters are considered in terms of permits, accessibility, and stakeholder proximity. Additional criteria include evidence of acroporids, low macro-algae cover, crustose coralline cover, presence of diadema and parrotfish/surgeon fish, solid/fixed substrate, and the potential for natural reef regeneration based on larvae dispersal maps. Table 11.2 summarizes the selection criteria for coral nurseries and outplanting sites.

FoH primarily works with *Acropora palmata, Acropora cervicornis, Acropora prolifera, Dendrogyra cylindrus, Montastraea cavernosa, Orbicella annularis* and *O. faveolata* (Figure 11.17). The three main outplanting techniques to degraded reefs include: cementing of coral fragments, nailing of ropes of coral, and micro-fragmenting corals in 5 cm or greater lengths and cementing (Figure 11.18).

Table 11.2 FoH coral nursery and outplant site selection criteria

Nursery Site Selection Criteria	Outplant Site Selection Criteria
• Accessibility (fuel considerations) • Optimal depth 2–5 m • Clear, good water quality and flow (presence of healthy corals) • Protection from high surge (leeward side of cayes, nestled among large coral heads) • Sand and/or rubble substrate or sparse seagrass and sand (test with probe and mallet) • Permanent residents on caye or nearby • MPA status/protection • Permission/endorsement from managers/co-managers if in an MPA • Stakeholder support • Proximity to outplant site and cross reference with outplant site selection criteria	• Accessibility (logistics for long-term monitoring) • Evidence of acroporids (dead and alive) • Clear, good water quality and flow (presence of healthy corals) • Low macro-algae cover • Crustose coralline cover • Presence of diadema • Presence of parrotfish/surgeon fish • Solid/fixed substrate (for rubble, domes can be used to plant coral) • No-take (replenishment) zone status • Site is strategically located to promote natural reef regeneration based on larvae dispersal maps • Stakeholder support

FoH continuously adapts and changes methods, depending on mother nature and with the intention of reducing steps and materials. While outplanting is usually done by cementing on old dead coral, a 2009 earthquake resulted in underwater cliffs/landslides where reefs were—exposing dead *A. cervicornis* rubble. So, domes were placed on the remaining seascape with single genets of each species, again in close proximity. Since 2017, FoH has worked with Dr. David Vaughan of Plant a Million Corals, adapting his micro-fragmentation methodology to use in both in situ versus land-based nurseries and also to directly outplant to degraded reefs (Figure 11.19), therefore, bypassing any nursery time.

Monitoring methods have already been discussed for LBCNP, and Table 11.3 summarizes those with more details on material needs.

Elkhorn Coral
Acropora palmata

Pillar Coral
Dendrogyra cylindrus

Staghorn Coral
Acropora cervicornis

Great Star Coral
Montastraea cavernosa

Fused Staghorn Coral
Acropora prolifera

Lobed Star Coral
Orbicella annularis

Figure 11.17 Types of corals outplanted by FoH in Belize since 2010 (not shown is *O. faveolata*).

Belize: Fragments of Hope

Figure 11.18 Main outplanting methods used by FoH today: (a) cementing: a *porcupine* or *rosette* method putting many fragments in a cement mound, (b) planting ropes onto substrate: ropes can be placed directly on dead reef with cement nails, (c) micro-fragmenting: corals are cut to ~5 cm with a diamond edge saw and cemented onto degraded reef.

Figure 11.19 *A. palmata* micro-fragments directly outplanted at south Silk Caye (a) at time of outplant in March 2019 and (b) 13 months later in April 2020.

Table 11.3 Summary of main monitoring activities performed by FoH and general considerations needed for implementation

Monitoring for:	Considerations:
Survivorship: number of corals outplanted and survival over time by species, genet, site, age, outplant method, etc.	*Frequency:* Ideally, monthly, (combined with nursery monitoring)—at least for the first six months. Special attention to spawning (if funded) and bleaching months (mandatory). *Materials:* Camera (software, laptop, and, especially, an external hard drive). Slates, pencils, and extra cable ties. *Photomosaics:* Track percentage of coral cover. The cameras are expensive, the protocol is time-consuming, and the analyses performed by the University of Miami (who developed it) come with a large service fee. Separate funding would need to be sourced to implement this method at new sites.
Growth: Once an acroporid is >6 months, it is very difficult to measure growth. If there were baseline Point Intercept Transects used in AGRRA and MBRS surveys data on your site, that may be useful but not completely accurate for growth. The easiest would be to select representative individual corals for long-term growth rate measurements.	
Bleaching/Disease: We want to know which genets perform better over time (are more resilient or resistant to bleaching and/or disease events). You must keep track of which genets are outplanted and where to collect these crucial data.	
Predation: Removal of coral eating snails, fire worms, and other coral predators, provided it is permitted.	
Biodiversity: Baseline fish surveys on unrestored sites can be compared to restored sites.	
Spawning: During variable small windows around the full moons of July–September. This monitoring requires extra funds because of the complicated logistics.	

COMMUNITY INVOLVEMENT

Based on stakeholder consultations with community members on the Placencia Peninsula and other places in Belize, FoH's approach to restoration includes (1) the development of a training and certification program for Belizeans, (2) the employment of only Belizeans, often certified tour guides and fishers in restoration activities, (3) the design of restoration as an additional income, especially during periods of slow tourism and outside of main fishing seasons, (4) the hosting of other restoration practitioners and researchers to exchange knowledge and co-create solutions for quantifying improved reef functions, and (5) education and outreach through local and international channels to build capacity on reef restoration.

The certification course, vetted by the Belize Fisheries Department, is held annually and targets Belizeans. Since 2016, 71 persons have been certified (Figure 11.20). Once certified in coral restoration, FoH provides a stipend equivalent to a dive master's pay that is seen as a supplemental alternative livelihood income. Training is offered in the evenings as much as possible to better accommodate tour guides and working women. Recognizing that overnight stays are sometimes required for sites further away or for coral spawning observations will

Figure 11.20 (a) Group picture after completion of FoH coral restoration workshop in January 2019. This workshop introduced micro-fragmentaion and certificates were signed by Ms. Beverly Wade (BFD Administrator), Dr. David Vaughan (Plant a Million Corals), and Lisa Carne (FoH). (b) Group picture after first vetted FoH training course in January 2016. Participants included tour guides, fishers, the Belize Fisheries Department, and University of Belize staff.

influence who does restoration work from a gender standpoint; FoH focuses the majority of its work closer to home. So far, 19 women have been certified by FoH, and some were supported to complete dive master training, thereby allowing higher paying jobs. At the 23rd Conference of Parties, the UN Secretariat for Climate Change awarded FoH a Momentum for Change, Lighthouse award under the Women for Results category. In 2018 FoH Founder and Executive Director Lisa Carne was given a *Women as Agents of Change* award from the Global Environmental Facility (GEF) Small Grants Programme in recognition of her outstanding work empowering women in the marine environment.

FoH's youth camps in the three Placencia Peninsula primary schools integrated Sandwatch, a United Nation's Educational, Scientific, and Cultural Organization program to engage youth on coastal challenges and climate change (Cambers and Diamond 2010), with tours of the mangroves in the Placencia Lagoon and replenished coral reefs at LBCNP. In addition to over 300 student participants between 2015 and 2019 in those camps, FoH created and distributed ~2,500 coloring books, highlighting the critically endangered acroporid corals as seen at FoH sites. For these coloring books, also available on the FoH website for free download, they worked with a local artist and various scientists and educators to inspire the next generation of marine conservationists. In 2018 the Placencia Village Council awarded FoH honors for "exemplifying Placencia da fu wi, now and forever in the field of the environment."

NEXT STEPS

With coral restoration efforts at 13 different cayes in Belize (23 nurseries), FoH will continue to analyze the coral genetic data collected with bleaching, disease, growth, survivorship, and temperature. FoH has collaborated with community members, government officials, the private sector, practitioners, scientists, and engineers from around Belize and the world, many times using LBCNP as a space for convergence and as a motivating factor for further research and financing for coral restoration. Through these partnerships, FoH hopes to quantify the value that increased coral cover brings to tourism, fisheries, shoreline protection, and local livelihoods.

FoH has initiated collaborations with Dr. Steve Schill from The Nature Conservancy, using drone orthomosaics to map shallow corals at the species level.

The diversity of coral restoration sites provides more opportunities to explore the influence of various parameters—like nutrient concentrations, sponges, and macroalgae—on coral restoration. Integration of value-added ecosystem services and products to support livelihoods, while improving reef health, are of great interest to FoH. An example of this is combining crab (*Maguimithrax spinosissimus*) stock enhancement with coral restoration for added benefits of the crabs controlling algae growth, while increasing a commercial species population for local fishermen.

FoH envisions teams of trained coastal community members to assist with its nurseries. In addition to completing FoH's coral restoration certification program, community members will gain experience and knowledge by working with FoH. The vision is that they monitor nurseries and outplants with minimal supervision and eventually take over ownership and responsibility for nurseries in their home/work areas. FoH is also interested in continued partnership with the local educational institutions—like the University of Belize and junior colleges—to train the next generation of Belizeans.

The Meso American Reef Restoration Network, comprised of representatives from Belize, Guatemala, Mexico, and Honduras, has been reinvigorated. In addition to knowledge sharing and co-creation, FoH is particularly interested in reef rescue initiatives with this network. For example, if a hurricane impacts Belize, neighboring groups can quickly come to assist if they know where sites are, and vice versa. In many instances, disturbed corals need to be turned upright and/or stabilized to increase survivorship. COVID-19 has added another dimension to existential threats that impact the work. Coral restoration is considered an essential service in Belize and FoH has continued to work with permission through *State of Emergency* orders. With the tourism industry being crippled by COVID-19, more opportunities to employ already trained community members on coral restoration are needed. FoH hopes to explore sustainable financing mechanisms that would ensure that those who are certified in coral restoration (by default this means registered Belizean tour guides, fishers, and divers) do not have to abandon this field.

CONCLUSION

The information shared in this chapter summarizes results from many trials and errors over ~10 years of work in the field. Some factors that have contributed to FoH's success include Belize's low population density, protection of grazers, and enforcement of no-take zones. Also, FoH's site selection criteria, *mother* coral selection criteria, outplanting outside of hurricane season, use of the same practitioners, and the fostering of community participation contribute to their success. Most important, it is patience and local support that guide the work. While local threats from dredging, pollution, and anchor damage are real, the environmentally conscious community in Belize continues to grow, as do mechanisms to address these issues—giving some hope that such threats will be reduced significantly in the future.

Figure 11.21 shows photographs of a reef near LBCNP in 2010, a reef site that was reduced to 6% coral cover after Hurricane Earl at LBCNP, and of that restored reef site 10 years later. How does one know when one's restoration work is done? How does one quantify this restoration, and share with stakeholders and colleagues? While data and photographs like that shared in this chapter are helpful, nothing compares to first-hand observations, and FoH will continue

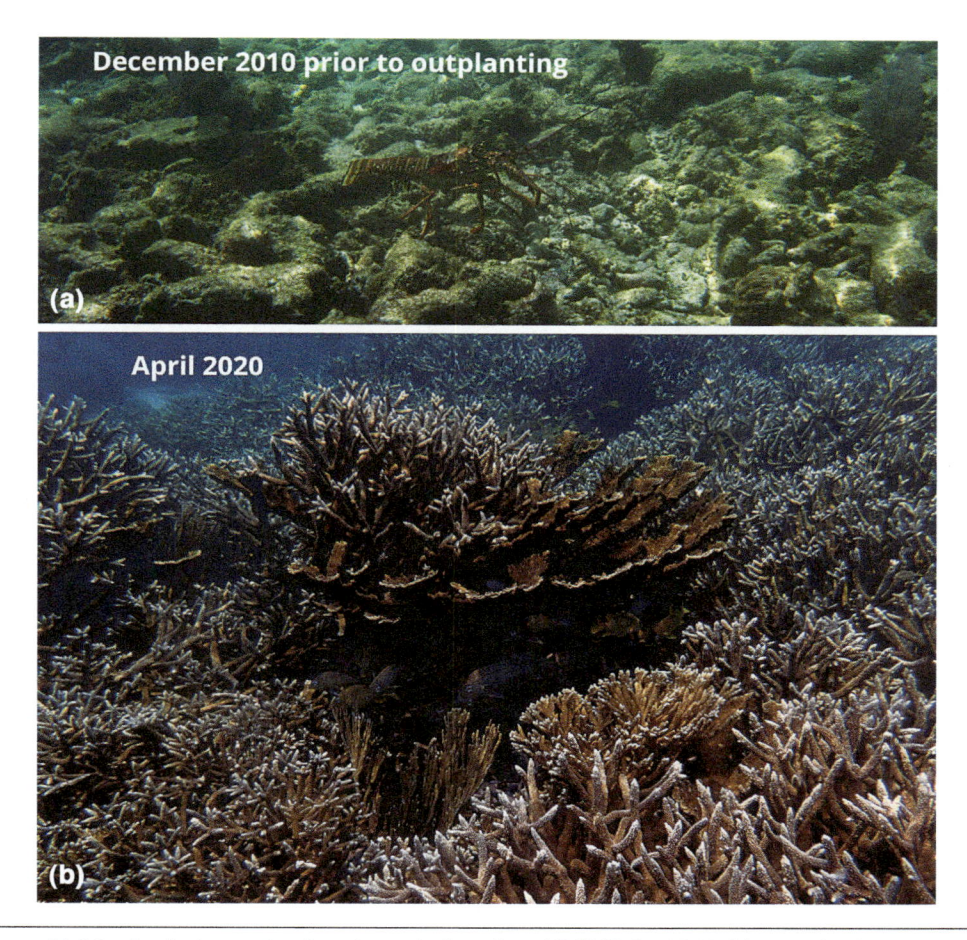

Figure 11.21 A photograph of a degraded reef at LBCNP in 2010 (a) at sub-site 13 prior to outplanting and (b) a photograph of sub-site 13 in April 2020, 9.5 years after FoH outplanted corals at this site.

to facilitate visitors, especially other practitioners and researchers, who are interested in coral restoration. After all, seeing is Belizeing.

ACKNOWLEDGMENTS

FoH's work was made possible through funding from the Caribbean Community Climate Change Center, Global Environment Facility Trust Fund (GEF Small Grants Programme), the Inter-American Development Bank, Marine Conservation and Climate Change Adaptation Project, Private Donations, the World Bank, World Wildlife Fund, the Adaptation Fund, MAR Fund, Ray Caye, and in-kind use of catamarans from the Moorings Belize. FoH also acknowledges the following individuals in alphabetical order by first name: Arthur Gleason, Ph.D., University of Miami; Austin Bowden-Kerby, Ph.D., Corals4Conservation; Beverly Wade, The Belize Fisheries Department; Christine Prouty, Ph.D., University of South Florida; Claire Paris, Ph.D., University of Miami; Diego Lirman, Ph.D., University of Miami; Emily Peters, Brigham Young University; Harold Hudson, aka Florida's *Reef Doctor*; Iliana Baums, Ph.D.,

Penn State; Janie Wulff, Ph.D., Florida State University; Jason Spadero, Ph.D., The College of the Florida Keys; Karina Scavo, Boston University; Les Kaufman, Ph.D., Boston University; Nadia Bood, World Wildlife Fund; Nicole Fogerty, Ph.D., University of North Carolina; Patricia Bencivenga, Citizen Science GIS; Steve Schill, Ph.D., The Nature Conservancy; Timothy Hawthorne, Citizen Science GIS; and Walter Vergara, World Resources Institute, along with all FoH reef restoration practitioners, past and present. Dr. Trotz is supported by the National Science Foundation (NSF) under Grants No. 1735320 and 1243510. Any opinions, findings, and conclusions or recommendations expressed in this material are those of the authors and do not necessarily reflect the views of any of the funders.

REFERENCES

Cambers, G. and P. Diamond. 2010. "Sandwatch: Adapting to climate change and educating for sustainable development." ISBN:978-92-3-104179-2. Collation:136 p., illus.

Healthy Reefs Initiative. 2018. "Mesoamerican reef report card: An evaluation of ecosystem health." http://www.healthyreefs.org/cms/wp-content/uploads/2012/12/2018-MAR-Report-Card-Web.pdf.

Klomp, K. D., K. Clarke, K. Marks, and M. Miller. 2003. "Condition of reef fish on Jamaica's north coast signals late stages of overexploitation." In: Proceedings of the 54th Gulf and Caribbean Fisheries Institute. November 2001. Providenciales, Turks and Caicos. R. L. Creswell. (ed.), pp. 592–608. Fort Pierce, FL: Gulf and Caribbean Fisheries Institute.

Spadaro J. A. 2019. "Cryptic herbivorous invertebrates restructure the composition of degraded coral reef communities in the Florida Keys, Florida, USA." Doctor of Philosophy (PhD), Dissertation, Biological Sciences, Old Dominion University. doi: 10.25777/fg35-1j72 https://digitalcommons.odu.edu/biology_etds/86.

12

INDIAN OCEAN: SEYCHELLES

Sarah Frias-Torres, Claude Reveret, Phanor Montoya-Maya, and Nirmal J. Shah

ABSTRACT

The challenges of coral reef restoration are magnified in Small Island Developing States (SIDS) due to their limited resources in infrastructure, material supply, and local knowledge capacity. Yet, SIDS are strongly dependent on coral reefs as a source of food, income, and coastal protection. Here, we discuss the lessons learned through implementing a large-scale coral reef restoration project in the Republic of Seychelles, Indian Ocean. We used the coral gardening process with midwater ocean nurseries and transplantation of nursery-grown corals directly onto the degraded reef. We present biomimicry solutions to scale up restoration using limited resources, including: coral self-attachment in nursery and transplantation phases, animal-assisted cleaning of nurseries and corals before transplantation, and restoration with breeding-size coral colonies. We also completed giant clam rewilding, restoration tailored to the needs of a hotel resort, and capacity building for national and international restoration practitioners. As large-scale coral reef restoration becomes a more widespread active conservation strategy, we encourage scientists and practitioners to apply our solutions or develop improved protocols based on them.

INTRODUCTION

The Need for Coral Reef Restoration in Seychelles

In 1998 an El Nino event coupled with the Indian Ocean Dipole (Graham et al. 2006) resulted in both the highest seawater temperature anomaly recorded to date in 50 years and coral bleaching and mortality worldwide. Coral reefs in the Indian Ocean were severely impacted (Sheppard et al. 2005). At a regional level, mortality was recorded at 30% (Obura 2005), with a reduction of live coral cover of 80–95% at the most heavily impacted reefs, such as in those located in Seychelles (Spalding and Jarvis 2002; Spencer et al. 2000).

Within the granitic islands of Seychelles, the 1998 mass bleaching event decreased live coral cover to less than 3% in some areas, with no depth refuge from temperature-induced coral mortality (Graham et al. 2006, 2007). Rapid algal colonization occurred shortly after the corals died (Spalding and Jarvis 2002), along with a gradual shift of the impacted reefs into rubble and algal dominated communities, and a collapse of structural complexity (Baker et al. 2008). During the following decade, recovery was extremely slow (Graham et al. 2006, 2007; Mumby and Steneck 2008). Live coral cover remained very low, even 16 years after the mass bleaching event, with less than 1% of the benthos composed of fast-growing branching species (Harris et al. 2014). Recovery within Seychelles was patchy, with significant spatial heterogeneity. In 2011, a survey of 21 coral reef sites between Mahe and Praslin had 12 sites with signs of recovery: average live coral cover of 23% and macro-algal cover of less than 1%. However, nine of the sites had shifted toward macro-algal dominated reefs, with an average of less than 3% live coral cover and macro-algal cover of 42% (Graham et al. 2015).

Coral reef degradation and limited recovery threaten the economy of Seychelles. The island nation is the third-largest consumer of fish per capita in the world because people rely on fish as their main protein source. Most of the fish consumed are caught in coral reefs and associated habitats. Seychelles depend almost exclusively on tourism and fisheries for foreign revenue (Jennings et al. 1996; Shareef and McAleer 2008). Tourism contributes directly to revenue, stimulates other commercial sectors that support the entire tourism industry (Spalding et al. 2017), and is critical in the financing of protected areas (Gössling 2002).

The loss of coral reef structure caused by bleaching-induced mortality also impedes the ability of reefs to provide coastal protection and sustain the white sandy beaches favored by the tourism sector (Sheppard et al. 2005). The beaches of Seychelles are classified among the most attractive in the world and are of crucial importance for the local economy, but the loss of coral reefs is expected to have future negative impacts on the entire beach habitat (Sheppard et al. 2005). Therefore, in the long term, bleaching events causing mass coral mortality and the subsequent marine environmental deterioration in Seychelles can substantially influence tourist arrival (Spalding et al. 2017). The predicted increase in both frequency and severity of coral bleaching events will further worsen these interconnected problems.

From 2011 to 2015, the United States Agency for International Development (USAID), through its Development Grant Program (DGP), funded the Reef Rescuers project to ensure that coral reefs in Seychelles continue to provide the local population with vital biological, ecological, and socioeconomic goods and services and to maintain resilience capability. The project was awarded to Nature Seychelles, the largest and oldest environmental nongovernment organization in the Seychelles archipelago, with experience in environmental conservation and management. The main project goals were to: (1) undertake vulnerability assessments and stakeholder consultations on coral reef restoration, (2) generate a stock of coral colonies for reef restoration, (3) initiate seascape restoration of selected coral reef habitats as a model for Seychelles and the region, (4) build stakeholder capacity in Seychelles and the region and generate a pool of skilled persons for sustained coral reef restoration, and (5) produce a green business plan to ensure financing and long-term sustainability.

The coral reef restoration activities that were implemented during the Reef Rescuers project followed the four basic principles of ecological restoration (Table 12.1) to increase sustainable and valuable outcomes (Suding et al. 2015). These four basic principles are:

1. *Restoration increases ecological integrity*—restoration initiates or accelerates recovery of degraded areas by prioritizing the complexity of biological assemblages, including species composition and representation of all functional groups, as well as the features and processes needed to sustain these biota and to support ecosystem function.
2. *Restoration is sustainable in the long term*—restoration aims to establish systems that are self-sustaining and resilient; thus, they must be consistent with their environmental context and landscape setting. Once a restoration project is complete, the goal should be to minimize human intervention over the long term. When intervention is required, it should be to simulate natural processes that the landscape no longer provides or to support traditional practices of local communities.

3. *Restoration is informed by the past and future*—historical knowledge, in its many forms, can indicate how ecosystems functioned in the past and can provide references for identifying potential future trajectories and measuring the functional and compositional success of projects. However, the unprecedented pace and spatial extent of anthropogenic changes in the present era can create conditions that depart strongly from historical trends. Often, then, history serves less as a template and more as a guide for determining appropriate restoration goals.
4. *Restoration benefits and engages society*—restoration focuses on recovering biodiversity and supporting the intrinsic value of nature. It also provides a suite of ecosystem services (e.g., improved water quality, fertile and stable soils, drought and flood buffering, genetic diversity, and carbon sequestration) that enhance human quality of life (e.g., clean water, food security, enhanced health, and effective governance). Restoration engages people through direct participation and, thus, increases understanding of ecosystems and their benefits, which thereby strengthens human communities.

The purpose of this chapter is twofold. First, we describe and summarize how we completed large-scale coral reef restoration at a degraded reef site in Seychelles and two small-scale restoration projects. Second, we synthesize and evaluate what we learned from the effectiveness of the methods used and provide guidelines for future work.

Table 12.1 Application of the four guiding principles of ecological restoration (Suding et al. 2015) to the large-scale coral reef restoration actions in Seychelles by the Reef Rescuers project

Restoration Principle	Application in Seychelles
Increase ecological integrity	Complexity of restored coral assemblages, prioritized by transplanting 45 species of 3 growth types (branching, massive, and encrusting).
Long-term sustainability	Restored coral reef consistent with species composition found in healthy site used as reference and designed to minimize human intervention in the long term.
Informed by the past and future	Historical knowledge of the existence of a diverse coral species composition in the restored site prior to degradation and intervention; transplanted corals mostly grown from fragments of 1998 El Niño survivors, potentially adapted to new warming events.
Benefits and engages society	Build stakeholder capacity in Seychelles and the region and generate a pool of skilled people for sustained coral reef restoration.

LARGE-SCALE CORAL REEF RESTORATION PROJECT IN SEYCHELLES

The Reef Rescuers team consisted of four staff members and four to six volunteers throughout the project. The permanent staff included: Chief Scientist/Project Coordinator, Technical/Scientific Officer, Dive Leader, and Boatman/Maintenance Technician. The volunteers were qualified scuba divers who assisted as scientific divers. Each volunteer group remained with the project for three months, at which time, a new group of volunteers joined the project. The volunteer rotation system fulfilled two of the main objectives of the Reef Rescuers project, namely to (1) build stakeholder capacity and (2) generate a pool of skilled persons for sustained coral reef restoration. We trained 43 volunteers over the entire project. All scuba diving operations were completed with six divers, working in three pairs. The total dive time per day was three hours, during a five-day workweek.

The project site was a continuous fringing reef on the southwest side of Cousin Island Special Reserve, a land and sea no-take, fully protected and enforced reserve (Figure 12.1). The reef was approximately 400 m long and 30 m wide (ca. 1.2 ha) with a depth range of 6.5 m–13 m. A 40-m-long section of the coral reef, at its southernmost end (4°20′09″S, 55°39′32″E), survived the 1998 mass coral bleaching event. This surviving section became the reference healthy site (ca. 0.12 ha)—a site that represented the target healthy conditions and was untouched throughout the project. Coral cover in this section of the reef had a good recovery from less than 15% in 2012 to less than 35% in 2014, and was dominated by *Acropora* (e.g., *A. appressa, A. cytherea, A. humilis, A. hyacinthus*) and *Pocillopora* (*P. grandis* and *P. verrucosa*) species. Coral cover in the remainder of the reef (ca. 1 ha) was less than 3%. A 50-m-long section of the reef, northwest (4°20′08″S, 55°39′30″E) of the healthy site, was selected as the control degraded site (ca. 0.13 ha)—an untreated site of degraded conditions and untouched throughout the project. Here, a mix of consolidated rubble, unconsolidated rubble, and sand dominate the substrate; and the coral cover has remained unchanged since 2012. A 150-m-long section of the degraded reef, north (4°20′04″S, 55°39′25″E) of the degraded site, was targeted for restoration through coral transplantation. This was the transplanted site (0.52 ha), where the substrate resembled the degraded site in 2012. All three study sites were separated by arbitrarily defined 50-m buffer zones (Figure 12.2(a), (b), (c)).

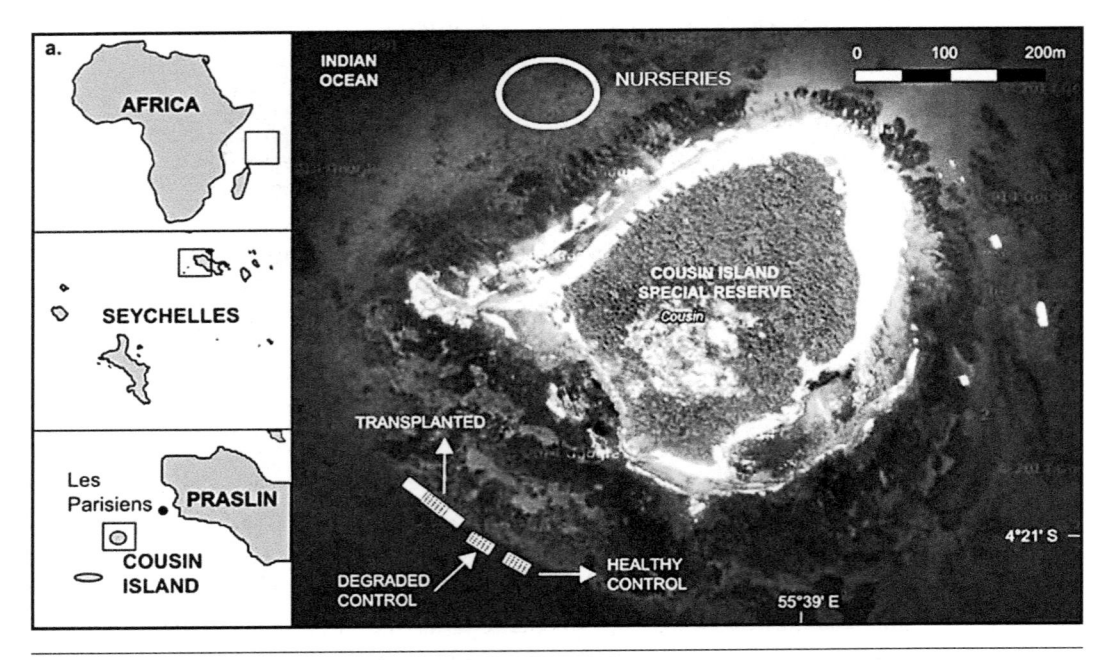

Figure 12.1 Study area—geographic location of the granitic islands of Seychelles, Cousin Island Special Reserve, coral donor site (Les Parisiennes), nursery site, and the three study sites: reference healthy, control degraded, and transplanted site.

Figure 12.2 Seascape overview of (a) reference healthy, (b) control degraded, and (c) transplanted site after completion of restoration (photo credit: Nature Seychelles).

We used the *coral gardening* concept (Rinkevich 2006) of asexual restoration in coral reefs. First, we generated a stock of farmed corals in underwater nurseries until they reached a threshold transplantation size. Second, we transplanted the nursery corals onto degraded reefs. To generate the stock of farmed corals, we targeted donor corals that had survived the 1998 mass bleaching event. When branching and tabular coral species were selected, fragment extraction was limited to a maximum of 10% of the colony to avoid damage to the donor. Massive and encrusting species were small and fragmenting could cause substantial damage to the donor colony. In this case, the whole colony was harvested and fragmented to fill the nurseries; during the transplantation phase, colonies were replaced in the donor site to compensate for the initial loss. We also used corals of opportunity, including entire coral colonies or fragments from larger colonies that were detached due to either human activities (e.g., anchor damage) or natural environmental damage. To obtain coral fragments, we used cutter pliers, chisel, or hammer and chisel—depending on the strength of the coral colony (Figure 12.3).

Figure 12.3 Collection of donor coral fragments (photo credit: Nature Seychelles).

Popular underwater nursery designs, such as the coral tree nursery model that is widely used in Florida, the Caribbean, and other regions (Nedimyer et al. 2011), were not adequate due to the projected scale of the restoration effort, the small dive team, the need for a low-cost strategy, and the limited resources of a state considered to be one of the SIDS. Instead, we scaled up the design of rope nurseries that were previously developed by Israeli scientists (Levy et al. 2010).

The nursery site was a sandy area on the northwest side of the island at approximately 1 km from the nearest coral reef. At this site, we built nine midwater rope nurseries and three midwater net nurseries. Each rope nursery consisted of five high-pressure PVC pipes (HP PVC), 600 mm × 64 mm in size, placed approximately 4 m apart, to which 20-m-long ropes were perpendicularly attached. Each rope held 80–150 corals, totaling approximately 5,000 corals in each rope nursery (Figures 12.4 and 12.5(a), (b)). Each net nursery consisted of a 6 m × 6 m frame constructed from PVC pipe, layered with a recycled 5.5-cm-mesh tuna net. Each net nursery held approximately 480 corals (Figures 12.6 and 12.7(a), (b)). All rope and net nurseries were attached to the seafloor at an 18 m depth by anchor lines and kept at a depth of 8 m below the sea surface using recycled plastic jerrycans as buoys and filled with air from the scuba tanks (Figure 12.8(a), (b)).

The combined stock in all the rope nurseries was over 40,000 coral fragments of branching and tabular species, including: *Acropora hyacinthus, A. cytherea, A. vermiculata, A. abrotanoides, A. appressa, Pocillopora verrucosa, P. indiania, P. damicornis, P. grandis, Stylophora pistillata,* and *S. subseriata*. In net nurseries, the corals were a mix of roughly 50% branching/tabular, 30% massive/submassive, and 20% encrusting growth forms (Table 12.2). During the nursery

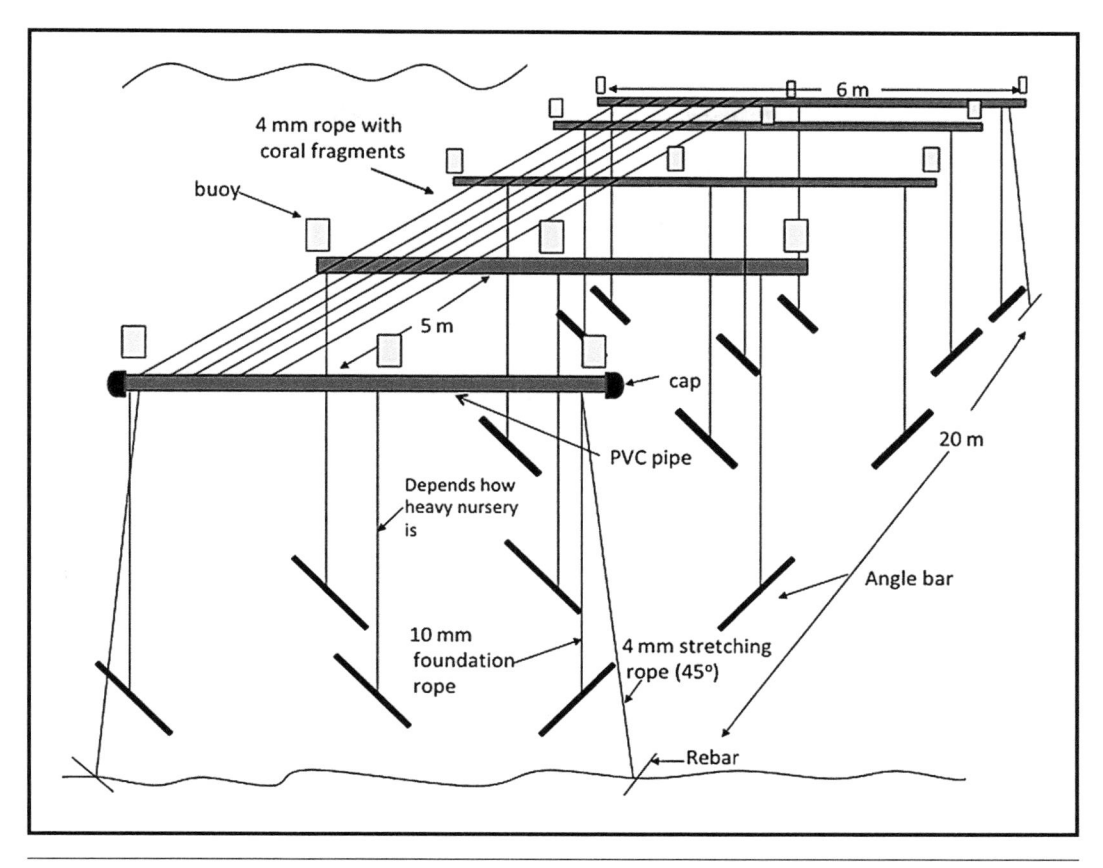

Figure 12.4 Schematic drawing of the midwater rope nursery (photo credit: Nature Seychelles).

phase, a hurricane destroyed one rope nursery and the corals were lost. An invasive sponge killed half the corals in another rope nursery. Our remaining stock of branching and tabular corals in rope nurseries was approximately 32,000 corals.

The reef-transplanted site, located on the southwest side of the Cousin Island Special Reserve, consisted of a degraded coral reef impacted by the 1998 mass coral bleaching event (Spalding and Jarvis 2002; Spencer et al. 2000) as well as the 2004 Indian Ocean Tsunami (Jackson et al. 2005). At this site, a gentle slope (roughly 25 m) extends to a depth of 13 m. The seabed then flattens out and consists of a mixture of sand and coral rubble interspersed with granite outcroppings. The coral colonies grown in the midwater rope nurseries were transplanted to this degraded reef (see *Biomimicry Applications and Inventions* herein). Between November 2011 and June 2014, a total of 24,431 nursery-grown coral colonies were transplanted in this section in an attempt to assist in natural reef recovery. The dominant transplanted coral genus was *Pocillopora*. However, 10 different branching/tabular species were transplanted in this site: *Acropora cytherea, A. damicornis, A. formosa, A. hyacinthus, A. abrotanoides, A. lamarki, A. vermiculata, Pocillopora damicornis, P. indiania, P. grandis*, and *P. verrucosa* (species identification after Veron 2000 and nomenclature after the WoRMS [www.marinespecies.org]).

We enhanced the structural complexity of a degraded reef by the addition of nursery-grown adult coral colonies (>15 cm diameter) at high densities (4–5 colonies per square meter). This

Figure 12.5 Rope nursery: (a) diver working on the nursery and (b) corals have grown over the rope section and self-attached within one month of placement (photo credits: (a) Mia Tranthem and (b) Nature Seychelles).

Figure 12.6 Building of a midwater net nursery (photo credit: Nature Seychelles).

intervention resulted in a rapid increase in live coral cover of locally dominant and pioneering species at the transplanted site, from 3% in 2012 to about 15% in 2014 when transplantation was finished, along with an immediate increase in the structural complexity of the site. A six-month coral settlement study in 2014 showed total spat density at the transplanted site (123.4 ± 13.3 spat m^{-2}) was 1.8 times higher than at the healthy site (68.4 ± 7.8 spat m^{-2}) and 1.6 times higher than at the degraded site (78.2 ± 7.17 spat m^{-2}). Two years after the first transplantation, the total recruit density was highest at the healthy site (4.8 ± 0.4 recruits m^{-2}), intermediate at the transplanted site (2.7 ± 0.4 recruits m^{-2}), and lowest at the degraded site (1.7 ± 0.3 recruits m^{-2}). The results suggest that large-scale coral restoration may have a positive influence on coral settlement and recruitment, with a stronger influence on coral settlement (Montoya-Maya et al. 2016a).

Two events tested the resilience of the coral reef transplanted site. First, in October 2015, a large-scale harmful algal bloom (HAB) was observed in the inner granitic islands of Seychelles, with widespread fish kills of coral reef species. Within the marine reserve of the Cousin Island Special Reserve, the HAB event resulted in coral bleaching mortality at the reference healthy site, on average 9.5% (±3.7 SE) and reached up to 16% within one transect. In contrast, no dead coral colonies were observed in transects at the transplanted site (Montoya-Maya et al. 2016b). Second, the 2014–2017 global coral bleaching event (Eakin et al. 2019) impacted the

Figure 12.7 Net nursery community: (a) endangered Humphead Parrotfish (*Bolbometopon muricatum*) were common visitors in the net nurseries but did not predate on the nursery corals and (b) overview of the coral community in the nursery (photo credits: C. Reveret).

Figure 12.8 The basic anchoring and buoyancy elements of midwater floating nurseries: (a) diver hammering anchor bar at 18 m depth in a sandy area of the coral nursery site and (b) diver filling up recycled jerrycan with air from scuba tank (photo credits: Nature Seychelles).

Table 12.2 Coral species grown at midwater rope and net nurseries within the marine reserve of Cousin Island Special Reserve. Scientific names of corals follow the World Register of Marine Species (WoRMS) (WoRMS Editorial Board 2016)

Growth Type	Species Names
Branching/Tabular	*Acropora abrotanoides, A. appressa, A. cytherea, A. humilis, A. hyacinthus, A. muricata, A. vermiculata, A. cf verweyi, Isopora brueggemanni, Pocillopora damicornis, P. grandis, P. indiania, P. verrucosa, Stylophora pistillata, S. subseriata*
Massive/Submassive	*Acanthastrea brevis, Astrea curta, Astreopora myriophthalma, Coscinaraea monile, Cyphastrea sp., Dipsastraea cf favus, D. lizardensis, Favites cf flexuosa, F. cf pentagona, F. vasta, Galaxea fascicularis, Goniastrea edwardsi, Goniopora tenuidens, G. pedunculata, Hydnophora exesa, H. microconos, Lobophyllia hemprichii, Paramontastraea serageldini, Pavona decussata, P. explanulata, Platygyra acuta, P. cf crosslandi, Porites lobata*
Encrusting	*Echinophyllia aspera, Echinopora hirsutissima, Favites pentagona, Leptastrea purpurea, Leptoseris incrustans, Psammocora haimiana, Turbinaria irregularis*

transplanted and reference healthy sites in two phases. Initial observation during the March to May 2016 coral bleaching season revealed that in the monitored plots, up to 80% of the nursery-grown coral transplants bleached, but only 10% died, and the rest recovered from bleaching. In contrast, in the healthy reference site, up to 50% of the corals bleached, but up to 25% of the bleached corals died. These early results suggested the corals in the transplanted site showed overall heat resilience, capable of recovering after bleaching (Montoya-Maya et al. 2016b). As the global coral bleaching event progressed, live coral cover decreased across all sites. Surviving heat-resilient corals were identified; fragments were collected, grown in midwater ocean nurseries, and transplanted in the restoration site between 2017 and 2018. Initial monitoring showed signs of recovery and the positive effects of coral transplantation were still observed, with juvenile coral density and fish density at the transplanted site being higher than at the control degraded site (Anstey et al. 2018).

SMALL-SCALE CORAL REEF RESTORATION PROJECTS IN SEYCHELLES

Coral reef restoration focuses on scleractinian corals, excluding other groups that provide structural complexity to these threatened ecosystems. Giant clams share the role of ecosystem engineers alongside corals in the Indo-Pacific, but overfishing has caused widespread local extinctions. To test whether giant clam restoration is feasible, a total of 150 captive-bred, adult giant clams (*Tridacna maxima*), 4–10 years old with a shell length of 99–198 mm, were deployed to the healthy reef (reference site) and the restored reef site, at 6 m and 12 m depths, at the Cousin Island Special Reserve in two sequential experiments (Figure 12.9(a), (b), (c)). Giant clam survival was monitored for up to 20 weeks and it was consistently higher at the coral transplanted site than at the reference healthy site. Sources of mortality included octopus predation and dislodgement by wave swells. The first 11 weeks were a critical time to monitor post-deployment success and mortality stabilization. This monitoring period offered guidance about the sites and depths with the best survival for transplanted adult giant clams. These results show that captive-bred, adult *T. maxima* survive restoration in the wild (Frias-Torres 2017).

Figure 12.9 Giant clam (*Tridacna maxima*) restoration with captive-bred adults: (a) one wild giant clam, *Tridacna maxima*, shell length 35 cm, was found at the reference healthy site, confirming historical accounts that these giant clams were once common at Cousin Island, (b) captive-bred *T. maxima* tagged and ready for relocation to the coral restoration site, and (c) diver measuring tagged giant clams that were relocated to the site (photo credits: (a, c) C. Reveret and (b) S. Frias-Torres).

With additional support from the United Nations Development Program (UNDP) and Global Environmental Fund (GEF) Tourism Partnership Programme, we implemented a coral reef restoration project at the Constance Lemuria 5-star resort in Praslin Island. The aim was to restore a shallow (1–3 m) degraded patch reef at a bay (Petite Anse Kerlan) within the hotel premises. The restored reef required easy snorkeling access to hotel guests. At this bay, we transplanted 2,015 nursery-grown corals of branching (4 genera, 15 species), massive (16 genera, 23 species), and encrusting (7 genera, 7 species) growth types (Table 12.2). Here we transplanted all the corals grown in the net nurseries and over 500 corals from the rope nurseries. Monitoring 345 days post-transplantation showed that survival ranged from 16.6% to 83.3% in branching corals and 50% to 100% in encrusting and massive corals. Growth was not significant (Frias-Torres et al. unpublished data).

BIOMIMICRY APPLICATIONS AND INVENTIONS

In resource-limited SIDS, such as Seychelles, recycling and upcycling materials to build our ocean nurseries was not enough to achieve large-scale coral reef restoration. We had to rely on biomimicry to provide sustainable and scaled-up solutions. Biomimicry aims to find solutions that are inspired by nature to develop innovative and sustainable techniques to solve complex problems (Benyus, 2002). The biology of scleractinian corals and the ecology of coral reefs have unique adaptations that provide opportunities for biomimicry-based solutions in the context of scaling up coral reef restoration.

Coral Self-Attachment in Nursery Phase and Transplantation Phase

The coenosarc is a continuum of living tissue on the surface of the coral colony that connects individual polyps that are hosted in their corallite skeleton with spaces between polyps (Ruppert et al. 2004). The existence of this living surface layer is critical in low-cost large-scale coral reef restoration. To attach thumb-sized coral fragments (nubbins) to our rope nurseries, one person spliced the 4-mm-diameter rope open by twisting the rope in the opposite direction to its natural coil, creating a hole in the rope that was large enough to place a coral nubbin through to secure it. After inserting the coral nubbin into the spliced rope, we released the rope fragment and it automatically returned to the twisted configuration. With this technique, a team of two people on the boat deck attached about 400 nubbins per hour, while two scuba divers received the rope underwater as it was being filled with corals and attached the rope to the nursery. Within one month of insertion, the coenosarc of each nubbin grew over the point of contact with the rope and achieved self-attachment. This biomimicry solution increased nubbin stability and reduced project costs because no additional connectors were needed to attach the nubbin to the nursery rope. Successful application of such a nursery self-attachment technique allowed us to build a nursery stock of up to 40,000 branching and tabular corals in eight rope nurseries, each nursery hosting 5,000 corals (Figure 12.5).

After corals grew in the nurseries for one year, they were transplanted onto the degraded reef. We used two methods of transplantation. First, we extracted ropes full of corals from the nurseries (Figure 12.10) and nailed the ropes onto the degraded reef. This is a fast method to secure the corals onto the degraded reef that had been used successfully in the Red Sea by teams at the Haifa Institute of Oceanography. The success of this technique relies on stable conditions so that corals have direct and constant contact with the substrate. Under these stable conditions, the coenosarc grows over the points of contact between the coral and the substrate and results in self-attachment of the coral within one month of nailing the rope.

The rope nailing technique failed in Seychelles. The restoration site had regular swells of different intensity, and the nailed ropes did not guarantee the stable conditions needed for coral self-attachment. For this reason, we developed a cementing technique, where corals were cemented directly onto the granite or limestone substrate (Figure 12.11(a), (b)). We used a unique cement mix that was developed by one of us (C. Reveret). Briefly, Portland marine cement was mixed with Sikacrete,® UCS—a stabilizer powder that increases cohesion and reduces washout when cement is applied underwater. The Sikacrete® to marine cement ratio used is proportional to the expected wave energy at the transplanted site. The cement mix was prepared onboard the boat before diving and distributed in pastry bags for transport. Before cementing the corals to the substrate, we cut them from the nursery rope. Then, we used a brush to scrub the targeted attachment site for each coral, to remove sand or other elements that may impede proper cement adhesion. Once the coral was positioned in the target site, we applied the cement mix using the pastry bag to the areas of the coral in direct contact with the substrate, the contact patches. The cement cured within one hour. Within one month, the corals had grown over the cement patches and made contact with the substrate, achieving self-attachment (Frias-Torres et al. 2019). Our technique of cementing coral transplants directly to the hard substrate has recently been validated by Unsworth et. al. (2020).

Figure 12.10 From nursery to transplantation site: diver detaches a nursery rope that will be towed by a boat to the transplantation site (photo credit: Nature Seychelles).

Figure 12.11 Cementing nursery corals at the transplantation site: (a) after brushing attachment site to secure proper cementing, diver deploys small amounts of cement mix with a chef pastry bag to secure the coral onto the substrate and (b) cemented submassive Pocillopora coral shows cured cement on the lower left quadrant (photo credit: Nature Seychelles).

Self-Cleaning Nurseries

Midwater coral nurseries are open to recruitment of reef organisms, and they can function as artificial reefs or fish-aggregating devices, due to an increase in the available substrate for reef organisms, structural complexity, and attraction of organisms from natural reefs (Abelson 2006; Shafir and Rinkevich 2010a). In coral gardening, cleaning the midwater coral nurseries from biofouling algae and sessile invertebrates (including sponges, hydroids, bivalves, barnacles, and tunicates) is essential to avoid space competition with corals and coral death. Nursery cleaning requires a considerable allocation of the time invested in the total restoration project (Shafir and Rinkevich 2010b; Johnson et al. 2011).

In the net nurseries, we regularly attached GoPro Hero™ cameras to monitor fish activity without diver interference and conducted standard diver-based video transects. These observation protocols allowed us to quantify that two types of reef fishes recruited to midwater coral nurseries—transient and resident. Transient species included Ephippidae—Longfin Batfish (*Platax teira*); Labridae (Scarinae)—the endangered Humphead Parrotfish (*Bolbometopon muricatum*); and Siganidae—Forktail Rabbitfish (*Siganus argenteus*). Resident species included Pomacentridae—Two-Bar Damselfish (*Dascyllus carneus*), Regal Damselfish (*Neopomacentrus cyanomos*), and Blue-Yellow Damselfish (*Pomacentrus caeruleus*); Gobiidae—Eyebar Goby (*Gnatholepis cauerensis*), Michel's Ghost Goby (*Pleurosicya micheli*); and Monacanthidae—Longnose Filefish (*Oxymonacanthus longirostris*). Large fishes that were observed feeding at the net nurseries included *B. muricatum*, *S. argenteus*, and *P. teira*. Fish were observed feeding on macroalgae (*B. muricatum* and *P. teira*), epilithic algal turfs (*S. argenteus*), plankton (*D. carneus* and *P. caeruleus*), and coral polyps (*O. longirostris*).

Overall, the fish assemblages included three trophic levels, from herbivores to omnivores. Fishes capable of limiting algal growth included *B. muricatum* and *P. teira* feeding on macroalgae and *S. argenteus* feeding on epilithic algal turfs. Based on video observations, *B. muricatum* did not predate on the nursery corals, and there was a lack of the characteristic scarring left by this parrotfish. Similar midwater coral nurseries evolved into floating-reef ecosystems over five years in the Gulf of Eilat, Red Sea (Shafir and Rinkevich 2010b). The presence of fish assemblages, and their predatory effect on biofouling, reduced the amount of effort that was necessary to clean the nurseries (Figure 12.12). Diver cleaning effort for the nursery with the highest

Figure 12.12 Biomimicry solution for nursery cleaning: Forktail Rabbitfish (*Siganus argenteus*) are frequent visitors of the net nurseries and feed on epilithic algal turfs (photo credit: H. Goehlich).

fish abundance was 36.3% of the time required for the nursery with the lowest fish abundance. Fish assemblages recruited to the net nurseries reduced projected cleaning time by 60% (Frias-Torres et al. 2015).

Animal-Assisted Cleaning Before Transplantation

Large-scale coral reef restoration presents both technical and behavioral challenges. We crossed a threshold of new fish behavior once we reached 10,000 corals transplanted. Fish abundance started to interfere with our activities. While cleaning the biofouling organisms at the midwater rope nurseries, we found that barnacles attached to the nursery ropes and to the coral/rope boundary were difficult to remove. After cementing nursery-raised corals to the restoration site and before the cement mix had enough time to cure, a mob of fish rammed the newly cemented corals to feed on mobile invertebrates or any leftover barnacles recruited during the nursery phase. The ramming fish species included the Sky Emperor (*Lethrinus mahsena*), Tripletail Wrasse (*Cheilinus trilobatus*), Titan Triggerfish (*Balistoides viridescens*), and Flagtail Triggerfish (*Sufflamen chrysopterum*). Dislodgement by fish activity required cementing each coral again. As the number of coral transplants increased, we discovered that up to 16% of newly cemented corals were impacted by the fish mobs. We had to find a solution to avoid delays in our restoration schedule.

Our biomimicry inspiration was the cleaning stations at coral reefs where fish, sea turtles, sharks, and rays congregate to be cleaned of parasites by cleaner fish and shrimps (Gorlick et al. 1987; Losey et al. 1994; O'Shea et al. 2010). Therefore, we systematically investigated the ability of coral reef fish to provide animal-assisted cleaning of coral nursery ropes before transplantation (Frias-Torres and van de Geer 2015). As a result, we eliminated diver-assisted cleaning in this phase; instead, we attached a nursery rope filled with corals, 0.3 m above the seabed, at a *cleaning station* located at the base of the mooring lines that were used by the divers to reach the transplanted site (Figure 12.13). After 48 h at the cleaning station, the ropes and coral/rope interface were free of barnacles and other biofouling organisms. The corals were also free of mobile invertebrates (except *Trapezia* sp. crabs). Once we started using the cleaning station protocol, the rate of coral detachment due to fish attacks fell from 16% to zero. This cleaning station technique could be included as a step before coral transplantation worldwide based on location-specific fish assemblages and during the early nursery phase of sexually produced juvenile corals.

Figure 12.13 (see facing page) Biomimicry solution in an animal-assisted cleaning station: (A) barnacle predation at the transplantation site—the circle shows a clump of barnacles before (left) and 48 h after placement (right), (B) Titan Triggerfish, *Balistoides viridescens*, shown in the foreground of the experimental setup, and (C) reef fish lined up and feeding on the 0.3 m coral rope at the transplantation site (photo credit: C. van de Geer).

Indian Ocean: Seychelles

Restoration with Breeding Size Coral Colonies

We rapidly increased the structural complexity of a degraded reef by the addition of nursery-grown adult coral colonies (>15 cm diameter) at high densities (four to five colonies per square meter). We found that coral transplantation with colonies large enough to reproduce promotes natural recovery due to higher structural complexity, self-recruitment, and recruitment of non-transplanted species. We quantified spatial differences in natural coral recruitment and juveniles after transplantation by comparing two untouched sites, a reference (healthy target condition) and control (degraded untreated condition) with the transplanted site. Coral recruitment was assessed more than 14 months after the first transplantation using a single tile deployment. Six months after tile deployment, total spat density at the transplanted site was 1.8 times higher than the healthy site and 1.6 times higher than the degraded site, but the magnitude of variation in coral recruitment between the transplanted site and the degraded site was up to six times higher for coral families other than the outplanted families Pocilloporidae and Acroporidae (Montoya-Maya et al. 2016a).

We propose three reasons to explain the increase in coral recruitment at the transplanted site. First, the coral transplants increase the local production of coral larvae. The coral colonies were large enough at transplantation time (>15 cm) to have a high probability of being mature (Babcock 1991; Montoya-Maya et al. 2014) and there were gravid colonies at the transplanted and healthy sites (P. H. Montoya-Maya, personal communication, February 2014). It is possible that the majority of larvae settling at the transplanted site were locally produced by the dominant transplanted coral genus Pocillopora. This genus included brooding species with larvae that can settle very close to parental colonies (Gorospe and Karl 2013). Second, the transplanted site attracted more coral larvae from elsewhere due to an increase in settlement cues. The transplanted site had an area three times larger than the two control sites, high species diversity, and coral cover. These conditions may offer more available space and signal more favorable settlement, survival, and growth conditions to incoming coral larvae (Kingsford et al. 2002; Sponaugle et al. 2002; Vermeij 2005; Edwards and Gomez 2007; Suzuki et al. 2008; Nakamura and Sakai 2010; Dixson et al. 2014) when compared to the reference healthy and degraded sites. The higher recruitment of acroporids at the healthy site and of pocilloporids at the transplanted site—where their respective coral cover and adult densities were higher (Frias-Torres et al. unpublished data)—also add support to this statement. The lower number of total recruits at the healthy site, where the coral structure is more complex than at the other sites, may be explained by an increase in recruit mortality from fish predation and grazing (O'Leary and Potts 2011) due to having a more diverse fish community than the two other sites (Frias-Torres et al. unpublished data). Further, a positive relationship between adult cover and recruitment rates (spat tile^{-1}) was found for pocilloporids in the Inner Seychelles (Chong-Seng et al. 2014). Enhanced settlement cues at the transplanted site due to the large-scale nature of the restoration project explain the overall higher number of coral spat and the higher number of spat from non-transplanted families compared to the degraded site. Third, both self-recruitment and attraction from elsewhere increased overall recruitment at the transplanted site. Such interaction of self-recruitment and attraction to increased coral recruitment has been suggested at a previous coral restoration study in Kenya (Mbije et al. 2013). We suggest future research could use techniques to identify immigrant and locally produced spat (e.g. assignment tests, Broquet and Petit 2009) to determine the real effect that coral transplants have in local seeding or larval attraction from elsewhere.

Coral transplantation with large adult colonies may help in accelerating the natural recovery of a degraded reef by improving its structural complexity. This will explain the differences in the number of coral juveniles between the transplanted and degraded sites, along with the steady uptrend in the density of coral juveniles at the transplanted site over the sampling period when compared to the other two sites. Therefore, physical (e.g., varying sizes and growth forms of coral transplants on sites) and biological (e.g., including fish, snails, and any other reef organism known to help coral recruit survival) complexity should be promoted in reef restoration projects to enhance the survival of settlers (Biggs 2013).

CAPACITY BUILDING: EMPOWERING THE END USER

In addition to on-the-job training in coral reef restoration for 43 volunteer scientific divers, we developed certified training modules based on our experience. First, we wrote a Toolkit to compile all methods and lessons learned during the restoration experience. Second, we developed and implemented a pilot six-week training program for scientists, managers, practitioners, and local communities in need of a solid foundation on coral reef restoration. The course curriculum required previous knowledge of basic coral reef ecology, the scientific method, and scuba diving certification. We tested the Toolkit on the training program audience and asked for their input to improve the text. We used the Toolkit as a textbook for the pilot training, where participants gained hands-on experience on how to complete a coral reef restoration project using the coral reef gardening method, how to build midwater nurseries and how to cement corals to a degraded reef site, along with learning the design, logistics, and evaluation that are required to develop their coral reef restoration projects.

In 2015 six international trainees participated in the pilot training program to learn and practice low-cost, field-tested restoration methods and to practice troubleshooting problems that they encountered in field conditions. Their input improved the final version of our Toolkit on large-scale coral reef restoration (Frias-Torres et al. 2019). Today, most of the trainees from the pilot training are working on coral reef restoration projects around the world.

After the pilot training, former Reef Rescuers staff implemented similar training workshops in the Maldives and Seychelles where 56 people trained in large-scale coral reef restoration. Two trainees from previous workshops initiated or enhanced successful projects in several island resorts in Fiji, Indonesia, Maldives, and Seychelles—and three trainees initiated professional careers in coral reef restoration or founded their coral reef conservation organizations.

Since completion of the Seychelles coral reef restoration projects shown here, the Reef Rescuers core staff team expanded work at a regional and global level: P. Montoya-Maya implemented Colombia's largest coral reef restoration project to date with the participation of 28 local fishermen and a community of volunteer scuba divers; C. Reveret joined two coral reef restoration projects (Guadeloupe, Caribbean, and Tamatave, Madagascar) and coral transplantation monitorings (Halul Island, Qatar); S. Frias-Torres continued to develop biomimicry solutions to scale up coral reef restoration, led efforts to fund research in coral temperature tolerance, and in collaboration with N. Shah and with support from the United Nations Development Program, secured USD 10 million from the Adaptation Fund to implement large-scale coral reef restoration across Mauritius and Seychelles over a five-year timeline.

SUMMARY

An evaluation of the coral reef restoration projects completed in the Republic of Seychelles leads us to the following conclusions:

- The highest priority to ensure the long-term persistence of coral reefs is to transition to an economy based on renewable energy sources and to protect reefs from environmental degradation. Meanwhile, we need to expand the field of coral reef restoration towards a holistic approach that is focused on biodiversity to restore the whole ecosystem, and on ecosystem engineers with tolerance to one or several environmental stressors, including high temperature, disease, and sedimentation.
- The first option, before attempting restoration, is to let nature take its course and allow the degraded coral reef to recover by itself after removing local stressors. If there is no evidence of natural recovery or a path towards recovery within a reasonable timeline (e.g., 5 to 10 years), then active restoration is needed.
- Biomimicry solutions allow scaling up of coral reef restoration. At every step in the process of coral gardening, from ocean nurseries to coral transplantation onto the degraded reef, biomimicry solutions allow the development of new techniques that are suitable for large-scale coral reef restoration with the limited resources found at SIDS.
- Local stressors (pollution, overfishing, habitat destruction) must be nonexistent or minimal to quantify recovery in the reef that is targeted for restoration. Otherwise, local stressors become confounding factors that influence the variables measured to evaluate restoration success.
- Coral transplantation with nursery-grown, breeding-size colonies facilitates the rapid transition in a degraded reef, from an empty, cleared state to the three-dimensional complexity needed for ecosystem restoration. The increase in coral recruitment at the transplanted site is explained by an increase in the local production of coral larvae by the coral transplants, the attraction of more coral larvae from elsewhere due to an increase in settlement cues, or a combination of both.
- Coral reef restoration must focus on the coral reef habitat, including diverse ecosystem engineers that provide structural complexity (scleractinian corals, giant clams, giant sponges) and ecological relationships at the community level. Specifically, for scleractinian corals, single species monocultures should be avoided. Instead, restoration using multiple species with diverse growth forms achieves a more realistic approach similar to the species composition of the reference healthy site.
- Success of coral reef restoration is measured by how similar transplanted areas are to the reference healthy site. To quantify progress, an effective long-term research and monitoring strategy needs to be included as part of the restoration program at relevant time scales and intervals—for example, two, five, and ten years post-restoration activity.
- Restoring a coral reef adapted to climate change is feasible. Coral donors can be selected among survivors of previous bleaching events so that transplants from nursery-grown corals show heat resilience during new bleaching events. However, if we aim for effective coral reef restoration in the current and future climate-change scenarios, we need to focus research on the underlying reasons for temperature tolerance in corals. Then, we would apply the results to develop field-deployable tools that allow us to precisely identify corals with higher temperature tolerance, so we can use them as donors for future restoration actions.

RECOMMENDED FUTURE RESEARCH

Restating the evolutionary biologist Theodosius Dobzhansky, nothing in Restoration Ecology makes sense except in the light of global climate change. Mass coral bleaching events that are linked to El Niño–Southern Oscillation have intensified since 1998, and if the observed background changes continue under future human-caused climate change, more frequent strong El Niño events are anticipated (Wang et al. 2019). Projections from the Intergovernmental Panel on Climate Change (IPCC) on the impacts of average temperature increase above preindustrial levels show that if we do nothing to stop burning fossil fuels: at a 1.5°C increase, 70% of the world's coral reefs will be lost by 2100; but at a 2°C increase, virtually all coral reefs are lost by 2100 (Hoegh-Guldberg et al. 2018). If we aim for effective coral reef restoration in the current and future climate change scenarios, we need to focus research on the underlying reasons for temperature tolerance in corals. Then, apply the results to develop field-deployable tools that allow us to identify corals with higher temperature tolerance so we can use them as donors for future restoration actions. However, the recent stony coral tissue loss disease (SCTLD) outbreak in Florida (Aeby et al. 2019) and the Caribbean (Alvarez-Filip et al. 2019) is a stark reminder of evolutionary trade-offs because corals that can survive higher temperatures can also be more susceptible to disease. Therefore, future research in coral reef restoration must take a holistic approach focused on biodiversity, where diagnostic tools are available to identify not only high temperature tolerance but also response to disease and sedimentation.

Socioeconomic research is needed to develop structures and mechanisms that will make coral reef restoration a long-term sustainable enterprise and an income generator for local communities. We need to develop equivalent income streams, similar to those found in marine conservation, through jobs in ecotourism, marine protected areas, and other activities. Unless we develop socioeconomic strategies that benefit local communities, with the involvement of the public and private sector, coral reef restoration will continue to rely on short-term grants and donations, and the ability to implement comprehensive restoration strategies will be limited.

We also recommend pursuing ecosystem-level metrics for the evaluation of restoration success, including (1) genetic tools to identify immigrant and locally produced spat (Broquet and Petit, 2009) to quantify the effect that coral transplants have in local seeding or larval attraction from elsewhere, (2) quantification of complexity (e.g., rugosity) to evaluate coral settlement and recruitment on transplanted sites with varying levels of structural complexity, and (3) quantification of fish biomass linked to fish movement between restored and non-restored sites using diver-based surveys combined with baited remote underwater video stations (Currey-Randall et al. 2020) and recording of soundscape ecology (Freeman and Freeman 2016).

Finally, we encourage the cross-pollination of ideas among scientists and practitioners of coral reef restoration across geographic regions. In addition to publishing in peer-reviewed scientific journals, we have presented the work shown here at several regional and international coral reef scientific conferences, including the 2014 Ocean Sciences Meeting, the 2015 Aquatic Sciences Meeting, the 2013 and 2015 Western Indian Ocean Marine Science Association Scientific Symposium, the 2016 International Coral Reef Symposium, the 2016 International Marine Conservation Congress, the 2018 Society for Ecological Restoration Australasia, and the 2018 Reef Futures Conference. Our work has also been covered extensively by African and European broadcast media, CNN International, Canadian Radio, and Reuters. However, we see that the work completed and the solutions achieved in low-income countries are systematically ignored by scientists and practitioners in high-income countries. As a result, we encounter many cases of *reinventing the wheel* when the technique has already been tested through the scientific method in a different part of the world. To advance the science and practice of coral reef restoration, we must bring down the barriers of knowledge exchange and implementation, and work as a truly international community.

ACKNOWLEDGMENTS

We thank the team of volunteer scientific divers for their help during our fieldwork. We also thank Kerstin Henri, Director of Strategic Operations of Nature Seychelles, for managing the Reef Rescuers project. Funding to Nature Seychelles was received through the USAID Reef Rescuers Project 674-A-00-10-00123-00. Additional funding was received through the UNDP/GEF Tourism Partnership Small Grants Program. The funders had no role in study design, data collection and analysis, decision to publish, or preparation of the manuscript. The statements, findings, conclusions, and recommendations shown here are those of the authors and do not necessarily reflect the views of USAID, UNDP/GEF, or Nature Seychelles.

REFERENCES

Abelson, A. 2006. "Artificial reefs vs coral transplantation as restoration tools for mitigating coral reef deterioration: Benefits, concerns, and proposed guidelines." *Bulletin of Marine Science* 78(1), 151–159.

Aeby, G. S., B. Ushijima, J. E. Campbell, S. Jones, G. J. Williams, J. L. Meyer, C. Häse, and V. J. Paul. 2019. Pathogenesis of a Tissue Loss Disease Affecting Multiple Species of Corals Along the Florida Reef Tract. *Frontiers in Marine Science* 6 (November), 1–18. https://doi.org/10.3389/fmars.2019.00678.

Alvarez-Filip, L., N. Estrada-Saldívar, E. Pérez-Cervantes, A. Molina-Hernández, and F. J. González-Barrios. 2019. "A rapid spread of the stony coral tissue loss disease outbreak in the Mexican Caribbean." *PeerJ* 2019(11). https://doi.org/10.7717/peerj.8069.

Anstey, P. C. Shute, P. Montoya-Maya, N. Shah, S. Frias-Torres, and K. Henri. 2018. "Positive effects of long term, large-scale coral reef restoration prevail beyond natural disturbances [abstract]." In: Book of Abstracts, Reef Futures 2018: A Coral Restoration and Intervention-Science Symposium; 10–14 December 2018, Key Largo, FL, USA.

Babcock, R. C. 1991. "Comparative demography of three species of Scleractinian corals using age- and size-dependent classifications." *Ecological Monographs* 61(3), 225–244. https://doi.org/10.2307/2937107.

Baker, A. C., P. W. Glynn, and B. Riegl. 2008. "Climate change and coral reef bleaching: An ecological assessment of long-term impacts, recovery trends and future outlook." *Estuarine, Coastal and Shelf Science*, 80(4), 435–471. https://doi.org/10.1016/j.ecss.2008.09.003.

Benyus, J. M. 2002. "Biomimicry: Innovation inspired by nature." In *Ecos Science for Sustainability* (Issue 129). Perennial. https://doi.org/10.1071/EC129p27.

Biggs, B. C. 2013. "Harnessing natural recovery processes to improve restoration outcomes: An experimental assessment of sponge-mediated coral reef restoration." *PLoS ONE* 8(6). https://doi.org/10.1371/journal.pone.0064945.

Broquet, T. and E. J. Petit. 2009. "Molecular estimation of dispersal for ecology and population genetics." *Annual Review of Ecology, Evolution, and Systematics* 40(1), 193–216. https://doi.org/10.1146/annurev.ecolsys.110308.120324.

Chong-Seng, K. M., N. A. J. Graham, and M. S. Pratchett. 2014. "Bottlenecks to coral recovery in the Seychelles." *Coral Reefs* 33(2), 449–461, https://doi.org/10.1007/s00338-014-1137-2.

Currey-Randall, M. Cappo, C. A. Simpfendorfer, N. F. Farabaugh, and M. R. Heupel. 2020. "Optimal soak times for Baited Remote Underwater Video Station surveys of reef-associated elasmobranchs." *PLoS ONE* 15(5). https://doi.org/10.1371/journal.pone.0231688.

Dixson, D. L., D. Abrego, and M. E. Hay. 2014. "Chemically mediated behavior of recruiting corals and fishes: A tipping point that may limit reef recovery." *Science* 345(6199), 892–897. https://doi.org/10.1126/science.1255057.

Eakin, C. M., H. P. A. Sweatman, and R. E. Brainard. 2019. "The 2014–2017 global-scale coral bleaching event: Insights and impacts." *Coral Reefs* 38, 539–545. https://doi.org/10.1007/s00338-019-01844-2.

Edwards, A. J. and E. D. Gomez. 2007. "Reef restoration concepts and guidelines: Making sensible management choices in the face of uncertainty." Coral Reef Targeted Research and Capacity Building for Management Programme.

Freeman, L. A. and S. E. Freeman. 2016. "Rapidly obtained ecosystem indicators from coral reef soundscapes." *Marine Ecology Progress Series* 561, 69–82. https://doi.org/10.3354/meps11938.

Frias-Torres, S. 2017. "Captive bred, adult giant clams survive restoration in the wild in Seychelles, Indian Ocean." *Frontiers in Marine Science* 4(APR), 1–12. https://doi.org/10.3389/fmars.2017.00097.

Frias-Torres, S., H. Goehlich, C. Reveret, and P. H. Montoya-Maya. 2015. "Reef fishes recruited at midwater coral nurseries consume biofouling and reduce cleaning time in Seychelles, Indian Ocean." *African Journal of Marine Science* 37(3), 421–426, https://doi.org/10.2989/1814232X.2015.1078259.

Frias-Torres, S., P. H. Montoya-Maya, and N. J. Shah. 2019. "Coral reef restoration toolkit: A field-oriented guide developed in the Seychelles Islands." Nature Seychelles. https://doi.org/10.31230/osf.io/8eua9.

Frias-Torres, S. and C. van de Geer. 2015. "Testing animal-assisted cleaning prior to transplantation in coral reef restoration." *PeerJ* (9), e1287. https://doi.org/10.7717/peerj.1287.

Gorlick, D., P. Atkins, and G. Losey. 1987. "Effect of cleaning by Labroides dimidiatus (Labridae) on an ectoparasite . . . ." *Copeia* (1), 41–45. http://www.jstor.org/stable/1446035.

Gorospe, K. D. and S. A. Karl. 2013. "Genetic relatedness does not retain spatial pattern across multiple spatial scales: Dispersal and colonization in the coral, Pocillopora damicornis." *Molecular Ecology* 22(14), 3721–3736. https://doi.org/10.1111/mec.12335.

Gössling, S. 2002. "Global environmental consequences of tourism." *Global Environmental Change*, 12(4), 283–302. https://doi.org/10.1016/S0959-3780(02)00044-4.

Graham, N. A. J., S. Jennings, M. A. MacNeil, D. Mouillot, and S. K. Wilson. 2015. "Predicting climate-driven regime shifts versus rebound potential in coral reefs." *Nature* 518(7537), 94–97. https://doi.org/10.1038/nature14140.

Graham, N. A. J., S. K. Wilson, S. Jennings, N. V. C. Polunin, J. P. Bijoux, and J. Robinson. 2006. "Dynamic fragility of oceanic coral reef ecosystems." *Proceedings of the National Academy of Sciences*, 103(22), 8425–8429. https://doi.org/10.1073/pnas.0600693103.

Graham, N. A. J., S. K. Wilson, S. Jennings, N. V. C. Polunin, J. Robinson, J. P. Bijoux, and T. M. Daw. 2007. "Lag effects in the impacts of mass coral bleaching on coral reef fish, fisheries, and ecosystems." *Conservation Biology* 21(5), 1291–1300. https://doi.org/10.1111/j.1523-1739.2007.00754.x.

Harris, A., S. Wilson, N. A. J. Graham, and C. Sheppard. 2014. "Scleractinian coral communities of the inner Seychelles 10 years after the 1998 mortality event." *Aquatic Conservation: Marine and Freshwater Ecosystems* 24(5), 667–679. https://doi.org/10.1002/aqc.2464.

Hoegh-Guldberg, O., D. Jacob, M. Bindi, S. Brown, I. Camilloni, A. Diedhiou, R. Djalante, et al. 2018. "Impacts of 1.5°C global warming on natural and human systems." In *Global warming of 1.5°C. An IPCC Special Report.* IPCC Secretariat.

Jackson, L. E., J. V. Barrie, D. L. Forbes, J. Shaw, G. K. Manson, and M.Schmidt. 2005. "Effects of the 26 December 2004 Indian Ocean Tsunami in the Republic of Seychelles." Report of the Canada-UNESCO Indian Ocean Tsunami Expedition 19 January–February 2005 (Issue Open File 4539).

Jennings, S., S. S. Marshall, and N. V. C. Polunin. 1996. "Seychelles' marine protected areas: Comparative structure and status of reef fish communities." *Biological Conservation* 75(3), 201–209. https://doi.org/10.1016/0006-3207(95)00081-X.

Johnson, M. E., C. Lustic, E. Bartels, I. B. Baums, D. S. Gilliam, L. Larson, D. Lirman, et al. 2011. "Caribbean acropora restoration guide: Best practices for propagation and population enhancement." The Nature Conservancy.

Kingsford, M. J., J. M. Leis, A. L. Shanks, K. C. Lindeman, S. G. Morgan, and J. Pineda. 2002. "Sensory environments, larval abilities and local self-recruitment." *Bulletin of Marine Science* 70(1), 309–340.

Levy, G., L. Shaish, A. Haim, and B. Rinkevich. 2010. "Mid-water rope nursery-testing design and performance of a novel reef restoration instrument." *Ecological Engineering* 36(4), 560–569. https://doi.org/10.1016/j.ecoleng.2009.12.003.

Losey, G. S., G. H. Balazs, and L. A. Privitera. 1994. "Cleaning symbiosis between the Wrasse, Thalassoma duperry, and the Green Turtle, Chelonia mydas." *Copeia* 1994(3), 684. https://doi.org/10.2307/1447184.

Mbije, N. E., E. Spanier, and B. Rinkevich. 2013. "A first endeavour in restoring denuded, post-bleached reefs in Tanzania." *Estuarine, Coastal and Shelf Science* 128, 41–51. https://doi.org/10.1016/j.ecss.2013.04.021.

Montoya-Maya, P. H., A. H. H. Macdonald, and M. H. Schleyer. 2014. "Estimation of size at first maturity in two South African coral species." *African Journal of Marine Science* 36(4), 513–516. https://doi.org/10.2989/1814232X.2014.980848.

Montoya-Maya, P. H., K. P. Smit, A. J. Burt, and S. Frias-Torres. 2016a. "Large-scale coral reef restoration could assist natural recovery in Seychelles, Indian Ocean." *Nature Conservation* 16, 1–17. http://natureconservation.pensoft.net/articles.php?id=8604.

Montoya-Maya, P. H., C. Reveret, S. Frias-Torres, K. Henri, and N. J. Shah. 2016b. "Coral gardening as a MPA management tool: A success story in the Republic of Seychelles (Abstract ID: 29441)." In: Book of Abstracts, 13th International Coral Reef Symposium, 19–24 June 2016, Honolulu, HI, USA.

Mumby, P. J. and R. S. Steneck. 2008. "Coral reef management and conservation in light of rapidly evolving ecological paradigms." *Trends in Ecology and Evolution* 23(10), 555–563. https://doi.org/10.1016/j.tree.2008.06.011.

Nakamura, M. and K. Sakai. 2010. "Spatiotemporal variability in recruitment around Iriomote Island, Ryukyu Archipelago, Japan: Implications for dispersal of spawning corals." *Marine Biology* 157(4), 801–810. https://doi.org/10.1007/s00227-009-1363-2.

Nedimyer, K., K. Gaines, S. Roach, C. R. Foundation, and G. Street. 2011. "Coral Tree Nursery ©: An innovative approach to growing corals in an ocean-based field nursery." 4(4), 442–446.

Obura, D. O. 2005. "Resilience and climate change: Lessons from coral reefs and bleaching in the Western Indian Ocean." *Estuarine, Coastal and Shelf Science*, 63(3), 353–372. https://doi.org/10.1016/j.ecss.2004.11.010.

O'Leary, J. K. and D. C. Potts. 2011. "Using hierarchical sampling to understand scales of spatial variation in early coral recruitment." *Coral Reefs* 30(4), 1013–1023. https://doi.org/10.1007/s00338-011-0789-4.

O'Shea, O. R., M. J. Kingsford, and J. Seymour. 2010. "Tide-related periodicity of manta rays and sharks to cleaning stations on a coral reef." *Marine and Freshwater Research* 61(1), 65–73. https://doi.org/10.1071/MF08301.

Rinkevich, B. 2006. "The coral gardening concept and the use of underwater nurseries." In: W. Precht (ed.), *Coral Reef Restoration Handbook* (pp. 291–301). CRC Press. https://doi.org/10.1201/9781420003796.ch16.

Ruppert, E. E., R. S. Fox, and R. D. Barnes. 2004. *Invertebrate Zoology: A Functional Evolutionary Approach*. Thomson-Brooks/Cole. https://books.google.com.co/books?id=A3opAQAAMAAJ.

Shafir, S. and B. Rinkevich. 2010a. "Integrated long term mid-water coral nurseries: A management instrument evolving into a floating ecosystem." *Mauritius Research Journal* 16, 365–379.

———. 2010b. "Constructing and managing nurseries for asexual rearing of corals." In: A. J. Edwards (ed.), *Reef Restoration Manual*. pp. 49–72. Coral Reef Targeted Research and Capacity Building for Management Program.

Shareef, R. and M. McAleer. 2008. "Modelling international tourism demand and uncertainty in Maldives and Seychelles: A portfolio approach." *Mathematics and Computers in Simulation* 78(2–3), 459–468. https://doi.org/10.1016/j.matcom.2008.01.025.

Sheppard, C., D. J. Dixon, M. Gourlay, A. Sheppard, and R. Payet. 2005. "Coral mortality increases wave energy reaching shores protected by reef flats: Examples from the Seychelles." *Estuarine, Coastal and Shelf Science*, 64(2–3), 223–234. https://doi.org/10.1016/j.ecss.2005.02.016.

Spalding, M. D., L. Burke, S. A. Wood, J. Ashpole, J. Hutchison, and P. zu Ermgassen. 2017. "Mapping the global value and distribution of coral reef tourism." *Marine Policy* 82(May), 104–113. https://doi.org/10.1016/j.marpol.2017.05.014.

Spalding, M. D. and G. E. Jarvis. 2002. "The impact of the 1998 coral mortality on reef fish communities in the Seychelles." *Marine Pollution Bulletin* 44(4), 309–321. https://doi.org/10.1016/S0025-326X(01)00281-8.

Spencer, T., K. A. Teleki, C. Bradshaw, and M. D. Spalding. 2000. "Coral bleaching in the southern Seychelles during the 1997–1998 Indian Ocean Warm Event." *Marine Pollution Bulletin* 40(7), 569–586. https://doi.org/10.1016/S0025-326X(00)00026-6.

Sponaugle, S., R. K. Cowen, A. L. Shanks, S. G. Morgan, J. M. Leis, J. Pineda, G. W. Boehlert, M. J. Kingsford, et al. 2002. "Predicting self-recruitment in marine populations: Biophysical correlates and mechanisms." *Bulletin of Marine Science* 70(1), 341–375.

Suding, K., E. Higgs, M. Palmer, J. B. Callicott, C. B. Anderson, M. Baker, J. J. Gutrich, et al. 2015. "Committing to ecological restoration." *Science*, 348(6235), 638–640. https://doi.org/10.1126/science.aaa4216.

Suzuki, G., T. Hayashibara, Y. Shirayama, and H. Fukami. 2008. "Evidence of species-specific habitat selectivity of Acropora corals based on identification of new recruits by two molecular markers." *Marine Ecology Progress Series* 355, 149–159. https://doi.org/10.3354/meps07253.

Unsworth, J. D., d. Hesley, M. D'Alessandro, D. Lirman. 2020. Outplanting optimized: Developing a more efficient coral attachment technique using Portland cement. *Restoration Ecology* https://doi.org/10.1111/rec.13299.

Vermeij, M. J. A. 2005. "Substrate composition and adult distribution determine recruitment patterns in a Caribbean brooding coral." *Marine Ecology Progress Series* 295, 123–133.

Wang, B., X. Luo, Y.-M. Yang, W. Sun, M. A. Cane, W. Cai, S. W. Yeh, and J. Liu. 2019. "Historical change of El Niño properties sheds light on future changes of extreme El Niño." *Proceedings of the National Academy of Sciences* 116(45), 22512–22517. https://doi.org/10.1073/pnas.1911130116.

WoRMS Editorial Board. 2016. World Register of Marine Species. Available from http://www.marinespecies.org at VLIZ. Accessed 2016-12-21. doi:10.14284/170.

13

ACTIVE CORAL REEF RESTORATION IN EILAT, ISRAEL: RECONNOITERING THE LONG-TERM PROSPECTUS

Yael B. Horoszowski-Fridman and Buki Rinkevich

ABSTRACT

Over the last decades worldwide, coral reef degradation and the failures of traditional management approaches have raised the need for innovative active reef restoration approaches in order to accelerate local, regional, and global-scale solutions to this pressing ecological calamity. The *coral gardening* notion, a two-phase practice adapted from forestation principles and methodologies, has been applied on a small scale in a highly degraded reef site in Eilat (Red Sea, Israel), in an attempt to test the long-term impact of repeated transplantation measures as a novel coral reef restoration tool. Nursery-bred colonies of seven locally common branching species (*Stylophora pistillata, Pocillopora damicornis, Acropora variabilis, A. humilis, A. pharaonis, A. valida, Millepora dichotoma*) and one massive species (*Dipsastraea favus*) were transplanted during three transplantation sessions (1.5 year intervals) onto six denuded coral knolls. The 1,400 farmed transplants were secured to the knolls using an underwater drilling methodology that increased transplantation efficiency, as compared to gluing/cementing approaches, and enabled the transplantation on vertical facets for maximum coverage of the target area. Over six years of in situ detailed monitoring and almost 15 years prospectus from initiation, revealed the capacity of nursery-bred transplants to acclimate and thrive in the new environment of a degraded reef. First, no signs of stress that could be related to the relocation of coral colonies from the protective coral nursery into the degraded site were observed, and over the long term, the nursery-bred transplants had slightly lower survival rates than the highly adapted, naturally growing colonies at the experimental site. Preliminary results suggest that repeated transplantations (i.e., adding transplants onto plots upon which coral transplants are already present) may enhance transplant survival. Despite the new challenging conditions of the degraded reef area, the farmed transplants continued to grow at enhanced rates, characteristic of those recorded in the coral nursery. In addition, *S. pistillata* transplants exhibited higher reproductive capacities than the

(continued)

naturally growing colonies at the reef that were maintained for at least eight reproductive seasons post-transplantation (the monitoring period). Though fish corallivory had inflicted damages to the branching species transplants (primarily shortly after their transplantation), causing tissue losses, colony breakage, and in some cases, even coral detachment, mortality was not associated with fish attacks, and most of the colonies had regenerated lost parts. In contrast, fish predation was highly detrimental for the massive D. *Favus* transplants and resulted in fast mortality. In order to reduce post-transplant detachment resulting from fish attacks and aggravated by scuba diving activity at the restoration site, we replaced the former nursing methodology of attaching nubbins onto plastic pegs with the insertion of nubbins into wall anchors, a method proven as being highly successful in substantially reducing post-transplantation coral detachment. Due to the ecosystem engineering properties of corals, the nursery-grown transplants created, in the transplantation site, new living spaces for reef fauna, colonized by an increasing number of coral-dwelling invertebrates and fish. The long-term successful integration of nursery-grown transplants in a highly impacted reef site, the high reproductive outputs of the farmed transplants, and their ability to provide new habitats for coral-associated organisms, all reveal the ecological engineering potential of the marine silviculture approach to generate new reef zones, reinforce coral reproduction, and support the biodiversity of degrading reefs. In addition, major project activities (e.g., creation stocks of corals, nursery maintenance, and transplantation) were assisted by local community volunteers—incorporating reef restoration into citizen science and establishing nonprofessional groups of participants with basic knowledge in coral reef biology and ecology.

INTRODUCTION

The worldwide decline of coral reefs over the past decades, despite extensive conservation efforts, has prompted the development of active reef restoration measures aiming to accelerate recovery and to prevent the loss of habitat structure and ecosystem function (Fine et al. 2019; Randall et al. 2020; Rinkevich 2020). Most reef restoration activities rely on coral transplantation acts, thanks to the fast replacement of lost populations, in order to circumvent the slow natural regeneration processes, dependent on natural coral recruitment (Young et al. 2012; Lohr et al. 2015; Ladd et al. 2018). Of the emerging restoration techniques, the *gardening coral reefs* approach (Rinkevich 1995, 2000, 2005a, 2014, 2015, 2017, 2019a, b, 2020) is gaining increased attention as it overcomes major drawbacks encountered with early restoration initiatives that were based on transplanting whole colonies or coral fragments directly from donor to denuded sites (Lirman and Schopmeyer 2016). The coral gardening methodologies and concepts are derived from forestation (Rinkevich 1995; Epstein et al. 2003; Horoszowski-Fridman and Rinkevich 2017), incorporating silviculture principles and theories into the underwater forestation, forming a coral restoration toolbox that is centered on ecological engineering tools (Rinkevich 1995, 2000, 2005a, 2014, 2015, 2019a, b, 2020; Epstein and Rinkevich 2001; Mbije et al. 2010, 2013; Linden and Rinkevich 2011, 2017; Horoszowski-Fridman et al. 2011, 2015; Chou 2016; Horoszowski-Fridman and Rinkevich 2017; Rachmilovitz and Rinkevich 2017; Linden et al. 2019; Rosado et al. 2019). It consists of two successive phases: (1) the generation of pools of coral colonies from coral fragments/nubbins that are reared in underwater coral nurseries to plantable size and (2) the transplantation of nursery-bred colonies onto degraded reefs.

Due to the protected environmental conditions in the coral nurseries, the nubbins that are clipped off of donor colonies, corals of opportunity, or sexual recruits can survive and flourish (Epstein et al. 2001; Shafir et al. 2001, 2006a, b, 2009; Bongiorni et al. 2003, 2011; Monty et al. 2006; Shafir and Rinkevich 2008, 2010; Shaish et al. 2008; Levy et al. 2010; Mbije et al. 2010; Linden and Rinkevich 2011, 2017; Omori 2011; Guest et al. 2014; Ng and Chou 2014; Barton et al. 2017; Linden et al. 2019), and the farmed colonies can be further pruned to alleviate collection pressure from degraded wild stocks. This approach is suitable for common and rare/endangered species alike (Lirman et al. 2010), enabling the fast establishment of large, sustainable stocks of new corals that are amenable for restoration (Rinkevich 2014; Schopmeyer et al. 2017). The transplantation of healthy, large colonies rather than coral fragments can increase the transplants' ability to acclimate on degraded reefs and will potentially contribute to local coral reproduction, thereby contributing to the ecosystem's services, preventing phase shifts and species loss, and reinforcing natural reef recovery.

This restoration act was designed to test long-term gardening prospectus on a highly degraded reef area in the northern part of the Red Sea (Eilat, Israel; 29°30′N; 34°57′E), assessing nursery-grown corals' ability to acclimate and thrive on degraded reefs. The coral reef of Eilat, once classified among the most diverse reefs of the world, has been degrading over the past five decades as a result of the combined effects of global climate changes and anthropogenic activities (Rinkevich 2005b). In particular, the rapid development of Eilat city, accompanied by increased loads of pollution, accidental sewage spills and overflows, industrial installations, and shoreline modifications, have all contributed significantly to the reef's deterioration (Zakai and Chadwick-Furman 2002; Rinkevich 2005b). An additional threat causing extensive coral damage stems from the flourishing tourist industry established in Eilat, that has led to an intensive recreational diving pressure (of the world's most dived reefs with over 250,000 dives per year on a less than 12 km shoreline; Zakai and Chadwick-Furman 2002).

Farmed coral colonies of seven locally common species were used to restore highly degraded coral knolls at the northern part of Eilat Bay. The farmed colonies originated from Eilat's underwater coral nursery floating at a depth of 6–8 m (12–14 m above the seafloor), away from the reef and recreational activities (Shafir et al. 2006a, b; Shafir and Rinkevich 2008, 2010; Figure 13.1(a), (b)). The gentle sway of the nursery in the water column results in enhanced water flow around the developing colonies, increasing oxygenation and planktonic supply while reducing the effects of sedimentation (Rinkevich 2006). Due to the several kilometers distances between the nursery and the closest natural reefs and as a result of the intensive care during nursery rearing (Figure 13.1(b)), colonies in the nursery were maintained under the most favorable conditions for coral survival and growth (Rinkevich 2006; Shafir et al. 2006a, b; Horoszowski-Fridman et al. 2015). The assigned transplantation site at the natural reef, named *Dekel Beach*, is located 2.7 km south of the coral nursery between the commercial and naval ports of Eilat. This site (imposed on us by Israeli Ministry of the Environment's permit) is under intense and continuous anthropogenic pressures and subjected to particularly high levels of recreational diving activities due to its proximity to a popular diving center (Figure 13.2). The first 18 m depth of this reef is characterized by a moderate sandy slope with scattered, emerged, hard-bottom knolls populated by various coral coverage, from entirely bare to almost-covered knolls (though the latter are quite rare).

Figure 13.1 Coral farming at the Eilat midwater, floating coral nursery: (a) trays with coral fragments glued on plastic pegs at the initiation of coral culture and (b) trays with fully developed branching colonies, reared at the coral nursery from small fragments. Intensive care is provided to the growing colonies during farming and the nursery-bred colonies are frequently inspected for coral competitors and predators that are removed when spotted.

The nursery-bred colonies were transplanted in three sessions in 1.5 year intervals. During the first session, 554 colonies of the two branching species, *Stylophora pistillata* and *Pocillopora damicornis*, were transplanted onto five large denuded knolls at a depth of 7–13 m, aligned from north to south on a 200 m stretch (Horoszowski-Fridman et al. 2015). A further 300 farmed colonies of six branching coral species, *S. pistillata*, *P. damicornis*, *Acropora variabilis*, *A. humilis*, *A. pharaonis*, and *A. valida*, were transplanted during the second transplantation session onto two of the five previously transplanted knolls. In addition, we transplanted 10 colonies of massive species *Dipsastraea favus* and the scleractinian hydrozoan *Millepora dichotoma* (n = 10) to explore technical transplantation aspects. At the third transplantation session, 530 colonies of the aforementioned branching species were split between the two repeatedly transplanted knolls and a sixth bare knoll, not yet transplanted. A long-term monitoring act tracked the performance of transplants at their new degraded reef environment, the recruited coral-dwelling invertebrates and fish, and the contribution of *S. pistillata* transplants to larval pools.

Figure 13.2 Intense anthropogenic footprint induced at Dekel Beach, Eilat: (a), (b), (c) imported sand, artificially deployed onto the seashore for touristic purposes; (d) immediately upon deployment, the sand is suspended in the water column and drifts away from the beach; (e) one month after sand deployment, the sand is still suspended in the water column, causing turbidity observed as deep as 15 m; and (f) high levels of recreational diving activity at Dekel Beach, which is a popular diving center.

TECHNIQUES AND METHODS

The farmed corals were first generated asexually by repruning the initial nursery-grown coral stock that was already established at the coral nursery (Shafir et al. 2006a, b; Shafir and Rinkevich 2008, 2010; Horoszowski-Fridman et al. 2015). The donor colonies were pruned by electrician's wire cutters providing fragments of 1–5 cm in size. The fragments generated for the first transplantation session were all glued onto flat surfaces of plastic pegs (plastic nails 9 cm long with 2 cm diameter flat surface heads; Shafir et al. 2006a, b). However, following a post-transplantation detachment problem that was noticed at the first session, a new rearing support, made up of plastic wall anchors (8–12 mm diameter), was tested in addition to pegs at the next two transplantations. These fragments were partially inserted into the hollow expansion anchors and, when needed, further secured with a small amount of epoxy glue (AquaMend; Figure 13.3(a)). The new colonies were reared in the nursery on trays constructed of 50 × 30 cm PVC frames with stretched plastic nets (0.25 cm^2 mesh size) according to the protocol of Shafir et al. (2006a, b; Figure 13.3(b), (c), (d)). Coral competitors and predators were frequently removed, and the numbers of colonies per tray was adjusted every three to four months to regulate the space between the corals and to optimize growth conditions. The farmed colonies were maintained at the nursery for a period of eight to 24 months, growing back into fully developed branching colonies (Figure 13.3(d)).

Before transplantation, the nursery-bred corals were prepared for transplantation by a team of volunteers (Figure 13.4(a)). The plastic pegs and wall anchors were cleaned of settling algae and other sessile fouling organisms (Figure 13.4(b)) using forceps, dish-pads, and scratching dental tools—and coral predators, such as *Drupella* and *Coralliophila* gastropod snails, were

Figure 13.3 Generation and maintenance of new coral colonies at Eilat's coral nursery: (a) new fragments of *Stylophora pistillata* pruned from the previously established nursery coral stock and reared on expansion wall anchors. The fragments are partially inserted into the anchors and further secured with a small amount of epoxy glue. Periodically, (b) fouling organisms will grow on the rearing support; (c) they are removed and cleaned using dish-pads and various dental scratching tools. (d) Coral predators are removed and parts of colonies exhibiting partial mortality are trimmed off the colonies using electrician's wire cutters, while colonies grow back into fully developed branching colonies.

removed when they were found. The prepared colonies were then arranged on trays placed in plastic containers that were filled with seawater and transferred by boat from the coral nursery to the restoration site (Figure 13.4(c), (d).

In order to evaluate the influence of transplantation on the coral transplants' growth, a subset of colonies in the first transplantation session were incubated prior to outplanting with 15 mg/L Alizarin Red S for 12 hours (from sunrise to sunset). They were immersed in aerated tanks that were placed in plastic containers with continuous water flow to maintain constant water temperature during Alizarin incubation and shed by plastic nets of 0.25 cm^2 mesh size to avoid excessive radiation between 10 a.m. to 2 p.m. Some of the incubated colonies were kept at the nursery after transplantation, serving as controls.

The colonies were transplanted onto the denuded knolls by scuba diver volunteers. The 3D structure of the bare knolls at the restoration site necessitated the development of a transplantation technique that enables coral transplantation not only on flat surfaces but also on vertical facets, hardly feasible with traditional gluing/cementing techniques. Therefore, we explored a new transplantation methodology that secured nursery-rearing supports (pegs/anchors) within holes made in the knoll substrates (Horoszowski-Fridman et al. 2015). Holes were drilled in

Figure 13.4 Preparation of the farmed corals at the nursery before their transfer to the restoration site: (a) trays with grown nursery-bred corals are selected for transplantation and taken for preparation; (b) the nursery-rearing supports (peg/anchor) of the selected colonies are cleaned of fouling organisms, and the colonies are scattered on the tray and checked for the presence of coral predators that are removed when found, then the corals are arranged on trays for transfer to the restoration site; (c) the coral trays are placed in plastic containers filled with seawater for boat transfer; and (d) the farmed colonies are then transferred from the coral nursery to the restoration site by boat.

the knolls' hard substrates using pneumatic drills powered by scuba tanks (Figure 13.5(a)). A minimal amount of epoxy glue (AquaMend) was placed at the bottom of each hole and the nursery-rearing supports were inserted in the holes, ensuring a strong attachment of the corals to the substrata and a close contact between the colony and the rock (Figure 13.5(b), (c)). Each colony was tagged with a numbered plastic strip for future monitoring.

Figure 13.5 The transplantation procedure: (a) holes drilled in the knolls' hard substrates using a pneumatic drill powered by a scuba tank; (b) the nursery-rearing support of an *Acropora variabilis* transplant is inserted into a drilled hole, resulting in close contact between the colony and the rock; and (c) a bare knoll covered with nursery-grown coral transplants.

Each volunteer prepared up to 15 colonies per hour during the nursery-preparation phase prior to coral transplantation. Transplantation operations at the restoration site, including drilling, epoxy glue mixing, colony tagging, and colony anchoring, lasted one to two minutes per transplanted colony. A 12 L aluminum scuba tank compressed to a pressure of 200 bars enabled the drilling of ca 30 holes in the hard-calcareous knolls' substrates. Simultaneous drilling and outplanting was found as the most efficient way of transplanting the colonies. Whenever large substrate areas were drilled prior to the insertion of the colonies, there was a problem with spotting the predrilled holes.

MONITORING

Monitoring was conducted monthly in situ by scuba divers during the first year of onset, every two to four months for the next six years (Figure 13.6), and occasionally in the following years, with visual observations supplemented by underwater digital photography. The monitored parameters included coral survival, detachment rates, partial colony mortality, coral growth, the number of fish bites, and the presence of corallivorous gastropods. Monitoring also included a follow-up of key coral-dwelling invertebrates and fish residing in the colonies and new recruits. A group of naturally growing corals of the same species and approximate sizes as transplants was tagged and monitored in parallel to the farmed transplants, serving as on-site controls.

Growth was monitored and compared by sampling the Alizarin Red S transplants and nursery controls 18 months following transplantation. The colonies were immersed overnight in a 50:50 freshwater and bleach (sodium hypochlorite) solution to eliminate the tissue, washed, and left to dry. They were weighed and measured for their width, length, and height with an electronic digital caliper. The new skeletal additions appearing after the Alizarin red marks

Figure 13.6 Monitoring of nursery-grown transplants and naturally growing colonies by in situ visual observations—recording coral survival, detachment, partial colony mortality, coral growth, fish bites, and coral-dwelling invertebrates and fish, as well as gastropod corallivorous in the colonies.

were cut, and the colonies were weighed and measured again, allowing the calculation of colony diameter and ecological volume of both the initial and the grown structures (Horoszowski-Fridman et al. 2015).

Reproduction of *S. pistillata* transplants, a brooding hermaphroditic coral species, was monitored and compared to naturally grown colonies at the restoration site during six reproductive seasons (within a period of eight years) following the first transplantation session. Planula larvae traps were placed on a total of 290 transplants and 126 natal controls during the peak spawning months (April to June; Amar et al. 2007; Linden et al. 2018; Shefy et al. 2018; Figure 13.7(a)). Each plankton trap consisted of a plankton net sleeve of 120 µm mesh size glued to a plastic funnel, which was connected by its tip to a plastic container (Amar et al. 2007; Figure 13.7(b)). The center of the container's lid was replaced by a plankton net similar to the trap's sleeve. During collection, the devices were placed over the colonies from dusk to dawn, trapping the released planulae in the plastic containers. The containers were drained of water, concentrating the planulae over the lid, and planulae were washed out into a wide petri dish. They were counted under a stereomicroscope in the field and released back to the water column above the transplanted knolls (Horoszowski-Fridman et al. 2011).

Figure 13.7 Monitoring of the reproductive outputs of *Stylophora pistillata* colonies at Dekel Beach. (a) Planula larvae collection devices placed over nursery-grown transplants and naturally growing colonies on a transplanted coral knoll. (b) A closer look of a collection device placed over a transplanted colony on the restored knoll. The device is made of a plankton net sleeve glued to a plastic funnel, connected by its tip to a plastic container, in which the released planulae are trapped.

COMMUNITY INVOLVEMENT, VOLUNTEERS, AND CITIZEN SCIENCE

Volunteers served as a substantial part of this restoration act. At the coral nursery, volunteers actively participated in the fragmentation of donor corals, assisted in fragments' rearing and general maintenance (e.g., removal of competing algae and sessile organisms from nursery trays, cleaning corals' supports, spotting and removal of coral predator gastropods, etc.), and helped in the preparation of farmed colonies for transplantation (Figure 13.8(a), (b)). Volunteer participants also assisted in the transplantation procedures at the restoration site, including drilling the substrate, colony attachment, and colony tagging (Figure 13.8(c), (d)). All of the participants were qualified scuba divers and were mainly composed of diving instructors from local diving centers, undergraduate students of the Israel maritime college (Ruppin Academic Center), research students of other disciplines, and enthusiastic scuba divers of the local community or visiting tourists. The participants were given on-site training and since the project employed mostly low-tech activities, their performance and outputs quickly equaled that of

Figure 13.8 Volunteer involvement in all stages of the project: (a) volunteers participating in coral rearing and maintenance at the coral nursery, (b) participants preparing farmed colonies for transplantation prior to their transfer from the coral nursery, (c) local diving instructors participating in coral transplantation—drilling holes in the knoll with a pneumatic drill, and (d) a group of scuba diving volunteers transplanting nursery-grown *Pocillopora damicornis* colonies.

scientific experts. The constant involvement of volunteers in this study resulted in high economic value savings by reducing substantial workforce costs that are normally associated with restoration activities (Edwards et al. 2010a; Rinkevich 2017). Their high performance and the lack of a need for extensive training indicates that reef restoration by the gardening methodology is providing an excellent platform for citizen science (see Hesley et al. 2017), decreasing restoration costs, alleviating workforce bottlenecks, and further engaging local communities in the conservation and restoration of marine resources (see also Mbije et al. 2010).

The involvement of volunteers in the study also created educational opportunities by establishing nonprofessional groups of participants with basic knowledge in coral reef biology and ecology and, most important, increasing sensitization to reef degradation and nature conservation. In addition, the location of the project in front of a diving center generated much interest among the scuba instructors and tourist divers and helped raise public awareness of reef degradation. Explanatory posters were hung at the diving center, informing the public about the ongoing project at the site (Figure 13.9). The diving instructors increased their attention toward the improvement of underwater behaviors of trained divers (e.g., more emphasis on buoyancy skills during training, enhancing environmental awareness at the pre-dive briefings). Exposing the reef users, such as the scuba diving and snorkeling communities, to restoration activities, increases their commitment to nature conservation, as was seen during this project.

Figure 13.9 (see facing page) An explanatory poster (in Hebrew) informing the public about the ongoing project at Dekel Beach. The poster depicts a brief background on reef degradation and the coral gardening methodology, explaining the rationale behind the research. The content is aimed at engaging divers and asking for their cooperation. The text on the poster reads: "Attention, please, we're planting! The reef in Eilat has been degrading for the past 40 years. As part of innovative research, we apply a novel active reef restoration approach to rehabilitate the reef. Similar to forest restoration, the first phase consists of rearing new coral colonies in a coral nursery, where the colonies are protected from predators and reef users. In the second phase, the farmed corals are transferred back to the degraded reef to fill in the voids that have opened in it. The transplanted corals create a new living space, attracting a wide variety of fish and reef organisms. This process leads to the formation of a live and diverse reef. Transplanting nursery-farmed corals was conducted for the first time in the world *here, at Dekel Beach*. This project's success will constitute a substantial breakthrough for reef restoration. Dear diver, *YOU* have an important role in the project's success!!! Diving in close proximity to corals harms them: *Keep a distance of at least one meter from the experimental knolls! *Do not touch the corals or the knolls! Touching corals damages them. *Watch your fins! A small kick can break the coral. *Pay attention to buoyancy! Swimming next to the sand and kicking it can cover and kill the corals. Thank you for your cooperation! Enjoy the dive."

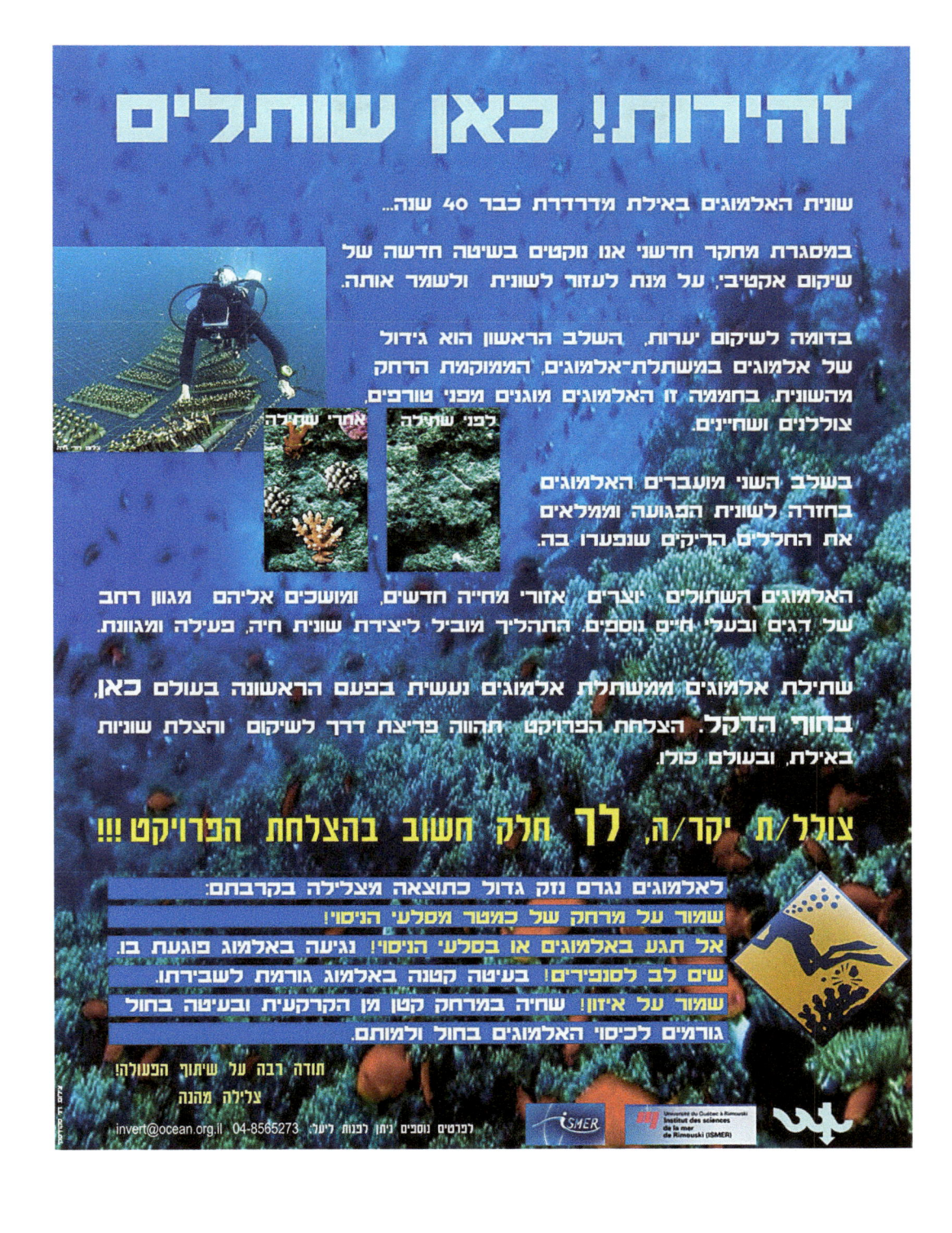

Active Coral Reef Restoration In Eilat, Israel: Reconnoitering the Long-Term Prospectus

MAJOR OUTCOMES AND DISCUSSION

This study reveals a simple transplantation approach, yet a very important technical improvement—the insertion of nursery-raised corals into predrilled holes, a process that increased transplantation efficiency (30 transplants/hour) compared to the commonly used gluing/cementing methods (five to six transplants/hour; Edwards et al. 2010b). It further enabled the transplantation of colonies on vertical facets of the substrate that are highly inconvenient with the traditional gluing techniques, allowing maximum coverage of the restored area. This method does not require any prior preparation of the substrate (e.g., scrubbing with a wire brush; Dizon et al. 2008), thus reducing the time of work while narrowing damages that could be inflicted on the substrate adjacent to the transplants.

The nursery-bred transplants have shown the capacity to acclimate to the new environment following their relocation from the protective coral nursery conditions. Over the short term, no signs of stress that could be related to the transfer of corals or their manipulation during the transplantation were observed—a result supported by the survivorship rates during the first four months post-transplantation (exceeding 95% for all species in three transplantation sessions), equalizing the survival rates of naturally growing colonies at the site (Horoszowski-Fridman et al. 2015; and unpublished). Over the long term, the nursery-bred transplants had slightly lower survival rates as compared to the natal colonies [first transplantation: 32% in transplants (n = 554) vs. 43% in natal colonies (n = 76) after 6 years; second transplantation: 48% in transplants (n = 300) vs. 50% in natal colonies (n = 103) after 4.5 years; third transplantation: 47% in transplants (n = 488) vs. 66% in natal colonies (n = 72) after 3.2 years; all species and all knolls pooled together; unpublished]. It should be noted, however, that just the opposite of the natal colonies which represent the most successful naturally recruited genotypes and are the only survivors of years of anthropogenic pressures at Dekel Beach, the farmed transplants were pampered under improved environmental conditions at the coral nursery, thus encountering environmental stressors only after transplantation. Yet, since none of the transplanted colonies originated from the natural reef, each surviving transplant is a net addition to the local coral populations.

As early as one hour after transplantation, the transplants attracted high attention from local fish, causing numerous fish bites that were inflicted by Scaridae and Chaetodon species (Horoszowski-Fridman et al. 2015; Figure 13.10(a), (b), (c)). These fish attacks removed various portions of the colonies, from a single portion of a branch to all branches of a colony (up to approximately 90% of the colony's volume), leaving only the basal part (Figure 13.10(d), (e)). In some cases, the intense fish corallivory even led to the detachment of transplants from the plastic-peg supports. However, with time, most damaged corals undertook regeneration processes and regained colony spatial complexity (Figure 13.10(f)). It was further recorded that the mortality of branching species was not linked to fish predation (Horoszowski-Fridman et al. 2015), while the pilot transplantation with the massive *D. Favus* revealed, within one-month of post-transplantation, the deaths of four out of the 10 transplants following parrotfish attacks that removed tissue and substantial parts of the colony's skeleton (Figure 13.11(a), (b), (c)) and three colony detachments. Four months post-transplantation, all of the remaining colonies were grazed and dead. In *Millepora dichotoma* transplants, the coral-associated fauna was the target for corallivory fish, further resulting in colony detachment (Figure 13.11(d), (e)).

Scuba diving was another factor causing coral detachment, due to contact by divers, scuba gear, and fins with the transplanted knolls that became points of attraction. Up to 10 times

Figure 13.10 Fish attacks on nursery-grown transplants at Dekel Beach: (a) a *Chlorurus gibbus* parrotfish biting nursery-grown coral transplants on a restored knoll; (b) a *Chaetodon austriacus* attacking *Acropora* transplants; (c) *Chaetodon paucifasciatus* nibbling the tissue of a *Dipsastraea favus* transplant; (d) branches of a *Stylophora pistillata* transplant broken by a parrotfish and scattered on the knoll next to the colony; (e) an *S. pistillata* transplant that lost most of its branches as a result of parrotfish corallivory; and (f) the complete regeneration of a damaged *S. pistillata* colony following fish bites—the coral tissue grew and covered the broken skeleton.

enhanced detachment was recorded for the transplants, compared to naturally growing colonies (Horoszowski-Fridman et al. 2015). Transplants were attached to plastic pegs by a thin layer of calcium carbonate, thus more susceptible to detachment, leaving just the basal pegs firmly attached to the knoll. To solve this issue, in the following transplantation sessions, we used wall anchors with partly inserted fragments, enabling further extension of the coral skeleton on the wall anchors, firmly embedding the anchors within coral skeletons (Figure 13.12(a), (b)). This resulted in significantly reduced detachment losses (<5% detachment with anchors vs. 18–22% with pegs, seven post-transplantation months; Figure 13.12(c), (d)).

Despite the stressed conditions encountered at the transplanted reef, the farmed colonies maintained enhanced growth rates and reproductive output at the same levels as at the coral nursery (Horoszowski-Fridman et al. 2011, 2015). *S. pistillata* and *P. damicornis* transplants showed an average of 2.3- and 1.8-fold annual increase in ecological volumes, respectively, at Dekel Beach, which is the same rates as the colonies at the coral nursery, where they are maintained under ideal conditions (Horoszowski-Fridman et al. 2015; Figure 13.13). *S. pistillata* transplants further revealed more enhanced reproductive activities than natal colonies. A higher percentage of transplants released planula larvae (91±2.1% transplants vs. 34±7.6% natal colonies, a multiyear average for six examined reproductive seasons), shedding 2.6–22.5 times more planulae per colony compared to natal colonies, throughout the studied period (11.6±1.8 planulae/transplant vs. 1.5±0.3 planulae/natal colony; Horoszowski-Fridman et al. 2011; 2020).

Figure 13.11 Fish attacks on *Dipsastraea* and *Millepora* farmed transplants: (a) a *Chlorurus gibbus* parrotfish attacking a *Dipsastraea favus* transplant, removing coral tissue and substantial parts of the colony's skeleton; (b) a close look at a *D. favus* transplant, partially grazed by fish that have also crashed some of its skeleton; (c) the bare white skeleton of a transplanted *D. favus* colony after the whole tissue was consumed by fish within two days after its transplantation; (d) nursery-grown *Millepora dichotoma* transplants harboring *Pteria* bivalves (red circles); and (e) an *M. dichotoma* transplant detached from its peg (red arrows) as a result of fish predation on an associated *Pteria* bivalve (red circle) that was attached to the colony.

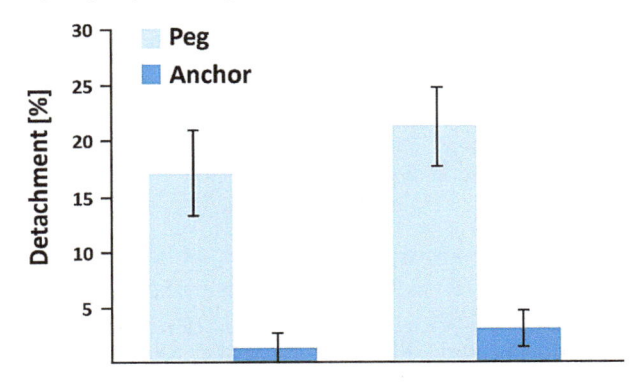

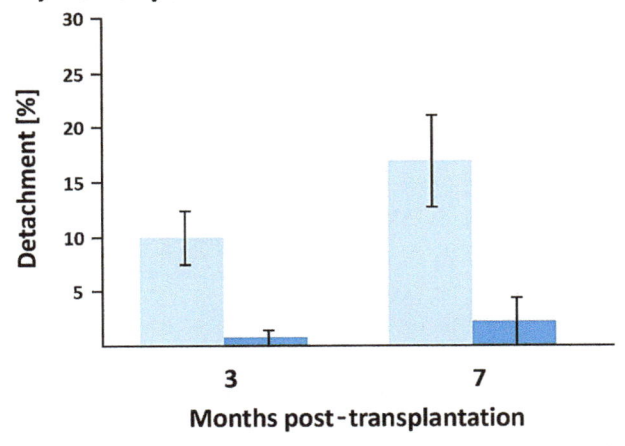

Figure 13.12 Comparison of post-transplantation detachment from two nursery-rearing supports: (a) a *Stylophora pistillata* transplant reared on a plastic peg; (b) an *Acropora variabilis* transplant reared on an expansion wall anchor; graphs depicting the detachment from pegs and wall anchors in (c) *S. pistillata* and (d) *Pocillopora damicornis* transplants after three and seven months post-transplantation.

Figure 13.13 The growth of a farmed *Pocillopora damicornis* transplant, 18 months after transplantation onto the knoll, revealed by Alizarin Red S staining. The pink Alizarin marks in the coral's skeleton (pointed out by red arrows in the image on the right) indicate the colony's dimensions prior to transplantation (left). The white portions located above the Alizarin stain (right) are products of growth at the restoration site.

The transplantation of nursery-grown corals further stimulated reef fauna assemblages (Figure 13.14), probably by the creation of new ecological niches available for colonization by coral-associated invertebrates and fish, and with time, increasing numbers of coral-dwelling organisms were recorded (Horoszowski-Fridman et al. 2015). This included numerous invertebrate species such as *Trapezia*, *Cymo*, and *Tetralia* crabs, *Spirobranchus* worms, *Alpheus* shrimp, and *Lithophaga* bivalves (Figure 13.15(a), (b), (c)), as well as various coral-dwelling fish species such as *Gobiodon*, *Dascyllus*, *Chromis*, and *Pseudochromis* (Figure 13.15(d), (e), (f), (g)).

Figure 13.14 The impact of transplants on reef fauna: (a) a bare zone of a degraded knoll prior to its coverage by *Acropora* transplants; (b) a few days after transplantation; (c) three months after transplantation; and (d) one year after transplantation. The addition of the farmed transplants onto the degraded knoll created new ecological niches that, with time, were colonized by an increasing number of coral-dwelling fish.

Active Coral Reef Restoration In Eilat, Israel: Reconnoitering the Long-Term Prospectus 359

Figure 13.15 Coral-associated invertebrates and fish observed in nursery-bred *Stylophora*, *Pocillopora*, and *Acropora* transplants at Dekel Beach: (a) *Spirobranchus* (Annelida) in *Pocillopora*; (b) *Cymo* sp., a decapod crustacean in *Stylophora*; (c) *Trapezia cymodoce*, a decapod crustacean in *Pocillopora*; (d) a young *Dascyllus trimaculatus* in *Pocillopora*; (e) several fish species (*Dascyllus marginatus*, *Gobiodon citrinus*, *Chromis flavaxilla*) inhabiting the living space of an *Acropora* transplant; (f) *Dascyllus marginatus* in *Stylophora*; and (g) schools of *Chromis viridis* in *Acropora* transplants.

The influence of the farmed transplants on the abundance and distribution of reef-dwelling species reflects the ecosystem engineering abilities (Jones et al. 1994) of these branching coral species, by modifying the biological, chemical, and physical environments (Wild et al. 2011; Horoszowski-Fridman et al. 2015, 2017; Rinkevich 2020). We also documented improved survivorship in the repeated transplanted knolls [74% (n = 172) vs. 31% (n = 316) survival after 3.2 years of repeated vs. single transplantation acts; all species pooled together; unpublished]. This resembles silviculture approaches, where plantation of various trees and plants are often used as first steps for changing the physical and chemical conditions of degraded sites, facilitating the establishment of subsequent transplantations (Horoszowski-Fridman et al. 2017).

CONCLUSIONS

We urgently need novel restoration approaches to accelerate recovery trajectories and sustain reef populations. This long-term monitoring (>6 years; sporadically up to 15 years) of 1,400 nursery-bred coral colonies, transplanted on a highly disturbed reef zone in Eilat, has shown promising, long-term results (Figure 13.16). The farmed colonies were capable of acclimating, thriving, growing, and reproducing following their transition from the near-idyllic nursery conditions to the real degraded reef environment. The farmed corals continued to grow on the reef at enhanced rates, similar to those documented at the coral nursery. In addition, they have shown higher reproductive outputs compared to natal colonies, maintained for at least eight years following transplantation to the challenging reef conditions. Together, this may reveal the possible enduring impacts of nursery conditions on the fitness and ecological traits of the transplants, an aspect that should be further investigated. Moreover, the augmented reproduction of nursery-grown transplants highlights their ecological engineering capacity to increase natural reef resilience by contributing to the local larval pool for reseeding degraded reefs. The presence of the nursery-grown transplants added onto the degraded zone has also created new living spaces at the reef (Figure 13.16), which were quickly colonized by coral-dwelling organisms, increasing the number of coral-obligatory invertebrates and fish on restored knolls. Thus, coral transplantation not only restores coral community but further enhances the whole biodiversity, owning to the ecosystem engineering capacity of coral transplants.

The marine silviculture approach has surfaced as an effective ecological engineering method to generate new reef areas and to support reef-associated communities at degrading reef locations. With the maturation of the methodology and the advances in its practical aspects, the time has come to deepen our understanding on conceptual challenges that have emerged in reef restoration. These include concerns associated with the use of clonal transplants of asexually propagated corals; implications related to the genetic diversity of farmed corals and their influence on the adaptability to future environmental and climatic challenges; how to harness biological interactions and functional diversity in restoration schemes; the influence of the attributes of transplanted species on the biodiversity of reconstructed reefs; the integration of transplanted reefs within the landscape to maximize intervention outcomes, and more (Horoszowski-Fridman et al. 2017; Bulleri et al. 2018; Ladd et al. 2018; Baums et al. 2019; Rinkevich 2020). The next pressing challenge—expanding farmed coral transplantations to ecologically meaningful scales—should not be confronted without substantial consolidation of these still-lacking rationales.

Figure 13.16 A restored knoll at Dekel Beach, 11 years after the transplantation of 300 nursery-grown corals from six branching coral species (*Stylophora pistillata*, *Pocillopora damicornis*, *Acropora variabilis*, *Acropora humilis*, *Acropora pharaonis*, *Acropora valida*), farmed at Eilat's midwater coral nursery. This complex spatial structure that was created by the farmed transplants growing on the restored knoll harbors a diverse community of reef-associated organisms. This knoll is at the same high biodiversity state today—15 years post-transplantation.

ACKNOWLEDGMENTS

We thank the many divers and non-diver volunteers who assisted with nursery rearing, coral preparation, and coral transplantation throughout the course of this project. We also thank the participants of the Reefres 2008 coral transplantation workshop (Eilat, Israel) for assisting with the second transplantation session. We are grateful to Naomi S. Zamir for her linguistic help and Prof. Naomi Ori and her lab members (HUJI) for their hospitality during the preparation of this manuscript. This study was supported by the AID-MERC program (no M33-001), by the North American Friends of IOLR (NAF/IOLR), and by the Israeli-French High Council for Scientific & Technological Research Program (Maïmonide-Israel).

REFERENCES

Amar, K. O., N. E. Chadwick, and B. Rinkevich. 2007. "Coral planulae as dispersion vehicle: Biological properties of larvae released early and late in the season." *Mar. Ecol. Prog. Ser.* 350, 71–78.

Barton, J. A., B. L. Willis, and K. S. Hutson. 2017. "Coral propagation: A review of techniques for ornamental trade and reef restoration." *Rev. Aquacult.* 9, 238–256.

Baums, I. B., A. C. Baker, S. W. Davies, A. G. Grottoli, C. D. Kenkel, S. A. Kitchen, I. B. Kuffner, et al. 2019. "Considerations for maximizing the adaptive potential of restored coral populations in the western Atlantic." *Ecol. Appl.* 29, e01978.

Bongiorni, L., D. Giovanelli, B. Rinkevich, A. Pusceddu, L. M. Chou, and R. Danovaro. 2011. "First step in the restoration of a highly degraded coral reef (Singapore) by in situ coral intensive farming." *Aquaculture* 322-323, 191-200.
Bongiorni, L., S. Shafir, D. Angel, and B. Rinkevich. 2003. "Survival, growth and gonadal development of two hermatypic corals subjected to in situ fish farm nutrient enrichment." *Mar. Ecol. Prog. Ser.* 253, 137-144.
Bulleri, F., B. K. Eriksson, A. Queirós, L. Airoldi, F. Arenas, C. Arvanitidis, T. J. Bouma, et al. 2018. "Harnessing positive species interactions as a tool against climate-driven loss of coastal biodiversity." *PLoS Biology* 16, e2006852.
Chou, L. M. 2016. "Rehabilitation engineering of Singapore reefs to cope with urbanization and climate change impacts." *J. Civil Eng. Arch.* 10, 932-936.
Dizon, R. M., E. J. Edwards, and E. D. Gomez. 2008. "Comparison of three types of adhesives in attaching coral transplants to clam shell substrates." *Aquatic Conserv: Mar. Freshw. Ecosyst.* 18, 1140-1148.
Edwards, A. J., J. Guest, B. Rinkevich, M. Omori, K. Iwao, G. Levy, and L. Shaish. 2010a. "Evaluating costs of restoration." In: *Reef Rehabilitation Manual*. A. J. Edwards (ed). Coral Reef Targeted Research & Capacity Building for Management Program, St. Lucia, Australia. pp. 113-128.
Edwards, A. J., S. Job, and S. Wells. 2010b. "Learning lessons from past reef-rehabilitation projects." In: *Reef Rehabilitation Manual*. A. J. Edwards (ed). Coral Reef Targeted Research & Capacity Building for Management Program, St. Lucia, Australia. pp. 129-164.
Epstein, N., R. P. M. Bak, and B. Rinkevich. 2001. "Strategies for gardening denuded coral reef areas: The applicability of using different types of coral material for reef restoration." *Rest. Ecol.* 9, 532-442.
———. 2003. "Applying forest restoration principles to coral reef rehabilitation." *Aquatic Conserv: Mar. Freshw. Ecosyst.* 13, 387-395.
Epstein, N. and B. Rinkevich. 2001. "From isolated ramets to coral colonies: The significance of colony pattern formation in reef restoration practices." *Basic Appl. Ecol.* 2, 219-222.
Fine, M., M. Cinar, C. R. Voolstra, A. Safa, B. Rinkevich, D. Laffoley, N. Hilmi, et al. 2019. "Coral reefs of the Red Sea—challenges and potential solutions." *Regional Stu. Mar. Sci.* 25, 100498.
Guest, J. R., M. V. Baria, E. D. Gomez, A. J. Heyward, and A. J. Edwards. 2014. "Closing the circle: Is it feasible to rehabilitate reefs with sexually propagated corals?" *Coral Reefs* 33, 45-55.
Hesley, D., D. Burdeno, C. Drury, S. Schopmeyer, and D. Lirman. 2017. "Citizen science benefits coral reef restoration activities." *J. Nat. Conserv.* 40, 94-99.
Horoszowski-Fridman, Y. B., J. C. Brêthes, N. Rahmani, and B. Rinkevich. 2015. "Marine silviculture: Incorporating ecosystem engineering properties into reef restoration acts." *Ecol. Eng.* 82, 201-213.
Horoszowski-Fridman, Y. B., I. Izhaki, and B. Rinkevich. 2011. "Engineering of coral reef larval supply through transplantation of nursery-farmed gravid colonies." *J. Exp. Mar. Biol. Ecol.* 399, 162-166.
———. 2020. "Long-term heightened larval production in nursery-bred coral transplants." *Basic. Appl. Ecol.* 47, 12-21.
Horoszowski-Fridman, Y. B. and B. Rinkevich. 2017. "Restoring the animal forests: Harnessing silviculture biodiversity concepts for coral transplantation." In: *Marine Animal Forests: The ecology of benthic biodiversity hotspots*. S. Rossi, L. Bramanti, A. Gori, and C. Orejas (eds). Springer International Publishing AG. pp. 1313-1335.
Jones, C. J., J. H. Lawton, and M. Shachak. 1994. "Organisms as ecosystem engineers." *Oikos* 69, 373-386.
Ladd, M. C., M. W. Miller, J. H. Hunt, W. C. Sharp, and D. E. Burkepile. 2018. "Harnessing ecological processes to facilitate coral restoration." *Front. Ecol. Environ.* 16, 239-247.
Levy, G., L. Shaish, A. Haim, and B. Rinkevich. 2010. "Mid-water rope nursery—testing design and performance of a novel reef restoration instrument." *Ecol. Eng.* 36, 560-569.
Linden, B., J. Huisman, and B. Rinkevich. 2018. "Circatrigintan instead of lunar periodicity of larval release in a brooding coral species." *Scientific Reports* 8:5668, 2018. doi:10.1038/s41598-018-23274-w.
Linden, B. and B. Rinkevich. 2011. "Creating stocks of young colonies from brooding-coral larvae, amenable to active reef restoration." *J. Exp. Mar. Biol. Ecol.* 398, 40-46.
———. "Elaborating of an eco-engineering approach for stock enhanced sexually derived coral colonies." *J. Exp. Mar. Biol. Ecol.* 486, 314-321.
Linden, B., M. J. A. Vermeij, and B. Rinkevich. 2019. "The coral settlement box: A simple device to produce coral stock from brooded coral larvae entirely in situ." *Ecol. Eng.* 132, 115-119.

Lirman, D. and S. Schopmeyer. 2016. "Ecological solutions to reef degradation: Optimizing coral reef restoration in the Caribbean and Western Atlantic." *PeerJ* 4:e2597.

Lirman, D., T. Thyberg, J. Herlan, C. Hill, C. Young-Lahiff, S. Schopmeyer, B. Huntington, et al. 2010. "Propagation of the threatened staghorn coral *Acropora cervicornis*: Minimize the impacts of fragment collection and maximize production." *Coral Reefs* 29, 729–735.

Lohr, K. E., S. Bejarano, D. Lirman, S. Schopmeyer, and C. Manfrino. 2015. "Optimizing the productivity of a coral nursery focused on staghorn coral *Acropora cervicornis*." *Endanger. Species Res.* 27, 243–250.

Mbije, N. E. J., E. Spanier, and B. Rinkevich. 2010. "Testing the first phase of the 'gardening concept' as an applicable tool in restoring denuded reefs in Tanzania." *Ecol. Eng.* 36, 611–750.

———. 2013. "A first endeavour in restoring denuded, post-bleached reefs in Tanzania." *Estuar. Coastal Shelf Sci.* 128, 41–51.

Monty, J. A., D. S. Gilliam, K. Banks, D. Stout, and R. E. Dodge. 2006. "Coral of opportunity survivorship and the use of coral nurseries in coral reef restoration." *Proceedings of 10th International Coral Reef Symposium*, 1665–1673.

Ng, C. S. L. and L. M. Chou. 2014. "Rearing juvenile 'corals of opportunity' in in situ nurseries—a reef rehabilitation approach for sediment-impacted environments." *Mar. Biol. Res.* 10, 833–838.

Omori, M. 2011. "Degradation and restoration of coral reefs: Experience in Okinawa, Japan." *Mar. Biol. Res.* 7, 3–12.

Rachmilovitz, E. N. and B. Rinkevich. 2017. "Tiling the reef—exploring the first step of an ecological engineering tool that may promote phase-shift reversals in coral reefs." *Ecol. Eng.* 105, 150–161.

Randall, C. J., A. P. Negri, K. M. Quigley, T. Foster, G. F. Ricardo, N. S. Webster, L. K. Bay, et al. "Sexual production of corals for reef restoration in the Anthropocene." *Mar. Ecol. Prog. Ser.* 635, 203–232.

Rinkevich, B. 1995. "Restoration strategies for coral reefs damaged by recreational activities: The use of sexual and asexual recruits." *Rest. Ecol.* 3, 241–251.

———. 2000. "Steps towards the evaluation of coral reef restoration by using small branch fragments." *Mar. Biol.* 136, 807–812.

———. 2005a. "Conservation of coral reefs through active restoration measures: Recent approaches and last decade progress." *Environ. Sci. Technol.* 39, 4333–4342.

———. 2005b. "What do we know about Eilat (Red Sea) reef degradation? A critical examination of the published literature." *J. Exp. Mar. Biol. Ecol.* 327, 183–200.

———. 2006. "The coral gardening concept and the use of underwater nurseries; lesson learned from silvics and silviculture." In: *Coral Reef Restoration Handbook*. W. F. Precht (ed.). Boca Raton, FL, CRC Press. pp. 291–301.

———. 2014. "Rebuilding coral reefs: Does active reef restoration lead to sustainable reefs?" *Curr. Opinion Environ. Sustainability* 7, 28–36.

———. 2015. "Climate change and active reef restoration—ways of constructing the 'reefs of tomorrow'." *J. Mar. Sci. Eng.* 3, 111–127.

———. 2017. "Rebutting the inclined analyses on the cost-effectiveness and feasibility of coral reef restoration." *Ecol. Appl.* 27, 1970–1973.

———. 2019a. "The active reef restoration toolbox is a vehicle for coral resilience and adaptation in a changing world." *Journal of Marine Science and Engineering* 7, 201. doi:10.3390/jmse7070201.

———. 2019b. "Coral chimerism as an evolutionary rescue mechanism to mitigate global climate change impacts." *Global Change Biol.* 25, 1198–1206.

———. 2020. "Ecological engineering approaches in coral reef restoration." *ICES J. Mar Sci.* doi:10.1093/icesjms/fsaa022.

Rosado, P. M., D. C. Leite, G. A. Duarte, R. M. Chaloub, G. Jospin, U. N. da Rocha, J. P. Saraiva, et al. 2019. "Marine probiotics: Increasing coral resistance to bleaching through microbiome manipulation." *ISME J.* 13, 921–936.

Schopmeyer, S. A., D. Lirman, E. Bartels, D. S. Gilliam, E. A. Goergen, S. P. Griffin, M. E. Johnson, et al. 2017. "Regional restoration benchmarks for *Acropora cervicornis*." *Coral reefs* 36, 1047–1057.

Shafir, S., S. Abady, and B. Rinkevich. 2009. "Improved sustainable maintenance for mid-water coral nursery by the application of an anti-fouling agent." *J. Exp. Mar. Biol. Ecol.* 368, 124–128.

Shafir, S. and B. Rinkevich. 2008. "The underwater silviculture approach for reef restoration: An emergent aquaculture theme." In: *Aquaculture Research Trends*. S. H. Schwartz (ed). Nova Science Publications, New York, NY. pp. 279–295.

———. "Integrated long term mid-water coral nurseries: A management instrument evolving into a floating ecosystem." *Mauritius Res. J.* 16, 365–379.

Shafir, S., J. van Rijn, and B. Rinkevich. 2001. "Nubbing of coral colonies: A novel approach for the development of island broodstocks." *Aquarium Sci. Conser.* 3, 183–190.

———. 2006a. "A mid-water coral nursery." *Proc. 10th Intern. Coral Reef Symp.*, pp. 1674–1679.

———. 2006b. "Steps in the construction of underwater coral nursery, an essential component in reef restoration acts." *Mar. Biol.* 149, 679–687.

Shaish, L., G. Levy, E. Gomez, and B. Rinkevich. 2008. "Fixed and suspended coral nurseries in the Philippines: Establishing the first step in the gardening concept of reef restoration." *J. Exp. Mar. Biol. Ecol.* 358, 86–97.

Shefy, D., N. Shashar, and B. Rinkevich. 2018. "The reproduction of the Red Sea coral *Stylophora pistillata* from Eilat: Four decades' perspective." *Mar. Biol.* 165, 27.

Wild, C., O. Hoegh-Guldberg, M. S. Naumann, M. F. Colombo-Pallotta, M. Ateweberhan, W. K. Fitt, R. Iglesias-Prieto, et al. 2011. "Climate change impedes scleractinian corals as primary reef ecosystem engineers." *Mar. Freshwater Res.* 62, 205–215.

Young, C. N., S. A. Schopmeyer, and D. Lirman. 2012. "A review of reef restoration and coral propagation using the threatened genus Acropora in the Caribbean and Western Atlantic." *Bull. Mar. Sci.* 88, 1075–1098.

Zakai, D. and N. E. Chadwick-Furman. 2002. "Impacts of intensive recreational diving on reef corals at Eilat, northern Red Sea." *Biol. Conserv.* 105, 179–187.

14

ACTIVE REEF RESTORATION IN THE MEXICAN CARIBBEAN: 15-YEAR TIMELINE

Claudia Padilla-Souza, Jaime González-Cano, Juan Carlos Huitrón Baca, and Roberto Ibarra-Navarro

ABSTRACT

In Mexico, the first actions to restore damaged coral reefs began in 2004, encouraged by the necessity to rescue corals that were affected by storms and hurricanes. Then in 2009, greater reef interventions were undertaken. The first great achievement was the establishment of marine coral nurseries, which allowed having corals available for restoration actions on a scheduled basis. Later, land-based coral nurseries offered new opportunities to produce and grow coral colonies, including sexual recruits by laboratory-assisted reproduction. At this point, the main work consisted of developing techniques to produce and outplant corals for active restoration.

From 2012–2016, important advances were made in the restoration of coral reefs impacted by ship grounding. The most important lesson learned at this stage was that the single action of outplanting corals in deteriorated areas generates a chain of events—both in the structure and the function of the reef—that helps to reverse the progress of degradation. The restoration project started outplanting *Acropora cervicornis* colonies, due to their ease of production and rapid growth, which made it possible to increase significantly their coverage in the entire area of intervention. Colonies of *Acropora palmata* began to be outplanted later, in 2014, mainly because they take longer to grow in the nurseries. Sites where *Acropora cervicornis* were outplanted had a significant increase in coral coverage during the first two years; however, their growth decreased gradually afterward. More interesting, two years later a new increase in coverage was observed—even without a new outplanting intervention—and an impressive recovery of the area occurred. This fact suggests that changes in the abundance of this species naturally occur in cycles of approximately two years. On the other hand, *A. palmata* colonies have shown slower growth rates, although they are becoming even more robust. Furthermore, a great milestone occurred when colonies of *A. palmata* that had been outplanted in a pilot test in 2011 reached sexual maturity and started releasing gametes in 2016. Now, it has been shown that most of the colonies that were outplanted in 2014 are producing gametes already. Another four species were also outplanted in this project: two massive corals (*Montastraea cavernosa* and *Orbicella annularis*) and two branched corals

continued

(*Porites porites* and *Agaricia agaricites*). Massive coral colonies took a much longer time to grow in the field nurseries, and when outplanted in the reef, their growth was slow as well, although their survival has been high. The other branched species displayed a rather slow growth, and some of them suffered partial mortality due to algal overgrowth. Although the project faced several challenges, the overall results are considered very successful since it has positively impacted the characteristics of the reef. The first observed impact was the increase in coral coverage (more than 6% gain), accompanied by a change in the abundance of coral species where reef builders were dominant, followed by an increase in substrate complexity, and finally, the fish biomass and diversity doubled. Even with these good results, the impact of the interventions is still limited—the number of outplanted coral colonies was small (2,500 corals), in an area of only 700 m^2.

Currently, restoration efforts and techniques have improved and many of the reef restoration challenges have been solved; however, there is an urgent need to scale up the production and outplanting of colonies to achieve greater results from coral reef restoration activities. One excellent approach for *scaling up* is through the implementation of *micro-fragmentation*, which is a very efficient technique for working with massive corals. With improvements in coral production, new restoration techniques are needed to increase the number of outplanted colonies and the variety of coral species, as well as the extent of the restored area. More recently, a new challenge has occurred due to stony coral tissue loss disease (SCTLD), and some trials to rescue live tissue from those colonies suggest that ex situ conservation is feasible and necessary. In addition, a specific monitoring tool to measure the efficiency of restoration actions is needed. Finally, involvement of the community in coral reef restoration is becoming increasingly important, through the training of community brigades and their participation in massive coral outplanting events.

INTRODUCTION

Degradation of coral reefs around the world has increased in recent years, causing the loss of their structure and functionality (McField et al. 2020). More than ever, there is a strong conviction about the urgency of implementing ecological restoration actions to recover these characteristics, as well as the environmental services they provide (Ladd et al. 2018; Foo and Asner 2019).

In Mexico, reef restoration actions started in the National Park named Costa Occidental de Isla Mujeres, Punta Cancún y Punta Nizuc (COIMPCPN-NP)—which is administrated by the National Commission for Natural Protected Areas (CONANP)—one of the most visited places in the country, located in the Mexican Caribbean. Due to its geographic location, this national park is constantly exposed to the impacts of hurricanes, representing one of the main threats to the reefs. Nautical activities are another source of stress and damage to the reefs, and ship groundings have been another permanent concern for the national park's managers. First actions were carried out after a disturbance when three hurricanes hit Quintana Roo between 2004 and 2005. This stage of the project involved stakeholders, dive guides, and managers in an intense effort to mitigate the damages that occurred at the reef. The work focused on the rescue of coral colonies and their reattachment to the substrate, using the materials and knowledge that was available at that time.

Later, the National Institute of Fisheries and Aquaculture (INAPESCA) and CONANP established a working collaboration to face new challenges through coral culture in tanks at INAPESCA's facilities in order to expand and to improve the marine nursery of CONANP in the field. Thus, the challenge of restoring reef areas that were damaged by ship grounding was taken. Two sites were chosen: Manchones Reef and Cuevones Reef—two of the most important reefs within the park because of their visitation and high coral coverage. Both areas were seriously damaged by three hurricanes and ship groundings, respectively. Before 2004, Manchones Reef was dominated by massive live colonies of *Acropora palmata*, but approximately 30% of them were destroyed due to the impact of hurricanes. At Cuevones Reef, a cruiser caused a severe nautical accident in 1997 with a recorded loss of 100% of the coral cover in several areas, previously dominated by *Acropora palmata*. Other species, such as *Orbicella annularis* and *Porites porites*, were also affected. The magnitude of the destruction was so high that managers and users decided to close the area to all activities except scientific research, and it still remains closed. In both cases, the damages extended to the rocky basement, fragmenting it into so many pieces that in some areas the restoration actions could not be performed for several years because they had to wait for the substrate to reconsolidate.

TECHNIQUES AND METHODS

The employed methods and techniques are presented in the following sections. These are grouped into five periods, depending on the activities that were carried out and the restoration concepts that were considered in each stage.

2004–2005 PERIOD

The first important effort to rescue and reattach corals to the substrate was carried out between 2004 and 2005 when COIMPCPN-NP was impacted by three major hurricanes (Ivan, Emily, and Wilma). The range of damage was very high, especially for Acroporids, and the destruction effects were cumulative because the reef had no chance for recovery in such a small period between impacts.

At the beginning, it was necessary to clean the debris that were brought to the reefs by the strong winds and surge and to rescue the broken corals and reattach them to the marine substrate. This work was coordinated by the national park staff with the participation of about 47 divers from the tour operator community of Cancun and Isla Mujeres. Several stakeholders collaborated with vessels, crew, dive tanks, and fuel to make the rehabilitation efforts possible (Figure 14.1).

There was a close collaboration within the Cancun and Isla Mujeres communities, and they shared some of their knowledge with the national park staff. In fact, some techniques and efforts were improved with the seamanship experience of these people, working as fishermen and dive masters. Among their recommendations was the use of tarred yarn, a very resistant fiber that is used to manufacture fishing nets, like the ones used for shrimping. Since this thread proved to be very useful, long lasting, easy to get, and cheap, the decision was made to use it as one of the basic materials to reattach fragments of corals. After the cleaning activities, the divers focused on reattaching the fragments and colonies to the substrate using the thread and plastic ties, trying to increase the survival chances of each fragment. The second step was cementing the fragments to make it permanent and more stable. The thread that was used lasted a long time and looked in good shape after many years under sea conditions.

Another material that the fishermen suggested was the use of iron rods, like the ones used in construction. These materials also proved to be very useful in making solid attachments of big pieces of coral; by drilling both the coral and the rock substrate and then filling it firmly with cement (Figure 14.2).

Figure 14.1 It is quite helpful when stakeholders are able to scuba dive and participate in the rehabilitation programs for coral reefs.

Figure 14.2 Different materials are used to facilitate the fixation of coral fragments onto the substrate, even iron rods that go through big pieces of coral as shown here.

Since the dominant species within the park boundaries is *Acropora palmata*, the most evident destruction and damage was received by it. This is the reason we decided to focus mainly on *A. palmata*, although the rescue and restoration considered other species, like *Orbicella annularis* and *Montastraea cavernosa*. The federal budget for the restoration project at that time was USD $25,000 and 2,200 hours/month of underwater work was estimated.

2005–2009 PERIOD

Several months after the impact of hurricanes, the work focused on the creation of a monitoring program to record the condition of a test group of corals. The growth of these corals was measured by fixing plastic ties around the tips of several coral branches. With ties as a reference, the growth of corals was measured every two months. The average growth per month was estimated as 1 cm/month (Figure 14.3).

In this period the team began the first tests using concrete structures to act as fixed bases for corals in a nursery (Huitrón-Baca, et al. 2011). The first ones were elaborated as experimental and control sets to evaluate the effects of sedimentation on corals due to a beach rehabilitation project in the hotel zone of Cancun in 2006. This first design of concrete blocks as a nursery for corals failed. Concrete structures were too close to the sea bottom, hence the moving sand around the blocks caused an abrasive effect over the coral tissue. It was concluded that this structure design generated low survival of coral fragments (Figure 14.4).

Figure 14.3 Plastic ties were fixed to the tips of several coral branches and used as a reference to measure the corals' growth rate.

Figure 14.4 The first coral nursery design to hold coral fragments in concrete structures had the columns very close to the bottom and the movement of sand produced abrasion to the corals.

2009–2011 PERIOD

In 2009 an extensive nursery was constructed at Bahia de Isla Mujeres over a sand bank named Bajo Pepito. For this coral nursery, the concrete structures included longer and hence taller PVC pipes to keep fragments away from the harmful effects of the sand. These new structures with taller pipes seemed to achieve the goal. Corals grew with fewer problems, and at higher survival rates. This operation, however, required divers to frequently clean and maintain the entire nursery (Figure 14.5(a), (b)).

Initially, the fragments of corals for the nursery were collected in different areas from natural broken branches. Different areas were visited, especially after storms and bad weather conditions. In other cases opportunity fragments came from the groundings of two vessels. In these two cases, the main goal was to recover as many live coral pieces as possible. The divers selected the healthiest fragments and took them to the nursery. During the traveling, several water changes took place to avoid stress. Once at the nursery, the branches were carefully fragmented into smaller pieces and fixed to the top of the PVC pipes. The nursery needed frequent maintenance to avoid the growth of fire coral, sponges, algae, or the sand deposits over the corals. By 2011, the staff of the national park transplanted 862 corals that were grown at the sea nursery in Bajo Pepito—293 colonies of *Acropora cervicornis* colonies and 569 colonies of *A. palmata*.

Figure 14.5 A PVC pipe was included in the design of modules to keep fragments away from the sand: (a) a panoramic view of the nursery complex in Bajo Pepito, Isla Mujeres, at the time it was installed and (b) two years later.

2012–2016 PERIOD

During this period, the aquaculture systems were diversified, the capacity of marine nurseries was increased, and the restoration sites were intervened with programmed and consecutive outplanting interventions in two sites affected by ship groundings. The production and culture of corals were carried out in three different culture systems, each one adapted for specific processes (Table 14.1).

Table 14.1 Characteristics of aquarium systems for coral culture at the INAPESCA—used during the 2012–2016 period

Culture System	# Tanks	Type	Size and Volume	Configuration/ Operation
Controlled Culture System (CCS)	4	Life support system with closed flow, artificial lighting control, biological, and mechanical filtration. Chiller and design of water movement with waves.	4.00 × 1.00 × 0.35 m, volume of 1,400 l each. Artificial lighting of halogen 250, 400 y 1,000 w—20,000°k.	Closed systems with partial changes of seawater (50% every 3 days). Temperature is controlled 27–28.5°C, water discharge every 2 min by 2″ pipe at a speed of 100 l/min.
Outdoor Culture System (OCS)	8	Open flow culture systems with sunlight under shade roof.	1.60 × 1:00 × 0.35 m, volume of 560 l each.	Water flow open at speed 3.7–4.0 l/min.
Marine Culture System (MCS)	50	Concrete plates with PVC pipe for growing corals at sea.	0.50 × .50 × 0.25 m, capacity for 20/30/36 coral fragments.	Concrete plates installed in a sand area.

Techniques of Coral Production

The production of coral colonies was through clonal propagation and sexual reproduction. The clonal propagation was carried out both in controlled culture system (CCS) and outdoor culture system (OCS) aquariums, and also in the marine culture system (MCS), in seven semi-annual production events. In total, 6,572 colonies were produced in both systems: 2,781 in the CCS/OCS and 3,791 in the MCS. Production focused on the species of the genus *Acropora*, which represented 60% of the total production (Figure 14.6(a), (b)).

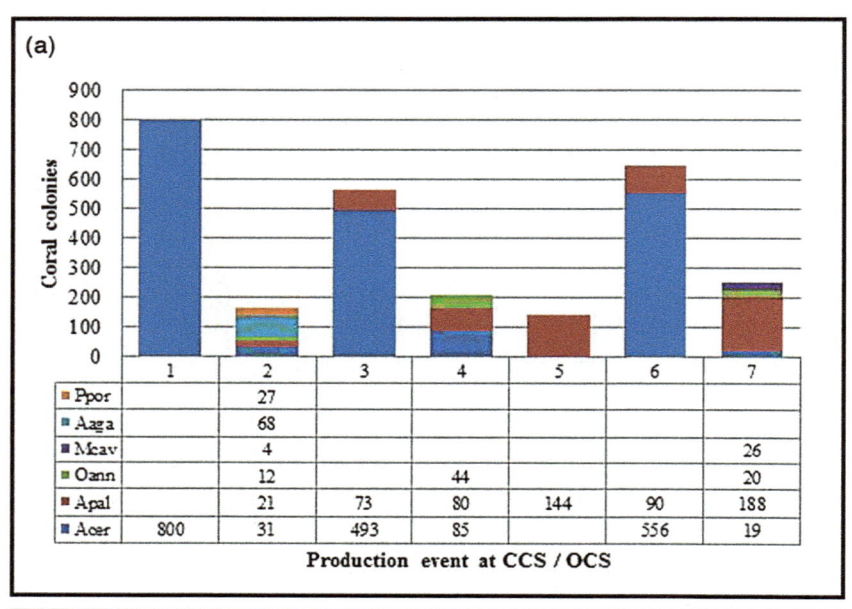

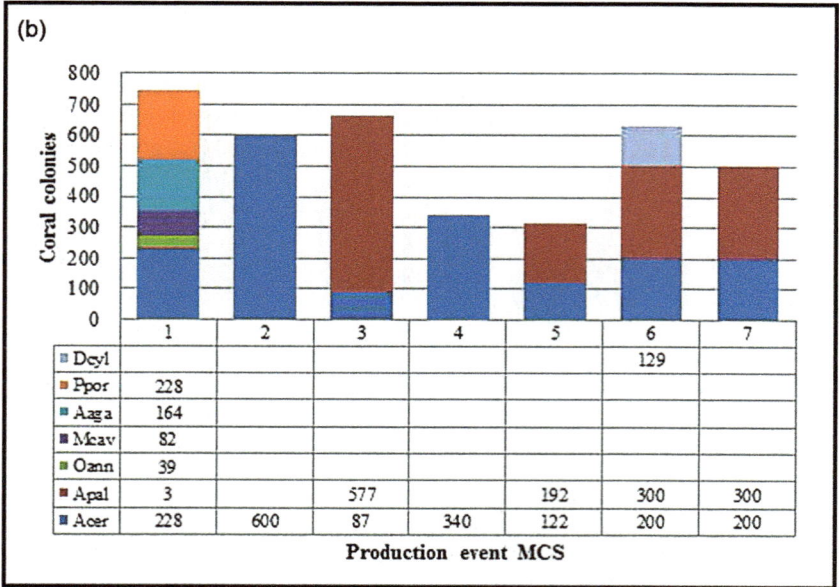

(a) Production event at CCS / OCS

	1	2	3	4	5	6	7
Ppor		27					
Aaga		68					
Mcav		4					26
Oann		12		44			20
Apal		21	73	80	144	90	188
Acer	800	31	493	85		556	19

(b) Production event MCS

	1	2	3	4	5	6	7
Dcyl						129	
Ppor	228						
Aaga	164						
Mcav	82						
Oann	39						
Apal	3		577		192	300	300
Acer	228	600	87	340	122	200	200

Figure 14.6 Production of coral colonies by clonal propagation in seven semi-annual events: (a) the number of colonies produced per species in CCS/OCS and (b) MCS is shown.

For the production of corals by sexual reproduction, gametes were collected from 10 colonies of *Acropora palmata* at El Bajito Reef in the COIMPCPN-NP during the reproductive season of years 2014 and 2015. Protocols were established and applied for *in vitro* fertilization. Embryonic development was monitored and larval culture was performed. The settlement of coral larvae and their metamorphosis process was promoted by exposing hard substrates. Settled sexual recruits were monitored and finally, live and artificial food was supplied to cultured sexual recruits (Figure 14.7(a), (b)).

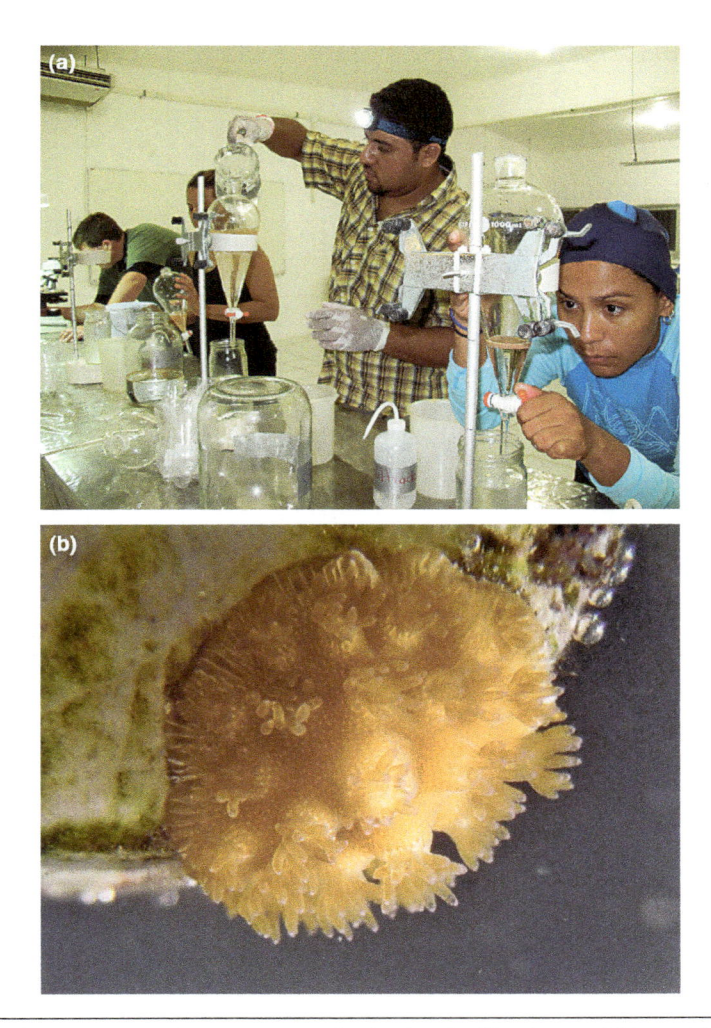

Figure 14.7 (a) Cleaning *A. palmata* gametes for *in vitro* fertilization and (b) a settled sexual recruit at six months old.

Actions for Reef Restoration

The active restoration efforts considered a surface of 350 m² as a restoration area in each of the two reefs—Cuevones and Manchones. In both areas, events for the outplanting of corals were carried out every six months, transplanting 180 to 300 coral colonies per event per site. Between October 2013 and April 2016, a total of 2,507 colonies were outplanted (51%

Acropora cervicornis, 23% *Acropora palmata*, 7% *Montastrea cavernosa*, 8% *Orbicella annularis*, 7% *Porites porites*, and 4% *Undaria agaricites*). In each event 30% of the colonies were tagged in order to monitor the survival and growth of the coral colonies that were transplanted in the restoration areas (Table 14.2).

Table 14.2 Restoration actions at two sites, Cuevones Reef and Manchones Reef. The number of colonies per species outplanted at each site and event is shown

Site	Species	Oct. 2013	Apr. 2014	Aug. 2014	Mar. 2015	Jul. 2015	Apr. 2016	Total
Cuevones Reef	Acer	300	180		85	90	72	727
	Apal				85	90	31	206
	Mcav			77			48	125
	Oann			24	22		37	83
Manchones Reef	Acer	300	110		67	90	70	637
	Apal				118	90	34	242
	Mcav						26	26
	Oann				22		56	78
	Ppor		70	180				250
	Aaga			133				133
Total		600	360	414	399	360	374	2507

Acer = *Acropora cervicornis*, Apal = *Acropora palmata*, Mcav = *Montastraea cavernosa*, Oann = *Orbicella annularis*, Ppor = *Porites astreoides*, and Aaga = *Agaricia agaricites*

Effects of Active Reef Restoration

During a period of 31 months, the increase in coral coverage due to the outplanted corals and active restoration was measured. In Cuevones Reef the coverage increase was estimated at 4.76% while Manchones Reef showed a higher percentage of 5%. In both cases, estimates considered only six species (Table 14.3).

Cuevones Reef initially had a low coral cover (8.94%), with dominance of the *Porites astreoides* species being a pioneer species of encrusting growth with low contribution to the

Table 14.3 Increase of coral cover due to active restoration by the outplanting of corals in two reefs of the COIMPCPN-NP

	Cuevones Reef		Manchones Reef	
	Total coral coverage (%)	Coral coverage of species involved in the active restoration* (%)	Total coral coverage (%)	Coral coverage of species involved in the active restoration* (%)
Initial (2012)	8.94	3.9	2.55	0.6
Final (2016)	12.6	8.6	8.62	5.9
Total Increase in Coverage	3.66	4.76	6.07	5.36

*Outplanted species: *Acropora cervicornis*, *Acropora palmata*, *Orbicella annularis*, *Montastraea cavernosa*, *Porites astreoides* and *Agaricia agaricites*

accretion of the reef structure. Reef builders *Acropora* spp. and *Orbicella* spp. were also registered, but with low cover (3.9%). Active restoration in this reef consisted of outplanting mainly *Acropora cervicornis* in the deepest parts, along with some events of outplanting *Orbicella* species, as well as *Acropora palmata* in the shallow areas. At the end of the intervention, coral cover reached 12.6%, representing an increase of 3.66% of the total achieved coral, where 4.8% of cover resulted from the species involved in the restoration actions. This difference is due to a gradual decrease in the cover of *Porites astreoides*, which in total represented 1.1% (Figure 14.8).

Manchones Reef also presented very low coral cover (2.55%), with high dominance of *Porites astreoides*, since the presence of other coral species only represented 0.6%. Active restoration in this site consisted of several events of outplanting *Acropora cervicornis* at the entire area because it was the most abundant species in this place, along with a few events of outplanting *Acropora palmata* colonies only in the shallow areas of the reef unit. Also, a few colonies of other species such as *Montastraea cavernosa, Orbicella annularis, Porites porites,* and *Agaricia agaricites* were outplanted in a scattered way in the area. As a result of the restoration actions in this site, a total coral cover increase of 6.1% was achieved. This includes a 5.4% increase in the coral coverage of the intervened species, since the *Porites astreoides* species presented a slight increase of 0.7% (Figure 14.9).

In addition, both restoration sites had a considerable increase in the richness of fish species two years after the outplanting of coral colonies, recording an increase of 17 species for Cuevones Reef and 20 species for Manchones Reef; which represents approximately twice the number of species in each site. In both sites, the number of commercially important species increased with a spillover effect to the region. In Cuevones Reef there was an increase in the number of fish in the Haemulidae and Lutjanidae families, finding schools of 20 or more

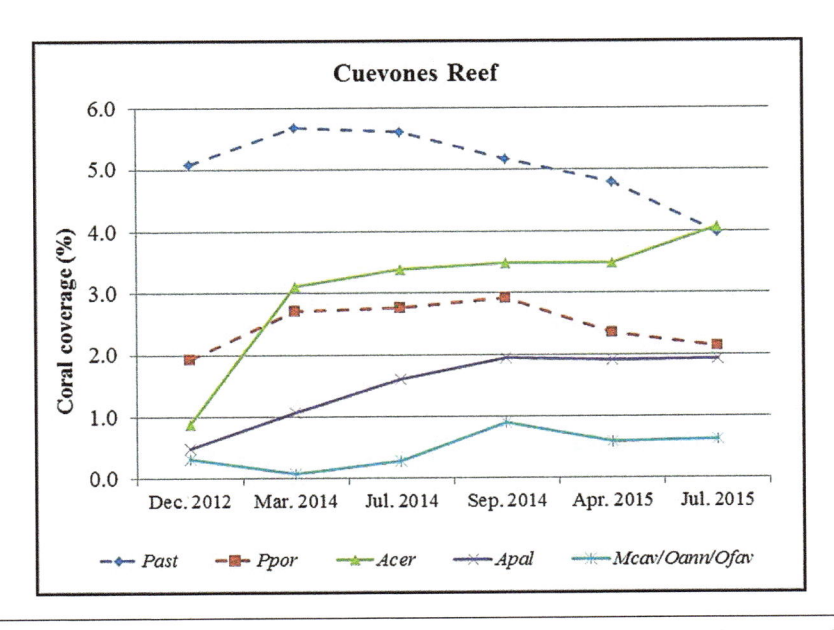

Figure 14.8 Increase in coral cover through the events of outplanting at Cuevones Reefs. The solid lines represent coral species that were outplanted during the restoration actions. The dotted lines correspond to pioneer species that were not intervened. PAST = *Porites astreoides*, Ppor = *Porites astreoides*, Acer = *Acropora cervicornis*, Apal = *Acropora palmata*, Mcav = *Montastraea cavernosa*, Oann = *Orbicella annularis*, and Ofav = *Orbicella faveolata*.

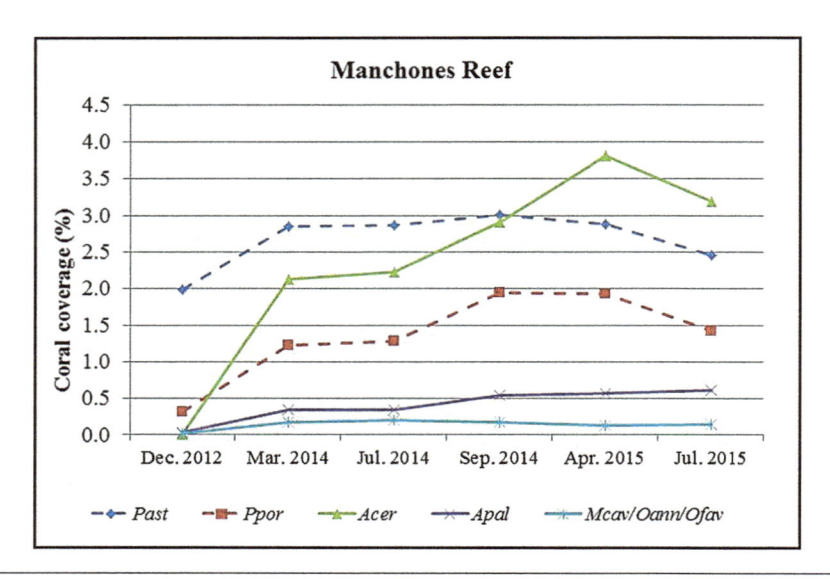

Figure 14.9 Increase in coral cover through the events of outplanting at Manchones Reefs. The solid lines represent coral species that were outplanted during the restoration actions. The dotted lines correspond to pioneer species that were not intervened. PAST = *Porites astreoides*, Ppor = *Porites astreoides*, Acer = *Acropora cervicornis*, Apal = *Acropora palmata*, Mcav = *Montastraea cavernosa*, Oann = *Orbicella annularis*, and Ofav = *Orbicella faveolata*.

individuals. The number of herbivore species of *Scarus* spp. and *Sparisoma* spp. increased from two to seven species, although their abundance was still low because most individuals were juveniles. In Manchones Reef a significant increase was observed in the species of the Haemulidae family, with the presence of frequent large schools in the area. The number of herbivore species of the genera *Scarus* spp. and *Sparisoma* spp. also increased in this site, from four species at the beginning, to a record of seven at the end (Figure 14.10).

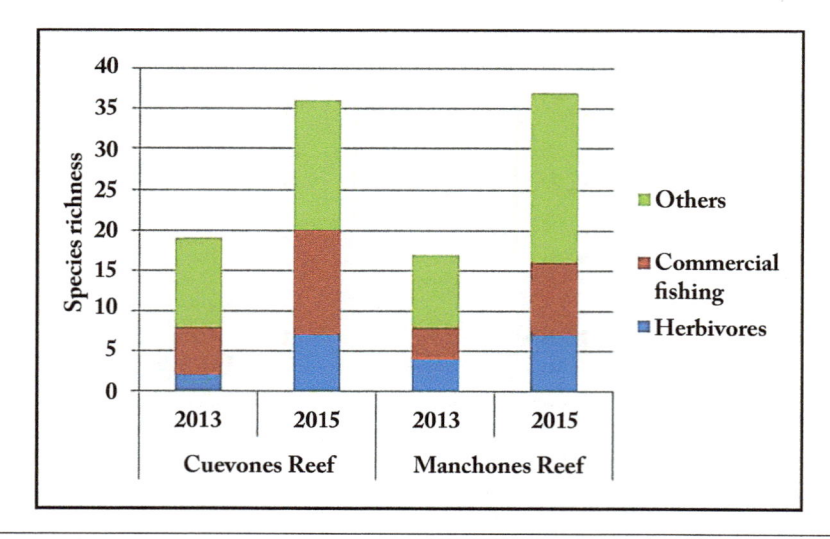

Figure 14.10 Increase in fish species richness at two restored sites. The number of species in three categories is shown, at the beginning of the restoration (2013) and at the end of the events of coral outplanting (2015).

2017–2022 PERIOD

This period began in 2017 with a project carried out by INAPESCA for the production of coral colonies and reef restoration, with financial support from the Government of the State of Quintana Roo. The goal of this project is to produce 265,000 coral colonies in six years. To accomplish the task, culture systems in the research center were modified and expanded in order to increase the capacity of production and to develop new processes for coral production (Table 14.4).

Table 14.4 Coral culture systems installed at the INAPESCA in 2017—description of the function, configuration, and use by coral production area

Culture System	Area	# of Tanks	Function	Size and Volume	Configuration/ Operation
Controlled Culture System (CCS)	Recovery area	8	Recovery and shelter systems for healthy corals: fragments, micro-fragments, or sexual recruits, after a production process.	1.60 × 1.00 × 0.35 m, volume of 560 l each.	Filtered water flow, aeration, indoor natural lighting, and temperature control with daily water exchange of 40–50%.
	Quarantine area	4	Recovery and shelter systems for healthy tissue from coral colonies affected by SCTLD under quarantine.	1.00 × 1.00 × 0.60 m, volume of 600 l with 3 separate compartments each.	Filtered water flow, aeration, artificial led lighting, and temperature control with daily water exchange of 40–50%.
	Reception area of collected samples	3	First preparation of the coral collection: cleaning and disposal of unwanted material through cutting processes before entering the recovery area.	1.60 × 1.00 × 0.35 m, volume of 560 l each.	Raw water flow, aeration, indoor natural lighting, temperature control with daily water exchange of 40–50% for acclimatization.
	Treatment area	4	Recovery and shelter systems for sick/damaged corals: fragments, micro-fragments, or sex recruits, under treatment.	0.35 × 0.70 × 0.40 m, volume of 98 l each.	Filtered water flow, aeration, indoor natural lighting, and temperature control with daily water exchange of 40–50%.
	Sex recruits area	1	Closed flow systems for larval development, settlement, and culture of sexual recruits.	4.00 × 1.00 × 0.35 m, volume of 1,400 l.	Incubators with partial water replacements of 50–70% every 3 days, indoor natural lighting, partial temperature 27–28.5°C.

Continued

Culture System	Area	# of Tanks	Function	Size and Volume	Configuration/ Operation
Outdoor Culture System (OCS)	Genetic bank area	8	Life-support systems of fragments, micro-fragments, or sex recruits of the genetic bank.	1.60 × 1.00 × 0.40 m, volume of 640 l each.	Filtered water flow, aeration, outdoor natural lighting with shade, temperature control with water replacements 40–50% every 3 days.
	Massive cultivation area	3	Life-support systems of fragments, micro-fragments, or sex recruits in massive cultivation.	4.00 × 1.00 × 0.35 m, volume of 1,400 l each.	Filtered water flow, aeration, outdoor natural lighting with shade, temperature control with water replacements 40–50% every 3 days.
Marine Culture System (MCS)	Old marine nursery	100	Concrete plates with PVC pipe for growing corals at sea.	0.50 × 0.50 × 0.25 m for 20/30/36 corals each.	Concrete plates installed in a sand area.
	New marine nursery	20	PVC racks for growing corals at sea.	0.50 × 0.50 m for 50 corals each.	PVC racks in a modular nursery installed in sand or hard substrate

Scaling Up Production Through Micro-Fragmentation

To scale up coral production, we considered the implementation of the micro-fragmentation technique, developed by Dr. David Vaughan, researcher at Mote Marine Laboratory and Aquarium in Florida, USA. This technique consists of cutting the coral fragments into smaller pieces. The polyps in these very small fragments survive as independent colonies. It has been demonstrated that fragments immediately start a regeneration process by healing the edges where the cut was made and maximizing the growth rate. In this way it is possible to scale up the coral production, as well as the reef restoration, by outplanting corals in less time than with traditional fragmentation techniques. An additional benefit is that this technique allows the production of corals of massive species (Figure 14.11).

With this vision, the project focused on improving production lines for the processes of micro-fragmentation, reaching a production of 32,880 coral colonies in 2018. At the end, with the experience acquired, we were able to produce cohorts of 3,000 micro-fragments in just one day and install them in the facilities (Figure 14.12).

Active Reef Restoration in the Mexican Caribbean: 15-Year Timeline

Figure 14.11 Stock of colonies of massive coral *Montastraea cavernosa* produced by the micro-fragmentation method.

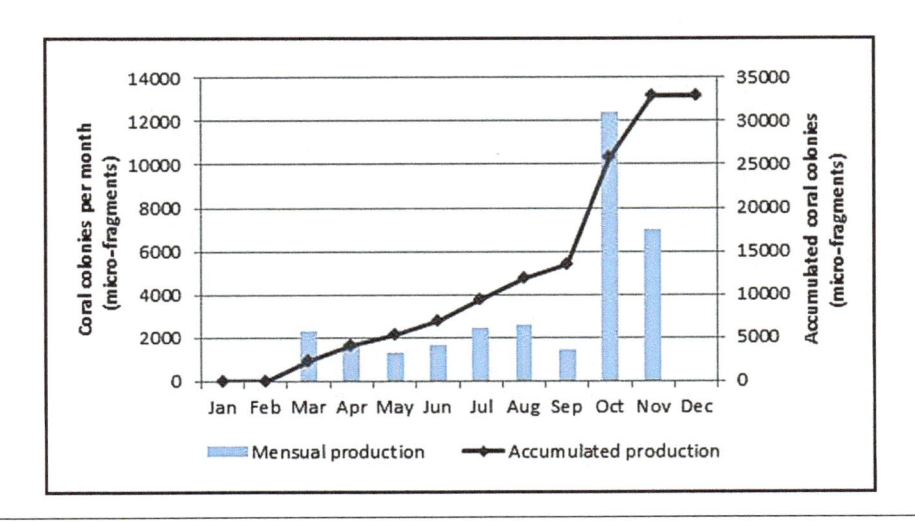

Figure 14.12 Coral colonies produced by micro-fragmentation at the INAPESCA in 2018.

New Reef Restoration Techniques

The production of coral colonies from micro-fragmentation requires the development of new techniques to outplanting these corals, but also allows more sophisticated reef restoration processes to be implemented. In the following sections, the most important aspects are briefly discussed.

Outplanting Micro-Fragments on the Marine Substrate

The micro-fragments can be outplanted directly on the marine substrate in order to promote the increase of coral cover. A pilot trial of this technique was carried out with massive species at the Manchones Reef in the Isla Mujeres Bay in October 2019. Thirty-four plates of coral tissue with 272 micro-fragments of the genus *Orbicella* spp. were outplanted directly on the reef substrate, covering a total area of 1 m^2 with the plates. This technique can also be used in branched species that do not form large colonies. A pilot trial was also undertaken in Manchones Reef, Isla Mujeres, with the outplanting of 650 micro-fragments of *Acropora cervicornis* species on the marine substrate in the windward side of Cuevones Reef, Punta Cancun, covering an area of 37.6 m^2 (Figure 14.13(a), (b)).

Figure 14.13 First trial of outplanting micro-fragments on the marine substrate with (a) massive coral *Orbicella annularis* and (b) branched species *Acropora cervicornis*.

Coating *Acropora Palmata* Skeleton

For branched species, such as *Acropora palmata*, the production of small colonies is used to coat skeletons of this same species that still remain in the reef. The structural complexity of the site remains and the cover of living coral tissue is recovered.

A pilot test was implemented in Manchones Reef, Isla Mujeres, with the outplanting of 232 colonies of *Acropora palmata* from two different genotypes in an area of 260 m^2. These colonies were fixed on skeletons of *Acropora palmata* with the intention of coating these structures with live coral tissue. The result was very encouraging; in three months the fragments began to fuse, and in less than one year they had already coated bigger areas of the skeleton (Figure 14.14(a), (b), (c)).

Figure 14.14 New restoration technique to cover coral skeletons with small fragments of *Acropora palmata*: (a) at the beginning of the intervention, (b) three months later the fragments were fused, and (c) one year later the coral tissue was covering a part of the skeleton.

Following the pilot trial in 2019, 7,104 fragments of *A. palmata* were outplanted to coat skeletons in nine different reefs, using four to seven genotypes per site (Table 14.5).

Table 14.5 Fragments of *Acropora palmata* outplanted over coral skeletons in 2019, with the intention to cover them

Marine Protected Area	Site (Reef)	Amount of Colonies	Amount of Genotypes	Date
Isla Contoy-NPA	Ixlache Barlovento	644	7	Jul. 2019
COIMPCPN-NPA	Arrecife Garrafón	700	4	Aug. 2019
Puerto Morelos Reef-NPA	Tanchacte encallamiento	800	5	Feb. 2019
	Tanchacte desove	700	5	Mar. 2019
	Arrecife Caracol	170	1	Jul. 2019
	Arrecife Caracol	1,040	5	Sep. 2019
	Bocana	1,800	7	Sep. 2019
Akumal	Media Luna Norte	450	5	Jul. 2019
	Media Luna	800	5	Jul. 2019

Coating Artificial Structures with Micro-Fragments

The tissue plates produced by micro-fragmentation can be used to coat artificial substrates, specifically designed for each species, in order to simulate larger coral colonies that provide structural complexity in the intervened sites. This new technique will allow corals to generate colonies that will grow and reach sexual maturity faster than wild colonies. The success of these actions indicate that coral reefs may be restored in less time and more efficiently.

In addition, a pilot trial was conducted considering 300 outplanted micro-fragments of *Orbicella annularis* on an artificial structure on the windward side of Cuevones Reef. The area covered by this structure was approximately 3 m². Subsequently, the artificial structure was modified. The new modules were reduced in size to make them easier to carry, handle, and deploy. These new structures of 30 cm in diameter and 18 cm in height were successful. In each structure, 10 plates with five micro-fragments—a total of 50 micro-fragments per structure—were attached (Figure 14.15(a), (b)).

Figure 14.15 Artificial structures designed for outplanting micro-fragments: (a) a structure covered with 300 micro-fragments and (b) a smaller structure with 50 micro-fragments on each one.

In 2019, 75 artificial structures of the new design were fixed at six sites and covered with micro-fragments of seven different species. A total of 3,750 micro-fragments were outplanted (Table 14.6).

Table 14.6 Micro-fragments of seven species outplanted on artificial structures at six sites in 2019

Marine Protected Area	Site (Reef)	Species	Amount of Artificial Structures	Amount of Genotypes	Amount of Micro-Fragments
Isla Contoy-NPA	Ixlache	OANN	9	7	450
		OFAV	4	4	200
		MCAV	3	3	150
		SSID	3	3	150
		SINT	1	1	50
Akumal	Media Luna	OANN	2	2	100
		OFAV	1	1	50
		MCAV	4	4	200
		SSID	3	3	150
	Morgan	OANN	3	3	150
		MCAV	4	4	200
		SSID	3	3	150
	La Isla	PCLI	1	1	50
		PAST	1	1	50
COIMPCPN-NPA	Garrafon	OANN	6	4	300
		OFAV	4	4	200
		MCAV	8	5	400
		SSID	5	4	250
		SINT	1	1	50
		PCLI	1	1	50
		PAST	1	1	50
Playa del Carmen	Chunzumbul	PCLI	5	2	250
		PAST	2	1	100

OANN = *Orbicella annularis*, OFAV = *Orbicella faveolata*, MCAV = *Montastraea cavernosa*, SSID = *Siderastrea siderea*, SINT = *Stephanocoenia intersepta*, PCLI = *Pseudodiploria clivosa*, and PAST = *Porites astreoides*.

Restoration of the Reef Crest

The success in the production of micro-fragments and their outplanting in the reef encouraged the generation of even more innovative techniques that allow better results at outplanting more corals—faster and at a lower cost. Therefore, new concepts emerge to address the restoration of the reef crest through the multiple-cutting technique and assisted dispersion in situ as well as ex situ.

Multiple-Cutting
In May of 2018 researchers of INAPESCA and Mote Marine Laboratory designed a new technique named *multiple-cutting* to scale up and reduce the reef restoration cost. During October 2018, a pilot trial to explore the use of this technology was conducted at Manchones Reef in Isla Mujeres Bay and Cuevones Reef in Punta Cancun under the supervision of Dr. David Vaughan. This technique consists of cutting small fragments of previously outplanted colonies and attaching them near the donor colony, with the intention of propagating their tissue and dispersing their genome, as it normally occurs in the natural environment (Bothwell 1981; Padilla and Lara 1996). In this way, as the fragments grow, they will fuse together into bigger colonies (Bak and Criens 1982) and eventually form coral barriers. After two days of work at the restoration sites, 1,083 micro-fragments of *Acropora palmata* were produced and outplanted. An area of 726 m^2 was covered by this technique (Figure 14.16).

Figure 14.16 New *multiple-cutting* technique applied to a colony of *Acropora palmata*. New small fragments can be seen on the substrate under the colony.

Assisted Dispersion of Acropora *spp.*
From the implementation of the multiple-cutting techniques, a new concept was developed by the work team for the restoration of the reef crest through the assisted dispersion of *Acropora* spp. The concept takes advantage of the high regeneration capacity of these species (Bak 1983). In general, it is possible to harvest 100 to 300 micro-fragments from a big (>1 m diameter), healthy coral colony, under the premise that collecting this must to be less than 1% of the total living tissue to inflict a relatively low effect. When using this practice, results showed that colonies recovered well from their lesions in less than 15 days; the tissue loss takes about three to five months to recover, and even generates a profuse growth, which is similar to the pruning effect on trees. The fragments that are obtained can be outplanted in adjacent areas to the donor colony to reinforce their biomass within the *Acropora* patch. On the other hand, fragments can be outplanted in the bordering areas of the patch to increase its size, being in both cases an in situ assisted dispersion. Also, it is possible to transfer the fragments to other reef patches, with the intention to rehabilitate damaged areas with low or no presence of *Acropora* spp. in an assisted dispersion ex situ to recover coral cover, to increase the genetic diversity, and/or to rescue the coral structure. The great advantage of this new technique is that the coral nurseries are not needed, decreasing costs significantly.

Use of King Crab to Reinforce Herbivore for an Integral Reef Restoration

A field pilot trial was performed in collaboration with the Healthy Reef for Healthy People Initiative (HRI) to evaluate the synergic effect of herbivorous organisms, such as king crab (*Maguimithrax spinosissimus*), with the outplanting of corals in more integral reef restoration projects. For this, 200 coral colonies of *A. cervicornis* were planted in four reef patches within a total area of 200 m^2. One month later, 28 crabs were transferred into two of those patches; they were distributed equally in numbers with the same sexual proportion in each one. The effect of the crab's presence in outplanted coral sites showed a significant decline in turf and macroalgae cover, followed by an increase in crustose coralline algae cover, a species considered a precursor for coral larvae settlement. These favorable results encouraged the team to start a crab farming project in 2019, which is currently being implemented.

Conservation Ex Situ as an Action Against SCTLD

SCTLD has caused massive mortality in several coral species in the Mexican Caribbean since it was first detected in July 2018. Trying to control this situation, tissue of most affected species has been rescued. Again, field pilot trials were considered and four fragments of *Orbicella annularis* with healthy coral tissue were rescued from diseased colonies. These samples were maintained in the aquariums under controlled conditions. After a quarantine period of more than 40 days, it was observed that all of the fragments had recovered and none of them presented lesions. Subsequently, four colonies of *Dendrogyra cylindrus* from Cozumel Island with SCTLD were rescued. After a 71-day period of quarantine, two genotypes showed tissue survival greater than 75%, while the other two colonies were already in very poor condition and had shown a major death in the rescued fragments. Those first experiences indicated that the success of rescuing tissue depends on the species and the initial condition of the diseased colony.

MONITORING THE EFFECTIVENESS OF RESTORATION ACTIONS

The methods of monitoring restoration actions has changed over time. Initially, methods to assess a reef's conditions were to directly measure the reef by using quadrants and visual censuses to evaluate coral coverage and the biomass of ichthyologic fauna (Table 14.7).

Currently, ecological restoration has begun to implement actions to recover both the structure and the functionality of the reef to achieve long-term success. However, specific monitoring to assess the effect and/or effectiveness of restoration actions does not exist; hence, it has been proposed that evaluation must consider the effect of the restoration efforts from an integral ecosystem point of view. Following this idea, since 2017, the team is working to adapt the International Principles and Standards for the practice of ecological restoration that was developed for the Society for Ecological Restoration (SER) (Gann et al. 2019) to Coral Reef Ecosystems. These standards will be used to evaluate a site before, during, and after the restoration actions, using the recovery wheel tool, through six main ecosystem attributes: absence of threats, physical conditions, species composition, structural diversity, ecosystem functionality, and external exchanges; it considers a range of zero to five to evaluate their recovery (Figure 14.17(a), (b)).

Table 14.7 Monitoring methods applied to evaluate the effectiveness of the restoration actions in the different periods

Period	Type of Monitoring	Method	Elements to Evaluate
2006–2007	Monitoring the growth in reef restoration actions	Measurement of coral branches	• Growth of fixed new coral colonies
2012–2014	Monitoring the growth in reef restoration actions	Photoquadrants 0.5 m^2 every 3 months	• Growth of fixed new coral colonies
2012–2013	Monitoring the environmental condition	Strickland and Parsons 1972; Parsons et al. 1984; Morris and Riley 1963; Lorenzen et al. 1976	• Temperature, salinity, dissolved oxygen, nitrates, nitrites, reactive, chlorophyll-a
2012–2014	Monitoring the survival rate in reef restoration actions	Live colonies account	• Survival of fixed new coral colonies
2012–2016	Monitoring the coral cover recovery due to restoration activities	Photoquadrants 1 m^2 every 6 months Visual census by fish community (AGRRA 2005)	• Coral cover per species increase • Fish biomass

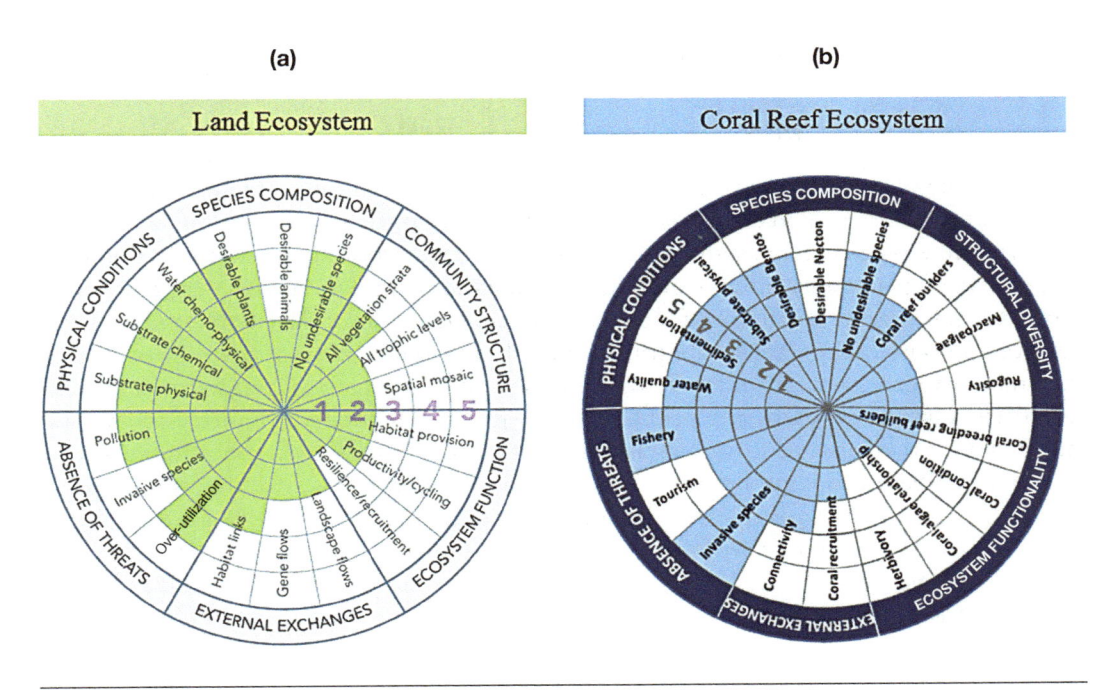

Figure 14.17 The ecological recovery wheel (a) for a land ecosystem taken from Gann et al. (2019) and (b) the proposed changes to implement in coral reef ecosystems.

COMMUNITY INVOLVEMENT, VOLUNTEERS, AND CITIZEN SCIENCE

Stakeholders and the community have been involved in coral reef conservation since the 1970s. They organized and pressed for the creation of the first national parks in the Mexican Caribbean. The aim was to prevent deterioration of the coral reef units and to control entry in the number of permits and to regulate visitors' activities in the water. Although reef restoration subprograms were incorporated into the management programs of all marine protected areas, most of the reef restoration activities started in 2004.

Between 2004 and 2005 the trajectory of three hurricanes exerted enormous damages upon the reef units, mostly on the northern coast of the Mexican Caribbean. Reef coral cover and structural complexity was lost. After Hurricane Ivan in 2004, a first action plan was established. After the event, it considered the closing of all reef units to visiting tourists which would reopen contingent upon the results of the assessment of damages. Depending on these results, the different reef units could be opened according to tourism activities. Before any assessment, the following actions should take place: (a) removal of debris and objects, (b) rescue of live fragments to avoid tissue loss or abrasion, (c) carrying the live fragments to safe places in order to maintain high survival rates and maintain them before their reattachment, and (d) assess damages to reef units.

In the Mexican Caribbean, as in other reef areas in Mexico, there is no volunteer program. Most of the participation has been paid and is enhanced considering that the sooner the problem is solved, the better, in order *to return* to normal activities. In 2005 CONANP provided contingency funds that were used to restore impacted reef units of the national parks of Isla

Mujeres, Cancun, and Puerto Morelos. Between 2005 and 2018, several government funds through CONANP were assigned to community members to develop and implement reef restoration projects. These low-budget projects were used in an effective way and have contributed to the learning and building capacity of the community to restore reef units.

Though some efforts have been conducted by local non-governmental organizations (NGOs) and research centers, most of the reef restoring activities have been supervised and implemented by CONANP and INAPESCA. This has been possible because restoring is an essential part of the protected areas management programs and INAPESCA contributes with two biological stations to conduct and test new techniques, both in the laboratory and in the field. This knowledge has increased with the contribution of local citizens from the communities, results from other parts of the world, contributions of campaigns, and to the increasing concern and awareness of the population who now live in the Quintana Roo State and see the importance of having a healthy reef and benefit from the environmental services it provides.

Thanks to hurricanes and the efforts to restore the impacted areas, true understanding and communication became possible between stakeholders and authorities in the Mexican Caribbean. The need to work together to restore the reefs impacted by natural phenomena had a greater and more positive effect than by training courses or surveillance by the authorities due to the destruction inflicted by hurricanes; a better relationship exists between the protected areas' staff and stakeholders. Even better, three scuba diving instructors enrolled with the national park staff and became park rangers.

In 2018 The Nature Conservancy and the Government of the State of Quintana Roo created a trust for the management of coastal areas to start the first parametric coral reef insurance policy in the world. To implement this instrument, an early warning protocol and immediate response to the impact of tropical cyclones on the reefs of the national park of Puerto Morelos Reef were developed (Zepeda et al. 2019). This includes the actions to be taken before, during, and after a hurricane. To apply the actions of this protocol, INAPESCA participated in the training of community brigades in Puerto Morelos, Isla Mujeres, and Isla Contoy in order to execute the actions provided in the protocol for the rapid evaluation of the impact of the cyclones and the primary response actions in the reef. For example, recently, the community brigades participated in a massive outplanting of corals, allowing the restoration efforts to be extended.

Things are changing in the Mexican Caribbean—climate change, problems of white syndrome, and massive beaching of mats of sargassum (*Sargasssum* spp.) are now impacting reef formations in a drastic way. More than ever, involvement of the community is needed and new restoration techniques are being designed to facilitate it. Micro-fragmentation (Page et al. 2018) and a scaling-up technique that was developed in 2018 by researchers of INAPESCA and the Mote Marine Laboratory called *multiple-cutting* or *assisted dispersion* could enhance the involvement of the community and make restoration efforts more effective and less costly.

As it was early in 1970, it is still necessary to continue the involvement of stakeholders and the community. It is also very important to create awareness in all visitors to the Mexican Caribbean. Action plans need to be revised and training courses for stakeholders are essential as part of the restoration program. Only in this way can we see that it would have a real impact in the conservation of coral reefs in the most visited areas of the Mexican Caribbean.

DISCUSSION

Current degradation of coral reefs makes it essential to implement restoration actions in order to maintain their structure and functioning. However, the condition of reefs has been decreasing rapidly while the challenges regarding reef restoration have increased. The most urgent problem that needs to be attended is the scaling up of coral-fragment production and their outplanting to achieve a greater impact on reef restoration actions and contribute to its resiliency. The first approach to do this has been through micro-fragmentation techniques, which also allows working more efficiently with massive corals (Page 2013; Page et al. 2018). Along with the production of corals, it is necessary to develop new restoration techniques that accelerate the rates of outplanting of corals in the field, to increase the quantity and variety of coral species, and to apply scaling-up techniques in order to achieve more extensive areas of intervention and increase coral reef coverage. Thus, the micro-fragmentation allows the production of coral tissue plates that can be used to cover both natural and artificial structures in the reef, with the intended benefit being to retain the rugosity of the site in the first case, or to increase it in the second case. Also, the micro-fragmentation technique can be used with branched species, like *Acropora palmata*, since many small fragments of a large colony can be obtained and outplanted directly in the reef substrate. Fragments obtained by this technique can be used to coat coral skeletons or to be outplanted in the substrate. One great advantage is that they no longer require fragments to be kept in marine nurseries or land-based tanks. Now, it is important to consider that the criteria for outplanting those fragments have implications for the restoration effect that we intend to achieve. Therefore, it is possible to outplant the fragments right next to the donor colony by in situ assisted dispersion to promote the formation of ramets of new cohorts, which make feasible the fusion of the colonies during their growth, with the main purpose being to reinforce the biomass into the reef patch. However, the fragments can be outplanted on the border of the patch to extend it in size or they can be transferred to other sites by ex situ assisted dispersion to recover damaged areas. It is important to say that these kinds of interventions are faster, cheaper, and can cover larger areas in less time. They also have a more direct and specific effect on the maintenance and recovery of the reef structure. In addition, they contribute to incremental coral coverage. In this sense, an encouraging attempt is the use of king crabs to reinforce herbivores in the intervened sites to get a synergistic effect that achieves an integral restoration of the site.

CONCLUSIONS

Reef restoration actions in the Mexican Caribbean began in 2004. The lessons learned throughout this time have been several and diverse. A relevant fact has been the inter-institutional collaboration to form a solid working group, enhancing the participation of the interested and trained community. The exchange of international experiences to share successes and failures has allowed for the strengthening of the group's capabilities. With regard to coral production and restoration actions, the techniques have been diversified, so there are different options to be applied and, therefore, new ways to implement reef restoration are conceived and new concepts are necessarily created. In this sense, we agree with Randall et al. (2020) that a combination of restoration approaches will deliver the greatest benefits.

Thus, previous knowledge of the specific conditions of the site to be restored becomes an important guide to intervention decisions. For example, in some highly degraded sites, it would be recommended to make initial interventions with pioneer coral species, such as *Porites astreoides*, in order to promote the consolidation of the substrate; or in places where the sedimentation and growth of algae are high, the intervention could initiate with *Acropora prolifera* that rapidly changes the substrate and generates new niches. In both cases, it is necessary that subsequent interventions consider more robust corals species. This is a new idea of intervention, through a succession restoration that allows gradual changes to be generated in highly deteriorated sites, where otherwise it would be a mistake to outplant coral colonies of great reef builders species at the beginning of the restoration actions. Finally, a new concept is to establish a network of functional restored areas, as a large-scale restoration measure, which can function as sources of recovery for nearby sites, due to the impossibility of restoring each area of the reef one inch at a time.

In order to scale up the intervention to restore coral reefs, the active participation of the community is fundamental. For this, in the northeast coast of the Mexican Caribbean, community brigades have been trained. Main courses were based on primary restoration techniques that were related to the early warning protocol and immediate response to the impact of tropical cyclones (Zepeda et al. 2019), which is also the reference for the world's first parametric insurance policy for coral reef restoration reefs. After the training process, these people participated in reef restoration activities, facilitating massive interventions where up to 3,000 corals were outplanted in just one day. However, there is a great need to continue and expand these efforts to increase the number of trained people to collaborate in restoration intervention in the future.

Unfortunately, while different methods and techniques are tested for reef restoration with much success, coral reefs are confronting a new problem that threatens their existence due to the massive mortality of corals influenced by SCTLD. At the moment, efforts by the working group have been focused on the rescue of healthy living tissue that can still be found in diseased colonies in order to establish a genetic bank for the ex situ conservation of most affected species. To reinforce these efforts, collaborations between institutions are being established for the conservation of the most affected species' genome through cryopreservation techniques.

It is true that sometimes it seems that degradation of the reefs is greater than the achievements obtained through restoration interventions. However, at this moment, there is already a capacity built among different institutions and organizations to guide coral production efforts to form banks of successful genotypes and to identify the most resistant ones; with restoration actions planned specifically for the type of environment and the degree of deterioration of the area to be intervened. All of these actions must necessarily be focused on adapting to climate change for long-term usefulness.

There is still much to learn—and areas that still need to be addressed. One is the economic valuation of damages, and the other is assessing a detailed cost of coral production along with the costs and benefits of restoration interventions, as well as valuating the environmental services that reef ecosystems provide. These results represent a very useful technical element for the economic valuation of damages, compensations, and fines.

In Mexico, there is a clear understanding of the reef degradation problem. Therefore, different government research institutions and NGOs are working on building capacity and coordinating efforts to implement a strategic plan to restore the coral reefs of the Mexican Caribbean.

Through this initiative, the hope is to strengthen the capacities in order to make reef restoration a successful activity to counteract future sources of impact.

ACKNOWLEDGMENTS

The authors acknowledge our institutions, the Instituto Nacional de la Pesca y Acuacultura (INAPESCA) and Comisión Nacional de Áreas Naturales Protegidas (CONANP), for the support to carry out this project since 2004. Also, this project has had external financial support from the Department for Environment, Food and Rural Affairs from the UK (DEFRA), Comisión Nacional de Biodiversidad (CONABIO) (JA-009), and the Government of the Quintana Roo State. Techniques for producing sexual recruits were initially learned from Dr. Anastazia Banaszak, a scientist at the National Autonomous University of Mexico (UNAM). Thanks to Melina Soto for the first review of the manuscript. We thank all members of the staff who have been participating for all of these years—technicians, students, and captains—for their work, ideas, and passion to restore our reefs even more and better every time.

REFERENCES

Atlantic and Gulf Rapid Reef Assessment (AGRRA). 2005. "AGRRA Methodology: Version 4.0, June 2005." *In*: M. McField and P. R. Kramer. 2007. Healthy Reefs for Healthy People: A guide to indicators of reef health and social well-being in the Mesoamerican Reef Region. UIT contributions by M. Gorrez and M. McPherson. pp. 208.

Bak, R. P. M. 1983. "Neoplasia, regeneration and growth in the reef-building coral Acropora palmata." *Mar. Biol.*, 77:221–227.

Bak, R. P. M. and S. R. Criens. 1982. "Experimental fusion in Atlantic Acropora (Scleractinia)." *Mar Biol. Lett.* 3:67–72.

Bothwell, A. M. 1981. "Fragmentation, a means of asexual reproduction and dispersal in the coral genus *Acropora* (Scleractinia: Astrocoeniida: Acroporidae)—a preliminary report." Proc. 4th Int. Coral Reef Symp., Manila, 2:137–144.

Foo, S. A. and G. P. Asner. 2019. "Scaling up coral reef restoration using remote sensing technology." *Front. Mar. Sci.* 6:79. doi:10.3389/fmars.2019.00079.

Gann, G. D., T. McDonald, B. Walder, J. Aronson, C. R. Nelson, J. Jonson, J. G. Hallett, et al. 2019. "International principles and standards for the practice of ecological restoration." Second edition: November 2019. *Society for Ecological Restoration*, Washington, D.C. 20005 USA. https://www.ser.org/page/SERStandards.

Ladd, M. C., M. W. Miller, J. H. Hunt, W. C. Sharp, and D. E. Burkepile. 2018. "Harnessing ecological processes to facilitate coral restoration." *Front. Ecol. Environ.* 16, 239–247. doi:10.1002/fee.1792.

Lorenzen, M. W., D. J. Smith, and L. V. Kimmel. 1976. "A long term phosphorus model for lakes." Application to Lake Washington. In: *Modeling the Biochemical Processes in Aquatic Ecosystems* 75–91. R. P. Canale (ed). Ann Arbor Science Publishers, Michigan.

McDonald, T., G. D. Gann, J. Jonson, and K. W. Dixon. 2016. "International standards for the practice of ecological restoration—including principles and key concepts." *Society for Ecological Restoration*, Washington, D.C.

McField, M., P. Kramer, A. Giró-Petersen, M. Soto, I. Drysdale, N. Craig, and M. Rueda-Flores. 2020. "2020 Mesoamerican Reef Report Card. Healthy Reefs Initiative." www.healthyreefs.org.

Huitrón Baca, J. C., J. González-Cano, and A. Vega Zepeda. 2011. "CASE STUDY 3: *Acropora* Restoration in Isla Mujeres National Park, Mexico." In: *Caribbean Acropora Restoration Guide: Best Practices for Propagation and Population Enhancement*. M. E. Johnson, C. Lustic, E. Bartels, I. B. Baums, D. S. Gilliam, L. Larson, D. Lirman, et al. (eds.). The Nature Conservancy, Arlington, VA.

Morris, A. W. and J. P. Riley. 1963. "The determination of nitrate in seawater." *Analytica chimica acta* 29:272–279.

Padilla-Souza, C., J. González Cano, A. Banaszak, H. Hernández Arana, and R. Raigoza Figueras. 2018. "Programa interdisciplinario de restauración activa para compensar daños antropogénicos en arrecifes coralinos del caribe mexicano." Instituto Nacional de Pesca y Acuacultura. Informe final SNIB-CONABIO, proyecto No. JA009. Ciudad de México.

Padilla-Souza, C. and M. Lara-Pérez-Soto. 1996. "Efecto del tamaño de las colonias en el crecimiento de *Acropora palmata* en Puerto Morelos, Quintana Roo, México." *Hidrobiológica* 6(1–2):17–24.

Padilla-Souza, C., E. Ramírez-Mata, M. Soto, J. González-Cano, and R. Ibarra-Navarro. 2017. *Programa de restauración de arrecifes coralinos: El caso de dos áreas afectadas por encallamiento.* Proceedings of the 69th Gulf and Caribbean Fisheries Institute. November 7–11, 2016. Grand Cayman, Cayman Islands. pp. 352–361.

Page, C. A. 2013. "Reskinning a reef: Mote marine scientists explore a new approach to reef restoration." In: *Coral: The Reef and Marine Aquarium Magazine* pp. 72–81.

Page, C. A., E. M. Muller, and D. E. Vaughan. 2018. "Microfragmenting for the successful restoration of slow growing massive corals." *Ecological Engineering* 123, pp. 86–94. doi.org/10.1016/j.ecoleng.2018.08.017

Parsons, T. R., Y. Maita, and C. M. Lalli. 1984. "A manual of chemical and biological methods for seawaters analysis." *Second Edition, Pergamon Press*, Oxford, England, pp. 173.

Randall, C. J., A. P. Negri, K. M. Quigley, T. Foster, G. F. Ricardo, N. S. Webster, L. K. Bay, et al. 2020. "Sexual production of corals for reef restoration in the Anthropocene." *Mar. Ecol. Prog. Ser. Vol.* 635:203–232. https://doi.org/10.3354/meps13206.

Strickland, J. D. H. and T. R. Parsons. 1972. "Practical handbook of sea water analysis." *Second Edition, Fisheries Research Board Canadian Bulletin*, Ottawa, Canada, pp. 311.

Zepeda-Centeno, C., C. Padilla-Souza, J. C. Huitrón-Baca, M. Macías-Constantino, E. Shaver, G. Nava-Martínez, and M. A. García-Salgado. 2019. "Early warning and rapid response protocol: Actions to mitigate the impact of tropical cyclones on coral reefs." *The Nature Conservancy*, 69 pgs.

15

ACTIVE CORAL REEF RESTORATION IN AUSTRALIA

Adam Smith, Nathan Cook, and Johnny Gaskell

ABSTRACT

The growing interest in coral reef restoration projects is relatively recent in Australia. It reflects a sense of urgency for action to confront the declines in coral reef health and tourism amenity, and an increase in funding opportunities and management support. This case study shares knowledge from eleven small-scale projects that have been deployed in the Great Barrier Reef Marine Park (GBRMP) between 2017–2020. The methods vary from transplant, nursery, and/or outplanting of coral larvae, fragments, or colonies.

Arguably, the first active coral reef restoration project was led by the Reef Restoration Foundation at Fitzroy Island, Cairns, and was comprised of 1,000 coral fragments in 10 coral tree nurseries. The largest active coral reef restoration project in Australia involved the restoration of damage caused by Cyclone Debbie utilizing bulldozers to relocate an estimated 400 tons of large coral bommies from the intertidal beach to subtidal at Manta Ray Bay. Several larval enhancement projects have collected millions of larvae and deployed them over an area between 25 and 100 m^2. These projects have involved collaboration between research scientists, tourism businesses, management agencies, and citizen scientists. Ecological research on survivorship and growth of coral has been conducted for all projects. Social research is being undertaken at one of the projects in the Whitsunday region.

Definition: Bommie

Australian—an outcrop of coral reef, often resembling a column, that is higher than the surrounding platform of reef and which may be partially exposed at low tide. The word is derived from the French bombax and is sometimes spelled bombie, but more commonly bommie. The term is not normally used in scientific papers but is usually understood to describe anything from a single coral boulder to a large reef structure.

In 2017 the Great Barrier Reef Marine Park Authority (GBRMPA) held a summit to discuss new priorities and one of the outcomes was to encourage active, localized coral reef restoration. In 2018, the Great Barrier Reef (GBR) Restoration Symposium was attended by over 300 people to share knowledge. Also in 2018 the GBRMPA published guidelines on perceived low, medium, high, and very high risks for various methods of reef restoration. A key success factor for all of these projects has been the collaborative, positive attitude and focus on good science, education, and action that has empowered diverse stakeholders with a common interest on restoring reef health.

INTRODUCTION

Coral reefs occur throughout tropical and temperate Australian waters with at least 400 species. This case study focuses on the GBR, the world's largest coral reef ecosystem, ranging over 2,300 km, 14 degrees in latitude, and comprising more than 2,900 separate coral reefs. The species diversity, habitat value, and natural beauty of coral reefs are major contributors to the reef's outstanding universal values as a world heritage area and the GBRMP.

The GBR is an ecosystem under global and local pressure. Long-term datasets indicate hard coral cover has significantly declined over the past 30 years. Between 1986 and 2014, though, there have been some periods of recovery; the overall average hard coral cover in the region is estimated to have declined from 28 to 13.8 percent and the rate of decline has increased substantially in recent years (De'ath et al. 2012).

Every five years, the GBR outlook report is prepared. In 2009 the GBR was considered to be at a crossroad, with decisions made in subsequent years likely to determine its long-term future (GBRMPA 2009). In 2014 the outlook for the GBR was assessed as poor (GBRMPA 2014) and in 2019 as very poor (GBRMPA 2019). The GBR has been severely impacted by two years of major coral bleaching, cyclones, a 50% decline in coral, and an 89% decline in coral larvae settlement (GBRMPA 2019).

Australian coral reefs have a long history of indigenous use, coral reef science, management, aquaculture, and sustainable industries. Australians have been involved in artificial reefs, oyster reefs, the transplantation of mangroves and seagrasses, seaweed removal, Crown of Thorns Starfish (COTS) removal, and other interventions to assist the environment and community. Coral reef restoration research and active reef restoration projects were rare in Australia until 2017 because we generally had healthy and well managed reefs. Global climate change, declining water quality, overfishing, coastal development, and other factors have resulted in cumulative impacts to coral reefs. The *Reef 2050 Plan* highlighted the need to restore the resilience of all ecosystems in the face of current and future threats such as climate change. The *2017 Reef Blueprint* established that the GBRMPA's approach moving forward would be to adopt additional measures to not only protect and mitigate but to support reef recovery, including the establishment of restoration demonstration site(s) to test, improve, and where appropriate, scale up restoration methods.

Australia has been quick to respond to reef decline and the community and industry desire for reef restoration. In 2017 Australia committed $100 million dollars to reef restoration over a 10-year period, which is arguably the single largest reef restoration investment in the world.

TECHNIQUES AND METHODS

The primary aim of coral reef restoration in Australia is to test techniques and methods, improve knowledge, and improve the health of recently degraded coral reefs in terms of ecosystem structure and function. A secondary aim is to assist reef-related industries such as tourism and education. In addition, some projects aim to involve citizen scientists and community volunteers to provide opportunities for hands-on involvement encouraging behavioral change beyond the restoration project. The focus of this chapter is on the secondary aim and the involvement of tourism, citizen scientists, and volunteers in active hands-on restoration projects.

Reef restoration techniques in Australia include simple *coral gardening, bommie tipping*, floating trays with rope, floating trays with plugs, coral trees, and electrolysis (see Table 15.1). These diverse methods have been led by scientists and supported by citizen scientists, businesses, snorkelers, divers, tourists, and the general public. Complex reef restoration techniques such as nurseries and larval enhancement require planning, costly infrastructure, experience, and skill that are generally led by scientists. One of the coral reef restoration projects in Australia associated with *bommie tipping* has been led by the state government (Table 15.1). Currently there is no specific requirement in Australia for preferred methods, techniques, locations, or a requirement for formal training in science or reef restoration.

There have also been several active coral reef restoration and relocation projects as a result of damage to coral from ship groundings, navigation channels, and marinas and tourism developments in the GBR (Marshall et al. 2002; Smith et al. 2002). Historically, the earliest confirmed

Table 15.1 A list of coral reef restoration projects, locations, and methods in the GBR region

Year	Technique	Location	Who	How	What	Why
1940s	?	Turtle Bay, Cairns	Yarrabah Traditional Owners	Coral gardening	?	?
2003	Transplant	Agincourt Reef, Cairns	Reef Biosearch	Coral gardening	Outplant 99 colonies	Research
2017–2019	Coral Trees	Fitzroy Island, Cairns	Reef Restoration Foundation	Coral gardening	Nursery 1000, outplant 96	Research
2017	Larval enhancement	Heron and One Tree Island	Southern Cross University	Harvest coral spawn	Coral bommie	Research
2017	Boulder placement (bommie tipping)	Manta Ray Bay, Whitsundays	QPWS	Bulldozer	Relocate 400 tons habitat	Cyclone Debbie
2018	Larval enhancement	Vlasoff and Arlington Reef, Cairns	SCU, UTS, JCU	Harvest coral spawn	Nursery, outplant	Research
2018–2020	Coral nursery	Blue Pearl and Manta Ray Bay, Whitsundays	Reef Ecologic	Floating trays, discs, and ropes	Nursery 425 corals, outplant 88	Cyclone Debbie
2018–2020	Coral nursery	Opal Reef	UTS, Wavelength	Floating trays	Nursery, outplant	Bleaching
2018–2020	Mineral accretion	Agincourt Reef #3, Cairns	Reef Ecologic, Quicksilver	Electrolysis	Outplant 288 colonies	Cumulative impacts
2019	Onshore raceway	Lovers Cove, Daydream	Daydream Island Resort	Coral plugs, spiders	Outplant 30 colonies	Cyclone Debbie
2019–2020	Coral Trees	Moore Reef, Cairns	Reef Restoration Foundation		Permitted but not installed	Research

KEY: QPWS = Queensland Parks and Wildlife Service, SCU = Southern Cross University, JCU = James Cook University, UTS = University of Technology, Sydney indigenous planting of coral for reef restoration was in the 1940s at Turtle Bay, Cairns (personal communication, Gudjugudju, in Burrows et al. 2019) (Table 15.1). We have collated a total of 11 case studies of coral reef restoration (Figure 15.1; Table 15.1). There are currently eight active reef restoration projects (Table 15.1) that we will briefly discuss in the following sections. All of

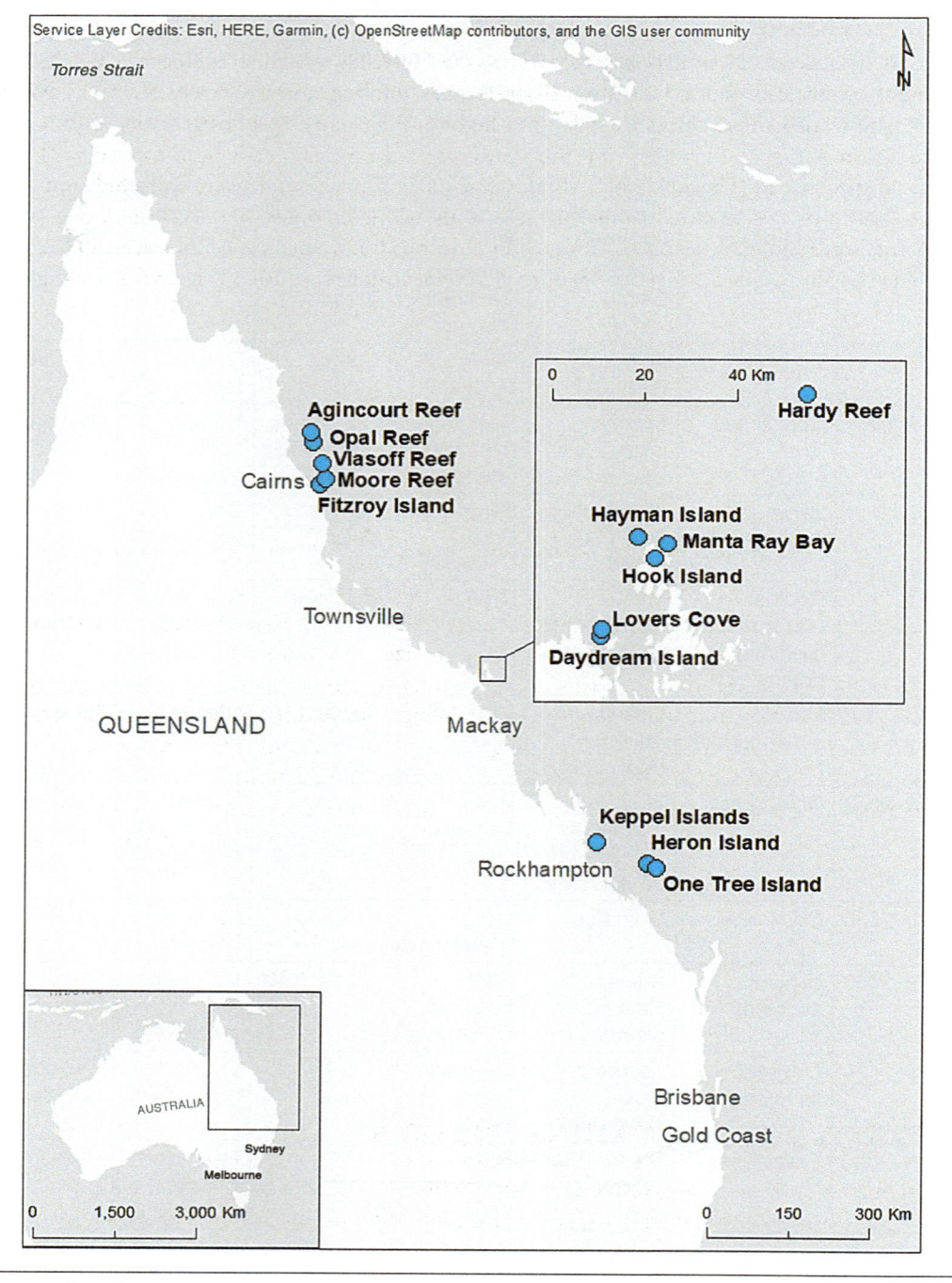

Figure 15.1 Map of active reef restoration projects in Australia.

the case studies are from the GBR, Queensland, and Australia. To our knowledge, there are no active or published coral reef restoration projects in other states of Australia.

AGINCOURT REEF, CAIRNS 2003

One of the first active reef transplantation and restoration projects was conducted as a pilot program conducted at Agincourt Reef, Cairns, in 2003. Ninety-nine live coral colonies and fragments were transplanted to three discrete sites totaling approximately 80 m^2 (Laycock 2004). The transplanted corals included the taxonomic groups: Staghorn *Acropora* (n = 51); Bottle Brush *Acropora* (n = 19); Corymbose *Acropora* (n = 21); *Pocillopora* spp. (n = 2); and *Sinularia* spp. (n = 6) (Laycock 2004; Monkivitch 2008). Donor corals were collected from sites within 200 m of the intended transplant site. Only whole colonies were collected, and when fragments were generated, a colony provided numerous fragments. Colonies were 15–30 cm in diameter for all species other than staghorn *Acropora* which were 30–50 cm and a select group of 50–100 cm fragments were used. Attachment was through a mixture of 3:1 cement/plaster after preparation of the natural reef surface, including scrubbing and chiseling. The transplanted corals were monitored weekly for three weeks, then at four-to-six-week intervals for seven months. Monitoring included attachment state, estimates of the percentage of live tissue area (%LTA), counts of growing tips, measurement of colony height and width, and a statement of general condition.

MANTA RAY BAY, WHITSUNDAY ISLANDS 2017

Following severe coral damage from ex-Tropical Cyclone Debbie, the Queensland Parks and Wildlife Service (QPWS) undertook a very large-scale coral restoration project involving the relocation of stranded *Porites* bommies ranging in size from 0.5 m–2.5 m in diameter. This project initially involved discussions of the feasibility of intervention works between QPWS and GBRMPA and commercial operators in the Whitsundays during the weeks following the cyclone event (mid-April 2017). The next stage was site assessment (through a series of swim transects) conducted by QPWS that observed less than one percent of live coral remaining, dominated by both encrusting and massive coral life-forms. Consequently, an authorization under Section 5.4 of the *GBRMP Zoning Plan 2003* for the purpose of such intervention works to relocate coral bommies back below the low-water mark to increase substrate for potential coral larval settlement in the future and fish habitats was granted. In terms of in-field operations scheduled over a two-day period, an estimated 100 cubic meters of dead coral substrate, equaling approximately 400 tons, were removed and placed back into the water below the low-water limit. A follow-up site assessment after these works was undertaken by QPWS in the following weeks to ensure that substrates were stabilized for in-water safety activity considerations. A full description of this project can be found in McLeod et al. (2019).

FITZROY ISLAND, CAIRNS 2017–2019

In December 2017, the Reef Restoration Foundation, in collaboration with a team of volunteers, local businesses, organizations, and researchers, established the first coral nursery on the GBR. The project was implemented in the shallow fringing reef around Fitzroy Island, 25 km east of Cairns (see Figure 15.1).

The Reef Restoration Foundation team utilized the coral tree (Nedimyer et al. 2011) method that is popular throughout Florida and the Caribbean. Six coral nursery trees were initially deployed just offshore from the island in a depth of between 6 and 14 m (Figure 15.2). Upon establishment, the team installed and stocked six coral nursery trees with 240 coral fragments from 24 mother colonies of the genus Acropora. After seven months, 96 coral fragments were outplanted into experimental quadrats, four additional trees were added, and all trees were restocked with 1,000 fragments. Early results indicate a high survivorship of greater than 85% on both the nurseries and the outplant sites.

Corals at Fitzroy Island have been outplanted using a range of methods including nail and cable tie, putty, and cement (Figure 15.3(a), (b), (c)).

Figure 15.2 Coral tree nursery at Fitzroy Island, Cairns.

Figure 15.3 Outplant methods including (a) the nail-and-tie method, (b) putty, and (c) cement.

BLUE PEARL AND MANTA RAY BAY, WHITSUNDAY ISLANDS 2018–2020

Following ex-Tropical Cyclone Debbie, Townsville-based marine research organization Reef Ecologic developed coral nurseries utilizing two different methods of nursery rearing—discs and rope. The aluminium coral nursery frames ranged in size from 2.4 m × 1.2/2.0 m onto which coral nursery fragment discs (Figure 15.4) were placed or ropes holding coral fragments were tied. In December 2018 a total of four nursery trays were deployed at two locations—Blue Pearl and Manta Ray Bay in the Whitsundays Region—collectively containing 425 coral fragments from over 10 different species. In August 2019 this project was expanded with the addition of ten nursery frames and the propagation of 1,245 coral colonies at Blue Pearl Bay (n = 495) and Manta Ray Bay (n = 750). Extensive consultation and subsequent involvement by local community members in the establishment and maintenance of the coral nurseries illustrates a shifting paradigm in both the acceptance of reef restoration activities and the ability to enable community stewardship in the GBR.

Figure 15.4 Researcher measures coral survivorship at the coral tray nursery, Whitsunday Islands.

AGINCOURT REEF #3, CAIRNS 2018–2020

One of the largest tourism operators in the Cairns-Port Douglas region, Quicksilver Connections, partnered with Reef Ecologic to implement an innovative reef restoration project at Agincourt Reef #3. This project represented an ideal opportunity to assist the recovery of a small section of degraded reef that is important to the socioeconomic values of the tourism business. The tourism site is based on a floating pontoon visited by 200–300 tourists each day and snorkelers and scuba divers undertake their activity close to the pontoon (Figure 15.5). The site has suffered from the cumulative effects of multiple bleaching events and cyclonic activity, with few signs of recovery.

Researchers collected partial colonies from a reef that was approximately 200 m away from the pontoon. Six steel mesh replicates were propagated with eight fragments from six species providing a total of 48 fragments per frame. The total number of fragments propagated was 288. Researchers securely attached individual coral fragments—each no larger than 5 cm in length—to the steel mesh frames using flexible 1–2 mm steel wire and pliers. Wire was wrapped around the fragment and the ends twisted to shorten the length of the wire and thus tighten the connection. It is important to ensure a tight attachment to prevent movement and encourage rapid accretion onto the frame. If a fragment was loose, a second piece of wire was attached.

Once the mesh frames were installed, they were connected to a low-voltage current to increase the alkalinity of the frames which enabled the precipitation of minerals from the surrounding seawater (Figure 15.6). This method has been trailed to examine whether the electrolysis provides enhanced growth and resilience to the corals on the frames. The installation of a small mineral-accretion project on the GBR represents an innovative approach to reef restoration and small-scale stewardship actions.

Figure 15.5 Tourism operations including catamarans, pontoons, glass-bottom boats, and diving provide opportunities for scientists and tourists to visit the GBR and learn about reef restoration.

Figure 15.6 In-water experimental setup showing the junction box, electrical cables to the anode and cathode, and the cathode mesh.

LOVERS COVE, DAYDREAM ISLAND, WHITSUNDAYS 2019

In 2019, custom-built coral raceways were developed on Daydream Island in the Whitsundays (Figure 15.7) to facilitate the initial growth stage of fragments that were to be used for restoration at one of the cyclone-damaged sites off the island. The raceways were uniquely designed to create optimal conditions for coral growth and operated on a fully flow-through raw water system. This allowed the coral fragments to grow in identical water parameters to what they experienced in the wild without the influence of predation and storm interference. Corals were held in the raceways for three to six months and were closely monitored until they were ready to be outplanted. The Daydream Island Marina is the key donor site for the initial trials that were testing two methods of restoration.

The first method of restoration used at Daydream Island involved the direct outplanting of corals that had been naturally fixed to cement discs. The disks are attached onto bare reef structures using various attachment techniques in order to fast track the initial recruitment stage on the natural reef.

Active Coral Reef Restoration in Australia

The second method involved the use of custom-designed spider frames (Figure 15.8(a), (b)) that were positioned over the seabed that consisted of mostly rubble or sediment. Both of these methods are being monitored using citizen science where tourists are able to contribute to long-term data using a newly developed iPhone app called *Coral Whitsundays*. To date, the results have been very promising with a survival rate of more than 95%.

Figure 15.7 Coral fragments and coral plugs in the raceway at Daydream Island.

Figure 15.8 (a), (b) Coral spiders designed for reef restoration and citizen science at Daydream Island.

VLASOFF AND ARLINGTON REEF, CAIRNS 2018–2019

In 2018 and again in 2019, the Larval Enhancement Project (Figure 15.9) was a collaboration between researchers Peter Harrison (Southern Cross University), Katie Chartrand (James Cook University), David Suggett (University of Technology, Sydney), and the GBRMPA, Queensland Parks & Wildlife Service, as well as other key industry partners. This partnership relied on logistical support from local tourism and other reef-based industries. Aroona Boat Charters, Argo Expeditions, and Biopixel donated key vessel and crew support during the mass spawning to assist with rearing and settling the coral larvae safely onto the reef. Coral larvae were collected during the annual mass spawning event, which typically occurs in November. The coral eggs and sperm are collected during mass spawning and then combined in enclosures on the reef to produce coral larvae for release onto damaged sections of reef.

Figure 15.9 Floating laboratory established offshore at Cairns that contains millions of coral larvae prior to reseeding damaged reefs.

MONITORING

Monitoring coral restoration projects typically involves a three-stage monitoring program corresponding to: (1) quantifying baseline benthic habitats and occasionally baseline fish communities, (2) measuring the biological response of coral nursery and/or transplants (e.g., survival, initial growth post-transplantation, and fusion of fragment to substrata), and (3) measuring longer term biological, social, and economic benefits of the project (Hein et al. 2017).

A summary of results from Laycock (2004) for the early research at Agincourt Reef demonstrated that after approximately seven months, 96 of the 99 corals were alive (96% survival). Stable or positive increments in %LTA were recorded for 68% of corals. Approximately 83% of the colonies had increased in size and 62% of corals had both a combined increase in %LTA and an increase in colony dimension (Figure 15.10). All mortality was attributed to attachment failure. There were 27 attachment failures due to wave action during two cyclones (14 cases), dislodgment by falling rubble, and dislodgment by foraging fish.

Figure 15.10 Indicative transplant growth, an *Acropora* staghorn colony (a) at initial transplant and (b) after seven months—note colony extension, basal die-back, and increased number of growing tips.

Monitoring of baseline coral abundance and diversity through Reef Health Impact Surveys (RHIS) has been conducted at coral reef restoration sites at Fitzroy, Agincourt, Blue Pearl, and Manta Ray Bay (Cook and Smith 2018). Monitoring of baseline fish abundance and diversity has been conducted at Fitzroy Island. Regular monitoring of coral survivorship and growth occurs at all sites (Figure 15.11). The experimental design for outplanted corals at Fitzroy Island involved replicate baseline surveys of fish and coral at control and treatment sites (Figures 15.12 and 15.13) (Cook and Smith 2018; Cook et al. 2018).

Figure 15.11 Snorkeler and scuba diver monitoring the survival of coral on trays in Blue Pearl Bay.

There have been small, pilot baseline social surveys of coral reef restoration projects in Australia. Following participation in the reef restoration projects, Daydream Island aquarists and volunteers were asked a series of questions to measure their enjoyment and inspiration gained from participation (Figure 15.14).

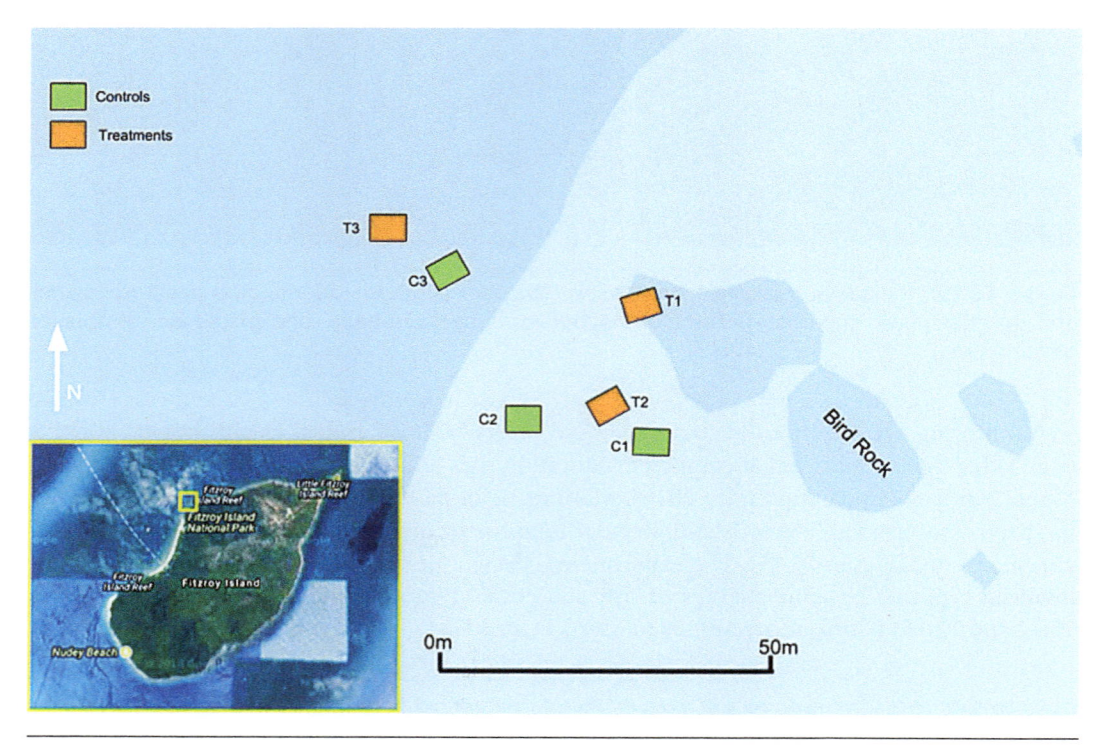

Figure 15.12 The experimental design of outplanted corals at Fitzroy Island involved three replicate quadrats for control and treatments.

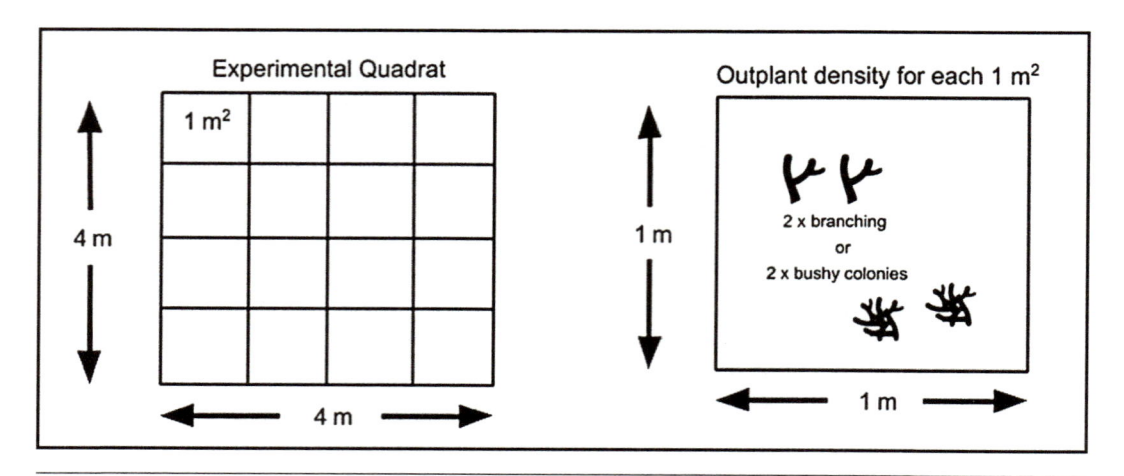

Figure 15.13 The study design of a 4 × 4 m experiment site with four corals transplanted in each 1 × 1 quadrat at Fitzroy Island.

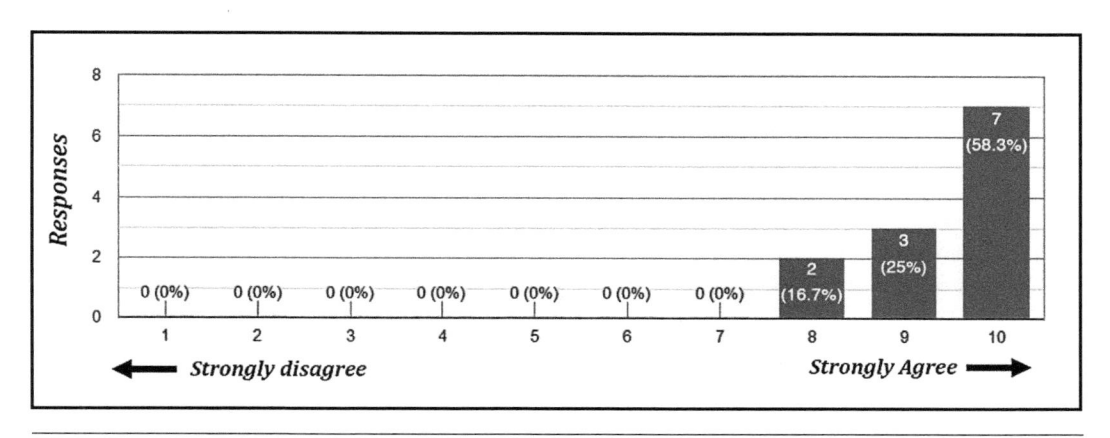

Figure 15.14 A pilot study of reef restoration volunteers (n = 12) who were asked to respond to the statement, "participation in the reef restoration activities was inspiring." Responses: 0 = strongly disagree, 10 = strongly agree.

COMMUNITY INVOLVEMENT, VOLUNTEERS, AND CITIZEN SCIENCE

A successful reef restoration project requires the involvement and support of multiple stakeholders. The GBR tourism industry has been actively involved in caring for reefs by removing COTS, *Drupella* snails, and occasionally assisting with *coral gardening* projects or the relocation of corals at tourism sites such as underwater observatories, snorkel trails, and popular dive sites following a disturbance such as a cyclone.

In 2017, following extensive damage from ex-Tropical Cyclone Debbie, local tour operators had tears in their eyes as they surveyed their broken reef for the first time. "It's worse than we thought it would be," a female crew member told news.com.au as the team searched in poor visibility for snorkeling spots that were still viable just days after the cyclone. "It's not even in long pieces, it's completely ground up. It's just barren. This is mother nature in all her wrath." While people are not usually permitted to touch the coral, Whitsunday tourism operators were given a special four-week authorization by GBRMPA to flip bommies (outcrops) that had been displaced to give the colonies a chance at survival (Reynolds 2017).

Reef restoration projects in Australia are generally led by scientists and/or government in collaboration with the tourism industry and citizen scientists (Figure 15.15(a), (b), (c)). This may be due to the complexity, time, and cost of environmental assessment and permit processes. There has been one not-for-profit company, the Reef Restoration Foundation, that has initiated a project which involved over 50 volunteers in nursery maintenance, outplanting, and citizen science. To date, there has been limited involvement in Australia of sectors such as traditional owners, recreational and commercial fisheries, and nontourism businesses. However, this is changing with increased emphasis on collaborative mapping and sharing of traditional knowledge with scientific knowledge and an emerging coral project in the Keppel Islands (Figure 15.1).

Several three-to-four-day *Introduction to Reef Restoration* and *Reef Restoration and Leadership* courses have been delivered by Reef Ecologic to stakeholders in the GBR region between 2018–2020 to share knowledge about coral species, reef restoration methodology, and project

Figure 15.15 (a), (b), and (c) Volunteers assist with many aspects of coral reef restoration projects throughout the GBR region.

planning. These courses involve the online training modules developed by the Reef Resilience Network in 2019 (Reef Resilience 2019), lectures, field assessment techniques, and project management skills.

Citizen scientists from the tourism industry have been an invaluable resource for checking the status of the Whitsunday Reef Recovery projects (Figure 15.15). The tourism industry visits these sites on a weekly basis—compared to a monthly or longer temporal scale for scientists. The tourism operators have been able to observe and take underwater video footage of the coral nurseries to share the status of corals in the nurseries and infrastructure. For example, the failure of the biodegradable ropes that were holding corals in one research experiment was disclosed to scientists who were able to respond quickly to the situation rather than wait for the next monitoring trip. The rare predation of outplanted corals by Bumphead Parrotfish (*Bolbometapon muricatum*) was also photographed and reported by the tourism industry (Figure 15.16(a), (b)).

An information display has been designed to share knowledge of the reef restoration project at Agincourt Reef (Figure 15.17(a), (b)). There are many other communication tools used by industry and citizen scientists including websites—Facebook, Instagram, Linkedin, and WhatsApp—and events to get involved and describe the process.

Figure 15.16 (a) Bumphead Parrotfish on the reef and (b) healthy outplanted coral before and after predation by Bumphead Parrotfish.

Figure 15.17 (a) An information display located on the tourist pontoon (b) describes the collaboration between tourism and researchers for reef restoration.

GOVERNANCE OVERVIEW

The Australian pioneers of coral transplantation and the links to coral management were Vicki Harriot and David Fisk. They published "Coral transplantation as a reef management option" for the GBRMPA in 1988. There are several other publications including GBRMPA (n.d.) and Michalek-Wagner (2001) that collate knowledge and make policy recommendations to the Australian Government.

In November 2019 Australia established the Australian Coral Restoration Consortium Regional Group with a mission to "foster collaboration and technology transfer among coral restoration scientists, practitioners, and managers, and to facilitate a community of practice that will advance coral restoration to keep pace with rapidly changing ocean and environmental conditions."

PERMITS AND GUIDELINES

Collecting coral in Australia requires one or more permits from either the state or federal government, depending on location. These may include fisheries departments or marine parks. The most common permits are for research or aquaculture. There are limits in permits that restrict the location, time, species, and number of coral, as well as reporting requirements. It is generally a three-to-six-month process to apply for and obtain a permit. The length of the permit is typically one, three, or six years.

The decline of coral reefs and the increasing importance of adaptive management and reef restoration has focused the GBRMPA on providing further guidance regarding coral restoration activities. The recent consultation and publication of *Applications for restoration/adaptation projects to improve resilience of habitats in the GBRMP* by the GBRMPA (2018) provides a guideline for different activities that are perceived to be low, medium, and high risk. The guidelines inform restoration and/or adaptation projects that are designed to improve the resilience of GBR habitats, while ensuring they do not have a disproportionate adverse impact on the ecological, biodiversity, heritage, social, or economic values of the marine park.

The Reef 2050 Plan highlights the need to restore the resilience of all ecosystems in the face of current and future threats, such as climate change. In 2017, as a response to unprecedented coral bleaching and mass mortality, the GBRMPA held a summit and published the GBRMPA Reef Resilience Blueprint (2017). This document identified 10 key initiatives that were focused on actions to deliver maximum benefits for reef resilience. One of the initiatives was the broad scale implementation of active, localized restoration. This priority initiative focuses on three activity areas: testing, improving, and scaling up local-scale reef restoration methods—based on the best available science—for potential application across the resilience network that is facilitating the opportunities for community and industry participation in local-scale restoration, and for researching and developing large-scale restoration methods.

To achieve these initiatives and protect the reef, the GBRMPA:

- Developed guidance on restoration activities in the GBRMP
- Established restoration demonstration site(s) with supporting communication material to test, improve, and where appropriate, scale up restoration methods
- Developed guidance for community participation in restoration activities, including *reef restoration toolkits* to support localized restoration activities and support the establishment of a research program on large-scale restoration methods

The GBRMPA permission system provides an avenue to enable restoration and adaptation projects to occur within a strong framework for assessing and managing risks while maintaining environmental protection and understanding public views about such activities.

Given the degraded condition in many areas of the marine park, the GBRMPA recognized that, in certain circumstances, risks associated with intervening may be outweighed by the risks of doing nothing (Table 15.2). Nonetheless, the GBRMPA takes the view that interventions should be implemented in a staged way, with low-risk interventions implemented and assessed for effectiveness first, while higher-risk interventions will require pilot studies and proof of concept before they are considered for full-scale implementation.

Table 15.2 Extract from the GBRMPA (2018) of types of reef restoration and/or adaptation activities, perceived risks, and the management agencies' likely assessment approach. Individual project risk will be determined using the managing agencies' risk assessment procedure for the permissions system. Note that the risk rating of any given activity type may be elevated if the activity is proposed in a location of particular ecological, social, economic, or cultural sensitivity

Activity	Examples	Likely Assessment Approach/Permit	Mitigation
Reorienting coral colonies and/or affixing broken coral fragments	Overturning (righting) coral upended by cyclones or other destructive forces and returning coral bommies to the water at the same place/reef (does not include translocation between reefs). Reattaching coral fragments/colonies to the substrate with adhesive (e.g., epoxy cement) following an incident (e.g., ship grounding or cyclone). Such actions will most likely not involve moving the coral to a holding/staging area prior to reattachment.	Routine/tailored assessment/permit depending on whether the request is proactive or reactive.	
Habitat stabilization/ substrate consolidation	Stabilization of coral rubble and could include mesh frames/coral spiders. This will increase the solid reef base after an incident and may also include the removal of algae to prepare the surface and/or enhancement of crustose coralline algae growth.	Tailored assessment/permit depending on the scale and materials used to stabilize.	
Fragmentation/ transplantation of corals to transplant within same reef complex (with or without coral nursery stage)	Local scale restoration of a site using healthy fragments from a different site within the same reef complex to support quicker recovery. Could include a nursery stage on either racks, trees, or other. May also include Biorock (mineral accretion for substrate stabilization or recovery) and coral gardening.	Tailored assessment/ permit including considerations for research equipment.	Corals must be transplanted within the same gene pool. Limits for coral take apply—see research guidelines. Some research equipment may require a deed. Research equipment must be removed at permit expiry (except for those that are meant to incorporate into the reef habitat, i.e., Biorock).
Coral larval reseeding within same reef complex	Local scale larval collection and distribution within the same reef complex.	Tailored assessment/permit.	Conditions dependant on the type of equipment used to collect and distribute coral larvae.

Examples of medium-risk projects include coral translocation, small artificial reefs (<20 m^2), assisted gene flow, and ultra-thin film for shading (GBRMPA 2018). Examples of high-risk projects include medium and large artificial reefs, installation of large infrastructure/facilities, hybridization, geo-engineering, large-scale coral aquaculture operation, introduction of biological and/or chemical control mechanisms for COTS and Drupella, coral feeding and probiotics, assisted migration, genetic engineering and synthetic biology, and employment or use of potentially toxic chemicals. Examples of very high-risk projects include introduction of nonnative species, introduction of natural or bioengineered pathogens or viruses, and use of materials that may introduce marine pests or artificially increase endemic species to outbreak levels (GBRMPA 2018).

Examples of projects that would be unlikely to get a permission in the GBRMP include:

1. Introduction of chemicals or minerals to encourage localized phytoplankton blooms
2. Introduction of natural or bioengineered pathogens as biological control agents (e.g., viruses)
3. Use of material that is likely to introduce marine pests
4. Introduction of genetically modified material
5. Projects that may artificially increase endemic species to outbreak levels (e.g., *Drupella* spp.)
6. Projects that increase risks to protected species
7. Medium risk projects that have no *proof-of-concept*
8. High-risk projects that have not undergone a GBR specific research *pilot study*
9. Reef intervention projects in the Marine National Park Zone, unless those projects are directly associated with nearby tourism activities (demonstrated by consultation or partnerships) or meet the requirements for conduct of research in that zone
10. Restoration and/or adaptation pilot studies in the preservation zone
11. Commercial reef intervention projects that involve collecting coral from Public Appreciation Special Management Areas, Scientific Research Zones, Buffer Zones, or the Marine National Park Zones for the purposes of transplanting/translocating elsewhere in the marine park.

THE REEF RESTORATION AND ADAPTATION PROGRAM

In January 2018, the Australian government provided $6M to establish the Reef Restoration and Adaptation Program (RRAP). Led by the Australian Institute of Marine Science (AIMS), the consortium included: the Commonwealth Science and Industrial Research Organisation, James Cook University, The University of Queensland, Queensland University of Technology, the GBRMPA, and the GBR Foundation.

Over 18 months, RRAP conducted the world's most rigorous and comprehensive investigation into medium- and large-scale reef interventions (Figure 15.18), drawing on more than 150 experts from more than 20 organizations across the globe. The aim was to study the feasibility of intervening at-scale on the GBR to help it adapt to, and recover from, the effects of climate change.

The study found successful intervention was possible and could double the likelihood of sustaining the reef in good condition by 2050. But time is of the essence; the longer we wait, the more expensive and difficult it will be to successfully intervene at any scale—and the greater the risk that the window of opportunity will close. The RRAP Concept Feasibility Study found

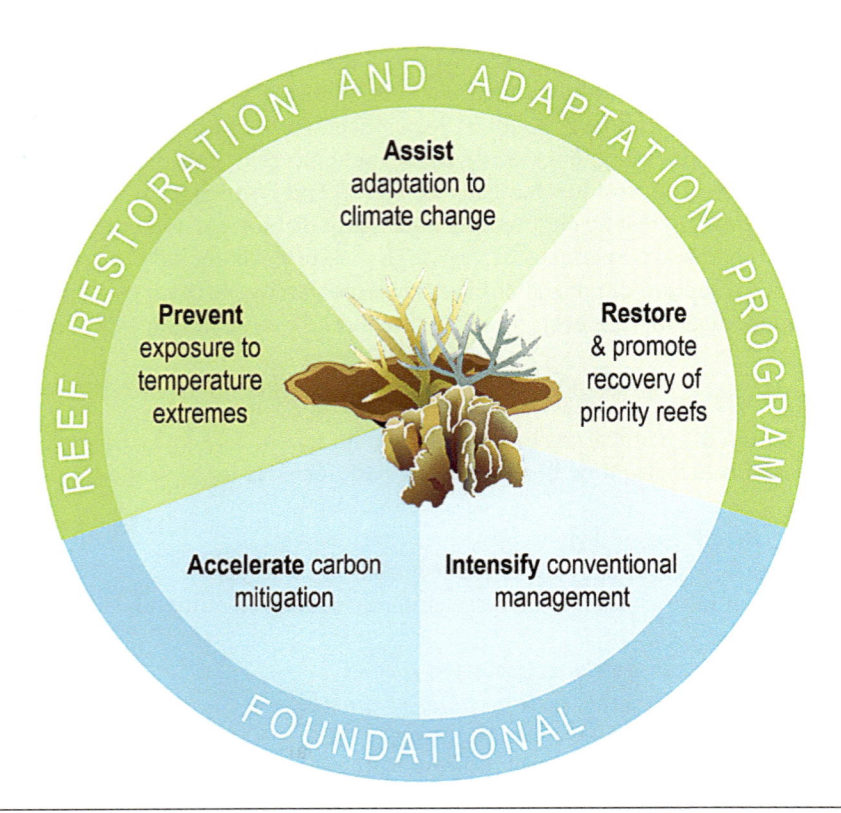

Figure 15.18 The foundational objective of Australia's Reef Restoration and Adaptation Program.

there was no single silver-bullet solution—rather a range of methods would be needed to work together to provide compounding benefits, along with ongoing best-practice reef management and emissions reduction.

At the time of writing, the consortium was embarking on a concerted, 10-year research and development (R&D) program to rigorously risk-assess, test, develop, and, if necessary, deploy a toolkit of novel interventions to help keep the reef resilient and sustain critical reef functions and values in the face of climate change. The interventions would be implemented at an effective scale if, when, and where it was decided that action was needed. They would help the reef help itself by harnessing and enhancing natural processes such as the reef's connectivity and natural variability.

The RRAP R&D Program is believed to be the world's largest effort to help a significant ecosystem survive climate change, and would place Australia as the global leader in coral reef adaptation and restoration. The program was approved to receive funding from the Reef Trust Partnership program to be supplemented by in-kind contributions from partner organizations as well as philanthropy.

DISCUSSION

Australia has been a late starter in reef restoration research and projects compared to the Caribbean, the Red Sea, and other parts of the Pacific. Australian scientists, managers, and businesses have collaborated and learned from experienced scientists from other countries and projects and have recently trailed several coral restoration methods in the GBRMP. Through the research of Peter Harrison, Australia is a leader in coral larvae enhancement methods or capturing larvae and containing the settlement on reefs.

Critical questions for marine park management, scientists, tourism industry, conservationists, and the community involved in coral reef restoration include: (1) what is our long-term vision? (2) how do we measure success? and (3) at what temporal and geographical time frames? Ultimately, current and future coral reef restoration research, education, tourism, or aquaculture must have a social license to operate and add value for the environment and stakeholders.

CONCLUSION

The planning and hosting of the July 2018 GBR Restoration Symposium in Cairns involved over 300 attendees and resulted in excellent knowledge exchange and collaboration that greatly assisted Australian coral reef restoration practitioners. The 2018 GBR Restoration Symposium was a watershed opportunity for multiple Australian and international stakeholders to gather and share knowledge and discuss issues, management, and future plans.

There have been a small number of scientists, managers, and businesses who have successfully pioneered reef restoration methods and projects in the GBRMP. There have been several detractors of reef restoration who believe that the research effort and funding can be spent in better ways. We are now at a critical time to focus on a significant scaling up of projects and funding of coral reef restoration. It is anticipated that the majority of future projects will be based on a solid research foundation and a low risk in partnership with tourism industries in locations such as Port Douglas, Cairns, and the Whitsundays. It is anticipated that some future projects will also occur as a response to a local disaster such as a cyclone, a ship grounding, or the coral bleaching of an important tourism site. The GBRMPA has been proactive and consultative in developing guidelines that specify the risks of various methods, which is a transparent approach that will greatly assist future coral reef restoration projects and proponents. However, the complexities, time, and costs associated with permit applications to start a project is a discouraging issue for many companies and individuals.

In 2018–2020, we estimate that there are between 100–150 people with experience in coral reef restoration projects in the Australian region. These include scientists, hands-on practitioners, or people who have completed training courses. If we are to make a major difference, it is anticipated that we will have to rapidly increase the number of experienced people and coral reef restoration projects. A desired future project will be to design and implement coral restoration demonstration sites where people can view the methods and learn from experts so that they can be involved in future projects. We anticipate that this will involve several coral reef restoration courses designed for university students, schools, scuba divers, scientists and citizen scientists, managers, and innovators.

ACKNOWLEDGMENTS

The authors wish to acknowledge the sharing of knowledge with a range of organizations including the GBRMPA, Queensland Parks and Wildlife Service, James Cook University, Southern Cross University, Australian Institute of Marine Science, Reef Restoration Foundation, and many amazing tourism operators and citizen scientists.

REFERENCES

AIMS. 2018. "Reef Restoration and Adaptation Program. Helping the Great Barrier Reef resist, repair and recover." https://www.aims.gov.au/reef-recovery/rrap.

Burrows, D. W., J. Purandare, L. Bay, N. Cook, D. Koopman, S. Long, P. Lundgren, et al. 2019. "Symposium report: Great Barrier Reef restoration symposium, 2018." *Ecological Restoration and Management.* https://doi.org/10.1111/emr.12368.

Cook, N., G. Molinaro, J. Gaskell, B. Cockerell, B. Buchan, A. Skeer, A. Keynes, et al. 2019. "Coral gardening edu-tourism project." Installation report. Manta Ray bay and Blue Pearl Bay. https://www.researchgate.net/publication/336736877_Coral_Gardening_Edu-tourism_Project_Installation_Report_Manta_Ray_Bay_and_Blue_Pearl_Bay.

Cook, N. and A. Smith. 2018. "Fitzroy Island Coral Nursery. Outplanting report and scientific baseline surveys." Report to Reef Restoration Foundation, Cairns.

Cook, N., A. Smith, I. M. McLeod, S. Christie, and G. McKenna. 2018. "Fitzroy Island Coral Nursery: Baseline Report to the National Environmental Science Programme." Reef and Rainforest Research Centre Limited, Cairns, 30 pp.

De'ath, G., K. E. Fabricius, H. Sweatman, and M. Puotinen. 2012. "The 27-year decline of coral cover on the Great Barrier Reef and its causes." *Proceedings of the National Academy of Sciences*, 109(44), pp. 17995–17999.

GBRMPA. (n.d.). Guidelines for Coral Transplantation at tourism sites. http://elibrary.gbrmpa.gov.au/jspui/bitstream/11017/873/1/coral-transplantation-1.pdf.

———. 2018. "Applications for restoration/adaptation projects to improve resilience of habitats in the Great Barrier Reef Marine Park." http://elibrary.gbrmpa.gov.au/jspui/bitstream/11017/3420/5/v1-Applications-for-restoration_adaptation-projects-%28Joint%29.pdf.

———. 2019. "Great Barrier Reef Outlook Report 2019, GBRMPA, Townsville." http://elibrary.gbrmpa.gov.au/jspui/bitstream/11017/3474/10/Outlook-Report-2019-FINAL.pdf.

Hein, M. Y., B. L. Willis, R. Bedeen, and A. Birtles. 2017. "The need for broader ecological and socioeconomic tools to evaluate the effectiveness of coral restoration programs." *Society for Ecological Restoration* pp. 1–11. https://doi.org/10.1111/rec.1258.

Laycock, P. 2004. "Window dressing selected sites associated with reef based tourism. A pilot study investigating the use of transplanted coral." A report to the Great Barrier Reef Marine Park Authority. *Reef Biosearch*, Port Douglas. 21 pages plus appendices.

Marshall, P., C. Christie, K. Dobbs, A. Green, D. Haynes, J. Brodie, K. Michalek-Wagner, et al. 2002. "Grounded ship leaves TBT—based antifoulant on the Great Barrier Reef: An overview of the environmental response." *Spill Science & Technology Bulletin*, Vol. 7, Nos. 5–6, pp. 215–221.

McLeod, I. M., D. W. Williamson, S. Tayler, M. Srinvasan, M. Read, C. Boxer, N. Mattocks, and D. Ceccarelli. 2019. "Bommies away! Logistics and early effects of repositioning 400 tons of displaced coral colonies following cyclone impacts on the Great Barrier Reef." *Ecological Restoration and Management.* https://doi.org/10.1111/emr.12381.

Michalek-Wagner, K. 2001. "Coral reef restoration: Scope and limitations of reef restoration as a management tool." DRAFT.

Monkivitch, J. 2008. "Activity-specific guidelines: Tools to maximise Environmental Impact Assessment outcomes: A case study of coral transplantation from the Great Barrier Reef Marine Park, Australia."

Nedimyer K., K. Gaines, and S. Roach. 2011. "Coral Tree Nursery©: An innovative approach to growing corals in an ocean-based field nursery." *AACL Bioflux* 4(4):442–446.

Reef Resilience Network. 2019. "Restoration online course." http://reefresilience.org/online/.

Reynolds, E. 2017. "Great Barrier Reef as you've never seen it after Debbie reduced it to rubble." https://www.news.com.au/technology/environment/natural-wonders/tragic-barrier-reef-as-youve-never-seen-it-after-debbie-reduced-it-to-rubble/news-story/4fe66356bfcfaa8bf503a7d77e15db78.

Smith, A., P. Marshall, C. Christie, and J. Storrie. 2002. "Environmental management of a shipping accident in the world's largest marine park." *Australian Journal of Environmental Management*. Volume 9.

16

REEF RESTORATION IN THE EASTERN TROPICAL PACIFIC, A CASE STUDY IN GOLFO DULCE, COSTA RICA

J. A. Kleypas, T. Villalobos-Cubero, J. A. Marín-Moraga, Á. Teran, J. Cortés, and J. J. Alvarado

ABSTRACT

Coral reef restoration is a fast-growing area of research in many parts of the world. However, coral propagation and reef restoration in the eastern tropical Pacific (ETP) have been very limited (Guzmán 1991; Liñan-Cabello et al. 2010; Tortolero-Langarica et al. 2014; Nava and Figueroa-Camacho 2017; Lizcano-Sandova et al. 2018; Tortolero-Langarica et al. 2019). Compared to other reefs worldwide, the ETP is a region with low coral biodiversity and less-developed reef frameworks (López-Pérez 2017). However, the coral reefs here persist in an environment characterized by wide fluctuations in temperature, pH, and salinity. Reefs in the Golfo Dulce of Costa Rica appear to be particularly resilient. During the 2016 warming event, almost all corals in Golfo Dulce were severely bleached for three to four months, but most survived. It is unclear whether the reasons for this are biological (corals conditioned to withstand extremes, high food availability) or physical (nutrients, mixing). For whatever reason, the resilience of these corals is a sound reason for developing techniques for their propagation and outplanting. We describe here the results from the first three years of coral propagation in an underwater nursery in Golfo Dulce and pilot outplanting at several sites on Golfo Dulce reefs. We also provide a summary of what was learned about reef propagation and restoration techniques for the major ETP corals, as well as some unanticipated challenges of reef restoration in general.

INTRODUCTION

Eastern Tropical Pacific

Coral reef ecosystems of the ETP extend from the Gulf of California to Ecuador, including the oceanic islands of Revillagigedo, Clipperton, Cocos, Malpelo, and Galápagos. The recent and comprehensive book *Coral Reefs of the Eastern Tropical Pacific* edited by Peter Glynn, Derek

Manzello, and Ian Enochs (2017a) provides extensive background on these reefs, and we summarize some of the Glynn et al. (2017b) points here, particularly those that are relevant to current-day restoration efforts.

Oceanographic conditions along the ETP coast are driven by local winds (including strong seasonal gap winds), eddies, and interaction with the eastern boundary currents. Surface waters are typically warm and have relatively low salinity and pH (Fiedler and Lavín 2017; Glynn et al. 2017b). Regions of seasonal upwelling can bring much cooler, low pH waters to the surface, such that many corals along the ETP are exposed to highly variable conditions and high rates of bioerosion (Alvarado et al. 2017). The ETP is strongly affected by the El Niño Southern Oscillation (ENSO), and warm ENSO events have caused widespread mortality of ETP corals in the years 1982–1983 and 1997–1998, which caused massive coral bleaching and mortality (Cortés et al. 1984; Glynn 1984; Jiménez 2001), and most recently in 2016 (Alvarado et al. 2020).

ETP reefs are isolated from most other Pacific reef regions by the Eastern Pacific Barrier, a vast expanse of ocean separating the Central and Eastern Pacific, across which few dispersing larvae can survive. Only 47 species of scleractinian corals have been identified in the ETP (Cortés et al. 2017), compared to about 72 species in Hawaii, and more than 600 in the Coral Triangle (Veron et al. 2015). The main coral genera of the ETP are *Pocillopora*, *Porites*, *Pavona*, and *Gardineroseris* (Glynn et al. 2017b).

The isolation has resulted in a shift in life-history strategies of ETP coral species from those of their western Pacific counterparts, favoring autotrophic larvae that can travel long distances (Baird et al. 2009). In the western Pacific, *Pocillopora damicornis* is usually a monthly brooder, but in the ETP it appears to be a monthly broadcaster. Similarly, while species within the genera *Porites* and *Pavona* normally spawn annually, in the ETP they appear to spawn over several months (Glynn et al. 2017c). This shift in spawning strategies likely reflects natural selection within a patchy geographic distribution of reefs and an environment with frequent disturbances (Glynn et al. 2017c).

Regardless of the rather harsh environment and low coral diversity of ETP reefs, there are many reasons to study their capacity for reef restoration. First, these reefs and coral communities support high-marine biodiversity (Cortés 1997; Cortés et al. 2017) and thus are essential in the life support of the tropical marine ecosystems here. Second, the corals appear to be resilient; they have demonstrated an ability to survive months of severe bleaching and an ability to recover (in terms of coral cover) following bleaching events, despite the low rates of coral recruitment (Glynn et al. 2017c). Third, the relative ecological simplicity of these systems, at least in terms of coral diversity, allows one to more easily understand the response of the system to restoration.

In addition, for the Costa Rican Pacific, the additive impacts of pollution, invasive species, etc., are relatively low. In Costa Rica, marine conservation is gaining attention similar to that applied to their terrestrial environments; e.g., the recent decree by the Costa Rican government to protect Costa Rican coral reefs—"Promotion of restoration and conservation initiatives for the recovery of coral ecosystems" (Executive decree N°41774-MINAE, June 6, 2019). This case study describes findings from the first three years of a coral propagation and outplanting project in Golfo Dulce, a small embayment of the Costa Rican Pacific (Cortés 2016).

Study Site

The Golfo Dulce is a deep basin with a shallow sill at the entrance and is rimmed by a shallow, narrow shelf (Hebbeln and Cortés 2001; Cortés 2016) that supports several coral reefs and coral communities (Figure 16.1). The main impacts on these reefs are sedimentation from land and

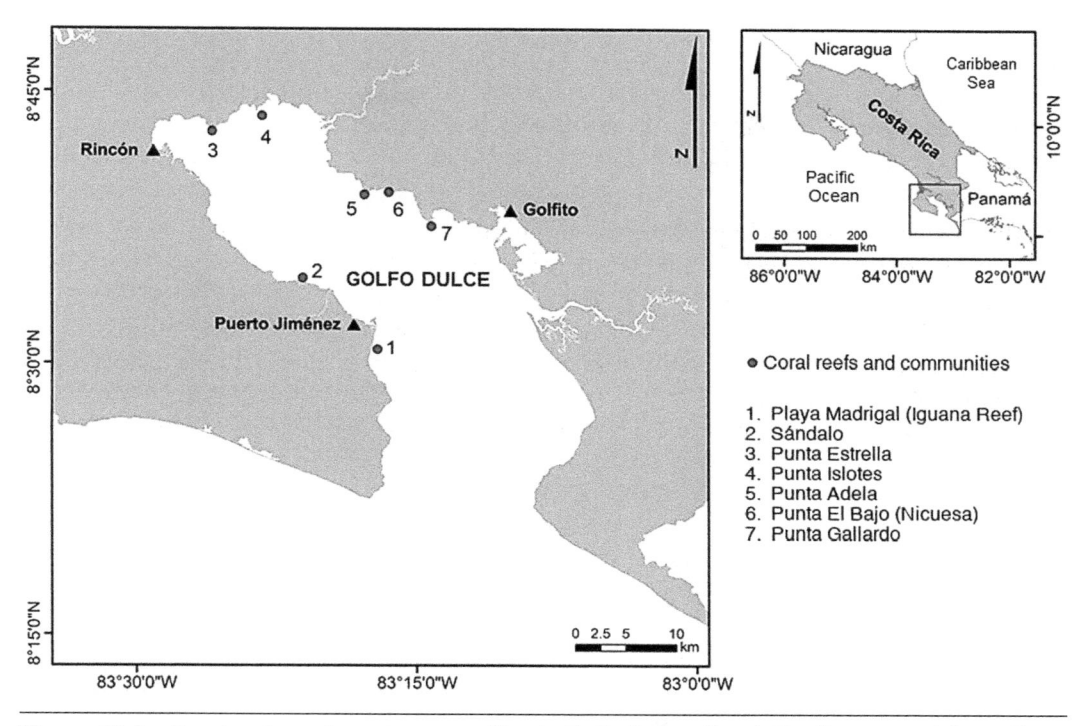

Figure 16.1 Coral reefs and coral communities in Golfo Dulce, South Pacific coast of Costa Rica. This figure is modified from Cortés (1990). Numbered locations show areas with coral reefs and coral communities. The underwater nursery is located near Punta El Bajo (Nicuesa).

warm water events. While the threat of sedimentation has decreased due to improved land-use practices, the threat of climate change continues to increase. In fact, the start of the restoration effort was delayed for many months because of severe bleaching of Golfo Dulce corals between February and May of 2016. Several potential outplanting locations were identified based on previous studies by Jorge Cortés and Juan José Alvarado, whose combined body of work on Golfo Dulce corals and reefs document their historical development as well as recent cycles of degradation/recovery (Cortés and Murillo 1985; Cortés 1990; Cortés 1991; Cortés 1992; Cortés et al. 2010; Alvarado et al. 2015).

In September 2016 a pilot coral restoration project was installed in Golfo Dulce, Costa Rica (Villalobos-Cubero 2019). The goal of the project was to evaluate propagation and outplanting techniques of fragments obtained from the most common species: *Porites lobata* and *P. evermanni*; *Pavona gigantea* and *P. frondifera*; and *Pocillopora* spp. (tentatively identified as *P. damicornis* and *P. edouxi*). Specimens of *Psammocora* spp. were also propagated on an experimental basis, but were not a target for restoration. The propagation was restricted to an in situ nursery located near 8°39.3'N, 83°16.3'W. The underwater nursery initially consisted of four tree structures in which fragments were closely monitored for growth in relation to orientation, initial fragment size, position (depth) within the tree, and temperature. During the third year the nursery was expanded to include four additional tree structures and two rope structures.

TECHNIQUES AND METHODS

Several members of the restoration team received training at the Mote Marine Laboratory in coral propagation and reef restoration techniques, and adapted the coral tree technique described by Nedimyer et al. (2011) that is widely used in the Caribbean (Schopmeyer et al. 2017) for propagation of ETP coral species. Construction of rope structures followed the description in Frias-Torres et al. (2018). Each structure was placed approximately 3–5 m from the surface, in waters 8–12 m deep. A single tree held approximately 150 *Pavona* and *Porites* fragments or 72 *Pocillopora* fragments. Each rope structure had a capacity of 200 *Pocillopora* fragments.

Coral donors were identified across several different reefs in Golfo Dulce and were marked with a numbered plastic tag nailed into adjacent hard substrate. Photographs, date of sampling, depth, and GPS coordinates of each donor were recorded. Samples of *Porites* and *Pavona* were obtained with hammer and chisel, and samples of *Pocillopora* were obtained by breaking a few branches from the colony. Less than 10% of a colony was taken from each donor, and when possible, fragments of opportunity were obtained, assuming they were derived from the nearest colony.

Pocillopora samples were further fragmented to approximately 2–4 cm long branches, and each labeled fragment was suspended in the tree structure with monofilament (Figure 16.2(a)). A few fragments were first glued onto ceramic discs, which were then suspended with

Figure 16.2 (a) Tree structure for growing branching corals; (b) rope structure for growing branching corals; and (c) growth of *Pocillopora* fragment over polypropylene line.

monofilament, but this step was deemed unnecessary after a few months. *Pocillopora* were also grown in rope structures by inserting fragments directly between the twines of twisted rope (Figure 16.2(b), (c)). The project first tested natural fiber rope, such as hemp and manila (⅜" wide), but these disintegrated within three months, so all lines were replaced with nylon or polypropylene rope. Fragments of the same donor were segregated by rope, so that a single donor label was required for each rope. Regardless of the method, all fragments overgrew the line or rope within one to two months.

Porites and *Pavona* samples were micro-fragmented using a Gryphon Aquasaw with a diamond blade, and each micro-fragment was attached to a ceramic disk with thick super glue. These were then placed in small egg-crate trays that were suspended in the tree nursery with monofilament line (Figure 16.3(a)). All ceramic disks were labeled and recorded according to donor. Most coral fragments had grown over the exposed skeleton of the micro-fragments and onto the ceramic disc within one to two months. Early deployments of *Porites* and *Pavona* experienced heavy mortality caused by triggerfish bites (*Balistes polylepis*). Plastic mesh grid (1×1 cm squares) was placed over coral trays to eliminate fish predation (Figure 16.3(b)). While these grids resolved the fish bite problem and increased survivorship, they also became overgrown with algae and other fouling organisms, requiring frequent cleaning (Figure 16.3(c)).

Figure 16.3 (a) Tree structure for growing massive corals; (b) egg-crate tray with ceramic disks holding *Porites* fragments and protected with plastic grid; and (c) growth of *Pavona* fragments after 10 months.

MONITORING

Several nursery structures were fitted with HOBO® Water Temp Pro v2 data loggers that were set to record the temperature every 10 or 15 minutes. The same type of sensor was also placed at each outplant site. The data documented similar temperature fluctuations across all sites, although deeper sites were slightly cooler than shallower sites. Of note in this region are periods of strong temperature fluctuations that coincide with the tidal cycle (Figure 16.4); these events appear to reflect cool water intrusions at a depth that contributes to the formation of a shallow thermocline. Because the sensors remain at a fixed level that is relative to the bottom, the vertical rise and fall of the thermocline are reflected in the temperature record. During periods with a strong thermocline, the nursery corals experience twice-daily temperature fluctuations of up to 9°C.

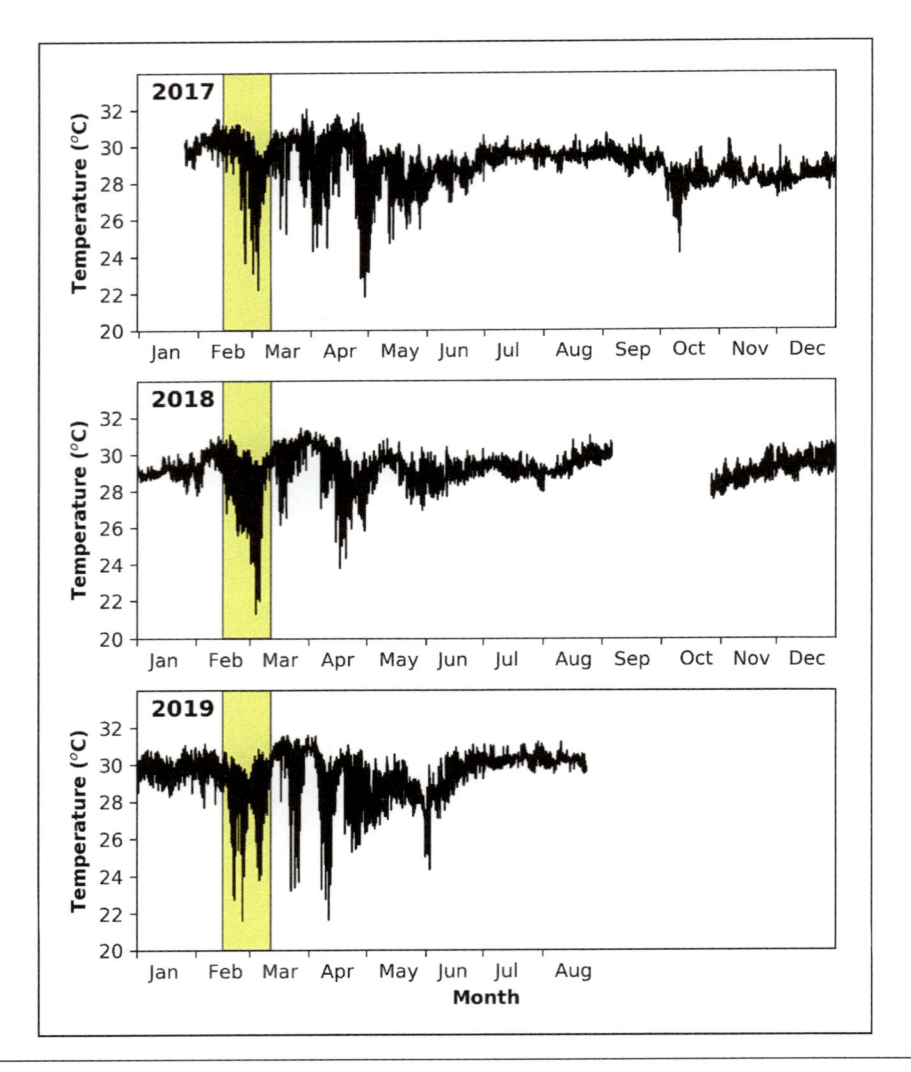

Figure 16.4 Monthly temperatures (°C) at the Golfo Dulce coral nursery, February 2017 through August 2019 (from HOBO® temperature sensors placed on the top branch of Tree 2 in the nursery).

Fragment growth was monitored with a combination of monthly photographs and Vernier caliper measurements. Photographs of each disk were analyzed using ImageJ software (Schneider et al. 2012), in which the area of the fragment was calibrated to the known area of the disk (Figure 16.5(a)). Branching coral growth was more problematic, and several techniques were tested, including wet weight, volume displacement, photography against a scaled background, and direct measurement of coral height and width. Monthly photographs of *Pocillopora* fragments provided the valuable information regarding both coral size and health, but they were not as quantifiable as taking three-dimensional measurements (Figure 16.5(b)). The three-dimensional measurements were converted to *coral volume* following the technique described by Salinas-Akhmadeeva (2018), and was considered representative of the *ecological space* occupied by the coral.

Growth and mortality of fragments in the nursery varied greatly with species. *Pocillopora* fragments had very low mortality, and grew to outplantable size within 8–12 months. *Pavona* fragments also had very low mortality (5%), and within 6–10 months, often grew rapidly over and beyond the ceramic disks, including over fouling organisms such as barnacles and serpulid worms. In contrast, fragments of the most common species in Golfo Dulce, *Porites* spp., had high mortality rates (average 70%), even when grids were used to eliminate *B. polylepis* bites. The high mortality was suspected to be a problem associated with the very small polyps of *Porites*, which decreased their ability to compete with rapidly growing fouling organisms. This species was also commonly used by invertebrates as a substrate for laying their eggs. *Porites* spp. grown in a land-based aquarium facility by one of us (Marín Moraga) with highly filtered water experienced very low mortality rates, which is evidence that fouling organisms have a negative impact on fragment propagation in this species. *Porites* fragments of opportunity that were placed directly on dead coral surfaces at Punta Adela reef in Golfo Dulce, particularly those protected with plastic grid, also had low mortality rates, perhaps because the grid allowed small grazing fish into the mesh enclosures.

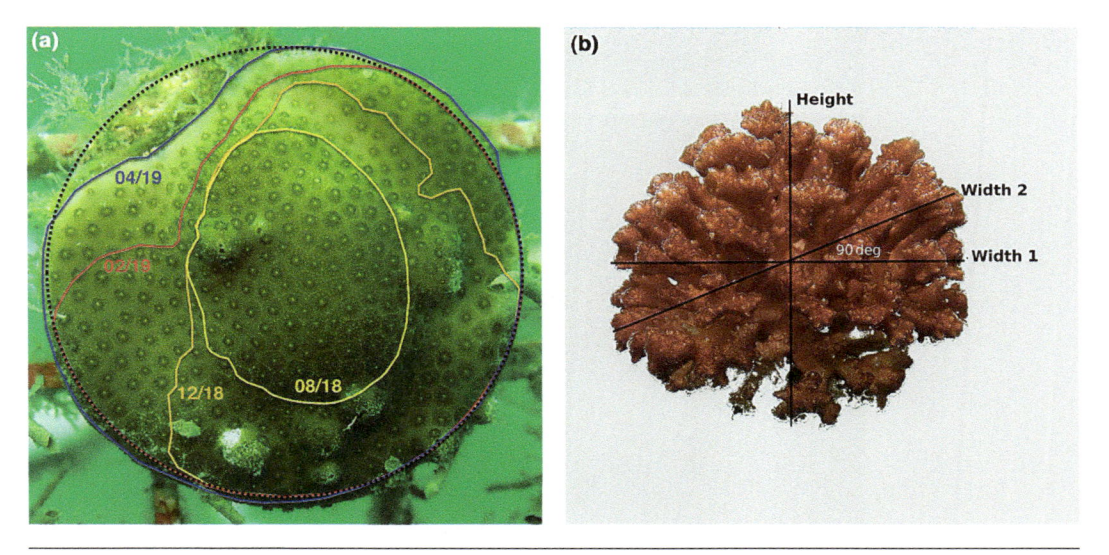

Figure 16.5 (a) Example of area determination over time using ImageJ software. Solid colored lines correspond to growth edge of fragment for a particular month/year; black dashed line shows outline of ceramic disk. (b) Three-dimensional measurements of the branching coral *Pocillopora* sp.

Test outplantings began once the corals had grown to a sufficient size—about 6–8 months for *Pavona* and *Porites* and about 8–12 months for *Pocillopora*. Test outplantings were first performed on the same reefs as the original donors, then monitored for a year or more to evaluate the outplanting method as well as the health and growth of the outplants. *Pavona* and *Porites* fragments were outplanted by inserting the stem of the ceramic disk into a hole that had been drilled into the substrate (following the protocol of the Mote Marine Laboratory); underwater epoxy (AquaMend®) was used to hold the fragment in place if the stem did not fit snugly into the hole. The coral fragments were typically outplanted in clusters of 10 or more from the same donor to evaluate the fusion process between the fragments (Figure 16.6). Occasionally, fragments were planted randomly and alongside small fragments of opportunity that were epoxied directly to a bare coral substrate on the reef.

Pocillopora fragments were initially outplanted using the *nail-and-zip-tie* technique; underwater epoxy was occasionally used to stabilize unstable colonies. For *Pocillopora* grown in rope nurseries, the entire rope was transported to the outplant site and tacked to the substrate using

Figure 16.6 (a) *Pavona gigantea* outplants at Punta Gallardo, June 27, 2017; (b) The same *P. gigantea* outplants on July 28, 2018.

fence staples to secure the rope to the substrate (i.e., U-shaped, double-pointed nails). Test outplantings were performed at five locations: Punta Gallardo, Punta Adela, Punta Islotes, Punta Bejuco, and Sándalo Reef. Between three and 10 colonies were outplanted in small clusters with spacing of 10 cm to 1 m. Recent outplantings with higher numbers of corals have focused on the Punta Islotes and Punta Bejuco reefs. Initial survival rates of *Pavona* outplants were low (~53%) (Villalobos-Cubero 2019) and reflect almost total mortality of outplants on crystalline versus carbonate rock surfaces at Punta Gallardo; mortality rates decreased with later outplants on old reef substrate at Punta Islotes and Punta Bejuco (Table 16.1). Most *Pavona* outplants extended their growth over the substrate within a few months, and many were fused with neighboring colonies within one year. The initial *Porites* outplants had a low survival rate (41–64%; Table 16.1), which appeared to be due to *algal gardening* by damselfish that smothered the outplants. Placing grids over the coral outplants for 6–12 months greatly reduced this mortality (Figure 16.7(a)). *Porites* outplants also fused if they were from the same donor, but outplants from different donors were obvious by a distinct line of competition between abutting colonies (Figure 16.7(b)). Survival rates of *Pocillopora* outplants improved from 65% to more than 90%, probably because of better outplanting techniques that prevented colonies from becoming dislodged from the surface. *Pocillopora* grew rapidly over the zip ties but often required several months to grow solidly over the substrate and appeared to fuse with the substrate more rapidly when epoxy was used (Figure 16.8(a), (b)). Outplanting rope segments with multiple coral colonies (Figure 16.8(c)) proved to be a more efficient outplanting

Table 16.1 Percentage of outplant survival for the first three years of the Golfo Dulce Project. Outplant sites are listed from left to right in order of dates of the first outplantings. Note: Punta Bejuco is located about halfway between Punta Estrella and Islotes

Species	Punta Gallardo	Punta Adela	Islotes	Punta Bejuco
Porites spp.		64	41	100
Pavona gigantea	53		67	100
Pocillopora spp.	65		100	95

Figure 16.7 (a) Caged *Porites* spp. outplants at Punta Adela reef, June 30, 2017. (b) some of the same *Porites* spp. fragments, October 15, 2019 (the cage was removed in January 2018). Note the boundary between two lower colonies where fragments from different donors were outplanted adjacent to each other.

Figure 16.8 (a) *Pocillopora* colony (P4) outplanted on May 5, 2018, using nail and zip tie, and showing two fragments from the colony epoxied to substrate. (b) P4 on October 15, 2018. (c) *Pocillopora* colonies (Donor 12) from the rope structures outplanted on December 11, 2019, by stapling the rope to the substrate and stabilizing colonies with epoxy when necessary.

method, but this recently employed technique will require further evaluation regarding the impact on survival rates of the colonies. The shallowest *Pocillopora* outplants on the old reef flat of Punta Bejuco (1.6–2 m depth) experienced more paling, bleaching, and mortality than *Pocillopora* outplanted in waters 3–8 m depth.

Based on genetic analyses of 21 samples from *Porites* colonies on a shallow local reef (Punta Adela) and five fragments in the coral nursery, the *Porites* colonies in Golfo Dulce are predominantly *P. evermanni*. The Punta Adela sampling followed the methodology for a previous study at a nearby reef in Golfo Dulce (Boulay et al. 2014), which showed a 1:2 ratio of *P. lobata* to *P. evermanni*. In contrast, only one of the colonies from the shallower Punta Adela reef, and none of the nursery corals, was *P. lobata*. Sampled colonies of *P. evermanni* displayed good genotypic diversity, however, with 18 genotypes represented among the samples.

COMMUNITY INVOLVEMENT, VOLUNTEERS, AND CITIZEN SCIENCE

Educating and engaging local communities about coral reef restoration was a priority from the beginning of the operation. Research to understand how persons from local communities use and perceive Golfo Dulce reefs was begun several months before the establishment of the coral nursery (Villalobos-Cubero 2019). The results revealed strong differences in perception about coral reefs between fishermen, people working in tourism, and non-reef users. Interviewees confirmed a high frequency in visitation to coral reefs and communities in the gulf, mainly for snorkeling. Their perceptions were that sedimentation and agrochemical pollution were the main factors affecting corals in the area. About two-thirds of the interviewees considered the lack of information as a strong obstacle for conservation and management initiatives, and the project's work within these local communities has proceeded to close that gap through scientific and public talks, presentations in schools, and participation in coastal clean-up events. All interviewees acknowledged the value of coral reefs and the need to protect them, but they did not support the formation of new marine protected areas or restrictions to the use of these ecosystems. The project also collaborated with a local non-governmental organization (NGO) and an ecolodge to train six persons from nearby communities in open-water diving and safe coral gardening and monitoring; these trainees participate regularly in restoration activities, as permitted by space on the boat.

The project has received hundreds of unsolicited requests to volunteer or intern, and many such requests are from local communities. The project is dedicated to creating ways to include stronger participation with volunteers and interns; however, the remoteness of the Golfo Dulce, the lack of local diver support, and the cost of boat rentals have so far postponed the implementation of a safe and affordable volunteer/intern program. The project has also formed the basis for several undergraduate and graduate research projects to evaluate propagation and outplanting techniques—and to follow changes in community structure, immunological responses in corals, and techniques for tracking coral growth.

DISCUSSION

The Golfo Dulce restoration project is the first large-scale evaluation of an underwater coral nursery as a tool to accelerate coral propagation and restoration in the ETP. It was founded with a vision to restore reefs in a scientifically supported way and to serve as an example for other coral restoration projects in the ETP. The project is guided by the four principles of successful restoration outlined in Suding et al. (2015) and aims to (1) be informed by historical data and future forecasts, (2) ensure ecological integrity, (3) engage and benefit local communities, and (4) be sustainable over the long term. The project is still evaluating the long-term stability of restoration, e.g., tracking recruitment of corals and other marine organisms at restoration sites, but overall, the project has been successful. A total of 1,500 colonies of seven coral species were propagated in the Golfo Dulce nursery, and about 300 were outplanted and are being monitored. The current standing stock of propagated corals in the nursery is maintained at 1,000–1,200 corals. While the overall numbers are small, the project has tested multiple techniques in both propagation and outplanting, and has set a baseline for continued research and scaling up while adhering to the principles of successful restoration.

We found that all coral species except *Porites* were easy to propagate and outplant. *Pavona* species grew well on ceramic disks, and *Pocillopora* grew equally well in tree and line structures. The choice of structure is a balance between efficiency (line nurseries are most efficient) and research (ease of moving coral fragments for experiments).

One of the biggest successes of the project so far is the ability to propagate more than a thousand colonies of *Pocillopora*, a species that had become difficult to find in the natural environment of the gulf. Our goal with this species is to re-establish a self-sustaining and genetically diverse population in Golfo Dulce.

CONCLUSION

Adhering to the Suding et al. (2015) principles has required a slower approach than many other projects—and less emphasis on scaling up. However, we feel that establishing a restoration project in the ETP, where very few coral restoration studies have been undertaken, was necessary within both the ecological and societal approaches. This slow approach to develop responsible practices allow us to expand the effort in a manner that is suitable for both research and effective ecological restoration. One of the biggest challenges in Costa Rica is the demand that is associated with Principle 3; there is a genuine desire among many individuals, businesses, NGOs, and the government to *be part of the solution* to the coral reef crisis, and much of the project's time and effort has necessarily gone toward guidance and training of other coral restoration projects in Costa Rica.

ACKNOWLEDGMENTS

This project was initially funded through an award from the Heinz Foundation, and has continued through funding and support from the University of Costa Rica and particularly the Centro de Investigación en Ciencias del Mar y Limnología, and Fundación Fundecooperación of Costa Rica. The first author is supported by the National Center for Atmospheric Research, which is largely funded by the National Science Foundation. We are particularly grateful to Dr. David Vaughan and the Schmidt Foundation for securing travel and tuition support to attend a training workshop at Mote Marine Lab, and for Dave's continued consultation for the Golfo Dulce project. Substantial logistical and monetary support has also been provided by Nicuesa Rainforest Lodge and by Tom and Jillon Weaver.

REFERENCES

Alvarado, J. J., A. Beita, S. Mena, C. Fernández, and A. Guzmán. 2015. "Ecosistemas coralinos del Área de Conservación Osa, Costa Rica: Estructura y necesidades de conservación." *Revista de Biologia Tropical* 63 (Supplement 1), 219–259.

Alvarado, J. J., B. Grassian, J. R. Cantera-Kintz, J. L. Carballo, and E. Londoño-Cruz. 2017. "Coral reef bioerosion in the Eastern Tropical Pacific." In: *Coral Reefs of the Eastern Tropical Pacific: Persistence and Loss in a Dynamic Environment*. P. W. Glynn, D. P. Manzello, and I. C. Enochs (eds). pp. 396–403. Dordrecht, The Netherlands: Springer Science+Business Media.

Alvarado, J. J., C. Sánchez-Noguera, G. Arias-Godínez, T. Araya, C. Fernández-García, and A. G. Guzmán. 2020. "Impact of El Niño 2015–2016 on the coral reefs of the Pacific of Costa Rica: The potential role of marine protection." *Revista de Biologia Tropical*, 68 (Supplement 1), S271–S282.

Baird, A. H., J. R. Guest, and B. L. Willis. 2009. "Systematic and biogeographical patterns in the reproductive biology of scleractinian corals." *Annual Review of Ecology, Evolution, and Systematics* 40, 551–571.

Boulay, J. N., M. E. Hellberg, J. Cortés, and I. B. Baums. 2014. "Unrecognized coral species diversity masks differences in functional ecology." In: *Proceedings of the Royal Society B-Biological Science,* 281, doi:10.1098/rspb.2013.1580.

Cortés, J. 1990. "Coral reef decline in Golfo Dulce, Costa Rica, Eastern Pacific: Anthropogenic and natural disturbances." Unpublished Ph. D. Thesis, University of Miami, Miami, FL, USA.

———. 1991. "Los arrecifes coralinos de Golfo Dulce, Costa Rica: Aspectos geológicos." *Revista Geológica América Central* 13, 15–24.

———. 1992. "The coral reefs of Golfo Dulce, Costa Rica: Ecological aspects." *Revista de Biologia Tropical,* 40, 19–26.

———. 1997. "Biology and geology of eastern Pacific coral reefs." *Coral Reefs* 16, S39–S46.

———. 2016. "The Pacific coastal and marine ecosystems." In: *Costa Rican Ecosystems.* M. Kappelle (ed). pp. 97–138. Chicago and London, University of Chicago Press.

Cortés, J., I. C. Enochs, J. Sibaja-Cordero, et al. 2017. "Marine biodiversity of Eastern Tropical Pacific coral reefs." In: *Coral Reefs of the Eastern Tropical Pacific: Persistence and Loss in a Dynamic Environment.* P. W. Glynn, D. P. Manzello, and I. C. Enochs. (eds.). pp. 203–250. Dordrecht, The Netherlands: Springer Science+Business Media.

Cortés, J., C. E. Jiménez, A. C. Fonseca, and J. J. Alvarado. 2010. "Status and conservation of coral reefs in Costa Rica." *Revista de Biologia Tropical* 58 (Supplement 1), 33–50.

Cortés, J. and M. M. Murillo. 1985. "Comunidades coralina y arrecifes del Pacífico de Costa Rica." *Revista de Biologia Tropical* 33, 197–202.

Cortés, J., M. M. Murillo, H. M. Guzmán, and J. Acuna. 1984. "Pérdida de zooxantelas y muerte de corales y otros organismos arrecifales en el Caribe y Pacífico de Costa Rica." *Revista de Biologia Tropical* 32, 227–231.

Fiedler, P. C. and M. F. Lavín. 2017. "Oceanographic conditions of the eastern tropical Pacific." In: *Coral reefs of the Eastern Tropical Pacific. Persistence and loss in a dynamic environment.* P. W. Glynn, D. P. Manzello, and I. C. Enochs (eds). pp. 59–83. Dordrecht, The Netherlands: Springer Science+Business Media.

Frias-Torres, S., P. H. Montoya-Maya, and N. Shah (eds). 2018. *Coral Reef Restoration Toolkit: A Field-oriented Guide Developed in the Seychelles Islands.* Mahe, Republic of Seychelles, Nature Seychelles.

Glynn, P. W. 1984. "Widespread coral mortality and the 1982–1983 El Niño warming event." *Environmental Conservation* 11, 133–146.

Glynn, P. W., D. P. Manzello, and I. C. Enochs. (eds.) 2017a. *Coral Reefs of the Eastern Tropical Pacific. Persistence and Loss in a Dynamic Environment.* Dordrecht, The Netherlands: Springer Science+Business Media, p 657.

Glynn, P. W., J. J. Alvarado, S. Banks, et al. 2017b. "Eastern pacific coral reef provinces, coral community structure and composition: An overview." In: *Coral Reefs of the Eastern Tropical Pacific: Persistence and Loss in a Dynamic Environment.* P. W. Glynn, D. P. Manzello, and I. C. Enochs (eds). pp. 107–176. Dordrecht, the Netherlands: Springer Science+Business Media.

Glynn, P. W., S. B. Colley, E. Carpizo-Ituarte, and R. H. Richmond. 2017c. "Coral reproduction in the Eastern Pacific." In: *Coral Reefs of the Eastern Tropical Pacific: Persistence and Loss in a Dynamic Environment.* P. W. Glynn, D. P. Manzello, and I. C. Enochs (eds). pp. 435–476. Dordrecht, The Netherlands: Springer Science+Business Media.

Guzmán, H. M. 1991. "Restoration of coral reefs in the Pacific of Costa Rica." *Conservation Biology* 5, 189–195.

Hebbeln, D. and J. Cortés. 2001. "Sedimentation in a tropical fjord: Golfo Dulce, Costa Rica." *Geo-Marine Letters* 20, 142–148.

Jiménez, C. 2001. "Seawater temperature measured at the surface and at two depths (7 and 12 m) in one coral reef at Culebra Bay, Gulf of Papagayo, Costa Rica." *Revista de Biologia Tropical* 49 (Supplement 2), 153–161.

Liñan-Cabello, M. A., L. A. Flores-Ramirez, M. A. Laurel-Sandovala, E. García-Mendoza, O. Soriano-Santiago, and M. A. Delgadillo-Nuño. 2010. "Acclimation in *Pocillopora* spp. during a coral restoration program in Carrizales Bay, Colima, Mexico." *Marine and Freshwater Behaviour and Physiology* 2010, 1–12.

Lizcano-Sandova, L. D., E. Londoño-Cruz, and F. A. Zapata. 2018. "Growth and survival of *Pocillopora damicornis* (Scleractinia: Pocilloporidae) coral fragments and their potential for coral reef restoration in the Tropical Eastern Pacific." *Marine Biology Research* doi:10.1080/17451000.17452018.115 28011.

López-Pérez, A. 2017. "Revisiting the Cenozoic history and the origin of the Eastern Pacific coral fauna." In: *Coral Reefs of the Eastern Tropical Pacific: Persistence and Loss in a Dynamic Environment*. P. W. Glynn, D. P. Manzello, and I. C. Enochs (eds.) pp. 35–57. Dordrecht, The Netherlands: Springer Science+Business Media.

Nava, H. and A. G. Figueroa-Camacho. 2017. "Rehabilitation of damaged reefs: Outcome of the use of recently broken coral fragments and healed coral fragments of pocilloporid corals on rocky boulders." *Marine Ecology Progress Series* doi:10.1111/maec.12456.

Nedimyer, K., K. Gaines, and S. Roach. 2011. "Coral Tree Nursery©: An innovative approach to growing corals in an ocean-based field nursery." *Aquaculture, Aquarium, Conservation & Legislation Bioflux* 4, 442–446.

Salinas-Akhmadeeva, I. A. 2018. "Relación entre la talla de colonias coralinas y la diversidad de peces, como guía para la restauracón de arrecifes." Licenciatura Thesis, Universidad Nacional Autónoma de México, Morelia, Michoacán, México. pp. 61.

Schneider, C. A., W. S. Rasband, and K. W. Eliceiri. 2012. "NIH Image to ImageJ: 25 years of image analysis." *Nature Methods* 9, 671–675.

Schopmeyer, S. A., D. Lirman, E. Bartels, et al. 2017. "Regional restoration benchmarks for *Acropora cervicornis*." *Coral Reefs* 36, 1047–1057.

Suding, K., E. Higgs, M. Palmer, et al. 2015. "Committing to ecological restoration." *Science* 348, 638–640.

Tortolero-Langarica, J. J. A., A. P. Rodríguez-Troncoso, and A. L. Cupul-Magañab. 2014. "Restoration of a degraded coral reef using a natural remediation process: A case study from a Central Mexican Pacific National Park." *Ocean and Coastal Management* 96, 12–19.

Tortolero-Langarica, J. J. A., A. P. Rodriguez-Troncoso, A. L. Cupul-Magana, L. C. Alarcon-Ortega, and J. D. Santiago-Valentin. 2019. "Accelerated recovery of calcium carbonate production in coral reefs using low-tech ecological restoration." *Ecological Engineering* 128, 89–97.

Veron, J., M. Stafford-Smith, L. DeVantier, and E. Turak. 2015. "Overview of distribution patterns of zooxanthellate Scleractinia." *Frontiers in Marine Science* 1, art. 81, doi:10.3389/fmars.2014.00081.

Villalobos-Cubero, T. 2019. "Manejo integrado y restauración de arrecifes coralinos en Golfo Dulce, Pacífico Sur, Costa Rica." Unpublished Master of Science, Universidad de Costa Rica, San José, Costa Rica, p. 96.

17

LINE ISLANDS, KIRIBATI

Austin Bowden-Kerby, Taratau Kirata, and Laurence Romeo

ABSTRACT

On Kiritimati (Christmas) and Tabuaeran (Fanning) Atolls, Line Islands, Kiribati, over 90% of corals on reefs died from bleaching caused by hot water during a globally unprecedented ten-month period in 2015–2016. Branching corals were particularly impacted with some species becoming locally extinct. The ongoing project focuses on the restoration and facilitated natural recovery of the branching *Acropora* and *Pocillopora* coral species. Encouraging findings of initial recovery are reported, which are proceeding through three processes: surviving adult colonies, colony regeneration from surviving micro-tissue fragments deep within the coral colony (*resurrection corals*), and larval recruitment from larvae coming in on the currents from other islands, or what may be a form of stress-induced asexual larvae formation resulting from *polyp bailout*. We have succeeded in finding a small number of adult *Pocillopora* and *Acropora* colonies that resisted the bleaching, and we are propagating bits of these within a coral nursery in the hope of growing thermally resistant *super corals*, to begin the process of facilitated restoration and long-term adaptation of the corals to a hotter climate. Through these humble efforts, the Line Islands have become the leading edge in the battle against permanent damage to one of the planet's main life-support systems. Additional resources and partnerships must be found to support this work. This strategy of securing and propagating the *super corals* is also being carried out in Fiji, Samoa, and Tuvalu, and must be expanded to other areas to assist the long-term adaptation of corals and coral reefs to increasing temperatures.

INTRODUCTION

Kiritimati, or Christmas Atoll (Figure 17.1(a)), and Tabuaeran, or Fanning Atoll (Figure 17.1(b)), in the Line Islands, Kiribati, experienced mass coral bleaching in 2015 and 2016 due to extremely hot waters caused by a strong El Niño event, superimposed onto increased ocean temperatures due to climate change. Oceanic temperatures remained over the bleaching threshold for corals (>30°C) continuously for some 14 months, with considerably hotter patches within enclosed lagoons. This is the first time in recorded history that coral reefs anywhere have experienced such hot water for such long a time. In 1997–1998 these islands experienced nine months of bleaching, which was the former global record. Kiritimati may thus be an important window into the future of coral reefs globally.

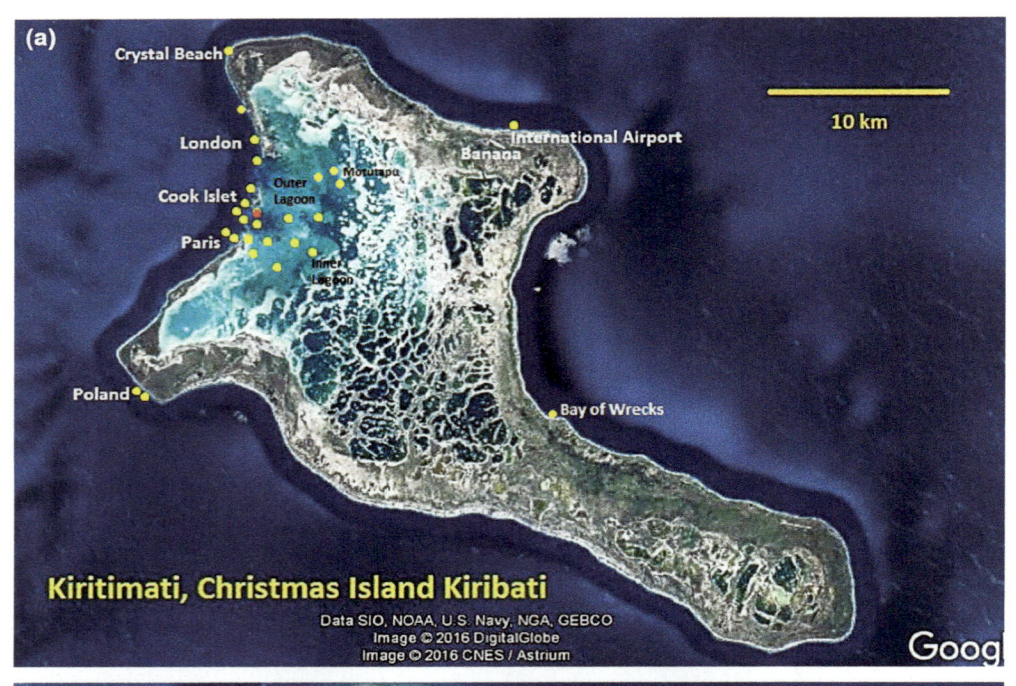

Figure 17.1 (a) Overview of Kiritimati, showing survey sites as yellow dots and the Cook Islet nursery in red. The atoll is over 50 km long and has the largest land mass of any atoll on the planet. The population of around 7,000 mostly lives in the London/Tabwakea and Banana areas, with an additional settlement at Poland, while Paris is an uninhabited area. (b) Fanning Atoll 200 km away, showing the approximate area surveyed. (See Figure 17.16 for relative locations.)

This coral project began in June 2016 and initial surveys found that an estimate of more than 90% of lobate and massive corals and more than 99.9% of all branching corals had died (Figures 17.2(a), (b)), undoubtedly affecting the quality of habitat for small fish and crustaceans. This level of coral death due to bleaching is among the first for an entire coral reef system. The inner lagoon was hit particularly hard, with virtually all corals dying while the outer reef slope and outer lagoon had up to 10–20% survival of massive corals in limited areas. Since June 2016, six trips have been made to Kiritimati to survey for surviving corals and to work on coral restoration alongside the Line Islands Fisheries Department. One trip was made to Tabuaeran, as well. This chapter discusses the results and findings of the work, along with the future plans and needs for coral recovery and restoration in the Line Islands.

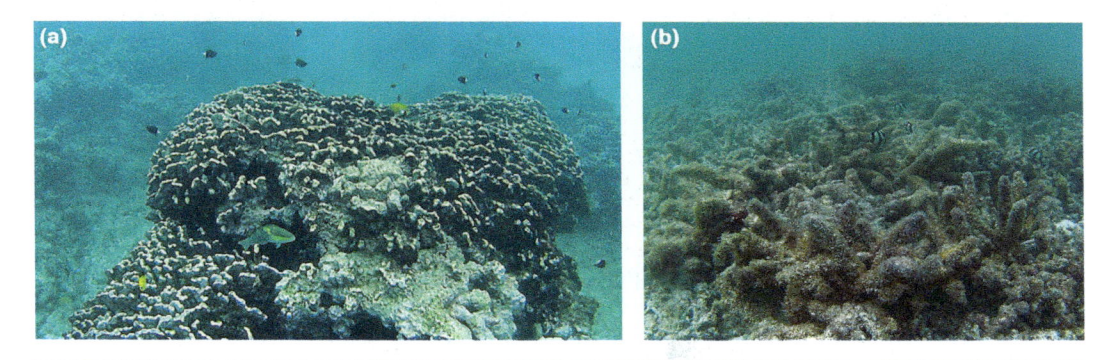

Figure 17.2 (a) Very large, completely dead *Pocillopora* colony of the fore reef, kept clean by fish grazing. (b) Completely dead staghorn coral thickets of the shallow inner lagoon, June 2016. Live coral associated damselfish were still present, but have since all disappeared.

CORAL NURSERY ESTABLISHMENT

A coral nursery was established in the proposed Cook Islet Conservation Area in mid-June 2016, focused on the preservation and increase of branching corals that had survived. In the initial June trip, only two *Acropora* corals could be located in spite of three days of searching. Of these, one colony was a small remnant of a much larger adult colony that had died (Figure 17.3) and one was a small 5 cm juvenile.

Only four surviving adult *Pocillopora* colonies could be located at that time—one at Paris and three at the pass near the coral nursery (Figure 17.4). Extensive searching of the lagoon and shallow outer reef slope found expanses of dead corals, with only a few partially alive massive *Porites* and *Pavona* corals remaining, most with only patches of live tissue.

Fragments of the four *Pocillopora* colonies and all of the two surviving *Acropora* corals found in June 2016 were brought into the nursery. The juvenile *Acropora* coral was collected along with the rock it had settled on, and the surviving branches of digitate *Acropora* were brought in and re-fragmented into seven pieces. A bright purple plating *Montapora* that had survived in the extreme conditions of the inner lagoon were also included—the only non-massive super coral we could find surviving in that zone (Figure 17.5). The surviving massive corals were not sampled because it would have involved thousands of collections; rather, we chose to focus on the more vulnerable branching coral genera.

Follow-up trips were made in November 2016 at four months, in May 2017 at eleven months, in April 2018 at twenty-two months, in December 2018 at two and a half years, and in

Figure 17.3 The last standing *Acropora* coral remnant that could be found, from a shallow tide pool at Cook Islet, June 2016. Greater than 90% of the original colony had died.

Figure 17.4 Map of the Cook Islet Conservation Area, Christmas Island, Kiribati—an important seabird nesting island. The location of surviving adult and juvenile corals found at eleven months is marked. *Pocillopora* super corals and colonies regenerating from remnants are in pink. On the fourth trip, at 22 months, many of the outer reef areas at 3–4 meters depth (not marked here) had become colonized with juvenile *Acropora* recruits.

Figure 17.5 The plating coral, *Montipora petula*, at two and a half years in the nursery, with two-year-old Pink *Pocillopora verrucosa*, and various younger digitate *Acropora* corals.

November 2019—additional corals were added to the nursery each time, with the corals thriving and growing within the nursery (Figure 17.6(a), (b), (c)).

In November 2016, additional reefs were searched, in hopes of finding more surviving corals. A scoping of the outer lagoon reefs opposite the pass found no *Acropora* corals, but many other coral species were found to be alive and healthy there, including several massive species such as *Porites*, submassive *Pavona*, and a few *Leptoserus* brain corals, as well as *Fungia*, *Heliofungia* and four adult colonies of *Pocillopora*. On a site visit to the Crystal Beach fringing reef, 8 km north of the pass and in clear waters with abundant fish and sea urchins, one juvenile *Acropora* coral was found with a few massive species, but no living *Pocillopora* corals were seen. The big waves and strong surge confined this search to the reef flat. An attempt to access the reefs of the north coast in November failed due to high surf.

At 11 months, a few coral colonies were removed and reattached to give more room for growth because contact was causing *Pocillopora* to kill the purple *Montastrea* colonies. A bright purple genotype of *Pocillopora* was also brought in. At 22 months, the initial *Pocillopora* colonies had grown too big for the table, 25–35 cm in diameter, which was sagging and in danger of collapse. The table was reinforced and the original *Pocillopora* corals were outplanted to the reef nearby using cement or were placed in shallow reef crevices (discussed later).

Two 40–50 cm colonies of pink *Pocillopora* have thus far been found, one to the north of Cook Islet in April 2017 and another on the outer reef flat at Crystal Beach in May 2018, and three and five samples respectively were taken and included in the nursery.

Other than cleaning some hydroids and a bit of *Caulerpa* seaweed from the nursery table, the nursery did not require cleaning due to the high numbers of herbivorous surgeonfish at the site. However, one of the tables became too heavy and collapsed in 2019, which required an intervention.

Figure 17.6 (a) The Cook Islet coral nursery, showing corals overgrowing the cable strap that secured them to a cement disc and the underlying plastic mesh (left) and the one problematic patch of hydroid, which was removed. (b) Seven *Acropora globiceps* coral colonies at 22 months, grown from a single survivor of that species, planted with *Pocillopora*. Robust health is striking, even without maintenance or care. (c) Twelve coral fragments harvested from a 60 cm bleaching resistant *Pocillopora eydouxi* "super coral" and planted in the coral nursery. Photo is at eleven months.

LARVAL-BASED CORAL RECRUITMENT

Searching for corals on subsequent trips became more and more encouraging as juvenile *Acropora* corals began recruiting. In November 2016, we found three ~3 cm *Acropora* recruits near the coral nursery, as well as another 47 juvenile *Acropora* corals in an enclosed reef bay to the north of Cook Islet (Figure 17.7(a), (b)). These abundant juvenile *Acropora* corals provide hope for recovery of the coral population over time.

Numerous adult and juvenile *Pocillopora* corals were also observed in this same coral cove area. Massive *Porites* and *Pavona* corals were the most common corals of the area. Perhaps this rather warm bay has favored bleaching resistance through selection pressure, resulting in higher coral survival?

The fact that the *Acropora* recruits were closely associated with living adult *Pocillopora* colonies and surviving massive *Pavona* corals may indicate that these adult corals are serving as a settlement signal for the coral larvae. Tridacnid clams are also particularly abundant at the site and might potentially be a settlement signal. On the May 2017 trip, we found that these juvenile

Figure 17.7 (a) Searching for and finding juvenile *Acropora* corals on the reef north of Cook Islet, Kiritimati; (b) note the blue juvenile coral colony among the dead coral rocks.

corals had grown to 8–12 cm in size, with some smaller corals of the 2–4 cm size also found, although no adult corals of any *Acropora* species could be found on Kiritimati that could serve as parent stock, both by our own searching of the shallows and by asking divers of the aquarium fish trade who dive daily on many deeper sites west and south of the island.

Further searching in November 2016 resulted in finding 11 juvenile *Acropora* colonies on the Paris reef slope, located in 3 m of water at the top of reef spurs. The new recruits were found among several surviving adult *Pocillopora* colonies which had been overlooked in June; however, no juvenile corals and no *Pocillopora* corals were found in shallower waters at that site.

On the outer reef slope off London during this trip, 1 km north of the pass but still under the influence of warm water leaving the lagoon, 14 juvenile *Acropora* corals and about six adult-sized *Pocillopora* colonies were found, but no massive corals were seen alive. This is a very dead coral reef, but with abundant herbivorous fish and some black-spined sea urchins.

The presence of juvenile *Acropora* corals of multiple species gave us hope for the future recovery of the coral reefs on Kiritimati. Their 3–5 cm size-range indicates that they are about one year old. The discovery of so many juvenile corals is a very exciting development in the recovery of the reefs. We now have multiple genotypes of three of the missing *Acropora* species, which gives potential for successful spawning and the formation of planktonic coral larvae in the future, enabling the wider recovery of these locally endangered species through natural larval recruitment processes, and eventually leading to the recovery of this badly damaged coral reef system.

The numerous juvenile corals found on the November 2016 trip must have been present during the initial June 2016 visit, although too small at that time to be seen easily. We can only assume that their parents all died in the mass bleaching shortly after they spawned, or perhaps they came in as larvae from another area—possibly Fanning Atoll—which is over 250 km upcurrent. Another possibility is that the polyps detached from the stressed corals and set out as asexual planula larvae, through a process called polyp bailout. Such asexual larvae contain the symbiotic algae and could therefore possibly swim into shaded microhabitats of the reef, potentially settling temporarily and remaining viable until the waters cooled off, at which point they could emerge and settle on the exposed parts of the reef (https://reefbites.wordpress.com). Regardless of origin, these baby corals are exceedingly precious and important to the recovery of the reefs.

MAY 2017 NURSERY EXPANSION USING THREATENED *ACROPORA* RECRUITS

The May visit found all of the corals in the Cook Islet nursery healthy and growing well. The large school of surgeonfish initially seen at the site were still present and had maintained a high level of cleanliness on the nursery table without any maintenance. No parrotfish bitemarks or any sort of physical damage was apparent.

The juvenile corals seen in November were revisited, and while they had increased in size, they were still too small for trimming and not growing as fast as the corals in the nursery. Many were seen with fresh parrotfish wounds and missing branch tips, which appeared to be the main reason for their slower growth. Some of the corals were also being overgrown by *Caulerpa* seaweeds, which were removed. It appears that the corals have recruited in two events, as there seemed to be two fairly distinct size classes, a 20–40-mm-size class and 80–120-mm-size class. Photographic data on colony size was taken but has yet to be analyzed; however, predation by parrotfish may affect the size class data.

Due to the ongoing damage resulting from the high abundance of parrotfish in the juvenile coral site, plus a lack of branches long enough for trimming, a decision was made to remove entire colonies—those that could most easily be chiseled off of the hard coral substrate and brought into the expanded coral nursery (Figure 17.8), away from the threat of so many large parrotfish and overgrowth (Figure 17.9).

A total of 63 colonies were moved in this way and planted to a new nursery table, which was filled to capacity. This collection represents about 10% of an estimated 600 juvenile *Acropora* recruits to the cove (Figure 17.10(a), (b), (c)).

The new nursery table is located parallel to the initial table and 2 m apart, and the tables were secured to one another by 3 m metal bars for added strength and to allow space for rope

Figure 17.8 Removing juvenile corals with a hammer and chisel. Note the two surviving lobate coral colonies nearby.

Figure 17.9 New coral table planted with juvenile corals collected from the field—with the older nursery table in the foreground, planted with three pink *Pocillopora* corals, taken from the first surviving colony of this color morph found thus far at the *coral cove* location where the abundant juvenile *Acropora* population is found.

Figure 17.10 (a) Close-up of the coral nursery—new corals in the foreground on a table and a line in the middle containing small broken bits from the juvenile corals, which otherwise would likely die. (b) Close-up view of the newly planted juvenile corals, some planted to cement cookie bases for easy removal when mature and some planted onto plastic mesh secured over 2×2 inch iron mesh. While uncertain due to small size, many individuals appear to be *A. nasuta, A. tenuis, A. selago*, or *A. globiceps*. (c) The coral tables in December 2018, with crowding clearly apparent, ready for trimming in the planned January 2019 visit.

culture of staghorn corals, as is the common setup in our other sites in the South Pacific and the Caribbean.

No mortality occurred over 19 months in spite of parrotfish bites to corals at positions located toward the edges and ends of the table, with corals growing an estimated 5–10-fold over the period in spite of the damage and their sometimes growing together and competing with each other for space (Figure 17.10(c)).

THE DISCOVERY OF REGENERATING CORAL COLONIES VIA SURVIVING TISSUE FRAGMENTS

In spite of the difficulty of accessing the reef front zone, site visits were made in May 2017 to the shallow (less than 0.5 m) reef flat zone at Poland on the southwest of the atoll, at Crystal Beach on the northwest, and to the reef flat at the airport on the northeast of Kiritimati (Figure 17.11). After extensive searching, we found multiple small *Acropora* colonies regenerating in the northern two of the three sites, at Crystal Beach and at the airport reef, all in direct association with dead *Acropora* colonies. In the 2018 visits, additional regenerating populations were found west of the airport. Rather than being larval recruits, these *resurrection corals* appear to have regenerated from micro-tissue remnants on much bigger micro-atoll coral colonies in the extreme shallows, all very near the shore. Anywhere from one to 20 small colonies were found per remnant population, with all multiple colonies within a population having identical and distinct coloration—yellow with green polyps, blue tipped, purple, cream, or brown—and representing what appears to be more than one tightly branched coral species (Figure 17.12). These remnant colonies were always found on dead *Acropora* branches of similar growth form,

Figure 17.11 Airport reef flat, with the location of remnant *Acropora* corals marked. An estimated 700 m of the nearshore was surveyed and six to seven genotypes found of what appears to be *A. trnuis* and perhaps one or two other species.

most often on the dead colony edges (Figure 17.13). Single colonies with these characteristics are also assumed to be remnants, although that is uncertain (Figure 17.14). From the appearance of the remnant colonies, it seems that small areas of coral tissue must have survived in the shaded depths of the original larger colonies, or perhaps on the colony edges under shaded overhangs.

Figure 17.12 Remnant colonies of *Acropora*, possibly *A. nasuta*, with over 15 small colonies of identical form and coloration found in this immediate location.

Figure 17.13 Remnant colonies on the edges of a once much larger reef flat colony of *Acropora*. Over one year since the die-off, coraline algae are infilling between the dead branches and overgrowth of algal turf is making the original skeleton more and more difficult to discern.

Figure 17.14 Solitary coral assumed to be a remnant *resurrection* coral growing from within the deep branches, rather than a sexual recruit—note the old, dead *Acropora* skeleton.

A total of what is thought to represent six different genotypes of coral were found at Crystal Beach, with eleven found at the airport reef flat, indicating that there could be thousands of genotypes of reef-flat-adapted *Acropora* corals surviving on Kiritimati, a very promising finding that indicates a slow recovery of formerly abundant species in progress.

Resurrection coral colonies were collected from Crystal Beach in May 2018 and from the airport in December 2018 (Figures 17.15(a), (b)) and brought into the coral nursery. Recovery via resurrection corals is patchy and is not everywhere. A similar extensive search at the Poland reef flat on the south of the atoll found no such remnants in spite of an abundance of dead *Acropora* skeletons.

Figure 17.15 (a) December 2018, two years post bleaching, with the *resurrection* corals growing, spreading, and gradually rejuvenating the original coral colony on the reef flat. (b) Close-up of the *Acropora* resurrection corals at two years post bleaching. Note the *Pocillopora* larval recruit toward the top of the photo. Surviving *Pocillopora* corals have the ability of reseeding the reef with asexually generated, internally brooded, coral larvae. Such recruits would have the same internal algae and thus the same thermal tolerance as their mother.

TABUAERAN FINDINGS

A trip to Tabuaeran, also known as Fanning Atoll (Figure 17.1(b)), some 200 km from Kiritimati (Figure 17.1(a)), was carried out in May 2017 to assess the impact of the mass bleaching there, and to seek out staghorn corals that had apparently become extinct on Kiritimati. Due to logistics and time (Figure 17.16), only one scoping trip into the lagoon was possible, accompanied by the local Fisheries officer. We surveyed a transect of lagoon reefs from north to south. The devastation of many of these reefs was virtually complete—almost no corals were found alive and some of the very biggest *Pocillopora* coral heads we had ever seen were completely dead. However, on four reefs, among the devastation of dead and standing colonies, we found four surviving staghorn coral, *Acropora muricata*, as well as *A. vaughani* and possibly one or two other *Acropora* species to be confirmed at a later date.

The fact that no coral-killing crown of thorns starfish were seen and only a few *Drupela* snails were present may have been significant in the survival of these corals after the demise of a conservatively estimated 90% of the coral population in the lagoon.

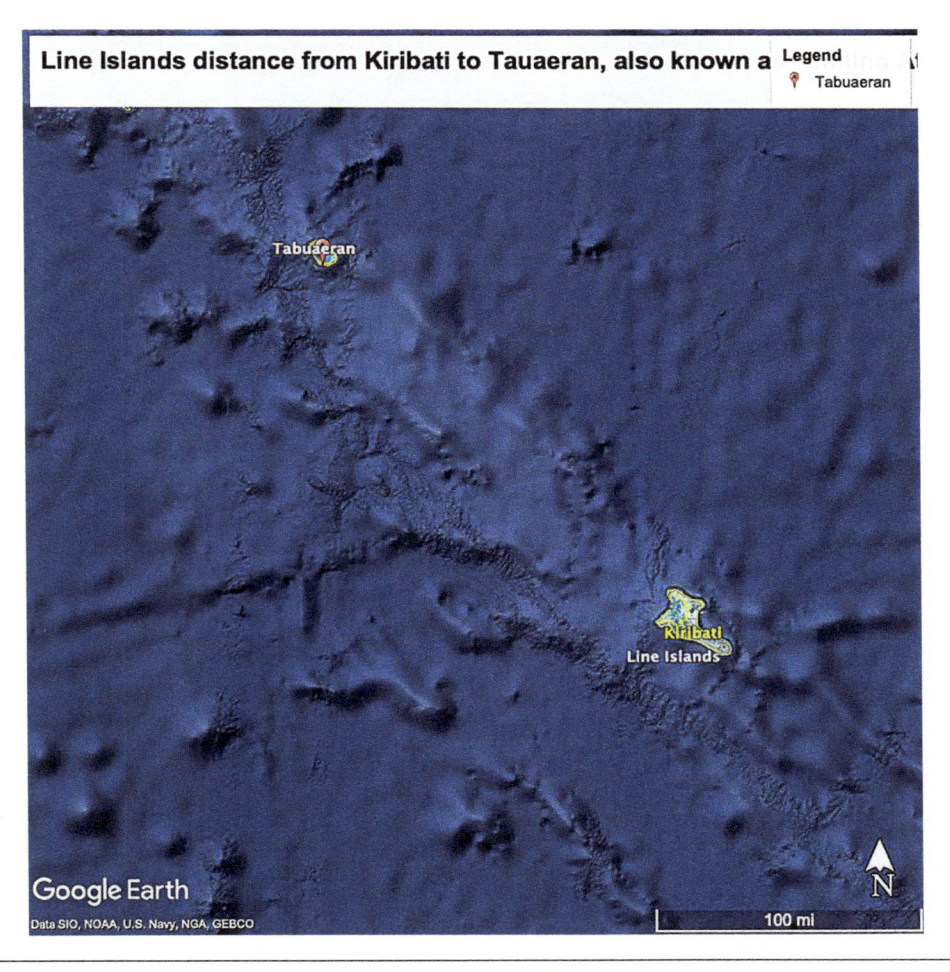

Figure 17.16 Tabuaeran or Fanning Atoll, showing the distance of over 200 km from Kiritimati Atoll, making multiple trips and monitoring difficult.

Due to the rough seas, and despite two attempts, we were unable to get out to the oceanic outer reefs; however, several fishermen confirmed that while most of the corals are now dead, some living corals of the sorts that are often blue or purple—the *Acropora* corals—continue to survive. While this must be confirmed at a future date, the hypothesis that the small juvenile corals coming into Kiritimati are from Tabuaeran has been strengthened.

Samples of 10 cm coral branches were taken from each of the staghorn coral populations that we found and put onboard in a shaded bucket filled with seawater changed several times during the day. The purpose was to collect as diverse a set of corals as possible for inclusion in the coral nursery on Kiritimati, the volume of which amounted to about half of a four-gallon bucket full, and representing both fine and robust branched species and a diversity of color morphs within each species. It is impractical at this point to create a coral nursery or gene bank on Fanning Atoll, as it is quite difficult and expensive to travel to for follow-up.

The sampled corals were immediately taken to shore and planted onto ropes that were then temporarily strung between existing metal stakes in the subtidal zone near the main settlement. These planted ropes were removed two days later, three hours before the flight back to Christmas Island, carried onboard in a bucket, and periodically sprinkled with seawater during the 45 minute flight. We were met by Kiritimati Fisheries officers upon landing, and the corals were rushed to a waiting boat and taken into the coral nursery and planted by simply tying the ropes onto the expanded nursery structure (Figure 17.17).

Moving corals between ecoregions is not promoted in our work. However, our underlying assumption with moving these corals is that the corals of Fanning are quite close to Christmas Island geographically, existing mere days upcurrent, so that they share the same ecoregion with Christmas Island.

Figure 17.17 Overview of the expanded and completed coral nursery at the Cook Islet site, Christmas Island, June 1, 2017, with table cultures for tight-branched *Acropora* and *Pocillopora* coral species and with roped cultures for the open-branched staghorn *Acropora* species.

The corals suffered no mortality despite the stress of collection and transport, and all corals were thriving when visited a year later (Figure 17.18). However, growth at one year was disappointing, as the corals had only doubled or tripled in size, less than the expected ten to fifteen times increase that is typical of staghorn corals when using similar methods globally. The reason for this slow growth soon became apparent, as numerous parrotfish bites covered the corals, with the staghorn corals particularly targeted (Figure 17.19). The *Acropora* corals on the tables were also impacted (Figure 17.20).

Two of the staghorn ropes were moved to a new nursery site at Motutapu reef where parrotfish are scarce, and the positive results were seen six months later in Figure 17.21; however, the problem of parrotfish predation seemed to have lessened by December 2018.

Figure 17.18 Rope nursery planted in May 2017 with several species of bleaching-resistant staghorn corals brought from Fanning Atoll to the Christmas Atoll nursery (as seen in Figure 17.17) showed good growth one year later, in May 2018.

Figure 17.19 Parrotfish bite marks clearly visible in May 2018, resulting in slower growth, but no mortality occurring.

Figure 17.20 Corals on the nursery table after one year, some damaged by parrotfish bites.

Figure 17.21 Cook Islet nursery at 17 months, December 2018. Comparatively, the staghorn coral lines moved to Motutapu and grew with more positive results due to less predation by parrotfish.

DISCOVERY OF SURVIVING STAGHORN CORALS ON A KIRITIMATI REEF FLAT

In December 2018, while scoping for regenerating corals on the reef flat, a remnant population of thick branched, blunt-tipped, staghorn corals (*Acropora robusta*) was discovered to the west of the airport at Crusher Reef. This area has the widest reef flat on the island (Figure 17.22).

Line Islands, Kiribati

Among the dead and standing coral colonies scattered on the reef flat (Figure 17.23) were a few surviving branches, plus one coral thicket was alive on all sides that looked to be a true *super coral*, not suffering from any significant mortality during the bleaching (Figure 17.24). Surviving *Acropora globiceps* remnants were also found (Figure 17.25).

Figure 17.22 The reef flat at Crusher Reef with remnant staghorn corals marked.

Figure 17.23 Dead and standing *Acropora* and *Pocillopora* corals nearly three years after their death in 2015–2016. A living massive *Porites* colony is in the foreground.

Figure 17.24 Three color morphs of regenerating/remnant *Acropora robusta* staghorn corals, each thought to be a different coral genotype, found in December 2018 among dead and standing coral colonies of the same species on the shallow reef flat at Crusher Reef, Kiritimati.

Figure 17.25 *Acropora globiceps* colony remnant in the foreground, plus smaller "resurrection coral" emerging towards the background, both on a former large colony at Crusher Reef flat.

OUTPLANTING OF CORALS FROM THE NURSERY

In May 2018 the original nursery table was being weighed down by heavy adult-sized corals, which had grown from small fragments over the two years. All of the original 24 colonies of four genotypes had survived and grown 20–30 cm in diameter at 22 months (Figure 17.26). These *Pocillopora* corals were harvested and planted nearby. Some were cemented securely to dead corals, but as that proved difficult due to the motion of the currents, the majority of the colonies were then planted without any attachment onto the reef about 30 m away. Each of these colonies were set within the grooves of a large dead lobate coral head into a 3–4 m circular area (Figure 17.27). In December, six months later, all colonies were healthy, with no mortality or partial mortality, and most of the colonies had self-attached firmly to the substrate. Two colonies had turned sideways, but most were still in the base-down position. This genetically diverse cluster should be ready and able to spawn, and is located where they can continue to serve as mother colonies for trimmed fragments in the coming months and years.

An experimental outplanting of small 2–3 cm branches of *Acropora selago* corals, trimmed from colonies growing on the nursery table, was also tried in May 2018. Multiple branch tips of the same genotype were set together into balls of wet cement that were placed on dead corals near the nursery; however, parrotfish bit the branches completely off within 48 hours. It was thought that the corals were dead. However, in December, some five months later, we found that tiny micro-fragments of flesh had survived and grown together to form viable patches of live coral tissue 5–10 cm wide (Figure 17.28).

Branches were seen forming in the tissue discs, and an upright elongation was expected in the coming months, which did not occur as parrotfish continued to graze the corals. The tightly branched growth form of this species on the nearby elevated nursery table appears to protect coral branches from being bitten off, but this protection is lost when branches are taken out and planted on the rocks below. The first major outplanting of *Acropora* took place in March 2020 using the pegged rope method, with the corals growing on the nursery ropes trimmed (Figure 17.29) and branches woven into 5 mm ropes.

Figure 17.26 *Pocillopora* coral colonies at 22 months ready for removal for outplanting.

Figure 17.27 Harvested *Pocillopora* corals are grown for 22 months; this is the result of the outplanting six months later—self-attached and healthy. Twenty-four colonies of four genotypes ~30 cm in diameter have now become a diverse cluster able to spawn and are located where they can continue to serve as mother colonies to produce trimmed fragments for more work.

Figure 17.28 *Acropora selago* planted and then bitten off by parrotfish (May 2018, top left). Surviving micro-fragments merge at six months, (Nov. 2018, top right), form branches (Nov. 2019, bottom left) and continue to struggle against parrotfish bites (March 2020, bottom right). Coral growth is suppressed over a 22-month period but note the adjacent *Tridacna* clam which recruited and grew rapidly over the same time period.

Figure 17.29 Trimming corals to prevent competition, while creating seed corals for outplanting; before (top) and after (bottom), March 2020.

More than 300 fragments in the 2–10 cm range were planted in this manner on ten outplanting ropes nailed into place on dead reef rock with concrete nails. The pegged ropes were all planted into shallow higher energy reef areas in an attempt to avoid parrotfish damage. Two sites were trialed, one with seven ropes near the coral nursery (Figure 17.30), and another with three ropes at Tabwakea village, in what is now a totally coral-free surf zone where it is too rough and shallow for parrotfish to live except on a rare calm day. Both efforts involved youth from the communities as an educational exercise (Figure 17.31).

Figure 17.30 Outplanting ropes nailed onto reef rock near the coral nursery. Parrotfish are abundant and their bite marks pock the rocks at this site, which may prevent outplanting success.

Figure 17.31 Youth involvement in the project of creating outplanting ropes at Tabwakea Village, Kiritimati, March 2020.

DISCUSSION

Is Adaptation of the Line Islands Corals to Climate Change Possible?

While the discovery of an ongoing and accelerating natural coral recovery process is encouraging, a big question is whether the juvenile corals that are recruiting or regenerating from surviving tissues, once they become adult colonies, will be better able to withstand future bleaching events than the corals that died out. The hope is that they are indeed more bleaching resistant, have more resistant algae, or have acquired them. The fact that newly settled juvenile *Acropora* corals initially have no symbiotic algae inside them and that they must take up the algae they need for photosynthesis from the water gives them a greater capacity to adapt. Assuming that the only corals left on the reef after 14 months of bleaching are bleaching-resistant individuals, it is hoped that the newly settled corals have acquired bleaching-resistant symbiotic algae (zooxanthellae) after settlement.

The first cohort of settled corals, which must have settled during the bleaching event, must have experienced warmer waters that were potentially filled with algae expelled during the bleaching. If the algae available were dominated by those dumped by the corals of the extremely hot inner lagoon, which would travel on tidal currents and exit the lagoon on either side of Cook Islet, they would potentially be available for acquisition by the juvenile coral recruits. The areas near where the two would pass do appear to have the highest densities of juvenile corals, which might help confirm this hypothesis. Genetic tests of the surviving corals to determine the specific algal clade and thermal tolerance regime should be done at some future date. Regardless, future bleaching events are inevitable, which will test the corals to determine if they are bleaching resistant or not.

The intention is that the coral nursery will serve as a gene bank of branching corals and their algae, especially the few individuals of *Acropora* and *Pocillopora* that have survived the mass bleaching, becoming a *Noah's Ark* of bleaching-resistant corals for the restoration of the reefs of Kiritimati. Our restoration strategy does not envision replanting large areas with corals, but rather to replant smaller patches of corals of multiple genotypes that are capable of spawning, in order to reboot sexual reproduction and the formation of coral larvae, so that nature can reseed the reefs naturally, over time (Figure 17.32).

The prediction is that bleaching temperatures will become more and more frequent in the coming years, and so it is questionable whether or not the reefs will be able to adapt to such increasing levels of stress. As sea level rises, healthy and growing corals are our best defense; thus, global warming must be controlled by greenhouse gas reductions for two reasons—coral reef health and to lessen sea-level rise. The future of Kiribati as a nation is gravely threatened, and international action is needed. Kiribati has been placed squarely in the forefront of the problem; therefore, Kiribati must become the leader in presenting the solutions. "The first shall be last and the last shall be first."

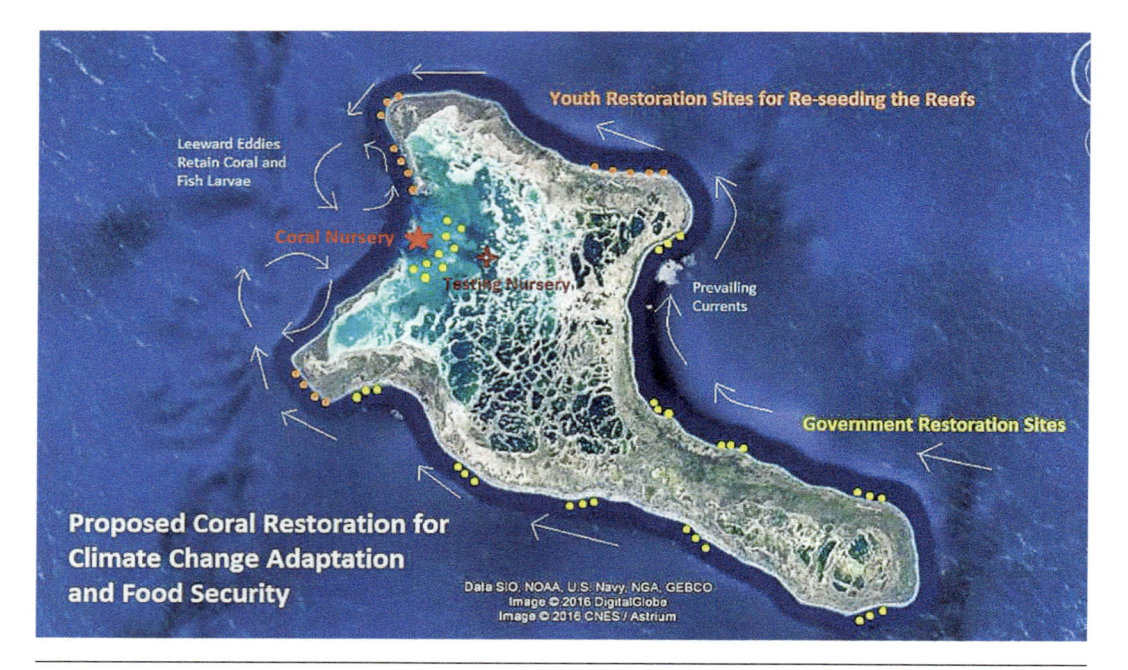

Figure 17.32 Proposed restoration plan for Kiritimati, Christmas Atoll, showing prevailing currents and proposed shallow water outplanting sites. An additional coral nursery is proposed for Motutapu to test samples of each coral genotype in warmer lagoon waters and enable the selection of the most resilient coral genotypes.

Protecting the Restoration Sites

Because this restoration work is so important to the future of the reefs of Kiribati, it is very important to set aside the main restoration reefs into no-fishing, marine protected areas (MPAs). This would strictly limit the number of people visiting the sites and placing fishing lines and nets, or stepping on the reefs, as this will break the regenerating corals. We also need a high density of grazing fish to clean the nurseries and the dead corals so that living corals thrive and so that once coral larvae are generated through spawning of restored coral populations, they can find a clean place to settle out on and grow. The ban on fishing should apply to all subsistence and commercial fishing activities in the restoration zone.

Controlled tourism activities and visits to the nursery and restoration sites should only be permitted on a case-by-case basis and the visitors should be well-controlled—taught not to stand on or kick the reef and not to wear any toxic types of sunscreen. Anchors should not be used on the reef, rather mooring buoys installed. Tourism activities might be used to generate income through fees or solicited donations to fund the work.

If possible, support for alternative livelihoods among the fishing families who have traditionally used this area should be given in the form of seaweed farming, other types of fishing, and perhaps poultry as an alternative to fish as a protein source.

PROPOSED 500-METER NO-GO AND NO-FISHING AREA AROUND COOK ISLET

In addition to providing extra protection to the nesting birds of Cook Islet, a 500-meter no-fishing area is needed in order to protect the corals on the reef (Figure 17.33) that were badly damaged in the 14-month 2015–2016 coral bleaching, in which an estimated 95% of the corals died. Abundant fish are needed to clean the dead coral skeletons of the reef and to help facilitate the recruitment of coral larvae. This recovery process fortunately is already occurring, with at least three *Acropora* corals now coming in on the currents as larvae, possibly from Tabuaeran, which was less badly impacted from the bleaching and mass mortality. The coral reefs around Cook Islet appear to have the highest remaining coral cover of any of the reefs of Kiritimati, with 10% cover in some areas; and as such, these reefs need protection from excessive boat anchors and related damage.

A process of outplanting the now rare branching corals has begun from the nursery, and these restoration patches require protection. The restoration strategy is to re-establish diverse breeding populations of rare branching corals within the protected area, which will facilitate a wider restoration of corals to the reefs of Kiritimati through the production of abundant coral larvae that will spread to nearby reefs through the currents. Establishing a no-take area is very important in securing breeding populations of not only corals, but also of tridacnid clams, reef fish, and other species in danger of over-exploitation, and would be a big step forward for conservation and the restoration of Kiritimati's wildlife.

Figure 17.33 Proposed no-take zone around the Cook Islet Conservation Area.

Ciguatera Fish Poisoning Outbreak Begins October 2018, Caused by the Death of the Coral Reefs

During the December 2018 trip to Kiritimati, we were informed that fish poisoning had recently become a problem, starting in late September and October. Even parrotfish have been affected, indicating a high density of the toxic dinoflagellates in the environment. The reported problem area is at Bay of Wrecks on the eastern side of the atoll and off of London.

Austin Bowden-Kerby had first-hand experience with this problem after eating reef fish at a local restaurant on December 8, suffering from repeated vomiting, itching (especially the hands and feet), and back and joint pains, requiring a visit to the hospital. Senior Nursing Officer Mrs. Ueata Maneaua was very helpful in going through the hospital records and reporting back to me that more than 10 severe cases had been admitted or treated at the hospital over the past two months, while in past years there might have only been one case every year or so. Since all out-patient cases are not recorded, those who were hospitalized may represent only a fraction of this developing problem. In September 2019, Taratau Kirata, a Fisheries officer and integral part of our team, was severely poisoned by ciguatera and required hospitalization.

Gambierdiscus toxicus, the toxic dinoflagellate microalgae responsible for ciguatera lives on dead corals and the surface of fleshy algae, and so is typically not a problem for live coral-dominated coral reef systems like those reported by Maragos in 1974. However, the reefs of Kiritimati have been transformed into dead coral reefs—an ideal habitat for the toxic algae species (Figure 17.34). Ciguatera is, thus, an entirely new health risk for the community and is directly related to the mass bleaching and death of the corals. With this new development, we can see that climate change is actively impacting both the food security and health of the Line Islands.

Figure 17.34 Dead corals make an ideal habitat for the toxic dinoflagellate microalgae *Gambierdiscus toxicus*, which lives on the surfaces of the dead coral rocks. They create a golden-brown film over the rocks, much like that pictured here.

With this new crisis, resources must be found to closely monitor the situation, to facilitate health statistics, to sample the physical environment for *G. toxicus* abundance, to map the fishing areas most affected, and if possible, to test the fish being caught. Community awareness must also become a priority once the facts are known, and measures to facilitate the recovery and restoration of the corals should be given proper attention and funding as the only recourse to diminishing the problem. Restoration of high coral cover back to the reefs is the only long-term solution.

Strategy for the Future

The corals within the nursery have now been grown into *mother colonies* and trimming has begun because colonies are overgrowing one another and competing for space in the nursery. A trip in December 2019 removed competing corals and started as a pilot *drop and scatter* transplantation of larger fragments on a nearby rubble bed. The goal is to trim the corals once or twice per year to produce hundreds of second generation coral fragments. These fragments will be replanted into restoration patches in limited areas on the main reef, both inside and outside the lagoon—initially in smaller numbers in order to test survival under parrotfish predation. Wherever the result is successful, the goal will then be to create diverse aggregations of each species with the goal being to restore reproduction among the corals and thus facilitate natural coral reef recovery. If after initial trials parrotfish predation is severe, an alternative strategy will be to focus the restoration into the shallow upcurrent reef flats of the main island, where parrotfish are considerably smaller and less abundant. Because the corals are so tightly branched due to parrotfish predation, we will only use the cementation method, plugging multiple 1–3 cm fragments into cement balls placed onto the substrate, while being careful to keep the branches that were trimmed from each mother colony separate from others, ensuring a single coral genotype in each cluster, so that the tissues can merge and form integrated colonies.

Because we have limited coral biomass to work with, we do not plan to replant extensive areas with corals, but rather to create numerous genetically diverse patches for each species within limited 3 × 3 meter areas in order to encourage spawning of adult colonies within a few years. By focusing the outplanting work on shallow reef flats that retain water during low tide, we will also be better able to involve the community in the work, using restoration as an educational tool and part of our efforts at supporting community-based management and the establishment of no-take MPAs.

CORAL REEF RESTORATION STRATEGY FOR KIRIBATI

Christmas Island, Kiritimati, is a very large atoll and millions of corals have perished in the recent mass bleaching event; therefore, it will be impossible to replant corals everywhere on the island's damaged coral reefs. This is not our strategy, rather our strategy is to help facilitate a natural coral recovery process. Because prevailing currents are from the east, where no coral reefs occur, the natural larval recruitment process will be limited or absent, unless and until we can re-establish local breeding populations of corals on the reefs of Christmas Atoll.

The reefs have essentially suffered an ecological extinction event of vital branching coral species, and major changes will likely occur in the coming years to the fish and other fauna. While a very few scattered and isolated adult colonies of *Pocillopora* have been found, only one adult-sized colony of the genus *Acropora* has been found. The ecological function of branching corals as a group is now essentially gone. Coral recovery of the *Pocillopora* species group may eventually occur on its own; however, it will be delayed and could take many decades since the surviving colonies are, for the most part, hundreds of meters apart from each other so that fertilization will not be likely. On the other hand, asexual production of larvae might help overcome this problem to a certain extent for this species group.

The situation with *Acropora* will take even more time since all of the existing corals are juveniles and will not spawn effectively for a few years. However, this recent find of numerous juvenile *Acropora* corals both recruiting from larvae and recovering from mostly dead colonies is very promising and offers hope for the future of these reefs. If left on their own, these corals have the potential to grow into a viable spawning population of *Acropora* corals of several species, but natural recovery processes might take several decades, and many more bleaching events will undoubtedly set back recovery, potentially preventing it altogether.

Our strategy will be to cultivate as much of the genetic diversity as possible within the nurseries, and then to use trimmed second generation branches to create discrete and genetically diverse patches of spawning corals at intervals along the wider reef to reseed the reefs naturally with larvae. Certainly, more colonies and additional species will be found in time, and pairing those surviving corals with different genotypes will help ensure effective spawning. Collecting and propagating additional coral samples within the nurseries will vastly increase the genetic and biological contribution that each of the surviving coral genotypes makes to the future recovery of the island's reefs. Our long-term goal is to have the coral nursery expanded to include hundreds of distinct genotypes of each surviving *Acropora* and *Pocillopora* species. Each genotype should be genetically tested for its algae symbionts to determine if the coral is sensitive to high temperatures or if it is bleaching resistant.

The coral restoration patches will serve as spawning aggregations for the natural production of coral larvae and should be located in areas where the currents are more likely to transport the larvae to other reefs—and not areas where they are more likely to be swept out into the deep ocean and lost. Some data on current flow would be helpful in developing this strategy and determining the best up-current locations.

Additional coral genotypes and species should be sought out, and additional nursery tables must be constructed as required. More *Pocillopora* corals should be included, with separate gene bank nurseries created, but only if additional financial and human resources can be found.

A high priority should be placed on creating a second duplicate nursery site, located in an area that is more sheltered from storm surges, which do occasionally reach these waters and could potentially severely impact the present nursery site. This secondary nursery, ideally, should be located in the sheltered lagoon, but in an area of good water circulation. Mother colonies of each of the *Acropora* corals should be trimmed and duplicated between the two sites as insurance against long-term loss. Over the years, as more corals are added to the gene-bank nurseries, the work will grow in importance and impact. The mother colonies should be trimmed over and over again, once or twice per year in order to maintain their vigor. Untrimmed corals lose their vigor, begin to grow more slowly, and can become susceptible to disease.

The coral restoration program should be expanded to Fanning and Washington Atolls as resources permit, and with the mass bleaching of the main Gilbert Islands, the need for the work throughout Kiribati has vastly increased. Community training and involvement may be possible, and youth would find the work encouraging and interesting as a service project.

Restoring and securing the original species of corals found on each island prior to the mass bleaching should be our long-term goal, with each species reproducing effectively and expanding its local range through natural larval recruitment processes. However, if after several years, a particular coral species can't be found on an island any longer, it should be assumed to be locally extinct and an effort to find and bring the species from other reefs of the same island group should be made, exchanging between nurseries if possible. If a coral species is composed of only a single or a few genotypes, more genotypes should be brought in from the nearest local source available, but never from different eco-regions.

Severe bleaching can be expected to come again to the Gilbert, Line, and Phoenix Islands in the coming years due to the rapidly changing climate and global warming. However, the corals that have survived the last hot water bleaching event are assumed to be bleaching resistant, offering some hope that adaptation is occurring. Our goal now is to propagate and replant populations of these bleaching-resistant corals, which will then spread into the environment and restore the reefs through natural larval production and recruitment processes. The restored reefs should, in turn, carry bleaching resistance adaptations and should be in a much better position to survive the hot water. Theoretically, the next mass bleaching will leave the reefs in a much less damaged position, and with many more unbleached corals.

This work gives us hope that we can help coral reefs survive into the future in spite of the severe challenges of climate change. Restored and bleaching-resistant coral reefs will, in turn, help secure the ecological, food security, and livelihood services that this precious ecosystem provides to the people of Kiribati and the world.

The work on Christmas Island goes beyond the simple recovery of this remote atoll's reefs; rather, if we can establish the effectiveness of this program on Christmas Island, it would be vastly relevant to all coral reefs of the nation and of the planet that are facing an uncertain future in a rapidly changing world. What better place to start this pioneering climate-change adaptation work?

As the work thus far has been entirely based on volunteerism, what is most important at this time is to identify funding for continuing and expanding this vital and unique program. The work should ideally expand to include more extensive reef surveys on all parts of the island, to try to identify more of the surviving corals, to expand the monitoring of restoration patches, to support the genetic testing of corals and their symbionts, to establish increased and intensifying nursery work, and to stimulate awareness raising work within the communities, nation, and region, as well as to secure the no-take status of Cook Islet Conservation Area and other areas as being special and sensitive to restoration and therefore of critical importance to the larger coral reef system and the nation of Kiribati.

CORALS FOR CONSERVATION'S CORAL REEF RESTORATION FOR CLIMATE CHANGE ADAPTATION STRATEGY

1. After prolonged mass bleaching temperatures, collect corals from among the few surviving remnants and increase their biomass within coral nurseries. If a severe mass bleaching event has not yet occurred, collect coral samples from heat stressed areas—shallow tide pools and closed lagoons.
2. Focus on *Acropora* species initially, as this group appears to be the most vulnerable to bleaching-induced extinction, and is vital as a fish habitat and for the geological processes vital for reef growth and atoll formation.

3. Using diverse coral samples, create gene bank nurseries located in cooler waters.
4. Restore reproductive coral patches to the reef using second-generation coral branches (Kufner et al. 2020).
5. Restored *Acropora* patches can create a strong settlement signal to attract coral larvae back to the reef (Dixson et al. 2014, Montoya-Maya et al. 2016).
6. Bleaching resistance becomes contagious as the super corals leak their super symbionts into the environment, which are picked up by juvenile corals, settle in naked, and only acquire their symbiotic algae from the environment through "horizontal transmission" (http://www.coralsoftheworld.org/page/algal-symbiosis/).
7. Up-scale the strategy in order to have a positive influence of significant scale.

List of Acropora Coral Species Found in the Line Islands with Comparisons to the Species List from Fanning Atoll by Maragos (1974)

- Species confirmed
    - *Acropora muricata* (synonym for *A. formosa*) staghorn coral of lagoons—dead and standing thickets of this species dominate the inner lagoon of Kiritimati, but now are apparently locally extinct. Found in the lagoon on Tabuaeran at several sites and brought into the Kiritimati nursery.
    - *Acropora vaughani* (similar to *A. horrida*)—forms bushy clumps on upper reef slope and lagoons; at a micro-level, it takes on a small staghorn growth form, often with blue tips. Absent from Christmas Island, collected in Fanning Lagoon and brought into the Christmas Island nursery.
    - *Acropora globiceps*—fat finger-like *Acropora*. Found as remnants of a large colony at Cook Islet and Crusher Reef flat, and some appear to be coming in as larval recruits. *Not found on Fanning by Maragos in 1974; recognized internationally as a threatened species.*
    - *Acropora robusta*—thick-branched, reef-front staghorn species.
    - *Acropora retusa*—Regenerating golden-brown or greenish corals found at Crusher and nearby reef flats as "resurrection" colonies, clearly showing the compact corymbose growth form of the original colonies. *Not found on Fanning by Maragos in 1974; recognized internationally as a threatened species.*
    - *Acropora cerealis* (synonym of *A. cymbicyathus*)—forms small tables with interlocking branches; cream with blue tips. Found as remnants on Tabuarean and brought into the Kiritimati nursery. Not yet found on Kiritimati.
- Species potentially found as new recruits
    - *Acropora tenuis*—delicate tubular branches similar to *A. nasuta*; upper reef slopes. It is a major component of the new recruits and the major recovering reef flat species regenerating from surviving micro tissues; colonies of purple, blue, pink, and brown.
    - *Acropora selago* (synonym of *A. delicatula*)—similar to *A. tenuis* but forming small tables; upper reef slopes and lagoons; coming in as new recruits. Colonies are a uniform grey color.

- Species not yet found
  - *Acropora florida* (synonym of *Acropora polymorpha*)—large upright staghorn corals with very short side branches.
  - *Acropora longicyanthus* (synonym of *Acropora syringodes*)—bottlebrush *Acropora* of lagoons.
  - *Acropora cytherea* (synonym of *A. reticulata*)—large, flat, table corals that are blue, cream, or brown; upper slopes and lagoons. The flat skeletons of this coral dominate some beaches and is a common construction material for walls and buildings.
  - *A. humilis* digitate corals with large axial polyps, commonly found on reef slopes and reef flats.
  - *Acropora corymbosa*—listed by Maragos, not presently considered a valid species and unsure which species this represents.

A synopsis report for Palmyra Atoll (Williams et al. 2008), a U.S. territory in the Northern Line Islands, and with considerable time spent on multiple collections over several years, gives a total of 38 species of *Acropora* for Palmyra, considerably more than the 11 *Acropora* species reported by Maragos for Tabuaeran in 1974. We have thus far only found a total of five *Acropora* species surviving on Kiritimati, with three additional species brought in from Tabuaeran, to make eight *Acropora* species in the coral nursery presently.

Two of the species found on Kiritimati, neither found on Tabuaeran by Maragos, have been recognized as being threatened corals internationally (*A. globiceps* and *A. retusa*); however, we consider the absence of so many coral species concerning. Even at the present low rates of recovery, there is a chance that two of the remnant *Acropora* species will in future years be able to reproduce and thereby recover on their own; however, when another mass bleaching hits, they might become locally extinct. It is vital, therefore, to maintain populations of *Acropora* species in cooler waters at the present Cook Islet South Pass, and to work on facilitating bleaching resistance in our restoration work.

We have developed an endangered species recovery plan focusing on restoring sexual reproduction in each species, hoping that the bleaching of the past will be rare and extreme occurrences. If it becomes the norm, repeated every few years, the reefs of Kiritimati may not have much hope. This is a similar approach being carried out with endangered *Acropora* corals in the Caribbean (Kuffner et al. 2020). Less precarious in their future survival and recovery are *A. selago* and *A. tenus* due to the presence of numerous juvenile colonies recruiting to reef flats and in the shallows, especially if this recruitment continues coming from an unknown larval source, whether sexual or asexual.

ACKNOWLEDGMENTS

This work was funded by grants from the Conservation Food and Health Foundation and Southern Cross Cable. Additional funding was provided by numerous small donations through Global Giving: https://www.globalgiving.org/projects/emergency-response-to-massive-coral-bleaching/. Boat, fuel, nursery materials, and staff were provided by the Kiribati Fisheries Department, kindly facilitated by Mr. Taratau Kirata, Senior Fisheries Officer. Accommodations were kindly donated during the initial two visits by Ereti Tekabwaia through the Tekabwaia lodge.

REFERENCES

Dixson, D. L., D. Abrego, and M. E. Hay. 2014. "Chemically mediated behavior of recruiting corals and fishes: A tipping point that may limit reef recovery." *Science* Vol. 345, Issue 6199, pp. 892–897.

Kohler, S. T. and C. C. Kohler. 1992. "Dead bleached coral provides new surfaces for dinoflagellates implicated in ciguatera fish poisonings." *Environ. Biol. Fish* 35, 413–416

Kuffner, L. B., A. Stathakopoulos, L. T. Toth, and L. A. Barlett. 2020. "Reestablishing a stepping-stone population of the threatened elkhorn coral *Acropora palmata* to aid regional recovery." *Endangered Species Research* Vol. 43: 261–273.

Maragos, J. E. 1974. "Reef corals of Fanning Island." *Pacific Science* Vol. 28, No.3, p. 247–255.

Montoya-Maya, P. H., K. P. Smit, A. J. Burt, and S. Frias-Torres. 2016. "Large-scale coral reef restoration could assist natural recovery in Seychelles, Indian Ocean." *Nature Conservation* 16:1–17.

Williams, G. J., J. E. Maragos, and S. K. Davy. 2008. "Characterization of the coral communities at Palmyra Atoll in the remote central Pacific Ocean." National Museum of Natural History, Smithsonian Institution, Washington, D.C., November 2008, 32 pp.

18

INDONESIA: MARS ASSISTED REEF RESTORATION SYSTEM

David J. Smith, F. Mars, *S. Williams, J. van Oostrum, A. McArdle, S. Rapi, J. Jompa, and N. Janetski

ABSTRACT

Mars Sustainable Solutions (MSS) is part of Mars, Incorporated—a privately owned company founded in 1911 that is widely known around the world for its chocolate and pet care brands. Mars has a long history of working within Indonesia, sourcing cocoa, coconuts, seaweed, and spices along with the local manufacturing of cocoa and confectionery products. Knowing how important coastal resources are for local communities within their supply chains, in 2006, Mars embarked on a long-term program of reef rehabilitation and restoration off the west coast of South Sulawesi within the Spermonde Archipelago. Through local and national collaboration, Mars has developed a rapid, cost-effective method to restore mobile, coral rubble beds that dominate many reefs in the region.

The Mars Assisted Reef Restoration System (MARRS) utilizes a hexagonal steel structure, termed a reef star, coated with resin and sand. Numerous reef stars are connected in situ to produce a strong web that is anchored to, and covers, the substratum in a predetermined and carefully planned build pattern. Corals of opportunity and locally harvested fragments are attached directly to the reef stars. A mixed coral assemblage is outplanted to match native reef assemblages. The restoration follows strict guidelines and standard operating procedures, which have been optimized to increase efficiency of deployment. An experienced team of builders supported by many members of the local community can deploy 350 reef stars in a day—resulting in well over 5,000 coral fragments being outplanted per day. Using this method, the collaborative team has restored approximately 4 ha of reef (approximately 450,000 coral fragments) across two island communities over an eight-year period.

The restoration of one of the islands, Pulau Bontosua, utilizes standard scientific principles to robustly test the performance of the technique over a five-year period. Coral cover has been raised from a site average of less than 10% to over 60% in two to three years, depending on the site. Fish abundance has increased four-fold in places over a three-year period and two-fold increases in biomass have been recorded in less than two years. The majority of the local community are supportive of restoration although views are sometimes mixed, highlighting the importance of including a strong social science element within coral restoration that is aimed at enhancing the welfare of dependent communities.

continued

> The Spermonde is an ideal location for restoration showing high levels of thermal tolerance and strong ecological connectivity. However, the MARRS technique has now been employed across Indonesia by multiple partners including the Indonesian Marine National Parks. The restoration program utilizes a supply-chain approach where each part of the process has been optimized to increase overall efficiency and different members of local communities are involved in different tasks to increase and widen participation. MARRS is an adaptable and flexible system that is particularly suited for mobile substrata but can be used in conjunction with other restoration techniques. The reef stars kick-start the natural ecological process, and if combined with correct governance, social and community support, and participation, they can be extremely effective tools to help restore the world's reefs.

INTRODUCTION

While the connection between Mars and coral reef restoration may not be an obvious one, it is a part of the company's long-standing commitment to work closely with local communities to solve complex problems and help sustain the livelihoods of people in their supply chains.

The Mars business and the many communities that it sources raw materials from depend on a healthy ocean. Since operating within Indonesia, the Mars team has noted significant declines in the availability of coastal fish products that support the food security of many of the people within its supply chains. This decline is due to several reasons, including the demise of coral reef systems and the fish populations they support. As the engines of marine biodiversity, the protection and restoration of coral reefs will have significant impact on the regeneration potential of tropical coastal ecosystems and on the services that they provide to local communities. The long history of working within Indonesia and the knowledge of how important coastal resources are for local communities within their supply chains stimulated Mars to embark on a long-term program of reef rehabilitation and restoration in 2006.

Mars started its restoration program within the Province of South Sulawesi off the coast of Makassar within the Spermonde Archipelago (see Figure 18.1), but has since broadened out to other regions of Indonesia, Australia, and Mexico. The Spermonde Archipelago, like many other coastal regions of Indonesia, historically suffered from intense blast fishing and coral mining (Sawall et al. 2013; Plass-Johnson et al. 2015). This activity has led to barren and highly mobile coral rubble beds with greatly reduced biodiversity. The goal of the Mars program was to develop a cost-effective, low-tech, and scalable solution to restore coral reefs that had been impacted by physical disturbance in areas dominated by rubble. The technique aims to rapidly kick-start the natural ecological recovery of damaged reefs by providing a stable platform for corals to grow, which in turn, provides habitat for numerous species of invertebrates and fish. The goal of the project was therefore initially to rehabilitate the system, which in time, and through natural ecological processes, would become restored to its predisturbed state. Furthermore, by increasing reef biodiversity, biomass, and productivity, a further goal was to demonstrate the value of a healthy restored coral reef system for local livelihoods. The program was developed and implemented in full partnership with the local community, government, and regional and international researchers.

Many restoration techniques were evaluated over the first few years of the program, which resulted in the development of the MARRS. MARRS uses a supply-chain approach, with each link in that chain representing a specific set of tasks—the delivery of which have been optimized

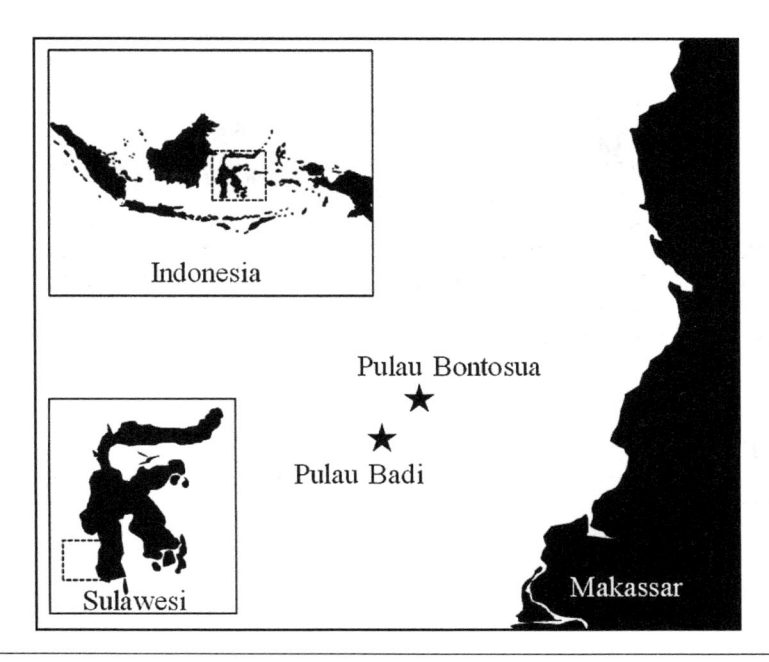

Figure 18.1 The Site of the Mars Coral Restoration Program within the Spermonde Archipelago, SE Sulawesi, Indonesia.

to maximize the efficiency and scalability of the technique. These links will be described here, along with examples of social and ecological performance of the technique and opportunities for the future.

THE RESTORATION SITE AND THE SPECIFIC RESTORATION PROBLEM

Two island communities have been directly involved with the MARRS restoration program, both of which are located within the Spermonde Archipelago. The Spermonde is a large patchy reef environment situated to the west of the city of Makassar and separated from the Strait of Makassar by a discontinuous barrier reef (see Kench and Mann 2017). Located around 119°6′52″E and 4°52′32″S, the archipelago consists of around 120 islands, many of which are densely inhabited, extending to approximately 60 km offshore. Being located within the Coral Triangle, the Spermonde is home to well-established and extremely diverse fringing, patch, and barrier coral reef systems, the health of which varies dramatically depending on location, distance to the nearest settlement, and the size of that settlement. Islands of the archipelago are located on a shallow carbonate platform covering approximately 2,500 km^2 and the total population is around 50,000. A detailed description of the geomorphology of the Spermonde is given by Kench and Mann (2017), but in its broadest terms, the archipelago can be divided into three zones—outer, middle, and inner zone—which have specific characteristics relating to water quality and exposure. Closer to the Sulawesi mainland, the reef systems run nearly parallel to the coast, but they become more disjointed further out to the edge of the platform. This case study describes restoration projects that were carried out at Pulau Badi which is located within the outer zone and Pulau Bontosua in the middle zone (see Figure 18.1).

Pulau Badi (4°58.061′S, 119°17.260′E) has a population of approximately 1,900 people across 460 households, the majority of which are heavily dependent on fisheries as a source of income. Local accounts suggest that the outer reef slope and flat were bombed around 30 years ago which, combined with other destructive fishing practices, the excavation of a boat channel, and coral mining for local house development, resulted in the near complete destruction of coral habitat, which had historically protected the island from erosion (Williams et al. 2019). Erosion is now one of the key issues facing the island, together with diminishing local fish stocks and poor income earning possibilities from the fringing reefs adjacent to the island. There has been no fish bombing at Pulau Badi for many years and the local people declared a relatively small area as a *Daerah Perlindungan Laut* (DPL)—in other words, a no-take zone, as part of the Coral Reef Rehabilitation and Management Project (COREMAP, World Bank 2005) in the mid-2000s to help fish stocks recover. Outside of this zone and prior to restoration, more than 80% of the reef crest and reef flat was mobile coral rubble with only 5–10% remaining live coral cover and a severely depleted fish community. In this initial stage of the restoration project, 2 ha of reefs at Pulau Badi were restored. Restoration was initiated in 2013 near the main island jetty and was continuous throughout the southeast side of the island. However, restoration *builds* were organized in discrete sections that were delineated in space and time (see Williams et al. 2019). Following the visible success of the Pulau Badi project, several other island communities expressed an interest in reef restoration.

In order to respond to these requests and select the next island community to work with, a multi-disciplinary team from the local university (University Hasanuddin) undertook a detailed study of several islands and posed a series of questions to the local leadership and wider communities. This was deemed essential to ensure that restoration was not just *needed* as determined through rapid ecological surveys, but was also *wanted* by local communities. The island of Bontosua (4°55.69′S, 119°19.254′E), which has a population of just 1,090 people in 270 families, was identified as being the most appropriate site for the next round of restoration due to both the need and desire expressed by the community for restoration. While the Pulau Badi restoration was based purely on the restoration of critical habitats only, the Pulau Bontosua restoration—in partnership with the local community and support of community leaders, plus input from numerous national and international scientific advisors—was designed as a large-scale scientific study following a blocked design.

The primary goal of the Pulau Bontosua restoration program was to restore coral communities, while the secondary goal was to complete the restoration in a standardized way using scientific principles to determine the ecological effectiveness of the MARRS technique and the impacts that coral restoration has on an island community. The study contained both positive (sites with best coral reef communities) and negative (sites deemed appropriate for restoration but left alone) control sites. Active restoration was undertaken in *experimental* blocks, delineated on the sea bed, each with a size of 50 × 20 m. Each block was started and finished within a set three-month period so that the influence of time on the ecological response could be determined and compared to controls. In addition to the establishment of significant coral nursery areas, at this point, nine of these blocks have been built since the initiation of the project in 2017 and further builds are planned in accordance with original agreements with the local community representatives. The ecological response of the Pulau Bontosua restoration was monitored using standardized operating procedures (see later text) and a team of researchers from University Hasanuddin (UNHAS) and the University of Rhode Island (URI) designed and implemented a social science program aimed at determining the impact of the restoration program on community livelihoods and the success of a community outreach program.

THE MARRS APPROACH

Successful implementation of the MARRS method requires careful site evaluation, planning, and the full engagement of all stakeholders. These include the local community—and their neighbors, who are often direct users of the same coral reef infrastructure—local and national governments, local researchers and academics, as well as scientific advisors in a range of topics. It also requires first-hand training with experienced practitioners to ensure that all key learning is transferred and that *shortcuts* or misunderstandings regarding the method limits do not result in project failure. The MARRS approach has been designed and optimized to be applicable in remote settings using easy-to-obtain materials and limited technological requirements. It has been designed to be effective with minimum resources required. However, correct and effective implementation of the program does require a detailed understanding of the technique and on-the-ground training. Without such training it is probable that the approach would not be effective and could cause further damage to the very system it is trying to restore.

Fundamentally, the MARRS approach is most effective and useful where coral rubble dominates. The method has been developed to allow rapid deployment of modular systems (reef stars—discussed later) in a web- or lattice-like structure that produces high physical integrity and stability. It is therefore most useful in areas where there are significant continuous rubble beds interspersed with coral or rock outcrops. Other requirements for restoration are also needed, such as a nearby stock of fish recruits and a suitable environmental setting—for example, good water quality, moderate water velocity, appropriate bathymetry, and the absence of stressors that may have originally caused reef destruction. However, reef stars can also be deployed in small patches and will complement other restoration techniques that may be focused on attaching corals to hard substrate through direct outplanting, including coral microfragmenting. In other words, the approach explained here can be considered in isolation for the right set of environmental conditions or as part of the larger restoration toolbox for a mixed environmental setting.

THE REEF STARS

The restoration of reefs within the Spermonde required a solution that stabilized the large, mobile rubble beds and provided coral with a stable platform to enable growth. The system needed to be flexible and adaptable to different physical habitat characteristics (e.g., large homogenous rubble beds or rubble beds mixed with coral outcrops of different sizes). Therefore, a modular approach was designed that built on designs used by others in the general restoration field. The individual modular elements are termed reef stars—previously *spiders* or locally known as *laba laba* (see Figure 18.2).

Reef stars are hexagonal units with an effective site footprint of approximately 0.74 m^2 when installed and consist of locally fabricated steel rod using specific and standardized dimensions. Reef stars are made by welding together 10 mm steel rods and coating them with a rust protecting layer including fiberglass resin and sand. Depending on availability, different sand types may be used, but always need to be biologically inert and allow for unimpeded coral growth and recruitment. The reef stars are made to a standard form (see Figure 18.2) but the height can be varied and depends on the environmental setting in which they are to be deployed. Each element of the reef star design has been optimized to limit material use and increase the ease and standardization of construction while ensuring physical integrity. The shape of the reef star also facilitates stacking, allowing for cheaper storage and transport.

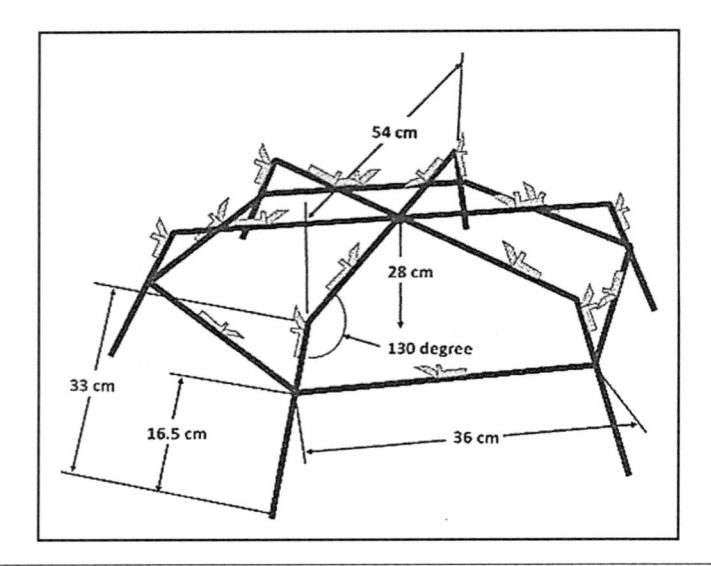

Figure 18.2 Standardized structure of the reef star. Attached coral fragments are depicted by small rectangular structures on reef star cross bars and upper legs (produced by Janetski and taken directly from Williams et al. 2019).

The reef stars can be fixed together to cover larger areas and, in some sites, several hundred are attached to form a web across large rubble beds. Current practice is to fix reef stars together at the intersection of two legs by using long-lasting, heavy duty cable ties (7–9 mm), the tails of which are cut off and recycled. New technologies are being tested to further reduce waste. In the Spermonde, the production of reef stars has been established as microbusinesses (within communities adjacent to the restoration sites). The steel structures are fabricated by one group and a separate community microbusiness then applies several coatings to the raw reef stars. The devolution of tasks has increased participation in the project, has diversified local income streams, and has increased efficiencies by having trained and experienced individuals focused on delivering specific tasks only. In this way, each local production unit can produce up to 1,000 reef stars per month.

THE RESTORATION BUILD

The restoration build process differed at Pulau Badi compared to Pulau Bontosua, the latter being designed as a scientific experiment and therefore more strict protocols in terms of areas of reef restored over specific time periods were employed. The Pulau Bontosua restoration was always undertaken in 50 m × 20 m blocks (see Figure 18.3(a)) equating to an area of 0.1 ha. Approximately 750 reef stars are deployed in each block depending on the extent of the coral damage in the block and on average between 300–350 reef stars are deployed in a single day—although this number has reached up to 660 in extreme cases.

Before the start of each build, a detailed block (50 m × 20 m) map is produced and used to plan the build. This map is generated by transect tapes being laid out on the seabed to delineate the block sides followed by vertical transects, which are run every 3 m along the horizontal resulting in 17 vertical transects each of 20 m length—the entire width of the block (see Figure 18.3(b)). The benthic characteristics of the site are determined along each transect line using

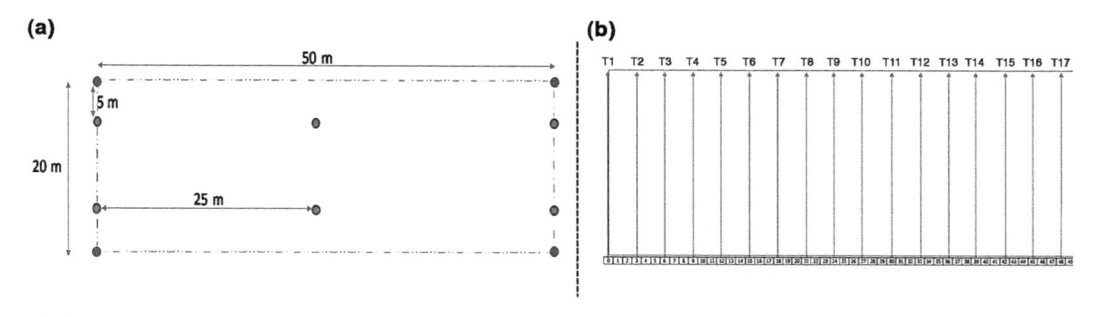

Figure 18.3 Schematic representation of the MARRS block design and approaches used for assessment: (a) the classic reef block dimensions and (b) vertical transects used for habitat assessment, build planning, and coarse monitoring of benthic structure.

a classical continual-line intercept technique but only using coarse life-forms and substratum categories. These vertical transects are monitored at other times as well (depending on monitoring frequency, but at least annually) as they provide an excellent overview of the entire block response (see later section on Ecological Monitoring). The block map enables the exact number of reef stars required for the build to be calculated (typically ±5%) and helps the build team to identify the best position to start and end the build, as well as the positioning and number of anchoring devices required. Trial and error shows that the best place to start the build is adjacent to an existing live coral reef structure and the healthiest fish community. The fish assemblage then moves into the reef star build area and helps keep the amount of maintenance required (cleaning) to a minimum (in essence, the existing fish community moves with the building process). Once the map has been produced, the actual build can be split into separate stages.

Stage 1: Collection of Coral

One of the benefits of working within the Spermonde, and Pulau Bontosua in particular, is that there are large healthy coral beds on submerged reefs near the degraded reef systems (e.g., within a few kilometers). These reef beds fall within the administrative jurisdiction of the Pulau Bontosua community and are termed the collection or donor sites. Collection of targeted coral species takes place the day prior to the start of the build and involves a team of trained individuals, including students from the UNHAS Faculty of Marine Science and Fisheries, to capture corals that have naturally fragmented from parent colonies.

The collection of corals occurs over large areas to maximize the chance of significant genetic diversity. For those species that do not naturally fragment but are in high abundance in natural reef systems, a direct harvesting approach is used applying the well-established 10% rule, which is that never more than 10% of the colony is extracted and should only be extracted from mature colonies that are free from any disease or signs of physiological stress such as abnormal depigmentation (i.e., sub-lethal bleaching or paling). Coral fragments are collected or harvested from corals at the same depth at which the restoration will take place—sometimes shallower but never deeper—to prevent any light induced stress that may be caused to the coral fragment when it is relocated to the restored site. The donor site is carefully monitored and a rotational system is used to prevent overharvesting from any one area. Great care is taken when extracting corals from the donor site to ensure that the ratios of coral that are taken roughly match the natural abundance of that coral species in the environment. Coral fragments (always greater than 10 cm but less than 20 cm in order to maximize coral biomass use without increasing coral mortality) are transported immediately back to the restoration site where they are kept in underwater baskets mimicking the same environmental conditions as the planned build. These corals represent the main stock of coral used in the restoration and will be entirely consumed during the build process, ultimately determining the exact number of reef stars installed on that build occasion.

Stage 2: Coral Attachment to Reef Stars

Stored corals are attached to reef stars the following day by trained members of the local community who are representing each of the six neighborhoods of Pulau Bontosua. The number of individuals involved varies slightly but is typically 36 people in six teams of six, together with an experienced trainer to ensure than any new people are trained prior to commencement. Individuals receive payment for their time through their neighborhood leaders by an amount agreed upon by restoration partners. Attachment of the corals starts early in the morning on floating pontoons (see Figure 18.4) located in the shallows adjacent to the restoration build site. Once coral fragments are attached to reef stars, they are immediately placed back in the water to reduce the amount of time that the coral fragments are exposed to the air. Corals are attached with thin cable ties that typically get covered by new coral growth within four weeks. Two cable ties are usually used to attach each coral in a predetermined and fixed pattern on each bar of the reef star, resulting in 15 coral fragments per reef star (taking approximately five minutes). Great care is taken to ensure that the fragment is securely attached along the greatest horizontal length of the fragment to ensure maximum contact with the reef star (as depicted in Figures 18.2 and 18.4). Trial and error have shown that this increases the speed at

Figure 18.4 Images of local community members participating in the Pulau Bontosua restoration program. Main image (a) shows community members attaching coral fragments to reef stars on floating pontoons the morning of the build. Inset (b) shows reef stars being coated. Inset (c) shows a close-up of a fully loaded reef star ready for deployment.

which the fragment adheres to the reef star, the speed at which new coral growth covers the cable ties that are used for the initial attachment, and overall, increases physical integrity and the sheer force that fragments can withstand once the reef stars are deployed. Proper training in the handling of coral, safe fragmenting, and the proper tying method are necessary to achieve good quality results with high survival of transplanted coral (greater than 95% survivorship in the Spermonde program). Excess plastic from the cable ties used to attach coral is cut and removed from the system post-deployment of the reef star. These off-cuts are taken back to the city for recycling. Biodegradable cable tie options (with the right physical properties, including *longevity*) are being tested, as are other attachment technologies to further reduce waste. Across 350 reef stars, 5,250 coral fragments are deployed in a single day session (highest number of corals deployed in a single day was 9,900) and each build is usually undertaken over two days until all collected coral fragments have been deployed. Therefore, typically, between 600 and 700 reef stars will be installed in one, two-day build session.

Stage 3: Installation of the Reef Stars

Installation of the reef stars requires *shuttling* of the completed units to the restoration site on a dive/speedboat, during which time the reef stars are out of the water. Therefore, shuttling times are kept to an absolute minimum. The fully loaded reef stars are stacked as much as possible in shade on the boat and continually sprayed with seawater. Within the Spermonde, the maximum time a reef star is out of the water is 20 minutes. When the boat arrives at the designated build site, if the build site is less than 4 m deep, a team of trained snorkelers, including students from UNHAS, accept the reef stars from the boat while in the water. They then move them to the appropriate location within the delineated reef build area and place them loosely on the seabed. The movement of reef stars from the boat to the appropriate location within the build area takes approximately 10 minutes using the *conveyer belt* unloading approach. Deeper sites require reef stars to be lowered to the build site by rope and, in this case, less reef stars are transported each time to minimize the length of time coral is exposed to the air.

Once the reef stars are delivered to the seabed, a team of highly trained scuba divers (usually four individuals per build, all of whom have completed the MARRS training program and deemed skilled enough to be part of the build team) interconnect all of the reef stars to form a continuous web (see Figure 18.5). The legs of the reef stars are bound together with heavy-duty cable ties, and stainless-steel anchors are installed in high impact areas on the outer margins of the built web (at every third reef star). Reef builds within the Spermonde usually occur over a four-day period (including coral collection, installation, and anchoring) with each build being separated by up to one month to coincide with the best tides (lowest tidal amplitude) and are seasonally dependent. Reef builds are exponentially more difficult in rough weather conditions (i.e., high tidal range, high exposure, and high current speed) and at most locations there will be an ideal *season* for restoration activity when the weather and tides are most conducive. In the Spermonde, this means that restoration activities are best planned between March and November, and typically scheduled for the new moon cycle. Within the Spermonde setting, this means that around 700 reef stars are deployed per month with approximately 10,500 coral fragments but this only represents two build days, one coral collection day, and one anchoring and quality control day—so only four in-water activity days. At this rate, one hectare of reef can be restored in approximately 40 in-water days if all materials are prepped and environmental conditions remain suitable. This timeline should be considered a theoretical maximum for any single small-build team and location.

Figure 18.5 Image (a) shows the site prior to restoration, (b) with reef stars deployed, and inset (c) shows a bird's-eye view (courtesy of the Ocean Agency).

Stage 4: Maintenance of the Restoration Build

The first stage of maintenance occurs on the final day of the build (e.g., day four in the case of Spermonde). Here, the team of trained divers inspects the entire build for physical integrity of the web, completes installation of the stainless-steel stakes that are used to anchor the web to the seabed, ensures that all excess plastic from cable ties are removed, makes certain that all coral fragments are securely attached, and confirms that there is no build material left within the site. Post-build, the learning from the Spermonde program suggests that, if corals have been collected correctly, stored appropriately, and fixed accordingly, and the reef star web is firmly installed in the right location, there is very little need for maintenance. Maintenance within the Pulau Bontosua scientific trial is only allowed over the first three months (the designated time given for the start and end of a single block build). However, in a restoration project that is not set up as a scientific trial, then maintenance could be more ongoing, as and when needed. The most important parts of maintenance within the Spermonde site have focused on two main areas:

1. *Checking for coral mortality and health*: any coral fragment that died during the restoration is recorded and replaced. Evidence from Spermonde suggest that mortality is low overall and is most likely to occur within the first week of installation. Dead or diseased coral fragments are removed and replaced; in the case of Spermonde, this has been less than 1% of relocated coral fragments.

2. *Management of macroalgae that attach to the reef stars*: this is particularly important in the early stages of restoration in the first few months following the build until a healthy population of herbivores become established within the newly restored reef. In the case of Spermonde, this normally takes up to three months and direct algal removal techniques are employed by a team of trained divers armed with a firm nylon bristle brush. Within Spermonde, this algal removal usually takes place one, two, and three months after the reef build. However, in more nutrified environments, the frequency of cleaning may have to be increased. Also, in situations where overpopulation of territorial, algae farming damselfish has occurred, there will be an increased algal load on reef stars and the decision may need to be made to either reduce the number of damselfish or increase the frequency of cleaning.

Although not an issue within the Spermonde, successful restoration may also require the removal of other pests that are detrimental to coral survival, such as a high abundance of the coral-eating snail, *Drupella*. The final stage of each build includes cautious quality control by trained divers to carefully inspect each build block for any loose coral fragments (which should be reattached), unsecured reef stars, or any debris. The approximate costs of restoring one hectare of reef in the Spermonde including preparation and maintenance is US $140,000.

MONITORING THE PERFORMANCE OF THE MARRS TECHNIQUE

Two main monitoring programs have been established by Mars and collaborators within the Spermonde to measure the performance of the restoration technique—one focusing on the social-economic impact (including fisheries) and a second focusing on the ecological performance of the restoration through detailed reef community monitoring.

Social-Economic Research and Monitoring Program

A team of researchers from UNHAS in collaboration with international researchers from URI developed and implemented a program of studies that were aimed at establishing firm baselines from which to measure impacts and to increase our understanding of the implications of coral reef restoration for local communities. More specifically, the study aims to assess levels of awareness of the restoration program (e.g., its goals, achievements, and aspirations), identify changes to community income and food availability, assess attitudes toward restoration over the lifetime of the program, and inform the program as to where improvements can be made. Classical fisheries' research techniques have also been used by collaborators to determine changes in fisheries' activity and to collect catch statistics.

Most of the commercial fisheries' activity at Pulau Bontosua is pelagic and not reef-based. However, many households do utilize local reef resources for subsistence. Social surveys implemented by the research team demonstrate how important it is to include a social science program within restoration projects. Detailed social analysis is required prior to and during site selection, project design, and during project socialization. Continued detailed monitoring is also required throughout the implementation of the restoration program with key findings being acted upon to increase the chances of long-term project success.

Initial outputs of mid-term social science reports from the Spermonde study have demonstrated how complex the situation can be in terms of community awareness, assessing socioeconomic benefits, and ensuring that the whole views of the community are considered when decisions are made on where and what should be restored. Within the Spermonde setting, complex interactions exist between different island communities, with fishers from one island having traditionally free access to reefs of another, despite that island community not necessarily fishing its own reefs (often with reciprocal free access being enjoyed). These complex traditional social networks were not fully understood at the time the restoration program was devised and initiated and is one of the main learning points of this program. Despite this, the research from the Spermonde suggest that the vast majority of individuals report positively on their experience of the restoration program. It also found that approximately 72% of respondents were of the opinion that the coral reef condition had increased around the island with the majority also predicting further improvement in the future. However, the fact that some members of the community had negative perceptions of the program cannot be overlooked since in these very small communities, individuals can have an exaggerated impact on project success. Such negative perceptions included (1) questioning why a company like Mars would be involved with coral restoration of their island, (2) what would the company demand in return, and (3) how this would impinge on their present and future access to reef resources of Pulau Bontosua. While Mars has been clear in its intentions, and as an example, had already *officially handed over* the previously restored reef at Pulau Badi, a few members of the community remain suspicious.

Within Spermonde, there has been a diverse attempt to engage the whole of the Pulau Bontosua community. The village head is directly engaged, as are locally elected leaders of each island district along with community leaders and elected representatives of the people. Town hall meetings and seminars have been delivered, and notice boards, pamphlets, and other techniques were employed to engage all members of the community. However, despite these efforts, there remains a section of society who are not aware of Mars' involvement or the goals of the project, suggesting that the approaches that are being used to ensure community-wide participation opportunities may not be fully effective. While some 55% of respondents reported that they did not feel they had an opportunity to be directly involved, scientists from the local university who conducted the most recent surveys, report that the general attitude of the community remains positive for coral restoration and the benefits it brings. The Spermonde program aims to do restoration where restoration is needed and, even more important, where it is wanted and will be supported over the long term. It is evident that a large amount of effort and expertise is required to deliver the social side of restoration during both the planning and the implementing stage. Research from the Pulau Bontosua program will allow Mars and others to build on existing approaches and increase the value of restoration to local communities.

Ecological Monitoring Program

Within the Spermonde program, significant effort has been placed on measuring the biological impact of restoration though a range of standard operating procedures (SOPs) that are designed to provide scientifically robust data that is resolute enough to detect annual changes in key ecological performance criteria. The SOPs outlined here are based on the standard restoration build approach that was used during scientific validation of the MARRS technique within the Spermonde—keeping in mind that the actual approaches used do vary with region, depending on the scale of restoration. In summary, monitoring within the Spermonde is based on the previously described *block* design (with each block taking no more than three months from start to finish). The three-month rule is needed where the aim of the restoration is to build replicate blocks and for scientific validation of the technique's performance in any given location. However, if scientific validation is not the focus of the restoration, then build times can and will probably vary depending on location, conditions, and resources. Under these circumstances, the three-month build time can be relaxed, but an activity build log is required, and all activities must be carefully documented. This is particularly important for those builds where time-zero data is needed (as is recommended). When scientific validation is required through dedicated monitoring, as in Spermonde, then we would recommend the time from start to finish of a build, regardless of how long that may be, is standardized so that when monitoring occurs, the time effect is minimal within any given sample (e.g., transect) and comparable between replicate samples. In the Spermonde project, *virtual* control builds are also established using the block (i.e., 50 m × 20 m) design. The basic experimental design is therefore two types of controls (positive and negative, n = 3 in both cases) and replicated restoration builds (n = 9 at the time of writing). The Spermonde restoration sites are dominated by large areas of coral rubble that is suitable for restoration, allowing for the relatively large block design. However, in other regions, individual restoration blocks are much smaller and sequential build approaches are used. In these locations, the Mars SOPS use the same sampling effort, but is divided across the sequential builds and the time effect is determined. The following is a brief overview of the techniques being used to monitor the restoration builds (also see Table 18.1 for a list of SOPs).

Table 18.1 List of standard operating procedures that are used to monitor the ecological responses of coral reefs being restored by the MARRS technique

Standard Operating Procedures
SOP 1. Introduction and background to block design
SOP 2. Environmental assessment prior to and during restoration
SOP 3. Habitat assessment
SOP 4. Monitoring of coral communities
SOP 5. Assessment of fish assemblage and biomass
SOP 6. Assessment of target invertebrate communities of ecological or economic significance
SOP 7. Agents of coral mortality
SOP 8. Site specific notes of special interest
SOP 9. Dive planning and responsibilities
SOP 10. Assessment of the impact of coral collection
SOP 11. Modifications to SOPs based on sequential builds
Appendix A: Crib Sheets to assist delivery of SOPs
Appendix B: In-water data sheets

Monitoring Frequency

The first monitoring takes place in the form of a rapid environmental assessment to determine the suitability of the site for restoration. The second form of monitoring is the prebuild mapping program, at which time all biological characteristics are determined (see Table 18.1). Time-zero represents a period within the first three months of the build and is aimed at capturing the restoration site at the time of initial placement of reef stars and, therefore, coral. By placing coral within the environment, we artificially increase live coral cover, and by including reef stars, we artificially increase habitat complexity. This has been shown in Spermonde to influence the initial fish community to the benefit of restoration, based on the need for grazing fish to provide grazing services as soon as the restoration build takes place. Sampling then occurs biannually for the first year, then annually thereafter.

SOPs (listed in Table 18.1) include initial site assessment and the detailed examination of environmental data including long-term temperature data and characterization of any thermal events. Temperatures are assessed through HOBO® data loggers at two depths spanning the depth range of the restoration block, but also at control and coral collection sites. Other environmental data collated should include key nutrients and estimates of turbidity (or at least light attenuation). Habitat assessment is undertaken during the prebuild survey and used to produce the previously mentioned habitat maps that are key for the design of the restoration build. However, the habitat assessments (vertical transects n = 17 per block; see Figure 18.3(b)) are also repeated at other monitoring periods. The key benthic life-forms are recorded across continual line intercept transects, as previously described.

A combination of techniques is used to assess the coral community. Two permanently located transects (5 m from the outer edge) are located within the restoration block (see Figure 18.3(a) and 18.6), parallel to the 50-meter block boundaries. High resolution photographs are taken every 1 m along each of these 50 m transects (alternatively on the upper then lower side of the transect; see Figure 18.6) representing independent quadrats (each being exactly 0.25 m^2). Images are analyzed back at the laboratory using the coral point count (n = 20 for counts per quadrat) software package with excel extensions (see Kohler and Gill 2006) using 20 point counts per quadrat, and subsequently the relative abundance of different coral species (if known, but always to genera) in each quadrat is determined. Consequently, throughout each block, 100 quadrats are analyzed using 2,000-point counts. As a backup to the 100 images, a continuous video is taken of each transect tape (so 2 × 50 m) to enable, if needed, a coarse analysis of communities using a line intercept transect technique.

Coral recruitment into the system is estimated in 10 quadrats on each transect in situ through a designated team using a magnifying glass (see Figure 18.6). This technique has a large error, which decreases with the size of the recruit. Therefore, size categories are used to partition counts up to 3 cm in diameter (<1 cm, 1.1–2 cm, 2.1–3 cm). The same 10 quadrats are used to estimate coral mortality or factors impacting coral health including the presence of corallivore activity, disease, or significant coral paling. In terms of paling, a semiquantitative scale is used at a 10% interval up to 50% paling, but a 25% interval thereafter.

Fish assemblage are determined on the same transects but using a size- and time-restricted belt transect. The two belt transects are 5 m wide and 50 m long—so 50% of each block is examined (i.e., 500 m^2 of a total block area of 1,000 m^2; see Figure 18.7) and the sampling effort is set at 20 minutes per transect. Fish species are recorded on an underwater slate or notebook, and the total length of the fish is estimated. If fish are within schools, only 20 of that school are sized. Fish lengths are converted into fish biomass using published algorithms (e.g., using Fishbase and other resources). Target invertebrates are estimated on the same belt transects (at a different time and always after fish surveys), but here the width of the transect is only 1 m.

Apart from these direct counts and assessments, all points of scientific interest are noted and recorded. Data is collected and analyzed within 48 hours of collection and entered into specifically designed spreadsheets and databases. The monitoring of transects is not considered complete until the data has been checked and backed-up on two different hard drives. SOPs also exist for dive planning, and crib sheets have been produced to aid divers in the water.

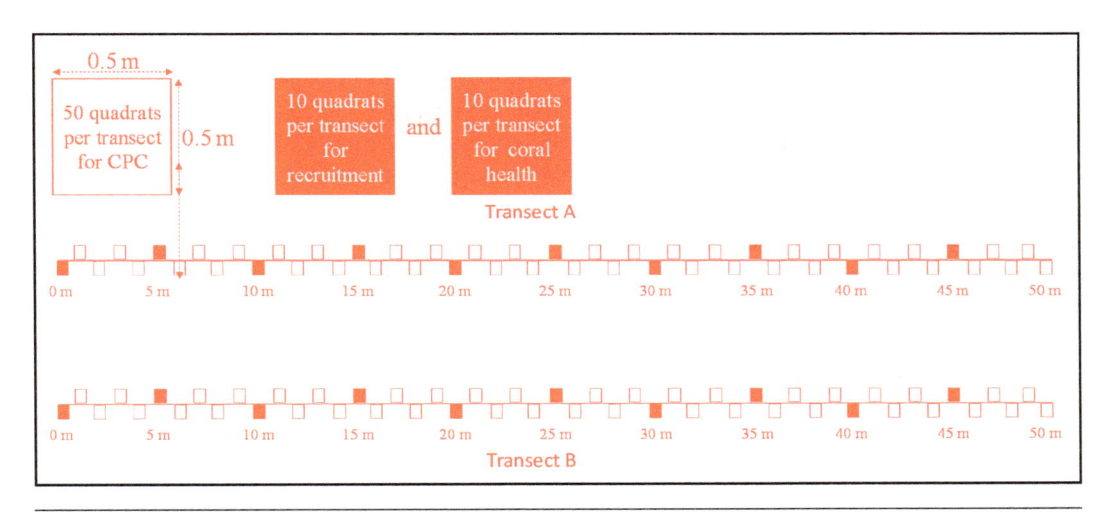

Figure 18.6 Schematic representation of the MARRS block design and approaches used for assessment. Photo-quadrats (0.25 m^2) used for coral assemblage assessment, recruitment, and health are depicted. Fifty quadrats used for coral assemblage (every 1 m along each transect) and 10 quadrats used (full boxes) for both recruitment (estimated in the size categories given) and health at 5 m intervals along each transect.

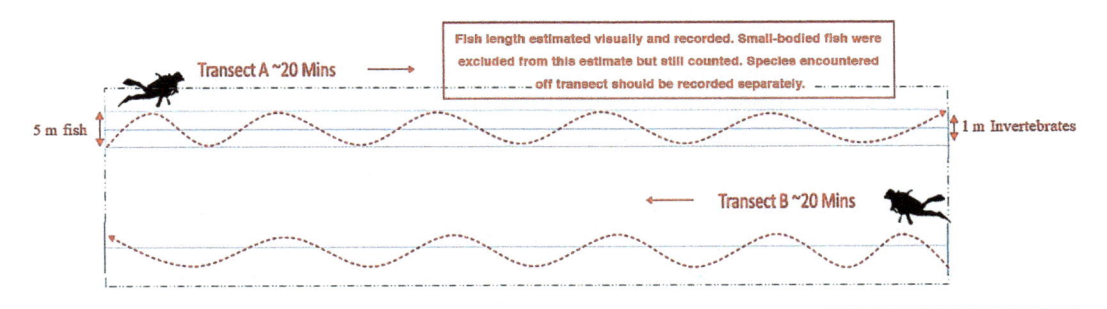

Figure 18.7 Schematic representation of the MARRS block design and approaches used for assessment. 50-m-long belt transects used for fish surveys (5 m width) and invertebrate surveys (1 m width). In both cases 20-minute survey time was used per transect, and in the case of fish transects, at least 15 minutes was allowed to elapse between the fish survey and any in-water activity. Fish and invertebrate surveys are carried out separately with fish surveys going first.

BRIEF OVERVIEW OF ECOLOGICAL RESPONSE TO RESTORATION

Within the Pulau Badi restoration project, maximum increases in coral cover were recorded to be from 10 to 60% over a two-year period, but on average, cover increased by around 40%. Gains in coral cover were mostly due to fast growing *Acropora* species, but overall, 42 species of Scleractinia corals were observed on or under reef stars by the end of the assessment period. Changes in coral cover over time were similar in shallow and mid-depth (2–3 m) yet slower at 4 m and below, but this corresponded to natural reefs in control sites. Interestingly, at the Badi site, the presence of reef stars facilitated native coral recruitment with new recruits settling onto the reef stars themselves but also onto underlying and previously unconsolidated rubble.

Despite the encouraging results at Pulau Badi, not all changes were positive; at one section there was a significant decrease in coral from 50 to 19% over a less-than-one-year period. It seems likely, according to anecdotal evidence, that this decrease was due to damage caused by illegal cyanide fishermen (Williams et al. 2019), which again highlights the need for restoration to include careful and community-sensitive management. Interestingly, and despite high seawater temperatures that exceeded the long-term mean temperatures by several degrees, very little (less than 5%) coral bleaching was observed at the restored reefs (see Williams et al. 2019). Clearly, reefs of this part of the Spermonde hold some thermally tolerant or protected coral species (or populations) and a greater understanding of what drives this tolerance from both a biological and oceanographic standpoint is needed and can help practitioners to identify the best locations for restoration. The Spermonde Archipelago appears to be one such location, and being adjacent to the Indo-Pacific throw flow, it is strongly ecologically connected.

Unsurprisingly, the fish assemblage responded positively to the restored coral habitat, both in terms of abundance and biomass. Maximum fish abundance recorded at Pulau Badi 45 months following restoration and as compared to negative controls, were more than four times higher (approximately 165,000 per ha as compared to 42,000 per ha), but at this stage of the restoration, program monitoring was more haphazard and less standardized. This increase in abundance drove a 1.4 increase in biomass from 1,600 to 2,220 kg ha^{-1}.

The Bontosua Restoration project is still at an early stage, but the results have been highly encouraging; a typical sequence of change can be seen in Figure 18.8. Coral cover has increased significantly across all restored reefs and positive change occurred within the first six months.

Figure 18.8 A typical timeline showing the dramatic changes to the reef, prebuild, time 0, and in the following months—8, 10, 16, and 26—within the Pulau Bontosua restoration site.

Over a 12–18-month period, coral increased from a starting value of around 15% to around 40% across all sites examined and coral survivorship was greater than 95%. As seen in the Badi site, significant changes in coral cover stimulated increases in fish abundance and biomass at Bontosua. Increases in abundance have not been so dramatic due to the relatively short timescale, but we have observed a 1.5 times increase in fish over one year (from approximately 25,000 to 36,000 individuals per ha) and a greater than 2.4 times increase in fish biomass over the same period (from 335 to 935 kg ha^{-1}). All signs suggest that the Bontosua restoration will be successful in increasing coral cover, restoring fish assemblages, and increasing fish biomass; and further research is underway to understand how the MARRS technique influences the functional ecology and diversity, as well as the long-term resilience of reefs.

FUTURE RESTORATION AND ACHIEVING SCALE THROUGH CATALYZING ACTION

Fundamentally, the Spermonde restoration program is aimed at increasing the quality of coral reef habitat for local communities (food and income, as well as for coastal protection), and has well-established procedures for monitoring the ecological and social success and failures, which should be used to inform future practices. However, the Spermonde program also aims to address other applied research questions that are key for restoration more generally. For example, how can we optimize restoration build design to maximize positive changes in fish biomass, how do we integrate high coral thermal tolerance into restoration design, how can build design and location increase the ecological footprint of restoration while not changing the physical footprint, and how can we decrease restoration costs by accelerating natural ecological recruitment and/or succession within restored environments. These and other questions are aimed at increasing the long-term acceptance, sustainability, and scalability of restoration initiatives. To achieve an even larger scale, the research from the Spermonde program must be adopted by willing partners, become part of the wider restoration toolbox, and be used alongside other restoration techniques when it is most appropriate to do so. To facilitate the use of the MARRS reef star approach, Mars has established a free training program in the Spermonde, where partners can learn about restoration techniques generally, understand where the MARRS technique fits in, and gain important practical experience regarding how to undertake each stage of the site selection, construction, and restoration using the MARRS method. Several partners from other countries—and notably from organizations within Indonesia including representatives from the 10 Indonesian marine national parks—have now been trained. Several of these partners have concluded that the MARRS approach is suitable for their specific restoration needs and reef star use has, therefore, spread to eight more sites in Indonesia, as well as Mexico, Maldives, and Australia.

It is important to understand that the Spermonde site represents an extremely diverse and productive ecosystem where coral growth is extremely rapid. It's an ideal place to demonstrate the potential for restoration and is extremely important globally. However, the use of reef stars in other locations may yield less rapid change due to those conditions that drive coral growth such as temperature and water quality.

The 14 years of learning by Mars, the employment of supply-chain thinking, and the optimizing efficiency of each individual step has led to a restoration approach that is cost effective, can be delivered at significant scale (particularly when used in conjunction with other restoration techniques, such as focusing on building larval source reefs), and can be combined with our latest knowledge of what drives thermal tolerance across coral species and regions. The MARRS technique is best used in areas that are dominated by or at least contain a high abundance of mobile coral rubble—but it can also be rapidly deployed in smaller patches within a reef mosaic consisting of mixed substrata, including in areas that have recently been damaged by boat strikes or high intensity storms. Opportunistic research, for example, demonstrated that reef stars remained fixed to the substrata in high intensity storms even when native reefs sustained significant damage; the reef stars actually collected loose rubble, leading to more rapid consolidation and colonization, including maintenance of reef height, which we know to be extremely important when it comes to resisting coastal erosion and flooding (see Beck et al. 2018). In the most basic sense, the reef stars are coral platforms that can be rapidly deployed as a strong interconnected web of varying sizes and shapes. This web disappears as attached and native corals growth over the structure, eventually leading to it becoming fully integrated into the reef system and non-observable (see Figure 18.9). The reef stars kick-start the natural ecological process, and when combined with the correct governance, social and community support, and local participation, they can be extremely effective tools to help restore the world's reefs.

Figure 18.9 Image (a) shows typical starting conditions (prebuild). Images (b), (c), and (d) are examples of changes to the reef environment at the Bontosua site between 24 and 36 months post-restoration, showing reef stars (red arrows) fully integrated into the reef. Images (b), (c), and (d) courtesy of the Ocean Agency.

ACKNOWLEDGMENTS

*Susan Williams is credited as an author because parts of this chapter contain materials that were documented by her, knowing that our long-term intention was to write such an overview. She is also honored in memorial for her contributions to this program and many of her other lifelong accomplishments.

REFERENCES

Beck, M. W., I. J. Losada, P. Menéndez, B. G. Reguero, P. Díaz-Simal, and F. Fernández. 2018. "The global flood protection savings provided by coral reefs." *Nature Communications* 9:2186.

Kench, P. S. and T. Mann. 2017. "Reef island evolution and dynamics: Insights from the Indian and Pacific Oceans and perspectives for the Spermonde Archipelago." *Frontiers in Marine Sciences*. 00145.

Kohler, K. E. and S. M. Gill. 2006. "Coral Point Count with Excel extensions (CPCe): A Visual Basic program for the determination of coral and substrate coverage using random point count methodology." *Computers and geosciences* 32:1259–1269.

Plass-Johnson, J. G., S. C. Ferse, J. Jompa, C. Wild, and M. Teichberg. 2015. "Fish herbivory as key ecological function in a heavily degraded coral reef system." *Limnology and Oceanography* 60:1382–1391.

Sawall, Y., J. Jompa, M. Litaay, A. Maddusila, and C. Richter. 2013. "Coral recruitment and potential recovery of eutrophied and blast fishing impacted reefs in Spermonde Archipelago, Indonesia." *Marine Pollution Bulletin* 74:374–382.

Williams, S. L., C. Sur, N. Janetski, J. A. Hollarsmith, S. Rapi, L. Barron, S. J. Heatwole, et al. 2019. "Large-scale coral reef rehabilitation after blast fishing in Indonesia." *Restoration Ecology* 27:447–456.

This book has free material available for download from the Web Added Value™ resource center at *www.jrosspub.com*

19

HURRICANE IMPACTS ON REEF RESTORATION: THE GOOD, THE BAD, AND THE UGLY

Jane Carrick, Caitlin Lustic, Diego Lirman, Stephanie Schopmeyer, Erich Bartels, Dan Burdeno, Craig Dahlgren, Victor Manuel Galvan, Dave Gilliam, Liz Goergen, Shannon Gore, Sean Griffin, Edwin A. Hernández-Delgado, Dalton Hesley, Jessica Levy, Kemit Amon Lewis, Shelby Luce, Kerry Maxwell, Samantha Mercado, Margaret Miller, Michael Nemeth, Carlos Toledo-Hernández, Claudia P. Ruiz-Diaz, Samuel E. Suleiman-Ramos, Cory Walter, Dana Williams

ABSTRACT

The impacts of hurricanes and tropical storms on coral reef organisms have been well documented. Impacts of storms on reefs have ranged from minor to devastating, with extreme cases resulting in the destruction of the reef framework. Coral taxa with shallow distributions and branching morphologies, like the Caribbean *Acropora palmata* and *Acropora cervicornis*, are especially susceptible to strong storms and experience severe fragmentation. Coral reef restoration, using both sexually and asexually produced corals, has undergone a dramatic expansion in both the number of projects and the number of corals being propagated and outplanted in recent years. Presently, programs around the Caribbean outplant tens of thousands of coral colonies grown within in situ and ex situ nurseries on a yearly basis. Here, we report the impacts of three major storms—Hurricane Matthew (Sept. 28–Oct. 10, 2016; max sustained winds = 165 mph), Hurricane Irma (Aug. 30–Sept. 12, 2017; max sustained winds = 180 mph), and Hurricane Maria (Sept. 17–Sept. 25, 2017; max sustained winds = 175 mph)—on reef restoration programs found along the path of these destructive storms, based on the collective observations made by reef restoration practitioners from the United States (Florida, the U.S. Virgin Islands, Puerto Rico), the Bahamas, the Dominican Republic, and the British Virgin Islands. The information evaluated includes impacts on different coral species, nursery types, and outplanted corals. The impacts on outplanted corals were also compared to impacts on wild colonies found in the same habitats. The goal of this collaborative effort was not only to document the impacts of the storms on restoration resources and corals, but also to highlight the lessons learned from these disturbances and suggest ways in which restoration programs

continued

can better prepare and mitigate the impacts of storms in the future. Our findings show that nursery damage was primarily due to wave/water energetic damage and sedimentation impacts, while damage to outplanted coral colonies were primarily due to fragmentation and sediment burial. Based on observed impacts, restoration program managers provide a suite of recommendations to mitigate future storm damages. These include modifying anchor deployments for floating structures, raising low-profile structures, and trimming nursery coral stock prior to a storm.

INTRODUCTION

Intense storms are important drivers of reef health, coral diversity and abundance, distribution, reef geomorphology, and even reef creation (Dollar 1982; Hubbard et al. 1991; Blanchon and Jones 1997; Perry 2001; Blanchon et al. 2017). Storms can also influence coral reproduction by creating new coral colonies through fragmentation and delaying sexual reproduction by causing tissue losses and reductions in the average size of colonies (Lirman 2000). The damaging impacts of hurricanes and tropical storms on coral reef organisms have been well documented in the literature (Woodley et al. 1981; Gardner et al. 2005) and have ranged from minor to devastating, with extreme cases resulting in the destruction of the reef framework (Gleason et al. 2007). Coral taxa with shallow distributions and branching morphologies, like the Caribbean *Acropora palmata* and *Acropora cervicornis*, have been shown to be especially susceptible to strong storms and experience severe fragmentation (Highsmith et al. 1980; Lirman 2000).

The impacts of storms, along with disease, temperature anomalies, and human factors such as eutrophication and overfishing, have led to the significant decline in coral abundance and condition over the past several decades. These declines have prompted the listing of seven species of Caribbean stony corals as threatened under the U.S. Endangered Species Act (Jackson et al. 2001; Aronson and Precht 2016). These declines have fueled a proliferation of coral propagation and reef restoration efforts across the Caribbean region that were focused initially on the genus *Acropora*, but now include several other taxa of framework-building coral species (Page et al. 2018). Coral reef restoration using both sexually and asexually produced corals has undergone a dramatic increase in both the number of projects and the number of corals being propagated and outplanted onto degraded reefs in the past 10 years. Presently, programs around the Caribbean grow and outplant tens of thousands of coral colonies from in situ and ex situ nurseries on a yearly basis (Lirman and Schopmeyer 2016). The location of in-water nurseries in generally shallow waters makes these programs susceptible to storm damage, thus requiring the development of best management practices to prevent and mitigate storm damage while balancing the reduction of other threats (NMFS 2015). While the initial emphasis of reef restoration efforts has focused on coral population replenishment, restoration researchers are now evaluating how restored reefs can be designed for the purpose of coastal protection, which, if successful, could mitigate the effects of storm-related wave energy and flooding on coastal communities (Ferrario et al. 2014; Beck 2016; Beck et al. 2018). However, restored coral populations and nursery resources must first be able to survive storm events before they can provide this protection.

Here, we document the impacts of three major storms—Hurricane Matthew, Hurricane Irma, and Hurricane Maria—on Florida and Caribbean reef restoration programs found along the path of these destructive storms. The information evaluated in this study include impacts on different coral species, nursery types, outplanted corals, and wild corals. The goal of this collaborative effort was not only to document impacts of the storms on restoration resources and corals at an unprecedented regional scale, but also to highlight the lessons learned from these disturbances and suggest ways in which restoration efforts can better prepare and mitigate the impacts of future storms.

METHODS

We surveyed regional restoration practitioners working on programs that were affected by hurricanes in 2016–2017 (Table 19.1, Figure 19.1). Impact surveys at each location that was included in this review were conducted as soon as conditions allowed after each storm. The impact data were collated through a questionnaire that was completed by each restoration practitioner from restoration programs in the United States (Florida, the U.S. Virgin Islands, Puerto Rico), the Bahamas, the Dominican Republic, and the British Virgin Islands (from here on, refer to Table 19.1 for restoration program abbreviations cited within the text). Each program manager was provided a survey requesting input on the type and extent of impacts, impact factors, structural failures and successes, and future recommendations. In addition, each program was asked to rank impacts and impact factors according to the severity of damages observed to nursery and outplanted corals, with 1 being least severe and 5 being most severe. To compare damages in both nurseries and outplant sites among programs, we used a simple stoplight severity score, with *green* being less than 10% colony loss; *yellow* being 10–50% colony loss; and *red* being more than 50% colony loss. When available, the impacts on outplanted corals were compared to impacts on wild colonies that were found in the same habitats. Even if the information reported here may be, in many cases, observational or anecdotal in nature, the findings and recommendations provided are based on the extensive collective knowledge shared by regional experts in the field of coral reef restoration through answering a common set of targeted questions. While the individual programs that were surveyed may publish more quantitative information and analyses independently at a later time, the conclusions reached here nevertheless provide a unique opportunity to evaluate the impacts of three severe storms on restoration efforts at an unprecedented regional scale.

Table 19.1 Damage reports provided by coral reef restoration practitioners from Florida, USA, and the Caribbean regarding reefs that were impacted by the 2017 hurricanes

Location	Organization	Storm(s)	Species* in nursery	Nursery structures	Nursery depth / depth range (m)	Nursery impact(s) (as reported)	Nursery impacts (descending order of severity from 5)	Outplant species*	Outplant method(s)	Outplant impacts	Outplant Impact source(s) (5 = most severe, 1 = less severe)	Wild reef damage(s)
Broward, FL, USA	Nova Southeastern University (NSU)	Irma	AC	PVC trees, PVC arrays, cement modules	6.7–7.9	Survival decreased over 2.5 mo. post-storm: modules survivorship [nursery 1] went from 92% to 72%, [nursery 2] went from 95% to 85%, trees were 76% to 58% and PVC arrays were 63% to 35%	(5) sediment movement causing decrease in colony health (4) disease/storm related	AC	Nail & cable tie, epoxy	>80% outplant colony loss	(5) physical damage (removal, fragmentation) (4) sediment burial (3) sand blasting (2) disease (1) debris	Complete loss of some AP colonies, movement of substrate, significant change in AC community at some sites, hundreds of loose gorgonians scattered at sites, beaches covered in sponges
Miami, FL, USA	University of Miami (UM)	Irma	AC, AP, OF, PD	PVC trees, cinder blocks	6.7–9.1	>50% trees lost, branch breakage	(5) sediment movement (4) water movement (3) algae entanglement (2) trap debris	AC, AP	Nail & cable tie, epoxy	>80% AC outplant removal, 50% AP removal	(5) physical damage (removal, fragmentation) (4) sediment burial (3) sand blasting (4) disease (5) trap debris	Sediment burial, fragmentation, colony removal, framework fracture, sand blasting
Key Largo, FL, USA	Coral Restoration Foundation (CRF)	Irma	AC, AP, OF, OA, MCo, DC, OD, SS, PP, PA	PVC trees, cinder blocks	4.6–9.1	>60% coral loss from structures. Structures with minor breakage but very little completely lost	(5) water movement (led to loss of stock) (2) sediment movement (3) trap debris entanglements	AC, AP	epoxy	(Not reported)	(5) physical damage (removal, fragmentation) (4) sediment burial (3) sand blasting (2) disease (1) trap debris	Sediment burial, fragmentation, colony removal, framework fracture, sand blasting

Continued

Hurricane Impacts on Reef Restoration: The Good, the Bad, and the Ugly

Table 19.1 *Continued*

Location	Organization	Storm(s)	Species* in nursery	Nursery structures	Nursery depth / depth range (m)	Nursery impact(s) (as reported)	Nursery impacts (descending order of severity from 5)	Outplant species*	Outplant method(s)	Outplant impact(s)	Outplant Impact source(s) (5 = most severe, 1 = less severe)	Wild reef damage(s)
Long Key, FL, USA	The Nature Conservancy (TNC)	Irma	AC	PVC trees, block modules	7.6–8.2	100% loss of corals, all trees missing, and 2/3 of the modules were missing but none had living tissue. Sand burial was not as much of an issue at Long Key	(5) wave action caused tree anchors to fail (trap rope/monofilament broke or entire anchor systems were gone) (4) sediment movement may have undermined the anchor systems (3) possible damage from trap debris	AC	(Not reported)	(Not reported)	(Not reported)	(Not reported)
Marathon Key, FL, USA	TNC	Irma	AC, OF, PC, MC	PVC trees, block modules	7.3–7.6	90% loss of AC, 78% loss of non-Acroporid stock. 18 out of 30 trees missing, remaining trees had missing branches, 30 of 46 modules were completely buried under sand and 13 were partially buried (only 3 unaffected)	(5) (water movement) wave action caused tree anchors to fail (trap rope/monofilament broke or entire anchor systems were gone) (4) sediment movement (most of the non-Acroporid stock on block modules were buried) (3) possible damage from trap debris	AC, OF, PC, MC	Nail & cable tie, epoxy	95% loss at offshore reef sites, 35–70% loss at mid-channel patch reef sites	(5) physical damage (mostly removal and to a lesser degree fragmentation) (4) sediment burial (3) sand blasting (2) trap debris (possible but not documented)	Colony detachment (present but loose) or removal, fragmentation, sediment burial, sand blasting, framework fracture
Summerland Key, FL, USA	Mote Marine Laboratory	Irma	AC, AP, OF, PC, MC, DC	PVC trees, cement/PVC modules	8.2	65% trees lost, 100% modules lost. 92.7% AC frags/97.8% AC TLE lost	(5) trap debris (4) sand movement (3) water/wave movement	AC	Nail & cable tie	Lower Keys (AC) loss = 92% of 2016 outplants, 99% of 2017 outplants	(5) Physical damage (removal/ fragmentation)	Physical damage (removal/ fragmentation)

Continued

Table 19.1 Continued

Location	Organization	Storm(s)	Species* in nursery	Nursery structures	Nursery depth / depth range (m)	Nursery impact(s) (as reported)	Nursery impacts (descending order of severity from 5)	Outplant species*	Outplant method(s)	Outplant impacts	Outplant Impact source(s) (5 = most severe, 1 = less severe)	Wild reef damage(s)
Key West, FL, USA	Mote Marine Laboratory	Irma	AC	PVC trees	8.2	25% trees lost. 32.1% AC frags/32.6% AC TLE lost	(5) trap debris (4) sand movement (3) water/wave movement	AC	Nail & cable tie, epoxy	Key West AC loss = 68% of 2016 outplants, 63% of 2017 outplants	(5) sand blasting (4) disease	Not reported
South Abaco, Bahamas	Perry Institute of Marine Science (PIMS)	Matthew (2016)	AC, AP	Line structures	4.6–10.7	Nonstructural damage, mortality of <10% of corals in nursery		AC, AP	Epoxy	Breakage of <10% of outplants	(5) fragmentation	Some AP toppled and broken, ~50% biomass of AC fragmented and scattered
Nassau, Bahamas	PIMS	Matthew (2016)	AC	PVC trees	9.1	23 out of 40 trees lost—only anchors remaining. Of surviving 17 trees, 50% had 1 or more arms snapped off, corals on remaining trees were fine.	(5) water movement	AC	Nail & cable tie, epoxy	loss of >90% outplants from 2 of 3 sites, loss of 25% at shallow site	(5) loss of reef structure (not just outplants) (4) sand blasting (3) burial in mud and debris at one site	Loss of large areas of reef structure—mounding corals toppled and hit other colonies knocking them down—large piles of rubble and swaths where reef structure toppled over wall. Burial in mud at one site
Andros, Bahamas	PIMS	Matthew (2016)	AC, AP	Line structures	4.6–10.7	Nonstructural damage, mortality of <5% of corals in nursery. Cannot attribute all losses to storms vs. other mortality sources. Only 2 fragments lost likely due to storms	No major damage	(Not reported)	Epoxy	n/a	n/a	Scattered AC colonies

Continued

Table 19.1 Continued

Location	Organization	Storm(s)	Species* in nursery	Nursery structures	Nursery depth / depth range (m)	Nursery impact(s) (as reported)	Nursery impacts (descending order of severity from 5)	Outplant species*	Outplant method(s)	Outplant impact(s)	Outplant Impact source(s) (5 = most severe, 1 = less severe)	Wild reef damage(s)
Andros, Bahamas	PIMS	Matthew (2016)	AC	PVC trees	10.7	Lost 1 of 6 trees, broken arms on 3 of remaining 5 trees	(5) water movement	(Not reported)	Epoxy	(Not reported)	(Not reported)	AC colonies fragmented and scattered at some sites, little impact to others
South Abaco, Bahamas	PIMS	Irma	AC, AP	Line structures	4.6–10.7	No damage to nursery, <2% of corals missing, another 2% dead from unknown sources (i.e., not necessarily storm related)	n/a	AC, AP	Epoxy	Breakage of 5% of outplants	(5) water movement	Minimal impact
Nassau, Bahamas	PIMS	Irma	AC	PVC tree	9.1	No damage to nurseries	n/a	AC	Nail & cable tie, epoxy	Breakage of 5% of outplants	(5) water movement	Minimal impact
Andros, Bahamas	PIMS	Irma	AC, AP	Line	4.6–10.7	No damage to nursery, loss of <5% of corals	No major damage		n/a	n/a	n/a	Minimal impact
Andros, Bahamas	PIMS	Irma	AC	PVC tree	10.7	No damage to nurseries or minimal loss of corals	n/a		Not reported	Loss of <10% of outplants	(5) sand blasting (4) sediment burial	Minimal impact—most impacts from Matthew in 2016
Punta Cana, DR	Puntacana Ecological Foundation	Irma, Maria	AC, AP, Por	A-frames, fixed-to-bottom structures	2.7–7.3	Burial and sand movement. Some infrastructure collapse	(5) sediment movement (4) overgrown frames that increased drag	AC, AP	Nail & epoxy	Two sites close to each other were buried in the sand	(5) sediment burial	n/a

Continued

Table 19.1 Continued

Location	Organization	Storm(s)	Species* in nursery	Nursery structures	Nursery depth / depth range (m)	Nursery impact(s) (as reported)	Nursery impacts (descending order of severity from 5)	Outplant species*	Outplant method(s)	Outplant impact(s)	Outplant impact source(s) (5 = most severe, 1 = less severe)	Wild reef damage(s)
Southern Puerto Rico	National Oceanic and Atmospheric Administration (NOAA) Restoration Center (RC)	Irma, Maria	AC, AP, DC	PVC trees, floating underwater coral apparatuses (FUCAs), benthic underwater coral apparatuses (BUCAs)	1.5–15.2	Minor physical damage to a few trees and FUCAs	(5) water movement (4) debris	AC, AP	Nail & cable tie, epoxy, cement	AP was fine; moderate damage to AC	(5) Physical damage (removal/fragmentation)	Fragmentation, colony removal, framework fracture, sand blasting
Eastern Puerto Rico	NOAA RC	Irma, Maria	AC, AP, DC	PVC trees, FUCA	3.0–9.1	Minor physical damage to a few trees and FUCAs	(5) water movement (4) debris	AC, AP, DC	Nail & cable tie, epoxy, cement	Severe impacts to AC; AP did ok	(5) Physical damage (removal/fragmentation)	Sediment burial, fragmentation, colony removal, framework fracture, sand blasting
Culebra, PR	NOAA RC	Irma, Maria	AC, AP, DC	PVC trees, A-frames, condos, stars, tables	3.0–9.1	Minor damage to trees, major damage to everything else; everything but trees were wiped out	(5) sediment movement (4) water movement (3) algae entanglement (2) debris	AC, AP, DC	Nail & cable tie, epoxy, cement	Severe (almost 100%) mortality for AC; AP did ok	(5) Physical damage (removal/fragmentation) (4) sediment burial	Sediment burial, fragmentation, colony removal, framework fracture, sand blasting
Culebra, PR	Sociedad Ambiente Marino (SAM)/ University of Puerto Rico (UPR)	Irma, Maria	AC, AP, OF, DC	PVC trees, horizontal line structures, PVC condos	3.0–12.2	>90% horizontal line nurseries lost, 100% PVC condominium units lost, <10% trees lost, multiple branch breakage	(5) coastal vegetation and algal entanglement (4) trap debris (3) water movement (2) sediment movement	AC, AP	Nail & cable tie	>90% outplant removal (AC), <10% removal (AP)	(5) physical damage (removal/fragmentation) (4) sand blasting	Fragmentation, colony removal, sand blasting, sediment burial, framework fracture

Continued

Table 19.1 Continued

Location	Organization	Storm(s)	Species* in nursery	Nursery structures	Nursery depth/depth range (m)	Nursery impact(s) (as reported)	Nursery impacts (descending order of severity from 5)	Outplant species*	Outplant method(s)	Outplant impact(s)	Outplant impact source(s) (5 = most severe, 1 = less severe)	Wild reef damage(s)
Little Thatch Island & Mount Trunk Bay, BVI	Association of Reef Keepers (ARK)	Irma, Maria	AC, AP	PVC trees, pucks	7.9–8.8	Complete loss	(5) wave energy	AC	Nail & cable tie	Complete loss	(5) removal (4) sand (3) debris	sediment burial, mechanical damage, coastal vegetation
St. Thomas, USVI	NOAA RC	Irma, Maria	AC, AP, DC	PVC trees and blocks	3.0–9.1	Minor damage to trees; blocks were a complete loss (burial by 2′ of sand)	(5) sediment movement (4) water movement (3) algae entanglement (2) debris	AC, AP, DC	Nail & cable tie, epoxy, cement	Severe damage to AC; minor damage to AP and DC	(5) Physical damage (removal/fragmentation)	Sediment burial, fragmentation, colony removal, framework fracture, sand blasting

*Species codes: AC = *Acropora cervicornis*, AP = *Acropora palmata*, DC = *Dendrogyra cylindrus*, MC = *Montastrea cavernosa*, MCo = *Millepora complanata*, OD = *Oculina diffusa*, OA = *Orbicella annularis*, OF = *Orbicella faveolata*, PD = *Porites digitae*, PP = *Porites porites*, PA = *Porites astreoides*, Por. = *Porites* NOS spp., PS = *Pseudodiploria clivosa*, SS = *Siderastrea siderea*

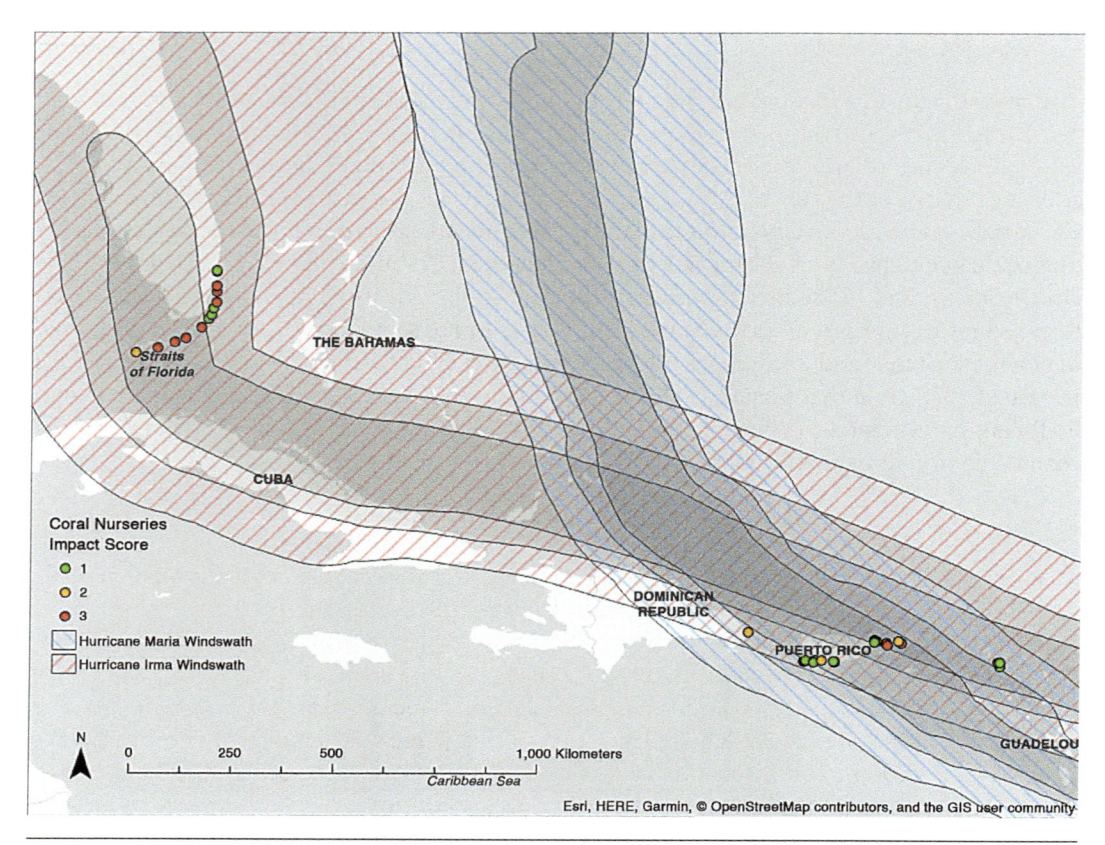

Figure 19.1 Map of all impacted nurseries in Florida and the Caribbean region. Nurseries are labeled (1–3) based on the impact score reported. An impact score of 3/red is equal to >50% mortality or loss of resources; 2/yellow is equal to 10–50% mortality or loss of resources; and 1/green is equal to <10% mortality or loss of resources. For the hurricane windswaths, the innermost gray swath is the extent of winds 64 mph or greater, the middle swath is the extent of winds 50 mph or greater, and the outermost swath is 34 mph or greater.

RESULTS

Impact Categories

The reported impacts were grouped primarily into the following four broad categories.

Physical Damage

During Hurricanes Matthew, Irma, and Maria, maximum sustained wind speeds reached up to 165, 185, and 175 mph, respectively. These systems caused high-energy waves, turbulent water, strong currents, and swells. As a result, in situ nurseries and outplants were subject to high fluid shear stress that resulted in coral fragmentation, coral removal, and breakage and removal of nursery platforms.

Sedimentation

The storms caused the suspension, movement, and deposition of high loads of sediments. Suspended sediments caused major physical damage to nursery corals, outplants, and wild corals via *sand-blasting* abrasion. In some cases, sediments remained on coral colonies several weeks after the passage of the storm, causing prolonged secondary impacts through shading and tissue burial. Sediment movement was the largest cause of damage to nursery platforms, especially in Florida where two types of impacts were documented: (1) burial of low-lying structures like cinder blocks, and (2) sediment washout resulting in the release of anchored floating structures. Some locations in Florida saw the loss of up to 1 m of sediments (the maximum depth of deployment of the sand anchors used to secure floating PVC trees to the bottom), causing the release of PVC trees that floated to the surface due to the buoyancy provided by their buoys. Sediment movement also affected outplanted and wild corals by burying colonies under more than 0.3 m of sediment in some reef areas.

Fishing Gear, Marine Debris, and Macroalgae

In Florida and in most nations of the Caribbean, the early weeks of lobster season coincide with hurricane season. During these months, commercial and private lobster fishermen deploy submerged lobster traps made of metal mesh, wire, wood, plastic, and/or netting. Traps are attached with rope or fishing line to a surface buoy and, in some cases, to each other, thereby forming a string of traps. Few of these traps are anchored securely in place and easily become projectiles in wind events exceeding 17 mph. These can significantly damage coral and other sessile fauna during storm events if not removed in time (Lewis et al. 2009). During Hurricanes Irma and Maria, fishing gear and debris caused significant physical damage to nursery structures and corals through direct collision and entanglement. Many nurseries also observed entanglement by macroalgae and coastal vegetation (e.g., mangrove debris, palm fronds). This caused breakage of some nursery structures and fragmentation of nursery and outplanted corals, and in some cases, covered entire fragments, essentially smothering polyps and reducing light availability.

Secondary Impacts

Restoration groups observed secondary impacts to their coral stock in both their nurseries and outplant sites in the weeks and months following a storm. Corals that remained in place after the storm showed reduced health. Open wounds in damaged coral tissue allowed for bacterial/pathogen colonization and increased disease prevalence. Environmental changes remained for weeks to months after the passage of the storms in most regions. Turbid coastal runoff exposed many sites to lower salinity and high nutrient and contaminant loads. Reductions in water temperature (a potential benefit of the passage of a storm, especially during bleaching season; Manzello et al. 2007) and reduced light penetration due to the resuspension of fine sediments were observed for up to three months post-hurricane. Several regions (e.g., BVIs, Miami) observed a bloom of cyanobacteria and macroalgae (*Liagora* spp., *Acrosymphyton caribaeum*, *Trichogloeopsis pedicellata*), occurring three to four weeks after the storms. Sediment suspension and algal overgrowth caused partial bleaching and partial coral mortality, as previously described by Knowlton et al. (1981) and Toledo-Hernández et al. (2018). Nurseries also accumulated decaying plant detritus transported from other areas in the weeks and months after a storm.

Impacts to Nurseries

Restoration practitioners were asked to list and rank the damage observed within their nurseries in order of severity, with 5 being the most severe impact (Table 19.1). The most severe impact across all groups was water movement and wave energy, which affected 14 out of 22 programs and had a median severity ranking of 3.5. Only six programs reported no damage to nursery structures and minimal loss of nursery coral stock (0–10%) (Table 19.2). Individual nurseries for each program were ranked by impact (low to high) and mapped against the paths of Hurricanes Irma and Maria (Figure 19.1). Nurseries with high impacts (greater than 50% damages) were highly spatially clustered (spatial autocorrelation analyses; Global Morans I, p = 0.0006). However, clustering was not explained by proximity to higher winds or proximity to the eye of the hurricanes (OLS r-squared = 0.008).

Table 19.2 Ranking of impact factors affecting nursery resources as reported by restoration practitioners

Nursery Impacts	Median	Number of Regions Affected (out of 22)
Water/Wave Energy	3.50	14
Sedimentation	3.00	11
Trap Debris	2.50	10
Entanglement	2.00	6
Disease	3.00	1
Unaffected (<10% loss of nursery resources)		6

Damage to Nursery Propagation Structures

The majority of the respondents utilize floating coral trees in their nurseries. Other nursery structures include low-lying cement blocks and modules, floating underwater coral apparatuses (FUCAs) (NOAA RC, Puerto Rico), lattice metal domes, rope tables, and floating line structures (Table 19.1).

Floating Structures

Floating PVC trees (Nedimyer et al. 2011) holding *Acropora* corals showed minor to severe breakage in every single program during Hurricanes Irma and/or Maria. Some of the most severe damages were recorded in the British Virgin Islands (ARK) and in Long Key, Florida (FWC), where all nursery trees were completely lost. However, in Culebra, Puerto Rico (SAM, NOAA RC), severe damage was seen on all nursery structures with the exception of trees; while over 90% of line nurseries were lost and 100% of PVC condominiums were lost, fewer than 10% of the nursery tree structures were lost (despite breakage of multiple branches) in this region.

Much of the damage to floating structures resulted from breakage. Breakage was caused by water movement as well as contact and entanglement with macroalgae, terrestrial vegetation, and marine debris, especially lobster traps and fishing line (Figure 19.2). The weakest points for the coral trees were the tree arms that were either completely removed or broken, usually at the point of attachment to the PVC spine (Figure 19.3(a)). In Marathon, Florida (FWC), all trees that were not removed entirely through Hurricane Irma had missing branches and in Nassau,

Figure 19.2 Entanglement by trap debris, fishing gear, and algae caused extensive damage. (Photos: (a) NOAA, St. Thomas, USVI; (b) CRF, Carysfort Reef Nursery, Upper Florida Keys; (c) CRF, Tavernier Nursery, Upper Florida Keys; (d) UM, Key Biscayne Nursery, Miami-Dade County.)

Bahamas (PIMS), 50% of trees that remained within nurseries through Hurricane Matthew (2016) had at least one arm snapped. In Puerto Rico, NOAA RC noted that fiberglass rods fared better than PVC arms on trees. In multiple nurseries, tree arms that survived the storm also saw breakage of the monofilament line that held the individual coral fragments (Figure 19.3(b)). Within one nursery in Miami, Florida (UM), coral size appeared to be a factor in branch breakage, with trees holding larger colonies experiencing higher breakage due to the higher profile and weight of the complex branching colonies. Another point of failure for the coral trees was the anchor lines, which, when broken, caused the complete loss of tree structures. One group

Figure 19.3 Multiple failure points on nursery structures resulted in loss of coral stock. (a) breakage of PVC or fiberglass arms at the point of attachment to spine; (b) breakage of monofilament loops, resulting in loss of individual fragments; (c) elbow joint with steel bolt of a surviving FUCA; (d) lifted or broken anchor lines resulted in fully intact trees floating away from the nursery like this tree from a UM restoration program—found by a citizen on Miami Beach following Hurricane Irma. (Photos: (a) FWC, Middle Florida Keys, FL; (b) CRF, Carysfort Reef, Upper Florida Keys; (c) NOAA, Shacks Nursery, Isabella, NW Puerto Rico; (d) UM, Miami-Dade County, FL.)

(FWC) that uses both sand anchors and column-block anchors for their trees reported that column-block anchors fared poorly compared to sand anchors in the Middle Florida Keys, though these differences are potentially attributed to the location of the nurseries and not the anchors used. Column-block anchors were deployed only within a nursery site that was further offshore and more exposed to wave action while sand anchors were only deployed within a nursery within the mid-channel region of the Middle Keys. At the offshore nursery, only four of 23 cement-block anchors remained after Hurricane Irma, compared to 12 of 30 sand anchors remaining in the mid-channel nursery. Many of the sand anchors that remained, however, broke at the point of attachment to the line at the base of the tree.

The FUCA nursery structures used in Puerto Rico (NOAA RC) largely escaped damage through Irma and Maria, but had some breakage at the *elbow joint* of the frame (Figure 19.3(c)). The FUCAs that were constructed with steel bolts broke less often than those that had PVC elbow attachments. Also, the one-quarter-inch parachute cord fared better than other lines used for nursery structures. In the Dominican Republic (PEF), floating rope structures performed poorly, though it was noted that the age of the lines as well as the amount of overgrowth on the lines by bivalves, fire coral, sponges, and hydroids may have contributed to the breakage.

One of the characteristics of the impacts of Hurricane Irma in Florida was the amount of sediment movement observed. While some reefs were blanketed by sediments that were carried by turbulent waters, others were scoured of sediments, exposing anchors and previously buried reef framework. While PVC trees and other floating nursery platforms are ideal for growing many corals within a limited benthic footprint (e.g., trees in Florida can hold more than 100 fragments), they were especially susceptible to sediment movement that uncovered and released the sand anchors that were used to secure these structures to the sandy bottom. In some nurseries, anchors were also broken or cut, either from contact with debris or from pulling due to shear stress. Once the anchors are cut or released by sediment loss, the buoyed structures float to the surface where they drift away from the nursery site. In Florida, all 10 nursery trees that had been deployed at a Miami Beach nursery (10 m of depth, anchors placed approx. 1 m deep into the sand; UM) were uprooted due to sediment movement and ended up structurally intact on a nearby beach with corals still attached (Figure 19.3(d)). An extreme example of the transport of nursery trees that had become unsecured from the bottom was documented in Florida, where coral trees from a nursery in the Lower Florida Keys were recovered in Cape Canaveral (more than 483 km/300 mi north of the nursery) with some surviving corals still attached. Also, floating coral trees, with surviving corals, made the voyage from St. Thomas in the U.S. Virgin Islands to the Exumas in the Bahamas (approximately 1300 km/800 mi).

Attached-to-Bottom Structures

Several restoration programs use nonfloating nursery platforms that are attached directly to the bottom (Johnson et al. 2011). These types of structures include cinder blocks, rebar frames, and PVC frames. Water movement was so powerful in some cases that cement modules were completely removed, as was the case for Mote (Summerland Key, Florida) and FWC (Long Key, Florida) who lost 100% and 66% of their modules, respectively. In some cases, these low-profile structures fared better than floating structures in the same region. One example comes from Miami-Dade County, Florida (UM), where all three nurseries that use floating structures had significant damage (with a complete loss of trees in two of the three nurseries), but the one nursery that had cement cinder blocks attached to the bottom with rebar experienced only minimal damage in the form of coral fragmentation and blocks turning on their sides. No burial or block removals were observed at this location, just five miles from a nearby nursery where all of the coral trees were lost. These different damage patterns can be explained by the patchiness in sediment movement patterns within small spatial scales. In one nursery in northwestern Puerto Rico, Hurricane Irma caused up to 0.5 m of previously buried frameworks to be exposed by sediment washout under a Benthic Underwater Coral Apparatus (BUCA) (Figure 19.4(a) (b)), anchored with rebar and cement cinder blocks. While this structure experienced washout of sediment, no burial of corals was observed which might otherwise have resulted in coral mortality.

By contrast, partial or complete burial of low-profile structures such as cement blocks, rebar modules, or PVC tables by sediments was observed by eight programs. While the structures were relatively unharmed, any attached corals that were covered by sediments had 100% mortality, as was the case in St. Thomas USVI, where all nursery blocks were covered by sediment. In Marathon, Florida, some cement blocks were buried by more than 0.6 m of sediment and buried coral fragments showed 100% mortality (Figure 19.4(c) (d)).

Figure 19.4 Sedimentation effects to nursery structures and coral stock. (a) BUCA prior to storm and (b) with exposed anchor system due to sediment washout post-storm; (c) block module before and (d) after excavation at Marathon, Florida. Buried coral fragments showed 100% mortality. (Photos: (a) NOAA, Shacks Nursery, Isabella, NW Puerto Rico; (b) NOAA, Shacks Nursery, Isabella, NW Puerto Rico; (c) FWC, Middle Florida Keys, FL; (d) FWC, Middle Florida Keys, FL.)

Impacts to Nursery Corals

The most common type of damage was breakage and removal of nursery corals from propagation structures. In addition, corals that remained attached to the structures often showed signs of sand blasting or abrasion, as evidenced by patches of exposed skeleton with damaged tissue. In all programs, corals that were broken or dislodged from nursery platforms that landed on the sediments had complete mortality due to burial or sand blasting (Figure 19.5). Damage to corals remaining on the structures was sometimes caused by the entanglement of algae (mainly

Figure 19.5 Multiple groups experienced high mortality of remaining coral stock within their nurseries post-storm. (a) Coral nursery tree in Miami-Dade County, FL, with >50% mortality; (b) sandblasting of *A. palmata* fragments on nursery tree; (c) disease and burial mortality of staghorn coral on a cement block nursery structure; (d) algae-related mortality; (e) intact coral fragments showing fragmentation and mortality. (Photos: (a) UM, Key Biscayne Nursery, Miami-Dade County, FL; (b) UM, Key Biscayne Nursery, Miami-Dade County, FL; (c) UM, South Nursery, Miami-Dade County, FL; (d) Claudia Ruiz-Diaz, SAM, Culebra, PR; (e) FWC, Middle Florida Keys, FL.)

Sargassum and filamentous red algae). Patches of bleached or dead tissue were observed after the removal of algae or debris at the points of contact (Figure 19.5(d)).

Two groups (ARK and SAM) noted that size did not appear to be a factor affecting survivorship of corals fragments, while two other groups (FWC and UM) observed that, on coral trees, smaller fragments fared better than larger fragments. Across all regions, survival of remaining nursery corals decreased over time after the storms. In the two and a half months following Hurricane Irma, NSU reported reduced survivorship of 15% (SE +/− 5.0) of module-attached corals across two nurseries, 18% of tree-hung corals, and 28% of corals on PVC arrays. Reduced survivorship is attributed to sandblasting and post-storm secondary effects (particularly disease), suspended sediments, and overgrowth by cyanobacteria and algae (Figure 19.5). NSU's two nurseries are located within the same sand channel, approximately 1 km apart, yet disease was more prevalent at one nursery than the other. The group reports that the only difference in the sites that could explain this is the sediment composition; the nursery with more disease had more rubble in the sand than the nursery with less disease prevalence.

In Puerto Rico, it was noted that *Orbicella faveolata* and *Dendrogyra cylindrus* had the highest survivorship within nurseries. Two groups (SAM and NOAA RC) reported that *A. palmata* survived better than *A. cervicornis*. This pattern was also true in the Upper Florida Keys (CRF) where *A. palmata* had higher rates of retention within nurseries compared to *A. cervicornis*, which experienced higher losses. In fact, *A. cervicornis* was reported to have the lowest survivorship of all nursery species, likely due to their brittle branching morphology which, while important in asexual reproduction, makes the species more susceptible to breakage-driven mortality (Gilmore and Hall 1976; Knowlton et al. 1981). Mote (Summerland Key, Florida) reported that, of the corals remaining in their nurseries, 97.8% of *A. cervicornis* total linear extension (TLE) was removed through fragmentation. In general, boulder and mounding corals also fared better than branching species in nursery sites maintained by FWC. Their fate, however, was related to whether or not these corals were propagated on the low-lying structures that were buried by sediments. The higher susceptibility of branching corals to storm impact compared to mounding corals has been reported in the past by Woodley et al. (1981).

Impacts to Outplanted Corals

Outplanted corals experienced impacts similar to those of nursery corals. Physical damage was the most severe and most frequent impact by a factor of two, with 14 (out of 22) programs reporting removal or fragmentation of outplanted corals, with a median impact score of 5 (Table 19.3). Restoration practitioners from NOAA and UM measured survivorship of staghorn corals that were outplanted four to eight months prior to Hurricane Irma at five sites in Miami-Dade County, Florida. The average survivorship of outplanted staghorn corals ranged from 4–14%, compared to 31% average survivorship of wild staghorn colonies at the same sites (Figure 19.6). Mortality included both the complete removal of corals as well as corals found still attached but without any living tissue. The few living outplants that remained within the plots were heavily fragmented, with most of the surviving corals having less than 10 cm of TLE after the storm (Figure 19.7).

Certain outplant methods appeared to perform better through hurricanes than others. In Puerto Rico (NOAA RC), outplants that were attached to the reef with cement did better than those attached with two-part epoxy. *A. palmata* fragments outplanted with cement were stable, while *D. cylindrus* fragments attached with epoxy were toppled over in the storm. Also, some coral species fared better than others as noted previously by Woodley et al. (1981). In

Table 19.3 Ranking of impact factors affecting outplanted corals as reported by restoration practitioners

Impacts to Outplanted Corals	Median	Number of Regions Affected (out of 22)
Physical damage	5.00	14
Sediment burial	4.00	8
Sandblasting	3.50	8
Disease	2.00	4
Trap Debris	1.00	5
Unaffected (no observed damage)		4

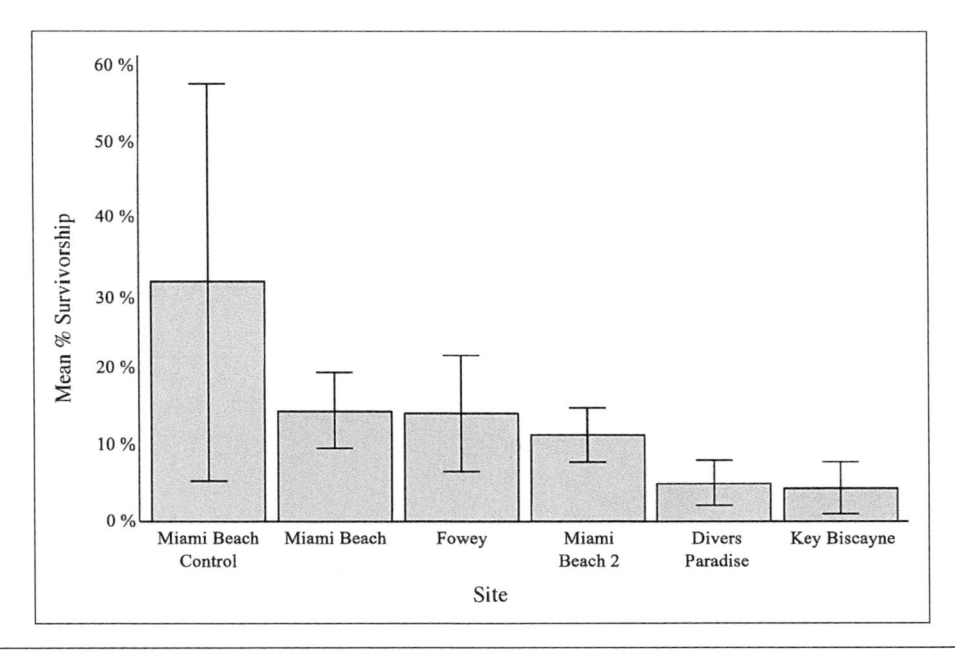

Figure 19.6 Percentage of survivorship of outplanted and wild (control site) *A. cervicornis* colonies after Hurricane Irma in Miami-Dade County, Florida, USA. Number of corals found before storm: control site (151 colonies within belt transects × 3 plots), Miami Beach (960 within 6 plots), Fowey (1,200 within 4 plots), Miami Beach 2 (1,200 within 4 plots), Divers Paradise (900 within 3 plots), and Key Biscayne (960 within 6 plots).

Culebra, Puerto Rico (SAM), *A. palmata* and *D. cylindrus* outplants had a higher survivorship than *A. cervicornis* outplants. As with nursery stocks, the low survivorship of *A. cervicornis* is not surprising because it is a species that is naturally prone to breakage. The pre-storm size of *A. cervicornis* outplants did not appear to be a factor in the likelihood of fragmentation since outplants of all sizes were broken. While *A. palmata* outplants were more prone to breakage at sizes greater than 50–75 cm TLE, surviving *A. cervicornis* outplants that had been fragmented to less than 15 cm TLE by the storm had a 90% mortality in the two to seven days after the storm (Toledo-Hernández et al. 2018). This pattern was similar to the post-storm mortality seen in nurseries, and could be due to scouring wounds or disease. In previous studies, rapid

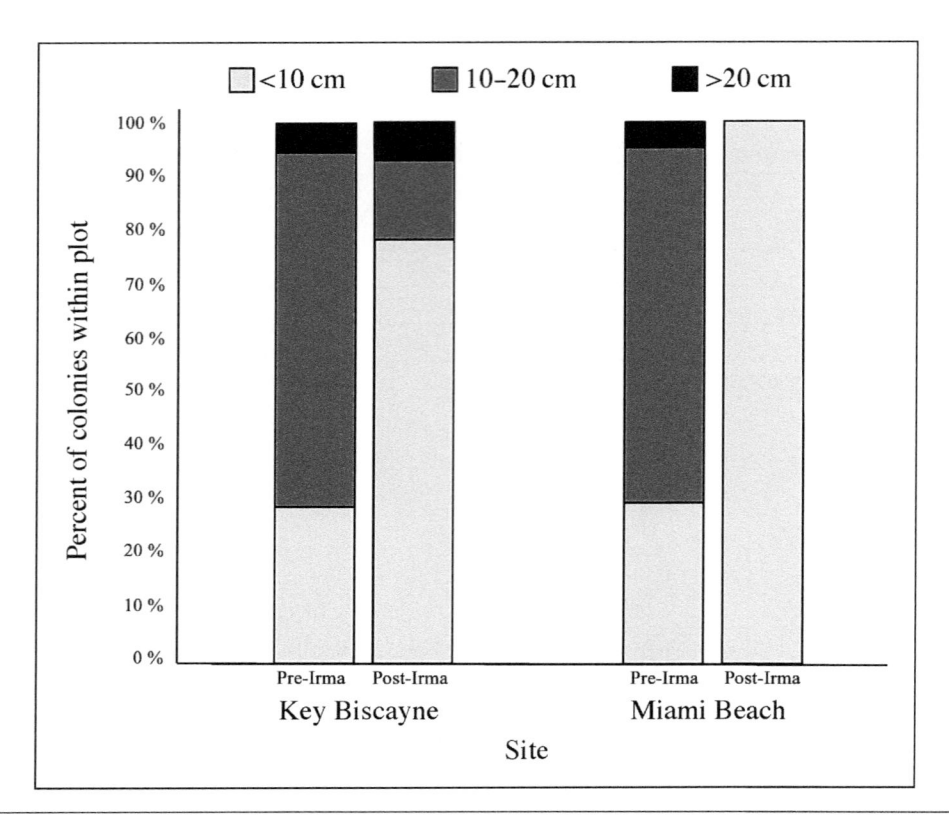

Figure 19.7 Size of *A. cervicornis* fragments before (Pre-Irma) and after (Post-Irma) the hurricane on two reefs in Miami-Dade County, Florida, showing the reduction in the average size of the surviving fragments.

tissue mortality—similar in appearance to the *white syndrome*—affected storm-fragmented *Acropora* species corals in the three weeks following a hurricane (Williams et al. 2008).

On a reef in the Lower Florida Keys (TNC, FWC, Mote) where corals from three species were outplanted—*A. cervicornis* (49 colonies alive prior to the storm), *M. cavernosa* (44 colonies), and *O. faveolata* (56 colonies)—Hurricane Irma caused tissue mortality (partial and total) as well as colony removal of outplanted colonies that had been planted 19 months prior. Colonies of *A. cervicornis* were attached with nails and epoxy, while colonies of the two massive species were attached with epoxy. The impacts of the storm were related to colony morphology as greater than 91% of the branching staghorn colonies were removed compared to 40% of *M. cavernosa* and 62% of *O. faveolata* colonies (Figure 19.8).

Outplant sites (as well as natural reefs) in Culebra, Puerto Rico (SAM), showed a survivorship gradient according to depth, with most of *A. cervicornis* removed from depths of less than 5 m, while colonies had a higher survivorship between 5 and 15 m. For *A. palmata*, 80% of colonies were lost at depths of less than 5 m but only 30–50% of *A. palmata* colonies were lost from sites found between 5 and 8 m in depth.

Figure 19.8 Damage to outplanted colonies; outplanted *O. faveolata* colony (a) July 2017, 2 months pre-Hurricane Irma and (b) October 2017, 1 month post-hurricane; (c) heavily fragmented and damaged *A. cervicornis* outplant post-storm and (d) remaining nails after *A. cervicornis* outplant completely removed from a reef in the Middle Florida Keys. (Photos: (a) TNC, Lower Florida Keys, FL; (b) TNC, Lower Florida Keys, FL; (c) UM, Miami-Dade County, FL; and (d) UM, Miami-Dade County, FL.)

Impacts to Wild Colonies

The removal of staghorn corals during Hurricane Irma was evident at all sites visited in Miami, Florida. At a site in Miami Beach that was tracked by affiliates at NOAA where *wild colonies* were tracked, 68% mortality (including dead and removed colonies) was observed (Figure 19.6). Many of the factors that affected outplanted colonies also appeared to affect wild colonies. For example, the depth gradient of outplant survivorship described in the previous section held true for wild *Acropora* as well, with coral survivorship being higher at a depth greater than 5 m. The morphology of wild corals played a role in survivorship. In the Middle Florida Keys (FWC) and the British Virgin Islands (ARK), mounding or boulder species survived better than branching species. Of the mounding corals tracked in the British Virgin Islands (ARK), *O. faveolata* had the highest survivorship.

In some cases, wild colonies experienced removal due to the fracturing of the reef substrate, resulting in toppled but otherwise intact colonies (Figure 19.9(a) (b)). Sandblasting of wild colonies was also observed on reefs throughout South Florida and the Caribbean (Figure 19.9(c) (d)). Burial was an issue on wild reefs as well, as evidenced by the amount of sediments and rubble deposited on Florida reefs by Hurricane Irma, burying low-profile corals (Figure 19.9(e) (f)).

Figure 19.9 Wild reefs showed heavy damage in some regions. (a) *D. cylindrus* colony in St. Thomas, USVI and (b) *A. palmata* colony toppled in Culebra, PR; (c) and (d) sandblasting caused tissue loss in wild corals; (e) sand and sediment inundation covering a reef; and (f) formerly healthy *A. cervicornis* thickets reduced to rubble post-storm. (Photos: (a) NOAA RC, St. Thomas, USVI; (b) NOAA RC, Culebra, PR; (c) FWC, Middle Florida Keys, FL; (d) FWC, Middle Florida Keys, FL; (e) UM, Miami-Dade Co., FL; and (f) UM, Miami-Dade Co., FL.)

The impacts of the storms were not limited to individual colonies; they also affected dense coral thickets that were, in some cases, reduced to rubble piles. Off the coast of Sunny Isles, Florida (just north of Miami), a healthy wild staghorn thicket measuring 10 m in diameter was completely removed by Hurricane Irma, leaving only rubble in its place. Meanwhile, in Broward County, Florida, off the coast of Ft. Lauderdale Beach, multiple similar thickets survived with minimal damage, illustrating the variability of storm effects within even a small geographical area (approximately 25 km).

LESSONS LEARNED: DAMAGE PREVENTION STRATEGIES

In light of the impacts observed, several recommendations can be made to improve storm preparations for coral nurseries and damage mitigation in the future:

- *Raising low-profile structures*: in general, structures that were higher off the substrate fared better than structures with low profiles placed close to the bottom. In cases where burial may be expected (e.g., nursery resources deployed within large sand patches), practitioners may consider raising their structures off the bottom either temporarily or permanently, by 0.6–1.0 m prior to a predicted storm or prior to hurricane season. This can be accomplished by raising the entire structure using cement blocks or by raising the corals using tall pedestals.
- *Deeper anchors*: due to sediment movement that lifted tree anchors and led to a complete loss of trees and other floating structures, it is recommended that anchors be installed as deep as practically possible into the substrate, and that anchors should penetrate hardbottom when possible. Deploying trees in hardbottom has the potential added benefit of promoting larval colonization from nursery stock parents to a nearby reef habitat. Structures that sit on the bottom should also be adequately anchored, including blocks, tables, and A-frames. This can be accomplished using rebar stakes, concrete weights, and sand anchors. Attachment to hardbottom, if possible, would limit impacts of sediment movement.
- *Redundant attachment points*: for nursery structures, it is recommended that multiple points of attachment are secured prior to a storm. This could include additional shackles, zip ties, and anchors for floating or low-lying nursery structures. Supplementary duckbill and rebar anchors were identified as particularly important components for securing floating structures and tables, respectively. Even heavy structures can be moved or flipped by water movement, so redundant attachment points are always recommended. To prevent trees with broken or exposed anchors from floating away, UM suggests tethering small groups of nursery trees together with a long line and attaching this line to a large, anchored central weight in advance of a storm.
- *Coral trimming and stock size*: because larger corals on nursery structures were more prone to breakage and entanglement, multiple restoration groups recommended trimming down coral fragments prior to storm season, especially for *A. cervicornis*. The best long-term management strategy is to outplant corals in the winter/spring prior to hurricane season to minimize potential losses. Fortunately, this strategy coincides with the common practice of avoiding outplanting during the warmer months of the year to mitigate thermal stress to new outplants.
- *Avoiding loss of genetic material*: in some cases, entire genotypes were lost from nurseries. To avoid loss of genotypic diversity, it is recommended that practitioners maintain a repository of each genotype from their nursery stock in land-based facilities that are equipped to deal with hurricane impacts. It is also recommended to spread each coral genotype across multiple individual structures, structure types, and nursery locations so that high redundancy is maintained even if multiple structures or entire nurseries are lost. Representative fragments of all stock genotypes can also be outplanted and tagged so that a genetic repository exists in situ, especially in deeper reef sites.
- *Removal of trap debris*: one of the main types of physical damage was caused by lobster traps moving through nurseries from nearby sand patches, breaking and removing nursery platforms. It was recommended that, where possible, restoration practitioners work

with local agencies and fishermen to create a spatial buffer around nursery or key outplant sites where no fishing gear is used, and/or attempt to have fishermen remove traps prior to a storm. For new nurseries, practitioners should consider nursery siting based on the level of fishing, particularly trap fishing, in the surrounding areas, and whether there are natural features like nearby reefs that could help protect the nursery site by trapping the moving debris.

- *Pre-storm cleanup*: much of the observed nursery damage was caused by debris. Many of these impacts may be unavoidable since it is very difficult to predict where debris will originate, as in the case of palm fronds and mangrove litter. However, where possible, practitioners should try to remove or secure any loose structures or items (e.g., old PVC, ropes and lines, tools) from nursery sites that could become debris during a storm.

- *Post-storm triage*: while it is not always possible or safe to return to nurseries immediately following a storm (especially in cases like Puerto Rico, where Hurricane Irma was closely followed by Hurricane Maria), loss of coral stock may be mitigated by returning to a nursery as soon as it is safe. This could allow for faster recovery of buried corals, mending of broken nursery structures, and disentanglement from debris, thus limiting secondary impacts.

- *Nursery and outplant siting*: though seemingly sheltered areas (e.g., inside lagoons) did not necessarily protect nurseries during storm conditions, it may be beneficial to place future nurseries at greater depths. It was noted that nurseries and outplant sites both fared significantly better at depths greater than 5 m and fared best at greater than 15 m of depth. If it is not feasible to maintain a deeper nursery year-round, moveable structures may be placed in deeper water for hurricane season. Alternately, a deep site could be maintained year-round as a grow-out and repository nursery with more frequent maintenance and outplanting from a shallower nursery. If nurseries must be sited in shallow water, it is advisable to consider storm impacts from various directions and all nearby sources of both land-based and ocean-based debris. As mentioned, fishing activity in the area should also be taken into account when siting new nurseries in order to avoid potential sources of debris. It was also recommended that nurseries be sited in areas with finer-grain sand because coarser sand or rubble caused severe sandblasting effects of nursery stock corals. In addition, it is important to consider outplant siting. FWC recommends that corals be outplanted to a distribution of offshore and nearshore sites to maximize overall success and mitigate losses as trade-offs in site selection may exist with various other stressors (e.g., higher potential for bleaching events in nearshore areas that may be conversely better protected from storm events).

- *Storm season protocol*: in Florida and the Caribbean, storms occur on a nearly annual basis. One of the most important strategies is to keep up with maintenance needs throughout the year instead of waiting for the threat of a storm. There is often little time ahead of a storm for nursery maintenance and restoration groups may not have the time or resources to complete storm preparation in time. Keeping up with basic nursery maintenance and increasing maintenance frequency in the months leading up to hurricane season is thus recommended. This includes checking all attachment points, maintaining buoyancy on floating structures, checking anchors, and replacing any nursery components that may appear worn. Keeping fragments in the nursery (particularly those hanging in the water column) at a manageable size where they aren't touching other fragments or nursery structures is a good practice in general, but is especially advisable during hurricane season. This can also be achieved by focusing outplanting just prior to hurricane season.

With some of the recommendations made here come potential risks as well—for instance, raising low-lying structures to prevent burial could be more likely to cause these structures to topple over. Tethering trees together may prevent tree removal but could cause severe damage to corals hitting each other or could create more debris to impact nearby structures if the tether does not hold. Clearly, not all of these recommendations are feasible for every restoration group, and not all recommendations will work for every nursery. Nevertheless, integrating a flexible storm preparedness protocol into restoration practices can help mitigate the impact of a severe storm. With the rising sea surface temperature and sea level comes the potential for stronger and more frequent storms (Emanuel 2005). If practitioners are to perform coral restoration effectively, best management practices must be implemented at every step, and storm preparation and damage mitigation are among the most important to prevent near-total losses (Hernández-Delgado et al. 2018).

CONCLUSIONS

The Ugly

The local impacts of the storms were catastrophic in some cases. Maximum damage was observed in Puerto Rico, particularly in SAM's Culebra nurseries, in which 98% (over 11,000 fragments) of *A. cervicornis* nursery stock perished across 75 non-tree nursery structures (line nursery structures and fixed structures). While 2% of the coral stock survived, none of the nursery structures remained functional (Toledo-Hernández et al. 2018). The severity of this damage is due to the combination of damages from Hurricanes Irma and Maria, which hit Puerto Rico just two weeks apart.

In the British Virgin Islands, ARK experienced the complete loss of their two nurseries. There and in the Dominican Republic, nurseries were entirely removed or severely damaged despite siting in sheltered areas (Little Thatch Island, Punta Cana). Finally, coral genotypes that only existed within nursery stocks have been lost across programs.

Florida also experienced severe losses in some areas. FWC's nurseries in the keys were hit particularly hard. Their nursery in Long Key, Florida, experienced 100% loss of corals with 100% of trees and 66% of block modules completely removed. Remaining modules had no living coral tissue. The same group lost 90% of *A. cervicornis* tissue and 78% of mounding species tissue in their Marathon, Florida, nursery, with 60% of trees lost and 65% of modules fully buried by sediment. Only three modules out of 46 were completely unaffected. In Miami (UM), two of four nurseries lost 100% of their coral fragments and nursery platforms. Moreover, losses to the outplanted and wild staghorn corals were significant. Many Florida reefs with five-to-seven-year-old outplants that were already contributing to reef structure and function lost all outplanted corals, setting back restoration efforts significantly.

The Bad

Storm damages were widespread throughout Florida and the Caribbean. A majority of restoration programs lost at least some amount of nursery resources. Burial and entanglement resulted in the mortality of substantial coral stocks throughout the region. Secondary effects, particularly low light, algal overgrowth, and disease, prolonged storm impacts for weeks to months in some locations. Resuspended sediments remained in the water column and led to severely reduced light levels, and heavy nutrient loads and poor water conditions led to algal overgrowth.

Disease was also seen in many areas a few weeks after the storm(s), thought to be a result of the turbid, sediment-loaded water and exacerbated in corals by sandblasting or fragmentation wounds. Post-storm triage proved to be very difficult and several groups were not able to assess and repair damages for months (and for this reason, it may have been difficult for these groups to differentiate direct storm damage with secondary impacts).

Spatial patterns were not readily apparent, due in part to confounding variation across different groups in storm impacts, nursery structure materials and designs, outplant techniques employed by different groups, and nursery and outplant site characteristics. Beyond that, damages could be variable in severity even within short distances and across identical structures. For instance, two nurseries run by the Mote Marine Laboratory located just 58 km from each other saw very different results in nursery tree loss—their nursery in Summerland Key, Florida, lost 65% of trees and 93% of *A. cervicornis* stock while their Key West nursery lost just 25% of trees and 32% *A. cervicornis* stock to Hurricane Irma.

The Good

Despite considerable damage to restoration at all scales, not all was lost. Six out of 22 programs reported that minimal-to-no damage was observed within nurseries (Table 19.2) and four out of 22 groups reported that minimal-to-no damage was observed within outplanting sites (Table 19.3). Across 22 programs, just over half (21 out of 41) of the nurseries observed *low* impact scores (less than 10% colony loss and nursery impacts) and six observed *medium* impact scores (10–50% colony loss and nursery impacts), meaning that much coral tissue was conserved despite considerable damage.

Depth provided some degree of protection from storm damage, resulting in lower damage levels to nursery and outplanted resources, as well as wild colonies. Wild colonies found deeper than 5 m survived the storms relatively well, including complex and susceptible branching *A. cervicornis* colonies. The patchiness of storm impacts, a common attribute of hurricanes, protected even some shallow habitats. For example, in Broward County, Florida, shallow (less than 10 m) wild *A. cervicornis* thickets were completely unscathed by Hurricane Irma, even when shallow thickets a few miles to the south in Sunny Isles were decimated.

In areas such as Puerto Rico, despite physical damage to colonies and reefs, many restoration practitioners were able to return to both the outplant sites and wild reefs to mitigate the damage shortly after the storms. In an example of strong collaboration after a storm in the United States, NOAA assembled a triage team consisting of volunteers from multiple government agencies, non-governmental agencies, and academic institutions that deployed within weeks of Hurricane Irma to assess damage, remove debris, relocate toppled coral colonies, and re-attach fragments to the substrate.

Groups that were able to return to their nurseries within two weeks following a storm were able to prevent further losses by recovering buried structures, disentangling debris, and replacing lost or broken anchors. Furthermore, though breakage of corals in outplant sites and nurseries may be an immediate loss to the restoration program, it is possible that a portion of these fragments may re-attach and may contribute to population recovery.

Almost two years later, the recovery of nursery resources is well underway in most regions, and lost structures are being replaced. Fragments of opportunity found on reefs are being collected to re-establish nursery stocks. The network of restoration scientists that exists in Florida and throughout the Caribbean proved itself invaluable; genets that might have otherwise been lost from one group's nurseries persisted because of the sharing of coral resources among partners. Restoration scientists are sharing lessons learned gained from their response to these acute disturbances and incorporating and sharing recommendations into their restoration frameworks. The silver lining is that, moving forward, restoration practitioners will be better informed and prepared to mitigate storm impacts.

REFERENCES

Beck, M. W. 2016. "Valuing the natural defenses of coastal ecosystems with a South Florida perspective." *The Nature Conservancy: Assessing Natural Coastal Defenses*.

Beck, M. W., I. J. Losada, P. Menéndez, B. G. Reguero, P. Díaz-Simal, and F. Fernández. 2018. "The global flood protection savings provided by coral reefs." *Nature Communications* 9(2186), 1–9. https://doi.org/10.1038/s41467-018-04568-z.

Blanchon, P. and B. Jones. 1997. "Hurricane control on shelf-edge-reef architecture around Grand Cayman." *Sedimentology* 44, 479–506. https://doi.org/10.1046/j.1365-3091.1997.d01-32.x.

Blanchon, P., S. Richards, J. P. Bernal, S. Cerdeira-Estrada, M. S. Ibarra, L. Corona-Martínez, and R. Martell-Dubois. 2017. "Retrograde accretion of a Caribbean fringing reef controlled by hurricanes and sea-level rise." *Frontiers in Earth Science* 5(October), 1–14. https://doi.org/10.3389/feart.2017.00078.

Dollar, S. 1982. "Wave stress and coral community structure in Hawaii*." *Coral Reefs* 1, 71–81. https://doi.org/10.1002/9781119117261.ch16.

Emanuel, K. 2005. "Increasing destructiveness of tropical cyclones over the past 30 years." *Nature* 436(7051), 686–688. https://doi.org/10.1038/nature03906.

Ferrario, F., M. W. Beck, C. D. Storlazzi, F. Micheli, C. C. Shepard, and L. Airoldi. 2014. "The effectiveness of coral reefs for coastal hazard risk reduction and adaptation." *Nature Communications* 5(3794), 1–9. https://doi.org/10.1038/ncomms4794.

Gardner, T. A., I. M. Côté, J. A. Gill, A. Grant, and A. R. Watkinson. 2005. "Hurricanes and Caribbean coral reefs: Impacts, recovery patterns, and role in long-term decline." Published by: Wiley on behalf of the Ecological Society of America Stable http://www.jstor.org/stable/3450998. Linked references are available. *Ecology* 86(1), 174–184.

Gilmore, M. D. and B. R. Hall. 1976. "Life history, growth habits, and constructional roles of *Acropora cervicornis* in the patch reef environment." *Journal of Sedimentary Petrology* 46(3), 519–522.

Gleason, A. C. R., D. Lirman, D. Williams, N. R. Gracias, B. E. Gintert, H. Madjidi, R. P. Reid, et al. 2007. "Documenting hurricane impacts on coral reefs using two-dimensional video-mosaic technology." *Marine Ecology* 28(2), 254–258. https://doi.org/10.1111/j.1439-0485.2006.00140.x.

Hernández-Delgado, E. A., A. E. Mercado-Molina, P. J. Alejandro-Camis, F. Candelas-Sánchez, J. S. Fonseca-Miranda, C. M. González-Ramos, R. Guzmán-Rodríguez, et al. 2014. "Community-based coral reef rehabilitation in a changing climate: lessons learned from hurricanes, extreme rainfall, and changing land use impacts." *Open Journal of Ecology* 4, 918–944. https://doi.org/10.4236/oje.2014.414077.

Highsmith, R. C., A. C. Riggs, and C. M. D'Antonio. 1980. "Survival of hurricane-generated coral fragments and a disturbance model of reef calcification/growth rates." *Oecologia* 46(3), 322–329. https://doi.org/10.1007/BF00346259.

Hubbard, D. K., K. M. Parsons, J. C. Bythell, and N. D. Walker. 1991. "The effects of Hurricane Hugo on the reefs and associated environments of St. Croix, US Virgin Islands—a preliminary assessment." *Journal of Coastal Research*, Special Issue (8), 33–48.

Jackson, J. B. C., M. X. Kirby, W. H. Berger, K. A. Bjorndal, L. W. Botsford, B. J. Bourque, R. H. Bradbury, et al. 2001. "Historical overfishing and the recent collapse of coastal ecosystems." *Science* 293(5530), 629–637. https://doi.org/10.1126/science.1059199.

Johnson, M. E., C. Lustic, E. Bartels, I. Baums, D. Gilliam, E. A. Larson, D. Lirman, et al. 2011. "Caribbean Acropora restoration guide: Best practices for propagation and population enhancement."

Knowlton, N., J. C. Lang, M. Christine Rooney, and P. Clifford. 1981. "Evidence for delayed mortality in hurricane-damaged Jamaican staghorn corals." *Nature* 294(5838), 251–252. https://doi.org/10.1038/294251a0.

Lewis, C. F., S. L. Slade, K. E. Maxwell, and T. R. Matthews. 2009. "Lobster trap impact on coral reefs: Effects of wind-driven trap movement." *New Zealand Journal of Marine and Freshwater Research* 43(1) 271–282.

Lirman, D. 2000. "Fragmentation in the branching coral *Acropora palmata* (Lamarck): Growth, survivorship, and reproduction of colonies and fragments." *Journal of Experimental Marine Biology and Ecology* 251(1), 41–57. https://doi.org/10.1016/S0022-0981(00)00205-7.

Lirman, D. and S. Schopmeyer. 2016. "Ecological solutions to reef degradation: Optimizing coral reef restoration in the Caribbean and Western Atlantic." *PeerJ* 4, e2597. https://doi.org/10.7717/peerj.2597.

Manzello, D. P., M. Brandt, T. B. Smith, D. Lirman, J. C. Hendee, and R. S. Nemeth. 2007. "Hurricanes benefit bleached corals." *Proceedings of the National Academy of Sciences of the United States of America* 104(29), 12035–12039. https://doi.org/10.1073/pnas.0701194104.

National Marine Fisheries Service. 2015. *Recovery Plan Elkhorn Coral (Acropora palmata) and Staghorn Coral (A. cervicornis)*.

Nedimyer, K., K. Gaines, and S. Roach. 2011. "Coral tree nursery©: An innovative approach to growing corals in an ocean-based field nursery." *AACL Bioflux* 4(4), 442–446.

Page, C. A., E. M. Muller, and D. E. Vaughan. 2018. "Microfragmenting for the successful restoration of slow growing massive corals." *Ecological Engineering* 123(September), 86–94. https://doi.org/10.1016/j.ecoleng.2018.08.017.

Perry, C. T. 2001. "Storm-induced coral rubble deposition: Pleistocene records of natural reef disturbance and community response." *Coral Reefs* 20(2), 171–183. https://doi.org/10.1007/s003380100158.

Toledo-Hernandez, C., C. Ruiz-Diaz, E. Hernandez-Delgado, and S. Suleiman-Ramos. 2018. "Caribbean Naturalist." *Caribbean Naturalist* 53, 1–6.

Williams, D. E., M. W. Miller, and K. L. Kramer. 2008. "Recruitment failure in Florida Keys *Acropora palmata*, a threatened Caribbean coral." *Coral Reefs* 27(3), 697–705. https://doi.org/10.1007/s00338-008-0386-3.

Woodley, J. D., E. A. Chornesky, P. A. Clifford, J. B. C. Jackson, L. S. Kaufman, N. Knowlton, J. C. Lang, et al. 1981. "Hurricane Allen's impact on Jamaican reefs." *Science* 214(4522), 749–755. https://doi.org/10.1086/275028.

20

BOLSTERING REEF RESTORATION EFFORTS: A MULTIFACETED APPROACH FROM REEF RENEWAL FOUNDATION BONAIRE

Francesca Virdis, Bridget Hickey, and Ken Nedimyer

ABSTRACT

Bonaire, a Dutch island in the southern Caribbean, has some of the most pristine coral reefs in the Caribbean, but a pair of powerful rogue hurricanes in 1999 and 2008 struck the coral communities on the leeward side of the island, leaving just sand and rubble in the place of once vast fields of staghorn and elkhorn coral. Seeing what was being done to try to restore reefs in the Florida Keys and elsewhere in the Caribbean, the owners of a local dive resort partnered with Ken Nedimyer and the Coral Restoration Foundation to start a program aimed at jump-starting the recovery of the popular nearshore reefs around Bonaire and Klein Bonaire. This chapter tells the story of Reef Renewal Foundation Bonaire and how the investment and vision of a local dive resort led to the development of a robust, highly successful restoration program that involves multiple dive operators on the island, along with local volunteers and hundreds of recreational divers.

INTRODUCTION

The island of Bonaire has long been known for its untouched nature and pristine reefs. Elkhorn (*Acropora palmata*) and staghorn corals (*Acropora cervicornis*) were once the most abundant and important species on Atlantic/Caribbean coral reefs in terms of building reef structure. This was no different in Bonaire, with the shallow-water plateau formerly densely populated by branching *Acropora* corals (see Figure 20.1). Detailed mapping published in 1985 indicated that both Bonaire and Klein Bonaire's shallow plateaus were home to expansive thickets of *A. cervicornis* and *A. palmata*. Studies showed that *A. cervicornis* comprised 28% of Bonaire's and 13% of Klein Bonaire's shallow reef terrace (see Figure 20.2(a), (b)). This accounts for

Figure 20.1 Old, expansive elkhorn thickets were once commonly found around the island of Bonaire and Klein Bonaire.

over 1.5 million square meters of coral coverage (van Duyl 1985). Local knowledge of these pre-decline populations has also been well documented through photographs and first-hand accounts from the diving population on the island at that time.

With the establishment of the Bonaire National Marine Park (BNMP) in 1979, Bonaire's surrounding reef systems have been well protected from boat anchoring, scuba diving salvage, and spearfishing, but even with these early conservation steps, the population of two iconic coral species, elkhorn and staghorn corals, underwent a precipitous decline. Data suggest the decline in Atlantic/Caribbean elkhorn and staghorn coral abundances were primarily the result of disease (Gladfelter 1982; NMFS 2015), and although disease was the primary cause of the initial decline (Peters 1983), multiple threats acting synergistically or cumulatively likely compounded impediments to the recovery of both populations. Later, two major hurricanes, Lenny in 1999 and Omar in 2008 (see Figure 20.3), decimated these important representatives of coral reefs and turned most of Bonaire's visually-stunning, shallow-water coral thickets into disperse patches and rubble (see Figure 20.4).

Recent studies in Bonaire (De Bakker et al. 2016) show dramatic changes in coral communities on the reef slopes since 1973. Cover and abundance declined for virtually all coral species. The data show a shift from communities dominated by framework-building species (i.e., *A. palmata*) to communities consisting of small, opportunistic species.

Recognizing that the problems at Bonaire's reefs were not unique, the owners of a local dive resort, Buddy Dive Resort, looked for solutions in the Caribbean and the Florida Keys and eventually reached out to Ken Nedimyer and the Coral Restoration Foundation for assistance in developing a coral restoration program on the island. Their shared concerns and hopes for coral reefs turned into a successful partnership, which jump-started the restoration program on Bonaire.

The project began with a small group of enthusiastic divers and one dive operation supporting coral restoration on Bonaire. They worked to obtain the required permits from the local government and garner the support of the BNMP. After two years of work, Coral Restoration Foundation Bonaire (now Reef Renewal Foundation Bonaire, RRFB) was founded in 2012,

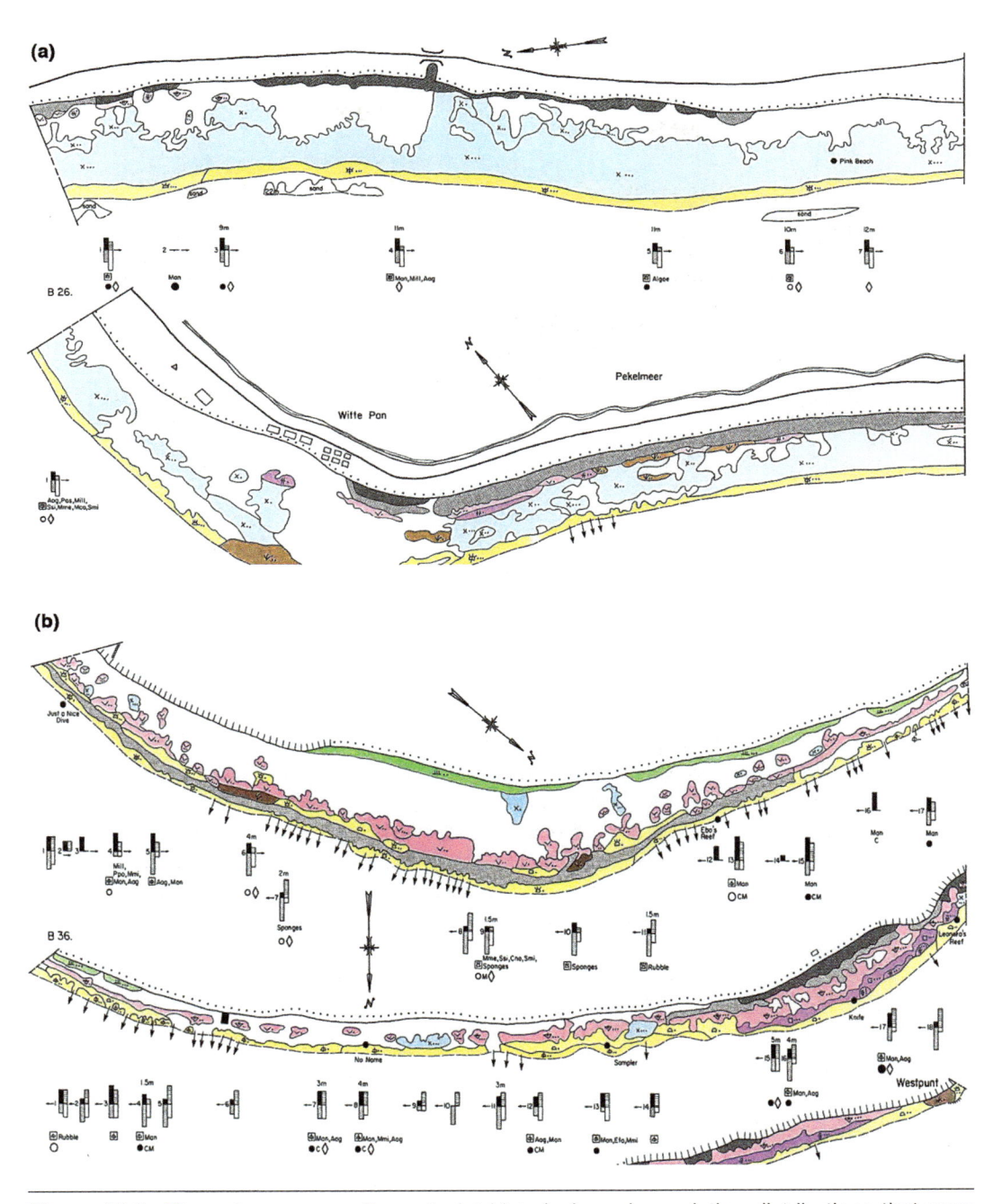

Bolstering Reef Restoration Efforts: A Multifaceted Approach 513

Figure 20.2 These two map sections depict historical coral population distributions that were mapped in the 1980s before most populations declined. This project mapped (a) the leeward side of Bonaire and (b) the coastline of Klein Bonaire. The blue distributions indicate populations of *Acropora cervicornis* and the pink regions indicate populations of *Acropora palmata* (van Duyl 1985).

Figure 20.3 Hurricanes, most notably Lenny in 1999 and Omar in 2008, contributed heavily to the local decline of Bonaire's shallow reefs.

Figure 20.4 Today, most shallow-water plateaus surrounding the island consist of sand and dead coral rubble; these flats provide little shelter for the marine life that once thrived there (photo credit: Reef Renewal Foundation Bonaire).

with the mission of restoring staghorn and elkhorn coral populations along Bonaire and Klein Bonaire by outplanting thousands of nursery-reared corals onto degraded areas of the reef. This initial support was the catalyst in transforming the foundation's mission from a hope to a reality.

After the foundation had been formed and permits obtained, the fieldwork could begin. Under the supervision of the managers of BNMP, corals were collected from widely scattered locations around the island with the hope that it would maximize genetic diversity. These corals—mainly fragments of opportunity or corals at risk—were tagged and taken to the nursery site for processing, where they would become the parent, or broodstock, colonies (see Figure 20.5).

To house these fragments, two in situ nurseries were developed. The first nursery was installed at Buddy's reef and was used primarily for training purposes and education. The second nursery was installed just off the coast of Klein Bonaire and functioned as a production nursery. Both nurseries utilized the coral tree nursery system developed in the Florida Keys by Ken Nedimyer and the Coral Restoration Foundation (see the narrative later on in this chapter for more details on the tree nursery design). With the nurseries installed, and the broodstock corals hanging and growing, it was time to cultivate the corals in the nursery.

After the first year of nursery operations, the team had successfully propagated and grown enough corals in the nursery to begin outplanting (see Figure 20.6). The first year began with outplanting at four different sites.

Criteria for selecting restoration sites included: water depth, water quality, bottom type, size of the area, competitor and predator abundance, wave exposure, current/historical presence of *Acropora*, human activities/impacts, and accessibility (Shafir et al. 2006; Smithsonian 2009; Johnson et al. 2011). These factors have proven reliable indicators, and are still taken into consideration today when selecting sites.

Figure 20.5 A couple of nursery trees at Buddy's reef that are holding the original broodstock corals collected from the reef (photo credit: Ken Nedimyer).

Figure 20.6 Full nursery trees at the production nursery on Klein Bonaire after successful propagation and growth (photo credit: Ary Amarante).

In the first seven years, RRFB has outplanted over 25,000 corals back to the reef at 12 different restoration sites, overseen eight different nurseries that contain 130 trees and over 15,000 corals, and collaborated with five local dive operators that curate nurseries and restoration sites on their house reefs and serve as centers of education for the foundation. (To see all of the foundation's current nursery locations and restoration sites, readers can visit the foundation's google maps page for up-to-date location information, as well as a detailed summary of the number of corals and species housed there.)

TECHNIQUES AND METHODS

Corals are grown on tree nurseries that are suspended above the bottom at a depth of 5–7 m. The tree nurseries are tree-like structures made of PVC and fiberglass that float mid-water, tethered to the seafloor in sandy patches using duckbill anchors, and buoyed at the top with subsurface floats. Trees in the nursery are spaced at least 3 m distance from each other. Corals are attached to the fiberglass branches of the tree with monofilament and aluminum crimp sleeves (see Figure 20.7). Design advantages of the mid-water tree nursery are:

- Ability to move with storm-generated waves, preventing damage to the tree structure or the corals
- Easily lowered or relocated temporarily prior to major storms
- Use of vertical space/reduced area occupation (versus frames/blocks that need extensive horizontal sandy/rubble areas)
- High water-flow circulation between corals and increased growth rates (versus reduced circulation when using blocks/frames)
- Low maintenance (versus high maintenance when using block/frames, having more microalgae accumulation and sand depositing)

This successful design is now being used in a slightly different capacity: as a *pop-up* nursery. A pop-up nursery is a temporary nursery that is installed directly at the restoration site where

Figure 20.7 A coral nursery tree filled with growing *A. cervicornis* colonies; the compact nature and the use of vertical space allows for thousands of corals to be grown densely in relatively small areas (photo credit: Beth Watson).

the corals will be outplanted. This design has shown a few key advantages, the first being that because the corals are grown in the same environmental conditions where they will get outplanted, oftentimes just a few meters from the restoration site, it allows for better acclimation to variations in conditions between sites. The pop-up design also simplifies outplanting logistics. Because there's no need to transport corals, dives can be more efficient, dedicating more time to the actual outplanting and less to harvesting corals from the nursery and preparing them for transport. It also adds flexibility into the dive plans. For example, because *A. palmata* grows in incredibly shallow water, if surges and waves are too great, the outplanting methods are rendered ineffective. With the nursery at the site, if conditions are poor and dives need to be canceled, it can be done without jeopardizing the health of the corals. Finally, once all of the corals have been outplanted, the nursery trees are easily removed, refurbished, and reused at the next pop-up location, leaving no visible trace of what was once there.

RRFB outplants corals using three different methods, dependent upon the available substrate. For hard, rocky bottoms, a two-part marine epoxy is used to attach nursery-reared corals directly to the substrate. Corals are planted in monoclonal clusters, and at least one coral in each cluster is marked with a tag that contains the genotype number and the cluster number. Within the clusters, the individual corals are placed in close proximity to each other so that within a year or two they will grow together into a fused thicket. This method can be used for both *A. palmata* and *A. cervicornis*, and has remained relatively unchanged in the time since it was implemented (see Figure 20.8).

When no hard substrate is available, elevated bamboo structures are built in sand/rubble areas to provide an area to attach corals. Corals are attached to the bamboo using tie wraps, and eventually it grows to cover the entire structure, even growing down to touch the bottom. Each bamboo structure is populated with a single genotype, forming monoclonal thickets (see Figure 20.9).

These square bamboo structures are not the first iteration of this outplanting method, with each new version getting a bit better. The first version of the structure method tie-wrapped

Figure 20.8 A diver preparing the substrate by scraping away algae before epoxying *A. palmata* colonies (photo credit: RRFB).

Figure 20.9 A diver ties *A. cervicornis* colonies to a bamboo structure over sand and rubble (photo credit: David J. Fishman).

A. cervicornis colonies to long rows of rebar elevated off of the bottom for protection from predation and sedimentation (see Figure 20.10a). To avoid the oxidation of the rebar and the unnatural look of long lines, the fiberglass square shape came next (see Figure 20.10b). Fiberglass, however, is an expensive material, so bamboo was quickly adopted as a cheaper and more environmentally friendly alternative (see Figure 20.10c). These bamboo structures are still elevated from the substrate and over time, they become totally overgrown, appearing to be small patches of corals. (see Figure 20.11).

Outplanting logistics and techniques are often considered the bottleneck of restoration efforts, requiring complex logistics, but also divers with good diving skills, dexterity, and precision. To increase the amount of corals outplanted per year and therefore enable larger scale reef restoration, the goal is to reduce costs and the time required to outplant the corals without adversely affecting coral survival and the overall success of the restoration site.

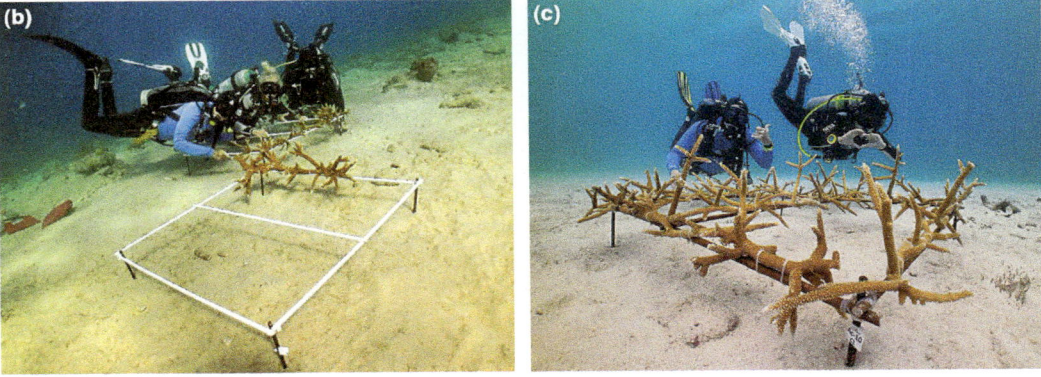

Figure 20.10 The evolution of the structure method of planting took place over the first few years: first (a) with long rows of rebar, then (b) square structures of fiberglass, and finally (c) square structures of bamboo (photo credit: RRFB).

Since 2019, RRFB, in order to increase outplanting efficiency, adopted a new outplanting technique for the majority of the outplanted *Acropora cervicornis* corals. In sheltered reef areas with limited wave and surge exposure and moderately complex topographies, coral clusters are outplanted by wedging and properly stabilizing them between dead corals and rubble, therefore the technique name *wedging* (see Figure 20.12).

Figure 20.11 Corals attached to the structures initially grow over the tie wraps that attach them to the structure in the first couple of weeks; they then begin growing over the entire structure (photo credit: RRFB).

Figure 20.12 Staghorn corals 12 months after being outplanted—*wedging* them between dead corals (photo credit: RRFB).

The newly adopted technique allowed for much shorter outplanting time, increased efficiency, and reduced labor and material (bamboo, epoxy, ties, etc.) costs that were otherwise needed using other techniques. When considering divers with an average level of experience, the technique allowed for an increase in the amount of corals that were outplanted per dive and per diver from approximately 25–30 to 75–80 corals.

Twenty-five genotypes have been collected of each *Acropora* species that RRFB works with, and they are strategically outplanted within restoration sites to increase not only colony abundance, but also genetic diversity at sites. These increases in genetic diversity within close proximity to one another will likely increase the chances of successful fertilization following reproduction events.

NEW TECHNIQUES: BOULDER CORALS AND LARVAL PROPAGATION

In 2019 RRFB started growing three species of boulder corals in its nurseries. These three coral species are among the most common reef-builders that make up Bonaire's reefs—lobed star coral (*Orbicella annularis*), mountainous star coral (*Orbicella faveolata*), and great star coral (*Montastraea cavernosa*). However, over the last decade, in Bonaire as well as throughout the greater Caribbean region, these coral species have experienced a decrease in cover and abundance on coral reefs.

After recent developments in Florida led to breakthrough methods of propagating boulder corals via fragmentation in both land-based and offshore nurseries, RRFB decided to incorporate these techniques to expand its restoration effort with a focus on the importance of species diversity. Using a modified coral tree nursery, which was installed the first week of October 2019 (see Figure 20.13), RRFB populated the four trees with 300 coral fragments. These fragments

Figure 20.13 Boulder coral nursery recently installed at Buddy's reef (photo credit: RRFB).

came from a few initial parent colonies that were collected by RRFB staff, under the supervision of the Bonaire National Marine Park, from four dive sites around Bonaire and Klein Bonaire.

After six months, 90.6% of the fragments survived and 9.3% of them self-attached by growing over the mounting cards (see Figure 20.14).

Over the coming years, RRFB will continue growing and propagating these boulder corals in their coral nursery with the goal of scaling up production to produce thousands of fragments a year. These fragments will be outplanted back onto the reefs at new and existing restoration sites around Bonaire as a part of the ongoing coral restoration effort.

In 2019, RRFB entered an exciting five-year partnership with SECORE International to bring the larval propagation method to Bonaire for the first time. For the past decade, SECORE International has been a leader in the study of the sexual reproduction of corals and has conducted pioneering research to develop novel methods for reef restoration. By taking advantage of corals' natural sexual reproduction, larval propagation has the ability to produce millions of genetically unique coral offspring (see Figure 20.15). During mass spawning events, coral gametes are collected using collection nets and taken back to the lab to be fertilized (see Figures 20.16 and 20.17). The resulting fertilized embryos are placed in floating pools to complete their development and settlement phase on special substrates designed by SECORE International. These are later outplanted onto the reef.

Over the last two years, staff from Reef Renewal Bonaire have attended two training workshops hosted by SECORE International in Curaçao to gain knowledge and practice the larval propagation technique in a hands-on setting with SECORE researchers.

In 2019, RRFB began the first phase of the larval propagation project on Bonaire, which included training workshops, spawning monitoring and collection, and first fertilization try-outs

Figure 20.14 Fragments of *Orbicella annularis* growing and self-attaching to the supporting cards (photo credit: RRFB).

Bolstering Reef Restoration Efforts: A Multifaceted Approach 523

Figure 20.15 Outplanted staghorn (*Acropora cervicornis*) coral colonies spawning in August 2018 at the Jeff Davis Memorial site (photo credit: RRFB).

Figure 20.16 RRFB staff places a net over a boulder brain coral (*Colpophyllia natans*) in order to collect the gamete bundles during an October spawning event at Buddy's Reef (photo credit: RRFB).

Figure 20.17 RRFB Project Coordinator Francesca Virdis inspects the gametes during the fertilization process (photo credit: RRFB).

of *Colpophyllia natans*. During the September and October 2019 spawning events, volunteer divers observed the spawning of dozens of boulder brain coral colonies (*Colpophyllia natans*) and were able to fertilize and produce an estimated 2.3 million *Colpophyllia* embryos, which were released back over the reef. In 2020 RRFB initiated the second phase of the larval propagation project utilizing floating pools to facilitate larval settlement on outplanting substrates.

MONITORING

Data are collected throughout the duration of the restoration process to ensure that both the genetic material and the corals themselves are properly tracked. During the collection process, donor colonies are photographed and GPS locations are recorded in order to be able to track colony health and return to the colony if needed. That corresponding genotype then enters the nursery where it is assigned a label; it is tracked and kept separate from all other genotypes of the same species to ensure the integrity of each genotype.

The outplant monitoring methods that are utilized by RRFB have evolved over time after testing what provides meaningful data and what is realistically achievable on a large scale. Different grant-funded projects have allowed the foundation to test different data collection methods and analysis to find a combination that best fits in both the short and long term.

Every coral that is outplanted is recorded and information about the outplanting is taken—including the date, the diver who outplants the corals, the site location, and the unique code for that cluster. At least one coral from each monoclonal cluster is tagged so that it can be found again later to be monitored (see Figure 20.18).

Figure 20.18 Divers perform in-water surveys to collect qualitative and quantitative data that are integrated with the information extrapolated via image analysis (photo credit: RRFB).

During the project financed by the Nature Fund from the Dutch government, a protocol was developed to monitor 100% of outplants—5,000 corals—split into 200 clusters of corals and spread evenly across four different restoration sites. Pictures of all the clusters over the four sites were taken five times over the course of the first year, then analyzed with CPCe, an image analysis software that was developed specifically for work with coral reef assemblages, using stratified random points to estimate coral cover and mortality (see Figure 20.19). Growth can also be extrapolated later. In addition, divers conducted corresponding in-water surveys at each interval to associate to qualitative observations of predation, disease, competition, etc., to mortality and to help give it context.

At the end of the one year, after completing this analysis for all 5,000 corals that were outplanted, the protocol proved to be too time-consuming on a large scale and over the long term, but provided useful information in this case because a comprehensive look comparing growth, cover, and genotypic performance between sites had not yet been completed. Applying this protocol in the future could still provide meaningful data regarding growth, coral coverage, and mortality if applied instead to a subset of outplanted structures.

Traditional coral restoration monitoring methods, even the ones employed during the Nature Fund project, have focused mainly on the growth and survival of individual coral outplants or individual clusters of outplants. This provides useful information for understanding the success of the individual outplants and comparing the performance of different genotypes in the short term. But over time (3–5+ years), it becomes difficult to keep track of these individuals as they fuse with other outplants of the same genotype, move about after storms, and/or fragment and create additional colonies.

Because of this, over the past few years, RRFB has worked to develop a monitoring protocol that would allow for meaningful and comparable results. To do this, two different time frames

Figure 20.19 Clusters of corals can be tracked and photographed over time to assess the coverage, growth, and health at various intervals (photo credit: RRFB).

are distinguished: short term and long term. Short-term monitoring methods (less than 1–2 years) can include in-water surveys, orthomosaics, and 3-D models. The goal is to assess the efficacy of the outplanting method, the individual coral, or the cluster performance. The long-term monitoring program (3+ years) is more focused on a larger scale, looking at the entire reef site to assess the overall project success. These methods then include orthomosaics, visual observations, and optional 3-D models.

With funding provided by a grant from the BEST 2.0 Programme, this photogrammetric monitoring protocol was developed to monitor the restoration site at different levels. For the coral cluster, it is possible to apply 3-D techniques to monitor growth in addition to giving a clear visual representation of the development of the colony over time. It's an accurate tool and allows for a comparison of metrics over time—volume, surface area, coverage, area base, height, width, and length—which proved to be a reliable ecological monitoring tool for outplanted *Acropora palmata* corals. 3-D measurements are incredibly helpful with corals in which linear measurements are not so helpful (see Figure 20.20).

This method offers multiple advantages over the existing approaches of measuring benthic features in hard-bottom underwater habitats. Measuring corals in situ is in fact labor intensive and time-consuming, especially if the goal is to measure every coral colony at an ecologically relevant scale (Young et al. 2017). Photogrammetric methods increase accuracy by reducing processing time and being highly efficient and cost-effective. Any measurement of spatial features within an underwater 3-D model reconstructed with this method is automated, thus

Bolstering Reef Restoration Efforts: A Multifaceted Approach 527

Figure 20.20 3-D models of individual clusters of corals can provide a finer-scale and more precise analysis of growth measurements; these models can be compared over time and retroactively analyzed to pull out new metrics (photo credit: RRFB).

significantly reducing post-processing time from multiple weeks of human time to hours of computation time.

Thanks to the same advances in imaging and image processing that helped make 3-D modeling a part of the monitoring protocol, orthomosaics of an entire restoration project can be created by swimming over a site and taking hundreds of pictures, then using specialized software to stitch these photos together (see Figure 20.21). The result is a high-resolution image that can be used to compare the growth and health of outplanted corals over time. Like 3-D models, orthomosaics can reduce the number of man-hours needed on-site, collect the same monitoring metrics that had been collected by previous monitoring methods, and offer the potential for the collection of new information retroactively.

Figure 20.21 Orthomosaics can be used as tools to see how entire reef sites change over time; these mosaics function as a snapshot in time and can be analyzed retroactively for new metrics (photo credit: RRFB).

Using orthomosaics, the long-term monitoring program expanded from colony-based monitoring efforts to monitor the site as a whole to get a better understanding of how thicket formation is occurring and how the thickets themselves are expanding or contracting. Orthomosaics provide a useful tool for measuring percentage of cover, expansion, and colony survival at a plot-patch reef scale and assessing changes in community structure.

COMMUNITY INVOLVEMENT, VOLUNTEERS, AND CITIZEN SCIENCE (IF APPLICABLE)

Throughout the first year of the project, the dive staff of Buddy Dive Resort and the resort itself supported the foundation in any way they could: from diving to maintain the nurseries and propagate corals and giving man-hours, tanks, and boats to facilitate the logistics of the fieldwork to providing financial support and raising awareness about the foundation through weekly public presentations and talks around the island. But with the initial set-up phase done, and the restoration efforts underway, it was understood that for this project to truly be successful, it needed as many volunteers and dive operations as possible on board.

Thanks to such a large diving community on Bonaire, both residential- and tourist-based, a large group of people who interact with the reef in a very intimate capacity already existed. Because divers already care about the reefs, they are eager to gain the knowledge and skills to go out and make an active difference. With this in mind, that small group of dedicated divers began training residents and tourists to start expanding the circle of volunteers. Divers were trained in all of the basic tasks and skills required to assist in the everyday maintenance of a coral nursery and the outplanting of corals back to the reef.

By the end of 2013, other dive operators who were concerned about the reefs started paying attention to the growing project and began to reach out to the foundation, asking how they could get involved. A smart, community-based business plan was put into place; dive operators could become involved in the program if they became active Dive Shop Members of the foundation. Dive Shop Members would pay monthly dues to RRFB, and these dues would be used to help keep the foundation's operations running and purchase the materials necessary for the foundation to continue and expand the restoration program. The Dive Shop Members would be trained to set up and maintain their own coral nurseries. After maintaining their nursery and propagating their corals, the Dive Shop Members and their staff would be trained in how to strategically outplant these corals to their house reef—restoring and creating even better dive sites for their guests and divers to enjoy. Dive Shop Members would also be able to teach their own guests how to help out and give back to the reefs. Through a paid certification course, guests become certified as Reef Renewal Divers, which empowers their guests to become volunteers who can help maintain the nurseries and outplant corals. This course not only allows the dive operators to generate revenue, offsetting the monthly dues paid to the foundation, but it also helps them with the task of maintaining the nurseries in general, generating much of the actual manpower of RRFB. Particularly unique to Bonaire, the dive and tourism industries are made up of a large majority of repeat guests who return year after year. Becoming Reef Renewal Divers was a perfect way for these guests to learn more about the underwater environment they appreciate so much and to give back and make a difference for healthier reefs that they could return to year after year.

The turning point for coral restoration on Bonaire was when the second dive shop, Great Adventures Bonaire, joined the effort in 2014. This was the first part of the shift toward community buy-in to the project. Great Adventures Bonaire also brought a unique reef environment and a new demographic of passionate divers to the foundation. Wanna Dive, Tropical Divers, and recently, Beyond the Corals, later gave their support and became Dive Shop Members, expanding the network of committed dive shops on the island to five as of 2020. The Dive Shop Members act as centers of education, involving the community directly and providing a way to be an active part of the solution (see Figure 20.22).

As the involvement grew from local and international dive communities, the education program grew on another front as well. RRFB began regularly hosting university students and recent graduates as part of its internship program. Interns are engaged by working side-by-side with staff in the field during restoration activities that provides them with an educational experience that augments their conservation, biology, and business management backgrounds. Working one-on-one with staff, interns also design, complete, and report on an individual project—expanding on their specific interests within coral restoration, nonprofit management, and conservation biology. In the first five years of the program, RRFB hosted 30 interns from several different countries around the world.

Figure 20.22 Enthusiastic Dive Shop Members before installing the nursery trees that they maintain, propagate corals on, and outplant corals from (photo credit: RRFB).

DISCUSSION

Coupled with the increasing involvement of volunteers, dive shops, and interns, RRFB secured its first larger grants. With all of this working synergistically, it was only natural that the amount of field work that got completed grew as well. The Nature Fund, allocated by the Dutch government, allowed for the outplanting of 5,000 corals, expanding the nursery capacity by over 50%, and the development of a comprehensive monitoring program. This fund also helped two additional dive shops to become members of RRFB, and provided operational funding to buy a boat and car for field work, as well as hiring a second full-time staff member. The fund from the Best 2.0 Programme from the European Commission also provided well-timed support, funding the development of a photogrammetry-based monitoring program and the actual tools and materials needed to implement the program, including the software, camera, training, etc. This program is comprised of reef-scale monitoring in the form of orthomosaics and coral-scale monitoring in the form of 3-D modeling of small groups of corals. Both techniques provide a more diverse set of data about how corals are performing and how the reefscape in general is changing with restoration.

Now with over 130 nursery trees in the water, housing over 15,000 corals, and institutional capacity built by an involved community and critical public funding, the number of corals outplanted to the reef has grown as well. In the first six years since outplanting began, over 25,000 corals have been outplanted back to 12 different restoration sites along the coasts of Bonaire and Klein Bonaire (see Figures 20.23 and 20.24).

The past three years have seen marked jumps in annual numbers—with the number of elkhorn corals planted in 2018, compared to the previous year, increasing by almost 350%. Certainly, all of this growth would not have been possible without the concerted effect of volunteers, funders, and Dive Shop Members. To date, more than 1,100 people have become certified Reef Renewal Divers. With their help and support the foundation has been able to accomplish quite a bit since its humble beginnings.

However, recognizing the urgency and complexity of the threats facing our reefs, RRFB is evolving and adopting a more comprehensive vision. Recognizing the successes of the past five years, RRFB has kept what works, but added new, cutting-edge techniques to give Bonaire's reefs a helping hand on an ecological scale, focusing on not only genetic diversity, but species

Figure 20.23 (a) and (b) Two-to-three-year-old outplanted *A. palmata* can be seen here; these colonies have encrusted bases and some have shown fusion (photo credit: RRFB).

Bolstering Reef Restoration Efforts: A Multifaceted Approach

Figure 20.24 Four-year-old *A. cervicornis* thickets at Tori's reef provide a ledge-like structure for fish to school under (photo credit: RRFB).

diversity as well. These new techniques and species are part of a broader, more inclusive reef restoration approach. Resilient reefs are complex ecosystems relying on both genetic diversity and a diversity of species. Regardless of the species of coral or the technique used to restore them, restoring Bonaire's coral reefs to the resilient, healthy ecosystems that they used to be will continue to be a community effort (see Figures 20.25, 20.26, 20.27, and 20.28).

Figure 20.25 A diver passes over outplanted corals at Jeff Davis Memorial site where their restored area covers around 2,500 m^2 (photo credit: David J. Fishman).

Figure 20.26 A panoramic view of outplanted corals at Jeff Davis Memorial site where their restored area covers around 2,500 m² (photo credit: David J. Fishman).

Figure 20.27 Divers work to complete an orthomosaic of a restoration site to better document changes in the reefscape over time (photo credit: David J. Fishman).

Figure 20.28 A panoramic view of outplanted corals at Jeff Davis Memorial site where the corals have been recorded spawning several years in a row now, completing the natural cycle (photo credit: David J. Fishman).

CONCLUSION—WORDS OF WISDOM FROM THE CASE STUDY

At this critical point in time when reefs are facing such large threats to reef ecosystems, we don't have any time to waste. RRFB agrees with many others around the world that now, more than ever, sharing knowledge and collaborating with other projects is particularly relevant given the urgency of reef conservation and restoration that we are now facing. That is why the foundation is working even harder to collaborate by sharing knowledge and techniques inter-organizationally to achieve restoration results at a meaningful scale and create practical solutions for problems at different stages in the restoration process.

Because resilient ecosystems are diverse ecosystems, RRFB also recognizes the necessity to integrate different techniques that address both genetic and species diversity. Threats to reef ecosystems must be addressed concurrently at different scales and in different arenas which is why reef restoration should also be paired with responsible environmental management.

ACKNOWLEDGMENTS

RRFB would like to thank its dedicated volunteers, its generous donors and sponsors, and its passionate Dive Shop Members without whom none of this would be possible.

REFERENCES

De Bakker, D. M., E. H. Meesters, R. P. M. Bak, G. Nieuwland, and F. C. VanDuyl. 2016. "Long-term shifts in coral communities on shallow to deep reef slopes of Curaçao and Bonaire: Are there any winners?" *Front. Mar. Sci.* 3:247. doi:10.3389/fmars.2016.00247.

Duyl, F. C. van. 1985. "Atlas of the living reefs of Curacao and Bonaire." (Netherlands Antilles).

Gladfelter, W. B. 1982. "White-band disease in *Acropora Palmata*—Implications for the structure and growth of shallow reefs." *Bull. Mar. Sci.* 32:639–643.

Johnson, M. E., C. Lustic, E. Bartels, I. B. Baums, D. S. Gilliam, E. A. Larson, D. Lirman, et al. 2011. "Caribbean *Acropora* restoration guide: Best practices for propagation and population enhancement." *The Nature Conservancy*, Arlington, VA.

National Marine Fisheries Service. 2015. "Recovery plan for Elkhorn (*Acropora palmata*) and Staghorn (*A. cervicornis*) corals." Prepared by the *Acropora* Recovery Team for the National Marine Fisheries Service, Silver Spring, Maryland.

Peters, E. C., J. J. Oprandy, and P. P. Yevich. 1983. "Possible causal agent of white band disease in Caribbean Acroporid corals." J. Invertebr. Pathol. 41:394–396.

Shafir, S., J. V. Rijn, and B. Rinkevich. 2006. "Steps in the construction of underwater coral nursery: An essential component in reef restoration acts." *Marine Biology* 149:670-87.

Smithsonian Institute. 2009. "*Acropora* coral conservation/restoration workshop report." Accessed Jan. 20, 2019.

Young, G. C., S. Dey, A. D. Rogers, and D. Exton. 2017. "Cost and time-effective method for multiscale measures of rugosity, fractal dimension, and vector dispersion from coral reef 3D models." *PLoS ONE* 12(4):e0175341.

21

PUNTA CANA, DOMINICAN REPUBLIC

Jake Kheel and David E. Vaughan

ABSTRACT

Active coral reef restoration in the Dominican Republic was initiated in 2005 and resulted in the eventual establishment of three restoration sites that were distributed in different regions of the country: Punta Cana, Sosua, and Montecristi. Reef restoration techniques and experience were brought in by Counterpart International under the leadership of Austin Bowden-Kerby. The Dominican Ministry of Environment and Natural Resources permitted the restoration activities and local partners supported the restoration work in each site.

In the region of Punta Cana, the Grupo Puntacana Foundation (GPCF) was the primary partner for a new restoration site with support from the private company Grupo Puntacana (GPC). Partners in Montecristi and Sosua were local dive shops. Coral gardening technologies and site selection were provided by Dr. Bowden-Kerby. Later, Dr. Diego Lirman from the University of Miami Rosenstiel School of Marine and Atmospheric Sciences contributed scientific monitoring, oversight, and formal publication of results. More recently, land-based nurseries have been built and experiments in micro-fragmentation have been initiated with support from Dr. David Vaughan and The Nature Conservancy (TNC).

The GPC nursery has experienced continually increasing production from 2005 through today. In addition, the original nursery in Punta Cana has led to the establishment of additional coral nurseries throughout the Dominican Republic and Haiti, the formation of a national coral restoration consortium, and numerous funded projects to expand nurseries, improve techniques, and involve tourists and fisher communities in restoration and tourism activities.

While the original nursery sites in Sosua and Montecristi have experienced difficulties with consistent oversight and management, a new restoration project in Bayahibe, under the management of the Dominican Foundation for Marine Studies (FUNDEMAR), has been successfully maintained for over five years and expanded into new restoration techniques. Coral restoration programs led by FUNDEMAR and the GPCF continue to enhance and provide reliable, fast growing, and genetically diverse species and technologies throughout the Dominican Republic, while promoting the natural recovery of coral reef services including reef-based fisheries, jobs, tourism, and shoreline protection.

The experience of the GPCF is a unique example of private sector involvement and leadership in coral restoration. But perhaps the most important indirect benefits being provided by gardening programs are economic services in the form of employment and enhanced tourism opportunities. In particular, it also provides important lessons for integrating local fisher communities in tourism and conservation jobs.

This chapter will give an overview of the GPCF's experience and lessons learned. The importance of incorporating value-added activities related to coral restoration will be discussed.

INTRODUCTION

Coral reefs in the Dominican Republic support important social and economic services for both fisheries and tourism (Wielgus et al. 2010). Tourism is one of the main economic activities of the Dominican Republic. In 2018, 6.6 million tourists visited the country of roughly 10 million people, representing an increase of 6.7% over the previous year and resulting in revenues of USD 7.5 billion.

Punta Cana (PC) is the most important tourism destination in the Dominican Republic and one of the most important in the Caribbean (World Travel and Tourism Council 2012). The region serves as an economic and employment engine for the entire country, providing an estimated USD 4 billion annually to the economy. Surveys indicate that 58% of visitors select beaches and climate as the main reason for visiting.

GPC is a resort development company that operates in the province of Altagracia, Dominican Republic. GPC is one of the Dominican Republic's biggest and most diversified companies. At the same time, GPC is noteworthy for its strong commitment to the sustainability of its namesake region, Punta Cana.

In 1969, North American investors acquired 48 km^2 of jungle in the eastern side of the Dominican Republic, at that time a very remote location. The area included 8 km of coastline and numerous white sand beaches. They were joined by local investors with the vision of developing tourism in the area. The expansion began in 1971 under the leadership of Dominican businessman Frank R. Rainieri and American investor Theodore W. Kheel.

For almost 50 years, GPC's businesses have had impressive growth and have been among the primary catalysts for the socioeconomic development of the region. Today, GPC consists of a multitude of companies, including hotels, the Punta Cana International Airport, real estate—most prominently the Puntacana Resort & Club and the Puntacana Village—residential communities of over 1,000 homes and condos, 45 holes of golf, restaurants, and aquatic activities. In addition, it ranks as one of the best Dominican companies in terms of employee satisfaction.

The Punta Cana International Airport, one of GPC's main revenue drivers, registered 3.9 million arriving passengers in 2018, more than half of the total arrivals to the Dominican Republic.[1] This makes Punta Cana International the busiest airport in the Caribbean.

Tourism in Punta Cana is heavily dependent on the coastal-marine ecosystem services that are provided by nearby coral reef ecosystems. These coastal-marine areas are major attractions that allow sunbathing on white sand beaches, swimming, snorkeling, diving, deep-sea fishing, catamaran tours, and other related aquatic sports.

In addition, coastal ecosystems provide seafood products served in GPC's restaurants and the region's hospitality industry in general. The presence of healthy ecosystems strengthens the resilience of the Punta Cana destination by protecting tourism infrastructure and services from hurricanes, storms, and floods and by reducing recovery time and expenses, thus supporting business continuity. Coral reef-based fisheries in the Dominican Republic provide protein to over 9,000 fishermen (Wielgus et al. 2010).

Healthy coral reef systems provide an important natural coastal defense against climate change by reducing wave energy, thus helping to protect thousands of people living in the area and hundreds of millions of dollars of coastal infrastructure. Reefs also provide several other

---

[1] Central Bank of the Dominican Republic (2020), *Flujo turístico: Llegada vía aérea 2018* [Microsoft Excel Spreadsheet]. Santo Domingo: Central Bank of the Dominican Republic. Available from: https://www.bancentral.gov.do/a/d/2537-sector-turismo [accessed February 10, 2020].

important ecosystem services (e.g., fisheries, tourism) that contribute to social resilience to climate change.

The climate has had a big impact on coral reefs with a special impact on one of the last major populations of staghorn corals *Acropora cervicornis*. By 2011, approximately 60–70% of these corals were dead or dying and by 2014 over 80% were dead from a combination of factors such as disease, predation, algal competition, and overfishing.

CORAL RESTORATION IN PUNTA CANA

Beginning in 2005, the GPCF, with support from GPC, initiated active reef restoration efforts by establishing a primary nursery and a dozen pilot coral outplant sites adjacent to the Puntacana Resort & Club. The initial experimental nursery consisted of an A-frame and table (Figure 21.1), rope (Figure 21.2), and A-frames seeded with locally recovered fragments of staghorn and elkhorn coral (*Acropora cervicornis* and *Acropora palmata* or together *Acroporid corals*) (Figure 21.3), with approximately ten different genotypes of coral. The nursery was situated in a protected sandy bottom substrate in the dive site known as *El Acuario*.

The site El Acuario was selected by Dr. Austin Bowden-Kerby, representing Counterpart International, for its excellent water quality, existing reef structure, and consistent presence of tourism activities. This site consists of two large reef outcroppings that provide a protected inlet where the nurseries are situated. Despite excellent reef structure and cave sites of interest for divers, the site had limited fish populations and poor coral cover.

Originally three to four in-water A-frame nurseries and one rope nursery were installed in the Acuario dive site. In different years, the number of A-frames has expanded to as many as

Figure 21.1 The initial experimental nursery in Punta Cana consisted of table, rope, and A-frame structures to grow the coral. (a) Here an A-frame with expanding wire to hold fragments. (b) Locally recovered fragments of staghorn and elkhorn coral (*Acropora cervicornis* and *Acropora palmata*), with approximately ten different genotypes, plus other massive corals were grown on the tables.

Figure 21.2 (a) Tables also hold ropes horizontally, thereby suspending staghorn corals above the sand. (b) Suspended ropes using floats and anchors to hold the ropes vertically in the location known as El Acuario.

25 individual frames but never fewer than 15 frames. Similarly, rope frames and tree frames have varied between two and five nursery types in different years. In general, strong currents, wave action, and seasonal storm events have made A-frames ideal nursery structures for the Acuario restoration site. The foundation continues to use rope and tree frames for specific experiments and coral species; however, the vast majority of Acropora tissue is cultivated in A-frames (Figure 21.3). The yearly biomass increase in the nurseries was estimated 8–10 times the original tissue, while 300+ fragments were outplanted to the reef. Mortality on frames and ropes were low (Young et al. 2012) and the primary concerns were damage by tourism activities (anchors damaging frames), predators, wave action, and bleaching.

During the ensuing 15 years, the Acuario site has provided continuous and reliable sources of fragments for reef restoration efforts in the Punta Cana region, while helping to avoid local

Figure 21.3 (a) A-frames made from expanding wire driven into the sand can hold staghorn corals attached with electrical tie-wraps. (b) Growth on the A-frame is thick and rapid.

extirpation of *Acroporid* corals. The site has been by far the most actively and consistently maintained site in the country, realizing continuous outplanting in the Punta Cana region, offering training and public awareness to practitioners throughout the Caribbean, and integrating local fishermen and tourists into restoration activities (see Figure 21.4).

Initially an experimental pilot project, this Punta Cana nursery gradually became an important example of in-water nurseries in the Caribbean, backed by continuous monitoring and scientific oversight. The program has been in place for more than 15 years and has outplanted greater than 15,000 staghorn corals onto reefs where this species had been eradicated previously due to algal overgrowth, overfishing, disease, and pollution (see Figure 21.5).

Figure 21.4 Map of Dominican Republic with the coral nursery locations.

Figure 21.5 Healthy staghorn corals outplanted from a Punta Cana Foundation nursery.

While restoration activities have led to increases of coral cover on local reefs and the recovery of *Acroporid* corals, restoration activities led by the GPCF have also facilitated the widespread expansion of coral restoration techniques in the Dominican Republic. Over a dozen nursery sites were established countrywide with over 20 unique genotypes and the largest genotype tracking effort outside of Florida. Over the last decade, advances have progressed by building long-lasting, hurricane-resistant, steel-bar tables to support nurseries and different culture methods; by adding rope culture, coral tree field nurseries, and land-based nurseries for other species; and by utilizing micro-fragmentation and sexual reproduction.

The GPCF nursery at El Acuario along with the foundation facilities has become a training hub that has received dozens of national and international interns, foundations, government representatives, and practitioners from throughout the Caribbean. The foundation hosted the Association of Caribbean Marine Laboratories annual conference in 2019, which brought together regional scientists and marine managers. The conference included a two-day coral restoration workshop. Mass outplanting events called *Coralmania* have been held on five separate occasions in Punta Cana and other sites, incorporating as many as 35 volunteers for outplanting. The Coralmania events produced between 1,500 and 3,000 coral fragment outplants, depending on the duration and number of participants (see Figure 21.6).

In Punta Cana, efforts have been made not only to restore endangered corals, but to integrate the fisher communities and visiting tourists in restoration activities. With support from the Interamerican Development Bank, the GPCF developed a Professional Association of Diving Instructors specialty diver certification that allowed visiting tourists to contribute to coral restoration while on vacation or visiting Punta Cana. The course, Coral First Aid, was developed with Blue Vision Divers, a local dive operator. The course certified over four dozen visiting tourists. More recently, TNC is expanding the concept of tourist involvement in reef restoration, creating the *Reefhabilitation* project with support from Booking.com. Reefhabilitation will expand and diversify opportunities for tourists to participate in coral restoration activities with initial pilots launching in the Dominican Republic.

Figure 21.6 The GPCF has become a training hub. Here the instructor (Victor Galvan) has disconnected the table top and brought it toward the surface to show the students the elkhorn *Palmata* fragments attached to the cement bases in the nursery located in El Acuario.

Perhaps the most important indirect benefit provided by gardening programs are economic services in the form of employment opportunities for local fisher communities. In 2015, the GPCF helped incorporate the Association of Artisans and Marine Services (ARSEMAR). The ARSEMAR provides a platform for hiring former and current fisherfolk and their families for tourism and conservation jobs. The association is an independent entity that contracts diverse services to GPC and the GPCF.

The GPCF has trained fishermen as boat captains and scuba divers, and has provided first aid training. Fishermen have been certified in coral restoration and hired to maintain nurseries, conduct coral outplanting, and reduce predators on coral nurseries (see Figure 21.7). Fishermen have been engaged in targeting invasive species, such as lionfish. Fisher families have been trained in creating artisanry from invasive lionfish with the foundation facilitating sales and marketing. More recently, the ARSEMAR has been hired to install and maintain mooring buoys, channel markers, and marine infrastructure such as wooden piers and docks. To date, over three dozen fishermen (about one half of the active local fishermen from the community of Juanillo) have been formally trained in different tourism and conservation skills and many work either on a part-time or full-time basis outside of artisanal fishing.

This economic activity was originally made possible by the establishment of the ARSEMAR's and the GPCF's efforts to include fishermen in conservation and tourism activities. Transitioning fishermen from harvesting to gardening has the added benefit of reducing the impacts of unsustainable fishing practices on the reefs that are being restored. It is estimated that each fisherman who is hired as a coral gardener keeps an estimated 12.5 lbs. of parrotfish per day on the local reefs, further improving reef conditions.

This program has also enhanced the local economy by restoring reefs that have become preferred dive sites that are used by local operators and hotels. The consistent presence of tourists at the Acuario site has limited the presence and spearfishing activities of artisanal fishermen. Studies have demonstrated that the Acuario site has some of the highest fish densities in the Dominican Republic, a direct result of coral restoration activities.

Figure 21.7 Fishermen have been certified by the GPCF in coral restoration. Here, trained divers pick and gather fragments of staghorn coral off of an A-frame nursery.

CENTER FOR MARINE INNOVATION (CIM)

The GPCF launched the Center for Marine Innovation (CIM) in 2018 as a center for exploring marine and coastal management, conservation, restoration, and education. The CIM is owned and operated by the GPCF within the Puntacana Resort & Club and works collaboratively with diverse partners, donors, and government institutions to achieve the following objectives:

1. Conduct scientific research and project implementation to support the development of practical tools that help reduce impacts on the coastal marine environment
2. Serve as a national and regional capacity building and environmental awareness training center for conservation and restoration
3. Develop collaborative relationships to improve, scale, replicate, and expand marine conservation and restoration programs in the Caribbean region
4. Develop alternative income generation opportunities for local fishermen and their families
5. Support the development of young science professionals through the foundation's internship program

The CIM sits on a half-acre site and includes a boat dock, classroom space, wet labs, external micro-fragmentation area with 10 raceway fiberglass tanks, two external 7,000-gallon circular retention tanks, an interactive tank hosting local marine species, an internal wet lab with space for 25 aquaria and micro-fragmentation space, 8 m^2 of work space, two work boats, dive equipment room, an ornamental fish nursery, and an administrative area (see Figure 21.8). It also hosted the outreach component and school visits as part of the Arrecifes del Futuro program.

Figure 21.8 Photos of the various points of interest in the CIM.

In 2019 the GPCF received a grant from the prestigious Caribbean Biodiversity Fund in the first round of the Ecosystem-based Adaptation Facility. The three-year project will greatly expand the foundation's efforts in micro-fragmentation, sexual reproduction of corals, and involvement of the local community in coral restoration.

DOMINICAN CONSORTIUM OF COASTAL RESTORATION

Following the early success of the GPCF's restoration activities, numerous restoration sites have been established by different organizations throughout the Dominican Republic with widely varying degrees of success and credibility. Over a dozen sites exist with in-water nurseries, though often without sustainable funding sources or staffing to supervise nursery maintenance or coral health, and with little to no effort dedicated to outplanting. Permitting by the Dominican Ministry of Environment and Natural Resources has been undertaken with little oversight and monitoring of new coral nurseries. By 2014, over 15 coral nurseries were reported throughout the country, though many did not have active oversight, maintenance, or outplanting programs.

The rapid expansion of nursery construction led the GPCF, FUNDEMAR, Counterpart International, and other institutions to lead an effort to create structured standards, parametric-based performance evaluations, and minimum requirements for managing nurseries. In 2017 the partners formed the Dominican Coastal Restoration Consortium as a collaborative effort to better manage coral nurseries and to facilitate the sharing of information and standardization of procedures and protocols in the Dominican Republic. The consortium, though not formally incorporated, was established with specific restoration objectives:

1. Establish a restoration network in the Dominican Republic to develop parametric measures and standardized procedures for nursery setup, maintenance, data collection, outplanting, information sharing, and nursery performance
2. Provide regular monitoring and performance results of the coral restoration programs within the network
3. Establish, maintain, and expand the network of coral nurseries in collaboration with local communities and institutions in order to increase threatened coral species populations, thereby preventing the species from a potential local or regional disappearance

Using the best available data, a set of parameters for the evaluation of each coral nursery has been established and used to gauge the performance of each member nursery. Standardized protocols are available digitally and on a developing platform for data collection, reporting, and information sharing. Training by its member institutions continues to take place, becoming a national and regional training hub for coral restoration and knowledge exchange. Efforts are currently underway to promote the development of similar consortiums in Costa Rica and Honduras.

THE NATURE CONSERVANCY

Beginning in 2015, TNC began to take an active role in bringing increased scientific, technological, and conservation expertise to restoration efforts in the Dominican Republic. In 2018, TNC formally established a *Coral Innovation Hub* in the Dominican Republic as part of its

Caribbean Coral Strategy, with the goal of developing and deploying scalable solutions to improve coral reef health and maximize the benefits that reefs provide to people and nature in a changing climate. TNC serves as a convener and catalyst to develop, integrate, and share the science and technology that is needed for upscale coral protection, restoration, and monitoring—and to put these innovations into action through meaningful community empowerment to promote the long-term recovery of coral reefs in the Caribbean and beyond.

To achieve this goal, TNC engages with organizations, governments, and communities in the Caribbean and across the globe to collaborate, share knowledge, combine resources, and build on one another's achievements. To address this challenge, TNC and partners have launched three Coral Innovation Hubs in key geographic locations across the Caribbean—the Bahamas, the Dominican Republic, and the U.S. Virgin Islands—in order to advance coral science, proactively share expertise, and promote rapid deployment in the Caribbean and around the world.

The Dominican Republic Coral Innovation Hub hired a country director for its coral efforts and has undertaken several important initiatives in collaboration with local partners. Some of the main projects under this Coral Innovation Hub include:

1. *REEFhabilitation*: the REEFhabilitation experience is a hands-on learning adventure where tourists can actively participate in coral restoration. Established by TNC, FUNDEMAR, and the GPCF, and supported by the Booking Cares Fund, this tourism product aims to contribute to scale coral restoration efforts and take advantage of the growing push for socially and environmentally responsible tourism and citizen science experiences.
2. *Aerial mapping*: TNC, local partners (GPCF, FUNDEMAR, and the Dominican Reef Network) and international partners (Asner Lab—Global Airborne Observatory and Planet Dove) are using cutting-edge technology to develop maps that allow visualization of coastal marine habitat in the Dominican Republic. These maps reveal in detail the location and condition of coral reef habitats. With this information available in order to guide conservation efforts, the Dominican Republic became the first country in the Caribbean to use this type of technology, with maps that are guiding coral restoration activities on the southeast coast of the island. This information serves as a baseline to monitor the survival of transplanted corals, observe how they can be affected by climate change, and measure the impact of hurricanes. This product also serves as a guide to define optimal ouplanting criteria to maximize coral outplanting survival and success.
3. *Outreach*: about two times per year, volunteers and multi-partner outplanting events are being carried out by the GPCF, FUNDEMAR, TNC, and partners to transplant thousands of coral fragments to the reef. These massive transplantation events bring scientists, restoration practitioners, and local communities together as volunteers to outplant thousands of coral fragments back to the reef in just a few days. It is also used as an outreach and engagement event with local tourism operators, government, nongovernmental organizations, and the local community.

THE MARINE SANCTUARY ARRECIFES DEL SURESTE

The Dominican Ministry of Environment and Natural Resources formally declared the Marine Sanctuary Arrecifes del Sureste as a marine protected area (MPA) in the Dominican Republic in 2009 under Decree 571-09. The sanctuary is almost 8,000 km^2, along approximately 120 km of the coast and encompasses coral reef ecosystems, several major urban centers, and two of the country's primary tourism centers that receive more than four million visitors annually. The present sanctuary is comprised of an Eastern Zone, a Central Zone, and a Southern Zone (see Figure 21.9).

On February 23, 2018, a renewable agreement for co-management—called the *Acuerdo de Co-manejo del Santuario Marino Arrecifes del Sureste*—was enacted for a period of 10 years. This agreement was a pioneering effort to implement marine management strategies with the direct and active participation of the tourism sector, local communities, and Dominican authorities. The agreement approved three distinct co-management bodies for the sanctuary, collectively referred to as *co-managers*: (1) Unidad Sur, (2) Unidad Centro, and (3) Unidad Este.

The GPCF, TNC, and FUNDEMAR have been the primary local partners who are driving the efforts to develop a co-management plan that incorporates strategies for marine conservation, local communities, and economic development. The other entities that comprise the co-managers of the Sanctuary *Arrecifes del Sureste* are the Ministry of Environment in the Dominican Republic, the Altagracia Tourism Cluster, the Altagracia Hotel Association, The Association of Aquatic Centers, the Central Romana Foundation, the Romana-Bayahibe Tourism Cluster, the Romana-Bayahibe Hotel Association, and the Blue Finance Foundation.

To date, no management plan is in place for waters within the sanctuary boundary, and there is an urgent need for the sanctuary to reduce spatial conflicts, address threats, develop zones for allowable activities, and identify (or purpose) regulations with local stakeholders for implementation. Primary local threats to the waters in the sanctuary include unsustainable tourism activities (e.g., high tourism rates with over 36,000 hotel rooms and numerous marine service providers), unsustainable coastal fishing practices, coastal erosion, increased sedimentation, and reduced water quality from issues associated with coastal development and public utilities (e.g., lack of water treatment facilities).

In the next two years, the waters within the sanctuary will be zoned based on objectives of the management plans, and designed with the best available science, stakeholder consultation, and local knowledge. The zoning framework may include conservation areas (e.g., seasonal and no-take zones), recreation and tourism, fishery, and transport areas—each with a regulatory framework and management strategy. Engagement and support of stakeholders and local communities is essential for a transparent, participatory approach.

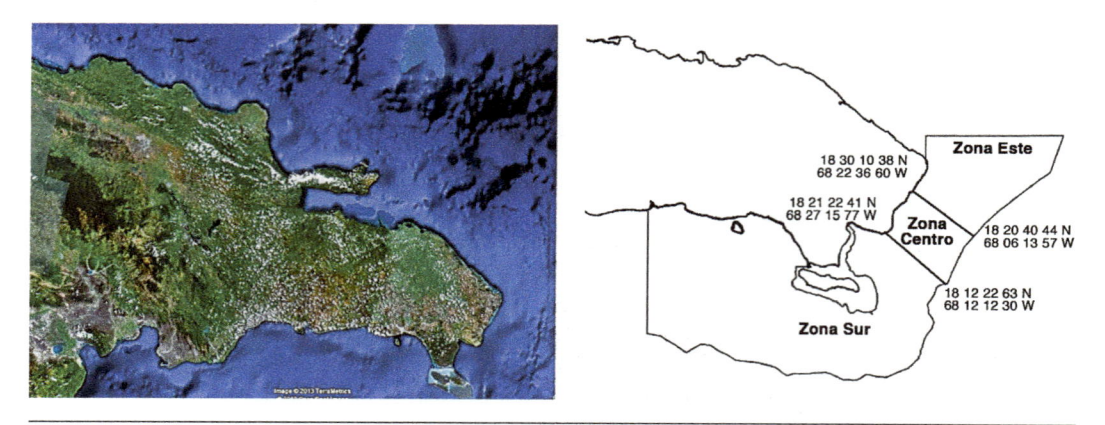

Figure 21.9 The Marine Sanctuary Arrecifes del Sureste was declared an MPA in the Dominican Republic in 2009 under Decree 571-09. The sanctuary is almost 8,000 km^2, along approximately 120 km of the coast.

The three co-management bodies have agreed to develop a management plan with active participation of local stakeholders. The management plan will include all areas of *Arrecifes del Sureste*, as well as habitat information to inform decision makers and stakeholders for an additional 4.5 km of coastal zone of Cabeza de Toro.

The Marine Sanctuary Arrecifes del Sureste represents the formalization of initial restoration efforts into a more comprehensive regional management plan. The sanctuary also demonstrates that early restoration efforts have proven to be consistent over time and have led to new and expansive efforts involving new partners in marine conservation. Specifically, early experiments in restoration have led to greater private-sector investment of time, resources, and political capital in protecting coral reefs.

DISCUSSION AND CONCLUSIONS

The Dominican Republic has been one of the prominent leaders in coral restoration in the Caribbean with the GPCF serving as a pioneer and active promoter of coral reef protection. Leveraging support from a private tourism company, GPC, the foundation is expanding restoration efforts by establishing new sites across diverse geographic locations, expanding partnerships, and using new and emerging restoration techniques. The involvement of the private sector has been a crucial aspect of coral restoration in the Dominican Republic. In addition to providing early seed capital, the private sector has allowed restoration to involve local fisher families and fisher communities by integrating them in conservation activities and tourism-related jobs.

More important, the foundation has committed to a collaborative strategy, involving key partners such as FUNDEMAR, TNC, and others in order to dramatically scale up restoration efforts with multi-species and technologies as a climate-change adaptation strategy. The goal is to restore corals and build the climate resilience of the Punta Cana community and communities across the Dominican Republic and the Caribbean region.

ACKNOWLEDGMENTS

To all of the people, entities, and organizations that helped to make the Dominican Republic a coral restoration reality.

REFERENCES

Bowden-Kerby, A. 2014. "Best practices manual for Caribbean *Acropora* restoration." *Puntacana Ecological Foundation*.

Weilgus, J., E. Cooper, L. Burke, and R. Torres. 2010. "Coastal capital: Economic valuation of coral reefs in the Dominican Republic." *World Resources Institute*. https://www.wri.org/publication/coastal-capital-economic-valuation-coral-reefs-dominican-republic.

World Travel and Tourism Council. 2012. Travel and Tourism—Economic Impact Dominican Republic WTTC. https://issuu.com/aibmarketing/docs/wttc_tourism2011.

Young, C. N., S. A. Shopmeyer, and D. Lirman. 2012. "A review of reef restoration and coral propagation using the threatened Genus *Acropora* in the Caribbean and Western Atlantic." *Bulletin of Marine Science* 88(4) 1075–1098.

SECTION IV

The Future of Coral Reef Restoration

22

EMERGING TECHNOLOGIES

David E. Vaughan and Ken Nedimyer

ABSTRACT

Technologies for coral restoration have been emerging quickly in the past few decades—and particularly in the last five years. In the beginning, coral restoration was simply the act of moving and dropping corals in predetermined locations in the ocean. Coral restoration has evolved significantly to an active process that includes the breaking of fragile branching corals (fragmentation), the growing of the massive coral species in nurseries on land using micro-fragmentation, the adoption of micro-fragmentation at sea, and continuing advances in the sexual reproduction for larval outplants. These techniques have all paved the way for new technologies in the future. We should strive to create emerging technologies to advance the production of corals for restoration at a larger scale with decreasing costs of production. In addition, we need new technologies to make advances in outplanting techniques and long-term monitoring. If we look at other types of aquaculture for species that are used in seafood production, we will see numerous technologies that can be adapted for coral to be grown at commercial scale. We will provide some of our insights for the purposes of stimulating new ideas with the new and innovative young technology developers. We can't wait to see what technologies will soon emerge.

INTRODUCTION

We, the authors of this chapter, have been pioneers in the development of—and transition to—active coral reef restoration. There was a time when coral restoration work was usually confined to vessel groundings and anchor damage. The technology was mostly comprised of techniques for the re-attaching of affected corals and stabilizing the reef itself in order to allow for natural recovery to take place over time. Since that time, we have witnessed great advances in coral restoration—through research and development, by trial and error, and some by mere accident. Presently, we sit perched to make more advances in both the equipment and refinement of new methods, so that corals can be grown for restoration at the scale needed and at the economic viability required. In this chapter we will explore emerging technologies for active coral restoration, including fragmentation and fragment growth, sexual recruit survival, field vessels and vehicles, substrate materials and adhesives, artificial reefs, the concept of the *pop-up* nursery, and increased production at scale.

NEW WAYS OF FRAGMENTING

In previous chapters asexual reproduction methods were covered and new ideas were mentioned that will be discussed more in-depth here. These newer ideas/techniques include: Frag-N-Fly, manual micro-fragmentation, field micro-fragmentation, and multiple cuttings. Fragment size and growth rates will also be discussed.

Frag-N-Fly

This technique allows for the reduction or elimination of the land-nursery phase. The cost savings for this procedure is tremendous. Most practitioners view land-based nurseries as too expensive due to the cost of waterfront property, permits, and operational costs—all of which are particularly daunting to early start-up operations. Land-based nurseries do have the advantage of being able to easily use electric saws, lights, pumps, etc., which are certainly harder to use underwater. Land-based nurseries also continue regardless of weather or sea conditions that can leave dive boat vessels in port. They also allow for unlimited work time without worry of dive-time limitations, and they can utilize the non-divers and less-trained volunteers. If the amount of time a coral spends in a land nursery is simply shortened, the cost per coral is less. For example, if a normal land-nursery phase for a coral is a full year and is then reduced to three months, there is now four crops per year; at one month, 12 crops per year; at one week, over 50 crops per year. Because the land-based nursery has the same fixed costs, shortening the time that is required for a coral to stay in the land-based nursery becomes one of the best ways to get to scale (Figure 22.1). This is where the concept of *Frag-N-Fly* comes in—where the coral is fragmented to the appropriate size and then outplanted very quickly or *on the fly*. In some situations, the coral can be fragmented on the boat near the outplant site, as demonstrated in Belize at Fragments of Hope (see Chapter 11), where their catamaran acts as a floating cutting platform and the cut fragments are returned directly back to the reef. This utilization of a stable vessel for cutting, combined with direct planting, has become very successful (see Figure 22.2).

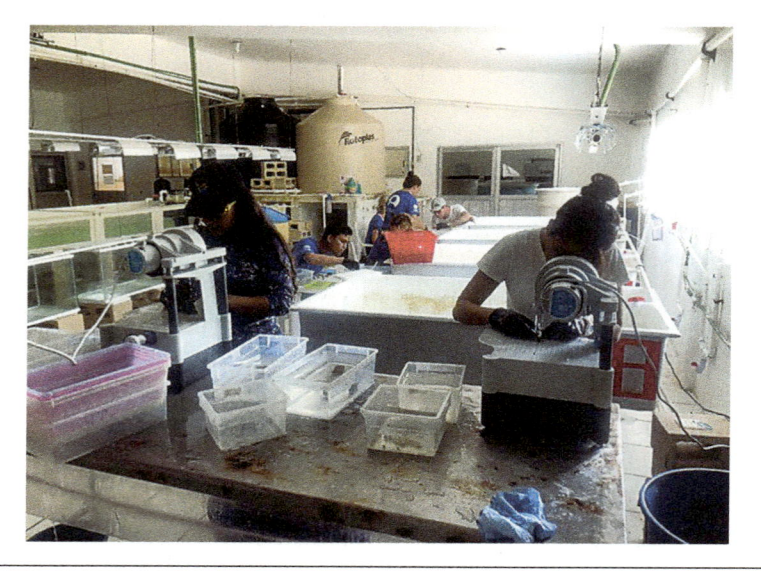

Figure 22.1 Small micro-fragments in a land nursery being cut on two diamond bandsaws, then rinsed and dried for attachment. They are then ready for immediate transport to either the land nursery tanks or into the field (photo at Puerto Morales, INAPESCA coral system).

Emerging Technologies 553

Figure 22.2 Vessel with small diamond bandsaw to provide fragmenting and micro-fragmenting in the field above the outplanting site (Belize-Fragments of Hope; photo by D. Vaughan).

Manual Micro-Fragmentation

The use of a set of manual clippers for either top-side cutting on a vessel or underwater cutting in a field-nursery is *manual micro-fragmentation*. This can be accomplished with simple hand-cutting tools to cut the outer growth area of a nursery-grown plug, or similar growth substrate, taking advantage of the thin new tissue from donor or brood-stock colonies. This allows field-nursery operators to use micro-fragmentation technologies without the required land-facilities costs. In a field nursery, the operator can cut the fragment either on the vessel or underwater, and then deposit it right back onto the nursery equipment (Figure 22.3).

Figure 22.3 Hand clippers used for manually cutting micro-fragments in the field (photo by D. Vaughan).

Multiple-Cutting in the Field

This emerging technology is one of my favorites as it can be implemented without any additional land equipment or costs. Furthermore, it can potentially increase the number of corals replanted exponentially. This can be done by simply using the existing field outplanted colony as a repeatable nursery tissue donor for *continuous broodstock* (Gonzales et al. 2018). Using these first fully grown outplants as the secondary nursery provider continues the potential for multiple fragments from the field outplants. The field outplant, if used for a second cutting or continued cuttings as a donor, helps produce fragments in the same location from recent outplants. This reduces travel distances, reduces the time and cost to grow the earlier stages, and increases the total number produced from the original planting. If every outplanted colony is used again in a year for clippings of 10 more fragments, and again after an appropriate amount of time to heal and grow back, you have a perpetual coral production machine. Theoretically, if 10 more fragments are possible after approximately two to three months, then in only 10 years that coral colony would produce another 100 colonies. Each of these, in turn, could do the same in a few years and fill in a reef over a decade of outplanting (see Figure 22.4).

Figure 22.4 Multiple-cuttings from a large elkhorn that was previously planted—now becoming the second nursery tissue by providing cut tips that are immediately planted alongside (circled). Growth of new colonies one year later are second generation and have the potential for more multiple-cuttings (bottom). (Cancun, CONAP and INAPESCA) (Photos: top, D. Vaughan; bottom, J. Gonzales and C. Padilla-Souza.)

REVISITING FRAGMENT SIZE

What is the smallest size fragment possible to cut and still thrive? One single polyp is the most likely answer today, but in the future, who knows? This will also depend on more accurate cutting tools as can be seen in other industries such as plant tissue culture and possibly by using automated cutting methods. Size is an issue where the donor tissue quantity is limited. In areas where there is substantial tissue to use (Belize, Indonesia, Australia), this may not be an issue at all. But in areas where corals have been reduced in numbers, and there exists permitting limitations/restrictions for taking more living tissue out of the wild, then cutting smaller pieces may be a future advancement. This could be especially important if a certain surviving strain or new sexually produced genotype or special cross is used to try and make as many new colonies as possible and as soon as possible. Presently, we use diamond bandsaws that were originally developed to cut coral rock into small jewelry pieces for earrings and bracelets. Future equipment may include laser cutting tools for industry or medical surgery. Robotics for cutting and automation for the procedures that are now done manually are also future possibilities.

REVISITING FRAGMENT GROWTH RATE

The optimization of environmental growing conditions will make the culture process even faster. This optimization will depend on understanding the biological mechanisms that result in faster growth and the ideal water quality parameters for this growth to occur. As mentioned before, aquaculture operations for other marine species must have improved growth rates and growing conditions first in order to optimize the speed and uniformity of growth rates. Environmental growing conditions can be optimized easily on land nurseries. Temperature control, salinity levels, pH, and the amount of calcium, alkalinity, and minor elements can be controlled. All home reef-tank aquarists watch these parameters closely and are adding calcium, iodine, and other micro-elements as you would vitamins and minerals for any animal feed; however, in this case, it is part of the water media. Lighting has been a huge item for reef-tank owners and public aquaria. Optimization of LED lighting and the control of light hours and spectrum has made an entire industry of equipment suppliers and their businesses abound.

FEEDS AND SUPPLEMENTS FOR CORAL GROWTH

If you have ever seen the artificial food isle in an aquarium store or are familiar with the size of the commercial feed products for aquatic organisms, you know the importance of feed and supplements. Aquatic organisms that are harvested in aquaculture—such as fish, clam, and oysters—must eat to survive. Consequently, feed and supplements are required in these aquaculture operations. Most reef-building corals, while they do filter food in the wild, do not have to physically eat in order to survive due to their partnership with the zooxanthellae algae that live symbiotically within them. The zooxanthellae live within the coral polyps, using sunlight to make sugar for energy that is transferred to the polyp, thereby providing nourishment. The coral polyp, in return, provides carbon dioxide to the algae, as well as a safe structure to live within. Therefore, appropriate lighting is extremely important for land-based nurseries. In all field nurseries, ambient sunlight is a given and is a natural supply of plankton, for filter-feeding is provided by Mother Nature.

Corals can survive with appropriate light, but may grow faster and hardier with food. In most land nurseries, natural sunlight alone provides the nutritional needs—only a few operations add supplemental feed. The quandary for land-based nursery operators is that supplemental feed for corals is general in nature and not a priority product for feed manufacturers because the demand is small relative to feed for other aquaculture species. Supplemental feed formulas tend to be for the aquarium trade and based on general theories of coral feeding preferences and less on actual research and development. For example, in the wild, many corals consume natural plankton such as copepods as their main diet and size preference—but that is not what is sold in the marketplace. Many formulas include ingredients such as generic (not species specific) phytoplankton that is too small for corals, egg yolk, brine shrimp, fish eggs, and fillers, many of which are never found as a source of nutrition for corals in the wild. Supplemental feeding of coral has shown potential in captive aquaria. For example, experimental trials with encapsulated aquaculture diets of shrimp larvae and brine shrimp have demonstrated appreciable growth in corals compared to when they grew with light alone. However, short-term feeding trials in small numbers of experimental tanks show that the logistics of large-scale production have issues that need to be considered. The addition of artificial or natural feeds to the culture tank now introduces the problems of wastes, discharge, and cleaning—like any other aquaculture feeding operation. The use of newly hatched brine shrimp that are native to the Great Salt Lakes into tanks that discharge into local coastal Atlantic and Pacific Ocean waters may be problematic because non-native species will then be introduced into local waters. There are many ways to filter, capture, and treat water before discharging it back into the environment, or a fully closed system can be used in which no discharge is created. Many *start-ups* may not have these capabilities or experience to handle the waste/discharge products effectively from the beginning, which could tarnish the entire industry.

Within the coral nursery industry, nutritional advances will hopefully be made, but because this industry tends to purchase feed in ounces (rather than pounds or tons as in other aquaculture industries), it will be hard to draw the attention of the commercial feeds industry research and development. Appropriate feed for tropical corals is definitely an area that needs to emerge if we want corals to grow more quickly for restoration purposes—or we will be left to use the generic feeds used in the home aquarium trade.

INCREASING THE SURVIVAL OF SEXUAL REPRODUCTION

In marine aquaculture, many types of fish and shellfish begin life in the tanks of a hatchery. This is where the fish and shellfish are spawned, hatched, and cared for. They remain at the hatchery until they are large enough to be transferred to a fish or shellfish farm, or released into the wild as part of a stock enhancement program. Commercial fish and shellfish farms require a steady, predictable source of juveniles from hatcheries in order to stay in operation. Many technological improvements in marine aquaculture production happens in the hatchery. This includes the maturation of adult broodstock out-of-season or on-demand, which is accomplished by controlling the environmental conditions such as temperature, seasonal light levels, lunar cycles, etc. In these aquaculture industries, many have tried to sidestep the land- and field-nursery stage and only add fertilized eggs or larvae to the ocean mix. This direct release of eggs and larvae into the ocean mix may not be the *best bang for the buck* since there is no way to determine the survival rate—and even Mother Nature's survival rate is low. For coral restoration efforts, mass spawning collections, larger larval-rearing vessels, and innovative ways to direct settlement onto predetermined reefs have all had some success and will continue to improve. The race is to do this in scale and economically.

The combination of using sexual reproduction for genetic diversity and for specific crosses should be coupled with improved ways to multiply these new, and possibly resistant, strains in sufficient numbers for nursery and outplanting purposes (see Chapters 8 and 9). All other marine aquaculture operations for fish and invertebrates have made their advances using these tools. The tools include: making genetic crosses, selecting for resilience, and creating genetically diverse individuals in the hatchery and nursery.

VESSELS AND VEHICLES USED IN ACTIVE CORAL RESTORATION

Predictions of the future include new styles of vessels that are not just adapted center-cockpit sportfishing vessels, but ones that will look more like commercial catamarans and barges. Vessels should be developed with larger payload capacity (not just a number of plastic buckets) and even larger, commercial style *live wells* for keeping corals alive and acclimated to local site conditions. Vessels with moving platforms or sections that can be lowered into position to provide corals to the nursery or planting personnel without requiring them to come up to the surface may become the future normal. A likely alternative that would improve field operations is to bring live corals up on a flooded platform to the working vessel where non-diving staff can clean, cut, or cement the corals in a comfortable, shaded area on deck. Underwater vehicles such as transport sleds, underwater scooters, etc., may become a working under-water transportation standard. Ideas and inspirations should be looked at through the marine technologies industry and the commercial fisheries and aquaculture industries. Technologies, equipment, and vessels for marine exploration are becoming available at an affordable level and could soon be modified and customized for reef restoration at scale (Vaughan et al. 2019).

SUBSTRATES AND ADHESIVES FOR CORAL ATTACHMENT

Coral producers are constantly looking for a better substrate to which they can attach the coral, along with a better adhesive to ensure the attachment. Substrates of concrete, ceramics, slate, and stone materials—of different shapes and sizes—are used around the world to attach a coral fragment to a base of some sort for handling. Some bases are made locally by hand, using concrete, and some are commercially produced imported ceramics which have the problem of scale to produce large numbers and end up having high costs. The bases are called plugs, pucks, and/or cookies and are currently used to describe various substrate sizes and shapes that are used in active coral restoration around the world. For example, pucks are made from concrete that is formed in Styrofoam cups and actually look like hockey pucks when ready to use as a substrate. Plugs have stems or projections on the underside to facilitate attachment to the reef structure. New development of hooks, pins, rings, and other devices are being invented to quickly attach coral to whatever you are attaching it to. The requirement of any substrate to be glued, cemented, or attached to the reef or hardbottom has strained the imagination of existing glues, epoxies, and cement mixtures—all with costs and speed of curing as diverse as the practitioners who use them. Hopefully new innovations will emerge.

MODULES AND COMPONENTS FOR TRANSPORTATION

Taking a lesson from the transportation industry for trans-modal shipping should be a direction for coral culture as well. The handling of transportation goods using pallets and containers could be a great model for the handling of corals from hatchery to nursery, nursery to the field, and onto vessels; special vehicles will help this industry to lower their costs, labor, and handling. Eventually, we can expect to see patch reefs and whole reefs being made and transported to the site—hopefully, in the near future.

INNOVATIVE AND EMERGING CORAL NURSERIES

The Pop-Up Nursery

This strategy and technique have had many reef enthusiasts interested in growing the corals in a nursery adjacent to or as close to the final outplanting location as possible. The term *pop-up nursery*, and the idea for it, was inspired by talks given at the November 2017 meeting in Ft. Lauderdale by Tom Moore from the National Oceanic and Atmospheric Administration and Dr. Andrew Ross from Sea Scape Caribbean. The concept presented was that a pop-up nursery is a midwater nursery structure adjacent to the outplant site that can be as simple as a piece of rope or a piece of bamboo onto which coral fragments are attached and allowed to grow. Once the corals have grown to a sufficient size, conceivably the entire structure could be outplanted onto the adjacent reef.

At the 2018 Reef Futures conference in Key Largo, I (Ken) teamed up with Andrew Ross and Bill Precht from Dial Cordy to present a broader application of how pop-up nurseries could be deployed as an effective, time-saving restoration tool. The presentation suggested a new way to design a restoration program where instead of growing most of the corals in large nurseries and transporting them by boat to a restoration site, the corals would be grown adjacent to the restoration site on midwater pop-up nurseries. These pop-up nurseries would be deployed temporarily at any particular site, and the structures themselves could be designed to grow a variety of different corals for different outplant needs (see Figure 22.5).

One simple design would be a biodegradable structure to which branching corals are attached and allowed to grow. The size and spacing of the corals would be such that the corals would quickly overgrow the structure, eliminating the need to clean anything during the grow-out period. The duration of the grow-out period will vary depending on the species, water depth, starting fragment size, and water temperature, but ideally the structure would be ready for outplanting at the end of a year. Outplanting would involve removing the floats and the tether lines, and laying the entire structure down on the reef at the targeted restoration site. If the structure is made out of biodegradable rope or segmented bamboo, it can be wrapped around features on the bottom to help hold it in place. If the structure is solid, such as a solid bamboo rod, it can be placed in natural depressions or gullies or it could be attached to the bottom or other structures with biodegradable rope. Prior to outplanting the structure, some of the branches of the coral could be pruned from the structure and used to populate another structure that will utilize the same tether line and the same float. This would allow multiple, successive deployments of pop-up nurseries at the same site using the same hardware and corals.

Another design would utilize either a polypropylene rope or a bamboo rod as the growing medium, and instead of outplanting the structure, corals would be pruned from the structure and outplanted onto the adjacent reef. Corals would be attached to the structure in such a way that they would overgrow the structure, eliminating any need to clean it. For most branching corals there could be one or two harvests per year.

Emerging Technologies

Figure 22.5 Example of a *pop-up* nursery of staghorn corals (photo by Ken Nedimyer).

Pop-up structures could also be designed to grow micro-fragments of nonbranching corals. These micro-fragments could then be outplanted onto the adjacent reef in clusters of identical genets so that they could fuse to form larger coral heads. Micro-fragments could be generated at a land-based facility, at a field nursery, or possibly at the site using corals of opportunity or corals that were produced on other pop-up nursery structures.

The advantages for using on-site pop-up nurseries over traditional regional nursery methods include:

- Greatly reduced maintenance time (virtually no cleaning after the first year)
- Reduced transport time and distance to the restoration site (meters instead of kilometers, minutes instead of hours)
- The corals grown on-site will adapt to local micro-biome of the reef before being outplanted, reducing stress to the coral and presumably increasing survival of the outplanted corals
- Low-cost materials
- Expedited outplanting when deploying the entire structure
- Accelerated growth rates (comparable to other midwater structures)
- Can be deployed in a wide variety of depths and water conditions. The structures bend with the waves, allowing them to be deployed in areas that receive extreme weather from time to time.
- Predators such as snails, worms, and crown of thorn starfish have a difficult time preying on the corals that are suspended midwater
- The individual structures can be spaced out to eliminate any entanglement hazard to megafauna

The Lay-Down Nursery

This strategy and technique have been shown to work with braided line nurseries by Austin Bowden-Kerby in the Dominican Republic and by Lisa Carne in Belize. Here, staghorn species are tied, wrapped, or inserted in between the braid strands of the poly rope and allowed to grow to size. Then the whole rope with its attached corals is laid out on the bottom as one planted line, using the whole string of corals (see Figures 22.6 and 22.7). If the line is actually grown at the location of the final plant, it is a *pop-up + lay-down scenario* and can save on transport distance, along with time and planting labor. The downside right now is the use of polypropylene or plastic rope and the stigma of putting more plastic in the ocean. Emerging biodegradable materials or equipment used for this process will go a long way in the future reduction of both costs and labor, while also being eco-friendly.

Figure 22.6 Lay-down nursery with staghorn corals connected with nursery line (Belize, Fragments of Hope, photo by D. Vaughan).

Figure 22.7 Staghorn coral nursery line pegged down on the bottom as a final plant (Belize, Fragments of Hope, photo by L. Carne).

The Transportable Nursery (Nursery-in-a-Box)

Land nurseries have always been looked at as too expensive, and were therefore ignored as a viable option. This was because early land-based nurseries were primarily developed in universities, agencies, or marine laboratories and could cost millions of dollars. Small-to-medium land-based nurseries can be made more simply and similar to small-farmer shellfish nurseries. A simple nursery needs basic components: a water source and pump including a general filtration, treatment, and distribution system that serves an array of coral raceway nursery tanks. A well-conceived size of operation can then be designed and engineered for the proper flow rates, pipe sizes, valves, fittings, and pumping requirements. These can be planned and designed by professionals and run by practitioners or culturists without any aquatic design experience and transported to a location for just thousands of dollars instead of millions. It can be fully created with parts purchased and constructed at a professional location—including the water supply system—and then transported in a shipping container to a remote or island location for installation. Once the container has arrived at its destination, the nursery can be set up again in just days, rather than months. Once the nursery is assembled, the empty shipping container can be used as an office, as part of the laboratory, for storage, or to even house live corals through hurricanes and otherwise disastrous events (Vaughan, personal experience) (Figure 22.8).

Figure 22.8 Transportable coral land-based nursery.

INCREASING CORAL PRODUCTION *AT SCALE*

How fast can you increase coral production at scale? This may depend on how quickly fragments in the land-based or field-based nurseries can grow and then get outplanted to the field with good survival. Decreasing handling time and/or distance from the final locations will help with the cost of labor. Automation may become a future player, as is seen in the land-nursery production of plants and animals in agriculture and aquaculture. Greenhouse production of plants in trays should be the best parallel example of how coral nurseries can emerge with newer and faster technologies. Large plant nurseries utilize tables with containers for growing, watering, and feeding—many of those operations include automatic sprinklers, automatic control of fertilizers, temperature, lighting, shade covers, etc. Many of these processes, equipment, supplies, and procedures could be implemented in land-based coral nurseries. Field nurseries for corals should also follow technological advances that have emerged in agriculture in the last 100 years and aquaculture in the last 30 years. Aquaponics is most likely the closest to land-based coral nurseries and the most recent to improve technologically for automation and optimization of growing conditions, maintenance and handling, and harvesting.

On-Site Population Enhancement

Ken Nedimyer proposes that another potential *simple* way forward to get to scale is the enhancement of existing coral reef populations or patch reefs. Three potential approaches are now being tested as strategies for easily increasing existing coral numbers. The first strategy, and probably the most obvious, is to look for loose fragments or orphaned colonies and simply attach them securely in a location where they will thrive. The second strategy is to trim some of the branches that are either damaged or at risk of breakage and re-attach the fragments in appropriate locations. The third strategy is to take some cuttings from some of those same at-risk branches and use them to jump-start production of additional fragments for future outplanting efforts. Implementing simple techniques like this through permitted trials could simplify and magnify reef restoration processes in the future.

Automation and Robotics

The area of advancement that is talked about often is pointing toward the use of underwater robots or drones to plant corals. This is fine in principal, but we first have to develop the correct process for a robot to follow. The technologies, equipment, and vessels for ocean exploration could soon be modified and customized for reef restoration production at scale (Vaughan et al. 2019). The potential for use of artificial intelligence (AI), remote sensing, satellite imagery, underwater photogrammetry and photomosaics, AUVs, SUVs, etc., to be used on a regular basis for all future underwater work is limitless. The following sections provide a quick-look at a few of these items.

Robots

For a land-based nursery process, robots could be used for any process that could be done faster or cheaper by machines. For field-based nurseries, robots could be used for cleaning, inventory, filming, and monitoring. For other aspects, such as outplanting, the use of robots has to be in the future not because of the inability to program a robot to do what a diver can do when it comes to physically placing a coral on a location with the appropriate cement or adhesive, but for the decision of where and how much to outplant, and then how to supply the required species of coral to the robot. Outplanting success and long-term monitoring can absolutely be assisted by robotics and this is the area that will need assistance once operations are scaled-up and multi-year monitoring starts to accumulate a very large amount of data.

Sensors and Monitoring Equipment

Sensor development has been advancing for underwater purposes—continuing to lower the purchase price, extending the equipment and battery life span, and improving the data download capacities. Temperature loggers are readily available, which is incredibly important since temperature is a key parameter in coral reef restoration efforts, particularly as climate change continues. Meters with which to measure pH are also widely available and should be utilized. There are and will be other innovative pieces of equipment including *eyes in, on, and under the water* to document what is happening when we are not there to observe, or the amount of time that is necessary to document the change (as in the *Chasing Corals* movie). Advances in underwater cameras such as the *GoPro* and others will allow relatively inexpensive ways to film, video, or use time-lapse photography at the nursery or outplanting site. Offshore aquaculture farms and ocean exploration processes utilize smart buoys, cameras, and telecommunications back to land headquarters for monitoring 24/7 without putting humans at risk. More advanced ocean-related industries that are involved with exploration and research will lead the way for equipment development that coral restoration practitioners should take advantage of.

A new technology company called *planblue* (www.planblue.com) provides a new and exciting seafloor monitoring technology. Its technology combines hyperspectral and RGB image processing with AI and underwater navigation. There are multiple advantages in combining these technologies. First of all, it allows seafloor monitoring to be objective. This ensures that we can standardize seafloor monitoring for the first time. Second, the monitoring process itself is optimized because the planblue technology cuts down the time needed for collecting and analyzing the data. Third, the technology collects a wealth of data, both in terms of quantity and quality since the technology does not subsample the seafloor. However, the largest advantage is that the technology can visualize the seafloor in such a way that anyone can understand its importance. Easy visualization of the seafloor is key in order to tackle critical global problems, such as coral health, plastic waste pollution, and other anomalies on the seafloor and the effects of climate change (see Figure 21.9). Easy visualization can also quickly validate coral reef restoration efforts to fast-track decision making and to validate and monitor coral restoration status with more information than a normal camera picture.

Figure 21.9 New camera technology using multi-spectrum imagery and underwater GPS location information by *planblue* (Prof. Tom Schils from the University of Guam, USA).

Artificial Reefs and Materials

The largest area of interest and advancement will be in the category of artificial reefs. The interest of the public and all coastal engineers of substituting the service that living coral reefs previously provided in shoreline protection with artificial reefs will outcompete the rate of coral growth and restoration. With increasing sea-level rise and more powerful and more frequent storms affecting the coastline of large populations, engineers will not wait for the reef restoration community to provide this shoreline protection all over the world. What would be advantageous is to include in the *gray* infrastructure (cement and concrete) the potential *green* infrastructure (corals and fisheries organisms) included in the design. Projects like "At the Water's Edge" (AWE) by The Nature Conservancy (TNC) in Grenada have shown progress in this direction of a hybrid artificial reef that can include coral additions to the mix (Figure 22.10).

Figure 22.10 Hybrid artificial reef that can include coral in Grenada as part of AWE by TNC have shown promise (photo by D. Vaughan).

SELECTIVE RAPID GROWTH CYCLE

Combining the methodologies that were described earlier in this book to reproduce corals both sexually and asexually for the purpose of rapidly growing selected corals for reef restoration has not been possible until recently. These methods include: the development of land and field nurseries (Chapter 5), the use of micro-fragmentation, and fusion (Chapters 6 and 7, for asexual reproduction); enhancement of settlement and survival with the use of hatcheries (Chapter 8 for sexual reproduction); and the new techniques for assisted evolution using the best management tools of genetics (Chapters 9 and 10). These methodologies can now be used in one cycle that we will call the selective rapid growth cycle (SRGC) for corals. The SRGC can be completed by using two different genotypes that have demonstrated resistance to disease and/or resilience to environmental stressors—as donor colonies for a quick cross and recombination. This will produce hardier outplants that will be better able to survive in just a few years. For example, if one genotype (A) shows resistance to a certain disease, and another genotype

(B) of the same species is resistant to bleaching, we can propagate both genotypes using micro-fragmentation to grow many micro-fragments. Then micro-fragments of genotype (A) can be grown close to one another so that they fuse together to make a larger colony that will reach sexual maturity size much more quickly. The same can be done with genotype (B). These two quickly grown colonies (A and B) can be positioned in close proximity to each other (either in the lab or outplanted) and recombination can take place naturally during a spawning event—or gametes can be collected and cross fertilization can be ensured in a laboratory (see Figure 22.11). SRGC has been proven to be successful in the past by producing a reproductive-size colony of *P. asteroides* in as little as 11 months that spawned and produced viable offspring in the lab (Vaughan, personal observation). Furthermore, the author Dave Vaughan, outplanted micro-fragments of *O. faveolata* to a field site in the Florida Keys each year from 2014 to 2017. These grew and fused to reproductive size (attaining the size of 25 to 75-year-old colonies) in less than five years. Dr. Hanna Koch (Chapters 9 and 10) was the first to observe a spawning event of these fused outplants in August 2020. Consequently, the use of the SRGC is a powerful tool that practitioners of coral restoration should use to greatly reduce the amount of time required to grow corals that are selected for preferred traits to sexual maturity.

The Selective Rapid Growth Cycle (aka the "Vaughan Cycle: frag-fuse-mature-spawn-cross-settle")

Figure 22.11 The SRGC, (a.k,a, *Vaughan Cycle*: *frag-fuse-mature-spawn-cross-settle*) can become a powerful tool by using micro-fragmentation and fusion to produce larger, mature-size colonies that reach reproductive size much earlier. Viable gametes from preferred genotypes can then be used in selected crosses in record time. From left to right—two separate genotypes (A and B) can be micro-fragmented and arranged in the size of a reproductive adult, so that upon fusion into one large colony, they can produce gametes for genetic crosses. Larvae of the new genotype (AB) can be produced and settled (photos by D. Vaughan and D. Mele).

CONCLUSION

In conclusion, the emerging and future technologies for the economic production of corals at scale, must be developed sooner, rather than later. The methods and materials used in existing marine aquaculture food-production systems can be adopted and tailored to help grow corals even faster, rather than relying on coral restoration as a stand-alone industry. All of the components—asexual reproduction, sexual reproduction, land-based systems, field-based systems, outplanting, and monitoring—are rapidly developing. These new technologies are and must be developed and quickly implemented in order to actively restore coral *at scale* on this changing planet.

ACKNOWLEDGMENTS

To all those giants in the industry whose shoulders we have stood on to get to this point—and to the future giants who will develop and advance the present technologies into the future.

REFERENCE

Vaughan, D., S. Teicher, G. Halpern, and J Oliver. 2019. "Building more resilient coral reefs through new marine technologies, science, and models." *Marine Technology Society Journal*. 53, 5:21–24.

23

MAKING RESTORATION MEANINGFUL: A VISION FOR WORKING AT MULTIPLE SCALES TO HELP SECURE A FUTURE FOR CORAL REEFS

Les Kaufman, Ilsa B. Kuffner, Tom Moore, and Tali Vardi

INTRODUCTION

If coral reefs continue to decline, society will lose important ecosystem services worth billions of dollars (Costanza et al. 2014), including coastline protection, food security, and economic (e.g., tourism) opportunities. There is hope, though. Many reefs around the world are doing okay, and even when degradation is pronounced, pockets and patches of reef remain where hard coral cover and individuals or populations of threatened coral species and other reef creatures survive despite continuing deterioration in ocean conditions (Guest et al. 2018). Right now, humans have a fleeting opportunity to intervene directly. While we mitigate climate change and coastal disturbances, active restoration of coral populations can, along with more advanced interventions that are currently in development, help corals sexually reproduce and successfully recruit to reefs, buying time and encouraging adaptation to changing conditions. In order to enact this vision, we need to work at multiple scales simultaneously. The concept of restoring reefs was developed years ago (Precht 2006), but in the past, efforts were mostly local-scale operations with a more focused purpose such as recovering reefs from boat groundings or other assaults. Currently, small scale, single-species restorations, mainly using coral fragmentation, continue to help floundering reefs hold on and keep valuable, endangered species alive until more significant investments can be made. Simultaneously, investment on the scale of thousands of kilometers is underway to intervene in the future of the Great Barrier Reef. There are restoration projects in progress at all levels of spatial scale, complexity, and investment in between those two extremes (Boström-Einarsson et al. 2020). Each of these levels is important to continue. We are making progress toward increasing the number and scale of reef stewardship and restoration projects. There is a chance to make a difference on regional and global scales, with the simple goal of ensuring that coral reefs still exist at the end of this century.

We stress that coral reef restoration is not a panacea. Of course, restoration must be couched in the context of, and not in lieu of, continuing global threat reduction and local management efforts to reverse the human impacts that are causing reef decline. Some areas of the world may not yet need, or be ready for restoration because local management actions have not yet been tried, nor have other interventions such as predator removal (e.g., crown-of-thorns starfish in the Indo-West Pacific) been recognized as a necessary prerequisite. However, after four decades of attempting to reverse coral reef ecosystem decline, focusing mostly on fishery regulations and marine spatial planning—for example, creating marine protected areas (MPAs)—the time has come to try new tactics (Anthony et al. 2017). While MPAs have shown success in rehabilitating fish stocks (Halpern and Warner 2002), positive effects on coral populations have not been realized (Toth et al. 2014; Bruno et al. 2019). The use of active coral restoration techniques, as outlined in this book, has gained recognition and validity throughout the world (van Oppen et al. 2017; National Academies of Sciences 2019). This chapter offers a vision of what coral restoration can look like along a continuum of increasing investment, spatial scale, and payoffs in the currency of ecosystem services.

Climate Predictions

The first question that people usually ask when they ponder the usefulness of coral-reef restoration is: "Why restore reefs if the ocean conditions that killed them in the first place have not been mitigated, and in fact, are getting worse?" This is a valid concern. Earth's climate is changing in ways that were set in motion centuries ago at the dawn of the industrial revolution, and humans continue to perturb the global carbon cycle at rates and on a spatial scale that is unprecedented in Earth's history (Mackenzie and Lerman 2006). Humans have moved hundreds of gigatons of carbon from where it was locked away in the Earth's crust as fossil fuels to the atmosphere, hydrosphere (oceans), and biosphere (land-bound vegetation) in nearly equal thirds. The consequences of this added carbon in the atmosphere (as carbon dioxide) and the ocean (as dissolved inorganic carbon) have direct impacts on coral reefs. Coral bleaching, the separation of dinoflagellate symbionts from their cnidarian hosts—most often in association with ocean warming—is now recognized as a primary cause of coral mortality around the globe (Hoegh-Guldberg 1999; Eakin et al. 2010; Hughes et al. 2017b). Ocean acidification is projected to accelerate dissolution and erosive processes on reefs (Enochs et al. 2016), cause declines in coral growth (Gattuso et al. 1998), and weaken reef framework (Wisshak et al. 2012; Fang et al. 2013). The combined effects of bleaching and ocean acidification that are projected for this century bring into question the future of coral reefs as geologic formations (Kleypas et al. 2001; Kuffner and Toth 2016), along with the survival of reef populations and associated species (Hoegh-Guldberg et al. 2007), which comprise at least 25% of all marine species (Fisher et al. 2015). Human activities have already contributed to warming the planet 1°C (1.8°F) (IPCC 2018). Because of lag times inherent in perturbations of the global carbon cycle and oceanic thermal inertia, humans have committed the Earth to an additional one degree centigrade of warming (for a total of 3.6°F) even if carbon emissions were stopped 20 years ago (Meehl et al. 2005; Wigley 2005; IPCC 2018). Coral reef persistence through these changes will require acclimation, adaptation, and reassembly by individuals, species, and communities, respectively. While suboptimal conditions for reefs presently pervade the globe and are predicted to persist, the occurrence of reefs doing unexpectedly well in pockets across the seascape offers hope that it is not too late to act (Guest et al. 2018). Restoration actions can multiply, expand,

and extend the lifetimes of these pockets. The result would be added value to people in the short term, and a more rapid rebound of the global coral reef estate in the future.

Sexual Reproduction and Adaptation

The demise of many of the world's coral reef ecosystems is due primarily to individual coral colonies dying en masse from bleaching and disease (Aronson and Precht 2006; Hughes et al. 2017a). Most reef-building corals reproduce via mass spawning, where colonies all release gametes together during specific times and seasons (Page, Fogarty, and Vaughan, Chapter 8 in this book). In a healthy population during mass spawning, there are enough individuals to ensure cross fertilization among different genetic strains (genets). When populations decline, sexual reproduction becomes more uncertain because compatible colonies are spread too far apart for gametes to meet and successfully fertilize (i.e., the *Allee effect*, Knowlton 2001). By intervening (Koch, Chapters 9 and 10 in this book) and increasing the number of genetically different corals of a particular species on a reef, restoration can help rebuild genetically diverse populations to maximize the potential for successful sexual reproduction in that species or population. This is an essential step in establishing self-sustaining populations of key framework-building corals (Randall et al. 2020). Further, recombination of genetic material is necessary for species to adapt to changing ocean conditions (Baums et al. 2019)(Koch, Chapter 10 in this book).

THE VALUE OF RESTORATION EFFORTS AT VARIOUS SCALES

Because of the lag in time between carbon emissions and subsequent climate impacts, there will be a gap—even with concerted efforts to lower greenhouse gas release—between the present when existing coral populations are threatened with extinction, and a future ocean that is once again hospitable to corals. The chapters of this book illustrate that the restoration of coral reef habitat is possible and the spatial scale of success is steadily increasing (Section III, Chapters 11–21 in this book). All of this is embedded in the larger context of arresting anthropogenic climate change while making local environments more conducive to coral reef recovery (Hughes et al. 2017a). Even considering climate change, it is critical for restoration to continue at the current (albeit small) scale, while other management actions continue—such as water quality and fisheries management—and large-scale coral reef ecosystem restoration is being investigated and planned for (Vaughan and Nedimyer, Chapter 22 in this book). This final chapter outlines the multiple steps along the way. We must maintain success at the local level while aiming for maximum impact at the ecosystem level. This is the trajectory we are suggesting for the coral reef restoration community, and the vision that we encourage for those who are new to the field.

A Continuum of Valuable Objectives

A comprehensive review of published literature, gray literature, and a survey of practitioners reveals that almost 70% of current restoration practice consists of coral gardening techniques or transplantation (Boström-Einarsson et al. 2020). Most of these efforts are directed to restoring local coral populations—usually of only one or a few species. However, restoration is steadily becoming much more than merely reattaching a limited number of asexually produced coral fragments of a limited set of one or two species (Precht 2006; Johnson et al. 2011; Rinkevich 2017; Boström-Einarsson et al. 2020), (Section II, Chapters 5–10, and Section III, Chapters 11–21 in this book). Restoration programs today exist along a continuum of objectives from supporting tourism to bringing back self-sustaining and functioning ecosystems (Shaver and Silliman 2017; Bayraktarov et al. 2019). The continuum of objectives or benefits relate to three basic parameters—spatial extent, complexity of the intervention (i.e., number of species or genotypes restored, substratum manipulations, genetic interventions—Chapter 9 in this book), and overall investment in terms of money and resources (Figure 23.1). The aim of this chapter is to leave the reader with confidence that thoughtful restoration can render critical ecosystem-service benefits all along the continuum. The benefits begin with even modest efforts, but then increase exponentially as the restoration increases in scope. Furthermore, an economy of scale can be achieved when practicing coral restoration at a larger scale because establishing the infrastructure is usually the most expensive and time-consuming element. Helping coral reefs to persist through the end of the century requires that we work at all scales simultaneously. Achieving many successes at a smaller scale will, in summation, contribute to the attainment

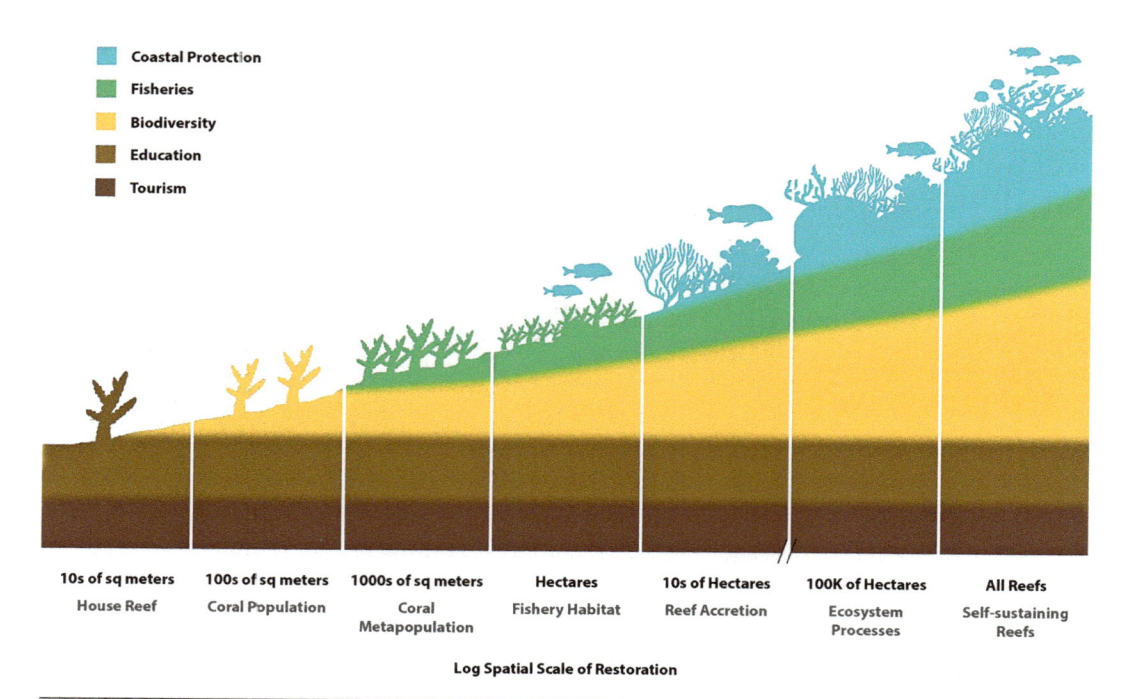

Figure 23.1 A conceptual representation of the increasing ecosystem service benefits that are accrued as the (log) spatial scale of restoration increases. The x-axis could have been represented by any number of other variables (e.g., cost, duration); but spatial scale was chosen as it probably represents the tightest correlation and it is easiest to visualize. The drawings at the top of each column hint at the level of effort (single species to full reef restoration) that is necessary for achieving the benefits. A more detailed explanation of what is needed can be found in the text and in Table 23.1, later on in this chapter. The first two columns represent the scale of current practices. Restoration projects or programs can fall anywhere along the continuum. Note that a fishery habitat restoration project would not necessarily be smaller than that for reef accretion. The primary difference between these two are the goals—fisheries/biodiversity accumulation versus the accumulation of reef structure for coastal protection. (Conceptual illustration by George Boorujy.)

of the end goal of restoring self-perpetuating, functioning reef ecosystems. We are not and cannot be doing all of this by ourselves. We have a powerful and resilient partner working with us: *nature*.

Baseline Conditions

Each restoration program's path depends on the starting baseline conditions of the particular reef ecosystem and the chosen objectives. Baseline conditions encompass considerations such as reef area, number of habitat zones represented, presence/absence of reef-associated habitats (seagrass, mangroves), island geography (low-island versus high-island), geologic makeup (carbonate atoll versus continental crust versus sedimentary), hydrologic setting (arid versus monsoon, etc.), and others aspects of the biophysical setting of a reef. Modern tropical reefs are complex systems that vary greatly in space and time. Any single coral reef at a given time represents one point on the spectrum of species composition and functional configuration that reefs in that location can express. Consequently, coral reef restoration might be able to consistently achieve certain broad goals, but the specifics of what is achievable will vary greatly according to baseline conditions. It may be impossible to restore most of what one reef was or can be, but some level of success is nearly always possible with clarity of purpose and scale (Figure 23.1).

Examples

Next, we provide seven examples of objectives that possess such clarity of purpose and scale for restoration programs. In general, the value of restoration increases exponentially with spatial scale, complexity, duration of effort, as well as time and money invested. In Figure 23.1, spatial scale is used as a proxy for all of these categories. Note that there are infinite intermediate steps along the spatial-scale axis where a restoration program could fit. These examples are made to complement and illustrate, not supersede, the objectives identified in other guides (e.g., Shaver et al. 2020). In each example, we outline the minimum of what is needed to achieve the specific goals (Table 23.1) and payoffs in terms of ecosystem services that success at this level should achieve (Figure 23.1).

1. House Reef

Vacationers traveling to tropical coastlines, as well as local people, seek beach and marine-related forms of relaxation. Snorkeling or diving to see brightly colored fishes and corals is an important part of these experiences. Many coastal hotels and resorts boast a *house* reef, a place where visitors can slip into the water without fuss and lavish in a blast of tropical marine diversity. Loss of a house reef portends serious economic impact if a resort's reputation rests on the environmental quality and recreational opportunities afforded by its setting. Publicly accessible reefs are also a great source of pride for communities that live near reefs, and local governments are increasingly interested in restoring habitats for enjoyment by their own citizens.

A restoration project to bolster a house reef or reinvigorate a local community's care and appreciation of their natural resource are examples of the smallest scale at which coral restoration is likely to deliver significant value in the short term. This type of restoration could be done with the least amount of effort by collecting *fragments of opportunity* and reattaching them to the substratum of a degraded reef. The next level of effort would be building a small in-water nursery for branching corals, fragmenting those corals, and attaching the fragments to the reefs.

Table 23.1 Rough guidelines of the *minimum* components that are needed to achieve the primary objective for each of the seven example objectives for restoration. This table is in no way a substitute for restoration planning and design-critical processes that would take place with local stakeholders, local ecological conditions, and local regulatory contexts in mind (as in Shaver et al. 2020)

Objective	CORAL Species	Genetics	Propagation Strategy	Morphology	Herbivores	Structural Augmentation
House Reef	minimum 1 species	3+ putative genotypes per 100 m²	asexual	branching	N/A	N/A
Coral Population	minimum 1 species	10+ putative genotypes per species				
Coral Meta-population	minimum 1 species	20+ putative genotypes per species		multiple	0–1 species	
Fishery Habitat	minimum 2 species	25+ known genotypes per species with broodstock rotation			1–2 species	
Reef Accretion	10% of native mix	50+ known genotypes per species with a genetic management plan and selection for diversity and conditions	asexual with larval augmentation		multiple species	if necessary to achieve goals
Ecosystem Processes	20% of native mix	75+ known genotypes per species with a genetic management plan and selection for diversity and conditions	asexual and larval	native mix		likely
Self-sustaining Reefs	50% of native mix	100+ known genotypes per species with a genetic management plan and selection for diversity and conditions	asexual, larval, and natural recruitment			

The resulting habitat quality is likely to depend on the availability of other healthy reef habitats that are reasonably close by, since many of the charismatic fishes and other animals (e.g., sea turtles) that people want to see would be moving among coral patches spread across the local region rather than permanently restricted to one reef. Potential payoffs include enhancement of citizen and visitor experiences, education of a broad audience (local and foreign) on the plight of coral reefs, and increased revenue from enhanced value of the visitor experience. Even this smallest level of restoration can function as part of a *seedbank* reef—in other words, as a source of genetic material and broodstock—if the corals are healthy enough to produce gametes and larvae. It may also contribute to the prevention of coastal erosion, particularly for reefs that are close to the shore. In addition, once a beachhead of hard corals and other structure-builders has been established, this small oasis can become a population node and stepping-stone for myriad other reef-associated organisms.

2. Coral Population

The threshold for local-scale (demographic) restoration is that a species or group of species have reestablished a secure and persistent population. This means that reefs can recover from local-scale perturbations within an area of interest, both through the recovery of surviving fragments and by larvae settling in from nearby subpopulations within a few years. There may be a need or a wish to define secondary goals such as the size of subpopulations or the genetic diversity of a population that relates to its resilience through time. Demographic restoration would surpass biomass and distribution thresholds that are associated with such factors as the Allee effect and recovery from severe storms, bleaching, disease, or other mass-mortality events. As such, the minimum level of effort on a patch reef scale, ~100m^2, would consist of: (1) a small in-water nursery that houses at least four genotypes (or putative genets based on local phenotypic knowledge) of a primary reef-building coral and (2) clustering outplants in groups of four to six different genotypes (Baums et al. 2019, Koch, Chapter 10 in this book). Ecosystem services restored at this scale should include those at the previous scale as well as additional biodiversity conservation, *passion* tourism such as underwater photography and scuba diving, and possibly some fisheries benefits. In addition, the restoration of a self-sustaining population means that this reef can then serve to rescue other nearby populations by providing larvae or habitat for settling recruits.

3. Coral Metapopulation

Restoration at this scale would be in the form of a network of connected populations that can absorb even higher levels of disturbance without shifting irreversibly into noncoral-dominated systems (i.e., they have some level of ecosystem resilience). This level of restoration necessitates promoting climate-resilient reefs (National Academies of Sciences 2019) at the levels of species, community, and metapopulation. Progress is being made in our understanding of the population genetics and functional genomics of corals—including resistance and resilience to high temperatures (Dixon et al. 2015), diseases, and combined stressors (Muller et al. 2018). Restoration at this level will benefit from cutting-edge research that evaluates locally available sources of genets for their genetic diversity and functional plasticity. This is of particular interest with regard to the ways that phenotypic variability corresponds with environmental variability in the complex array of biophysical settings found on reefs (Kenkel et al. 2013). The *minimum* steps necessary for this objective would be similar to those previously mentioned, repeated at least three times. Thus, (1) an in-water nursery of at least one primary reef-building coral with at least twelve genets of various physiological traits sourced from both local and distant reefs and (2) clustered outplants of at least four genotypes on each of three patch reefs. Ecosystem services restored at this scale should include those at the previous levels as well as increases to some fisheries services, biodiversity from obligate coral-associated species, and the beginnings of a reduction in subsequent restoration costs. Of course, increasing the size of each patch, the number and variability of each genotype, the number of coral species, and the number of patches would result in greater benefits.

4. Fishery Habitat

A distinct step-up in minimum effort is required to provide habitat at a scale sufficient to enhance reef fisheries that are important to local communities. In essence, restoration at this level seeks to reboot an entire coral reef community—that is, providing the shelter and sustenance to support populations of reef fishes, lobsters, and other coral reef fishery targets. Restoration at this scale involves multiple species of coral, and possibly also the restocking (or culling of, e.g., crown-of-thorns starfish) of non-coral species, such as herbivorous sea urchins, predators of coral predators (e.g., lobsters and hogfish that eat corallivorous snails), or any organism that contributes to critical ecosystem functions like grazing, production of suitable settlement habitat, and coral colony survival. However, if restoration promotes a settlement of key species, additional restocking efforts may not need to be carried out. We do not yet understand how succession works on many reefs, but continued restoration experience will help reveal these unknowns. In reef regions where there is a generally healthy ecosystem to begin with, bolstering the populations of multiple species of coral may be sufficient to re-attract a full complement of fishes and other reef species. The topographical complexity of reefs is likely to increase with restoration at this scale, thereby attracting cryptic organisms that fill out trophic webs and add complexity and needed redundancy in ecological functions. Restoration at this scale would pay attention to the biophysical setting and enabling conditions necessary for a wide array of ecologically important coral reef taxa, such as crustose coralline algae that are settlement cues for coral and other invertebrate larvae. In this phase, it becomes possible to tolerate ecological players that may be intolerable in a scenario that is characterized by smaller patches of this or that coral. For example, at a very low density of branching acroporid corals, algal-gardening damselfishes can have a devastating impact on populations of their host corals. In extensive thickets of these same corals, however, algal gardeners might actually *benefit* their host corals by defending a larger area of live coral from coral enemies such as excavators and borers. Ecosystem services restored at this scale include those at the previous levels as well as gains in fisheries, a steeper rise in biodiversity from volunteer recruitment, and ecological processes such as larval export and the beginnings of shoreline protection returning. Note that research and development of restocking programs for non-coral species can be costly.

5. Reef Accretion

Restoration at this scale requires the reestablishment of net-positive carbonate-accretion budgets. This is accomplished when the amount of calcium-carbonate rock and cemented sediments produced by corals and other calcifiers outweighs the amount that is lost from dissolution, erosion, and transport off the reef (Perry et al. 2018). The most important metrics for justifying public funding for coral-reef stewardship, in all forms, is return on investment. The value of the shoreline protection by U.S. reefs in terms of human lives and dollar amounts to an annual flood-risk reduction of more than 18,000 lives and 1.8 billion dollars (Storlazzi et al. 2019).

Returning reefs to positive accretion rates is no easy task, may not be possible in all locations, and will be particularly challenging in subtropical areas, such as Florida, where reef building largely ceased several thousand years ago (Toth et al. 2018). However, considering that reefs attenuate, on average, 97% of wave energy (Ferrario et al. 2014) and protect human lives and infrastructure (Storlazzi et al. 2019), restoring reefs could be far less costly than rebuilding the human communities they protect. Bolstering reef accretion and coastal protection will necessitate work with multiple reef-building coral species at higher densities than in previous steps, and will require focused restoration at the top of the reef crest where the bulk of wave energy dissipation takes place; alas, a challenging reef setting in which to work! Restoration at this level will also challenge us to stage coral communities that, on their own, can then restore coral reef architecture and geomorphology—a daunting but noble pursuit.

In certain locations, adding artificial reef structure could be an important interim step in preventing coastal erosion (Reguero et al. 2018). However, for the longevity of the project and to ensure multiple, additional ecosystem benefits (fisheries, tourism, biodiversity), an artificial reef structure would be complemented by active coral restoration to form a living, and thus, self-sustaining coral reef and not simply a series of concrete structures on the seafloor. This type of restoration would be accompanied by specific monitoring tailored toward measuring increases in topographical complexity and reef elevation. Providing evidence that restoration can attain positive reef accretion, and thus, geological function (Kuffner and Toth 2016), and deliver decreased risk to coastal human communities is of major importance in making the case for the cost-effectiveness of restoration (Reguero et al. 2018). Ecosystem services restored at this scale include those at the previous levels as well as enhanced coastal protection through increased reef elevation (Alvarez-Filip et al. 2009) and roughness (Quataert et al. 2015), beach replenishment via net positive sediment production, and further increases in biodiversity as ecological complexity rises in concert with physical complexity.

6. Ecosystem Processes

By this scale of restoration, many major ecosystem components and ecosystem resilience are being reestablished. Processes such as sexual reproduction, herbivory, recruitment, trophic dynamics, competition, niche partitioning, and population connectivity are returning, at least in some part, on a scale of hundreds of hectares. This scale and level of coral reef ecosystem restoration is still aspirational; it has not yet been done. However, the Reef Restoration and Adaptation Program (RRAP) in Australia is developing plans to do this for the Great Barrier Reef (Hardisty et al. 2019). RRAP is a $500M (AUS dollars) program and the plan includes deployment of sexually-derived coral larvae on a massive scale, analyses of heat tolerance and gene flow among coral populations to allow for future reef processes to continue through the coming decades of warming, prevention of bleaching during warming events, researching additional highly scientific and technological advancements, modeling exercises, and then eventually implementation. Although such a comprehensive program does not yet exist elsewhere, others are beginning to emulate it (e.g., Florida's Mission: Iconic Reefs, the UN Decade of Restoration, Blue Charter Program), and lessons learned from this program will be broadly applicable. Ecosystem services restored at this scale would include those at the previous levels, and these would now be, in part, self-sustaining systems. While these very large projects are exciting to think about, equal attention should be paid to efforts that are more modest in scale, but also more achievable and instructive in the short term, for the benefits of restoration in serving and educating local residents is not only necessary (Suding et al. 2015) but very valuable. The restoration of significant areas of Laughing Bird Caye National Park in Belize by Fragments of Hope (see Chapter 11 in this book), of large swaths of reef in Puerto Rico by NOAA and its partners, and other examples (see Chapters 14 and 18 in this book), are both illuminating and inspiring.

7. Self-Sustaining Reefs

This paragraph describes the level of restoration that should be the *ultimate and final goal*. Restoration of the global ecological-economic landscape in which coral reefs are embedded, including the whole human-biosphere system, is accomplished. All ecosystem services of coral reefs have been restored at this scale and restoration investments can cease. This level of restoration requires that fossil-fuel burning has arrested, global climate change is no longer primarily anthropogenic in nature, there is better fisheries management, water pollution is under control, there is more thoughtful coastal and watershed development, and region-wide ecosystem-scale restorations such as those described previously have been implemented in all reef regions (Hughes et al. 2017a). There is total and complete politico-economic restoration; that is, the Earth and all its human and nonhuman inhabitants are living in sustainable harmony. While this may sound like a pipe dream in the early to mid-21st Century, it could be possible to achieve in part, and any progress toward achieving it would be worth the resources expended.

CONCLUSIONS

Coral reef restoration is a very young but maturing set of tools with great potential in the fight to bridge the gap between the current phase of exponential anthropogenic climate change and a future when it has been arrested and reversed (Hoegh-Guldberg et al. 2008; van Oppen et al. 2017). Coral reef restoration can enable the species, relationships, and processes that constitute a coral reef system to cross this bridge from hostile to amenable ocean conditions for reefs, and to reassemble on the other side in some form capable of, once again, accreting calcium-carbonate edifices that keep pace with sea level and support the ocean's richest biological community. The methodical steps toward scaling up coral reef restoration are key to this grand vision of ecosystem repair and resurrection. Restoration cannot and will not solve all of the problems facing coral reef communities today, for it is not a substitute for the abatement of anthropogenic climate change—it is only an adjunct, but an important and legitimate one. Coral reef restoration can buy time—but it is *precious* time, and without it, we risk losing these systems.

DISCLAIMER

Any use of trade, firm, or product names is for descriptive purposes only and does not imply endorsement by the U.S. Government. We thank J. A. Kleypas and I. M. McLeod for their critical and constructive reviews that greatly improved our manuscript.

REFERENCES

Alvarez-Filip, L., N. K. Dulvy, J. A. Gill, I. M. Cote, and A. R. Watkinson. 2009. "Flattening of Caribbean coral reefs: Region-wide declines in architectural complexity." *Proceedings of the Royal Society of London*, Series B 276:3019–3025.

Anthony, K., L. K. Bay, R. Costanza, J. Firn, J. Gunn, P. Harrison, A. Heyward, et al. 2017. "New interventions are needed to save coral reefs." *Nature Ecology & Evolution* 1:1420–1422.

Aronson, R. B. and W. F. Precht. 2006. "Conservation, precaution, and Caribbean reefs." *Coral Reefs* 25:441–450.

Baums, I. B., A. C. Baker, S. W. Davies, A. G. Grottoli, C. D. Kenkel, S. A. Kitchen, I. B. Kuffner, et al. 2019. "Considerations for maximizing the adaptive potential of restored coral populations in the western Atlantic." *Ecological Applications* 29:e01978.

Bayraktarov, E., P. J. Stewart-Sinclair, S. Brisbane, L. Boström-Einarsson, M. I. Saunders, C. E. Lovelock, H. P. Possingham, et al. 2019. "Motivations, success, and cost of coral reef restoration." *Restoration Ecology* 27:981–991.

Boström-Einarsson, L., R. C. Babcock, E. Bayraktarov, D. Ceccarelli, N. Cook, S. C. A. Ferse, B. Hancock, et al. 2020. "Coral restoration—a systematic review of current methods, successes, failures and future directions." *PLoS ONE* 15:e0226631.

Bruno, J. F., I. M. Côté, and L. T. Toth. 2019. "Climate change, coral loss, and the curious case of the parrotfish paradigm: Why don't marine protected areas improve reef resilience?" *Annual Review of Marine Science* 11:307–334.

Costanza, R., R. de Groot, P. Sutton, S. van der Ploeg, S. J. Anderson, I. Kubiszewski, S. Farber, and R. K. Turner. 2014. "Changes in the global value of ecosystem services." *Global Environmental Change* 26:152–158.

Dixon, G. B., S. W. Davies, G. A. Aglyamova, E. Meyer, L. K. Bay, and M. V. Matz. 2015. "Genomic determinants of coral heat tolerance across latitudes." *Science* 348:1460–1462.

Eakin, C. M., J. A. Morgan, S. F. Heron, T. B. Smith, G. Liu, L. Alvarez-Filip, B. Baca, et al. 2010. "Caribbean corals in crisis: Record thermal stress, bleaching, and mortality in 2005." *PLoS ONE* 5:e13969.

Enochs, I. C., D. P. Manzello, G. Kolodziej, S. Noonan, L. Valentino, and K. E. Fabricius. 2016. "Enhanced macroboring and depressed calcification drive net dissolution at high-CO_2 coral reefs." *Proceedings of the Royal Society of London*, Series B 283.

Fang, J. K. H., M. A. Mello-Athayde, C. H. L. Schönberg, D. I. Kline, O. Hoegh-Guldberg, and S. Dove. 2013. "Sponge biomass and bioerosion rates increase under ocean warming and acidification." *Global Change Biology* 19:3581–3591.

Ferrario, F., M. W. Beck, C. D. Storlazzi, F. Micheli, C. C. Shepard, and L. Airoldi. 2014. "The effectiveness of coral reefs for coastal hazard risk reduction and adaptation." *Nature Communications* 5:3794.

Fisher, R., R. A. O'Leary, S. Low-Choy, K. Mengersen, N. Knowlton, R. E. Brainard, and M. J. Caley. 2015. "Species richness on coral reefs and the pursuit of convergent global estimates." *Current Biology* 25:500–505.

Gattuso, J. P., M. Frankignoulle, I. Bourge, S. Romaine, and R. W. Buddemeier. 1998. "Effect of calcium carbonate saturation of seawater on coral calcification." *Global and Planetary Change* 18:37–46.

Guest, J. R., P. J. Edmunds, R. D. Gates, I. B. Kuffner, A. J. Andersson, B. B. Barnes, I. Chollett, et al. 2018. "A framework for identifying and characterising coral-reef 'oases' against a backdrop of degradation." *Journal of Applied Ecology* 55:2865–2875.

Halpern, B. S. and R. R. Warner. 2002. "Marine reserves have rapid and lasting effects." *Ecology Letters* 5:361–366.

Hardisty, P. E., C. H. Roth, P. Silvery, D. Mead, and K. Anthony. 2019. "Investment Case: A report provided to the Australian Government from the Reef Restoration and Adaptation Program." https://www.gbrrestoration.org/reports, downloaded on September 3, 2020.

Hoegh-Guldberg, O. 1999. "Climate change, coral bleaching and the future of the world's coral reefs." *Australian Journal of Marine and Freshwater Research* 50:839–866.

Hoegh-Guldberg, O., L. Hughes, S. McIntyre, D. B. Lindenmayer, C. Parmesan, H. P. Possingham, and C. D. Thomas. 2008. "Assisted colonization and rapid climate change." *Science* 321:345–346.

Hoegh-Guldberg, O., P. J. Mumby, A. J. Hooten, R. S. Steneck, P. Greenfield, E. Gomez, C. D. Harvell, et al. 2007. "Coral reefs under rapid climate change and ocean acidification." *Science* 318:1737–1742.

Hughes, T. P., M. L. Barnes, D. R. Bellwood, J. E. Cinner, G. S. Cumming, J. B. C. Jackson, J. Kleypas, et al. 2017a. "Coral reefs in the Anthropocene." *Nature* 546:82–90.

Hughes, T. P., J. T. Kerry, M. Álvarez-Noriega, J. G. Álvarez-Romero, K. D. Anderson, A. H. Baird, R. C. Babcock, et al. 2017b. "Global warming and recurrent mass bleaching of corals." *Nature* 543:373–377.

IPCC. 2018. "Summary for Policymakers." In: V. Masson-Delmotte, P. Zhai, H.-O. Pörtner, D. Roberts, J. Skea, P. R. Shukla, A. Pirani, W. Moufouma-Okia, C. Péan, R. Pidcock, S. Connors, J. B. R. Matthews, Y. Chen, X. Zhou, M. I. Gomis, E. Lonnoy, T. Maycock, M. Tignor, and T. Waterfield, (eds.). Global Warming of 1.5°C. An IPCC Special Report on the impacts of global warming of 1.5°C above pre-industrial levels and related global greenhouse gas emission pathways, in the context of strengthening the global response to the threat of climate change, sustainable development, and efforts to eradicate poverty.

Johnson, M. E., C. Lustic, E. Bartels, I. B. Baums, D. S. Gilliam, L. Larson, D. Lirman, et al. 2011. "Caribbean *Acropora* restoration guide: Best practices for propagation and population enhancement." p. 54. *The Nature Conservancy*, Arlington, VA.

Kenkel, C. D., G. Goodbody-Gringley, D. Caillaud, S. W. Davies, E. Bartels, and M. V. Matz. 2013. "Evidence for a host role in thermotolerance divergence between populations of the mustard hill coral (*Porites astreoides*) from different reef environments." *Molecular Ecology* 22:4335–4348.

Kleypas, J. A., R. W. Buddemeier, and J. P. Gattuso. 2001. "The future of coral reefs in an age of global change." *International Journal of Earth Sciences* 90:426–437.

Knowlton, N. 2001. "The future of coral reefs." Proceedings of the National Academy of Sciences of the USA 98:5419–5425.

Kuffner, I. B. and L. T. Toth. 2016. "A geological perspective on the degradation and conservation of western Atlantic coral reefs." *Conservation Biology* 30:706–715.

Mackenzie, F. T. and A. Lerman. 2006. "Carbon in the geobiosphere—Earth's outer shell." *Springer*, Dordrecht.

Meehl, G. A., W. M. Washington, W. D. Collins, J. M. Arblaster, A. Hu, L. E. Buju, W. G. Strand, and H. Teng. 2005. "How much more global warming and sea level rise?" *Science* 307:1769–1772.

Muller, E. M., E. Bartels, and I. B. Baums. 2018. "Bleaching causes loss of disease resistance within the threatened coral species *Acropora cervicornis*." *eLife* 2018:7:e35066.

National Academies of Sciences, Engineering, and Medicine. 2019. *A Research Review of Interventions to Increase the Persistence and Resilience of Coral Reefs*. The National Academies Press, Washington, DC.

Perry, C. T., L. Alvarez-Filip, N. A. J. Graham, P. J. Mumby, S. K. Wilson, P. S. Kench, D. P. Manzello, et al. 2018. "Loss of coral reef growth capacity to track future increases in sea level." *Nature* 558:396–400.

Precht, W. F. 2006. "Coral Reef Restoration Handbook." CRC Press Taylor & Francis Group, Boca Raton, Florida, p. 363.

Quataert, E., C. Storlazzi, A. van Rooijen, O. Cheriton, and A. van Dongeren. 2015. "The influence of coral reefs and climate change on wave-driven flooding of tropical coastlines." *Geophysical Research Letters* 42:6407–6415.

Randall, C. J., A. P. Negri, K. M. Quigley, T. Foster, G. F. Ricardo, N. S. Webster, L. K. Bay, et al. 2020. "Sexual production of corals for reef restoration in the Anthropocene." *Marine Ecology Progress Series* 635:203–232.

Reguero, B. G., M. W. Beck, V. N. Agostini, P. Kramer, and B. Hancock. 2018. "Coral reefs for coastal protection: A new methodological approach and engineering case study in Grenada." *Journal of Environmental Management* 210:146–161.

Rinkevich, B. 2017. "Rebutting the inclined analyses on the cost-effectiveness and feasibility of coral reef restoration." *Ecological Applications* 27:1970–1973.

Shaver, E. C., C. A. Courtney, J. M. West, J. Maynard, C. Hein, C. Wagner, J. Philibotte, P. MacGowan, I. McLeod, L. Boström-Einarsson, K. Bucchianeri, L. Johnston, J. Koss. 2020. A Manager's Guide to Coral Reef Restoration Planning and Design. NOAA Coral Reef Conservation Program. NOAA Technical Memorandum CRCP 36, p. 120. https://doi.org/10.25923/vht9-tv39.

Shaver, E. C. and B. R. Silliman. 2017. "Time to cash in on positive interactions for coral restoration." *PeerJ* 5:e3499 https://doi.org/3410.7717/peerj.3499.

Storlazzi, C. D., B. G. Reguero, A. D. Cole, E. Lowe, J. B. Shope, A. E. Gibbs, B. A. Nickel, et al. 2019. *Rigorously Valuing the Role of U.S. Coral Reefs in Coastal Hazard Risk Reduction*. U.S. Geological Survey Open-File Report 2019–1027.

Suding, K., E. Higgs, M. Palmer, J. B. Callicott, C. B. Anderson, M. Baker, J. J. Gutrich, et al. 2015. "Committing to ecological restoration." *Science* 348:638–640.

Toth, L. T., I. B. Kuffner, A. Stathakopoulos, and E. A. Shinn. 2018. "A 3000-year lag between the geological and ecological collapse of Florida's coral reefs." *Global Change Biology* 24:5471–5483.

Toth, L. T., R. van Woesik, T. J. T. Murdoch, S. R. Smith, J. C. Ogden, W. F. Precht, and R. B. Aronson. 2014. "Do no-take reserves benefit Florida's corals? 14 years of change and stasis in the Florida Keys National Marine Sanctuary." *Coral Reefs* 33:565–577.

van Oppen, M. J. H., R. D. Gates, L. L. Blackall, N. Cantin, L. J. Chakravarti, W. Y. Chan, C. Cormick, et al. 2017. "Shifting paradigms in restoration of the world's coral reefs." *Global Change Biology* 23:3437–3448.

Wigley, T. M. L. 2005. "The climate change commitment." *Science* 307:1766–1769.

Wisshak, M., C. H. L. Schonberg, A. Form, and A. Freiwald. 2012. "Ocean acidification accelerates reef bioerosion." *PLoS ONE* 7:e45124.

EPILOGUE

Dear Reader,

As an emerging restoration practitioner, you are a noble hero. A spring of hope on a dark and dusty earth. Before you, we lay several options. The bigger your restoration—the better. The more species you cultivate and plant—the better. The more diverse your reef is—the better. If the fisheries come back—excellent. If you can support your local economy and educate your citizenry—amazing. If the corals you replanted begin mass spawning—success! If the fish that live on the reefs begin spawning—even better! If the reefs you planted are more resistant to bleaching than native reefs—a win! If you have restored a fully functioning reef ecosystem that spans several hundred kilometers—you deserve a prize. However, even the simple but noble practice of keeping fragmented coral species alive and cared for is a critical step on this journey. These words of inspiration, however, should not be taken to mean we should throw caution to the wind! A critical step in starting even the most modest restoration work involves getting the right training and guidance, plus careful planning. If you made it to the final chapter of this book, clearly you have done your part! We commend you. Good luck!

Tali Vardi

APPENDIX: NOTES FOR RECORD KEEPING

Donna Vaughan

WHY KEEP RECORDS?

It is important to keep detailed records of the corals in your care, whether they be in a land-based or field-based nursery—or outplanted at a restoration site. At times it may feel tedious, but recorded data will become important for future planning and decision making. Looking back on your records to determine trends that are not readily apparent in the day-to-day operations may solve any unexplained changes. Furthermore, when there is a change in staff, good record keeping ensures continuity of information within the system. Record keeping is also an accountability tool for your operations. Well-kept records can serve as visual evidence that your protocols are being followed. If you require technicians to sign off or initial the data sheets once tasks are performed, you may be able to determine who your best technicians are.

The type of records you keep will be determined by your system and protocols. As with most aquaculture systems, each is unique and may have different requirements for record keeping. This appendix is designed to be a starting point for the records that are necessary for each system. For example, you may do all of your tasks in the field and your record keeping may not be as detailed, although keeping track of the weather and water conditions is still valuable. It is difficult to predict what trends you may discover. When working with corals, it is highly recommended that you print your data sheets onto a form of waterproof paper that can be used in the rain or underwater. Later, the data can be logged into an electronic spreadsheet such as Excel.

Record keeping can give your system the information and details that are needed in order to bring success to your operation. Here we provide a basic overview of how to track important information through record keeping, which can be used to tailor your own record-keeping process. Examples of data sheets are included in this appendix and are also available for download through the Web Added Value (WAV™) section of the publisher's website (www.jrosspub.com/wav). These data sheets can serve as a template to work from as you tailor them to fit your specific needs.

DAILY ENVIRONMENTAL RECORDS

Environmental conditions can affect all parts of your operation. They may determine what exactly can be accomplished on any given day, as well as the growth of your corals. Weather events can have catastrophic implications for your entire project. Precautions can always be implemented if conditions are forecast, but the effects cannot always be predicted.

In today's world of climate change, what we have always known and depended on increasingly changes. We may at any time experience weather and water conditions that we have never seen before. It is, therefore, important to record these conditions—whether you operate a land-based nursery, a field-based nursery, or an outplant site—so that appropriate decisions can be made for the future. Your records may also help regulators when making future decisions regarding climate change. Watching these factors will help to indicate which of your corals are able to best survive these changes.

The parameters for environmental monitoring can be difficult to assess for field nurseries and outplant sites because they are not typically visited on a daily basis. For these sites, continuous temperature recorders can be installed and solar index recorders can be placed on land nearby. If governmental buoys are nearby, such as those deployed by the National Oceanic and Atmospheric Administration (NOAA), they can also provide information that may be helpful. Data collection buoys can now be purchased that currently monitor for several different parameters out in open water as well.

Data should be recorded daily (if possible) so that even small effects can be monitored. By keeping daily environmental data, you will be able to relate changes in the environment to coral growth and health. Basic data for daily environmental records may include: air temperature, rainfall, cloud cover (wind/velocity), water temperature, salinity, pH (all water parameters coming from the water source), noted observations, and the initials of the technician (Appendix 1A).

LAND-BASED NURSERY RECORDS

Daily: Land-Based Nursery

Once the frags (or sexual recruits) are located in the nursery, they should all be labeled so that they may be easily identified as to their group or genotype (see Chapter 5 in this book for labeling ideas). Data as to when they were put in the nursery should be at the top of all data sheets relating to that particular group. This baseline information is most important in recognizing how each group is doing compared to others that are growing in the nursery. Decisions on the *winners* will then be easily identified.

Depending on the protocols for your particular system, notes should be taken on whatever procedures are performed, each time they are accomplished. Data for raceway maintenance is typically entered once a day, depending on what the best management practices are for that particular system. Some nurseries want salinity and pH noted twice a day. Water chemistry parameters in the raceway can be used to compare with the same parameters in the source water. Furthermore, corals are sometimes moved from one tank to another; this needs to be noted, and their data sheets must move with them in order for the information to be valuable. Notes should be entered daily on anything of interest or concern; for example, when a particular coral starts to look like it is starting to decline in health. Daily parameters to record for raceway maintenance may include: date, the raceway identification, water temperature, pH, salinity, any maintenance procedure done, noted observations, and the initials of the technician (Appendix 1B).

Monthly: Land-Based Nursery

Because growth appears slowly, even in micro-fragmented corals, daily observations for growth can be hard to determine. Therefore, monthly measurements for growth are recommended and notes should be made at consistent intervals in order to see differences in growth rate. Measuring these differences can be difficult because of the three-dimensional growth that occurs. Growth can be observed by measuring the horizontal amount of coverage on the plugs that the corals are growing on or the amount of fusing that is occurring (see Chapter 5 in this book for techniques to measure coral growth). It is important to note these observations because the faster growers may be the *winners* for future fragmentations. If your protocol for planting is related to size, these measurements can help in determining planting, stocking, and fragmenting schedules. Monthly parameters to record may include: the current date, tray number, species, date of fragmentation or spawn, whether they are alive or dead, size, signs of disease or bleaching, noted observations, and the initials of the technician (Appendix 1C).

Mechanical Maintenance: Land-Based Nursery

Maintenance on a land-based nursery can be the key to success. A clear schedule must be adhered to so that nothing is overlooked. Days for back-flushing of the filtration systems and pump maintenance are of the utmost importance, and flow rates must be monitored as well. In some situations, supplies may be hard to obtain—and just one of these systems going down could be catastrophic. Consequently, your facility should have back-up pumps and they should be routinely checked as well.

Data sheets for maintenance may include: date, pump number, backwash, water flow, water pressure, any other parameters appropriate to your system, notes, and the initials of the technician (Appendix 1D).

OUTPLANTINGS AND FIELD NURSERY RECORDS

These records are probably the most difficult to keep as your project grows. One of the biggest questions still to be answered is how to measure growth in the field. The amount of documentation that you need for your reporting will determine how you might decide to make these measurements or observations (see Chapter 5 in this book for techniques on how to measure coral growth). Once these have been determined you will be able to identify groups in the field. Labels should be able to withstand the growing conditions in the field—keeping in mind ease of reading and allowing for the fouling organisms that will attach to the labels (see Chapter 5 in this book for labeling ideas).

A clear strategy should be developed for the procedures to be performed for each visit to the field—whether it be to a field nursery or an outplant site. If planting, the methods used should be thoughtfully determined. A clear checklist of materials needed should be made and checked prior to going to the field. A day that is wasted because of forgotten equipment must be avoided. If using drills, cameras, or anything that may require special attention, it is always a good idea to have back-up batteries, drill bits, etc., and any manuals that may help if the equipment should break down while in the field. If the procedure requires the cleaning of the field nursery, notes should be taken that can be referred to in the future as to how much unwanted growth has occurred. This will be helpful, especially if it can be related to certain conditions or seasons of the year. Again, this will help in knowing how much maintenance is required throughout the year.

Survival, evidence of disease/bleaching, and predation should always be noted. Comparisons of different sites can be made and future decisions will be much better informed. Parameters for data sheets used in either field nursery or outplant sites may include: date, location, species, frag or spawn, number alive, number dead, disease, bleaching, signs of predation, procedures, size, photo number, notes, and the initials of the field technician (Appendix 1E). While in the field, it is important to also complete a data sheet for the environmental conditions observed.

COSTS OF OPERATION

It is vital to keep records on the costs of your operation. The goal should be to produce corals at the lowest cost possible, while also allowing for the expansion of your system. While trying to operate in a cost-effective manner, keep economies of scale in mind. You may find that as you tweak the system, you spend less on either utilities, labor, or materials—or even all three. Therefore, it is important to correlate any changes in costs to changes made in the system. Whatever accounting system you use, the ability to correlate each expenditure directly to a particular operation (utilities, labor, materials) is essential. For example, changing to a more efficient pump may decrease your electric costs. As you relate these changes to your costs, you will be able to make more informed decisions going forward. You are essentially creating your own ecosystem and everything is related to the efficiency of your project.

CONCLUSIONS

Consistent record keeping is vital and can be the key to a successful operation. Before beginning, it is important to identify your goals. If you are growing coral for research and looking to write a scientific publication, you will have a larger amount of data that must be recorded. The records that are kept will be determined by your project design. If your goal is solely to restore a reef on a budget, your records may be less precise but still need to be kept so that you can best use the funds available. Records can also make the staff accountable for their responsibilities. With well-kept records you may identify procedures that need to be implemented either more often or less often. No matter what you decide, records are not useful unless you look back and correlate any changes with what was going on at the time of the change. Sometimes things can be revealed that could be the key to your success.

All of the recommendations for record keeping that have been suggested in this chapter are just that—recommendations. Every project is unique, as is every site, so tailor your record keeping to fit your needs.

ACKNOWLEDGMENTS

I would like to thank all of those scientists whom I have had the pleasure of working with and who taught me the importance of data and record keeping. These would include the Rutgers Marine Lab, AquaFarms, and Harbor Branch Oceanographic. Special thanks to Gef Flimlin and Kim Kosko for editing Record Keeping in Aquaculture. Thank you to the scientists at

Harbor Branch, Mote Marine, Fragments of Hope, and Plant a Million Corals Foundation for helping me with what is important with record keeping for coral restoration.

REFERENCES

Carne, Lisa. 2018. *Coral Reef Replenishment Manual.* Fragments of Hope.org and Belize Fisheries Department.

Vaughan, Donna. 1988. "Record keeping for aquaculture." NOAA Office of Sea Grant, Department of Fisheries, Grant No. NA85AA-D-SG04 (Project No. MM/1).

Appendix 1A Record of Daily Environmental Data

Date	Air Temp	Rainfall	Cloud Cover (%)	Wind (D/V)	Water Temperature	Salinity	pH	Notes	Initials

Appendix 1B Record for Daily Raceway Maintenance

Date	Raceway Identification	Water Temp	pH	Salinity	Maintenance Procedure	Notes	Initials

Appendix 1C Monthly Record for Coral Growth and Health

Date	Tray Number	Species	Date of Frag/Spawn	Number Alive	Number Dead	Size	Signs of Disease/Bleach	Notes	Initials

Appendix 1D Record for Mechanical Maintenance at Land-Based Nursery

Date	Pump Number	Backwash	Water Flow	Water Pressure	Maintenance Procedure	Notes	Initials

Appendix 1E Record for Field Nursery/Outplant Site for Coral Growth and Health

Date	Location/Site	Species	Date of Frag/Spawn	# Alive	# Dead	Size	Signs of Disease/Bleach Predation	Procedures	Photo Number(s)	Initials

GLOSSARY

Acclimatization: phenotypic adaptation in response to variation in the natural environment; it can alter performance and possibly enhance fitness, but it does not involve genetic change.
Active restoration: human intervention techniques that directly accelerate recovery of ecological systems.
Adaptive evolution: natural selection drives adaptive evolution by selecting for and increasing the occurrence of beneficial traits in a population.
Adaptive potential: the ability of populations/species to respond to selection via phenotypic or molecular changes.
AIMS: Australian Institute of Marine Science.
Allee effect: a feature of small populations whereby low density limits population growth.
Allele: one of two or more alternative forms of a gene that arise by mutation and are found at the same place on a chromosome.
Allozyme: allelic variants of enzymes encoded by structural genes.
Amplified fragment length polymorphisms (AFLPs): differences in restriction fragment lengths caused by SNPs (single nucleotide polymorphisms) or INDELs (insertion or deletion of bases in the genome of an organism) that create or abolish restriction endonuclease recognition sites.
Antagonistic pleiotropy: when one gene controls for more than one trait and can arise when alleles that have beneficial effects on one set of fitness components also have deleterious effects on other fitness components.
Aposymbiosis: a form of symbiosis in which two species live independently of each other, but their life cycles affect one another.
Asexual reproduction: a type of reproduction by which offspring arise from a single organism and inherit the genes of that parent only; it does not involve the fusion of gametes, and almost never changes the number of chromosomes.
Assisted evolution: a range of approaches involving active intervention to accelerate the rate of naturally occurring evolutionary processes to enhance certain traits of interest; such approaches may include acclimatization, experimental evolution of algal endosymbionts, manipulation of the host microbiome, interspecific hybridization, and intraspecific managed (or selective) breeding.
Assisted gene flow: the process of outcrossing colonies sourced from widely separated and environmentally divergent reefs to exchange potentially beneficial alleles among populations and produce offspring with increased phenotypic variation.
Backcross: to cross a hybrid with one of its parents or an organism with the same genetic characteristics as one of the parents.

Biomarkers: naturally occurring molecules, genes, or characteristics in a biological system used as indicators of exposure, effect, susceptibility, or disease; can be diagnostic or predictive.

Bleaching: the elimination of the algal symbiont from the coral polyp resulting in a white appearance.

BMCs: beneficial microorganisms for corals.

BNMP: Bonaire National Marine Park.

Bottom modules: cement base and PVC pipe or pedestals for holding corals in a field nursery.

Broadcast spawner: a mode of scleractinian coral sexual reproduction where colonies release gametes into the water column, typically during annual mass synchronized events, for external fertilization and development.

Brooder: a mode of scleractinian coral sexual reproduction involving internal fertilization and development; typically, fewer but larger larvae that may already have their algal symbionts are released and settle more quickly after release.

Broodstock: larger grown or donor coral tissue that will be fragmented again.

BRUVS: Baited Remote Underwater Video Stations.

CCS: Controlled Culture System.

CIM: Center for Marine Innovation in the Dominican Republic.

Clone (coral): colonies, produced via asexual reproduction (e.g., fragmentation), that are genetically identical to the parental (donor) colony.

Cluster: a distinct group of multiple colonies of the same species and genotype outplanted together to form a thicket.

Codominance: a relationship between two versions of a gene where neither allele is recessive and the phenotypes of both alleles are expressed.

Coenosarc: Living tissue between and connecting individual coral polyps.

COIMPCPN-NP: "Costa Occidental de Isla Mujeres, Punta Cancún y Punta Nizuc" National Park.

CONANP: National Commission for Natural Protected Areas (of Mexico).

Coral at risk: a healthy coral growing at the end of a dead colony. As the skeleton erodes and weakens, the healthy portion becomes *at risk* of breaking off of the mother colony.

Coral reskinning: coral micro-fragments that have grown together on the surface of older skeletal substrates, a technique that can be employed to put new tissue onto dead coral heads.

Coral trees: a branching pipe and rod arrangement for suspending corals off of the bottom for field nursery operations.

Corals of opportunity: coral fragments at risk of further endangerment from storm or damage that can be saved and used in a coral restoration nursery.

CPCe: image analysis software developed to estimate coral cover.

Cryopreservation: a process that preserves organelles, cells, tissues, or any other biological constructs by cooling the samples to very low temperatures.

DARP: Damage and Restoration Program in the Florida Keys National Marine Sanctuary Program.

de novo **mutation:** a newly arisen variant (mutation).

Demography: the branch of ecology that studies the growth and regulation of animal and plant populations, resulting from the individual processes of birth, death, immigration, and emigration in natural, managed, or artificial environments.

Diploid: (of a cell or nucleus) containing two complete sets of chromosomes—one from each parent.
Ecological restoration: the process of assisting the recovery of ecosystems that have been damaged, degraded, or destroyed.
Endolith: an organism (archaeon, bacterium, fungus, lichen, algae, or amoeba) that lives inside rock, coral, animal shells, or in the pores between mineral grains of a rock.
Endosymbiont: an organism that lives inside another organism (the *host*).
Epigenetics: the study of heritable changes in gene expression that do not involve changes to the underlying DNA sequence, so the phenotype may be altered, but not the genotype.
Epistasis: the interaction of genes that are not alleles, in particular the suppression or amplification of the effect of one such gene by another.
ETP: Eastern Tropical Pacific.
Fecundity: a measure of reproductive output and a fitness-related trait.
Field nursery: culture facilities in the ocean (in situ).
Fitness: refers to how well an organism is able to survive and reproduce in its environment.
Fitness trade-off: where a fitness benefit associated with one function (e.g., defense) is correlated with a fitness cost of another function (e.g., growth).
Founder effect: the reduced genetic diversity that results when a population is descended from a small number of colonizing ancestors.
Fragmentation: a type of asexual reproduction by cutting a portion of the living tissue off of a parent or donor colony to attach and grow into a new colony.
Fragment of opportunity: a coral fragment that is loose on the sea floor, usually broken off from another colony.
Fragments of Hope (FoH): a nonprofit, community-based organization in Placencia, Belize, that focuses on the challenge of coral reef restoration.
Frag-N-Fly: the immediate outplanting in the field or a field nursery after micro-fragmentation.
FRRP: Florida Reef Resiliency Program.
Fusion: combining or fusing the tissue coral fragments that are genetically identical (see re-skinning).
Gametes: eggs or sperm.
Gametogenesis: the process in which cells undergo meiosis to form gametes.
GBRMPA: Great Barrier Reef Marine Park Authority.
Gene expression: the process by which the instructions in DNA are converted into a functional product, such as a protein.
Gene flow: the movement of individuals, and/or the genetic material they carry, from one population to another; occurs via processes such as migration and dispersal.
Genetic adaptation: change or adjustment in structure or habits by which a species becomes better able to function in its environment, occurring through the course of evolution by means of natural selection.
Genetic architecture: the characteristics of genetic variation that are responsible for heritable phenotypic variability.
Genetic (population) bottleneck: occurs when a population is greatly reduced in size, thereby reducing genetic diversity.
Genetic diversity: refers to the amount of variation on the level of individual genes within a population, can be expressed as heterozygosity or allelic richness, and can differ among the genomes within a cell.

Genetic drift: the stochastic loss of allelic diversity at functional genes.
Genetic swamping: a process influenced by gene flow and reproduction where non-native species can bring about a form of extinction of native flora and fauna by hybridization and introgression, either through intentional introduction by humans or habitat modification, bringing previously isolated species into contact.
Genomics: the study of whole genomes of organisms, incorporating elements from genetics.
Genotype: the genetic constitution of an individual organism.
Genotypic diversity: the number of unique multilocus genotypes (MLGs), which varies on the level of whole organisms.
Genotyping: a type of molecular analysis that determines differences in the genetic makeup of an individual by examining the individual's DNA sequence using biological assays and comparing it with another individual's sequence or a reference sequence.
Gonochorism: a form of sexuality entailing separate sexes where—in the case of corals—colonies are either male or female.
GPCF: Grupo Puntacana Foundation for reef restoration in the Dominican Republic.
Grow-out: an extension of nursery operations or an area for growth and survival until ready for harvest or final restoration planting.
Hatchery: usually a land-based building, equipment, or area used to condition broodstock, and to spawn or hatch eggs and sperm in order to develop larval forms for settlement.
Heterozygosity: the condition of having two different alleles at a locus.
Holobiont: an assemblage of a host and the many other species living in or around it, which together form a discrete ecological unit.
Homeostasis: any self-regulating process by which biological systems tend to maintain stability.
HP PVC: high pressure PVC (polyvinyl chloride plastic pipe).
HRI: Healthy Reef for Healthy People Initiative INAPESCA: National Institute of Fisheries and Aquaculture (of Mexico).
Hybrid vigor (or heterosis): the tendency of a crossbred individual to show qualities superior to those of both parents.
Inbreeding depression: the reduced biological fitness in a given population as a result of inbreeding or breeding of related individuals.
Intraspecific genetic variation: the presence of genetically based variation among individuals of the same species.
Intraspecific hybridization: the breeding or mating between different subspecies or individuals of the same species but very different (e.g., distantly located) populations.
Introgression: the transfer of genetic information from one species to another as a result of hybridization between them with repeated backcrossing.
Isogenic fusion: fusion of the same genotypes of tissue into one colony; it is an important life history strategy for clonal organisms to increase shared resources.
Karyogamy: the fusion of cell nuclei (as in fertilization).
Kiribati: Line Island in the Pacific Ocean.
Kiritimati: Christmas Atoll in the Line Islands.
Land based nursery: culture facilities in indoor or outdoor tanks (ex situ).
Larval seeding: a coral restoration intervention that aims to speed the return of coral cover to a disturbed or damaged reef by increasing the number of available coral larvae for natural settlement, particularly where the reef has a low larval supply.

Laughing Bird Caye National Park: a United Nations World Heritage site in Belize that was directly hit by Category 4 Hurricane Iris in 2001.
Lay-down nursery: a line nursery that can be directly planted on the bottom as one piece instead of separate fragments.
Line nurseries: suspended monofilament lines that float off of the bottom. Also, a suspended or floating line of any type for attachment of corals for nursery operations.
Live rock: coral rubble or substrate with living encrusting and fouling organisms that are used in marine aquarium trade.
Local adaptation: occurs when a population of organisms evolves to be better suited to its local environment compared to other individuals of the same species.
Managed (or captive) breeding: may involve supportive breeding, which seeks to enhance population sizes by sampling a subset of individuals from a population for captive rearing and subsequent release; outcrossing between populations, which aims to introduce novel genetic variation within a species range; following reproduction between individuals from different populations; or hybridization between species, which uses sexual reproduction to create individuals with novel genotypes that are more fit than the parental species.
MARRS: Mars Assisted Reef Restoration System.
Maternal effect: a situation where the phenotype of offspring is determined not only by the environment it experiences and its genotype, but also by the environment and genotype of its mother.
MCS: Marine Culture System.
Meiosis: a type of cell division that reduces the number of chromosomes in the parent cell by half and produces four gamete cells; this process is required to produce egg and sperm cells for sexual reproduction.
Metabolomics: refers to the systematic identification and quantification of the small molecule metabolic products (the metabolome) of a biological system (cell, tissue, organ, biological fluid, or organism) at a specific point in time.
Metapopulation: networks of discrete populations distributed across fragmented landscapes, connected through dispersal (e.g., the movement of planktonic coral propagules by currents over varying spatial scales).
Micro-fragmentation: a type of fragmentation using smaller portions of living tissue to produce a larger number of fast-growing coral colonies, used for massive coral species as well as branching coral species.
Microbiome: the community of microorganisms—such as bacteria, archaea, fungi, as well as viruses—that inhabit an ecosystem or organism.
Microevolution: the change in allele frequencies that occurs over time within a population as a result of the processes of mutation, selection (natural or artificial), gene flow, or genetic drift.
Microsatellites (or simple sequence repeat, SSR): markers based on short, tandem repeat sequences (2–6 base pairs in length) interspersed in the genome.
Mixed provenance strategy: a strategy for sourcing stock corals for propagation from both locally sourced genotypes and ones from across an environmental gradient.
Molecular markers (or neutral genetic markers): fragments of DNA associated with a particular region of the genome.
Morphotype: any of a group of different types of individuals of the same species in a population; a morph.
MSS: Mars Sustainable Solutions.

Multilocus genotypes (MLGs): the unique combination of alleles across all loci.
Multiple-cuttings: The secondary use of an original outplanting as a second use donor for field cuttings.
Next-generation sequencing (NGS): a powerful technology that offers simultaneous sequencing of thousands-to-millions of nucleic acid sequences in a massively parallel way (*high throughput*).
NOAA: National Oceanic and Atmospheric Administration.
Nursery: a land-based or field-based system for protection and growth of juveniles into a size or age for final outplanting.
OCS: Outdoor culture system.
Outbreeding depression: occurs when crosses between two genetically distant groups or populations result in a reduction of fitness.
Outcrossing (or outbreeding): mating between unrelated individuals of the same species.
Outplant: the movement of corals from a nursery to the final field position.
Outplant site: the location in the sea where corals are planted.
PAM fluorometry: pulse-amplitude-modulated (PAM) fluorometry measures the photosynthetic efficiency of photosystem II (PS II) within the endosymbiotic Symbiodiniaceae that may be used as a quantitative measure of photoinactivation during coral bleaching; used as a proxy for photosynthetic function.
Parthenogenesis: a form of asexual reproduction in which growth and development of embryos occur without fertilization by sperm.
Phenotype: the set of observable characteristics of an individual resulting from the interaction of its genotype with the environment.
Phenotypic plasticity: the ability of one genotype to produce more than one phenotype when exposed to different environments, thereby allowing an individual organism to change its phenotypic state in response to variation in environmental conditions.
Photomosaics: utilization of multiple images to combine into one large patchwork of photos, such as to monitor a whole reef.
Phytoplankton: plankton consisting of microscopic plants.
Planulae: planktonic larvae.
Polymerase chain reaction (PCR): a widely used method that allows scientists to take a very small sample of DNA and amplify it to a large enough amount to study in detail.
Pop-up nursery: nursery structure at or immediately adjacent to the outplant site to alleviate transport time.
Proteomics: the study of proteomes and their functions.
RADseq (or RAD-tag sequencing): a sequencing strategy that can identify and score thousands of genetic markers randomly distributed across the target genome from a group of individuals using Illumina technology.
Recombination (genetic): DNA recombination involves the exchange of genetic material either between multiple chromosomes or between different regions of the same chromosome.
Recruitment: the process by which young individuals undergo larval settlement and become part of the adult population.
Reef stars: hexagonal, modular-designed, resin-covered steel rods, previously known as spiders, to support corals.

Re-skinning: coral fragments that are achieving rapid colony fusion back into a single colony on the surface of older skeletal substrates can be employed to put new tissue onto dead coral heads.

Restriction enzyme: a protein that recognizes a specific, short nucleotide sequence and cuts the DNA only at that specific site, which is known as a restriction site or target sequence.

RNA-Seq (or RNA sequencing): a sequencing technique that uses next-generation sequencing (NGS) to reveal the presence and quantity of RNA in a biological sample at a given moment, analyzing the continuously changing cellular transcriptome; see transcriptomics.

RRAP: Reef Restoration and Adaptation Program.

RRFB: Reef Renewal Foundation Bonaire.

Scleractinia: stony or hard corals—marine invertebrate animals in the phylum Cnidaria that secrete skeletons made of calcium carbonate; also known as reef-building (foundational) corals.

SCTLD: Stony Coral Tissue Loss Disease.

Selective breeding: crossing individuals to generate genotypes exhibiting certain desirable phenotypes and/or to increase genetic variation within offspring populations to be used for restoration.

Selfing (self-fertilization): the union of male and female gametes and/or nuclei from the same haploid, diploid, or polyploid organism; an extreme form of inbreeding.

SER: The Society for Ecological Restoration.

Sexual propagation (or assisted sexual reproduction): the process of producing, with some level of human intervention, more corals (genetically unique offspring) via sexual reproduction; see also selective or managed/captive breeding.

Sexual recruit: a coral offspring produced through sexual reproduction that has undergone larval settlement, metamorphosis, and formed a new genetically unique coral colony.

SIDS: Small Island Developing States.

Sikacrete: Trademark of a concrete powder stabilizer to increase cohesion underwater.

Simultaneous hermaphroditism: a form of sexuality where a single organism—or in the case of corals, a single colony—has both male and female sex organs and produces both types of gametes (eggs and sperm).

SNPs (single nucleotide polymorphisms): sites at which more than one nucleotide is found in a population (i.e., a single base-pair change via mutation); the most common type of genetic variation and commonly used as biological markers.

Soft sweep (from standing genetic variation): occurs when a previously neutral mutation that was present in a population becomes beneficial because of an environmental change.

Standing genetic variation (SGV): the presence of alternative forms of a gene (alleles) at a given locus in a population.

Symbiosis: the interaction between two different organisms living in close physical association, typically to the advantage of both.

Tabuareran: known in English as Fanning Island, it is an atoll that is part of the Line Islands of the central Pacific Ocean and part of Kiribati.

Transcriptomics: the study of the transcriptome—the complete set of RNA transcripts that are produced by the genome under specific circumstances or in a specific cell—using high-throughput methods, such as microarray analysis.

Transportable nursery: land-nursery equipment and a water system customized into a shipping container for transport and ready to use and operate as a lab and storage.

UNAM: National Autonomous University of Mexico.

USAID: United States Agency for International Development.

Zooxanthellae: single-celled dinoflagellate algae of the genera Symbiodiniaceae that live in symbiosis with diverse marine invertebrates including demosponges, corals, jellyfish, and nudibranchs.

INDEX

Page numbers followed by "*f*" refer to figures and those followed by "*t*" refer to tables.

Acclimatization, 148–149, 151*f*, 154–161, 155*f*, 158*f*
  acute preconditioning, 156
  chronic preconditioning, 156
  corals of opportunity, 156
  intragenerational, 156
  microbes and, 159–160
  transgenerational, 157–159
Acropora cervicornis, 7, 26, 46, 90, 91, 179, 180*f*, 191, 192*f*, 193–194, 246*f*, 251, 290, 294*f*, 296, 299, 305, 365, 370, 374, 374*t*, 375, 375*f*–376*f*, 380, 380*f*, 385, 484, 500, 501–502, 501*f*, 502*f*, 503*f*, 504*f*, 505, 507, 508, 511, 513*f*, 517, 518*f*, 519, 520, 537, 537*f*
Acropora digitifera, 261
Acropora millepora, 127, 178–179
Acropora palmata, 26, 60, 81, 91, 98, 98*f*, 113, 117*f*, 124, 125, 126*f*, 132*f*, 133*f*, 134, 135*f*, 138*f*, 139, 179, 180*f*, 183, 191–192, 193, 236, 239, 251, 288, 290, 290*f*, 293*f*, 296, 302*f*, 304, 307*f*, 365, 367, 369, 370, 373, 373*f*, 374, 375, 381–382, 381*f*, 382*t*, 384, 389, 484, 499*f*, 500–501, 502, 511, 517, 526, 537, 537*f*
Acropora sp., 71, 90–92
  assisted dispersion of, 385
  hybridization, 179–182
Acropora tenuis, 125, 173, 460
Acropora valida, 125
Acroporids, 300, 302*f*

Active restoration, 33–38. *See also* Passive restoration
  evolution, developmental steps, 34–35
  gardening tenet for, 35
  progression of, 36
  protocols, 37
  schematic illustration, 36*f*
Acute preconditioning, 156
Adhesives, 557
Aerial mapping, 545
Agincourt Reef, Cairns, 397, 401
Algal endosymbionts (Symbiodiniaceae), 161–168, 163*f*, 165*f*
  coral bleaching, 161–164
  manipulating, 164–166
Algal symbionts, 256–257
American Recovery and Reinvestment Act (ARRA), 15, 60
Animal-assisted cleaning, 330, 331*f*
Aplysina fulva, 299, 300*f*
Area required for land and field nurseries, 74
Argo Expeditions, 404
Aroona Boat Charters, 404
Artificial coral modules, 107–108, 108*f*
Artificial reefs, 564, 564*f*
Artificial structure, 382, 382*f*
Asexual propagation, 21
Assisted evolution, 117–118, 151–200
  acclimatization (nongenetic) processes, 154–161, 155*f*, 158*f*
  algal endosymbionts (Symbiodiniaceae), 161–168, 163*f*, 165*f*

concept, 151–154
  interspecific hybridization, 177–184, 180f, 181f, 183f
  intraspecific managed breeding, 184–200
  manipulating host microbiome, 168–177
Assisted gene flow (AGF), 243
Association of Artisans and Marine Services (ARSEMAR), 542
Association of Caribbean Marine Laboratories, 541
"At the Water's Edge" (AWE), 564, 564f
Australia, active coral reef restoration in, 393–415
  community involvement, 407–409, 408f, 409f–410f
  GBRMPA, 17, 393, 394, 397, 404, 407, 411–413, 412t
  governance, 410
  monitoring, 404–406, 405f, 406f–407f
  permits and guidelines, 411–413
  RRAP. See Reef Restoration and Adaptation Program (RRAP)
  techniques and methods, 394–397
Automation, 561–562

Bacteria. See Coral-associated bacteria; Microbes/microbiome
Barber, Todd, 9t, 11f, 19
Belize. See Fragments of Hope (FoH)
Belize Fisheries Department, 288
Biological filtration, 79
Biomarkers, 259–260
Biomimicry, 326–333
  animal-assisted cleaning, 330, 331f
  breeding size coral colonies, 332–333
  coral self-attachment, 326–327, 327f–328f
  self-cleaning nurseries, 328–330
Biopixel, 404
Blue Pearl Bay, Whitsunday Islands, 400
Bowden-Kerby, Austin, 9t, 11f, 12, 13f, 26, 61, 91, 290, 456, 535, 537, 560
Breeding, 184–200
  cryopreservation, 196
  ecosystem-based restoration, 195–196
  risks, 194–195
  timelines, 195
Breeding size coral colonies, 332–333

Broodstock selection, 190–191, 243–245
Buddy Dive Resort, 512, 528

Caribbean Coral Strategy, 545
Carne, Lisa, 10t, 288, 309, 560
Catastrophic changes, 44–45
Center for Marine Innovation (CIM), 543–544
Chaetomorpha linum, 302, 303f
Chartrand, Katie, 404
Chou Loke Ming, 15
Christie, Stewart, 20
Chronic preconditioning, 156
Cliona caribbaea, 299, 300f
COIMPCPN-NP. See Costa Occidental de Isla Mujeres, Punta Cancún y Punta Nizuc (COIMPCPN-NP)
Communication and education, 17–19
Comprehensive Environmental Response, Cleanup, and Liability Act, 16
CONANP. See National Commission for Natural Protected Areas (CONANP)
Continuous broodstock, 554
Continuum of objectives/benefits, 569–571, 570f
Cook, Nathan, 15
Coral-associated bacteria, 171–172
Coral-associated viruses, 172
Coral bleaching, 319, 321, 324, 335, 455, 478, 568
  algal endosymbionts (Symbiodiniaceae), 161–164
Coral colonies, 332–333
Coral farm, 48–49, 50f
  transformation into nursery, 52–59
Coral First Aid, 541
Coral gardening, 35, 341
  asexual propagation through, 124
  of asexual restoration, 317
  guidelines for, 238–239
  phases, 342–343
  silviculture principles and theories, 342
Coral Innovation Hub in Dominican Republic, 544–545
Coralmania, 541
Coral metapopulation, 573–574

Coral nursery. *See* Nurseries
Coral population, 573
Coral reef(s), 8
   assistance needed for, 146–151
   passion for, 43–44
   worldwide decline of, 342
Coral Reef Rehabilitation and Management Project (COREMAP), 466
Coral reef restoration, 8–10, 51
   communication and education, 17–19
   genetic risks to, 230
   hybridization and, 178–179
   indigenous people and, 10
   literature review, 21–26
   management support, 16–17
   private businesses, 19–21
   scientific pioneers, 10–16
   sexual reproduction for, 184–185
Coral Reef Restoration Program, 4
Coral Reefs of the Eastern Tropical Pacific (Glynn, Manzello, and Enochs), 417–418
Coral re-skinning, 104–107, 105*f*
Coral Restoration Foundation, 14–15, 20, 26, 60–61
Coral seedlings, 109–110, 110*f*
Coral self-attachment, 326–327, 327*f*–328*f*
Corals of opportunity, 115, 156
Coral Transplantation as a Reef Management Option (Harriot and Fisk), 17
Coral tree nursery model, 62–63
Cortes, Jorge, 90
Costa Occidental de Isla Mujeres, Punta Cancún y Punta Nizuc (COIMPCPN-NP), 366, 367, 373, 374*t*
Cousin Island Special Reserve, 316, 319
Cousteau, Alexandra, 4
Cousteau, Jacques, 4
Cousteau, Philippe, 4
COVID-19, 310
Cozumel, Mendez, 18
Cozumel Coral Reef Restoration Program, 18
Crustose coralline algae (CCA), 132–134, 133*f*, 297, 299
Cryopreservation, 196

Daerah Perlindungan Laut (DPL), 466
DAR Coral Restoration Nursery, 107, 111
Daydream Island, Whitsundays, 402–403, 403*f*
Daydream Island Marina, 402
Deep Water Horizon oil spill, 16
Dekel Beach, 343, 355
   anthropogenic pressures, 343, 345*f*, 354
   coral-associated invertebrates and fish, 358, 359*f*
   explanatory poster about ongoing project, 352*f*–353*f*
   fish attacks on nursery-grown transplants, 354, 355*f*
   recreational diving activity, 345*f*
   restored knoll at, 360, 361*f*
   Stylophora pistillata colonies, 350*f*
Dendrogyra cylindrus, 242, 385, 500
Development Grant Program (DGP), 314
Diadema antillarum, 224
Dipsastraea favus, 344, 354, 355*f*, 356*f*
Dive Shop Members, 528–529, 529*f*
Dobzhansky, Theodosius, 335
Dominican Coastal Restoration Consortium, 544
Dominican Republic, 535–547
Drone orthomosaics, 296

Eastern tropical Pacific (ETP), 417–418
Eco Koh Tao, 15
Ecological impact of nurseries, 86–87
Ecological recovery wheel, 386, 387*f*
Ecological restoration, 31–32
   active and passive restoration, 33–35
   core elements, 33*t*
Ecosystem processes, 575–576
Edwards, Alastair, 9*t*, 11*f*, 17, 18
Eilat, Israel, active coral reef restoration in, 341–361
   farmed colonies, 343–344, 344*f*
   monitoring, 349–350
   outcomes and discussion, 354–360
   techniques and methods, 345–349
   volunteers, 351–352
El Acuario, 537–541
El Niño Southern Oscillation (ENSO), 418
Enochs, Ian, 418

Equipment utilized in nurseries, 74–76, 74f
Evolutionary perspective, 225–229
Ex-Tropical Cyclone Debbie, 397, 400

Fanning Atoll. *See* Tabuaeran/Fanning Atoll
Feeds and supplements, 555–556
Field nurseries, 71
   area required for, 74
   designs, plans, drawings, and layouts, 80
   ecological impact, 86–87
   equipment utilized in, 74–76, 75f, 76f
   fouling, 81
   fusion, 111–112
   labels and tagging, 81–82, 82f, 83f
   location, 73
   measuring growth of corals, 84
   production capacity, 85–86
   safety concerns, 86
   supplies and materials, 77–79
   vessels and vehicles, 86
Filtration equipment, 79
Fish biomass, 299, 300, 301f
Fishery habitat, 574
Fish functional groups, 300, 301f
Fisk, David, 9t, 11f, 17, 26, 410
Fitness, 225
   factors driving reductions in, 229–237
Fitzroy Island, Cairns, 397–398, 398f–399f
Floating nurseries, 75
Florida Keys, 43–66
Fogerty, Nicole, 302
FoH. *See* Fragments of Hope (FoH)
Forest landscape restoration, 34
Fouling, 81
Founder effects, 232–233
Fragmentation, 21, 90–95
   Frag-N-Fly, 99, 99f, 552
   manual micro-fragmentation, 99, 100f, 553, 553f
   methods of, 92–95
   multiple-cutting, 99–100, 100f, 384, 384f, 554, 554f
   perceived potential risk of, 115
Fragment growth rate, 555
Fragment size, 555

Fragments of Hope (FoH), 287–310
   community involvement, 308–309
   LBCNP, 287, 288–304
   monitoring methods, 308t
   nursery and outplant site selection criteria, 304–305, 305t
   techniques and methods, 304–307
Frag-N-Fly, 99, 99f, 552
Functional restoration, 34–35
Fusion
   benefits, 104
   confusion, 114–115
   coral re-skinning, 104–107, 105f
   defined, 103–104
   field nurseries, 111–112
   genetic crosses, 117–118
   land nurseries, 110–111
   natural or artificial modules, 107–108, 108f
   process, 112–114
   seedlings, 109–110, 110f
   sexual maturity, 116–117
   tiling, 108, 109f

Gaines, Kevin, 63
Gambierdiscus toxicus, 456, 456f
Gates, Ruth, 10t, 11f
Gene flow, 223
Genetic adaptation
   hybridization and, 177–178
   standing genetic variation (SGV), 226–227
Genetic risks to coral reef restoration, 230
Genetics, 221–263
   algal symbionts, 256–257
   assisted gene flow (AGF), 243
   biomarkers, 259–260
   evolutionary perspective, 225–229
   founder effects, 232–233
   genotypic diversity, 230–232
   genotyping, 258–259
   holobionts, 255–256
   inbreeding and selfing, 234–236
   molecular markers, 257–259
   nursery and broodstock selection, 243–245
   omics, 260–261

outbreeding, 236–237
outplanting, 252–254
phenotypic variation, 251–252
scleractinian species, 239–254
sexual propagation, 245–251
sexual reproduction, 232
sourcing corals, 242
swamping, 233–234
target species, 242
Genotypic diversity, 230–232
Genotyping, 258–259
Gladden Spit and the Silk Cayes Marine Reserve (GSSCMR), 288
Gleason, Arthur, 290
Global Environmental Facility (GEF) Small Grants Programme, 309
Global Environmental Fund (GEF) Tourism Partnership Programme, 326
Global warming, 146–147
Glynn, Peter, 417
Goad, Alex, 20
Golfo Dulce, Costa Rica, 418–428
    community involvement, 427
    monitoring, 422–427
    techniques and methods, 420–421, 420f, 421f
Gomez, Eduardo, 9t, 11f, 17, 18, 21
GoPro, 563
Goreau, Tom, 9t, 11–12, 11f, 26
Great Adventures Bonaire, 529
Great Barrier Reef Marine Park Authority (GBRMPA), 17, 393, 394, 397, 404, 407, 411–413, 412t
Grupo Puntacana (GPC), 535, 536, 537
Grupo Puntacana Foundation (GPCF), 535, 537, 540–542, 543, 544, 545, 547

Habitat restoration, 35
Harbor Branch Oceanographic Institute (HBOI), 4
Hard hat diving, 10
Harriot, Vicki, 9t, 11f, 17, 26, 410
Harrison, Peter, 10t, 11f, 16, 125, 127, 404, 415
HBOI. *See* Harbor Branch Oceanographic Institute (HBOI)

Healthy Reef for Healthy People Initiative (HRI), 385
Healthy Reefs Initiative, 299
Hilbertz, Wolf, 9t, 11f, 12, 26
Holobionts, 255–256
House reef, 571, 572–573
Hurricanes and storms, 483–509
    damage prevention strategies, 505–507
    nurseries and, 494–500
    outplanted corals and, 500–502, 501f, 501t, 503f
    physical damage, 492
    secondary impacts, 493
    sedimentation, 493
    wild colonies and, 503–504, 504f
Hybridization
    Acropora genus, 179–182
    coral reef restoration and, 178–179
    genetic adaptation and, 177–178
    interspecific, 177–184, 180f, 181f, 183f

INAPESCA. *See* National Institute of Fisheries and Aquaculture (INAPESCA)
Inbreeding, 234–236. *See also* Self-fertilization (selfing)
Indigenous people, 10
International Coral Restoration Initiative (CRI), 4
Interspecific hybridization, 177–184, 180f, 181f, 183f
Intragenerational acclimatization, 156
Intraspecific managed breeding, 184–200

Kaufman, Les, 299
Koch, Hanna, 565
Koh Tao Dive Operators Club, 15

Labels and tagging, 81–82, 82f, 83f, 84f
Labrador Park, 15
Land nurseries, 72
    area required for, 74
    designs, plans, drawings, and layouts, 80
    ecological impact, 86–87

equipment utilized in, 74–76, 74f
fouling, 81
fusion, 110–111
labels and tagging, 81–82, 82f, 83f, 84f
location, 73
measuring growth of corals, 84
production capacity, 85–86
safety concerns, 86
supplies and materials, 77–79
vessels and vehicles, 86
Large-scale coral reef restoration project in Seychelles, 315–324
Large-scale harmful algal bloom (HAB), 321
Larval culture, 129–130
Larval development, 130–131, 131f, 132f
Larval enhancement experiments, 15
Larval Enhancement Project, 404
Laughing Bird Caye National Park (LBCNP), 287, 288–304. See also Fragments of Hope (FoH)
Lay-down nursery, 560, 560f
Lennon, David, 9t, 11f, 20
Line Islands, Kiribati, 431–461
   Acropora recruits, 438–440
   adaptation to climate change, 453, 459–461
   ciguatera fish poisoning outbreak, 456–457
   coral nursery, 433–435, 434f–435f, 436f
   larval-based coral recruitment, 436–437
   outplanting, 449, 449f–451f, 451, 452f
   proposed no-fishing area, 455, 455f
   protecting restoration sites, 454
   regenerating coral colonies, 440–442
   strategy, 457–459
Line Islands Fisheries Department, 433
Line nurseries, 61, 75
Literature review, 21–26
Live rock farm, 45–48

Management support, 16–17
Manta Ray Bay, Whitsunday Islands, 397, 400
Manual micro-fragmentation, 99, 100f, 553, 553f
Manuals, 17–18

Manzello, Derek, 417–418
Marhaven, Kristen, 18–19
Marine Conservation Group of the Nature Society (Singapore), 15
Marine protected area, 16
Marine Sanctuary Arrecifes del Sureste, 545–547, 546f
Marine species, 4
MARRS. *See* Mars Assisted Reef Restoration System (MARRS)
Mars, Frank, 20
Mars Assisted Reef Restoration System (MARRS), 463–480
   ecological response, 477–479
   future action, 479–480
   implementation of, 467
   monitoring performance, 473–476, 475t, 477f
   reef stars, 467–468, 470–471
   restoration build, 468–473
   supply-chain approach, 464–465
Mars Corporation, 20
Mars Sustainable Solutions (MSS), 463
Measuring growth of corals, 84
Meso American Reef Restoration Network, 310
Metamorphosis. *See* Settlement and metamorphosis
Mexican Caribbean, active coral reef restoration in, 365–391
   community involvement, 387–388
   monitoring, 386, 386t
   techniques and methods, 367–385
Microbes/microbiome
   acclimatization and, 159–160
   coral-associated bacteria, 171–172
   coral-associated viruses, 172
   coral core, 171
   manipulating/manipulations, 168–170, 173–174
   microhabitats, 172–173
Micro-colony fusion, 104. *See also* Fusion
Micro-fragmentation, 95–99, 378, 379f, 380. *See also* Fusion
   asexual propagation through, 124
   perceived potential risk of, 115

Index

scaling up production through, 378
sexual maturity with, 116–117
Microsatellites, 258
Millepora dichotoma, 344, 354, 356*f*
Miller, Margaret, 9*t*, 139
Mixed provenance strategy, 242–243
Molecular markers, 257–259
Montaestrea sp., 98
Montipora capitata, 116
Moore, Tom, 558
Mote Tropical Research Laboratory, 4
Multiple-cutting, 99–100, 100*f*, 384, 384*f*, 554, 554*f*
Multiple settlement and survival, 135, 136*f*
Museo Subacuático de Arte, 17

National Commission for Natural Protected Areas (CONANP), 366, 387–388
National Coral Reef Action Strategy, 16
National Geographic, 3
National Institute of Fisheries and Aquaculture (INAPESCA), 366, 371*t*, 377, 377*t*, 384, 388
National Marine Protected Area, 17
National Oceanic and Atmospheric Administration (NOAA), 15, 16, 90–91
The Nature Conservancy (TNC), 15, 544–545
Nature Fund, 525, 530
Nedimyer, Ken, 9*t*, 10*t*, 11*f*, 14–15, 14*f*, 43, 49*f*, 52*f*, 90, 420, 511, 515, 562
New Heaven Reef Conservation Program, 15
Nurseries
  broodstock selection, 243–245
  field. *See* Field nurseries
  land. *See* Land nurseries
  transformation into, 52–59

Ocean acidification, 146–147
Ocean Farming Systems, 44
Oil Pollution Act, 16
Omics, 260–261
On-site population enhancement, 562
ORA (Oceans, Reefs and Aquariums), 4, 72

Orbicella annularis, 242, 367, 382, 385
Orbicella faveolata, 46, 74*f*, 96*f*, 104*f*, 105, 106–107, 197–198, 240, 502, 503, 503*f*, 521, 565
Orbicella sp., 98
Outbreeding, 236–237
Outcrossing. *See* Outbreeding
Outplanting, 252–254
Outreach, 545

Paris, Claire, 302
Passive restoration, 33–34
  reef restoration, 37–38
Phenotypic plasticity, 148–149
Phenotypic variation, 251–252
Philippe Cousteau Foundation, 4
Phytoplankton, 556
Placencia Village Council, 309
Planblue, 563
Pocillopora damicornis, 344, 351*f*, 355, 357*f*, 358*f*, 361*f*, 418
Population persistence, sexual reproduction for, 184–185
Pop-up nursery, 558–559, 559*f*
Porites astreoides, 374–375
Precht, W. F., 9*t*, 11*f*, 17, 18, 63, 558
Private businesses, 19–21
Production capacity of nurseries, 85–86
Pulau Badi, 465–466, 477–478
Pulau Bontosua restoration program, 466
Pumps, 78–79
Punta Cana, 537–542

Queen of the Giant Clams, 15
Queensland Parks and Wildlife Service (QPWS), 397

Raceway ecology, 138–140
Reef accretion, 574–575
Reef Arabia, 20
Reef Ball Australia, 20
Reef Balls, 19
Reef-building corals, 148
Reef Crest, restoration of, 383
Reef enhancement units, 15
REEFhabilitation, 545

Reef Rehabilitation Manual (Edwards), 18
Reef Renewal Foundation Bonaire
  boulder corals, 521–522, 521*f*, 522*f*–524*f*
  Dive Shop Members, 528–529, 529*f*
  foundation, 512, 515
  larval propagation, 522, 524
  monitoring, 524–528
Reef Rescuers, 314–316, 333
  principles of ecological restoration, 314–315, 315*t*
Reef Resilience Network, 9*t*, 18, 26, 408
Reef Restoration and Adaptation Program (RRAP), 27, 413–414, 414*f*, 575
Reef stars, 467–468
  coral attachment to, 470–471
  installation of, 471
Resilience-based management (RBM), 254–255
Restore Act, 16
Revegetation, 34
Ridge modules, 20
Rinkevich, Baruch, 9*t*, 11*f*, 12, 14, 26, 108
Risks, breeding, 194–195
Roach, Stephanie, 63
Robots/robotics, 555, 562
Ross, Andrew, 61, 558

Scarus spp., 376
Schill, Steve, 296
Scientific pioneers, 10–16
Scleractinian species, 239–254
Scott, Chad, 15
Sea surface temperature (SST), 128
SECORE International, 21
Selective rapid growth cycle (SRGC), 564–565, 565*f*
Self-cleaning nurseries, 328–330
Self-contained underwater breathing apparatus (SCUBA), 10–11
Self-fertilization (selfing), 234–236
Self-sustaining reefs, 576
Sensors and monitoring equipment, 563, 563*f*
Settlement and metamorphosis, 132–134, 133*f*, 134*f*–135*f*

Sexual maturity with micro-fragmentation, 116–117
Sexual propagation, 245–251
Sexual reproduction, 123–141, 125*f*, 232, 569
  branching coral species, 124
  genetic variation and, 232
  increasing survival of, 556–557
  juvenile size, 137, 138*f*
  larval development, 130–131, 131*f*, 132*f*
  multiple settlement and survival, 135, 136*f*
  population persistence, 184–185
  post-settlement care, 136–137
  raceway ecology, 138–140
  settlement and metamorphosis, 132–134, 133*f*, 134*f*–135*f*
Seychelles, coral reef restoration in, 313–333
  biomimicry, 326–333
  capacity building, 333
  future research, 335–336
  large-scale project, 315–324
  need for, 313–315
  small-scale project, 324–326
Silviculture, 14, 360
Single nucleotide polymorphisms (SNP), 238, 258, 259, 261
Small-scale coral reef restoration project in Seychelles, 324–326
Society for Ecological Restoration (SER), 386
Sourcing corals, 242
Southern Environmental Association (SEA), 288
Sparisoma spp., 376
Spawning of corals, 128–129
Spermonde Archipelago, 463–464, 465*f*. *See also* Mars Assisted Reef Restoration System (MARRS)
  geomorphology, 465
  zones, 465
Spiders, 20
Sponge species, 299, 300*f*
SRGC. *See* Selective rapid growth cycle (SRGC)

Standard Tools for Acroporid Genotyping (STAG), 259
Standing genetic variation (SGV), 226–227
Sterilization, 79
Stony coral tissue loss disease (SCTLD), 200, 335, 385
Stress-tolerant corals, 200
Stylophora pistillata, 344, 346*f*, 350, 350*f*, 355, 355*f*, 357*f*
Substrates, 557
Suggett, David, 404
Sultan Shoal, 15
Sustainable Oceans International, 20
Swamping, 233–234
Sweeping tentacles, 112
Symbiodiniaceae. *See* Algal endosymbionts (Symbiodiniaceae)
Symbiodinium fitti, 193, 259
Symbiodinium genus, 161

Tabuaeran/Fanning Atoll, 431, 432*f*, 437, 443–445, 443*f*, 445*f*–446*f*. *See also* Line Islands, Kiribati
Tagging. *See* Labels and tagging
Tanks, 77, 77*f*
Target species, 242
Taylor, Jason deCaires, 9*t*, 11*f*, 17, 18
Technology, 551–565
Temperature loggers, 563
Thailand, 15
Tiling method, 108, 109*f*
Time-lapse photography, 563
Timelines, breeding, 195
TNC-NOAA Community-Based Restoration Program (CRP) Partnership project, 15
Transgenerational acclimatization, 157–159
Transplantation of coral fragments, 21
Transportable nursery, 561
Trees, 76
Tridacna maxima, 325, 325*f*
True, James, 15

"Underwater World of Jacques Cousteau," 3, 43–44
United Nations Development Program (UNDP), 326
United States Agency for International Development (USAID), 314
University Hasanuddin (UNHAS), 466
University of Rhode Island (URI), 466
U.S. Coral Reef Task Force, 16
U.S. National Academy of Sciences, 32
U.S. National Action Plan to Conserve Coral Reefs, 16

Vaughan, David, 10*t*, 11*f*, 15–16, 17, 18, 130, 134*f*, 137*f*, 305, 378, 384, 428, 535, 565, 565*f*
Verongula rigida, 299, 300*f*
Vessels, 86
Viruses. *See* Coral-associated viruses; Microbes/microbiome
Vision for future restoration, 567–576
　adaptation, 569
　baseline conditions, 571
　climate predictions, 568–569
　continuum of objectives/benefits, 569–571, 570*f*
　sexual reproduction, 569
Vlasoff and Arlington Reef, Cairns, 404

Wulff, Janie, 299

A Year on the Great Barrier Reef 1928–29 the Yonge Expedition, 10

Zooxanthellae, 555